Certification Study Companion Series

The Apress Certification Study Companion Series offers guidance and hands-on practice to support technical and business professionals who are studying for an exam in the pursuit of an industry certification. Professionals worldwide seek to achieve certifications in order to advance in a career role, reinforce knowledge in a specific discipline, or to apply for or change jobs. This series focuses on the most widely taken certification exams in a given field. It is designed to be user friendly, tracking to topics as they appear in a given exam. Authors for this series are experts and instructors who not only possess a deep understanding of the content, but also have experience teaching the key concepts that support readers in the practical application of the skills learned in their day-to-day roles.

More information about this series at https://link.springer.com/bookseries/17100

Developing Solutions for Microsoft Azure Certification Companion

Hands-on Preparation and Practice for *Exam AZ-204*

Brian L. Gorman

Apress®

Developing Solutions for Microsoft Azure Certification Companion:
Hands-on Preparation and Practice for Exam AZ-204

Brian L. Gorman
MajorGuidanceSolutions
Jesup, IA, USA

ISBN-13 (pbk): 978-1-4842-9299-0   ISBN-13 (electronic): 978-1-4842-9300-3
https://doi.org/10.1007/978-1-4842-9300-3

Managing Director, Apress Media LLC: Welmoed Spahr
Acquisitions Editor: Jonathan Gennick
Development Editor: Laura Berendson
Editorial Assistant: Shaul Elson
Copy Editor: Kezia Endsley

Cover designed by eStudioCalamar

Distributed to the book trade worldwide by Springer Science+Business Media New York, 1
New York Plaza, Suite 4600, New York, NY 10004-1562, USA. Phone 1-800-SPRINGER, fax (201)
348-4505, e-mail orders-ny@springer-sbm.com, or visit www.springeronline.com. Apress Media,
LLC is a California LLC and the sole member (owner) is Springer Science + Business Media
Finance Inc (SSBM Finance Inc). SSBM Finance Inc is a **Delaware** corporation.

For information on translations, please e-mail booktranslations@springernature.com; for reprint,
paperback, or audio rights, please e-mail bookpermissions@springernature.com.

Apress titles may be purchased in bulk for academic, corporate, or promotional use. eBook
versions and licenses are also available for most titles. For more information, reference our Print
and eBook Bulk Sales web page at http://www.apress.com/bulk-sales.

Any source code or other supplementary material referenced by the author in this book is available
to readers on GitHub. For more detailed information, please visit http://www.apress.com/
source-code.

Printed on acid-free paper

This book is dedicated to my wife Cassie and my children Kiera, Karson, Kreighton, and Kierstyn, who have all made many sacrifices to give me space and time to write, as well as for your daily, unceasing love, grace, patience, and encouragement. I would also like to dedicate this book to the many people who have helped me in my career through the years, given me opportunities, and believed in me even when I haven't always believed in myself.

Table of Contents

About the Author

 **Brian L. Gorman** is a Microsoft Azure MVP, developer, computer science instructor, and trainer. He has been working in .NET technologies as long as they have existed. He was originally MCSD certified in .NET 1 and recertified with MCSA: Web Apps and MCSD: App Builder certifications in 2019. From 2019 on, Brian has earned 11 Azure certifications, including the Azure, Security, and Data Fundamentals certifications, the Azure Administrator, Database Administrator, Security Engineer, and Developer Associate certifications, the Azure Solutions Architect and DevOps Expert certifications, and the IoT and Cosmos DB Specialty certifications.

Additionally, Brian became an MCT as of April 2019 and is focusing on developing and training developers with full-stack web solutions with .NET Core and Azure. Most recently, Brian has found purpose as an instructor for the Microsoft Software and Systems Academy (MSSA) in the cloud application development program.

In addition to working with .NET technologies, Brian was also an adjunct faculty member in the computer science department at Franklin University for over ten years, where his courses included data structures, algorithms, design patterns, and full-stack solutions in the computer science capstone practicum course. Brian has created many online technical training courses that can be found online on various platforms. Brian is also the author of the Apress books *Practical Entity Framework* and *Practical Entity Framework Core 6*.

About the Technical Reviewer

Gerald Versluis is a Senior Software Engineer at Microsoft, working on .NET MAUI. Since 2009, Gerald has been working on a variety of projects, ranging from frontend to backend and anything in between that involves Azure, ASP.NET, and all kinds of other .NET technologies. At some point, he fell in love with cross-platform and mobile development with Xamarin (now .NET MAUI). Since then he has become an active community member, writing, tweeting, and presenting about all things tech. Gerald can be found on Twitter @jfversluis, blogging at https://blog.verslu.is or on his YouTube channel at https://youtube.com/@jfversluis.

Acknowledgments

I would not have been able to write this book if it were not for a number of people who have both influenced and helped me throughout my career, as well as the multitudes of grace and support that I have received from my family throughout this process.

I'd like to begin by thanking Gerald Versluis for his hard work reviewing this material. It's been great to have a chance to work with him through this project and I'm very appreciative of the excellent feedback and suggestions he's provided along the way. This book would not be what it is without the hours of work he put into reviewing chapters, calling out questions, and making sure the content was accurate.

I'd like to next thank a few of the people who have believed in me as I've been working on building out Major Guidance Solutions and the unique Azure Training programs that I offer. Specifically, I'd like to thank Mike Cole, Javier Lozano, Alec Harrison, and Brian McKeiver, who either attended or sent their team through my Azure certification training program. I'd also like to thank John Unsen and his colleagues at VGM for giving me the chance to take them through this material as well as material on the Azure administration side in my Azure Expert Training programs.

I'd also like to thank the many friends and acquaintances I've made at various tech conferences in the past few years. I've learned so much from all of you, and I had a blast making music in the hotel Lobby in Lincoln. I'm looking forward to more of those fun times ahead!

Thank you to Apress and the team who have believed in me and have helped to make this book possible. Thanks to Jonathan Gennick and Jill Balzano, as well as to Nirmal Salvaraj and Shaul Elson for running the project, editing, and overseeing the entire schedule and process.

ACKNOWLEDGMENTS

I would be remiss if I didn't also thank Dustin Behn, the leader of the Inspired Nation, and his life coaching and his Emergence program. Thank you for coaching me these past few years and for helping me get out of my own way to do things like this book. I also want to say thanks to Dr. Ashley Lang of GoalDigger for helping me to identify my strengths and coaching me past the writer's block I was having early in the process of starting this book. Finally, I want to thank the staff and owners of Panther Lanes for providing some awesome pictures of a bowling alley to help illustrate partitioning of data in Cosmos DB (used in Chapter 2).

Introduction

The Azure Developer Associate Certification (AZ-204 at the time of this writing) is the premier Azure certification for developers. Adding the Azure Developer Associate Certification to your resume can be one way to set yourself apart from other developers applying for positions, or it can help you get noticed or qualify for promotions or raises. As such, it's definitely a great certification to earn and one that you most likely are interested in achieving if you are considering this book.

The main goal of this book is to help you prepare for that certification. Unlike most prep books, this book does not present practice questions. Instead, what you will find in the pages of this book are practical examples and discussions related to the important topics that could show up on your certification exam.

If you are mainly concerned about practice questions, you should invest your money in a MeasureUp (`www.measureup.com`) practice test, which is officially sponsored by Microsoft. Additionally, Microsoft has released some official practice assessments which can be found here: `https://learn.microsoft.com/en-us/certifications/practice-assessments-for-microsoft-certifications`. You can find the AZ-204 in the list to take the practice assessment.

As the book is written to aid you in developing solutions for Azure, the idea is that you can complete any chapter in any order, based on your needs and desires for studying the solution. The one exception to this is that a number of chapters rely on a provisioned app service with a default application (found in the source materials for this book). With that, while you can still jump around, you will need to first deploy the application and any features you turn on would need to also be provisioned (for example, you can't read from the app config and Key Vault if you haven't deployed them).

In general, if you work through this book, you'll experience similar material to what I would take you through if you were training directly with me in one of my Azure training programs, while also having an organized study guide for each of the topics and links to the official training modules in Microsoft Learn.

I'm confident that by completing modules on Microsoft Learn and the practical examples presented in this book on your own subscription, you will be well prepared to sit for the exam.

Finally, in order to ensure this book has what you are looking for, you can see all of the topics covered in this book by reviewing the chapters and topics in the table of contents. You'll find that the book lines up with the materials on Microsoft Learn and covers each of the major objectives listed on the exam page.

Preparing for the AZ-204 Exam

To complete this introduction, I'd like to take a moment to talk generally about Azure Certification exams and give you a bit of guidance to help you prepare for test day.

Important Microsoft Links

Before getting started, make a note of these invaluable links:

1. Azure Developer Exam (`https://learn.microsoft.com/en-us/certifications/exams/az-204`)

    This first link is your "home base" for Microsoft Learn materials around the AZ-204 Exam. This is where you can find all important links, including some of the following links, and also where you'll need to go to register for the exam.

Each chapter in the book lines up with this material and contains links to the various learning modules. As a static book can't keep up with live website changes, make sure to double-check this page if something doesn't line up after a few months.

2. AZ-204 Exam Study Guide from Microsoft (`https://query.prod.cms.rt.microsoft.com/cms/api/am/binary/RE4oZ7B`)

    This guide contains a bunch of the important links you'll want to review, including things like the change log, how to renew, how to view your Learn profile, and other important information about the exam.

    Along with this information, the documents have flat links to the major concepts you'll need to be in command of. Concepts as listed are also presented in more detail through the course of this book and in Appendix A.

3. Exam Sandbox (`https://aka.ms/examdemo`)

    If you've never taken an exam before with Microsoft, this site will be worth your time. In this exam sandbox, you'll learn what types of questions you may encounter, how to mark questions for review or feedback, and the general flow of an exam. Take a minute to do this so you can see how the pages flow, because it can be confusing and even scary with a feeling of "where's my score?" because just when you think you'll see it, you don't.

4. Schedule your Exam (`https://go.microsoft.com/
    fwlink/?linkid=2188679`)

    As with the other links, if something changes, this
    link is easily found on the main AZ-204 Exam page,
    where you can register for the exam.

5. Microsoft Certifications Practice Assessments
    (`https://learn.microsoft.com/en-us/
    certifications/practice-assessments-for-
    microsoft-certifications`)

    Find the practice assessment for AZ-204:
    Developing Solutions for Microsoft Azure and click
    the link to practice and discern your readiness for
    the exam.

Why Should You Get Certified?

I assume that since you are reading this, you are looking to get certified
and I don't need to convince you of all the benefits. Just in case you are
on the fence and reading this in a preview mode or still wondering if you
should take the exam, here are some benefits of certification validated in
this document: (`https://learn.microsoft.com/certifications/posts/
microsoft-learn-why-get-certified`):

- Enjoy potential career benefits like higher salary, more
  responsibilities, and/or promotion

- Publicly validate your knowledge of the topics and
  concepts

- Add the achievement to your resume to get noticed by
  hiring managers

- Become a Microsoft Certified Trainer (MCT)

I added this last one because if you are interested in becoming an MCT, this certification will be half of the qualification you need. You also need to get a valid technical training certification and then apply to the program, but this exam is one that qualifies you for the program.

Shameless Self-Promotion

I would also like to point you to a video that I made last year regarding the benefits of getting certified. In that video, I discuss the exam experience and talk about a number of additional resources you can leverage in your general study. You can find the video at https://training. majorguidancesolutions.com/courses/blog-posts-and-talks/ contents/622a5be022172.

Scheduling, Taking, and Passing the Exam

By the end of this book, you'll be confident and ready to schedule the exam. This last section will help answer many of your questions about the exam. I want to point out, however, that there are some things that I can't discuss due to the NDA requirements of the exam. This will hold true for you as well. For this reason, please do not ever ask me if "Topic X" will be on the exam, or things like "How many questions did you get on Topic Y?". These are pieces of information that cannot be discussed. I am confident that after working through this material, you will be prepared for the exam. These kinds of questions won't matter to you any more, because you'll be ready to display your knowledge when the exam starts.

Important   Always use your personal email for all exam registrations and badges. This will live with you forever, regardless of your company and/or affiliations with any institutions. With the exception of getting a free exam for military or education emails, you will want to ensure that you have *full* control over your information. It is *not* easy to transfer your certifications once an email has been used to take the exam.

Purchasing the Exam

This section guides you through the registration process.

Registering for the Exam

To register for the exam, you need to go to the exam home page (`https://learn.microsoft.com/en-us/certifications/exams/az-204`) and click the big yellow button that says Schedule Exam. Note that the cost of the exam (currently $165 in the United States) is also displayed here. Your cost may vary slightly. If you completed a cloud skills challenge, which are sometimes offered, or if you have received a voucher in another way, you will still need to register through this page and enter your voucher later.

Confirming Your Information

The next page asks you to confirm your information, including your name, address, email, and preferred language. You can typically take any of the exams in English or in a number of other languages based on what makes the most sense to you.

You are also asked to check a couple of boxes to opt in for some marketing and offers. You must check the box that reads "I have read and agree to the terms ...".

Leveraging any Discounts

If you have any discounts, such as program offers for military, education, etc., you may see those on this next page. If you do not have any discounts, you can check to see if you have by entering your email. If you have a discount, select it to apply the discount. If not, just move to the Scheduling page.

Note that vouchers are not entered on this page; they are entered at the end of the purchase process.

Scheduling the Exam

The next page allows you to choose how you will take the exam. Will you take the exam in a center or from home? Let's consider the potential benefits and drawbacks of each.

Taking the Exam at a Test Center

If you can do this, you might choose this option, especially if this is your first Microsoft exam.

The benefits of taking the exam at a test center are many:

- You get a live proctor

- You are in a secure testing location

- You get an ability to use a dry-erase scratchboard

- You can raise your hand to take a break

- If the center can't provide you with Internet access, you get to reschedule

Some of the drawbacks of using a test center are as follows:

- Limited appointment times and days

- You must drive there or get to the center

- It can potentially be more difficult to reschedule

When you choose the test center option, you get the benefit of having a live proctor. This means you can rely on the center for providing a secure location to take the test and you will have a bit more flexibility (you can raise your hand for a restroom break, for example). Your stuff will be locked in a cabinet somewhere so you can't get to it but you know it's safe. At a test center, you can use scratch-paper, and you don't have to worry about any problems connecting to the exam and/or getting rescheduled if something is wrong with the Internet.

Taking the Exam from Home

Once you have experienced an exam or if you need more flexibility, this is likely the best option for you.

Some of the benefits of taking the exam from home are as follows:

- Flexible scheduling, 24 hours, 7 days a week.

- You don't have to drive anywhere.

- You can easily reschedule up to 24 hours before the exam starts, as many times as you need, when you don't feel prepared or if you get sick or know that you won't be able to have a clean space to take the exam.

Some of the drawbacks of taking the exam from home are as follows:

- You must have a clean workspace (no other monitors plugged in, no paper in sight, if you have a whiteboard it must be wiped clean and out of reach, and all devices must be out of reach). I've been asked to remove a tissue box before, and one time the light behind me coming through the blinds was too bright so I had to prove the shade was down (you can't have a window behind you that someone could be looking through).

- You must be on camera at all times.

- You must have your microphone on at all times.

- You are responsible for proper Internet access.

- Your machine can't have any other services running, including anti-virus (it has blocked the exam software before and vice versa).

- If anyone enters the room during your exam, you are immediately disqualified.

- If anyone talks to you during the exam or if you talk out loud, you are immediately disqualified.

As you can see, it sounds pretty scary to take an exam from home with all the restrictions. That being said, it's actually a great experience and how I prefer to take exams at this point. I can schedule them at 10 PM when everyone is in bed, and I take them from a coworking office I rent for the three hours around the exam. Usually, there are no issues with anyone else even being in the building.

Home-Based Exam Test Program

If you choose the home-based exam, you need to run a system test on your computer. This will download the program used to run the test. Make sure you do this on the machine you intend to test from, from the location you intend to test from. You will also see information about the testing space and a short video on what to expect.

Bringing Your Photo ID

No matter where you take the test, you need a government-issued photo ID, such as a driver's license or a passport. In some instances, you may need a secondary validation method, such as a credit card with your name on it. If you are taking the test from home, you'll take an image of this ID and send it to your proctor. Be prepared with more than one ID just in case something doesn't work. I typically use my passport, but it is shiny and that can sometimes cause issues with the image, so my driver's license can back me up in that case.

Choosing Your Preferred Language

Next, you'll be prompted to pick the language you want to use for the exam. Pick the one that makes sense to you.

Confirming Your Choice and Agreeing to Terms

No matter which option you choose, you must confirm your consent on a couple of screens. The home option has a number of additional confirmations based on the fact that you agree to facial recognition and other privacy things. Agree to the terms and conditions of taking the test or you won't be able to complete the registration.

Make sure to read through these terms if you've never taken an exam before. There are a number of important pieces of information on these screens.

Included on these pages is all the pertinent information about the reschedule policy, how to check in, and all the acceptable forms of ID you can use.

Note that a number of the paragraphs have a checkbox next to them. You must manually check each one to prove you read the page.

Choosing Your Proctor Language (Home-Based)

If you are taking the home-based test, a second prompt will appear, asking if you want the proctor to speak English or another language like Japanese.

Confirming Your Time Zone and Selecting an Appointment Time (Home-Based)

If you are taking the exam from home, your next page has you confirm the time zone and select a date and time. You then get a default option for that day, but you can modify that by selecting to view all times. Make sure you find a time that gives you about 30 minutes before the exam to get set up and ensure you are where you need to be, logged in, and having gone through all of the sign-in requirements to take the exam.

Finding a Test Center (Test-Center)

If you are taking the exam from a test center, you next pick the center where you want to take a test, and then find their times and schedule your exam.

Completing the Exam Registration

When you have all of the details ironed out, book the exam and pay for it. You can choose to add a Measure-Up test at this point if you want, which is an additional fee but gives you 30 days to run practice test questions. This is optional, so do not feel like you have to purchase the practice test.

Taking the Exam

Taking the exam is the stressful part of this whole process.

I'm not going to go into the details of the exam (number of questions, etc.), as that is irrelevant. It's an exam with questions, you'll get enough to ascertain your knowledge and more than you likely want, but it can vary from test to test and the experience could be different from today to tomorrow.

Take the practice exam and know it will be similar to that experience, with questions that line up with the practice formats. Read the test as you go so you can get instructions as to how to answer each question. Is it single option? Do you need to have two answers? Does the answer need to be in order? That is all displayed on the screen as you go.

The main thing to know about this exam is that you need to allow for a minimum of three hours for the exam experience.

- 15-30 minutes prior to get set up/get to the center

- ~2.5 hours for the exam, feedback, surveys, and cleanup (you may be done much more quickly, depending on how well you know the material)

- 15-30 minutes or more after for celebration or reflection

When it comes to the exam, here are a few hints I can give you on how I work through any exam:

- Do not cram. You either know it or you don't. Cramming just stresses you out and taxes your brain. You're better off just watching a movie, playing a game, or reading for leisure and giving your mind a break the night before an exam.

- Be early. You will be nervous anyway, so just get there early and do some breathing exercises or meditation.

- Make sure you aren't hungry or lacking energy and that you won't have to go to the restroom during the test.

- Think logically. Use your skills to discern answers that can't possibly be correct and eliminate them. When presented with a question that you don't know, make your best guess, then mark it for review. Keep it in your mind, in case questions later in the exam help you remember the answer.

- Review every question at the end. If you know it, just skip through it. If you were uncertain, give it one last look (time permitting).

- Limit your feedback. Even though you can give feedback on any question, you only have five or ten minutes to do this. Choose wisely about what and how you will say what's on your mind regarding a question. If it was too hard, make it known. If you felt it wasn't relevant, then say that. If it was just confusing, then say that too.

- Some sections are one and done. This means you should take a bit longer on each and make sure you have read the question thoroughly every time you need to select an answer in case the question has changed and you didn't notice.

- If you get a scenario or a lab (not guaranteed but entirely possible), you will want to review it well. I generally approach these by reading the general information quickly, then looking at the question, then reviewing the scenario to ensure I can find the best answer to the question.

- Always try to find the best answer to a question, not just the one that looks right.

What You Should Do Immediately After the Exam

I have two things that I do immediately after an exam.

When I pass, I get a Reese's Peanut Butter cup and a Diet Mt. Dew. Yes, that is how I celebrate. You should reward yourself with something—coffee/tea/drink/sweet treat. You earned it, and you need to mark this moment with something you'll always remember. I also reflect during this time, mostly if there is something I know I can work on based on the questions I just reviewed.

When I fail, I reflect on the exam. What were the questions like? What gave me trouble (concepts/terms/services/etc.)? Is there a concept or term I had never heard of? What do I think I got right but I'm not sure about? Is there clearly something I need to get better at? I write it out so that I have a plan of attack, along with the exam report (covered later).

When You've Passed the Exam, What Happens?

At the end of the exam, you receive a score. Congratulations, you passed. The score report shows where you did well and where you did well enough. You get confirmation that you passed.

At a test center, you get to print this out and bring it home. Online, you just say "OK" and hope that it goes through (it always does, but it's still scary because you don't have that piece of paper).

Reviewing Your Email

Within a few hours, you'll get an email that congratulates you. In that email will be a link to claim your badge.

Claiming Your Badge

You do this via a website called Credly. Make sure you register ahead of time for this site and use your personal email. When you click the link to claim your badge, things will just work.

Sharing Your Badge

Do some shameless self-promotion and put that badge on your LinkedIn and Twitter accounts (and any other social media you want to share it on).

Reviewing Your Learn Profile

Ensure that your certification shows up on your Microsoft Learn Profile. This is also where you go to renew your certification each year (all exams that are not fundamentals must be renewed yearly).

Renewing is easy and free, so don't stress. You can take the renewal assessment over and over again, it's open book, and you don't pay anything to take it, so just make sure you do this so your certification doesn't expire.

Also note that you'll get an email 180 and 90 days out that reminds you to renew your certification. You can see what certifications need to be renewed in your Microsoft Learn Profile at any time.

What If You Didn't Pass the Exam?

Okay, it happens. You worked hard, showed up, and didn't pass. The first thing you need to do is give yourself some grace. These exams are hard and you may have to take them over to really understand what is being asked as well as the depth and breadth of the exam.

Do Not Be Defeated   You should not expect to pass every exam on the first try. Instead, use this moment to refocus and commit to doing the work to pass on your next attempt. Make that attempt soon (such as within four weeks). You have momentum and you need to use it now, or you will lose that momentum along with not passing the exam.

Reviewing Your Score

When you don't pass, you get your score. It will be less than the required 700 to pass, but it will likely be somewhere near that (hurting even more when it feels like just one more correct answer would have made the difference). No matter what, the report is now your best friend.

On the report, look for the "three areas you can improve." The report will show you your weaknesses in regard to the concepts on the exam. Use that to focus your efforts for your next attempt. You still want to review more than just these three things, but these are the "needle movers" that might take you over the hump to pass.

Review the bar chart and identify any other areas that hurt you.

You didn't get to write the questions down, but surely there was that one question you can remember that was about something you never expected. What was that again? Go read about it and make sure you won't ever be stumped on a question like that again. (Even if it that question doesn't show up in your retake, you learned something new and that's awesome.)

Scheduling Your Retake

Yes, it hurts, and yes, it is expensive. Even so, put that retake on your calendar right now, even if it's 30/60/90/120 days out. Put it on your calendar so you will force yourself to keep working on this. If you say, "I will do it later," then I promise you that two years later you'll be thinking about how you should retake that exam, but now it's potentially changed and you may have a lot more work ahead of you. I recommend retaking 28-42 days from the original failure (4-6 weeks, ideally). Anything earlier might be a futile effort, and longer than that you start to lose momentum and desire.

Please Share Your Results with Me

Okay, as I close this out, I assume you have purchased this book, and that you have taken the time to review it. I want to hear about how you did on the exam (good or bad). I would love to know your honest opinion of the text and how well you felt it prepared you for the exam. Please connect with me on LinkedIn (https://www.linkedin/in/brianlgorman) or Twitter (@blgorman).

If you passed the exam, let's celebrate. If you didn't, I want to help you get there, so please reach out so I can work with you to find ways to help you get over the final hump.

Also, one last thing. I struggle with social interactions, and I go to a lot of conferences and speak. If you happen to be at one and you would like to chat, please don't hesitate to talk with me if you see me in person. I would be honored to hear your story and find out more about how this book or anything else in your journey has helped you to move toward your goals.

Let's do this!

PART I

Develop for Azure

CHAPTER 1

Azure Storage Ecosystem: Overview and Development with Azure Blob Storage

Whenever I run an AZ-204 (Azure Developer Fundamentals) training session, I always start with Azure Storage. Storage is not necessarily sexy, and it's not the first thing you often think about when getting ready to study for an Azure exam. However, storage is the essential backbone to pretty much anything you do in Azure.

Do you need to work with the Azure cloud shell? You're going to need a backing storage account. Would you like to host a virtual machine (VM) in Azure? I bet you can already guess where your virtual disks are housed. Would you like to create a Big Data pipeline that utilizes a data lake? How about a simple Azure Function application? Perhaps you just need a place to share documents quickly and easily, with versioning capabilities and access restrictions. Maybe you would like to host a static website and/or a CDN for your static web assets. These solutions, and many more, require and/or leverage storage in some way.

© Brian L. Gorman 2023
B. L. Gorman, *Developing Solutions for Microsoft Azure Certification Companion*,
Certification Study Companion Series, https://doi.org/10.1007/978-1-4842-9300-3_1

Even though storage isn't likely the first thing on your mind (and may actually be the one thing where you think "I got this"), it is still a great place to start as a foundation for the rest of your learning. Additionally, storage is typically one of the easiest topics to master. For these reasons, it makes a great deal of sense to kick off with a review and exploration of Azure Storage.

Over the next few pages, you're presented with a high-level overview of many of the major concepts regarding Azure Storage that you will want to be in command of before sitting for the AZ-204 Exam.

General Information about Azure Storage

Almost everything you will encounter in Azure has some sort of hierarchy involved, and this will almost always play out in your development experience. Additionally, many services in Azure require a unique Fully Qualified Domain Name (FQDN). This is a name that is accessible from anywhere on the Internet, such as microsoft.com or yourcompany.org. For this reason, start to establish this pattern recognition now, as it will likely play out in one or many scenarios as you build code samples. Additionally, this knowledge of the hierarchy of services is a good thing to be in command of when you sit for the exam.

Azure Storage has a hierarchy that typically looks something like Account ➤ Type of Account ➤ Object. For example, Azure Blob Storage will always have an account that contains one or more containers, and each container has one or more binary large objects (blobs). A *blob* is typically a serialized binary object referenced in code via a byte array (byte[ ]). For example, any image or document serialized to a byte[ ] as well as strings and fully-serialized JSON objects all store one binary object. Consider the hierarchy presented in Figure 1-1, where each blob could be something entirely different, such as an image file, a Word document, or any other object as a byte[ ] of data.

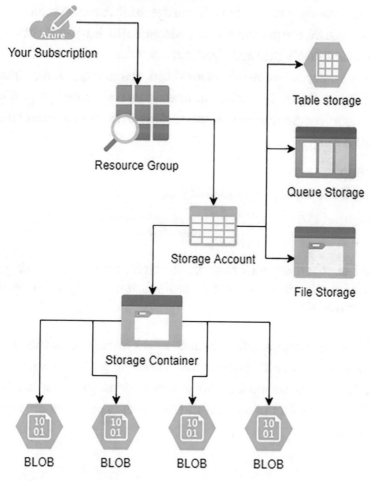

Figure 1-1. *A hierarchical representation of a storage account with
a container, some blobs, and some potential table, queue, and file
storage implementations*

Along with the hierarchy, the URL for each service is important,
because the public-facing URL for storage will make some of your data (set
by you) available over HTTPS protocols.

Since the Azure Storage account must have a unique FQDN across all
of Azure, you likely won't be able to create an account with a name such as
myStorage, since someone else has likely already used that name.

This would translate to `https://mystorage.blob.core.windows.net`.
With your FQDN, the pattern for accessing the URL is typically `https://`
`your-account-name.storage-type.core.windows.net/some-resource`,
where `your-account-name` is 3-24 lowercase characters that are either
a-z or 0-9 only. Figure 1-2 highlights how Azure will remind you when
your storage account name does not conform to the limitations of the
naming schema.

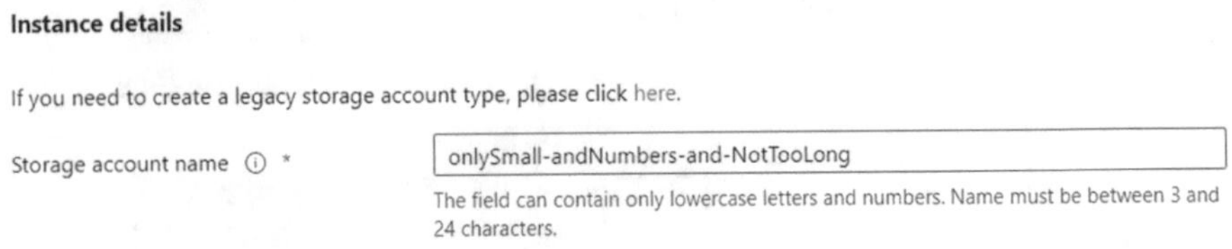

Instance details

If you need to create a legacy storage account type, please click here.

Storage account name ⓘ * | onlySmall-andNumbers-and-NotTooLong |

The field can contain only lowercase letters and numbers. Name must be between 3 and 24 characters.

Figure 1-2. *Creating a storage account with improper naming will generate an error in the portal. It reminds you when your account name is invalid*

All storage accounts will contain access keys that can be used to
connect to the storage account via the Azure Storage Software Developer
Kit (SDK). Keys can be rotated. The connection string is a combination of
the unique FQDN for the account and the primary or secondary key (see
Figure 1-3).

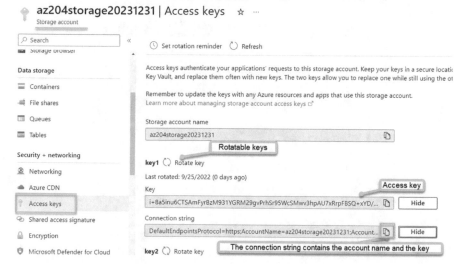

Figure 1-3. *Reviewing a storage account on the Access Keys blade to get the connection string. Note the ability to rotate the keys at will*

Types of Azure Storage

When it comes to storage, you might think mostly of blob storage. However, there are four types of storage that you can utilize within a storage account. The four types are *Containers*, *Tables*, *Queues*, and *File Shares*, as highlighted in Figure 1-4.

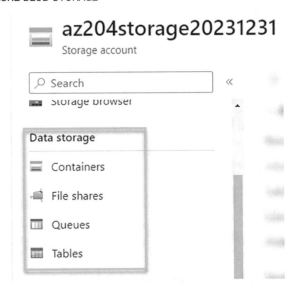

Figure 1-4. *The four types of storage are highlighted in the left
navigation menu on the storage account*

How you utilize storage is entirely up to you and your team. It's
important to note that there really are few restrictions when it comes to
how you structure your storage account. You can have one account for
container storage, another for table storage, and another for file or queue
storage. You can also have one storage account that has some combination
of one or more of each type.

The bulk of the AZ-204 material covers developing solutions against
Azure Blob Storage. For the most part, therefore, you'll home in on blob
storage in this review, but it's still a good idea to start with a look at each of
the four types of storage, so you can ascertain the correct type of storage
for any solution that might be presented, either on real-world projects or
on the exam.

Azure Container (Blob) Storage

As a developer, a great deal of the work you do with storage will likely be working with code against container (blob) storage. As mentioned earlier, a binary large object (blob) is typically an object that has been serialized to binary, leveraged as a *byte array* (byte[]), and then uploaded to or retrieved from storage as an immutable blob. Later in the chapter, you learn how to work directly with blob storage using code, and a challenge will follow for you to implement a solution utilizing C# and Azure Blob Storage.

In addition to understanding what a blob is, it is important to know how Azure Blob Storage stores different types of blobs, because the way blobs are stored determines the maximum size of the blob and how you can interact with the blob. There are three types of blob storage that you can select, and each type is important for various workloads.

Finally, it is important to understand that as you create a storage account, you also need to create a container in which to store your blobs. You can have many containers in a storage account, with different access levels and different default tiers. (Figure 1-5 shows a potential storage account with multiple containers.)

Figure 1-5.   *The storage account can have multiple containers. Each container can have its own public or private access*

Depending on your settings when you create the storage account, some system containers will be generated, such as the $logs container shown in Figure 1-5. These containers cannot be deleted. However, the contents of a $ container are mutable/able to be deleted, but you should do so with caution. The $logs container is where Azure Storage is logging requests, so if you delete/modify the logs, you are essentially removing the ability to trace through requests.

Block Blobs

The main type of storage you'll work with in typical code for interaction with Azure Blob Storage is the *block* blob. The blob itself that you upload is broken into chunks called *blocks*. This breaking up of the data is a mechanism to allow the throughput of the blob to be optimized over the network.

When you upload a blob to Azure Blob Storage, you can choose the size of the blocks, which can be anywhere from 64 Kilobytes (KB) in size to 100 Megabytes (MB) in size. The typical default for blocks is 4 Mebibytes (MiB) in size. The maximum number of blocks that can be utilized is 50,000. Therefore, if you choose a size of 64 KB, the maximum size of your blob in Azure Blob Storage is 64*50,000, which is 3,200,000 KB (or 3.2 GB). If you choose the maximum size of 100 MiB, you get 100 MiB* 50,000, which is 5,000,000 MiB, which translates to around 4.75 TiB (Tebibyte).

Recent updates to some tiers and preview versions put the block maximum size to up to 4000 MiB, making the maximum size a massive 190.7 TiB. If you want more information about these limits, you can read more at https://docs.microsoft.com/rest/api/storageservices/ Understanding-Block-Blobs--Append-Blobs--and-Page-Blobs.

The typical use case for block blobs will be for most of your typical objects that you store in the container. This can include images, videos, documents, and serialized objects. Figure 1-6 highlights some options when uploading a block blob.

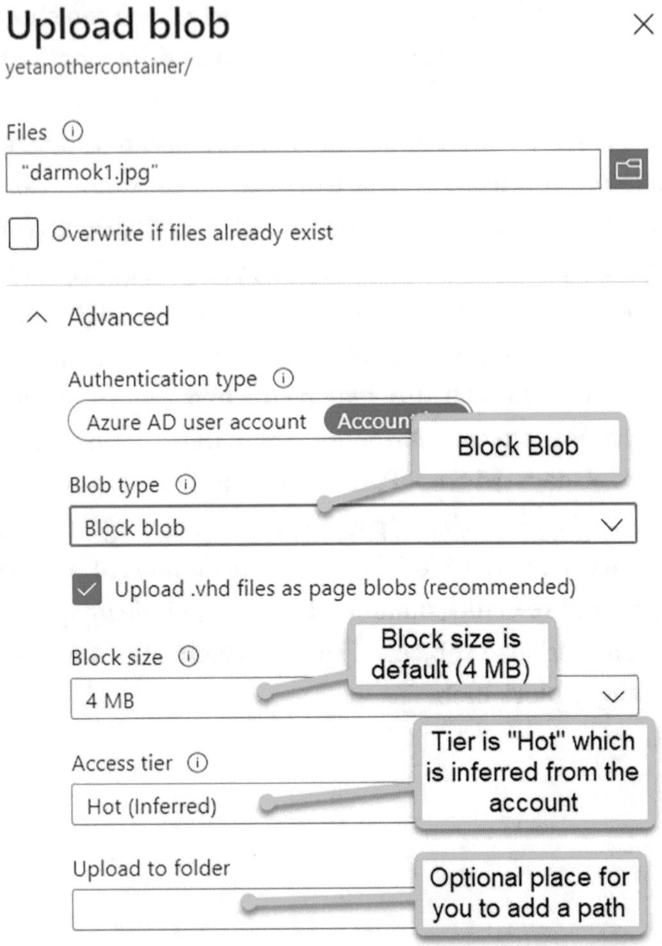

Figure 1-6. Creation of a block blob with options selected for the block size and initial tier. Callouts also note the ability to set a folder path

Append Blobs

The second type of blob storage that you can use is the *append* blob. The append blob is also a block blob but is optimized for only adding blocks to the end of the blob.

This *end-only* optimization creates an ideal scenario for utilization when writing to a log file, where you are continuously writing new information that is appended, and the original information is unchanged.

The append blob cannot modify the existing blobs, as it is optimized only to modify the blob by appending additional blobs to the end of the blob.

Page Blobs

Page blobs are a specialized storage type that is optimized for storing virtual disks. Typically, at this point, when you provision a new VM, you will utilize a managed disk and not worry about any of this underlying architecture, as Azure will now manage the storage of the disk for you. However, you may encounter legacy VMs in Azure or scenarios where an unmanaged disk was provisioned into a storage account. In any scenario, to be correctly applied, the storage account for the disk, whether managed or managed, should be stored as a page blob.

It is important to note that page blobs are stored in 512-byte pages. When writing to page blobs, the write operations are happening in 512-byte chunks and can utilize an offset to hit the specific pages. The maximum simultaneous write operation is 4 TiB. The maximum size for a page blob is 8 TiB.

Managed disks are typically solid-state drives (SSDs) and are going to reside in the premium tier to maximize throughput. An unmanaged disk can leverage standard storage or premium storage, depending on your need for throughput and the type of hard drive that is backing the compute for your machine.

Azure Table Storage

The second type of storage you may utilize is Azure *Table* Storage. If you are looking for a way to take advantage of quick, easy, and inexpensive key-value pair (KVP) NoSQL storage without utilizing a *Cosmos DB* account, then Azure Table Storage is your answer.

13

With a table storage account, you can utilize code to read and write and work with structured NoSQL data, which can be referenced by key and/or cluster index consisting of the primary key and row key. There are some great advantages to this approach and also some limitations. You'll take a closer look at the capabilities of the Table API for Cosmos DB in the next chapter, where you learn about a few of the benefits of switching to the Table API.

Should you already have a table storage account or just want to avoid using Cosmos DB, the good news is that now there is an SDK that lets you easily work against either table storage or the table API for Cosmos DB.

Good candidates for utilization of table storage include storing simple settings for users in your applications and using table storage to de-normalize data and quickly and easily make this data available to many applications.

Table storage is scalable, but you won't get the robust global replication you might need unless you move to Cosmos DB. In high-availability/high-throughput scenarios, you can make a read-only replica of your table storage in a secondary region, but you will only be able to write to the primary region.

The URL for table storage will follow a common pattern that you'll see for each of the storage types. The Table Storage URL always looks as follows:

```
https://<your-storage-account-name>.table.core.windows.
net/<table>
```

You'll see the contrast to this in the next section for the Cosmos DB, where `table.core.windows.net` becomes `table.cosmosdb.Azure.com`.

The hierarchy for table storage contains the top-level account, followed by the table. Within the table, you will encounter the entities, and within entities, properties. The properties are the NoSQL KVPs. When you build your code, you will need to connect to the account with a connection string, then leverage the table/entity/property.

Entities in Azure Table Storage are limited to a maximum size of 1MB.

Each property will have some common properties and then the data that can be anything you want it to be. The properties are a timestamp, a row key, and a partition key.

Designing Your Data

When it comes to working with data in a NoSQL document store, it is important to know that you aren't building relational data. As such, joining data across documents is not generally possible and a need to do so would be an immediate indication of a design flaw in the architecture.

Without a relational structure, what do you do with your data and how do you optimize it in certain scenarios? The answer to this question really depends on your application. Will you need to maximize for writing or reading? Will there be a ton of ad hoc or disparate queries against the data, or can you define a couple of queries that encompass the majority of your needs?

Both table storage and Cosmos DB rely heavily on partitioning data by utilizing the correct property as the partition key. Where the partition key comes in is how to efficiently group that data for your solution. Indeed, a Cosmos DB has the ability to do multiple indexes, where table storage only has one index, so already you might be thinking that would be a better place to store this data. You get a chance to dive deeper into structuring NoSQL data for optimization in the next chapter.

For this examination of table storage, know that the index is always the partition key and row key combined. With that knowledge, you can be assured that the best performance comes for a query when both are named directly, with no variability.

Azure Queue Storage

The third type of storage you need to be in command of is *Azure Queue Storage*. As you learn more about cloud-native, microservices, and serverless development, you will likely need a messaging solution to help communicate among disparate components. One option for a messaging solution is Azure Queue Storage. In a later chapter on messaging, you get a chance to dive deeper into Azure Queue Storage and see how it compares with the Service Bus Queue/Topic messaging service in Azure.

A couple of quick pieces of information about queue storage that you'll need to be aware of:

- You can store massive amounts of small messages in the Azure Storage Queue.

- Messages automatically expire after seven (7) days.

Azure File Storage

If you are like me and you see the word "File" followed by storage, you might think something like "This must be where I put all my files." Well, you are correct and incorrect at the same time. Azure File Storage is a solution that is designed to help a team migrate a Storage Area Network (SAN) drive from an on-premises data center into the cloud. Azure File Storage is not for storing the images and/or videos that you are hosting for public or private consumption from your website.

Therefore, to distinguish the correct scenario for utilization of Azure File Storage, it is important to remember that any file can also be a blob. For example, images or videos for a website will likely be stored as blobs in blob storage. If your scenario is creating a shared network storage solution in Azure, or the purpose is replacing a shared storage solution like Dropbox or OneDrive, then the correct solution is Azure File Storage.

Another important aspect of Azure File Storage is the fact that
Server Message Block 3.0 (SMB 3.0) protocols utilize it. This means that
any existing solution you have can easily be pointed at the Azure File
Storage solution and the code and/or settings you configured for existing
applications should just work. In addition to SMB 3.0, Azure File Storage
also utilizes the Network File System (NFS) protocol.

When you create your file storage, you'll need to choose which
protocol you want to use, as you can't utilize both in the same file storage
instance. You can, however, have side-by-side file storage implementations
in the same Azure Storage account.

Blob Storage

Table storage is covered in the next chapter and queue storage is covered
in Chapter 13. File storage is a bit outside of the scope of the AZ-204 Exam,
as file storage is typically more important for the administration and
solution architect paths. Therefore, the remainder of this chapter looks
exclusively at utilization of Azure Blob Storage, including how to work with
blob storage from C# code.

Storage Account Performance Tiers

When you provision an Azure Storage account, you'll need to configure
a number of options on it. One of the options you'll need to choose is the
correct performance tier. The choice of tier will have a direct effect on
pricing and the overall throughput of the storage account. There are two
tiers from which to choose when creating storage—*Premium* and *Standard*
(see Figure 1-7).

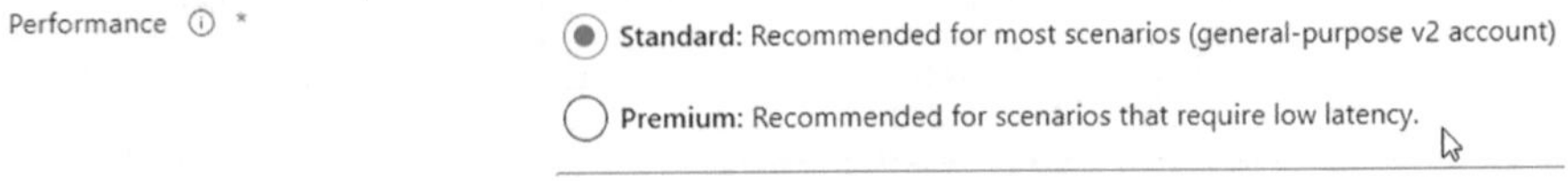

Performance ⓘ *   ◉ **Standard:** Recommended for most scenarios (general-purpose v2 account)

                               ○ **Premium:** Recommended for scenarios that require low latency.

Figure 1-7. *The two choices for storage performance tier are Standard and Premium*

Standard Tier

In general, standard storage is adequate for workloads that do not need a maximized throughput (low latency). For example, serving files and storing documents are great candidates for a standard account.

Premium Tier

Workloads that require a lower latency or a private network will be better served in a premium tier. Good use cases for a premium account include storing and accessing SSD disks, streaming larger audio and video files frequently, or building a private network endpoint to connect to storage from other Azure resources over a private connection.

Storage Account Redundancy

An additional choice when provisioning a storage account is the level of redundancy that you want. Do you need to have resilience across regions? Do you care to have resilience across zones within a region? Do you want both? In addition to resiliency, do you also need the ability to read the storage from a secondary region? These are the questions you need to answer when selecting the storage redundancy.

In general, all storage account blobs in the hot tier have an SLA of 99.9% (three nines). However, accounts with Read Access and Geo Redundancy (GRS-RA) have a Service Level Agreement (SLA) of 99.99%

(four nines) for read operations. Additionally, cool and archive storage
have a lower SLA of just 99 (two nines) for everything but GRS-RA, and
GRS-RA has a guarantee of 99.9% (three nines) for read operations. Also
note that availability (SLA)—the ability to access the service in Azure—is
not the same thing as durability of the objects, which is the integrity of
the data without loss or corruption. Figure 1-8 shows the options for the
storage account. Note that the option for Read Access is a checkbox that is
only available when one of the geo-replication options is selected.

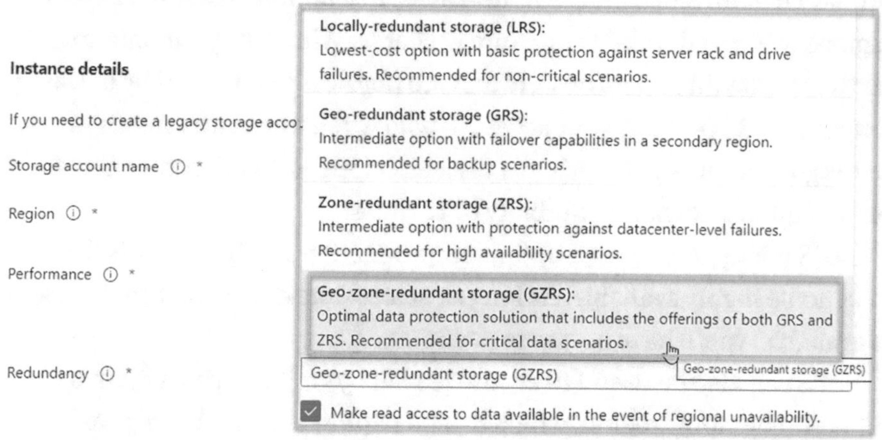

Figure 1-8. *The options for storage data resiliency and redundancy
are presented, with GZRS-RA selected in this image*

Locally Redundant Storage (LRS)

Locally Redundant Storage (LRS) is the least expensive and least resilient
storage option. With LRS, you get redundant storage within the data center
across three fault domains (three disks on different racks), but you do not
get any additional redundancy. As this option is not replicated to any other
regions (or zones), there is no option for read access at this level of storage.

Example scenarios where you might choose LRS are development and
test environments and any other solutions where high availability and
resiliency are not required. LRS guarantees at least 11 nines durability of
objects.

Zone-Redundant Storage (ZRS)

Zone-Redundant Storage (ZRS) uses the availability zones within your
primary region. Since ZRS requires zones, this option is only available in
regions where redundant zones are available. With ZRS, your data spans
across at least three data centers that are physically separated by at least
ten miles. ZRS protects your access to data when one center needs to
undergo maintenance or when a disaster happens and doesn't affect the
entire region. ZRS has a durability of 12 nines.

ZRS is a recommended option for production-ready accounts that
need to be highly available. As long as at least one data center in the region
is available, you'll have access to your data.

ZRS can also be useful to ensure resiliency while staying within a
limited geographic region, which can be required in some compliance
scenarios.

Geo-Redundant Storage (GRS)

Geo-Redundant Storage (GRS) is similar to LRS, as your data is once again
replicated to at least three fault domains in a single zone within your
primary region. Additionally, your data is also replicated to one data center
in a secondary region. Within the secondary region, your storage is also
replicated to three fault domains as LRS. GRS has a durability of 16 nines.

Scenarios for GRS include any solution that needs to be available in
case of a regional failure. Although the data is not available, if your primary
region fails, then the data in the secondary region can temporarily become
the primary region and your work can continue without interruption.

Geo-Zone-Redundant Storage (GZRS)

Geo-Zone-Redundant Storage (GZRS) is the next step in resiliency and availability. As you might expect at this point, GZRS is similar to ZRS, but also includes the failover (secondary) region. In this scenario, the primary region replicates the data across at least three data centers. The secondary region is again implemented as LRS, and the data in the secondary region is not available for read/write operations unless the secondary region is temporarily made primary during regional failures. GZRS has a durability of 16 nines.

Geo-Redundant Storage with Read Access (GRS-RA)

Geo-Redundant Storage with Read Access (GRS-RA) gives you the ability to have all of the benefits of GRS (including 16 nines durability) with the additional ability to read the data from the secondary region.

Geo-Zone-Redundant Storage with Read Access (GZRS-RA)

Geo-Zone-Redundant Storage (GZRS-RA) is similar to GZRS and also gives you the ability to read data from the secondary region.

Read-Access Storage and Development of Your Applications

With either the GRS-RA or GZRS-RA redundancy, your storage can be read by applications from the secondary region. In order to achieve this functionality, the primary URL for the storage account will be the same as the original storage account but will contain -secondary as part of

the account. The storage account keys will work in either the primary or
the secondary region, so you can use this knowledge to configure your
applications to read from the secondary region.

Blob Storage Tiers

Within a blob storage account, each individual blob can have one of three
tiers as an attribute to the blob. The tiers are *Hot*, *Cool*, and *Archive*.

Each of these tiers can exist in a single container, and containers can
have a default setting to be either hot or cool. If the default setting is hot,
then any blob uploaded to the container will be optimized for hot storage.
Service lifecycles can be used to move blobs from hot to cool, hot to
archive, cool to hot, and/or cool to archive. Moving a blob from archive to
either hot or cool requires some manual intervention.

One important point to remember is that while it may be the case in
many scenarios, moving between tiers is not a stair-stepping operation.
Blobs can be moved directly from hot to cool or directly from hot to
archive. Blobs can also be moved from archive to either cool or hot storage.
As expected, blobs can also be moved from cool to hot or archive storage.

When you create the storage account, you set the tier default, which
can be only cool or hot. Note that the default setting is not a requirement
for new blobs. When you upload a blob, you can specify a tier. Therefore,
the default storage tier will be leveraged for blobs that are uploaded
without specifically overriding the access tier (see Figure 1-9).

Figure 1-9. *Creating an account presents a chance to set the default
to hot or cool tier as the default access level for new blobs*

Hot Storage

Hot storage is an optimization for your blob that minimizes the cost for access and throughput. Since throughput cost is optimized, in the hot tier, the cost to store blobs is higher.

Consider a scenario where you have a document or image that will be accessed frequently throughout the day by multiple applications and/or users. This might include blobs like your web images, documents that are frequently reviewed, and other important, highly visible storage assets.

In this scenario, since the blob needs to be accessed often, your maximized cost option is to keep the blob in hot storage.

Cool Storage

Cool storage is an optimization for your blob that minimizes the cost of storage while allowing access to the blob. Since the storage is optimized, blobs in the cool tier are going to cost more to access. For this reason, you want to utilize cool storage when your document may have limited use or access but still needs to be readily available.

Consider a scenario where you have generated a monthly billing report and you need to keep the billing reports available even when they aren't utilized much after the first 30 days. In this scenario, users may need to review the document for historical purposes, but it's unlikely that the document would be reviewed more than once or twice in a longer period of time. In this scenario, cool storage would be a great solution.

Archive Storage

Archive storage is for the blobs you need to keep but don't need to access without special reasons for that access. There is no direct access to an archive storage blob. To review or utilize the blob, you must first hydrate the storage blob item back to the cool or hot storage tier. The hydration of a blob from the archive tier to either the cool or hot tier can take a significant amount of time. Prior to recent releases, this rehydration period was up to 24 hours. Now there are options whereby you can pay more to get the data more quickly. If you create a high-priority request and your data is less than 10 GB, you may see it within an hour. For a standard request, you should expect around 15 hours before rehydration is completed. You have no other control other than to place the request for rehydration.

Scenarios for the use of archive storage include legal holds for important documents to keep in case you need to validate a statement of work or some other legal arbitration. Additional reasons to keep blobs in archive storage could be backup operations and other automations that ensure that you never lose state or data from a point-in-time, while also maximizing your value for your storage expenditures.

As noted, archive is not available as a default setting. However, when you upload a blob, you can set its access level to any tier, including archive (see Figure 1-10).

Figure 1-10. *New blobs can be uploaded with any of the three access tiers*

Automation of Tier Placement

When you upload a blob into storage, if you don't set the tier, then the
default tier for the container will be used. Typically, the default tier will be
the hot tier. In many cases, you will likely want to automate the lifecycle
of blobs so that administrators or developers don't waste time checking
and manually moving blobs across tiers. For this reason, Azure Storage
accounts have the ability to create lifecycle management rules.

Creating a lifecycle management rule allows the blob to be
automatically moved to a different tier. There are two conditions you can
use to check for automatic handling, which are `if` conditions based on
the *last modified* date or the *created* date. You can use one of these trigger
conditions with a date window of *"more than x days ago"* to automate the
handling of the blob. Figure 1-11 shows a lifecycle rule on the container
that moves blobs to cool storage after 30 days.

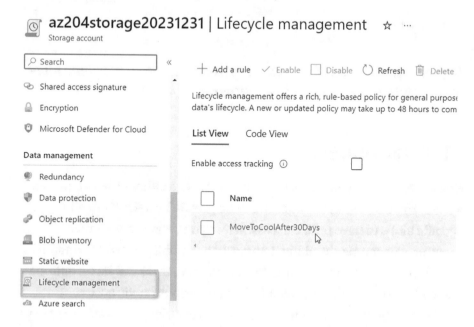

Figure 1-11. *A lifecycle access rule for blobs in the storage container
automatically moves blobs to cool storage 30 days after creation*

Handling the blob involves one of three options, which are *move to cool storage, move to archive storage,* or just *delete* the blob. Figure 1-12 shows the options when creating a rule.

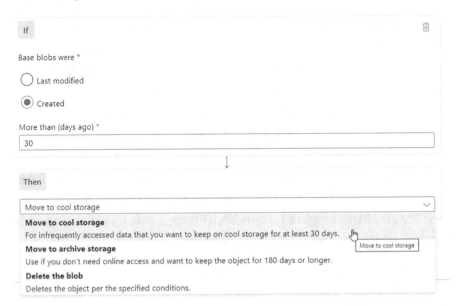

Figure 1-12. *Options for creating an automation rule include move to cool storage, move to archive storage, and delete*

Storage Access

Containers within your storage account can have either public or private access. You can also set a container to be private by default but allow specific blobs to have public access. When you create your storage account, you can set the ability to prevent any public access to containers and blobs. If you set the account level to private, there will be no option to make blobs or containers available for anonymous public access.

As you create your account, you also have options to create the storage account in a private network. When you place an account in a private network, only resources within that network or with configured access

through that network can access the storage account. The traffic on a
storage account with private access utilizes the Azure backbone and is
therefore more secure. If you do not utilize a private network, then traffic
for your storage account will typically go over the public Internet. Although
communication is encrypted and storage at rest is encrypted, you will
likely want to put sensitive accounts on a private network.

All blobs stored in container storage have the same URL pattern. The
pattern is the name of your storage account, followed by the blob storage
common URL, and then any information to identify the blob. This URL
always looks as follows:

```
https://<your-storage-account-name>.blob.core.windows.
net/<optional-folder/<blob-detail>.<blob-extension>
```

It is important to note that the storage account name is whatever you
created, but the folder structure is just a virtual identifier for the blob.
Unless you created a data lake storage (hierarchical), the "folders" are just
additional identifiers on the URL and every blob is stored at the same level
in the container.

Figure 1-13 shows options enabled for allowing public containers and
for allowing access via the key. Key access is required for working with the
SDK. Unchecking (disabling) either of these options will limit who can
access the blobs and how they are available.

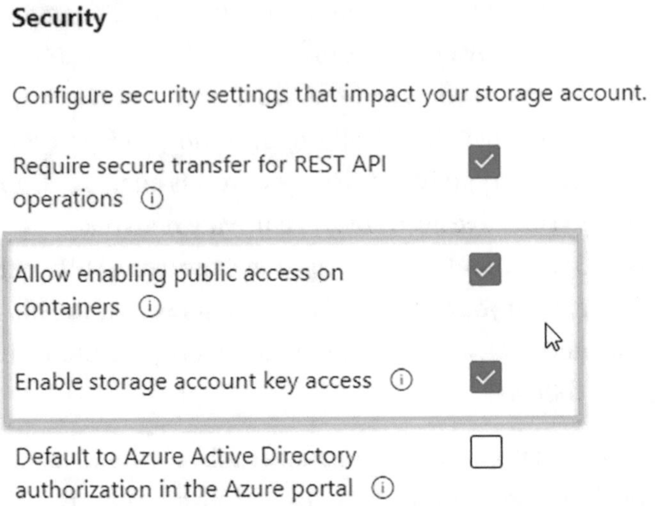

Security

Configure security settings that impact your storage account.

Require secure transfer for REST API
operations ⓘ

Allow enabling public access on
containers ⓘ

Enable storage account key access ⓘ

Default to Azure Active Directory
authorization in the Azure portal ⓘ

*Figure 1-13. The options to allow public access and key access are
enabled by default during account creation*

Public Access

As mentioned, when a storage account is created, as long as the option
to make containers public is allowed, containers can be set to a default
access level of public. When a container is public, all blobs in the container
are public. Typically, this is used in a scenario where you want to allow
anonymous read access to assets, such as images or videos for a website.

Private Access

In many scenarios you will want to ensure that blobs cannot be accessed
via anonymous requests. Setting private access will make sure that only
authorized users or applications can access your data.

As stated, the entire account can be locked into a private-only option
during creation, or you can ensure that access levels on a blob storage
container are set to private.

Shared Access Signature (SAS) Tokens

As mentioned, when a container is set to private access, there are a couple of ways to access the data. One way is to utilize the account keys and connection information and then utilize code with the Azure Storage SDK to access the data. Another way is to issue Shared Access Signature (SAS) tokens. The SAS token can be issued on an individual basis or can be issued per a shared access policy. Figure 1-14 calls out the left-nav menu items for each type of token at the container level.

Figure 1-14. *The left-nav menu contains links to create the SAS tokens individually or create a policy that can issue and revoke multiple tokens en masse*

When you create a token, you have the option to set things like the duration and specific rights for the token, such as read, write, and delete (see Figure 1-15). Tokens can be issued at the single-blob level or the container level. Single-blob tokens are useful for individual access to only one blob. Container-level tokens allow access to all blobs in the container with the permissions set during creation of the token.

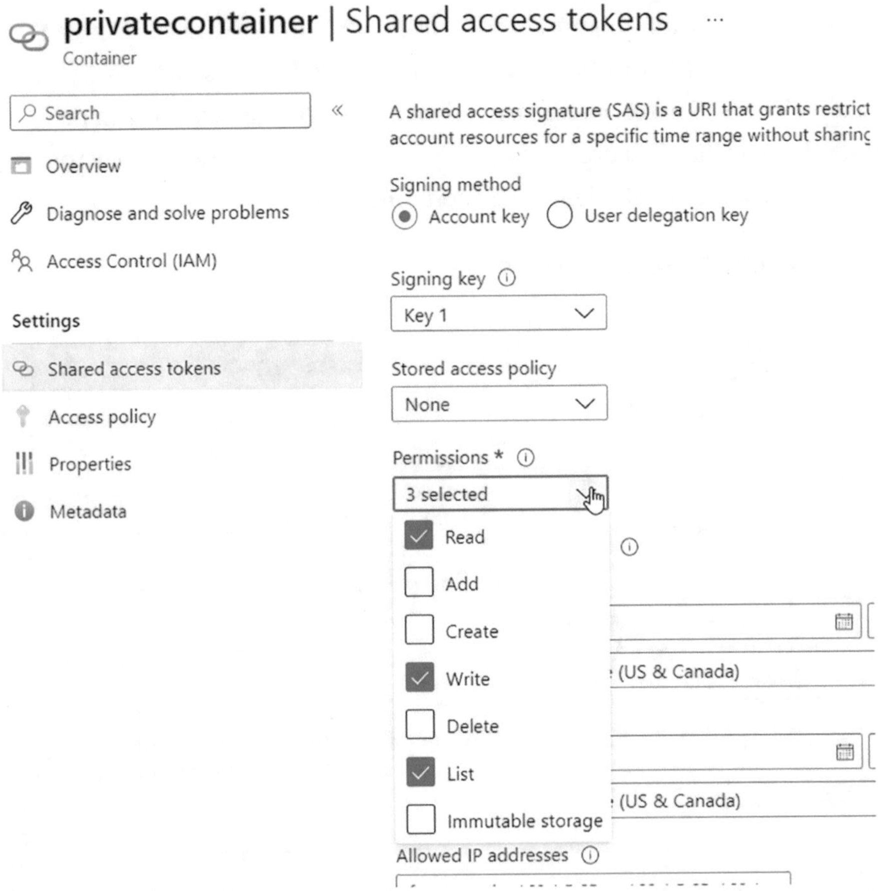

Figure 1-15. *Creating tokens allows you to set various options regarding the permissions, time of expiration, filtered IP addresses, and access protocols*

Individual (Ad Hoc) Tokens

Individual tokens can be for a single blob or can be issued for an entire
container. With an active token that has read access, anyone with the link
can access the blob(s) that are exposed by the token for read but cannot
modify them.

Individual (ad hoc) tokens are not manageable in Azure Storage
once they have been created. For this reason, the only way to invalidate
an active ad hoc token is to regenerate the key with which the token was
created.

Policy-issued Tokens

Policy-based tokens are valuable because they are not only going to
accomplish the access tasks as per any SAS token, but they are also issued
by a policy.

For this reason, if you have a lot of volatile tokens and you need to
rescind them for some reason, you can invalidate all tokens issued by
a policy. This is more powerful than individual tokens and can be safer
for business continuity for your customers, since keys don't have to be
regenerated.

To create a token via a policy, you must first create the policy. Tokens
in the policy share lifecycle and access permissions. Once the policy is
created, return to the menu to issue tokens and, in the appropriate drop-
down menu, select the policy you want to apply. Figure 1-16 shows the
creation screen for creating a new access policy.

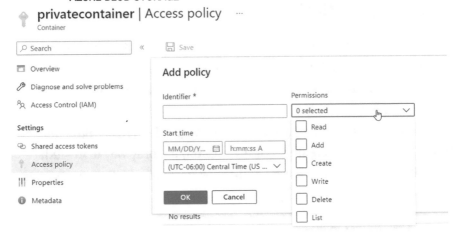

Figure 1-16. *Use the Access Policy menu to create a new policy for issuing a group of SAS tokens*

Working with the Azure Storage SDK

To complete this chapter, you'll want to gain a solid ability to work with the Azure Storage SDK. Therefore, this chapter wraps up by looking at the code that makes it possible to develop applications against Azure Blob Storage using the Azure Storage SDK.

The easiest way to learn this material is to reference the Microsoft Learn ecosystem and complete the learn modules. For many of the MS Learn activities, you must have an active Azure subscription. If you do not have a subscription, refer to Appendix A for information on how to get a free Azure trial account.

Working with Azure Storage from Code Using the .Net SDK

The rest of this chapter is a summary of the code and operations you need to be in command of in order to work with Azure Storage. You can find all code shown in the source files, which are located in the GIT repository for this book.

Creating the Account

As previously mentioned, when developing against Azure services with an SDK, you will almost always need to be in command of the hierarchy. For storage, you'll first need to create an account. The account will need to reside in a resource group in your subscription.

There are typically four ways to create resources in Azure—through the portal, through the REST APIs, through automation templates like ARM or Bicep, or through imperative commands using the Azure CLI.

1. Connect to Azure.

2. Navigate to the Storage Account blade and create a new storage account.

3. Use the Azure Portal, Azure CLI, or PowerShell to create a storage account with:

    a. A unique name that's 3-24 characters, lowercase or 0-9 only.

    b. Local Redundant Storage (LRS)

    c. Standard Tier (Gen Purpose V2)

    d. Ensure that enabling public access on containers and storage account key access are checked

    e. Utilize the hot tier for the default on the account

The end result should be a new storage account in Azure. Navigate to the Access Keys blade, as shown in Figure 1-17.

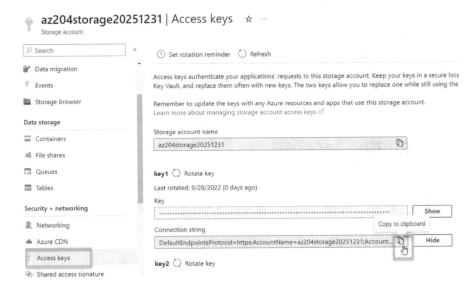

Figure 1-17. *A storage account exists that allows you to connect to it via the SDK using the connection string*

Copy the connection string to the clipboard for use in code.

Getting Connected to the Account

There are many languages you can use to work with an Azure Storage account via the Azure Storage SDK. This book assumes a primary approach with C# for snapshots of code, but you can also use Java, Python, JavaScript, C++, Go, PHP, and Ruby. Instructions can be found at `https://learn.microsoft.com/azure/storage/common/storage-introduction`.

1. Create a console project in C#, either in Visual Studio or Visual Studio code.

2. Import the `Azure.Storage.Blobs` SDK libraries.

3. Implement a methodology to get the connection string from a configuration file and place the connection string in your user secrets.

4. Create a folder called notes and place a file in that folder called affirmations.txt. To the file, add the following statement: "I'm going to pass the AZ-204 Exam soon!"

5. Set the TXT file properties to Content and Copy Always.

6. Use the following code to create the BlobServiceClient for the connection:

```
//get the connection string from config
var storageCNSTR = _configuration["Storage:
                    ConnectionString"];

//create blob storage client
var blobStorageClient = new BlobServiceClient
                        (storageCNSTR);
```

Creating a Container

With the application created and ready to connect, you can use this simple code to create a container named images:

```
//create notes container
var exists = false;
var containers = blobStorageClient.GetBlobContainers().
AsPages();
foreach (var containerPage in containers)
{
    foreach (var containerItem in containerPage.Values)
```

```
    {
        if (containerItem.Name.Equals("notes"))
        {
            exists = true;
            break;
        }
    }

    if (exists) break;
}
if (!exists)
{
    blobStorageClient.CreateBlobContainer("notes");
}
var containerClient = blobStorageClient.GetBlobContainerClient
("notes");
```

Uploading a Blob

Leverage the SDK to upload your text file:

```
//upload
var path = "./notes/affirmations.txt";
var blobClient = containerClient.
GetBlobClient("affirmations.txt");
var fileBytes = File.ReadAllBytes(path);
var ms = new MemoryStream(fileBytes);

blobClient.Upload(ms, overwrite: true);
```

Listing All the Blobs

To get a list of all the blobs in a container, use the following code:

```
//list blobs
exists = false;
foreach (var blob in containerClient.GetBlobs())
{
    Console.WriteLine($"Blob {blob.Name} found!
    {blob.Properties}");
    if (blob.Name.Contains("affirmations.txt"))
    {
        exists = true;
    }
}
```

Downloading a Blob

To download a blob from storage, use the following code:

```
//get blob
if (exists)
{
    blobClient = containerClient.GetBlobClient
    ("affirmations.txt");
    Console.WriteLine($"Blob {blobClient.Name} exists at
    {blobClient.Uri}");
    var downloadFileStream = new MemoryStream();
    blobClient.DownloadTo(downloadFileStream);
    var downloadFileBytes = downloadFileStream.ToArray();
    using (var f = File.Create($"{Environment.
    CurrentDirectory}/notes/affirmations-download.txt"))
```

```
    {
        f.Write(downloadFileBytes, 0, downloadFileBytes.
        Length);
    }
}
```

Modifying the Blob Metadata

To work with blob metadata, leverage the container to get blobs and then
set the specific blob metadata:

```
// metadata
foreach (var blob in containerClient.GetBlobs())
{
    Console.WriteLine($"Blob {blob.Name} found!
    {blob.Properties}");
    if (blob.Name.Contains("affirmations.txt"))
    {
        //add metadata
        blob.Metadata.Add("createdby", "yourname");
        blob.Metadata.Add("reason", "success");
        blob.Metadata.Add("filter", "important");

        //review metadata
        var metadata = blob.Metadata;
        foreach (var key in metadata.Keys)
        {
            Console.WriteLine($"Metadata {key} has value
            {metadata[key]}");
        }
    }
}
```

Deleting a Blob

To delete a blob, use the following code:

```
//delete blob
blobClient = containerClient.GetBlobClient("affirmations.txt");
blobClient.DeleteIfExists();
```

Deleting a Container

To delete a container, use the following code:

```
//delete container
containerClient.DeleteIfExists();
```

Review Your Learning

As an additional challenge, consider the following questions and determine how you would approach the potential solution(s). You can find answers to these questions in Appendix A at the end of this book.

1) How do you access a specific private blob and all private blobs in a container from the public URL?

2) What are some scenarios where you might make blobs public?

3) Can you put an Azure Storage account inside a private network?

4) What is the maximum size of a blob?

5) How do you move blobs from one tier to another?

6) Describe the process of rehydration of a blob from archive storage to any other tier?

Complete the AZ-204: Develop Solutions that Use Blob Storage Learning Path

To fully learn the material, I recommend taking the time to complete the MS Learn modules for Azure Storage found here:

- Develop solutions that use Azure Blob Storage: https://learn.microsoft.com/training/paths/ develop-solutions-that-use-blob-storage/

Chapter Summary

In this chapter, you learned about storage in Azure and how to utilize the storage SDK to work with blobs in Azure Container Storage.

After working through this chapter, you should be on track to be in command of the following concepts as you learn about Azure and prepare for the AZ-204 Exam:

- Know the four types of Azure Storage and what they are for.

- Understand what the various tiers are for in Azure Storage and how to optimize your utilization of each tier based on your application's needs.

- Understand how to automatically move blobs from one tier to another within your storage account, or move the blobs from one container or account to another container or account.

- Enable public and private access on blobs and
  containers and work with SAS tokens and policies to
  allow unique access to private blobs.

- Interact with Azure Blob Storage via the .NET SDK,
  including working with properties and metadata.

In the next chapter, you will learn about working with Cosmos DB and
Azure Table Storage for NoSQL data storage.

CHAPTER 2

Develop Solutions That Use Cosmos DB

About two years ago, I started learning about Cosmos DB and all the nuances that it contains. Even after all this time and an additional certification (DP-420), Cosmos DB is still an incredibly difficult topic to understand, and can be even more tricky to fully leverage correctly. Learning Cosmos DB is especially difficult for those who, like me, have been developing solutions utilizing relational database systems for more than just a couple of years.

Truth be told, relational developers like me love the structure of relations. We love the consistency of normalization and the ease of building high-performing queries that get our data quickly and efficiently to render to our clients. We are confident that our stored procedures are the only tool we need to manipulate the data, and, on rare occasions, we can even use a trigger if we have no other choice.

The good news is that some of these concepts do translate (in a way) into Cosmos DB. The bad news is that most operations are contradictory to how relational developers think about normalization and relational data, and that can make the barrier to Cosmos DB even greater.

Cosmos DB has a top-level account (like a server), with one or more databases, which store data in one or more containers (which you can think of a bit like a table). Cosmos DB has an Atomicity, Consistency, Isolation, and Durability (ACID) transaction capability that you can

B. L. Gorman, *Developing Solutions for Microsoft Azure Certification Companion*, Certification Study Companion Series, https://doi.org/10.1007/978-1-4842-9300-3_2

implement with the Cosmos DB SDK. You can even write stored procedures and triggers—albeit utilizing JavaScript as the development language.

For all of these reasons, in this chapter, I take the approach that you are fairly new to Cosmos DB and need to know how to utilize it effectively with code (for this exam and for some actual projects). I also present some of the major concepts around the optimization of these mysterious Request Units (RUs), and how they play out in both your analysis of your data and your overall cost for utilizing Cosmos DB. Even if you aren't a non-relational database developer by trade, this chapter will help position you for the knowledge around development with Cosmos DB.

In addition to those things, we also look at the specific pieces you need to be in command of for working with Azure Cosmos DB for the exam, and we compare working with Cosmos DB to working with Azure Table Storage.

Why Choose Azure Cosmos DB?

With the learning curve being somewhat steep, and the cost being another prohibitive hurdle, there must be good reasons to choose Cosmos, right?

Among the benefits of choosing Cosmos DB, you get the best possible throughput on your data with a 10ms guarantee for reads and writes on 99% of your requests. Additionally, Cosmos DB provides 99.999 (five nines) availability on accounts with multi-region read and write capabilities.

Cosmos DB also gives your applications the ability to write to any region or read from any region, all the while making sure to handle the replication within Cosmos itself. This means you don't have to do anything but configure the account and the rest of the replication and failover is taken care of for you.

Finally, Cosmos DB has the ability to scale to massive levels of throughput. Theoretically, you can get unlimited throughput if you configure the account correctly. However, there are ultimately physical and financial reasons that could prevent you from testing that theory (data centers have a physical capacity limit and the cost of scaling to unlimited throughput could be devastatingly astronomical).

All of this is to point out that even though there is a curve and a number of things that need to be considered, the move to Cosmos DB is a logical choice for today's cloud-native applications.

Azure Cosmos DB Hierarchy

As mentioned, there is a definitive structure to Azure Cosmos DB that gives you a foundation to build upon. This structure allows the Cosmos DB SDK to work in a similar manner to how the SDK utilized a structural approach to composing objects in the storage section of the previous chapter.

At the top level, you'll create a *Cosmos DB account*. In Azure, you can now create one free Cosmos DB account per subscription, with 1,000 RUs of manually provisioned throughput. Even if you don't understand exactly what that means, you can discern that it means you should be able to create an account and learn how to work with Cosmos DB in code, even making some mistakes, and likely not see a penny of expenditure on your Azure bill.

Once you've created an account, you'll leverage a similar concept to a database server with databases to create one or more *databases* in your account. Within each database, you can create one or more *containers*. Containers have *items*, which are the unstructured JSON documents that contain the data. In addition to items, containers hold the stored procedures, triggers, user-defined functions, conflicts, and merge procedures. Depending on the API chosen for Cosmos DB, the item structure differs internally based on the functionality implemented by the chosen API. Figure 2-1 shows a sample of this hierarchy.

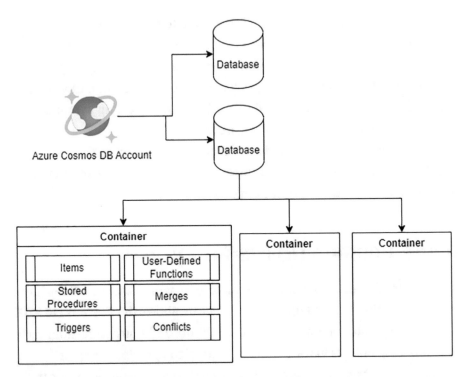

Figure 2-1. *The Cosmos DB hierarchy contains an account with one or more databases, where each database has one or more containers, and each container holds items, stored procedures, user-defined functions, triggers, conflicts, and merges*

Choosing the Correct API

Azure Cosmos DB currently supports six API offerings that you need to select from when creating an account. The offerings are based on specific concepts or technologies, and you need to be able to determine which one to choose in any given scenario.

The six APIs as of this writing are *Azure Cosmos DB for NoSQL (also known as SQL API), Azure Cosmos DB for Mongo DB, Azure Cosmos DB for Apache Cassandra, Azure Cosmos DB for Table, Azure Cosmos*

DB for Apache Gremlin, and *Azure Cosmos DB for PostgreSQL.* Before diving too deeply into these different APIs, the recommendation for all new development is to utilize Azure Cosmos DB for NoSQL. That being said, each of these APIs exists to fill specific needs. When you create a new Cosmos DB account, you need to choose the API for the account to match the needs of your application and/or the skill set of your team (see Figure 2-2).

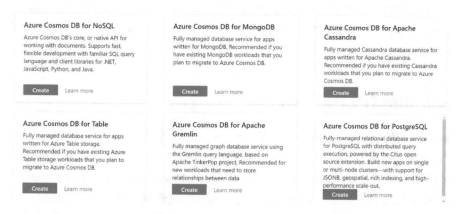

Figure 2-2. *The five APIs are presented for your selection during the creation of an Azure Cosmos DB account*

Cosmos DB for MongoDB

The API for MongoDB (`www.mongodb.com`) is exactly like it sounds. You will utilize this API any time it makes sense for you to have your application based on MongoDB but store your data in Azure Cosmos. By utilizing the MongoDB API, you can easily migrate your data and have plug-and-play capabilities to work with your data using the same code that existed prior to the migration.

Reasons to utilize this API are as described, with the migration of an existing project and minimal application changes. Additional reasons are for the creation of new projects that are multi-cloud and/or as part of a team of seasoned MongoDB developers.

Cosmos DB for Apache Cassandra

The Cassandra API (`https://cassandra.apache.org/`) is also exactly like it sounds. You will utilize this API any time it makes sense for you to have your application based on Cassandra, but store your data in Azure Cosmos. Cassandra is a columnar based NoSQL store, which is different from Azure Cosmos Core SQL and MongoDB.

Reasons to utilize this API are as described, with the migration of an existing project and minimal application changes or on teams of seasoned developers.

Cosmos DB for Table

Azure Table Storage was briefly discussed in the first chapter. The reason the Azure Table Storage API for Cosmos DB exists is so that you can easily migrate existing table storage to Azure Cosmos with no changes to your application. The same code that works against table storage will work against the Azure Cosmos DB Table API.

Reasons to utilize this API are to migrate your existing table storage solution to provide the additional ability to have global replication, multiple write regions, and complex indexes for more proficient query operations than what Azure Table Storage can offer.

Cosmos DB for Apache Gremlin (Graph)

Gremlin is a graph-traversal language for Apache TinkerPop (`https://tinkerpop.apache.org/gremlin.html`). In the typical Cosmos offering, you can't have graphs that can be traversed. An example of a graph that needs to be traversed is finding friends of your friends. In a social network, you have friends, and they also have friends (perhaps many are the same), so the graph can be traversed through these complex relationships to discern common friends or provide the ability to make recommendations as to friends you may know in the network. Another simple example is an organization hierarchy where there are complex relationships between employees, departments, and managers.

The reason to use the Gremlin API for Cosmos DB is to create relationships in your data that can be queried and traversed as a graph.

Cosmos DB for PostgreSQL

This offering gives you the ability to work with data from PostgreSQL for distributed tables and highly scalable applications. This offering is powered by the Citus open source extension for PostgreSQL. You can count on the latest features being available for this offering within a few weeks of them being released. Offerings include the ability to work with JSONB and use native partitioning; they are also fully capable of working with geographical locations in tables and queries.

Cosmos DB for NoSQL

The Cosmos DB for NoSQL API is the recommended API for most development. Although the name of the API includes SQL, this is not anything like a relational SQL Server offering.

The reasons to use the Core SQL API are many, but the standard recommendation from Microsoft is that you will mostly choose this offering. Unless you are doing multi-cloud, have a team of seasoned developers in another offering (MongoDB, PostgreSQL, or Cassandra), need a graph, or need to migrate an existing app from one of those technologies with minimal changes, Cosmos DB for NoSQL is the recommended choice. For this reason, the rest of the chapter focuses on the Cosmos DB for NoSQL offering.

Capacity Mode

When you create your Azure Cosmos DB account for Core SQL, you get to choose one of two capacity modes. The first mode is *Provisioned Throughput*. The second mode is *Serverless*. Figure 2-3 shows the optional choices during account creation.

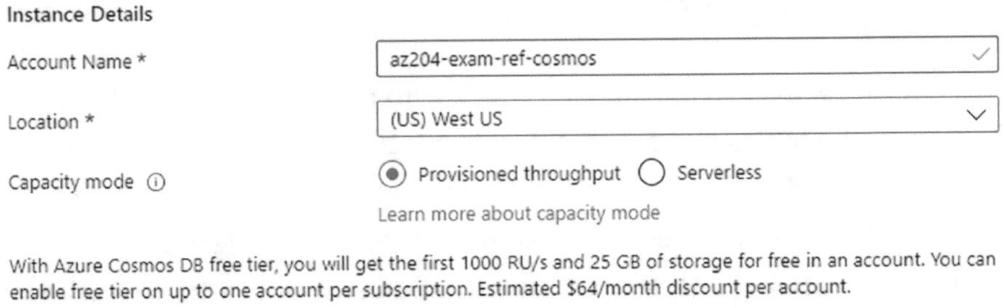

Instance Details

Account Name * | az204-exam-ref-cosmos   ✓

Location * | (US) West US   ⌄

Capacity mode ⓘ   ◉ Provisioned throughput   ◯ Serverless
                         Learn more about capacity mode

With Azure Cosmos DB free tier, you will get the first 1000 RU/s and 25 GB of storage for free in an account. You can enable free tier on up to one account per subscription. Estimated $64/month discount per account.

Figure 2-3. *Creation of an Azure Cosmos Core SQL account allows the option to select Provisioned Throughput or Serverless*

Provisioned Throughput

For most scenarios, you'll likely choose Provision Throughput. When you utilize this option, you will be reserving the RUs for your account. Because these RUs are reserved, your cost for the monthly utilization of the service will be predictable. Additionally, because of the reserved nature of the account, you will be billed for the reserved RUs for the month, even when you don't do anything with the database.

When provisioning your RUs for the service, you can also select options to automatically scale your account to respond to demand. This ability to automatically scale allows you to set a baseline for your normal operations but respond with additional throughput when necessary.

If you are concerned about the cost, you can also select an option to limit the total throughput on the account to prevent any accidental changes that would cause your cost to skyrocket, even when auto-scaling is utilized (see Figure 2-4).

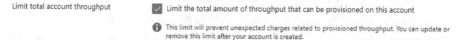

Figure 2-4. *The option to limit throughput on the account is checked*

To Share or Not To Share; That Is the Question

One of the more complex topics with Azure Cosmos DB is the idea of throughput and RUs. In addition to the complexity of having to discern how your account will be billed for utilization of storage, you also have to think about how the throughput can be distributed or reserved for specific databases or containers.

After choosing provisioned throughput, when it comes to provisioning throughput utilization, you need to determine if you want to share the throughput across all of the containers, or if you want to create a throughput that is manually set and individually consumed by a single container.

Consider a scenario where you provision 1,000 RUs for a single database. Inside the database are multiple containers. Each container can use up to 1,000 RUs, but the total consumption can't exceed 1,000 RUs. This means that in a shared scenario with uneven workloads, one or more containers could become resource hogs and block other containers from being performant.

Consider that instead of sharing throughput, the solution provisioned 500 RUs for the main container, and then 250 RUs each for the remaining two containers. In this scenario, the same amount of RUs would be utilized (1,000), but the containers that were previously blocked would be readily available. You should also recognize, however, that this means the container that was hogging 1,000 RUs is now limited to 500 RUs unless the container is allowed to automatically scale.

Serverless

In some scenarios, you may decide to utilize the Serverless offering. This works best when you are going to be using Cosmos DB in a bursting scenario. Perhaps you only need a few RUs in a month, and maybe they are all on the last few days of the month. In this scenario, rather than paying for Reserved Throughput, you might opt to use the Serverless offering.

A word of caution about this offering is worth noting, however. Although this offering is based on consumption and is offered to help you save money, incorrect utilization of this offering can result in even higher costs than you would have incurred had you just provisioned the account with reserved (provisioned) throughput. With the consumption model, you'll pay more per RU than you would have paid if they were reserved.

Autoscaling

As with everything in Azure, the cloud should be elastic and able to respond to your solutions as needed in a manner that gives you economies of scale at will. With Cosmos DB, you can set autoscaling rules on databases or containers to automatically respond to the critical needs of your application.

Global Distribution

One of the primary benefits of Cosmos DB is the fact that you can easily allow Cosmos DB to be replicated globally. When the solution is replicated, you will also need to select the correct consistency levels (covered in the next section).

Along with the ability to be replicated in multiple regions, you can select the option to allow multi-region writes. When you enable writing in regions other than the primary region, you need to configure your application to set the connection policy for multi-region writes, and you also need to make sure to configure the policy to use multiple write locations. Once deployed and set correctly, if you add replication regions for read and/or write operations, the application will be able to find and utilize the region that is closest to its deployed location. Adding replication and distribution adds costs, as the account goes from being billed at a single-region rate to a multi-region rate. In these scenarios, you will pay additional costs for the ability to read from each region, and even more to gain the ability to write to additional regions. More information on cost calculation can be found at `https://cosmos.azure.com/capacitycalculator/`. More information on configuring multiple write regions in your applications can be found at `https://learn.microsoft.com/azure/cosmos-db/how-to-manage-database-account#configure-multiple-write-regions`. Figure 2-5 shows options selected for Geo-Redundancy and Multi-Region Writes during account creation.

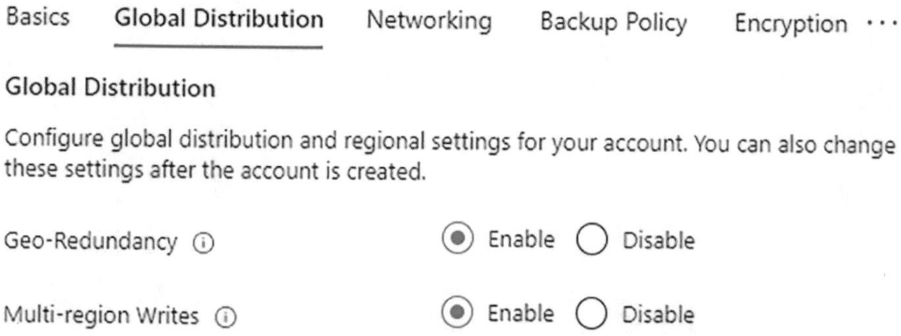

Basics	**Global Distribution**	Networking	Backup Policy	Encryption · · ·

Global Distribution

Configure global distribution and regional settings for your account. You can also change these settings after the account is created.

Geo-Redundancy ⓘ   ⦿ Enable   ◯ Disable

Multi-region Writes ⓘ   ⦿ Enable   ◯ Disable

Figure 2-5. *Geo-Redundancy and Multi-Region Writes are enabled during the creation of the account*

Consistency Levels

Since the nature of Cosmos DB is to be distributed, it's important to select and configure how your solution will respond and deal with data as it is replicated within the write region and out into any replicated regions.

Consistency is set at the account level and applies to all databases and containers in the account. You can change the consistency throughout the lifetime of your account as needed.

There are five consistency levels, with Strong being the most consistent and Eventual being the least. The other three are Bounded Staleness, Session (which is the recommended setting), and consistent Prefix. When using Strong or Bounded Staleness, the cost of your operation is doubled (for example, a query with a cost of 2 RUs is doubled to a cost of 4 RUs).

Overall, every consistency except for Eventual will preserve the order of the writes to the database.

Table 2-1 shows a quick overview of the five consistency levels, information about each, their effect on cost, and the ability to guarantee that data delivery happens in order.

Table 2-1. *A Quick Summary of the Five Consistency Levels in Azure Cosmos DB*

Consistency Level	Effect	Effect on Cost	Guaranteed Order
Strong	No dirty reads; all writes require replication to all regions	Doubles the cost of RUs for each query	Yes
Bounded Staleness	Data is consistent to a set time or number of versions	Doubles the RU cost for each query	Yes
Session	Read your own writes	None	Yes
Consistent Prefix	Transactional availability (falls to eventual when utilized in multiple regions)	None	Yes
Eventual	Immediate read results but could be stale. Results could also be out of order.	None	No

Strong Consistency

Strong consistency guarantees that there will never be any dirty reads of data for any application in any region. The problem with this consistency is that to make this promise, the data that is written cannot be read until the replication has been propagated successfully around the globe, which can lead to some noticeable latency for reads on recently written data.

Bounded Staleness

Like Strong consistency, Bounded Staleness is a highly accurate way to review the data with very little chance of a dirty read. This option is recommended when you need to guarantee order around the globe with a minimum amount of latency. With this option, you set either a time interval or a number of versions to force the read to take place. Whichever option is hit first will trigger the ability to work with the data. As the system is close to the trigger for time or versions, the system will ensure that writes can be guaranteed by throttling down the ability to perform new writes.

While the data is written within the staleness window, different scenarios will see different performance. Within the same region as the write, applications get Strong consistency, even in the staleness window. Other scenarios get Consistent Prefix consistency. If you are utilizing a multi-region write and the client is writing to multiple regions, then during the staleness window, you will have Eventual consistency.

Session Consistency

Session consistency gives applications in session the ability to read their own writes. The session consistency utilizes a session token to ensure applications have the correct ability to get the correct data.

Session consistency is typically the default scenario for most applications, as you'll get the best trade-off between data consistency and overall performance at this level, regardless of whether you are replicating data.

Consistent Prefix

Consistent prefix allows transactions to take place as a group and become available at the same time, once the transaction is completed. If a transaction is not used or the application is writing to multiple regions, then the consistency will fall to Eventual. In other scenarios, the writes will become available simultaneously. This is best visualized if you are using an Azure Function to monitor the change feed. Perhaps a category name has changed, and multiple documents need to be updated. In this consistency, within a transaction, all of the documents will be updated and available at the same time. Before they are available, all documents will show the original category name. After the transaction completes, all documents will show the new transaction name. Your solution is guaranteed to never have some documents with the original category name and others with the new category name.

Eventual

Eventual consistency will give your solution the highest level of throughput you can achieve. This performance, however, comes at the cost of data having the possibility of being a dirty read. After some time, the data will eventually be correct.

Networking

As with most offerings, creating a Cosmos DB account allows you to select how to connect to the Cosmos DB account.

The default connection is over All Networks, which is essentially the public Internet. A second option allows you to create a public-facing endpoint and set firewall rules and connect to a virtual network within your Azure subscription. A final solution is to utilize a private endpoint. The private endpoint also utilizes a private network in your Azure subscription. Since this is on a private network, you can limit traffic to Cosmos DB to internal or private IP addresses, preventing public access to your Cosmos DB. These network options are highlighted in Figure 2-6.

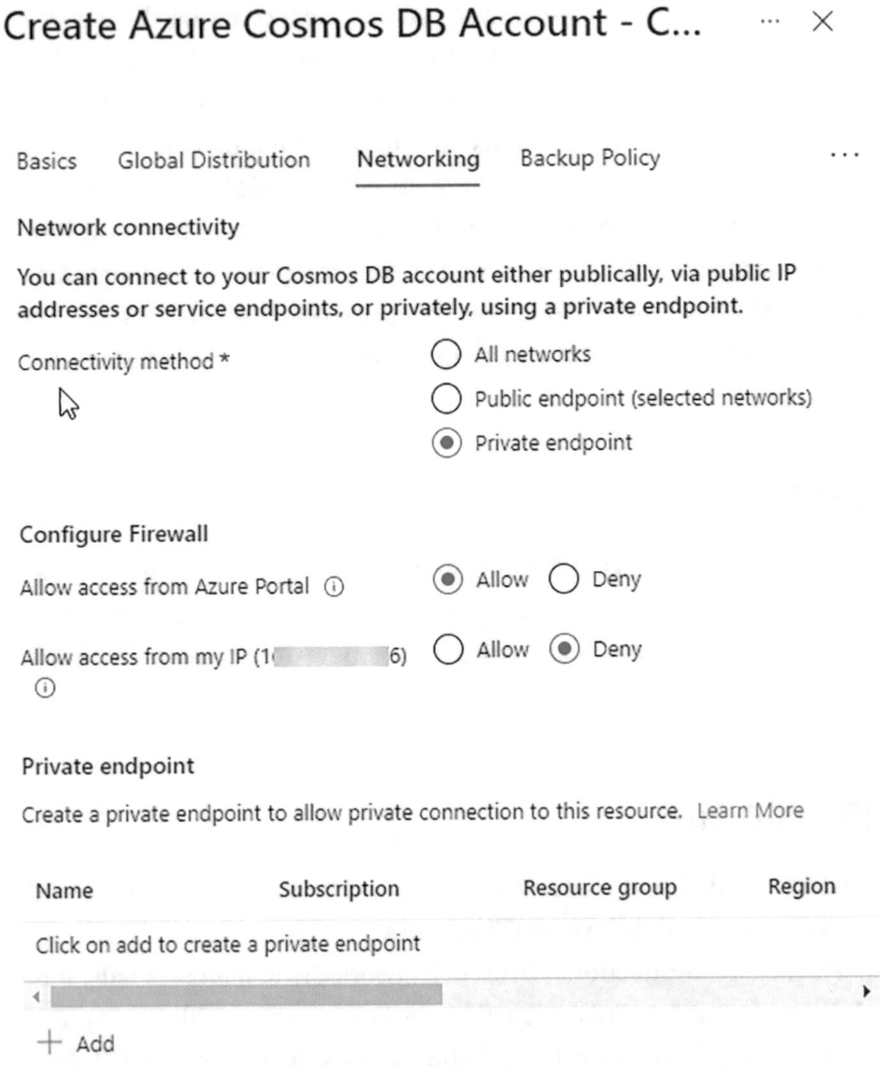

Create Azure Cosmos DB Account - C...   ···   ✕

Basics   Global Distribution   **Networking**   Backup Policy   ···

Network connectivity

You can connect to your Cosmos DB account either publically, via public IP addresses or service endpoints, or privately, using a private endpoint.

Connectivity method *

⃝ All networks

⃝ Public endpoint (selected networks)

◉ Private endpoint

Configure Firewall

Allow access from Azure Portal ⓘ   ◉ Allow ⃝ Deny

Allow access from my IP (1   6)   ⃝ Allow ◉ Deny
ⓘ

Private endpoint

Create a private endpoint to allow private connection to this resource. Learn More

Name	Subscription	Resource group	Region
Click on add to create a private endpoint			

◄   ►

+ Add

Figure 2-6. *The connectivity method can be set to one of three options. Choosing an option that requires a virtual network allows you to configure the virtual network*

Backup Policy

As you provision your account, you can set rules for the automatic backups. There are multiple configurations, including Periodic, Continuous (7 days), and Continuous (30 days). Each offering has a default or set backup interval and retention period. The maximum backup interval is 24 hours, and the minimum backup retention is two days. With minimal settings, there will be as few as just two copies of your data available.

The more backups you configure, the more cost you incur. An additional consideration is where to store the backups. Options exist to select Geo-Redundant backup storage (for multiple region storage) or you can choose to store Locally-Redundant backup storage (for single-region backups). See Figure 2-7.

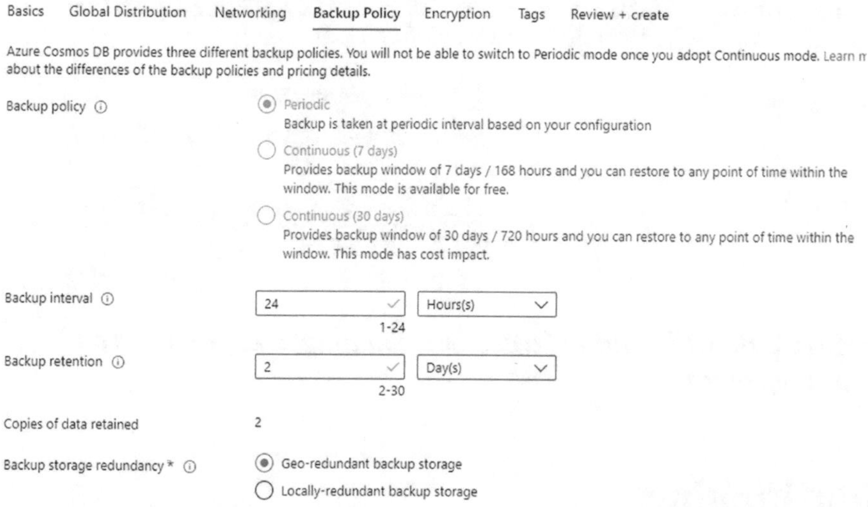

Figure 2-7. *The backup policy is easily configured during account creation*

Encryption

All data at rest in Azure is encrypted. If you do nothing to change the defaults, the encryption will be managed by Azure with an encryption key managed by Azure. If you would like more control, you can enable the option to utilize a customer-managed key. When you want to manage your own encryption key(s), you must store them in the Azure Key Vault and allow the service that needs the key to have the correct permission to read from the Key Vault (see Figure 2-8).

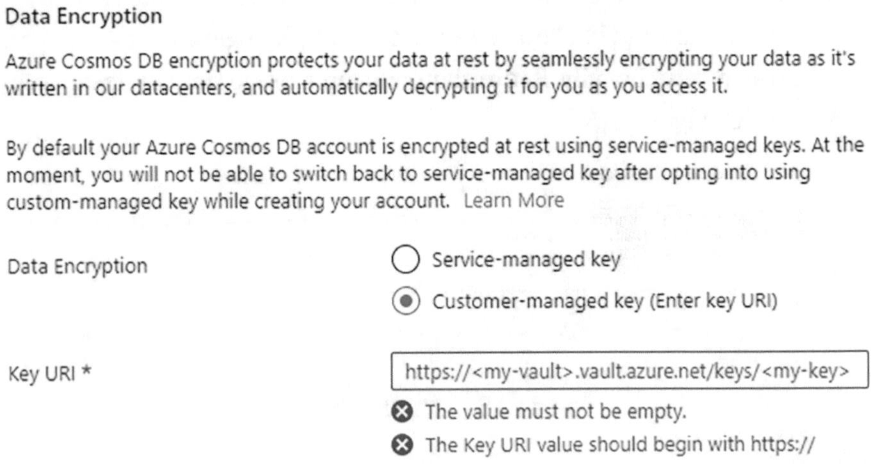

Data Encryption

Azure Cosmos DB encryption protects your data at rest by seamlessly encrypting your data as it's written in our datacenters, and automatically decrypting it for you as you access it.

By default your Azure Cosmos DB account is encrypted at rest using service-managed keys. At the moment, you will not be able to switch back to service-managed key after opting into using custom-managed key while creating your account. Learn More

Data Encryption   ◯ Service-managed key

                       ⦿ Customer-managed key (Enter key URI)

Key URI *   `https://<my-vault>.vault.azure.net/keys/<my-key>`

                       ✖ The value must not be empty.
                       ✖ The Key URI value should begin with https://

Figure 2-8. *Utilization of a customer-managed key requires a Key Vault reference*

Partitioning

Partitioning is the most critical concept to understand about Cosmos DB. Partitioning is also one of the most difficult concepts to understand when it comes to Cosmos DB. Indeed, the entire chapter could have focused solely on working with Cosmos DB partitioning. In the next few pages, I attempt to get you squared away on the most important aspects of partitioning. If you're like me, or if you are strictly used to working with relational data, you will likely find that this will be a good introduction, but you'll want to go deeper before implementing an entire production solution.

To get started, I'd like you to envision a bowling alley. In the bowling alley are many lanes, each with its own pins. For simplicity, assume this bowling alley has eight lanes (choosing eight is entirely for envisioning the solution and not at all to do with any limitations in Cosmos DB). At the end of each lane are a number of pins. Once again, a typical bowling alley lane has ten and only ten pins for an active first roll. When all the pins are ready, there are eight lanes, with ten pins each, for a total of 80 pins spread evenly in groups of ten across the eight lanes (see Figure 2-9).

Figure 2-9. *A bowling alley has many lanes with equal numbers of pins*

When it comes to working with Cosmos DB, there are two types of partitions. The two types are *logical* and *physical* partitions. The next sections break these down by continuing to use Figure 2-9.

Logical Partitions

In the bowling alley, the pins are separated evenly across the different lanes. If you will, imagine that each "pin" is really a JSON document that holds data. The logical placement of these documents is spread evenly across the lanes in Figure 2-9. Spreading the data evenly across logical partitions is an ideal goal.

Separating the data logically into partitions means that you have set your data in a way so as to optimize your read and write throughput and resource utilization to achieve the best possible use case.

Imagine the problems that would exist if one lane in the bowling alley suddenly had 50 of the pins, another had 30 pins, and the remaining 20 were spread across the last eight lanes. While a bowler might be able to get a strike more easily in a lane with just three pins, the lanes that have too many pins would be next to impossible to utilize for a normal game of bowling.

In Cosmos DB, when your logical partitioning structure is bad, you can end up with a hot partition. One cause of a hot partition can be that the data is not evenly distributed and, therefore, the majority of queries run against the data have to go against that one lane, thereby slowing everything down. Figure 2-10 shows a bowling alley with lanes having different numbers of pins placed, which is chosen to help envision uneven data distribution in Cosmos DB.

Figure 2-10. *Pins in a bowling alley where some of the lanes have all the pins and others have just a few is a simple way to view data that is not partitioned correctly in the Cosmos DB database*

No matter what, if you don't know anything else yet, one thing you must understand is that the logical partition is simply all of the data that has the same partition key grouped together.

Along with that grouping concept, you must remember that JSON documents don't need the same properties (columns). For example, if you have a partition key called LastName and three different documents have LastName, they can be grouped together as a logical partition on the LastName property, even if none of the other properties in the documents are the same and the data is completely different and used to model entirely different entities. Note that this partitioned data is also not relational data, so you should not think of this as a field on which you join data across documents. In a non-relational NoSQL Cosmos DB database, you do not ever join data across documents, even if they have fields that can be used as keys.

The fact that you can have data grouped in the same partition that is completely unrelated but has a common field, along with the fact that you don't relationally join documents for queries even if they have a shared key, are two reasons that it is incredibly difficult for a relational database developer to initially grasp the concepts of Cosmos DB. I hope that by pointing these out here, it helps to set the stage for you to grasp this disparity more quickly than I did.

Physical Partitions

In the bowling alley, the lanes are physically separated. In Cosmos DB, the physical partitions are also separated across different SSD physical storage and disk implementations within Azure data centers.

In the bowling alley, some machinery is handling pin placement. In Cosmos DB, the pin placement (if you envision pins as JSON documents) is handled based on how the Cosmos DB partitioning is set up. No matter how you set things up, there are two limitations you need to always remember that are directly related to physical partitions.

The first limitation is that any physical partition is limited to 10,000 RUs of throughput. Anything more than 10,000 RUs, and data must be split across partitions. The second physical limitation is that the document storage for a physical partition is 50 GB. If you have more than 50 GB of data, then you know for a fact you are on multiple physical partitions.

With logical partitioning, data is grouped together to maximize query throughput based on a common key field. However, if you set up the partition incorrectly, then the query won't perform well. For example, imagine what it would be like if the pins were uniquely colored, and the bowler, in order to get a strike, had to suddenly hit just the ten pins of a specific color that exist in placements across multiple lanes. This scenario is similar to what can happen when queries are utilized that span physical partitions.

For those of us who are familiar with relational data, one of the cardinal sins of querying data is called a table scan—where all the data in the table must be read to get accurate results for a particular query.

In Cosmos DB, one of the cardinal sins is a partition scan. In a cross-partition scan, like the multiple pins in lanes, data is not correctly placed in logical partitions as per the requirements of the query, and, therefore, the query must hit all the partitions to get the correct data result sets.

For example, a partition that has high cardinality (discussed in some following sections) will spread data (the pins) evenly across the partitions (lanes). However, if each lane contains a field such as "favorite color," then a query trying to find all the data where the favorite color is green will not perform well, since the data can (and likely will) exist in all the lanes.

One last thing you need to know about physical partitions is the fact that you have absolutely no control over them. All of the physical partitioning work is done by Azure and Cosmos DB. The only thing that you can control is the logical partition. By structuring your logical partitions correctly for your data, you automatically get the best physical partitioning that is available for your solution. If you structure your partitions poorly, your physical partitioning will also suffer as a result.

Partition Keys

To enable the correct placement of data, it is the responsibility of the Cosmos DB architect and/or developer to ensure that proper partition keys are chosen. The ultimate "correct" result may be a hard pill to swallow for relational database developers, because the logical partitioning of unstructured data may feel completely contrary to the typical patterns of a relational developer.

The most important aspect of choosing a partition key is how the queries will be used along with the nature of the data. Is your database read-heavy or write-heavy? Will you need to query against a secondary set of data? Can you group data by a partition key even if the data would be in different tables in a relational database? These things will play into your design decisions.

It's also important to note that you cannot change the partition key of a container once it is created. Therefore, if you make a mistake, or if you need a different partition key, your only option is to create a new container and migrate the data from the old container to the new container.

For the remainder of this discussion on partitioning, it would be helpful to have some JSON data to simulate important points regarding the structuring of logical and physical partitions using a partition key. Any Cosmos DB account can generate some sample JSON documents by using the Quick Start option from the Azure Portal (see Figure 2-11).

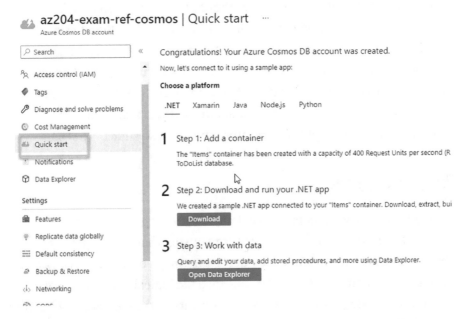

Figure 2-11. *Any Azure Cosmos DB account can utilize the Quick Start option to create a database with some items in place*

Creating a sample database and running code to populate items but not deleting them would generate and leave the following document (or something similar) in place:

```json
{
    "id": "Andersen.1",
    "partitionKey": "Andersen",
    "LastName": "Andersen",
    "Parents": [
        {
            "FamilyName": null,
            "FirstName": "Thomas"
        },
        {
            "FamilyName": null,
            "FirstName": "Mary Kay"
        }
    ],
    "Children": [
        {
            "FamilyName": null,
            "FirstName": "Henriette Thaulow",
            "Gender": "female",
            "Grade": 5,
            "Pets": [
                {
                    "GivenName": "Fluffy"
                }
            ]
        }
    ],
    "Address": {
        "State": "WA",
        "County": "King",
        "City": "Seattle"
    },
```

```
    "IsRegistered": false,
    "_rid": "fqFkAIOeqP+BhB4AAAAAAA==",
    "_self": "dbs/fqFkAA==/colls/fqFkAIOeqP8=/docs/
    fqFkAIOeqP+BhB4AAAAAAA==/",
    "_etag": "\"0000f903-0000-0700-0000-6343380f0000\"",
    "_attachments": "attachments/",
    "_ts": 1665349647
}
```

Note that this document has a `partitionKey` field, which is the same as the `LastName` field.

Using this document, consider the bowling alley to envision logical partitions (lanes) that now are being grouped, essentially by `LastName`. Assuming that the `partitionKey` and `LastName` fields are always the same would show you that there is likely to be a hot partition at some point. While the early performance of this data won't likely suffer, as the last names will mostly be disparate with a small set of data, consider the data for an entire state or the city of New York. Think about names like "Johnson," "Williams," and "Smith," which are the top three most common last names in the United States. These groupings would become disproportionately larger than the others as more names are added to the list. Eventually, the data may have to be split over physical partitions as well, which could further stress the system.

High Cardinality for Write-Heavy Workloads

Instead of using something that is not unique, such as just the last name, consider a solution where the `partitionKey` would have mapped to the last name and id (`Anderson.1`) of the document. In this case, every single document would have a unique ID, which would lead to a high cardinality.

As data is written to the database, the logical partitions would be evenly placed across the physical partitions (i.e., data as pins placed evenly across all the lanes and each bowler's pins are in their own lane as expected) and the system would not have any issues with hot partitions or cross-partition scans based on the unique ID as the partition key. In a write-heavy scenario, this would be an ideal choice.

Utilizing Your Query Filter as the Partition Key for Read-Heavy Workloads

In scenarios where you need to perform filtered queries, rather than using the ID, you would likely find better results by keeping the partition on the field that will appear in the query. For example, if the main segregation of data is the LastName, you will likely want to keep that as your partition key. A better solution is to still have the filter and the partition key have a higher cardinality to avoid the hot partition problem. As stated, however, this is not always possible. Ideally, fields like username and email both give you unique values that lend well to querying for data. However, lots of similar data on the partition key may still need to have a high cardinality.

Assume you have millions of IoT devices out in the universe and you utilize Cosmos DB to store the telemetry. Assume you need to find unique data by day and by device. Utilization of the time as a partition key is a really bad idea, because the data would all be from today so the logical partition would be a hot partition. Utilization of the device is not going to work because you might get more data from one device than you can store in one partition across time spans, like a couple of days, a week, or a month, which is a cross-partition scan.

The answer to this scenario is to use a synthetic partition key. With a synthetic partition key, you can group similar data together with what is essentially a composite key. For example, using the device ID and the timestamp as one field stored will correctly partition by device and day, and should solve the problems of hot partitions and cross-partition scans.

Indexing in Cosmos DB

What would happen, however, if your main use of this data is a query that needs to read from the data where `IsRegistered` is true? Knowing what you know already, the first problem (cross-partition queries) would exist if you used the `IsRegistered` field as a partition. With only two values, this is a terrible partition key. If the field is not a partition key, then any query that needs to read from the data is going to perform a cross-partition scan. The same issue exists when you need to order data. For example, what if you need to select from the items but you need to order by `LastName` and then by `Address.State`?

The answer for these scenarios is to build an index. As mentioned in the previous chapter, this is one area where Cosmos DB can vastly outperform table storage. With Cosmos DB, you can create composite indexes on your data to optimize query performance. Indexing is mostly outside of the scope of the AZ-204, so if you want to know more about it, you can read about indexing in Azure Cosmos DB at `https://learn.microsoft.com/azure/cosmos-db/index-overview`.

As a quick overview here, it's important enough to know that all data is automatically indexed in Azure Cosmos DB, on every property. The data is then searchable based on the fields in the document and organized as best as it can be by default for particular searches. When you create an index, you essentially help define the exact places for Cosmos DB to search when performing queries. For example, when needing to key on the `IsRegistered` field, you could create an index to maximize the throughput for queries that need to key on the `IsRegistered` field.

Cosmos DB Change Feed

The data in the Cosmos DB is not relational. As such, your data may be duplicated in multiple documents. For example, consider a scenario where you have a number of users, and they choose from one of three particular settings for a theme on your website. The data is easily managed in Cosmos DB, and the partition key is better for performance in this scenario if the unique user ID is utilized. The choice of "theme" is just duplicated all over the user profiles.

In a relational database, this theme would be an ID with a field for the display name used in a drop-down list, with important properties of the theme being stored in a relevant table, normalized as expected. In Cosmos DB, the document nests the theme information per user. What happens when you want to update the name of the theme site-wide? Or, what about changing one of the critical properties of the theme, such as the primary color? In this case, you need to update all of the non-relational, denormalized data. This update will certainly go across documents on multiple logical partitions and maybe even on multiple physical partitions. Additionally, the way the data is used means you need to affect the name of the theme anywhere it is nested as part of a document, which might be more than just within the user profile documents.

When this happens, you'll need to read important information from the Cosmos DB change feed and then you use a process (typically implemented in an Azure Function) to ensure that your data is updated appropriately as a response to the change feed.

More information about the change feed can be found at https://learn.microsoft.com/azure/cosmos-db/nosql/read-change-feed. You can also look at the basic information on that link about using the change feed processor. Additionally, if you really want to go deep with this, there is a lab for the DP-420 Exam that covers a similar scenario as mentioned previously, which can be found at https://microsoftlearning.github.io/dp-420-cosmos-db-dev/instructions/17-denormalize.html#prepare-your-development-environment. Although this level of knowledge may be overkill for the AZ-204 Exam, it can't hurt you to know how to do this and will likely be a fun challenge for you as a developer.

Utilizing .NET with Azure Table Storage and Cosmos DB via the Cosmos DB SDK

Now that the bases are covered with the inner workings of Cosmos DB, it's time to once again look at some code that will interact with the SDK to work with Cosmos DB. In addition to Cosmos DB, this code portion will also show table storage interaction. The best part of all of this is that the same code that works against table storage will work against Cosmos DB. If you are mostly concerned with the exam, remember that the ideal path is to migrate your table storage offering to Cosmos DB via the Table Storage API, so the primary focus is most likely to be working directly against Cosmos DB. As a developer, however, you should know how to use both, how to migrate from table storage to Cosmos DB, and when you should choose one offering over the other.

Azure Table Storage

To get started, create an Azure Table Storage account. If you don't know how to do this, follow the documentation at `https://learn.microsoft.com/azure/storage/tables/table-storage-quickstart-portal`.

Once you have a table storage account, leverage the project called `WorkingWithAzureTableStorage` found in the repository for this book under the materials for Chapter 2. For these examples, I'm working against the same storage account from the previous chapter, but you could easily create a new storage account to work with the code.

Compose the Client

As with other offerings, remember that you must build the hierarchy. For table storage, you need the account and connection string.

```
var storageCNSTR = _configuration["Storage:ConnectionString"];
```

You then need to get the table client to work with table storage:

```
var tableServiceClient = new TableServiceClient(storageCNSTR);
```

Create a Table

To create a table in table storage, make sure you have the connection string information and account in place and include the NuGet packages for the `Azure.Data.Tables`. With these in place, run the following code (must be in an asynchronous method):

```
//Create a new Table "Universities"
var tableClient = tableServiceClient.GetTableClient(
    tableName: "Universities"
);

await tableClient.CreateIfNotExistsAsync();
```

Add an Item to Table Storage

Once you have the table in place, you can add a JSON document to the storage. The JSON document's structure for use in table storage is stricter than is required for utilization in Cosmos DB. With table storage, every item must have a `RowKey` and a `PartitionKey` defined. Additional properties that must exist are an `ETag` and a `TimeStamp`. The `ETag` and `TimeStamp` fields are used to help the Table Storage API know if the data is concurrent with integrity. If another process modifies the data, the `ETag` will be different than what is being sent for update or delete operations. In this way, the system can know not to modify data when the field has been modified.

Using a defined object that implements the ITableEntity interface allows easy interaction with the table data. In the sample project, a class is defined to model the University that implements the ITableEntity interface.

```
var iowaStateUniversity = new University()
{
    RowKey = "iowa-state-university-ames-iowa",
    PartitionKey = "iowa-state-university",
    Name = "Iowa State University",
    Location = "Ames, Iowa",
    YearFounded = 1858
};

await tableClient.AddEntityAsync<University>(iowaState
University);
```

Get an Item from Storage

With table storage, you can leverage LINQ to query. The best performance will take place when getting the single entity utilizing the PartitionKey and RowKey together:

```
var isu = await tableClient.GetEntityAsync<University>(iowaState
University.PartitionKey, iowaStateUniversity.RowKey);
```

However, you can use other methods to accomplish the same task or get groups of items using LINQ. Note that both of these queries return a collection, so they must be further filtered in order to get a single result:

```
var secondIsu = tableClient.Query<University>(x => x.Name.
Equals("Iowa State University"));
```

```
//or

var anotherIsu = tableClient.Query<University>
                 (x => x.PartitionKey == "iowa-state-
                 university");
```

Delete Items

To delete items, you can run yet another asynchronous statement utilizing the Parti and RowKey of the item:

```
await tableClient.DeleteEntityAsync(iowaStateUniversity.
PartitionKey, iowaStateUniversity.RowKey);
```

You can further restrict this if you know the ETag, making sure you only delete items that have not changed since you last read them.

Azure Cosmos DB (Table API)

Working with Cosmos DB on the Table API is very similar to working with table storage in the initial setup; however, the ability to utilize the more robust ecosystem of Cosmos DB will allow your solution to work across regions and additional complex indexing when necessary.

Table Storage to Cosmos DB

To get started working with the sample code porting data from Azure Table Storage to a Cosmos DB Table Storage API, create a Table Storage API account to handle the migration of the code from using Azure Table Storage, as discussed previously, to utilize Cosmos DB on the Table Storage API. If you are unsure how to create a Cosmos DB Table Storage API Container, refer to https://learn.microsoft.com/azure/cosmos-db/table/how-to-create-container.

Once the account is created, take the original table storage app and change the connection string in the existing application to the new connection string for the table storage API Cosmos DB account you just created. The connection string can be found under the left-navigation item called Connection String (see Figure 2-12).

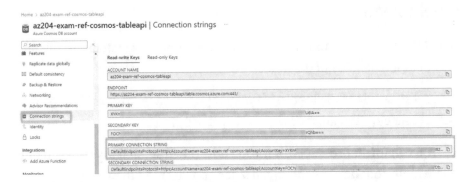

Figure 2-12. *The connection string for the new Table API Cosmos Account is under the Connection String left-navigation menu item*

Select Primary Connection String and use that in the code. Once the new connection string is in place, run the exact same code that was used for working with Azure Table Storage. The new Table API account should work with no code changes! You can then review the data in the Cosmos account using the Data Explorer (as shown in Figure 2-13).

Figure 2-13. *The Table Storage is easily ported to Cosmos Table API. The only change was to set the connection string to the new Table API Cosmos account. Then the code just works*

Azure Cosmos DB (SQL API)

Working with Cosmos DB and the SQL API is the primary focus for development and the recommended way to integrate your application with Cosmos DB for all new development work. Working with Cosmos DB on the SQL API follows the same types of patterns we've already established in previous work. Create the account, then get the connection string. Once you have that in place, you can easily integrate code.

As mentioned, there is a set of sample code that you can easily get from any Azure Cosmos DB account. If you simply create a Cosmos DB account, go to the Quick Start menu item (refer back to Figure 2-10), add the Items container, then download the sample code.

In addition to that sample code, refer to the sample code called WorkingWithAzureCosmosDB in the repository for this book under the Chapter 2 materials.

Once you have the application, make sure to create a Cosmos DB SQL API account. If you are unsure how to do this, follow the documentation at https://learn.microsoft.com/en-us/azure/cosmos-db/sql/quickstart-dotnet.

Once you have the account created, get the Primary Key and Endpoint URI using the portal. An easy way to find this is shown in Figure 2-14. Using the portal, navigate to the Keys left-navigation menu in the account.

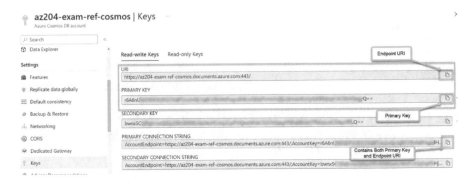

Figure 2-14. *Getting the connection string from the portal using the left-navigation Keys menu under the Azure Cosmos DB SQL API account*

Note that the connection string has both pieces of information, and the SDK has you compose objects using the two individual pieces. Or, you can just use the full connection string. Additionally, ensure you have the NuGet package called `Microsoft.Azure.Cosmos` included in your project in order to interact with the SDK correctly. For this example, ensure you are using the package that references the SQL API. The sample code already contains the proper references, but it's always wise to double-check what NuGet packages you are leveraging, because there are generally a number of packages that are named in a similar manner. Sometimes Microsoft will update to a new version and change the name as new iterations of .NET are released. For example, in the past you might have leveraged `Microsoft.Azure.DocumentDB` for similar operations, which is now deprecated since the latest version is called `Microsoft.Azure.Cosmos`.

Connect to the Cosmos DB Account

To get started, create the client with the following code utilizing a using statement:

```
using (CosmosClient client = new CosmosClient(endpointURI,
primaryKey))
```

Note that the remaining code for this section with operations against the database must be inside of this client block. Like other solutions with Azure and .NET, remember the composition hierarchy. Without a client, you can't perform operations like GetDatabase or GetContainer.

Create and Delete Databases

You can easily create databases with the following code (inside the client block):

```
var db = await client.CreateDatabaseIfNotExistsAsync
("Universities");
```

Deleting an existing database can be accomplished with this code:

```
var dbDeleteResponse = await client.
GetDatabase("Universities").DeleteAsync();
```

Create and Delete Containers

In the hierarchy, the account is provisioned, then one or more databases, then one or more containers per database. In the client block (account), with reference to a database, you can create a new container as follows:

```
//Create Container:
var containerProperties = new ContainerProperties();
containerProperties.Id = "Public";
containerProperties.PartitionKeyPath = "/Name";
```

```
containerProperties.IndexingPolicy.Automatic = true;
containerProperties.IndexingPolicy.IndexingMode = IndexingMode.
Consistent;

var container = await client
                    .GetDatabase("Universities")
                    .CreateContainerIfNotExistsAsync
                    (containerProperties, 400);
```

Note that the container properties were set, giving an indexing policy and partition key path in this creation. Throughput was provisioned to 400 RUs (see Figure 2-15).

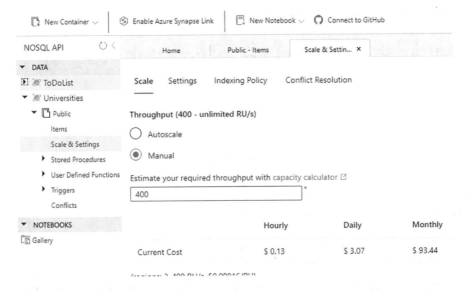

Figure 2-15. *The Database container is provisioned with 400 RUs*

The PartitionKey can be validated from the Settings tab, as shown in Figure 2-16.

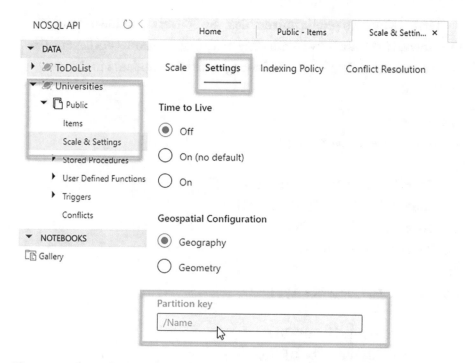

Figure 2-16. *The partition key is set as expected from the code*

Deleting a container works in a similar manner. Remember this code must also be in the code that has the using statement to create the client in order to work correctly:

```
//Delete Container
var containerToDelete = client.GetDatabase("Universities").
GetContainer("Public");
await containerToDelete.DeleteContainerAsync();
```

Insert and Update Items

To insert and update items, you can use the Upsert command, or you can use the Insert and Upsert commands in tandem. For this activity, all data is based on a prebuilt class called University that is part of the sample project.

First, define two public universities, the University of Iowa (Iowa City, Iowa, USA), and Iowa State University (Ames, Iowa, USA). Note: USA is purposefully omitted in the following code to be updated in the next command.

```
//Add Items
var isu = new University()
{
    Id = "iowa-state-university",
    Name = "Iowa State University",
    Location = "Ames, Iowa",
    YearFounded = 1858
};
var iowa = new University()
{
    Id = "university-of-iowa",
    Name = "University of Iowa",
    Location = "Iowa City, Iowa, USA",
    YearFounded = 1847
};
```

The Insert command requires checking for existence and trapping an exception, and it looks like this:

```
//create requires you prove it doesn't exist first:
try
{
    var isuExists = await containerInfo.ReadItemAsync<University>
                        (isu.Id, new PartitionKey
                        (isu.Name));
    Console.WriteLine("ISU Document existed, so not created");
}
```

```
catch (CosmosException cosmosEx)
{
    if (cosmosEx.StatusCode == System.Net.HttpStatusCode.
    NotFound)
    {
        var ISUDocument = await containerInfo.
        CreateItemAsync(isu);
        Console.WriteLine("ISU Document created");

        isu.Location = "Ames, Iowa, USA";
        await containerInfo.UpsertItemAsync(isu);
    }
}
```

Note the second part containing the Upsert:

```
isu.Location = "Ames, Iowa, USA";
await containerInfo.UpsertItemAsync(isu);
```

Alternatively, Upsert can be used to either Insert or Update as follows, without the need to check for existence:

```
var iowaDocument = await containerInfo.UpsertItemAsync(iowa);
```

After the insert/update, you should be able to query to see the two items in the database, as shown in Figure 2-17.

Figure 2-17. *The data exists after being added via code to the database container for Public Universities*

Query the Data via Code

One of the most frustrating things I've encountered about working with Cosmos DB is the query syntax and a few of its idiosyncrasies. Once you learn it, the syntax and inner workings make perfect sense. However, there is a very simple "gotcha" that I want to bring to your attention here. This is an important thing to understand about the structure of the queries, and it can save you hours of work.

Consider, if you will, the previous data. Suppose you only ran the data as presented so far, leaving the container, the two items, and the database intact. The query as presented in Figure 2-17 shows that the data exists:

```
SELECT c.Name, c.Location FROM c
```

Try the following queries on your own if you can. I also show you the results so you can see them here if you just want to take my word for it. The first query is as follows:

```
SELECT * FROM c
```

This query takes 2.28 RUs and returns both documents (see Figures 2-18 and 2-19).

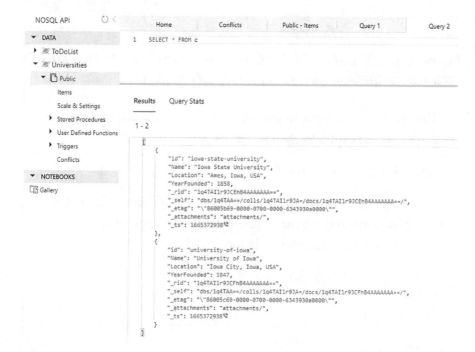

Figure 2-18. *The SELECT * FROM c query returns all data as expected*

Figure 2-19. *The SELECT * FROM c query runs in 2.28 RUs, which is pretty much the ideal processing time you can get in Cosmos DB*

This query is efficient and gets all the data. Compare it to the query we ran earlier, which explicitly names the fields:

```
SELECT c.Name, c.Location FROM c
```

This query gets the two fields for both items and runs in 2.29 RUs, which is pretty much the same as previously (RUs result shown in Figure 2-20; original result shown in Figure 2-17).

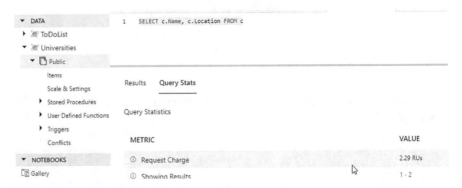

Figure 2-20. *The query with named fields runs in 2.29 RUs and gets the same results with just the named fields as expected*

Note specifically, however, that one query names the fields with an alias, while another one just uses the asterisk to get all fields.

You might be saying "yes, that makes sense." I agree with you. However, the following syntax is much more strict than in a typical T-SQL query you might be used to writing. For example, do you think the following query will return data?

```
SELECT c.* FROM c
```

If you answered "no, it will throw a syntax error" then you win. Figure 2-21 shows the result of this query.

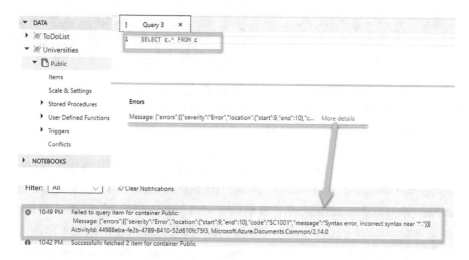

Figure 2-21. *The syntax error is shown for the SELECT c.* from c query*

In other words, if you want to use a wildcard asterisk, do not preface that asterisk with an alias.

Now what do you think will happen if you run this query:

```
SELECT Name, Location FROM c
```

If you stated "An error that says Name and Location can't be resolved, thereby making me think the fields aren't part of the document even though they are..." then you get the point well here (see Figure 2-22).

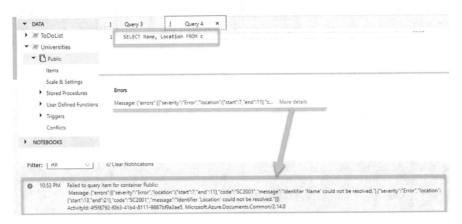

Figure 2-22. *The Name and Location fields are stated to be unresolvable. This can be confusing since they are valid fields. The problem is the lack of the alias*

Once again, the syntax here matters. The reason I'm calling this out is so you don't write code from .NET and run one of these queries and spend hours trying to determine what is wrong with your code only to realize it was a syntax error in the query. These seemingly conflicting values that work for the queries will make sense once you expect and/or experience them. Before they happen to you, especially if you are used to T-SQL, they may not be as apparent.

Now that you understand the syntax for the queries, it is time to finish up the code for working with Cosmos DB from the SDK.

Using a Point Read

The best way to get a single item is to perform a point read. To do this, you need to know the partition key and ID for the item. If the partition key is the item, you are already there. If the partition key is not the item, use both.

In this case, you need to get a point read on the specific university. This is done by creating the partition key using the string value, as shown in the following code:

```
var isuDoc = await containerInfo.ReadItemAsync<University>
                (isu.Id, new PartitionKey(isu.Name));
```

The result is a single document retrieved with the absolute best performance and RU utilization possible.

Using the Query Item Iterator

There are two ways to work with data results. The Query Item Iterator is the first. The next section leverages the LINQ version of the iterator.

To iterate results, utilize the query discussed earlier in code as follows:

```
//iterate all results
var query = new QueryDefinition("SELECT * FROM c");

using (var feed = containerInfo.GetItemQueryIterator<University>
(query))
{
    while (feed.HasMoreResults)
    {
        var allItems = await feed.ReadNextAsync();
        foreach (var item in allItems)
        {
            Console.WriteLine($"Next: {item.Name}, " +
                            $"founded {item.
                            YearFounded}, " +
                            $"is located in {item.
                            Location}");
        }
    }
}
```

This query returns results as expected, and iteration shows all the data from the container.

Using the LINQ Version of the Iteration for Query Syntax

The query iterator with raw SQL is great, but in the real world you'll likely want to use the LINQ version of this code as follows:

```
//use LINQ
var universities = containerInfo.GetItemLinqQueryable
<University>();
using (var feed = universities.ToFeedIterator())
{
    while (feed.HasMoreResults)
    {
        var data = await feed.ReadNextAsync();
        foreach (var item in data)
        {
            Console.WriteLine($"LINQ result: {item.Name}, " +
                            $"founded {item.
                            YearFounded}, " +
                            $"is located in {item.
                            Location}");
        }
    }
}
```

Delete Items from the Container

To complete this look at the code, the final thing that needs to be addressed is deleting items from the container (deleting containers and databases is addressed earlier).

To remove items from a container, use a point delete approach with the ID and partition key, similar to the point read:

```
var dIowa = await containerInfo.DeleteItemAsync<University>
                (iowa.Id, new PartitionKey(iowa.Name));
```

Review Your Learning

As an additional challenge, consider the following questions and determine how you would approach potential solution(s). You can find answers to these questions in Appendix A at the end of this book.

1) What is a logical partition in Cosmos DB? What are some good and bad partitions for write-heavy and read-heavy databases?

2) What is a physical partition in Cosmos DB? What are the physical partition limits?

3) Can a Cosmos DB be accessed from a private network?

4) What is the maximum size of a Cosmos DB document?

5) How do you calculate an RU?

6) When working with code against the Cosmos Database, what are two ways to connect to the account using keys?

7) What does it take to migrate a table storage application to a Cosmos DB Table API application?

Complete the AZ-204: Develop Solutions That Use Azure Cosmos DB

To fully learn the material, I recommend taking the time to complete the MS Learn modules for Azure Cosmos DB found here:

- Develop solutions that use Azure Cosmos DB:
  `https://learn.microsoft.com/en-us/training/paths/az-204-develop-solutions-that-use-azure-cosmos-db/`.

Chapter Summary

In this chapter, you learned about working with Cosmos DB in Azure. The discussion featured a number of important points regarding partitioning, consistency levels, capacity, global distribution, migration of table storage to a Cosmos Table API, and working with Cosmos DB from the .NET SDK.

After working through this chapter and the Microsoft Learn modules, you should be on track to be in command of the following concepts as you learn about Azure and prepare for the AZ-204 Exam:

- Understand the main API offerings for Cosmos DB, and why each one is useful, with the ability to choose the correct API.

- Understand the difference between Cosmos DB for NoSQL and Cosmos DB for Table.

- Understand and work with partitions within Cosmos DB.

- Utilize the correct consistency level in your solution.

- Interact with Azure Cosmos DB via the .NET SDK using the correct SDK for the scenario.

- Work with the Azure Cosmos DB Change Feed.

In the next chapter, you start the next section on working with Azure Compute by learning about implementing Infrastructure as a Service (IaaS) solutions.

PART II

Develop Azure Compute Solutions

CHAPTER 3

Implement Infrastructure as a Service (IaaS) Solutions

August 10, 2020. That date may not be very important to you, but for anyone that lived in Nebraska, Illinois, or Iowa, it was a day they'll never forget. It was especially difficult on farmers. On that day, out of pretty much nowhere, a land hurricane (known as a derecho—*day-ray-cho*) wreaked havoc for about 700 miles in a swath of 40 or more miles from top to bottom. An estimated 11 billion dollars in crops and other assets were lost. Something else was lost—power and internet. In a matter of 20 minutes, it was like going back to the dark ages, as all pipelines in and out were completely lost, and Internet was just gone. Do you know what still worked? All of Azure on the East and West regions of the United States, as well as the rest of their global regions.

Businesses that had only housed resources on premises in Des Moines were likely not able to continue their day-to-day operations. Businesses that had regional failovers and operations on any other valid region could continue serving their customers outside of the region.

© Brian L. Gorman 2023
B. L. Gorman, *Developing Solutions for Microsoft Azure Certification Companion*,
Certification Study Companion Series, https://doi.org/10.1007/978-1-4842-9300-3_3

Infrastructure as a Service (IaaS) is one of the primary ways that cloud migration can enable your business and your applications to continue working when the world is literally not working. Additionally, moving to the cloud allows your business to take advantage of cloud benefits like the economy of scale and leveraging operational expenditures over capital expenditures. Finally, with your resources deployed in the cloud, you don't have to go into an office at 2am to fix a broken network card, a failed hard drive, or a server that won't reboot.

For this exam, the IaaS component is composed of four key Azure infrastructure technologies and services. These four areas of concern are *Virtual Machines, ARM Templates, Azure Container Registry*, and *Azure Container Instances*. For purposes of brevity of the chapters and organization of the material, this chapter covers the virtual machines and ARM templates. Chapter 5 covers the Azure Containers ecosystem, focusing on the exam topics of the container instances and registries. As an update to this statement, from the time I originally wrote this until the time I'm doing the final proof, the exam has been updated. As of April 2023, the focus has shifted towards the containers ecosystem. In the official path you are no longer asked to train for virtual machines and ARM/Bicep Templates. An additional module on Azure Container Apps has been added. Even though the exam doesn't necessarily require this material, it is still worth your time as a developer to know how to do the things in this chapter. That being said, if your sole purpose is to prepare for the exam you can likely skim through this chapter quickly. If your end goal is the AZ-204 followed by the AZ-400, I would recommend you pay attention to this material in more detail as the infrastructure piece may still be a critical part of creating a robust DevOps solution.

Virtual Machines

Regarding the exam, there are a few things you need to be aware of regarding virtual machines. The next few pages cover the issues with some screenshots and discussions around the utilization and deployment of machines. I recommend that you try working through this on your own subscription as well, just to get the practice.

The main topics you need to understand are the resilience and redundancy of the Azure Data Centers for infrastructure deployments, specifically around virtual machines. Additionally, you need to understand the networking components enough to know how to provision, limit, and change access to the machine (especially around ports 22, 80, 443, 3389).

While you shouldn't technically have to memorize ports, any developer who has ever done a manual deployment to an on-premises machine should know at least three of those without having to think about what they are. Port 22 is for Secure Shell Protocol (SSH), which is the primary port for connecting to a Linux virtual machine. Port 80 is for Hypertext Transfer Protocol (HTTP) and port 443 is for Hypertext Transfer Protocol Secure (HTTPS). Both 80 and 443 are utilized for connecting to websites and other public endpoints via the Internet. Finally, port 3389 is for Remote Desktop Protocol (RDP), which allows you to connect to a Windows virtual machine.

I will also say a developer should know about either port 1433 or port 3306, or both. Both of these ports are critical for database interaction on standard server deployments, with port 1433 being the main port to communicate with MS SQL Server and 3306 being the main port for a standard MySQL deployment.

In addition to ports for networking, a developer should also understand simple concepts around load balancing to distribute traffic, which allows you to ensure that a fleet of machines can handle load, typically for what might be called a *server farm*.

A final concept that you need to be aware of with Azure Virtual Machines is the Desired State Configuration (DSC). With DSC, you can ensure that a machine has specific capabilities enabled or features installed. For example, ensuring that IIS is installed on a Windows Server deployment. DSC is also useful to minimize configuration drift, which allows you to ensure that a machine maintains a specific state, restoring features that were improperly disabled, or removing features that should not have been enabled automatically.

To get started learning about these concepts, first you need to take a step back to the Azure Fundamentals Exam (AZ-900) material around Azure Data Centers. The most important concepts can be found in this unit on Microsoft Learn: `https://learn.microsoft.com/training/modules/describe-core-architectural-components-of-azure/`.

Azure Physical Architecture

For purposes of learning, imagine that an Azure Data Center is a physical building or set of buildings on physical land in a major city, such as Des Moines, Iowa. Because this is a physical building, Microsoft has implemented and employed security measures and personnel to ensure that no unauthorized access is taking place at this building. When thinking about defense-in-depth, the outer layer of security is always the physical barriers. Additional concerns like power and maintenance are all handled by Microsoft and/or agents of Microsoft. With all of this, Azure can offer virtualized hardware and the consumers don't have to worry about any of the physical aspects of the deployment.

Inside the data center, there are racks of bare-metal servers, each with power and networking requirements. It is upon this backbone that you will deploy your virtual machine workloads to host your applications. You can also utilize this hardware to create a standardized image that all of your developers utilize every day for performing their daily work.

Fault Domains

To understand how you can achieve the greatest resilience, it's important to understand how the bare-metal servers work to distribute your virtualized workloads. The first concept to understand is a fault domain. You can think of a fault domain as a rack of servers sharing the same network and power sources. In this fault domain, you have many servers and many virtual machines on these servers. If someone trips over the power cord, unplugs the network connection, or a hardware failure happens, this fault domain is unable to continue backing virtual machines until the issue is resolved. Patching and/or updating with Windows Updates is yet another scenario that temporarily restricts the fault domain.

In a basic deployment of a virtual machine with no hardware infrastructure resiliency, your virtual machine is deployed on one single fault domain, within one physical data center for one region in Azure. Your SLA for uptime for connectivity in this scenario is typically three nines (99.9 percent). This means out of each day you should have connectivity for all but about 1.5 minutes. If the region your deployment is in becomes unreachable, you'll have a longer time before you get back to operational status.

Update Domains

In scenarios where you need to have the ability to connect to a machine but also allow for patching and Windows Updates to work, you need to place multiple machines in separate update domains. You can have multiple update domains on the same fault domain, and you can have update domains on different fault domains.

To utilize update domains for virtual machines within an Azure Data Center, you need to create an availability set.

Availability Zones

Within the Azure Region where at least three physical buildings that are a minimum of ten miles apart exist, you can create deployments utilizing availability zones.

To visualize this, imagine there are data centers for the Central U.S. region in Kansas City, Chicago, and Minneapolis. When you deploy your virtual machine (or other resources) utilizing an availability zone, your primary zone is one of the three locations. If the city where your resources are deployed loses power or Internet, your solution continues to work via one of the other two locations. In this scenario, the only time you should not have availability is when the entire region is unavailable.

Azure Regions

As a global solution, regions provide the ability to place resources closer to your customers. This can be a physical closeness or a closeness in terms of latency. Either way, when you need the best availability or resiliency, you'll utilize multiple regions in your solution.

For virtual machines, a common scenario is to have a primary region where the machine is always available. A secondary region is created by implementing an Azure Site Recovery services vault. In this scenario, the backup machine can easily become the primary machine in case of regional failure. The switch over can be either manual or automatic. The regional failover machine also serves as a backup in case of corruption on the primary region machine.

Azure Regions are typically paired together with regions at least 300 miles apart for the best redundancy solutions.

Azure Sovereign Regions

Although it's not likely super important to the AZ-204 Exam, it's important to know that there are multiple Azure Cloud offerings. Typically, you'll be working on the public cloud. However, if you are working for the U.S. Government, you might be utilizing the Azure U.S. Government cloud. If you are in Germany, another private cloud exists for sovereignty. China also has a sovereign region.

Sovereign regions are completely isolated from the public cloud and from one another. Therefore, by design, you should not be able to directly communicate with resources between different sovereign regions.

Deploying an Azure Virtual Machine

Deploying a virtual machine in Azure is straightforward. On the portal, you choose the subscription, resource group, and region for the deployment of the machine. You also need to give the machine a name.

Creating a Virtual Machine: The Basics

Windows machines are limited to 16 characters, while Linux machines can be named with up to 64 characters. The recommendation is to utilize a naming schema that illuminates the region, workload, and machine number to make it easier to identify what the machines are doing. Names like uscwebvm001 and noreudatavm025 are examples that help you note the regional deployment, workload, and machine number. Figure 3-1 shows the start of creating a new virtual machine.

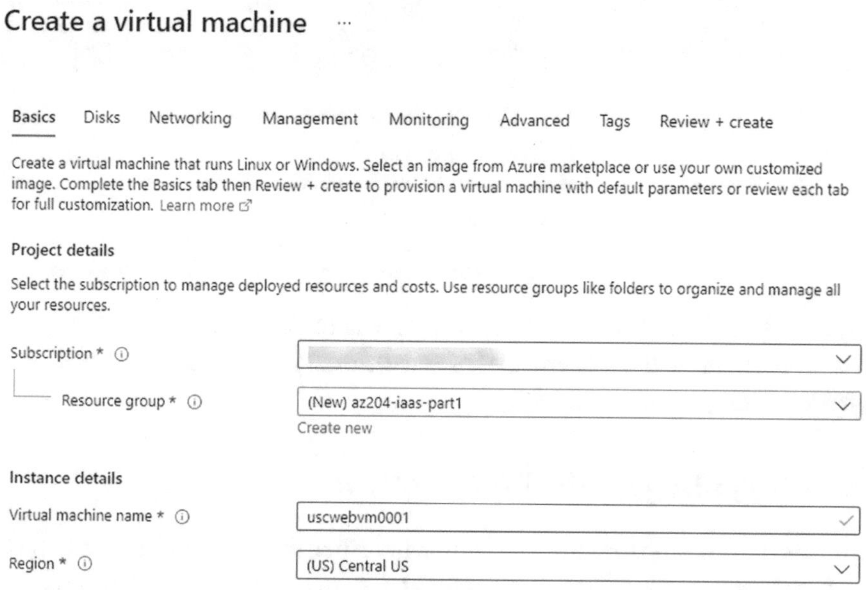

Create a virtual machine ···

| Basics | Disks | Networking | Management | Monitoring | Advanced | Tags | Review + create |

Create a virtual machine that runs Linux or Windows. Select an image from Azure marketplace or use your own customized image. Complete the Basics tab then Review + create to provision a virtual machine with default parameters or review each tab for full customization. Learn more ⬀

Project details

Select the subscription to manage deployed resources and costs. Use resource groups like folders to organize and manage all your resources.

Subscription * ⓘ
[_____ ⌄]

Resource group * ⓘ
[(New) az204-iaas-part1 ⌄]
Create new

Instance details

Virtual machine name * ⓘ
[uscwebvm0001 ✓]

Region * ⓘ
[(US) Central US ⌄]

Figure 3-1. *Creation of a virtual machine starts with the subscription, resource group, name, and region*

Availability Options

The next fields on the Basics tab allow you to determine your availability options, with choices for "No Infrastructure Redundancy Required," "Availability Zone" (Regional Separation Across Zones), "Virtual Machine Scale Set" (Zone and Fault Domain Redundancy), and "Availability Set" (Fault Domain Redundancy). For this deployment, no redundancy is selected. In a production scenario for a unique machine, you'll want to choose Availability Zone or Availability set (see Figure 3-2). If you have a fleet of identical machines (i.e., a server farm), you'll want to select the virtual machine scale set. As an added piece of information, Kubernetes clusters with nodes backed by virtual machines utilize virtual machine scale sets for the cluster nodes due to the ability to easily scale out on identical machines.

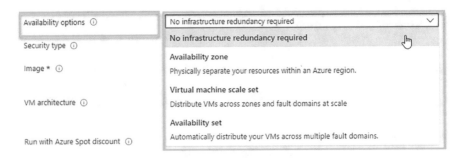

Figure 3-2. *The availability options for a virtual machine help you provision with the amount of redundancy and resiliency that is appropriate for your workload*

Security, Image, and Architecture

For this demonstration, the machine will utilize the standard security type and a Windows Server 2019 image (to simulate a production web server with IIS). Azure Spot discounts give you an ability to leverage reserved resources that are essentially not being used. They are very limited, however, when resources are in high demand, as is generally the case in a scenario like the first months of COVID-19 lockdowns, when all the world started working from home. During that time, you were not able to utilize spot instances because there were no resources available. Figure 3-3 shows the selections for Security Type, Image, Architecture, and Spot Discount.

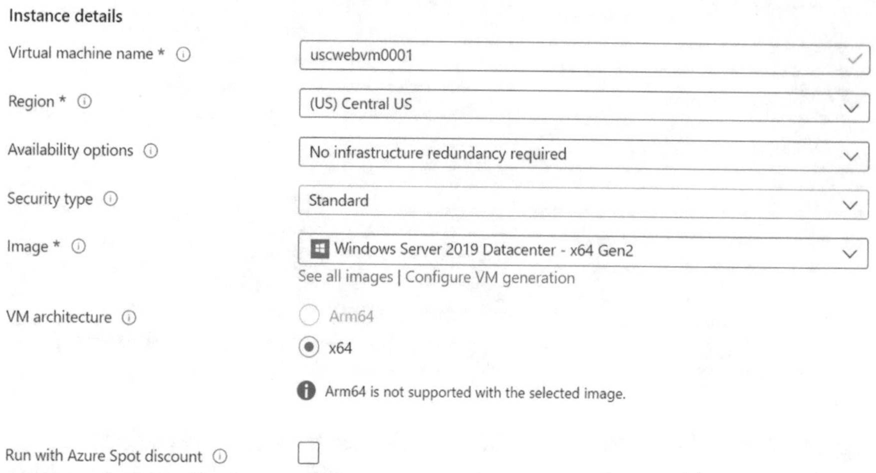

Figure 3-3. *Selecting the security type, image, architecture, and leaving the spot discount unchecked*

Virtual Machine Size

Another area to understand well are the workload sizes that are preconfigured by Azure. Each group has a specific purpose, and the goal is to help you create virtual machines that meet your needs and that are also cost effective.

Groups exist for general purpose workloads (D-Series), Batch (Burstable) workloads, (B-Series), High Memory (E-Series), GPU (F-Series), Storage (L-Series), and a few others (see Figure 3-4).

Select a VM size ...

Figure 3-4. *The various machine sizes are grouped according to potential workloads to aid with selection of the size for your machine*

Each offering allows you to select a number of vCPUs, RAM, disks, and IOPs. As you look through the offerings, you get estimated costs for the month. The cost is what you would pay if you left the machine running 24/7 for the whole month. You can save money by deprovisioning the machine when not in use. No matter how much you use it, you will pay some costs for storage, so a typical work machine might see 60-80 percent of the estimate, when shut down on nights and weekends.

Once you've selected the size for your machine, you'll see the estimated price, and then you'll need to enter a valid username and password combination for the administrator (see Figure 3-5).

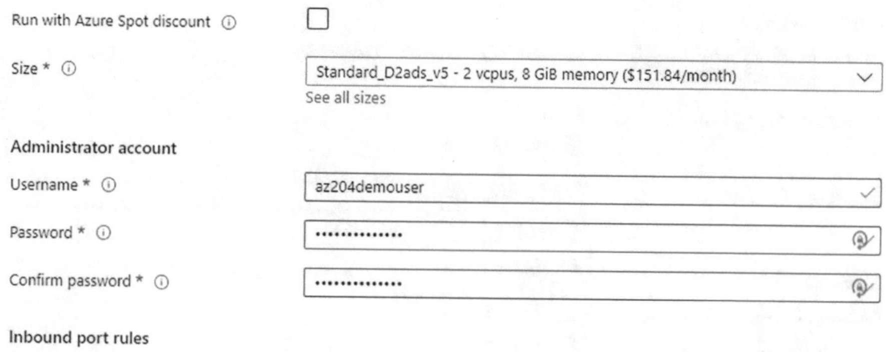

Run with Azure Spot discount ⓘ   ☐

Size * ⓘ   Standard_D2ads_v5 - 2 vcpus, 8 GiB memory ($151.84/month)   ⌄
See all sizes

Administrator account

Username * ⓘ   az204demouser   ✓

Password * ⓘ   ••••••••••••   ⊚

Confirm password * ⓘ   ••••••••••••   ⊚

Inbound port rules

Figure 3-5. *The size is selected, and a username and password are entered for the administrator*

Port Rules

In order to access the machine, ports need to be open. The default deployment state opens port 3389, but additional options exist for 80, 443, and 22. To be most secure, select None for public inbound ports, perhaps even closing off port 3389 (you can easily enable it later if you need to). If this machine is going to be exposed for web traffic, you can open ports 80 and/or 443 here. For SSH connections, you can open port 22. Any additional port configuration can only be configured after the machine is deployed. Figure 3-6 shows the options for port selection at this point.

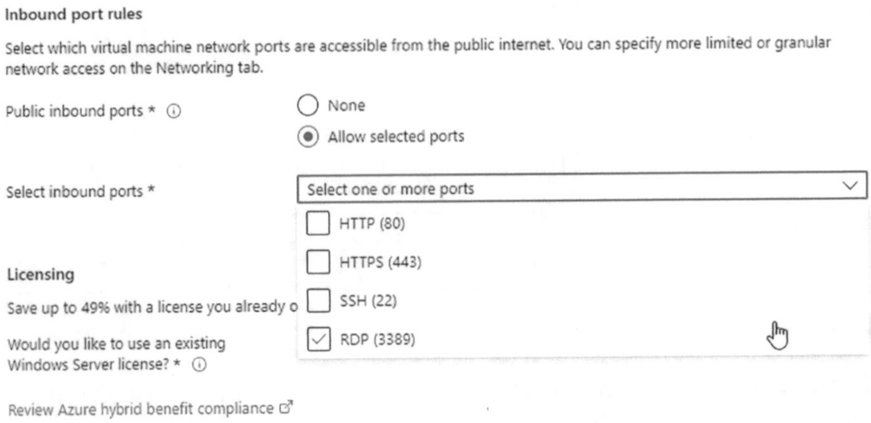

Inbound port rules

Select which virtual machine network ports are accessible from the public internet. You can specify more limited or granular network access on the Networking tab.

Public inbound ports * ⓘ   ○ None
                             ● Allow selected ports

Select inbound ports * | Select one or more ports   ∨ |

                          ☐ HTTP (80)

                          ☐ HTTPS (443)

Licensing

Save up to 49% with a license you already o ☐ SSH (22)

Would you like to use an existing   ☑ RDP (3389)
Windows Server license? * ⓘ

Review Azure hybrid benefit compliance ⬏

Figure 3-6. *During creation, on the Basics tab, options exist to open one or more ports for the machine*

For this deployment, no ports are opened during creation. After deployment, browsing to the networking blade will allow you to set the ports directly in inbound rules on the Network Security Group (NSG) for the VM.

Hybrid Licensing

One of the ways Azure lets organizations save money with virtual machines is to deploy and utilize existing licenses. On a Windows Server 2019 image, you must have a license. If you have corporate licenses, you can save 40-70 percent of the cost. If you do not check the box, the cost of the license is baked into your machine cost.

Disks

Currently you can utilize disks in one of two ways—managed or unmanaged. At this point, unless you have a serious reason not to, you should utilize managed disks.

Managed disks are automatically configured and deployed in Azure Storage for you by Azure and are encrypted by default. You can utilize your own key for encryption if you desire to do so. If you choose your own key, you must store the key in Azure Key Vault. Premium SSD Disks for virtual machines are only available as managed disks. If you want a standard hard drive, which you can deploy as managed or unmanaged, you can still choose one at the time of this writing. Unmanaged disks must be managed by you, so you need to create storage for the disk. Additionally, unmanaged disks are not encrypted by default, so you also need to ensure the disk is encrypted.

As you create your VM, about 12-15 resources are created. One option now available is to enable a pseudo-grouping of these resources. In the past, the only way to clean up a machine was to delete all the resources manually (or delete the resource group they were in). Now you can check a box for resources like the Network Interface Card (NIC) card and disks to associate with the VM for lifecycle management.

During disk creation, you can also choose to add disks for storage to attach to your machine. Figure 3-7 shows the disk selection screen.

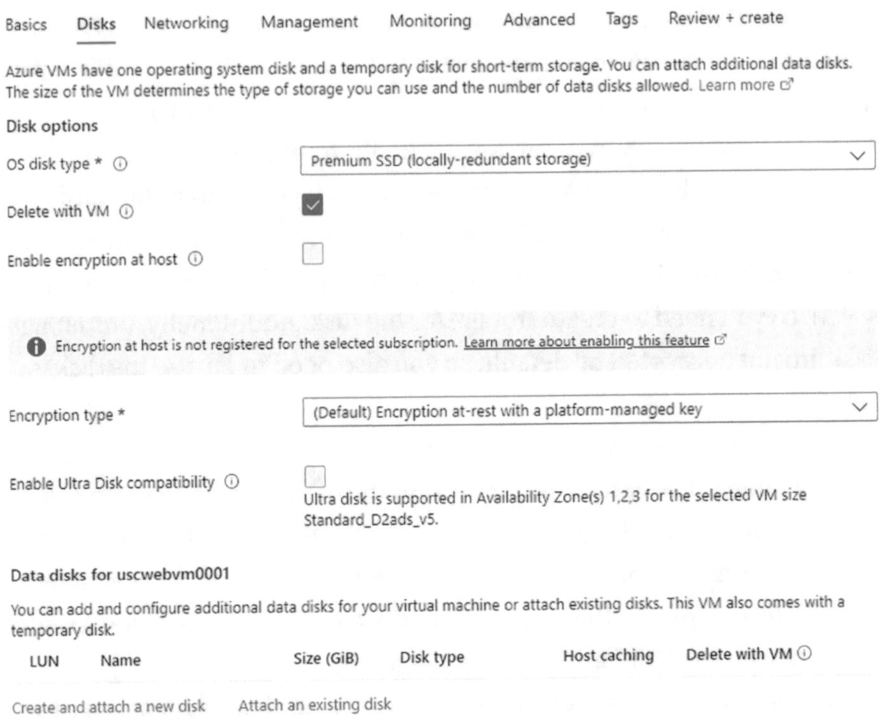

Basics   **Disks**   Networking   Management   Monitoring   Advanced   Tags   Review + create

Azure VMs have one operating system disk and a temporary disk for short-term storage. You can attach additional data disks. The size of the VM determines the type of storage you can use and the number of data disks allowed. Learn more ⬈

Disk options

OS disk type * ⓘ
> Premium SSD (locally-redundant storage)   ⌄

Delete with VM ⓘ
> ✓

Enable encryption at host ⓘ
> ☐

> ⓘ Encryption at host is not registered for the selected subscription. Learn more about enabling this feature ⬈

Encryption type *
> (Default) Encryption at-rest with a platform-managed key   ⌄

Enable Ultra Disk compatibility ⓘ
> ☐
> Ultra disk is supported in Availability Zone(s) 1,2,3 for the selected VM size Standard_D2ads_v5.

Data disks for uscwebvm0001

You can add and configure additional data disks for your virtual machine or attach existing disks. This VM also comes with a temporary disk.

LUN	Name	Size (GiB)	Disk type	Host caching	Delete with VM ⓘ

Create and attach a new disk   Attach an existing disk

Figure 3-7. *Creating the disk(s) for the virtual machine*

Networking

When a virtual machine is created, it must exist on a virtual network in Azure. Rules around IP addresses and virtual network interactivity in Azure are outside of the scope of the AZ-204 Exam; however, any good developer who is also responsible for DevOps should understand that the network allows resources to communicate privately. For example, if you want to create an additional VM for the data server (or a load balancer and a data server farm), the Web VM and the Data VM will need to be on networks that can communicate. This is typically done via subnets in the same virtual network but can also be done with Virtual Network Peering.

For the AZ-204 Exam, the number one concern is communication with the outside world. In other words, you should be ready to answer the question: How will your users connect to this machine? Once again, you have the choice to open ports 22, 80, 443, and 3389 for various connection options. Once again, you do not get the option to do any other port designations during the creation of the machine, but additional port changes can happen at any time after the machine is deployed.

The network rules can be configured against the machine directly using the NIC card attached to a Network Security Group (NSG). Every NIC card must have one NSG, but an NSG can have many NIC cards. NSG rules can also be applied to a network subnet, so a VM can actually be behind two sets of port rules. If both the subnet and the NIC have an NSG, then both of these NSGs must open the appropriate ports. If either blocks traffic, then the machine cannot be reached on the port. This is bidirectional for outbound ports as well. Figure 3-8 shows the Networking tab with a new virtual network, a default subnet, a public IP, the basic (new) NSG for the machine, and ports locked down so no access to this machine will be possible until the NSG is updated later.

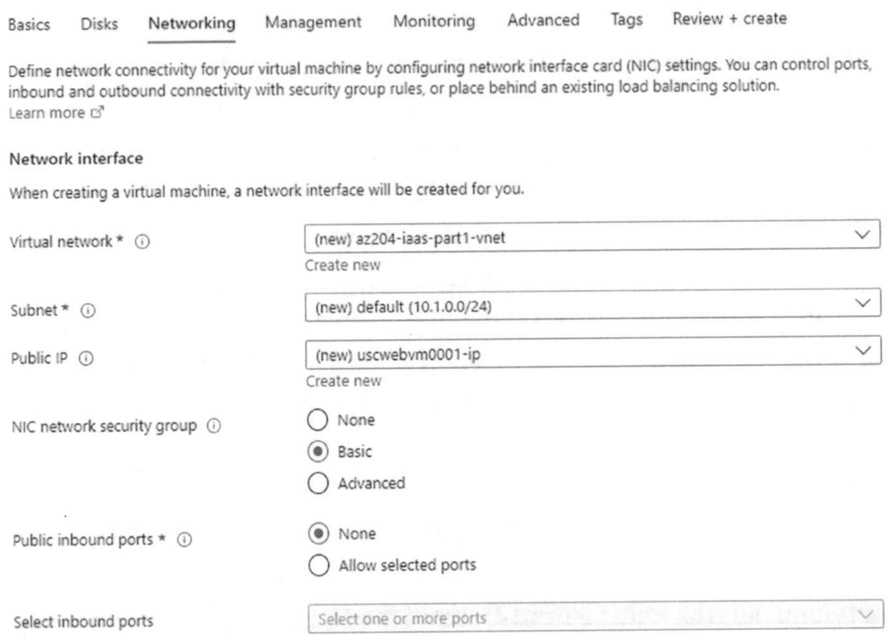

Basics   Disks   **Networking**   Management   Monitoring   Advanced   Tags   Review + create

Define network connectivity for your virtual machine by configuring network interface card (NIC) settings. You can control ports, inbound and outbound connectivity with security group rules, or place behind an existing load balancing solution.
Learn more ☐

Network interface

When creating a virtual machine, a network interface will be created for you.

Virtual network * ⓘ	(new) az204-iaas-part1-vnet ⌄
	Create new
Subnet * ⓘ	(new) default (10.1.0.0/24) ⌄
Public IP ⓘ	(new) uscwebvm0001-ip ⌄
	Create new
NIC network security group ⓘ	◯ None
	⦿ Basic
	◯ Advanced
Public inbound ports * ⓘ	⦿ None
	◯ Allow selected ports
Select inbound ports	Select one or more ports ⌄

Figure 3-8. *Creation of the networking portion of the virtual machine*

At the bottom of the Networking tab are options to associate the public IP and the NIC when the VM is deleted, as well as enable accelerated networking, which can give better throughput to the machine. Finally, options are provided to select a load balancer or an application gateway to be the entry point for public traffic.

A common scenario is to select an Azure Application Gateway for layer 7 route-based traffic direction for web applications and web APIs. For typical IP-based layer 4 routing, the Azure Load Balancer is a valid choice. Either option allows provisioning a gateway to a farm of machines for round-robin or other load-balancing strategies (see Figure 3-9).

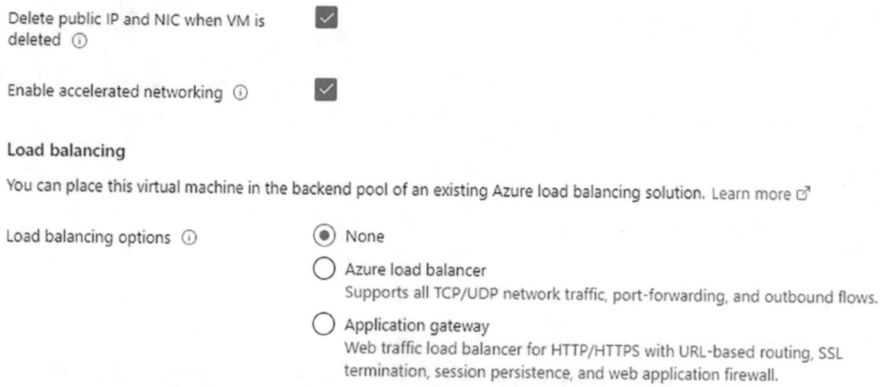

Delete public IP and NIC when VM is
deleted ⓘ   ☑

Enable accelerated networking ⓘ   ☑

Load balancing

You can place this virtual machine in the backend pool of an existing Azure load balancing solution. Learn more �

Load balancing options ⓘ   ⦿ None
                                      ○ Azure load balancer
                                        Supports all TCP/UDP network traffic, port-forwarding, and outbound flows.
                                      ○ Application gateway
                                        Web traffic load balancer for HTTP/HTTPS with URL-based routing, SSL
                                        termination, session persistence, and web application firewall.

Figure 3-9. *The final selections from the Networking tab*

Management

On the Management tab, you get to choose if you want to assign a
managed identity for the machine. You can also set options to log in with
an Azure AD account.

Additional options exist to enable auto-shutdown, backup, disaster
recovery, and patching selections. The auto-shutdown script is nice if
you have a machine that should not be left running all the time and could
potentially be left on by mistake, such as a developer machine or a test
server that doesn't need to run on nights and weekends.

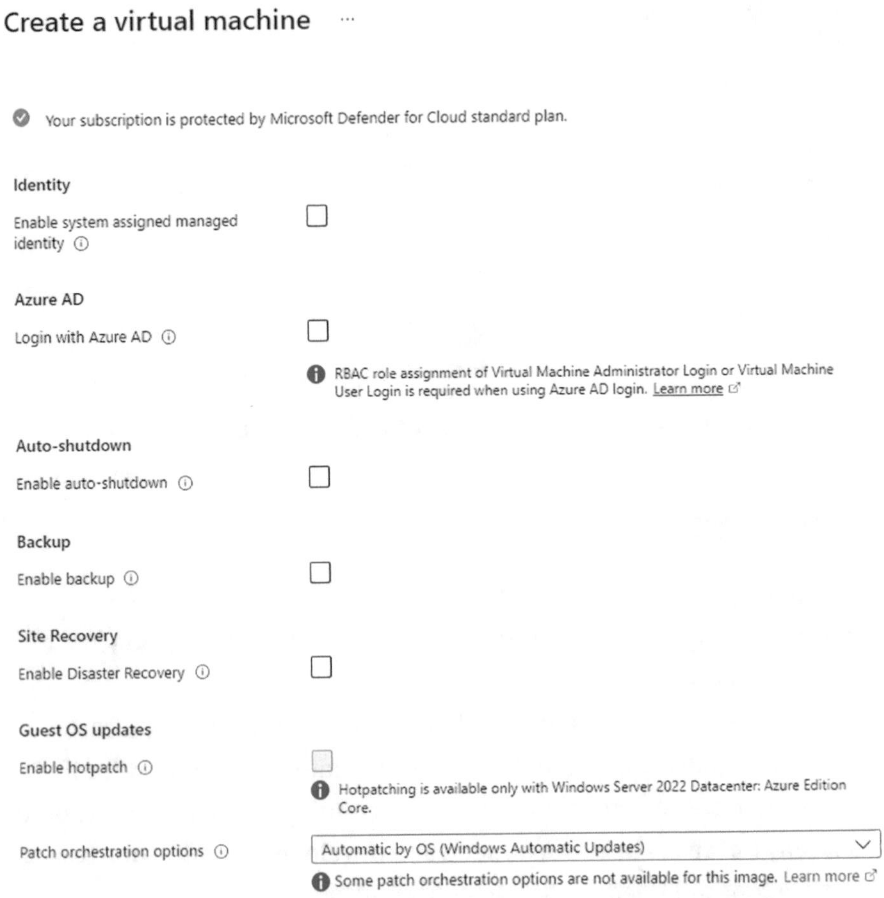

Create a virtual machine ···

✅ Your subscription is protected by Microsoft Defender for Cloud standard plan.

Identity

Enable system assigned managed
identity ⓘ ☐

Azure AD

Login with Azure AD ⓘ ☐

ⓘ RBAC role assignment of Virtual Machine Administrator Login or Virtual Machine
User Login is required when using Azure AD login. Learn more ↗

Auto-shutdown

Enable auto-shutdown ⓘ ☐

Backup

Enable backup ⓘ ☐

Site Recovery

Enable Disaster Recovery ⓘ ☐

Guest OS updates

Enable hotpatch ⓘ ☐

ⓘ Hotpatching is available only with Windows Server 2022 Datacenter: Azure Edition
Core.

Patch orchestration options ⓘ | Automatic by OS (Windows Automatic Updates) ⌄ |

ⓘ Some patch orchestration options are not available for this image. Learn more ↗

Figure 3-10. *These options allow you to select additional*
management options during deployment

Monitoring

On the Monitoring blade, you can select to enable Boot Diagnostics and
OS Guest diagnostics, as well as where to store the data.

Another monitoring tool exists that is not available here during
deployment but can be added to a deployed machine, called Virtual
Machine Insights (VM Insights). Similar to Application or Container

Insights, VM Insights is an agent you deploy to the machine to report metrics to Azure. By default, Azure will give you critical metrics about a VM whether you deploy VM Insights or not, but VM Insights can give you additional metrics and workbooks to visualize your VM metrics in more detail with ease. Once the machine is deployed, you can configure and deploy VM Insights. Figure 3-11 shows the monitoring options during deployment from the portal.

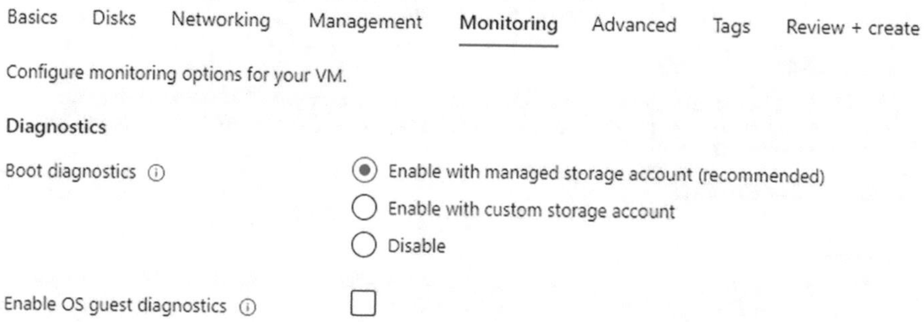

| Basics | Disks | Networking | Management | Monitoring | Advanced | Tags | Review + create |

Configure monitoring options for your VM.

Diagnostics

Boot diagnostics ⓘ
- ⦿ Enable with managed storage account (recommended)
- ◯ Enable with custom storage account
- ◯ Disable

Enable OS guest diagnostics ⓘ   ☐

Figure 3-11. *Monitoring options for diagnostics can be configured during deployment*

Advanced

You can take additional actions at the time of deployment around your virtual machine. You can add extensions like the Azure Pipelines Agent, the Custom Script Extension, Azure Performance Diagnostics, Network Watcher Agent, PowerShell Desired State Configuration, OpenSSH for Windows, Chef VM Extension, Octopus Deploy Tentacle Agent, a number of security and monitoring tools, and many more (see Figure 3-12).

You can deploy applications if you have preconfigured applications for VM Deployment. You can also execute a custom PowerShell script such as:

```
Install-WindowsFeature -name Web-Server -IncludeManagementTools
```

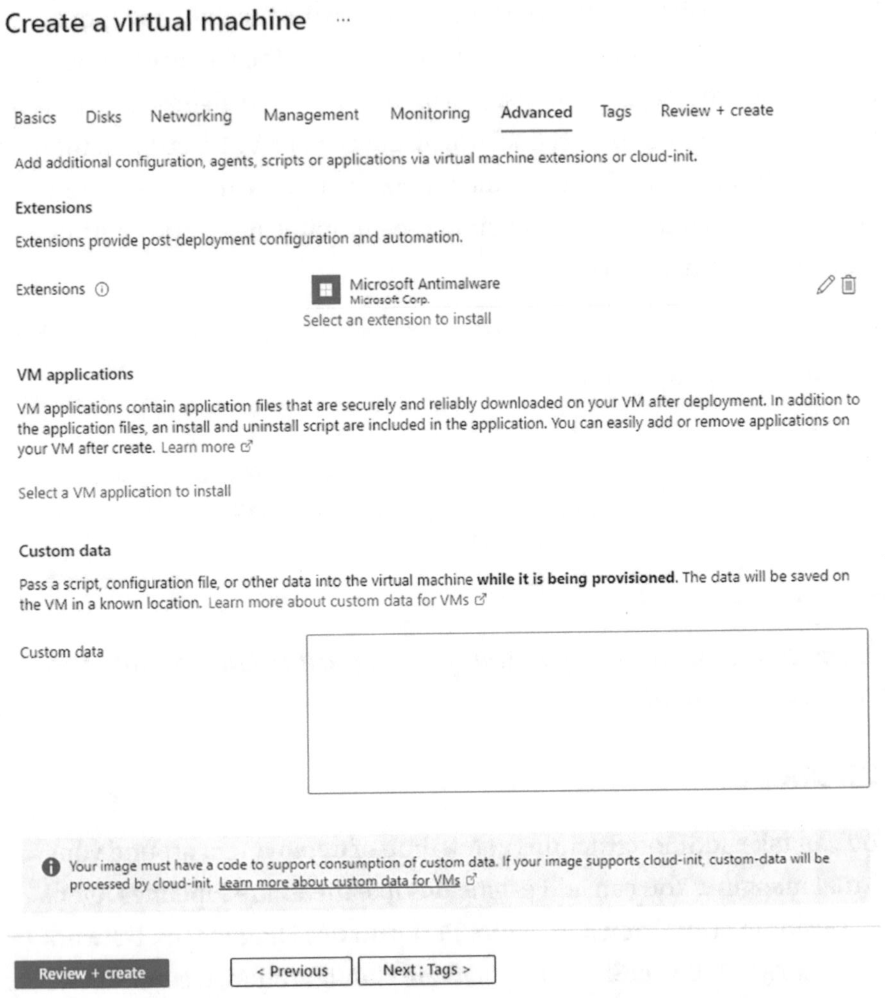

Create a virtual machine   ...

Basics   Disks   Networking   Management   Monitoring   **Advanced**   Tags   Review + create

Add additional configuration, agents, scripts or applications via virtual machine extensions or cloud-init.

Extensions

Extensions provide post-deployment configuration and automation.

Extensions ⓘ

　　　　　　　　　　　　　　🔲 Microsoft Antimalware　　　　　　　　　　　🖉 🗑
　　　　　　　　　　　　　　　　Microsoft Corp.
　　　　　　　　　　　　　　Select an extension to install

VM applications

VM applications contain application files that are securely and reliably downloaded on your VM after deployment. In addition to the application files, an install and uninstall script are included in the application. You can easily add or remove applications on your VM after create. Learn more ☐

Select a VM application to install

Custom data

Pass a script, configuration file, or other data into the virtual machine **while it is being provisioned**. The data will be saved on the VM in a known location. Learn more about custom data for VMs ☐

Custom data

ⓘ Your image must have a code to support consumption of custom data. If your image supports cloud-init, custom-data will be
processed by cloud-init. Learn more about custom data for VMs ☐

[Review + create]　　　　[< Previous]　　[Next : Tags >]

Figure 3-12. *Advanced options for deployment of a virtual machine—an extension for Microsoft anti-malware is included for deployment*

Final Checks

After the machine is configured for deployment, you get a review screen (shown in Figure 3-13) that allows you to validate the settings and shows a final, estimated price. You can review and then create the machine at will.

Figure 3-13. *The final review screen is shown, ready to create the virtual machine*

Restricting and Allowing Network Access to a Virtual Machine

With the machine deployed, currently there is no access to the machine. As a seasoned web developer, it's highly likely that you've remoted into a machine before to deploy applications and/or configure settings on a machine, or to review the IIS logs for potential attacks and additional errors. With that in mind, you likely want to enable RDP access over port 3389 or SSH on port 22.

To set networking rules around the machine, including enabling RDP on 3389 and/or SSH on port 22, on the blade for the machine select the Networking left-navigation offering to review the NSG rules for the machine NIC. Once again, in some scenarios, you need to also configure a subnet NSG, and you should be prepared to navigate this challenge with the subnet and NIC options for port access and what that means for traffic flow to and from your machine when both have rules configured.

On the Networking tab, you can set an inbound port rule (see Figure 3-14) and add your own IP address as the source. Additional sources can be other resources within your Azure subscription like an Application Security Group, or any other resource on the private network. For example, a Bastion server or another virtual machine (sometimes called a *jump box*) might be deployed into the private network to connect to the virtual machine via the private IP address. Note that all NSG rules have defaults at the lowest priority (highest numbers possible) that cannot be removed.

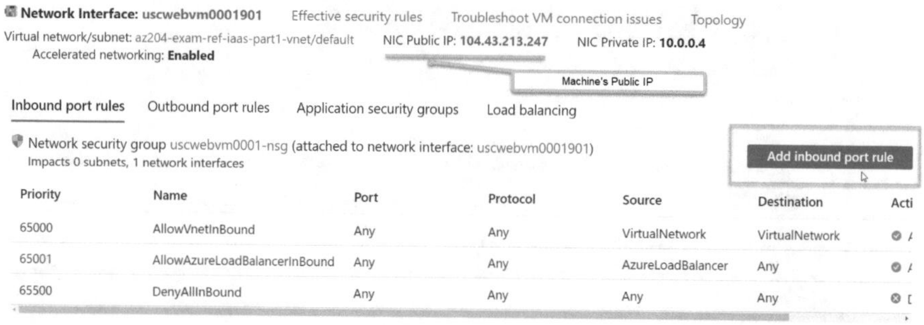

Figure 3-14. *The Network security group rules are shown with the ability to add inbound rules, review effective rules, add outbound rules, application security groups, and load balancing*

The rules at this level are much more configurable for all ports, and a number of common services are preconfigured for selection (see Figure 3-15).

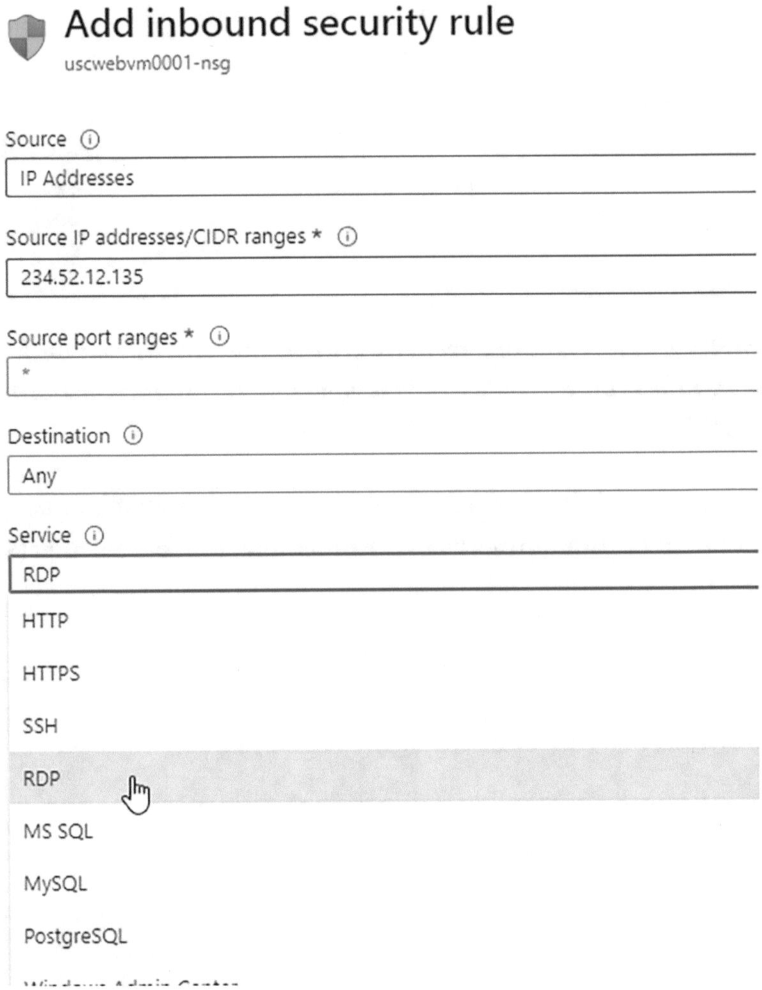

Add inbound security rule

uscwebvm0001-nsg

Source ⓘ

| IP Addresses |

Source IP addresses/CIDR ranges * ⓘ

| 234.52.12.135 |

Source port ranges * ⓘ

| * |

Destination ⓘ

| Any |

Service ⓘ

| RDP |

HTTP

HTTPS

SSH

RDP

MS SQL

MySQL

PostgreSQL

Figure 3-15. *Inbound rules can utilize pre-built configurations or can be customized for any valid port range*

You then select the action for Allow and set a priority. The lower the number for the priority, the higher the precedence. For example, priority 400 is very high and overrides any rule with a priority number greater than 400. Name the rule here (you can't rename it later). Give the rule a meaningful description. Figure 3-16 shows the remaining configuration.

Protocol

○ Any

⦿ TCP

○ UDP

○ ICMP

Action

⦿ Allow

○ Deny

Priority * ⓘ

| 400 |

Name *

| AllowCidrBlockRDPInbound |

Description

| Home Network Access |

Add   Cancel

Figure 3-16. *The Allow action is selected and priority is set to 400.*
The rule has been named and a description has been added

To serve web traffic, enable port 80 for inbound traffic and set the
priority to something like 500 (see Figure 3-17).

Inbound port rules	Outbound port rules	Application security groups	Load balancing

🔘 Network security group uscwebvm0001-nsg (attached to network interface: uscwebvm0001901)
   Impacts 0 subnets, 1 network interfaces

[Add inbound port rule]

Priority	Name	Port	Protocol	Source	Destination
400	AllowCidrBlockRDPInbound	3389	TCP	234.52.12.135	Any
500	AllowHTTPInboundPort80	80	TCP	Any	Any
65000	AllowVnetInBound	Any	Any	VirtualNetwork	VirtualNetwork
65001	AllowAzureLoadBalancerInBou...	Any	Any	AzureLoadBalancer	Any
65500	DenyAllInBound	Any	Any	Any	Any

Figure 3-17. *The network security rules are shown, allowing RDP and HTTP traffic to the web*

Effective Security Rules

As mentioned a few times previously, it's important to know what traffic can get to and from your machine. The networking blade has one more tab that is interesting, and it is the Effective Security Rules. In the Effective Security Rules, you can drill into the Associated NSGs (see Figure 3-18).

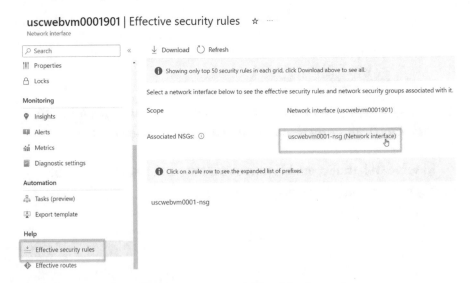

Figure 3-18. *The Effective Security Rules blade*

This tab helps you discern what traffic can get to your machine (see Figure 3-19). Any associated NSGs are shown here.

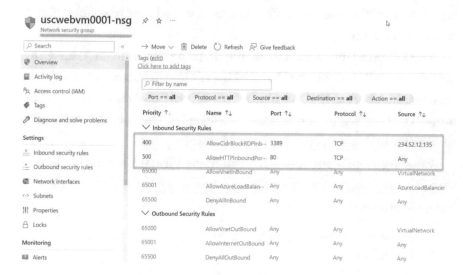

Figure 3-19. *The Effective Security rules are shown*

Implementing Desired State Configuration on an Azure Virtual Machine

The final thing that is important for developers to know about virtual machines around the scope of the AZ-204 Exam is the concept of the Desired State Configuration (DSC) for Azure Virtual Machines. The DSC is the number one tool to use for ensuring that your fleet machines have appropriate configurations (i.e., IIS Enabled, Containerization Capability, etc.). Additionally, DSC can be utilized to prevent configuration drift, ensuring that resources that are not supposed to be enabled are not.

During the deployment, I purposefully left off the IIS deployment script. However, consider the scenario where the machine needs to host a web application via IIS. In order to host the application, the machine must enable IIS. This is easily done by remoting to the machine and running a

PowerShell script or just turning it on via additional Windows features. But what happens if someone turns it off? What about the scenario where you have 100 fleet VMs. Do you really want to go to each one to enable IIS? Of course you do not.

The following interaction to enable IIS using DSC with an Azure virtual machine is well-documented here: https://learn.microsoft.com/powershell/dsc/quickstarts/website-quickstart?view=dsc-1.1. For purposes of brevity, this book simply enables IIS. The documentation also shows how to deploy a default page to the web server.

Creating a DSC configuration on an Azure Virtual Machine is a four-step process. First, you must create an Azure Automation Account (see Figure 3-20).

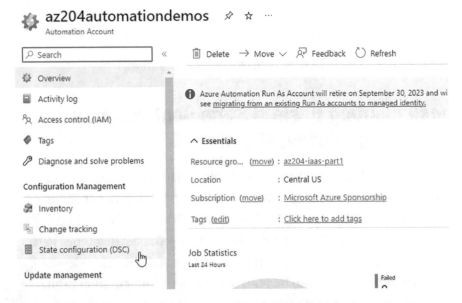

Figure 3-20. *In order to utilize DSC, you need an Azure Automation Account. The State Configuration (DSC) left-navigation menu then allows you to create DSC configurations and associate machines to the configurations*

Next, you must create a PowerShell script. For example, create a simple file called EnsureIIS.ps1 with the following script:

```
configuration EnsureIIS
{
    Node IsWebServer
    {
        WindowsFeature IIS
        {
            Ensure              = 'Present'
            Name                = 'Web-Server'
            IncludeAllSubFeature = $true
        }
    }

    Node NotWebServer
    {
        WindowsFeature IIS
        {
            Ensure              = 'Absent'
            Name                = 'Web-Server'
        }
    }
}
```

You then upload the script (see Figure 3-21) and create a manifest from the script Managed Object Format (MOF) file, as shown in Figure 3-22.

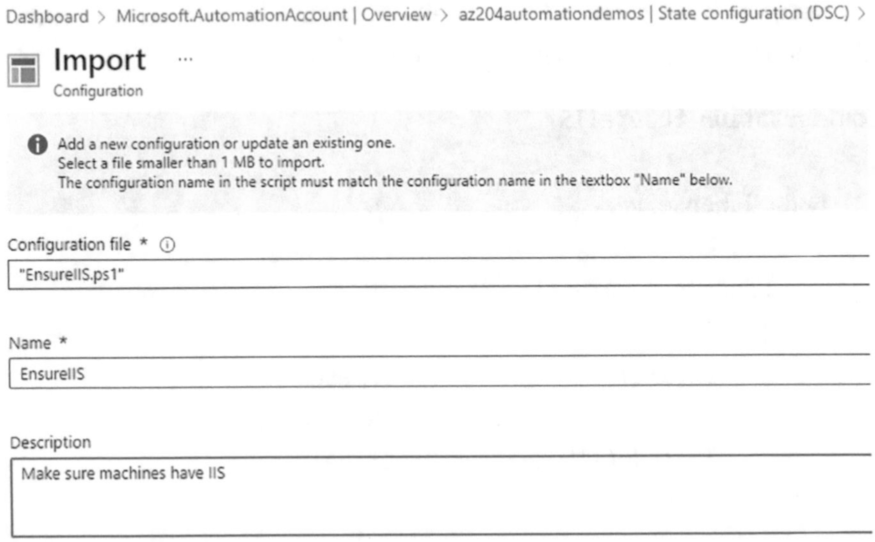

Dashboard > Microsoft.AutomationAccount | Overview > az204automationdemos | State configuration (DSC) >

Import
Configuration

ⓘ Add a new configuration or update an existing one.
Select a file smaller than 1 MB to import.
The configuration name in the script must match the configuration name in the textbox "Name" below.

Configuration file * ⓘ

"EnsureIIS.ps1"

Name *

EnsureIIS

Description

Make sure machines have IIS

Figure 3-21. Uploading a script to the Automation Account DSC on the Configurations tab

Creating the MOF file is as easy as selecting your script and compiling it, as shown in Figure 3-22.

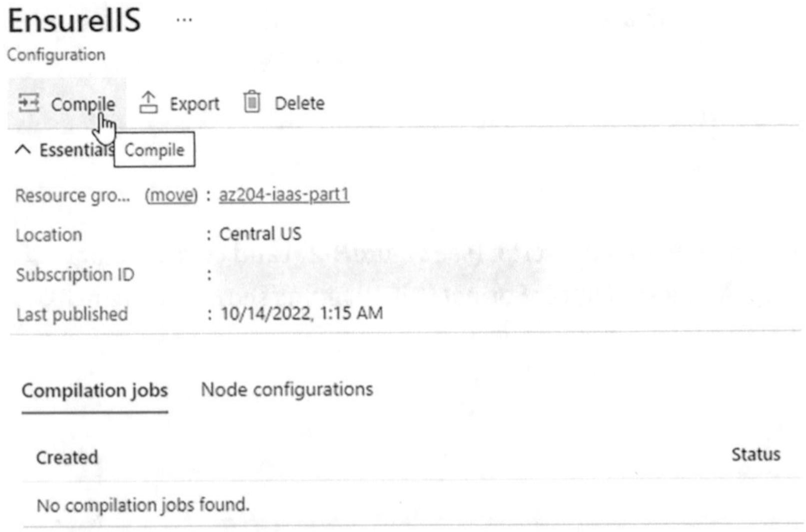

EnsureIIS
Configuration

⊡⊡ Compile   ⬆ Export   🗑 Delete

∧ Essentials   Compile

Resource gro... (move) : az204-iaas-part1

Location   : Central US

Subscription ID   :

Last published   : 10/14/2022, 1:15 AM

Compilation jobs   Node configurations

Created	Status
No compilation jobs found.	

Figure 3-22. Compiling the script

Finally, you add nodes that you want to manage by connecting to the VM Node and selecting the configurations to apply (see Figure 3-23).

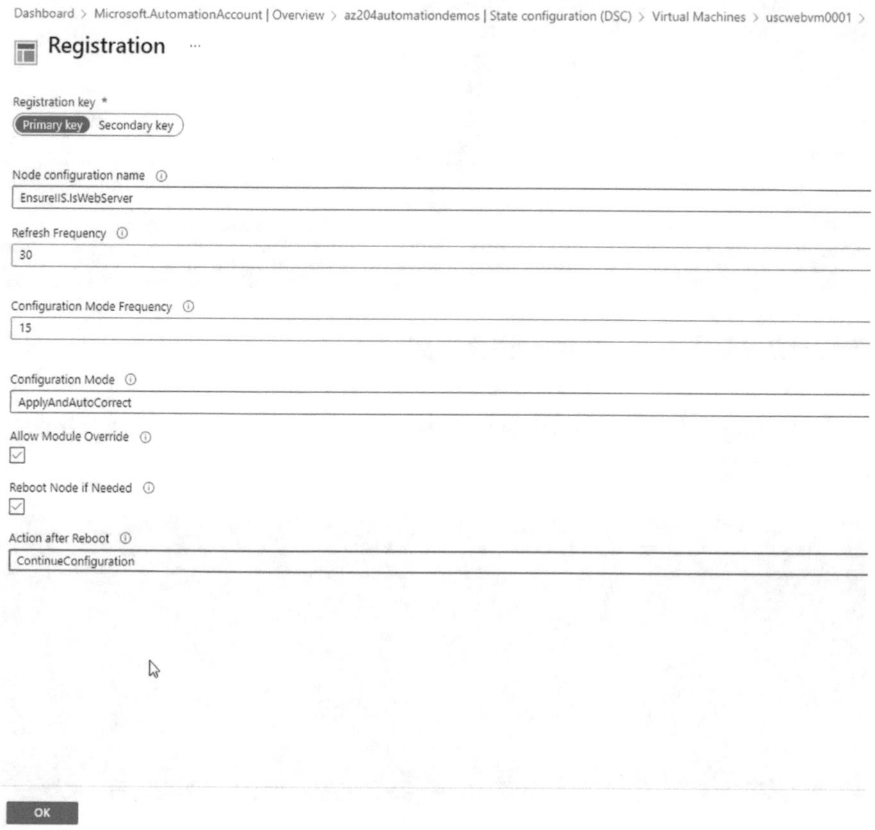

Figure 3-23. *Ensuring the node is set as a webserver*

After the DSC is created and applied, the node will show up as compliant (as in Figure 3-24).

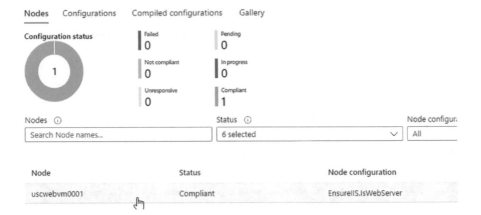

Figure 3-24. *The node is now compliant*

Browsing to the public IP also proves the node is compliant, as shown in Figure 3-25.

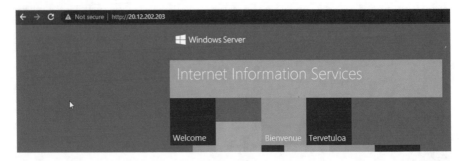

Figure 3-25. *The node now exposes the default IIS page, proving the web server tools are enabled and the route on port 80 is open as expected*

Azure Resource Manager (ARM) Templates and Bicep for Infrastructure as Code (IaC)

In addition to Infrastructure as a Service (IaaS), developers also need to have some experience with Infrastructure as Code (IaC). The tools you want to be in command of are traditional ARM templates and the newer Bicep templates. It's also important to understand how the ARM resources work in Azure.

Whenever you deploy anything into Azure—whether the deployment is manual via the portal, imperative via PowerShell or the Azure CLI, or automated via template deployments—the final result is that the commands are all essentially sent to the ARM REST API for execution. The advantages of using a template are maximum efficiency coupled with less chance for error.

Using the portal is great for one-off deployments, but repeating operations in the portal is more than tedious, it's a waste of time. Using an imperative approach is nice if you like declaring everything individually and then deploying in a procedural approach, but using scripts may have errors that aren't known until runtime and may have more errors with dependencies and configurations than anticipated. Using templates allows you to declaratively deploy an entire environment using parallelism whenever possible. Additionally, templates are fully evaluated before execution for potential errors. It's easy to set dependencies in templates. You can even use a main template to orchestrate deployments using additional templates.

Template Structure

The ARM template structure contains five major sections. Of these five sections, you should be able to recognize and use three of them regularly. The five major sections are *Parameters, Variables, Resources, Functions,* and *Outputs.* When working with templates, you will almost always use Parameters and Variables. You will always use the Resources section. Optionally, you might create a function, but using functions is fairly rare. The Outputs section is useful if you need to create a value during the deployment for use elsewhere in your solution, typically for use in another template as part of an orchestration.

VS Code for Templates

Before diving deeper, when working with ARM and Bicep templates, I highly recommend utilizing VS Code. The extensions for ARM (see Figure 3-26) are found at `https://marketplace.visualstudio.com/items?itemName=msazurermtools.azurerm-vscode-tools`. The extensions for Bicep (see Figure 3-27) are found at `https://marketplace.visualstudio.com/items?itemName=ms-azuretools.vscode-bicep`. You'll also find a few simple shortcuts that allow you to create a template in a matter of minutes. Couple that with the fact that the stubbed-out structure is free from errors and you have a powerful tool to get up and running quickly.

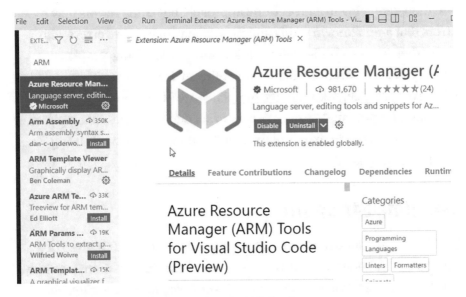

Figure 3-26. *The ARM extension in VS Code*

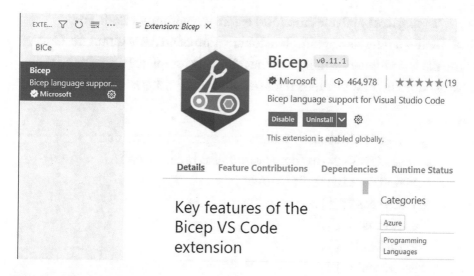

Figure 3-27. The Bicep extension in VS Code

ARM Templates

To get started, simply open VS Code with the ARM template extension installed, then create and save a file called azuredeploy.json. In that file, type **arm!** and then select the first item by checking the box to generate a new template (see Figure 3-28).

Figure 3-28. Starting a new ARM template by typing arm! in an azuredeploy.json file using VS Code

Typing **arm!** activates the ARM extension within VS Code and generates a new starter template for creation of an ARM template. Once the file is generated, you'll have the following template (the schema may vary based on new versions released after this writing):

```
{
    "$schema": "https://schema.management.azure.com/
    schemas/2019-04-01/deploymentTemplate.json#",
    "contentVersion": "1.0.0.0",
    "parameters": {},
    "functions": [],
    "variables": {},
    "resources": [],
    "outputs": {}
}
```

The major sections are included as expected. The schema determines the API version to use. For purposes of simplicity, delete the functions and outputs sections from this template to get a basic shell for a simple template.

Resources

The main section of any ARM template is the Resources section. In this section, you'll declare all of the resources you want to deploy. You will also set any dependencies in this area. You can also use this area to link to other templates or nest another template.

To create a storage account resource, expand the resources array and type **storage**. Then select the option to stub in a storage account resource (see Figure 3-29).

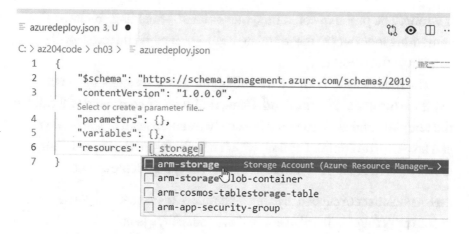

Figure 3-29. *Creating a storage account resource is accomplished using the arm-storage template*

The ARM template can be deployed at this point, but if anyone else in the world (outside of your subscription and resource group) has created a storage account called storageaccount1, then this template would fail. The template will also fail if you try to create a storage account with an invalid name (it must be between 3-24 characters, all lowercase, or 0-9). Change the name to something like mystorYYYYMMDD, where you replace YYYYMMDD with the current date. Additionally, change the SKU name to Standard_LRS and the tier to Standard if you want to avoid premium charges.

Validating ARM Templates

Because there are several things that can go wrong with a template deployment, it is possible to validate the template before attempting to deploy it.

As mentioned, if your storage account name is incorrect or the deployment can discern that it will fail to run to completion, then the validation of the template will let you know right away when something is wrong. The problem could be syntax-related—meaning you have something incorrect in the template itself—or it could be an issue like a conflict in the resources.

The main way to see if a template is going to work and what it will do is to utilize the What-if command. Using the What-if command will validate the template and also tell you what will happen. Instead of What-if, you can also use the Confirm option, which will show you the What-if and then let you choose to continue or cancel the group deployment.

```
New-AzResourceGroupDeployment -Whatif -ResourceGroupName "your-
resource-group" -TemplateFile "azuredeploy.json"
```

PowerShell has a command called Test-AzResourceGroupDeployment that you can also use, which can be used to simply validate the template and parameters to ensure there are no major errors.

Deploying ARM Templates

Once the template is validated, you can deploy it. Optionally, you can live dangerously and skip validation (which will happen during deployment anyway).

Open a shell in your browser to the Azure Portal by navigating to https://shell.azure.com. Make sure you are in the Bash terminal (you can do this in PowerShell too, but the syntax is slightly different).

To complete the following deployment, create a resource group for the new storage account and set the name of the resource group in a variable. Upload the azuredeploy.json file to create a basic storage account to your Azure subscription using the Upload/Download icon on the shell.

Once the file is uploaded, ensure that everything is in the correct folder (Note: You may need to move the file because the upload will be at the root of your home directory.) With everything in place, run the following commands (also found in the deployarmstorage.sh script in the resources for this chapter) to deploy the template using the Azure CLI (see Figure 3-30):

```
touch deployarmstorage.sh
code .
```

Once the code editor is opened, add the following lines to the script, making sure to replace the generic resource group name with your resource group name:

```
rg=<your-rg-name>
az deployment group create -g $rg --template-file
azuredeploy.json
```

Figure 3-30. *You can run deployments from your local machine or via the Azure Portal*

Save the file and exit the code with Ctrl+Q. If you forget to save, you'll be prompted to do so. This will close the code editor. Next, run the script with the following command:

```
bash ./deployarmstorage.sh
```

Once the deployment is completed, you will see output in the form of JSON that shows the new storage information, and you can easily review the account in the Azure Portal (see Figure 3-31).

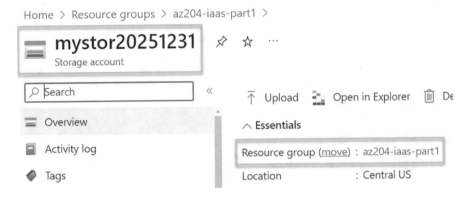

Figure 3-31. *The storage account is created as expected from the execution of the ARM template*

Parameters

In the template, the parameters and variables are empty. Perhaps you want to allow the deployment to change from one execution to another. For example, perhaps you'd like to make the name and the location into parameters. Parameters can have default values, a set of predefined options, and can be moved into a parameters file to easily configure a group of parameters.

Returning to VS Code, add parameters in the parameters section by typing **param** and selecting the new-parameter option (see Figure 3-32).

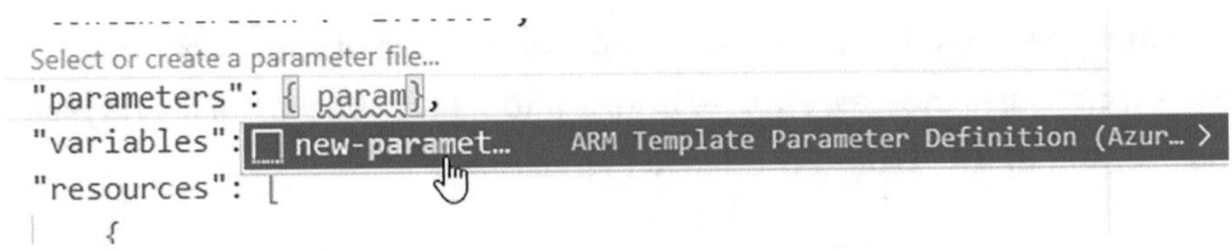

```
------------------------------------
Select or create a parameter file...
    "parameters": { param },
    "variables": [ new-paramet...    ARM Template Parameter Definition (Azur... >
    "resources": [
       {
```

Figure 3-32. *Use the VS Code extension to easily add parameters to your ARM templates*

Change the name of the parameter to name. Create a second parameter called location. For the name, do not specify any other changes. For the location, add an attribute called defaultValue with a value of [resourceGroup().location]. See Figure 3-33.

```
Select or create a parameter file to enable full validation...
"parameters": {
    "name": {
        "type": "string",
        "metadata": {
            "description": "description"
        }
    },
    "location": {
        "type": "string",
        "defaultValue": "[resourceGroup().location]",
        "metadata": {
            "description": "description"
        }
    }
},
"variables": {},
"resources": [
    {                        I
        "name": "mystor20251231",
```

Figure 3-33. *The Location and Name parameters are added to the template*

Next, leverage the parameters in the template by replacing the hard-coded name and location values in the resource for the storage account with the key string [parameters('parametername')]. The square braces in the JSON string are special and Azure knows to evaluate the text internal to the square braces as a function. The resource should now be as follows:

```
"resources": [
    {
        "name": "[parameters('name')]",
        "type": "Microsoft.Storage/storageAccounts",
        "apiVersion": "2021-04-01",
        "tags": {
            "displayName": "storageaccount1"
        },
        "location": "[parameters('location')]",
        "kind": "StorageV2",
        "sku": {
            "name": "Standard_LRS",
            "tier": "Standard"
        }
    }
]
```

Save and upload the file to Azure or just copy/paste the new file into the Azure location and rerun the template command. This time you will be prompted for the name (see Figure 3-34), since the name value is parameterized and no default value is provided.

Figure 3-34. *When a parameter exists with no default value, you must provide the value during deployment*

Variables

In this case, you've parameterized the name and allowed the location to be a parameter or to be set to the default location. What if you wanted to also create a default name but reuse this template to create different storage accounts? This can be done with a combination of parameters and variables.

Update the name parameter to have a default name value of `mystor`. Clearly this won't be unique, so running the deployment would likely fail. Sometimes you'll want to group resources together or have an ability to append a unique string to make a value unique.

In VS Code, in the variables section, type **var** to get the prompt to create a new variable. Select the new variable shortcut to create a new variable. When the variable is created, change the name to `storageAccountName` and set the value to `[concat(parameters('name'), uniqueString(resourceGroup().id))]`. Leverage the value in the resource name by changing it to `[variables('storageAccountName')]` (see Figure 3-35).

```
"parameters": {
    "name": {
        "type": "string",
        "defaultValue": "mystor",
        "metadata": {
            "description": "description"
        }
    },
    "location": {
        "type": "string",
        "defaultValue": "[resourceGroup().location]",
        "metadata": {
            "description": "description"
        }
    }
},
"variables": {
    "storageAccountName": "[concat(parameters('name'), uniqueString(resourceGroup().id))]"
},
"resources": [
    {
        "name": "[variables('storageAccountName')]",
        "type": "Microsoft.Storage/storageAccounts",
        "apiVersion": "2021-04-01"
```

Figure 3-35. *The storage name is now default and unique, but can still be set by the deployment if desired*

Make sure the updated code is in the Azure shell and run the command again without a name. This time the deployment works as expected. Additional runs would also work, as would explicitly naming the storage account.

Outputs

In some scenarios, you'll want to get the values back from the template for use in further deployments. Since the account name is unique and generated during deployment, you could return the value from the template for use elsewhere.

In VS Code, add the Outputs section back to the bottom of the template under the resources, before the closing squiggly brace. In the outputs section, type **new** and use the shortcut to get a new output (see Figure 3-36).

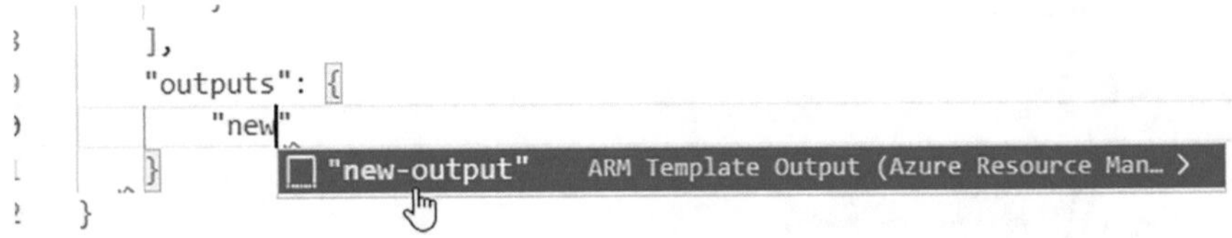

Figure 3-36. *The outputs section has a helper to create a new output*

Name the output storageAccountName and set the value to the storage account variable:

```
"outputs": {
        "storageAccountName": {
            "type": "string",
            "value": "[variables('storageAccountName')]"
        }
    }
```

Any template that called this template could utilize the outputs value to further work with automation.

Functions

Functions are utilized to perform repeated actions. For example, if multiple variables needed that unique string, one option is to build a user-defined function in the template that takes the value for the variable and concatenates it with the unique string to get the value. In this example from Microsoft Learn, `https://learn.microsoft.com/azure/azure-resource-manager/templates/user-defined-functions#use-the-function`, the code is doing this exact operation by replacing the previous example with a function and referencing the function call in the name of the resource. You can create and leverage a similar function in this template if you want to try it out yourself.

Bicep Templates

Like ARM templates, Bicep templates are IaC and they give you the ability to declaratively provision a group of resources. Indeed, if you have never worked with ARM, it is now recommended that you just learn Bicep. The good news is that you can easily write Bicep and then translate to ARM via a simple PowerShell command. A similar command exists to go from ARM to Bicep.

At the time of this writing and when I took the exam, Bicep wasn't really on the list of things you need to know. Going forward, I'd be surprised if it doesn't show up in the list of potential things you should be aware of.

The good news is that Bicep is much easier than ARM because it is human-readable and generally easy to use. Like ARM templates, you create resources and you can define parameters, variables, and even link to other Bicep templates (modules). Using VS Code, you can easily leverage the extension to quickly build a Bicep file that can be deployed to Azure.

Another thing about Bicep is that it is extremely similar to Terraform, which is one of the, if not the most, popular ways to automate infrastructure in multi-cloud and other non-Azure scenarios (so it is likely that you might know Terraform but not ARM or Bicep). In that case, Bicep will definitely be your best option.

Whether you learn Bicep or ARM for this exam, the concepts are the same. You must remember precedence (you can't create a container for blob storage without a storage account, and you can't create an app service without an app service plan). You must also remember the limitations around uniqueness of naming and any other naming restrictions. If you know that, either Bicep or ARM will help you build robust IaC solutions.

A Quick Bicep Example

To wrap up this look at IaC, I present the code from a basic Bicep file that does the same thing the ARM template in the previous example did. The following template will use parameters to create a unique storage account. You can review and compare the following syntax with what was done for the ARM template. If you'd like a deeper dive into learning Bicep, leverage this Learn module: https://learn.microsoft.com/training/paths/fundamentals-bicep/.

Here is the code for the Bicep deployment:

```
param name string = 'mystor'
param location string = resourceGroup().location
var storageAccountName = '${name}${uniqueString(resourceGro
up().id)}'

resource storageaccount 'Microsoft.Storage/
storageAccounts@2021-02-01' = {
  name: storageAccountName
  location: location
```

```
kind: 'StorageV2'
sku: {
  name: 'Standard_LRS'
 }
}
```

You can also find that code in the resources for this chapter in the azuredeploy.bicep file. Once you have the file uploaded to the correct folder, run the command highlighted in Figure 3-37.

```
brian@Azure:~/az-204/iaas-arm$ rg=az204-iaas-part1
brian@Azure:~/az-204/iaas-arm$ az deployment group create -g $rg --template-file azuredeploy.bicep
A new Bicep release is available: v0.14.46. Upgrade now by running "az bicep upgrade".
- Running ..
```

Figure 3-37. Utilizing the AZ CLI to deploy a Bicep template is similar to working with ARM templates

Final Thoughts about Template Deployments

To complete the look at IaC, it's important to know that there are two deployment modes. Almost all the deployments you will do are going to be of the Incremental type. These deployments were all incremental. In some cases, you may choose to do a Complete deployment. Using a Complete deployment is a dangerous operation, so you need to be certain when you want to perform a Complete deployment. For this reason, the default is set to Incremental, which is also why all the previous deployments were Incremental.

Incremental Deployments

As mentioned, most of your template deployments will be Incremental. In an Incremental deployment, Azure looks at the incoming template. If a resource exists in the template, the resource is created in Azure if it doesn't already exist. If the resource already exists, the resource is evaluated. If anything in the template is configured differently from the resource in Azure, then the resource will be modified to match the specifications as laid out in the template. This is a safe operation, as it's essentially an "Upsert" of resources to match the defined requirements in the template.

In an incremental deployment against a resource group in Azure, any resources not named in the template are completely ignored. All existing resources named are not deleted, but are modified if needed or left alone if configured as per the template. New resources named in the template are deployed as expected.

Complete Deployments

In some scenarios, such as a production environment, you may desire to have zero configuration drift. In other scenarios, you may want to clean up resource groups that have had some modifications that may not have been desired. An easy way to accomplish this is with a complete template deployment.

In a complete deployment against a resource group in Azure, any resources that exist in the resource group that are not named in the template are deleted. Any resources named in the template are modified or inserted as needed in the resource group. This is a potentially dangerous operation because resources not named will no longer exist after the deployment is finished.

Review Your Learning

As an additional challenge, consider the following questions and determine how you would approach potential solution(s). You can find answers to these questions in Appendix A at the end of this book.

1) What is a VM Availability Set? What is a VM Scale Set? How are VM Scale Sets and VM Availability Sets different? When would you use one over the other?

2) What are some of the main groups of VM compute configurations?

3) Which Azure disks are managed? Which are potentially unmanaged? What are some considerations to remember when utilizing an unmanaged disk?

4) How do you limit traffic to and from a VM in Azure? What are some common ports to be aware of?

5) What resources in Azure are necessary to deploy a VM with a desired configuration? What are the steps to ensure a VM has a feature enabled?

6) What are the main sections of an ARM template? How do you create and work with variables?

7) Working with Bicep, how do you configure a deployment for a new resource? How do you use variables?

8) What is the difference between an Incremental and a Complete template deployment?

Optional Training: Complete the Original First Two AZ-204: Implement Infrastructure as a Service Solutions Modules (no longer a the learning path for AZ-204 as of April 2023)

To fully learn the material, I recommend taking the time to complete the MS Learn modules for Implement Infrastructure as a Service solutions found here:

- Provision virtual machines in Azure: `https://learn.microsoft.com/training/modules/provision-virtual-machines-azure/`

- Create and deploy Azure Resource Manager templates: `https://learn.microsoft.com/training/modules/create-deploy-azure-resource-manager-templates/`

Chapter Summary

In this chapter, you learned about provisioning virtual machines for Infrastructure as a Service and working with Bicep and ARM templates for Infrastructure as Code.

After working through this chapter, you should be on track to be in command of the following concepts as you learn about Azure and prepare for the AZ-204 Exam:

- Work with Infrastructure as a Service, specifically creating and managing Azure Virtual Machines.

- Utilize ports for allowing inbound and outbound network traffic via Network Security Groups.

- Utilize Azure Automation to implement Desired State Configuration for virtual machines.

- Create and utilize ARM and Bicep templates to provision resources.

- Work with parameters and variables in ARM and Bicep templates.

- Understand the difference between Complete and Incremental deployments.

- Validate ARM templates.

In the next chapter, you learn about working with Azure App Service for hosting web applications.

CHAPTER 4

Create Azure App Service Web Apps

Traditional architecture requires a virtualized PC and IIS, Tomcat, or some other hosting agent. In those scenarios, you are responsible for making sure the operating system is patched. You must maintain the network where the virtual machine is deployed, and you must ensure that you've properly built regional failovers and backups into your business continuity and disaster planning. When you deploy your solution, you must maintain any SSL certificates and ensure that your network traffic is handled correctly.

What if you could forego most of that and deploy a website with baked-in disaster recovery, resiliency, backups, and even SSL certificates, hosted in the correct environment, with the ability to scale at will and deployment slots for modern deployment patterns like blue-green deployments?

The benefits of using Azure App Services are exactly what you can gain, along with speed of deployment. The Azure App Service is a platform as a service offering in Azure. This allows you to get up and running with ease; your main job is maintaining the code, handling or automating deployments correctly, and choosing if you want to scale manually or with automatic rules. Additionally, a couple of other choices allow you to determine how many deployment slots you can utilize, as well as the option to go for a shared hardware solution or an isolated plan if you want to ensure that your application is the only application running on the backing hardware.

© Brian L. Gorman 2023

B. L. Gorman, *Developing Solutions for Microsoft Azure Certification Companion*, Certification Study Companion Series, https://doi.org/10.1007/978-1-4842-9300-3_4

Before Getting Started

This chapter demonstrates the major features of the Azure App Service for which you need to be ready to answer questions on the exam, as well as work with the solutions in real life. To aid in the demonstrations used in this chapter, there is an application that utilizes .NET 6 and ASP.Net MVC. You are welcome to work with this code (found in the repository for this book or on my GitHub). For additional practice, you can try deploying other solutions with different technology stacks. It is also incredibly easy to create your own applications with the .NET CLI (for more information, review the material at `https://learn.microsoft.com/dotnet/core/tools/dotnet-new`).

Creating an Azure App Service

Deploying an Azure App Service (app service) can be easily accomplished via the Azure Portal, using imperative commands with the Azure CLI and/ or PowerShell, via ARM or Bicep templates, or via direct commands to the REST API.

All Azure App Services belong to an App Service Plan, which determines the overall compute for the services in the plan. If multiple app services are deployed to the plan, they share the compute thresholds of the plan, which can lead to issues if one of the hosted services becomes a resource hog. For this reason, it's a good idea to not mix workloads within an App Service Plan for production scenarios. Instead, spread your workloads into specific plans to ensure the best availability and utilization of the provisioned resources.

App Service Plans

App Service Plans can be created as stand-alone deployments. If your overall goal is to deploy an app service, you can typically deploy the App Service Plan along with the app service deployment.

Pricing Tier

Choosing the correct App Service Plan ensures that you maximize your utilization of the hardware while also managing your expenditures. If you are just one developer or in a very small shop, you might choose to deploy this as a free app service. A couple of other developments and shared solutions exist where you can slightly increase your expenditures and gain benefits like the ability to have a custom domain or have some deployment slots. Figure 4-1 shows how the testing and shared plans break down when creating an App Service Plan.

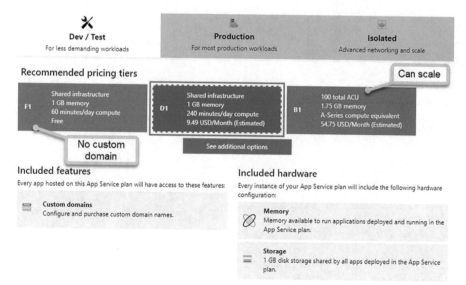

Figure 4-1. *The App Service Plan options for test include Free, Shared, and Basic*

In the Free plan, no custom domain is available, so the website is only available at the default `https://{your-app-service-name}.azurewebsites.net`. None of these dev/test plans offer deployment slots. The B1 plan is more expensive, but it can scale to three instances, whereas the other two plans cannot scale to meet demand.

In the production tier, the Standard (S1) plan is the first tier to offer deployment slots. From there—depending on how much memory and compute time you want, how many instances you want to scale to, and how many deployment slots you want—you can choose from a number of options, as shown in Figure 4-2.

Spec Picker

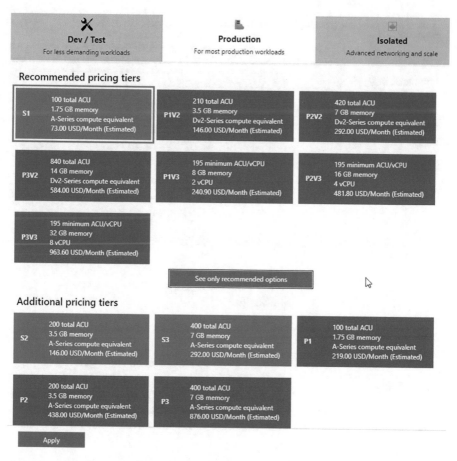

Figure 4-2. *The Standard and Premium plan offerings vary based on how much compute, how many slots, and how many instances you want to scale to during peak workloads*

The S1 plan is adequate for small production workloads, and it is the first plan to offer deployment slots, so the tier used to demonstrate concepts in this book deploys an S1 instance (see Figure 4-3). Outside of slots and scale, a free tier application could be used for the purposes of learning and testing.

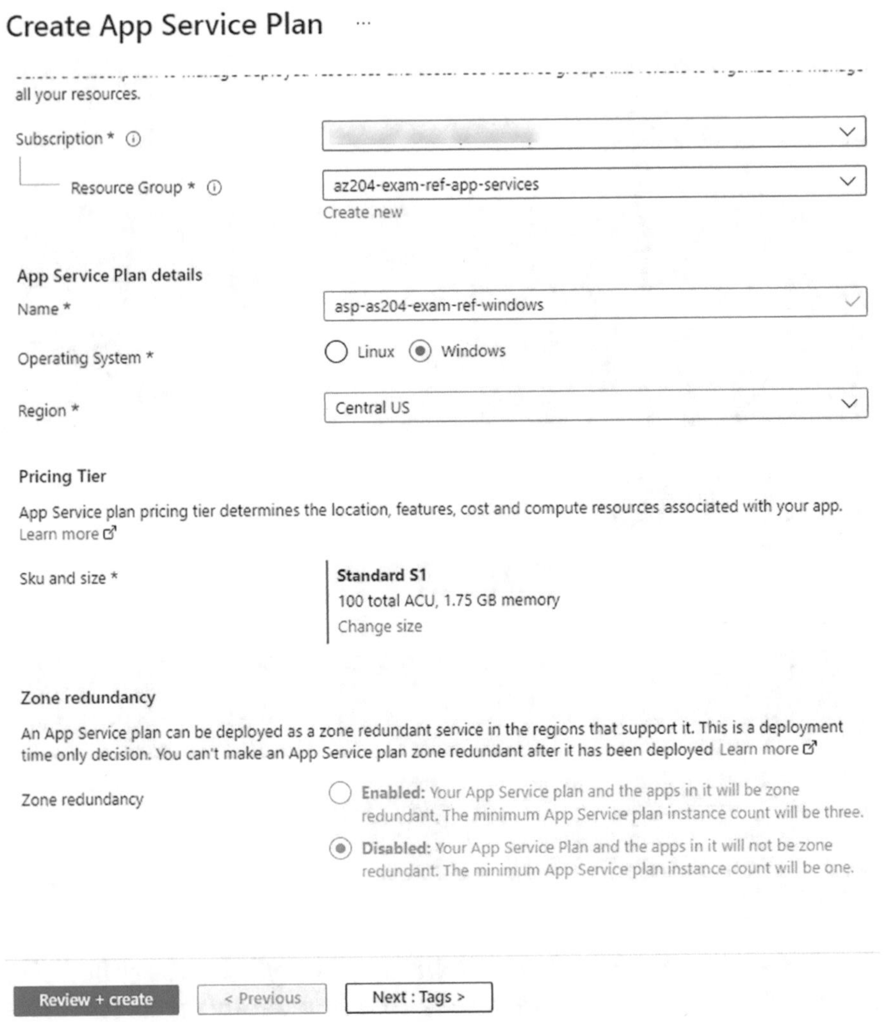

Create App Service Plan   ...

all your resources.

Subscription * ⓘ

[⌄]

Resource Group * ⓘ   [az204-exam-ref-app-services   ⌄]
Create new

App Service Plan details

Name *   [asp-as204-exam-ref-windows   ✓]

Operating System *   ○ Linux   ● Windows

Region *   [Central US   ⌄]

Pricing Tier

App Service plan pricing tier determines the location, features, cost and compute resources associated with your app.
Learn more ☐

Sku and size *   **Standard S1**
100 total ACU, 1.75 GB memory
Change size

Zone redundancy

An App Service plan can be deployed as a zone redundant service in the regions that support it. This is a deployment
time only decision. You can't make an App Service plan zone redundant after it has been deployed Learn more ☐

Zone redundancy   ○ **Enabled:** Your App Service plan and the apps in it will be zone
redundant. The minimum App Service plan instance count will be three.

● **Disabled:** Your App Service Plan and the apps in it will not be zone
redundant. The minimum App Service plan instance count will be one.

[Review + create]   [< Previous]   [Next : Tags >]

Figure 4-3. *An App Service Plan with the Windows operating system
is selected. Choosing Linux might be a better choice depending on
your workload and technology stack*

Additional offerings not shown are in the Isolated tier. You should
take a look at the various offerings, so you have a good feel for some of
the differences. The main difference with an Isolated instance is the

knowledge that your application is the only application on the physical hardware. Other plans share physical hardware to leverage the cost savings of sharing infrastructure with other Azure tenants.

In order to create an Isolated App Service Plan, you first need to create an App Service Environment (ASE). App Service Environments can be used for other deployments as well as the app service, including Azure Functions and Azure Logic Apps. ASEs are also great for high-throughput and scale workloads.

Operating System

Another consideration when deploying an Azure App Service Plan is the operating system to host the application. For most deployments, you can currently leverage the Linux operating system. Java, the LAMP stack, MEAN/MERN, and .NET can all run on Linux at this point. App Service Plans that are hosted on Linux are also ideal for containerized workloads.

In some scenarios, you may want to leverage the Windows operating system, such as when you are deploying a traditional .NET Framework application.

If you deploy your App Service Plan first, you need to choose the appropriate operating system during the creation of the app service in order to see your plan. If you are doing the plan deployment at the same time as the site deployment, you only need to choose the operating system once.

Redundancy

Zone redundancy can be used on premium and higher plans. With Zone redundancy, you can set the ability to use the zonal architecture of Azure. When you choose this option, the minimum amount of app services that are active is three. Three instances are required in order to have one instance available in each of the different redundancy zones within a region. The Free, Shared, Basic, and Standard plans do not support zone redundancy.

App Services

Whether you deploy your App Service Plan first or during the App Service deployment will be up to you. Either way, the main resource you want for hosting your web applications is the Azure App Service. The next sections review the options for the App Service deployment.

Name Your Application

In order to deploy your application, you must choose a name. Since the application is going to have a fully-qualified domain name, your application name must be unique to the world. There are a couple of other naming considerations due to the nature of FQDNs. For example, you can't start or end with a dash, and don't try to use any special characters, as only 64 alphanumeric characters and dashes are allowed (see Figure 4-4).

Figure 4-4.   *The creation of an app service requires a name that is unique and can be utilized as a fully-qualified domain name tagged with *.azurewebsites.net*

Once you deploy your application, the name will be part of the overall domain. Every app service shares a common base domain that includes your unique application name. For example, a website named az204examref20251231 after deployment would have this URL: `https://az204examref20251231.azurewebsites.net`.

Publish Type

After choosing your application name, you need to pick the way you will publish your code. The options are *Code*, *Docker Container*, or *Static Web App*, as shown in Figure 4-5.

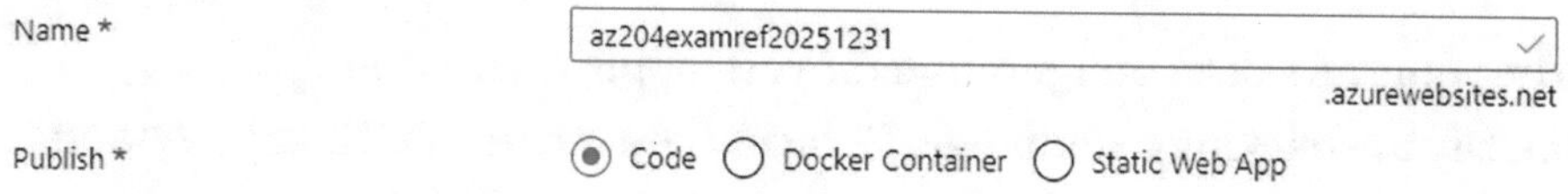

Name *	az204examref20251231 ✓
	.azurewebsites.net
Publish *	◉ Code ○ Docker Container ○ Static Web App

Figure 4-5. *Choices for publish type*

Code

Choosing Code is the traditional approach. In the code deployment, you can FTP your application, publish directly from Visual Studio, or set up automated deployments to pull from GitHub, BitBucket, Azure DevOps Repos, or another public, external Git repository.

Docker Container

Choosing a Docker Container deployment requires that your code be built into an image that can run in a container. You can publish your images to Azure Container Registry or Docker Hub. From there, setting the image to use for your App Service is easily configured, as is choosing the exact image and version tag for the image.

Static Web Application

When you deploy a static web application, you can choose either a Free or a Standard plan. The main difference is the number of staging environments you can have as well as the size of your application. Both plans allow for custom domains. Only the Standard plan has an SLA and allows for a private endpoint.

Deployment of a Static Web Application is based on your Git repository. Pointing your application to the branch of your choice allows for automated deployments every time you check changes into the branch.

Runtime Stack

The runtime stack configuration for your application allows you to specify the backing technology. Choices here include .NET, Java, Python, JavaScript/Node, Go, and Ruby. Based on your stack choice, the app service will automatically be provisioned with necessary technologies to host your application.

App Service Plan

Once again, either create a new plan at this point or utilize one that you have previously provisioned. As a reminder, the App Service Plan can host many different app services, but the best production scenarios will likely be based on the workload.

If you need to create a new App Service Plan, you can easily just click the Create New link and set the name. You'll need to choose the correct Sales Keeping Unit (SKU) for SKU and Size. If you choose an existing plan, only the plans from the operating system will be available, but the SKU and Size will match the plan chosen when the plan was created. Figure 4-6 shows the choices for Runtime Stack, Operating System, Region, App Service Plan, and SKU and Size.

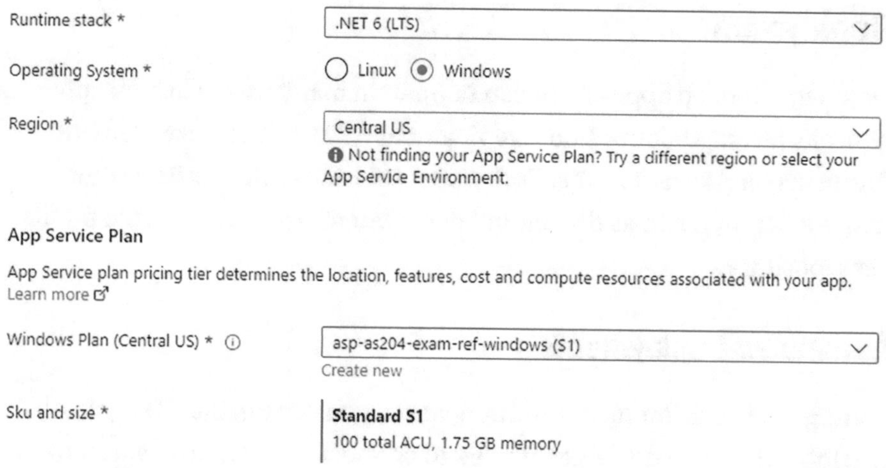

Runtime stack *	.NET 6 (LTS) ⌄
Operating System *	○ Linux ⦿ Windows
Region *	Central US ⌄
	ⓘ Not finding your App Service Plan? Try a different region or select your App Service Environment.

App Service Plan

App Service plan pricing tier determines the location, features, cost and compute resources associated with your app. Learn more ☐

Windows Plan (Central US) * ⓘ	asp-as204-exam-ref-windows (S1) ⌄
	Create new
Sku and size *	**Standard S1**
	100 total ACU, 1.75 GB memory

Figure 4-6. *The choices for stack, operating system, region, and the plan and SKU*

As this plan has been provisioned with the standard S1 SKU, the options for Zone Redundancy are automatically disabled and cannot be enabled (see Figure 4-7).

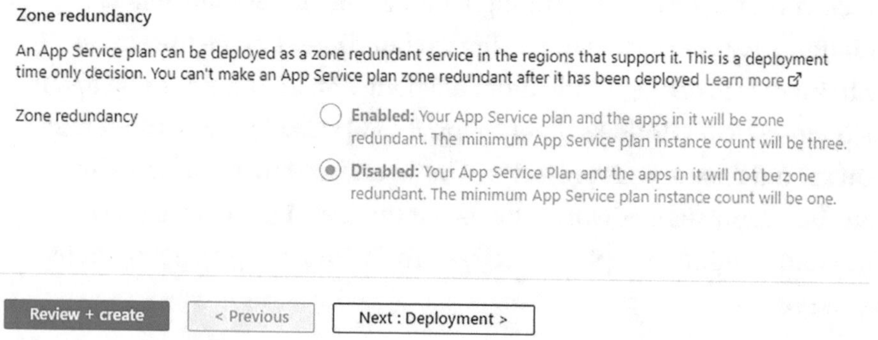

Zone redundancy

An App Service plan can be deployed as a zone redundant service in the regions that support it. This is a deployment time only decision. You can't make an App Service plan zone redundant after it has been deployed Learn more ☐

| Zone redundancy | ○ **Enabled:** Your App Service plan and the apps in it will be zone redundant. The minimum App Service plan instance count will be three. |
| | ⦿ **Disabled:** Your App Service Plan and the apps in it will not be zone redundant. The minimum App Service plan instance count will be one. |

[Review + create]   [< Previous]   [Next : Deployment >]

Figure 4-7. *Zone Redundancy is disabled when the App Service Plan is not at least at the Premium level*

Deployment

Deployment of an app service can happen in many ways. Current solutions typically leverage Continuous Deployment (CD), directly from GitHub, BitBucket, or Azure DevOps. Traditional solutions might utilize some manual deployment, as do manual deployments from an external public Git repository.

Automated Deployments

During the provisioning of the application, you can enable CD against GitHub. When you do this, you need to connect your Azure account to GitHub, and then choose the organization, repository, and branch for the code that will be deployed. Once the application is provisioned, a GitHub action is built that includes the necessary YAML to build and deploy your application.

The default YAML will not run unit tests. Additionally, the default YAML will utilize a Windows build agent when using a Windows runtime stack. If your code is .NET 6 or higher for a web project, you will at a minimum want to switch to an Ubuntu build agent, since the action will run orders of magnitude more efficiently on an Ubuntu build agent as opposed to a Windows build agent. It's important to remember that you should ensure your project will build on Ubuntu, because there may be circumstances where that is not the case. Figure 4-8 shows the configuration to deploy directly from GitHub using an action built by Azure.

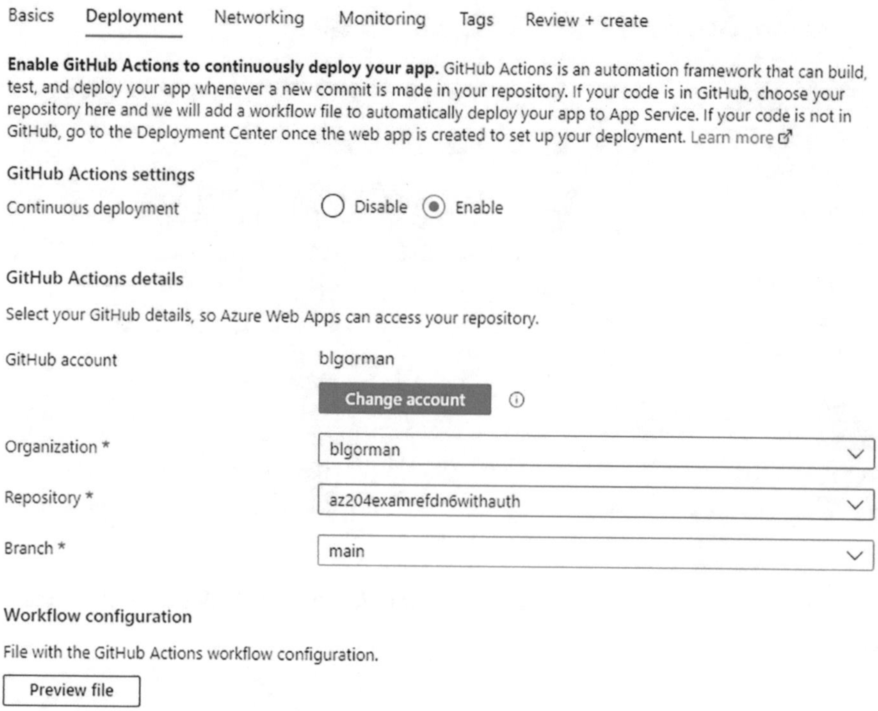

Basics   **Deployment**   Networking   Monitoring   Tags   Review + create

Enable GitHub Actions to continuously deploy your app. GitHub Actions is an automation framework that can build, test, and deploy your app whenever a new commit is made in your repository. If your code is in GitHub, choose your repository here and we will add a workflow file to automatically deploy your app to App Service. If your code is not in GitHub, go to the Deployment Center once the web app is created to set up your deployment. Learn more ⧉

GitHub Actions settings

Continuous deployment   ○ Disable ◉ Enable

GitHub Actions details

Select your GitHub details, so Azure Web Apps can access your repository.

GitHub account   blgorman

                                  [Change account]   ⓘ

Organization * | blgorman   ⌄ |

Repository * | az204examrefdn6withauth   ⌄ |

Branch * | main   ⌄ |

Workflow configuration

File with the GitHub Actions workflow configuration.

[Preview file]

Figure 4-8. *The automated deployment is set to utilize an existing GitHub repository*

Automated deployment can also be configured after the application is provisioned. When an application has not been set for CD during provisioning, visiting the Deployment Center blade gives you options for utilization of the four major Git locations, as well as the ability to use an external Git repository (see Figure 4-9).

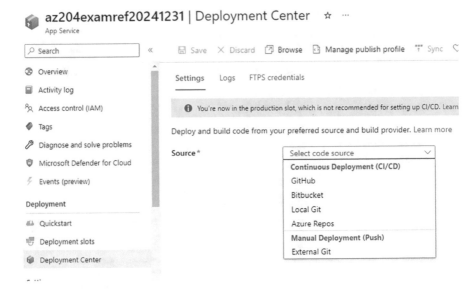

Figure 4-9. *You can configure CI/CD after an app service has been deployed*

Manual Deployments

When Automated deployment is not an option or was not configured, manual options for deployment exist. The first option is to provision utilizing FTPS.

On the Deployment Center blade in the app service, under the FTPS credentials, you can find your endpoint, username, and password for deploying an application (see Figure 4-10).

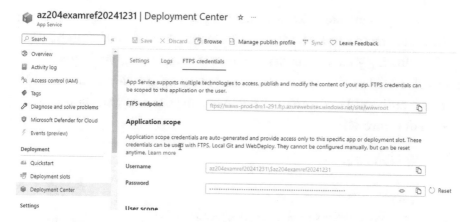

Figure 4-10. *The FTPS credentials can be retrieved for manual deployment from the Deployment Center*

Additional manual options for deployment exist, including right-clicking and publishing from Visual Studio or VS Code. In those scenarios, you need to connect to your Azure account and then you can easily create a publish profile or publish your build from your machine. While this is possible, it's not a recommended production solution due to security concerns and other DevOps principles that you would be missing out on by building an automated deployment.

Networking

The next blade for the App Service deployment is the Networking options. Here, only one option is available, and that is to enable network injection.

Essentially, without enabling any Internet limitations, your app service will be hosted on the public Internet. You can change any settings after deployment to make the application only able to be reached via a private endpoint, or to ensure that traffic only happens on a private network within your Azure tenant.

Here, if you enable network injection, you need to leverage an existing network or create a new one. This traffic is for inbound and/or outbound traffic, allowing your app service to connect to resources within your network. Enabling this option allows you to set up private endpoints and/ or direct outbound traffic to a subnet in one of your Azure networks, as shown in Figure 4-11.

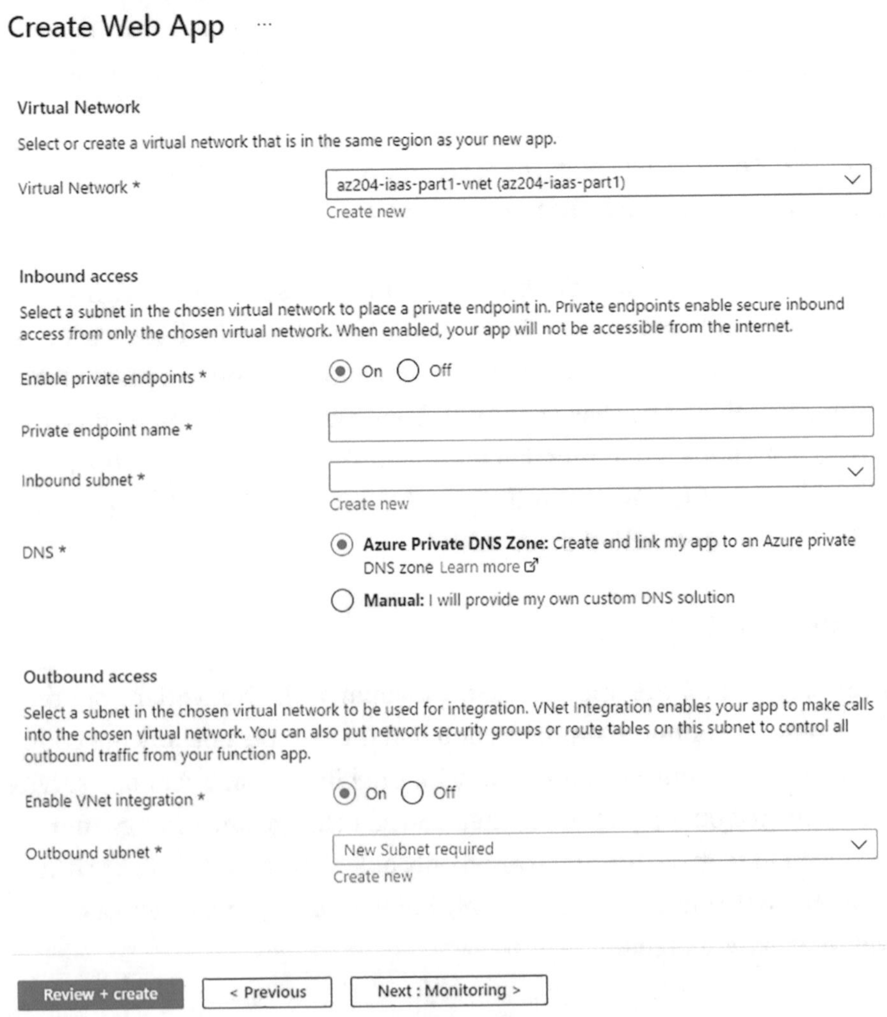

Create Web App   ...

Virtual Network

Select or create a virtual network that is in the same region as your new app.

Virtual Network *   az204-iaas-part1-vnet (az204-iaas-part1)   ⌄
                          Create new

Inbound access

Select a subnet in the chosen virtual network to place a private endpoint in. Private endpoints enable secure inbound access from only the chosen virtual network. When enabled, your app will not be accessible from the internet.

Enable private endpoints *   ● On   ○ Off

Private endpoint name *

Inbound subnet *   ⌄
                                    Create new

DNS *   ● **Azure Private DNS Zone:** Create and link my app to an Azure private
                           DNS zone Learn more ⌕

                         ○ **Manual:** I will provide my own custom DNS solution

Outbound access

Select a subnet in the chosen virtual network to be used for integration. VNet Integration enables your app to make calls into the chosen virtual network. You can also put network security groups or route tables on this subnet to control all outbound traffic from your function app.

Enable VNet integration *   ● On   ○ Off

Outbound subnet *   New Subnet required   ⌄
                          Create new

[Review + create]   [< Previous]   [Next : Monitoring >]

Figure 4-11. *The Networking options allow you to configure private inbound and outbound traffic to and from your app service*

To be clear, I'm not enabling any network traffic in my deployment, which is easily accomplished by leaving the network injection set to Off.

Monitoring

The most overlooked and most important aspect of the app service deployment is likely to be the monitoring of the application.

Enabling Monitoring, as shown in Figure 4-12, requires that you provision Application Insights, and you'll want to back that with a Log Analytics workspace. When you do this, you will have the ability to run Kusto Queries (KQL) against your logs to do spelunking into your application when things go wrong or to access other interesting metrics.

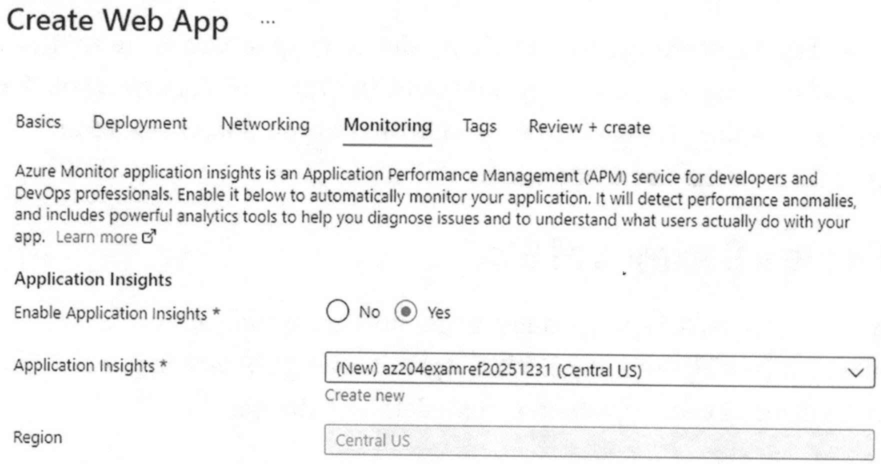

Figure 4-12. *Monitoring with Application Insights is enabled on the application*

In .NET, a simple setting and NuGet package allows you to instrument your applications for App Insights, which also allows you to write custom telemetry very easily from your applications. App Insights can also be configured to run from the JavaScript on your client side of the application.

Application Insights also gives you a number of additional tools you can use to see information about the utilization your website or just to perform simple health checks. More information on Application Insights is covered in Chapter 10.

After Provisioning

After provisioning your application, a number of configurations and settings will be essential to managing your application.

Deployment Slots

One of the most critical aspects of a production app service is the ability to deploy to application deployment slots. Utilization of slots gives you the ability to deploy production-ready code to a non-production location for quick integration and user testing.

Create a Deployment Slot

After your website is provisioned, when slots are available, you can create new slots (see Figure 4-13). Each slot gets its own public-facing URL, which is the name of your application plus a dash and the slot.

Figure 4-13. *The staging slot is added to the application. The slot gets its own URL and even has its own ability to be administered*

Swap Slots

A bit later in this chapter, you'll examine the configuration settings for things like environment variables and connection strings. When you consider configuration, note that slots can have settings that are always going to be at the slot level and others that can move with the deployment. For example, an environment variable that denotes a non-production slot would be *sticky* to the staging slot and will never move to production. A connection string that is the same in multiple slots could just move with the slot or be sticky with the slot. A key to a production API or a production database connection string that should be accessible only from production would need to be sticky to the production slot.

You can then point your repository to deploy to the slot, and when the time is right, you can press a button or automate the swap of the staging slot to production. If things go wrong, a simple press of the button swaps the slots back to their original places, as shown in Figure 4-14.

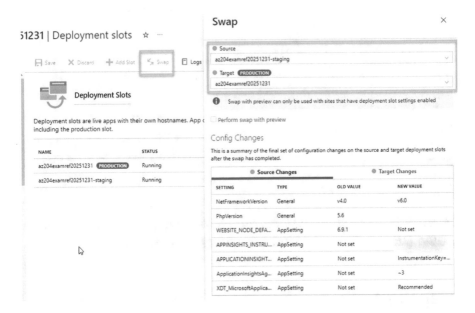

Figure 4-14. *You can swap slots, as shown with the staging and production slots in this example*

Simple Traffic Load-Balancing/Routing

One last benefit of swapping slots is the ability to direct part of the traffic to the slots. This is not as robust as a full routing solution can be, but it is a very quick way to direct a small percentage of traffic to the slot. While you have no control over which requests are routed, you can at least know that a percentage of traffic is hitting the next version of the site and you can get some immediate feedback if there are errors before sending the next version to the live placement with 100 percent of the traffic (see Figure 4-15).

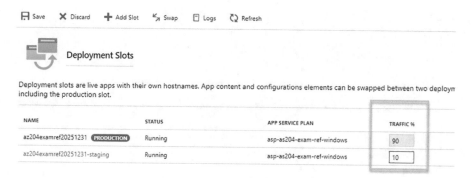

Figure 4-15. *The ability to route traffic by percentage to the slots is possible from the app service without having to deploy or leverage a full routing solution*

Automated Deployment Using the Deployment Slot's Publish Profile

Now that you have a public-facing deployment with slots, you can change your pipeline to deploy to Azure. DevOps work is a bit outside of the scope of the AZ-204 Exam, but it's still a great idea to know your deployment options in case some scenario might show up in the exam or at your place of work or for a client. For purposes of brevity, this book only covers deployment pipelines from GitHub actions, but you can easily translate this to your provider of choice.

When enabling a deployment from GitHub to your app service, the default setting is that Azure created a GitHub action that utilizes your App Service publish profile. This action leverages a secret that stores your publish profile at GitHub. The target for the deployment also names the Production slot (see Figure 4-16).

Figure 4-16. *The deployment pipeline is triggered by the push to the main branch and has a workflow_dispatch trigger that allows the pipeline to be manually triggered*

To determine the publish profile for the application, you can go to the app service and download the publish profile (shown in Figure 4-17), which is a bunch of XML with information about your application and permissions to deploy to it. This XML is exactly what is stored in your GitHub secrets.

Figure 4-17. *The publish profile can be retrieved from the App Service Overview blade*

Unfortunately, or perhaps mercifully, depending on your stance, the publish profile for your slot is not the same as your production slot. The name of the slot is added to the settings and a different password is also used. For this reason, it is not sufficient to just switch your YAML to point to the "staging" slot (see the error in Figure 4-18). You must also update the publish profile.

main_az204examref20251231.yml
on: push

✅ build   47s ●————● ❌ deploy   34s

Annotations
1 error and 14 warnings

❌ deploy
Deployment Failed with Error: Error: Publish profile is invalid for app-name and slot-name provided. Provide correct publish profile credentials for app.

Figure 4-18. *The slot has its own publish profile, so you must download that and store it in GitHub secrets*

You can either overwrite the initial secret, or you can create a new one and put the new publish profile in the new secret, then leverage the new secret from the YAML. For purposes of demonstration, I store my staging publish profile in a secret called STAGING_PUBLISH_PROFILE at GitHub (see Figure 4-19).

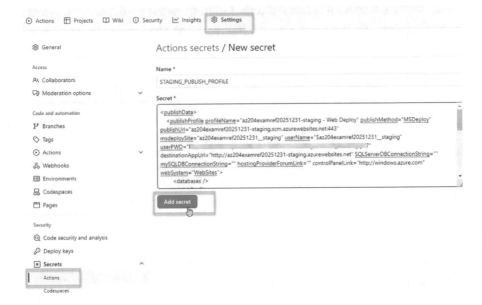

Figure 4-19. *Store the publish profile in a secret to utilize from the YAML in the pipeline*

After adding the secret, I ensure that the slot is set to Staging to match my slot name and that I've leveraged the correct secret, as shown in Figure 4-20.

```
37   deploy:
38     runs-on: ubuntu-latest
39     needs: build
40     environment:
41       name: 'Production'
42       url: ${{ steps.deploy-to-webapp.outputs.webapp-url }}
43
44     steps:
45       - name: Download artifact from build job
46         uses: actions/download-artifact@v2
47         with:
48           name: .net-app
49
50       - name: Deploy to Azure Web App
51         id: deploy-to-webapp
52         uses: azure/webapps-deploy@v2
53         with:
54           app-name: 'az204examref20251231'
55           slot-name: 'Staging'
56           publish-profile: ${{ secrets.STAGING_PUBLISH_PROFILE }}
57           package: .
58
```

Figure 4-20. *The application publish profile variable is updated and the slot is set to match my slot by name*

You'll also notice that I switched my deployment agent to ubuntu-latest for the performance reasons mentioned earlier. After making the changes, my application correctly deploys into the staging slot in my app service in Azure. If you want more information about working with YAML pipelines, you can find some resources at https://docs.github.com/actions/quickstart.

Additional Services

In order to make an application work, you often need to deploy additional resources. A few of these resources include Azure Storage, Azure Cosmos DB, Azure SQL, and/or Azure App Configuration.

Deploy an Azure SQL Instance

Azure SQL is not really part of the AZ-204 Exam, but it is yet another topic that you should understand enough to work with it, should you be presented with a question on the exam or encounter any real-world scenario.

For this application, a very simple and inexpensive database is required to back authorization (see Figure 4-21).

Figure 4-21. *The Basic Azure SQL Server costs less than five dollars per month and is very limited but sufficient for learning*

A couple of quick notes:

- You need to enable your IP address on the server firewall if you want to run queries within the portal or from SSMS on your machine.

- You need to enable the ability for other Azure services to connect to this server. Failure to allow other services will likely result in errors when making calls to the database due to access denied and/or server not found timeouts (see Figure 4-22).

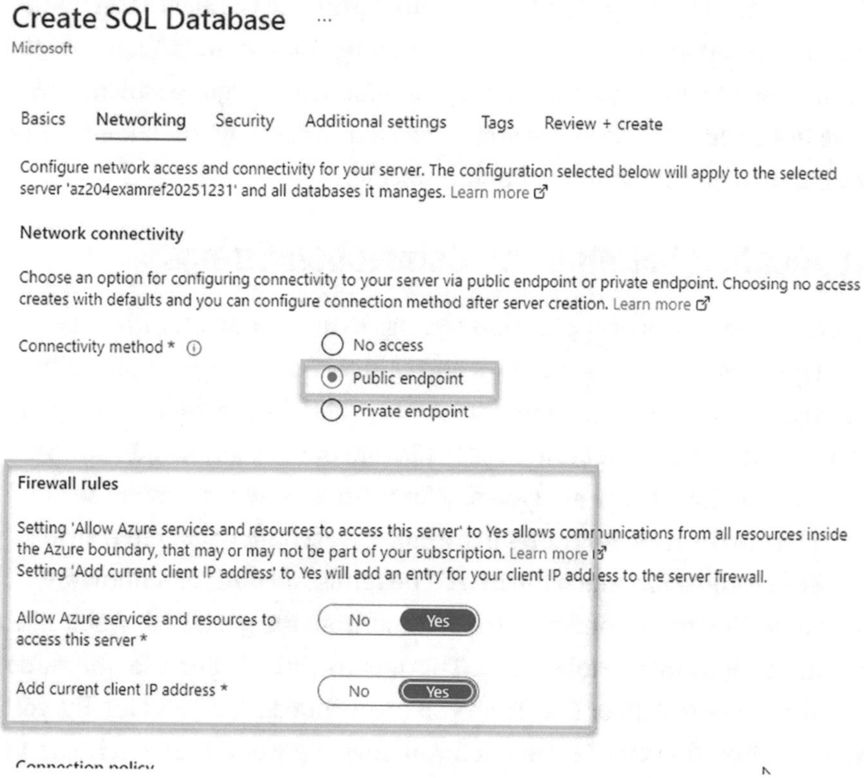

Create SQL Database ...
Microsoft

Basics	**Networking**	Security	Additional settings	Tags	Review + create

Configure network access and connectivity for your server. The configuration selected below will apply to the selected server 'az204examref20251231' and all databases it manages. Learn more ☐

Network connectivity

Choose an option for configuring connectivity to your server via public endpoint or private endpoint. Choosing no access creates with defaults and you can configure connection method after server creation. Learn more ☐

Connectivity method * ⓘ   ◯ No access
                            ⦿ Public endpoint
                            ◯ Private endpoint

Firewall rules

Setting 'Allow Azure services and resources to access this server' to Yes allows communications from all resources inside the Azure boundary, that may or may not be part of your subscription. Learn more ☐
Setting 'Add current client IP address' to Yes will add an entry for your client IP address to the server firewall.

Allow Azure services and resources to   (No   **Yes**)
access this server *

Add current client IP address *   (No   **Yes**)

Connection policy

Figure 4-22. *The Networking settings allow you to set the server firewall to allow Azure services and your local IP address. If you fail to do this, you can easily do this from the portal on the Server blade under the Server Firewall settings*

173

After creating the database, you need to get the connection string for use in the next section. If you want to create other resources to connect to, you need to get connection information or environment variable information for those resources, and you can then utilize the resources by configuring connection information in the configuration section. Chapter 8 goes deeper, with a couple of configurations for the Azure App Service and Azure Key Vault.

Configuration

With the application deployed and a database or other resources ready to go, a number of settings can be configured from the Configuration blade on the app service. It's important to remember that some settings can be configured to be sticky for both the production and staging (which could have been copied if the slot was created after the setting was added). Other settings can be configured to be slot specific.

Application Settings and Connection Strings

There are two types of application settings to be concerned with. The two types are Application Settings and Connection Strings. Application Settings are typically environment variables and they replace values you would find in the appsettings.json file that are not connection strings. The Connection Strings are typically for the database connection string and can also be used for things like a storage account connection string.

Before going too much further, I'd be remiss if I didn't mention the pain of setting these configuration settings from the portal. Most settings require a triple-save to take effect. This means you must first set the value and then choose Add or OK. Then you must choose Save, and finally, you must confirm the save. I cannot tell you how many development hours I've lost because I never chose Save and didn't navigate away from the page to receive the warning about the changes being unsaved. Although a triple save won't likely be something you would encounter on your exam, always keep this on your radar when you are working with configuration settings.

Connection Strings

During this first look at the app service, I'll set the configuration for the database to be connected to both the staging and the production slots. They will share the same database as configured (see Figure 4-23). This is accomplished by visiting both the production and staging slots, going to their configuration, and then scrolling down to the connection strings section to set the connection string. In this app, the connection string is named DefaultConnection.

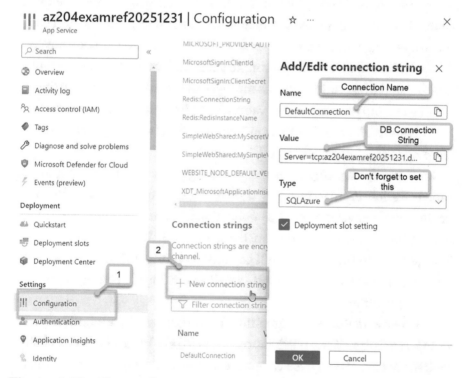

Figure 4-23. *The configuration is set for the database on the App Service Connection Strings section in the Configuration blade*

Note that the Deployment Slot Setting is checked here. This will make the setting sticky to the slot. Even though the values will be the same, this would easily allow you to use a different connection string for each environment in the future. Also, with them being the same, there is no need to swap it with the code, as both will be set to work equally well.

Application Settings

The application that is deployed has a couple of custom variables that can be set to easily see their values and settings from the Application Settings blade. These variables have a stub in the appsettings.json file and you can also leverage them from a user secrets file if you run the code locally. The variables are for showing a simple value and a secret value and will be populated from various places throughout the book to enhance the learning around how to retrieve values from different places such as the Configuration blade, an Azure App Configuration (see Chapter 8), and Azure Key Vault (also covered in Chapter 8).

In Azure, configuring the two App settings values on the Configuration blade will allow them to be easily shown. These entries can be used for proving which environment the application is in, or any other relevant information. When you read about using Key Vault and Azure App Configuration in Chapter 8, you'll get another look at injecting the secret value from a more secure location as well as sharing the shared value across applications.

On the Azure Portal configuration for the app service for both slots, I'm adding a setting for SimpleWebShared:MySimpleValue and SimpleWebSh ared:MySecretValue. These values are added to the application settings for the deployed app service, and they can override the values from the appsettings.json file. The really great thing is you can have different values in different environments, so the deployment slot matters and the text can remain for each slot, even when the application is swapped to a different slot. The Shared value will state the environment. The Secret will state where the secret is coming from. Figure 4-24 shows the settings on the production slot.

Figure 4-24. *The production slot sets the environment variables for the shared values. Both are configured as deployment slot settings*

With the application settings and connection strings in place, you can now view both applications. Users can be registered to the default ASP. NET Identity provider baked into the application, and the deployment slot environment variables will show their respective values (see Figure 4-25).

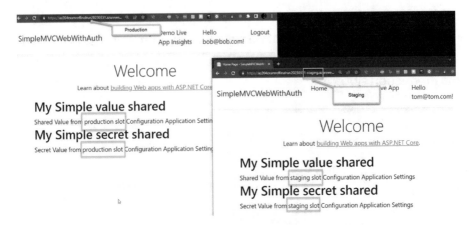

Figure 4-25. *The applications are deployed and working as expected. Users can be registered and environment variables are sticky to their slots*

General Settings

In addition to environment variables and connection strings, sometimes you'll need to change a few of the general settings for an application. There are a number of things that you can configure here, and when it comes time to take the test you should remember this page in case you are asked to tweak some settings.

The most important general settings are Stack and Version. Depending on what technology stack you are using, you can set the values here. You would have configured this typically during deployment, but in case things change, you can update them here (see Figure 4-26).

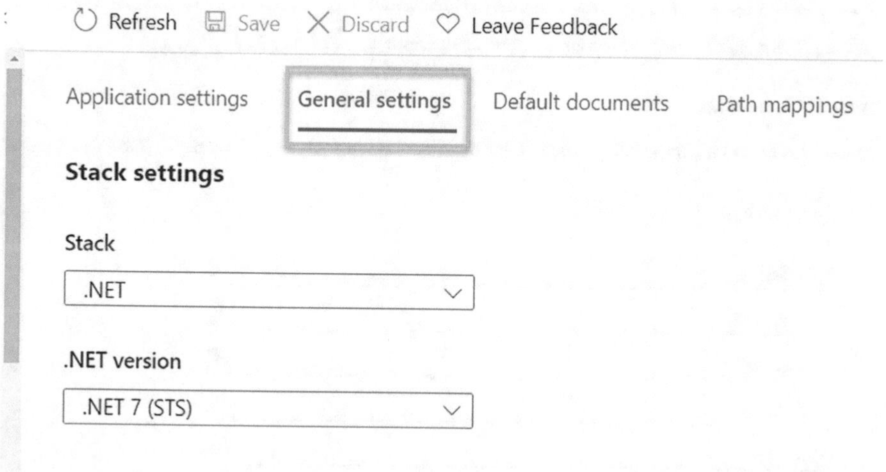

⋮   ○ Refresh   🖫 Save   ✕ Discard   ♡ Leave Feedback

| Application settings | General settings | Default documents | Path mappings |

Stack settings

Stack

.NET   ⌄

.NET version

.NET 7 (STS)   ⌄

Figure 4-26. *The application configuration General Settings tab allows configuring the stack and version for your application*

In addition to the stack, you can set the platform settings for the application. This section includes the bitness (32- or 64-bit), and for different settings like the Managed pipeline version, the FTP State and HTTP Version, as well as whether you'll allow web sockets. The next major setting of interest is the *Always On* setting. In standard and better SKUs, you can set Always On to the "On" value. When you do this, there is never a warm-up time for the first visit to your application, even if no one has accessed the site in some time. This Always On setting is not available on free SKUs. The setting is highlighted in Figure 4-27.

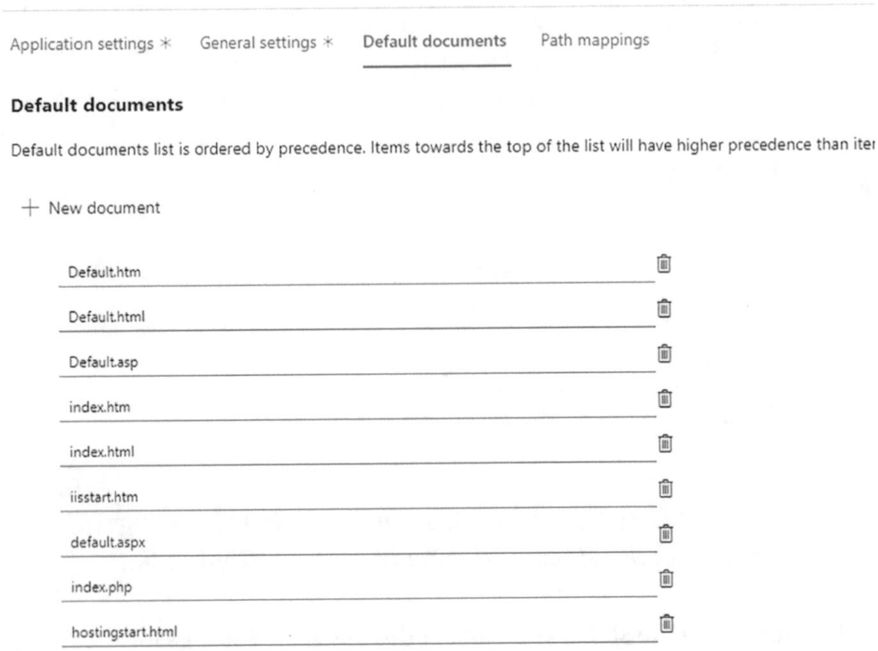

Application settings ✳   General settings ✳   **Default documents**   Path mappings

Default documents

Default documents list is ordered by precedence. Items towards the top of the list will have higher precedence than iter

+ New document

Default.htm

Default.html

Default.asp

index.htm

index.html

iisstart.htm

default.aspx

index.php

hostingstart.html

Figure 4-27. *The first part of the platform settings, with the interesting setting for Always On highlighted*

Additional settings exist for ARR Affinity, HTTPS Only (which should always be on at this point), and a Minimum TLS Version. Remember that by default, SSL is baked in and you don't need to do anything to leverage HTTPS for your app service (see Figure 4-28).

Figure 4-28. *The remaining platform settings, with the interesting setting for HTTPS Only set to On*

The next-to-last setting on this page includes the ability to allow remote debugging. When turned on, you'll also need to set the version of Visual Studio that will be attached to the app service for debugging.

The final settings are for configuring and utilizing client certificates. When set to Ignore, nothing is needed or done here. The Optional setting allows you to have SSO as a sign-on option, but also can be authenticated via a client certificate. For Allow, all requests must be authenticated and a client certificate can be used but the user can still fall back to SSO for your organization or application. When set to Require, all users must have a client certificate to connect to the application. Figure 4-29 shows the remaining options for the general settings on the application.

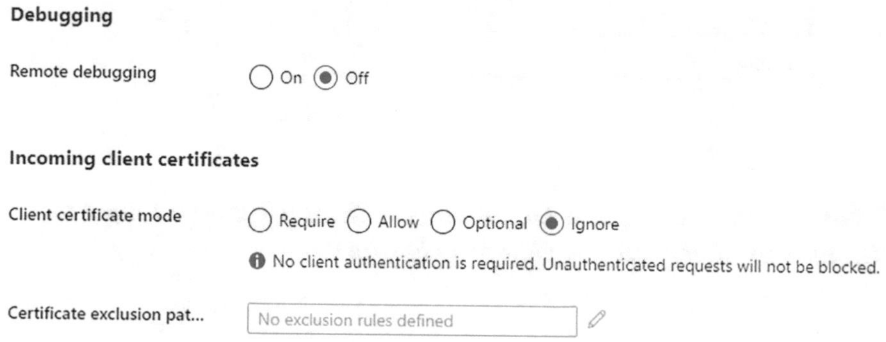

Debugging

Remote debugging   ○ On ● Off

Incoming client certificates

Client certificate mode   ○ Require ○ Allow ○ Optional ● Ignore

❶ No client authentication is required. Unauthenticated requests will not be blocked.

Certificate exclusion pat... | No exclusion rules defined | ✎ |

Figure 4-29. *The final settings for the General Settings tab*

Default Documents

If you've ever worked with IIS and set up a website, you'll likely remember the default documents settings. This setting in Azure is no different.

The Default Documents settings simply employs a list of potential files you could drop as your start page for your application. You can generally just leave this page alone, as most default documents are listed for almost all the web technologies. If you need a different start-up page, you can add it here as well (see Figure 4-30).

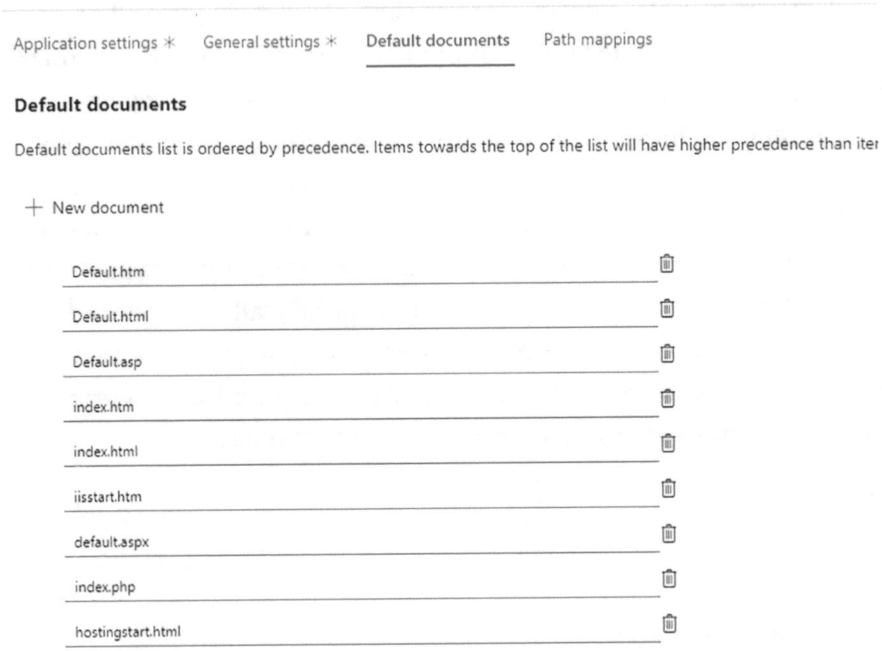

Application settings ✳   General settings ✳   Default documents   Path mappings

Default documents

Default documents list is ordered by precedence. Items towards the top of the list will have higher precedence than iter

+ New document

Default.htm	🗑
Default.html	🗑
Default.asp	🗑
index.htm	🗑
index.html	🗑
iisstart.htm	🗑
default.aspx	🗑
index.php	🗑
hostingstart.html	🗑

Figure 4-30.   *The Default Documents settings. Unless you need to change this page, you can generally ignore it*

Path Mappings

In more traditional web applications, there might have been scenarios where you had to handle some requests. In Java, this was typically done with Servlets. In .NET, this has been done with page-handlers. On the Path Mappings page, you can set customer handler mapping. You can also create virtual applications and directories.

Another reason you might come to this page outside of routing for handlers is to add a mounted Azure storage account. While this is currently in preview as I write this book, you can now mount storage directly to the app service for utilization within your application. Figure 4-31 shows the settings available on the Path Mappings blade.

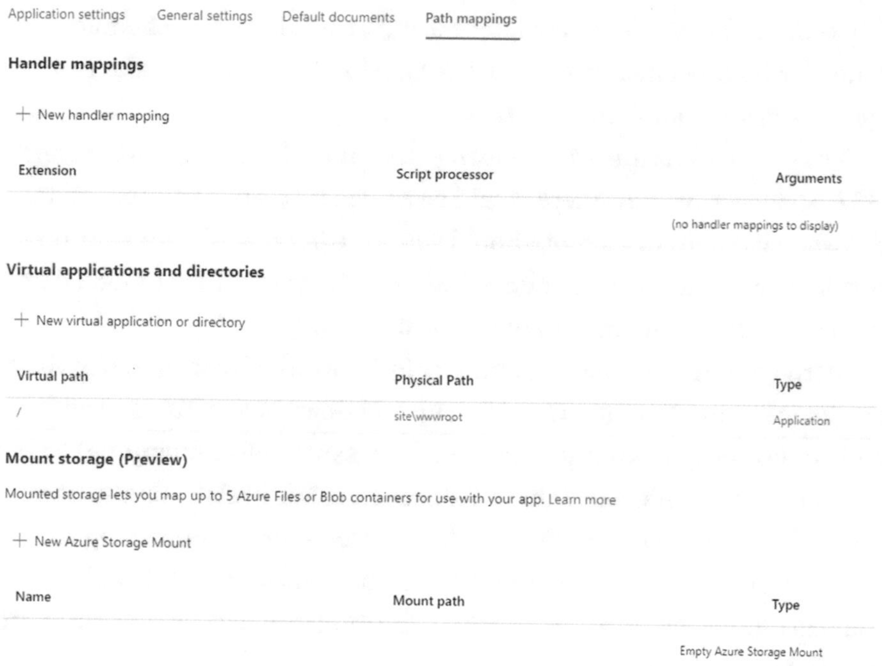

Application settings   General settings   Default documents   Path mappings

Handler mappings

+ New handler mapping

Extension	Script processor	Arguments
		(no handler mappings to display)

Virtual applications and directories

+ New virtual application or directory

Virtual path	Physical Path	Type
/	site\wwwroot	Application

Mount storage (Preview)

Mounted storage lets you map up to 5 Azure Files or Blob containers for use with your app. Learn more

+ New Azure Storage Mount

Name	Mount path	Type
		Empty Azure Storage Mount

Figure 4-31. *The path mappings options*

Scaling

At this point, your application is deployed, you have the configuration settings in place, and you have automated your deployments. You are now ready to go live, so you flip the switch and traffic starts flowing to your website. Everything is running great during your normal workloads. However, there are a couple of things that happen that cause you some pain.

The first thing that happens is that, every Monday morning when work resumes, your application gets a massive influx of traffic due to backorders over the weekend. Additionally, there are times when items are placed on discount. When popular items go on sale, your site gets quite a bit more traffic. Although some traffic loads can be predicted or anticipated for things like holiday sales or clearance events, there is no set schedule for general sales on items, so you must be able to respond to demand in a dynamic fashion for these scenarios.

Of course this is the exact reason you deployed in a standard or better SKU, because you knew there would be a need to scale your application. But when it comes to scaling, should you scale out or scale up? How do you know when to scale in or down? Should the scaling be automated or should you have someone manually push the trigger?

Perhaps you read that and don't really know what scaling out/in versus up/down means. Essentially, scaling up and down is one instance with more or less power. Scaling in and out is the same power (compute) with extra instances deployed. Behind the scenes, this is likely compute power backed by VMs in Azure in the data center. However, the only thing you need to worry about is the number of instances currently deployed to serve your customers. Azure will take care of the infrastructure for you, since this is a platform service.

As there are two types of scaling, you can choose which type to configure on the App Service blade. Scaling up allows you to change the SKU set on the App Service Plan. Scaling out allows you to set the number of instances when the plan allows for multiple instances. Note that, once again, these settings are plan specific, not app service specific. This is because the compute is based on the plan, not on the app service(s) deployed within the plan.

Autoscaling

In almost every production scenario, you'll likely want to utilize autoscaling. After all, the whole point of going to the cloud is to make it so you don't have to take calls at 2am because servers are down due to not enough capacity.

When you click the Scale Out (App Service Plan) option, you can choose *Manual Scale* or *Custom Autoscale*. If not set previously, the scaling is likely manual. Choosing the Custom setting allows you to build rules for automatic scaling.

Scaling can take place based on a metric, which is the best choice for handling dynamic scenarios. Your metric can be things like CPU utilization, HTTP queue length, TCP operations, socket counts, and data throughput. Choose the metric that makes sense for your scenario, in this case, likely CPU utilization or perhaps HTTP queue length. You then set the threshold to trigger an autoscale. This is all done by creating a rule (see Figure 4-32).

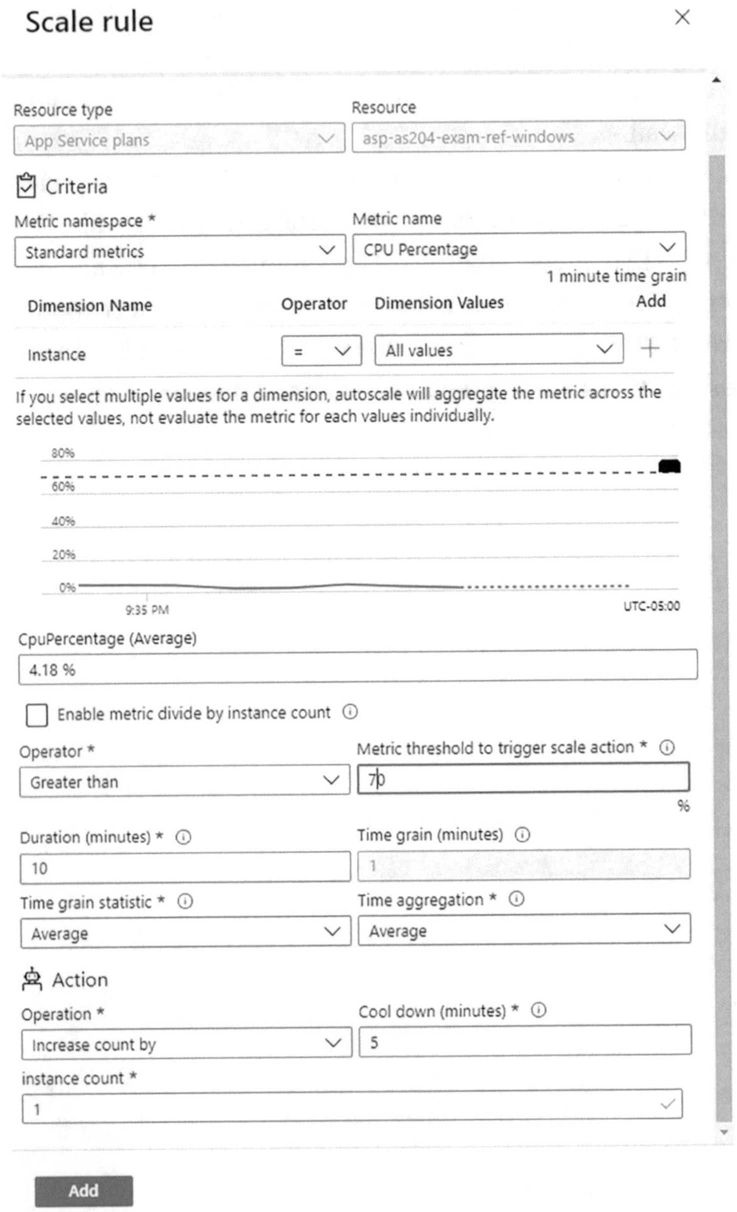

Scale rule   ✕

Resource type
[App Service plans   ⌄]

Resource
[asp-as204-exam-ref-windows   ⌄]

☑ Criteria

Metric namespace *
[Standard metrics   ⌄]

Metric name
[CPU Percentage   ⌄]

1 minute time grain

Dimension Name	Operator	Dimension Values	Add
Instance	[= ⌄]	[All values ⌄]	+

If you select multiple values for a dimension, autoscale will aggregate the metric across the selected values, not evaluate the metric for each values individually.

CpuPercentage (Average)
[4.18 %]

☐ Enable metric divide by instance count ⓘ

Operator *
[Greater than   ⌄]

Metric threshold to trigger scale action * ⓘ
[7p]
                                          %

Duration (minutes) * ⓘ
[10]

Time grain (minutes) ⓘ
[1]

Time grain statistic * ⓘ
[Average   ⌄]

Time aggregation * ⓘ
[Average   ⌄]

⧉ Action

Operation *
[Increase count by   ⌄]

Cool down (minutes) * ⓘ
[5]

instance count *
[1   ⌄]

Add

Figure 4-32. *Creating a rule for automatic scaling requires choosing a metric and then setting thresholds to trigger the scaling event*

What do you think would happen if this were the only rule you created? If you think about this, you'll likely quickly realize you will scale out, but you will never scale in.

For this reason, there are two rules to remember when creating scaling rules. The first rule is to always create your rules in pairs. If you create a scale out rule, you must also create a scale in rule if you want to respond to demand efficiently and bring the instance count back in when not necessary.

The second rule of creating autoscaling is to remember to utilize thresholds that don't create a scenario where you would scale back up after scaling down immediately. This is done by utilizing thresholds that are far enough apart that they can't create an auto-cycle scenario, where the solution continually scales in and then right back out. For example, utilize a 70 percent scale out rule and a 30 percent scale in rule. If an instance is running at 75 percent, a new instance is added. Suppose the workload is 40 percent on each for some time. If you scaled back in, 40 percent + 40 percent = 80 percent, and your app service would have to immediately scale back out. Therefore, 30 percent +30 percent = 60 percent, and your app service would be able to remain at one instance until the CPU goes above 70 percent again (see Figure 4-33).

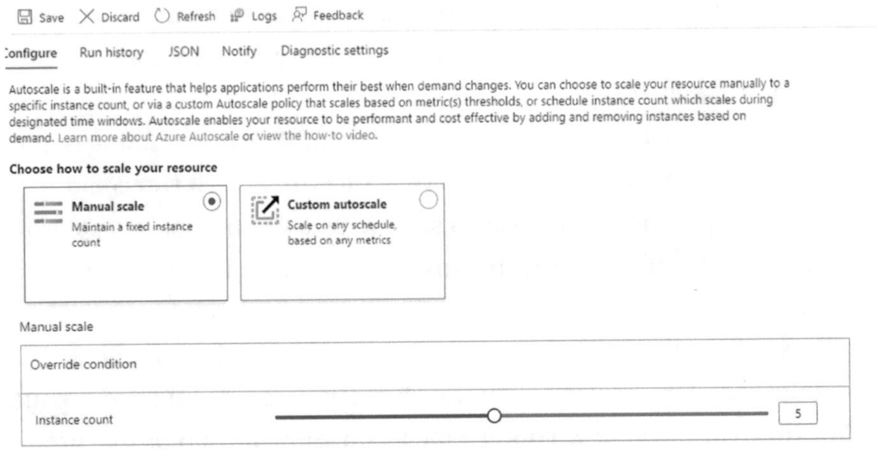

Figure 4-33. *Two rules are set to make sure that the app service can effectively scale out and back in*

Another setting exists on the Custom Autoscaling blade. As you likely want to ensure that your application is always effective, you can set a minimum number of instances. You can also set a maximum number of instances to ensure that you don't scale out uncontrollably. When these instance counts are effectively set, you will be ensured that your application is always running with a number of instances somewhere in your predefined range.

There is one other option that is a bit tricky. The *Default* instance count setting. For this setting, assume a scenario where, for some reason, the metric on which you are basing your scaling rules is unreadable. In this scenario, it's not certain whether you should scale in or scale out. If this scenario happens, then Azure will ensure you have at least the default number of instances running. Once the metric can be read, the normal thresholds and scaling in and out will happen based on the rules and ranges you have predetermined. Figure 4-34 shows a potential setup for this scenario.

Instance limits	Minimum ⓘ	Maximum ⓘ	Default ⓘ
	1 ✓	3 ✓	2 ✓

Figure 4-34. *Instance limits and a default are set for the autoscaling of this app service*

In addition to metrics, you can use a schedule to scale. On a schedule, you set the start and end dates for the scaling. This would be highly useful to scale the app service during the Monday morning rush and for holiday sales (see Figure 4-35).

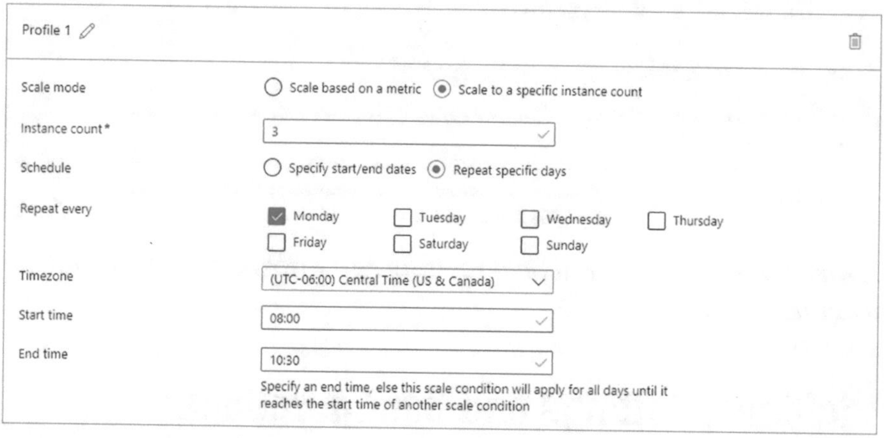

Figure 4-35. *Autoscaling can be set via a schedule to handle known and predicted periods of increased workloads*

Manual Scaling

Manual scaling allows you to set a number of instances that immediately takes effect. The benefits of this ability include the fact that you can quickly scale out if you don't have a rule and are experiencing unresponsive web pages due to traffic or other issues. The main drawback to this approach is that any autoscaling rules will immediately override any manual scaling as soon as they are evaluated.

The standard app service SKU has a maximum of ten instances. You won't be able to autoscale or manually scale past your maximum number of instances. The Manual Scale setting is shown in Figure 4-36.

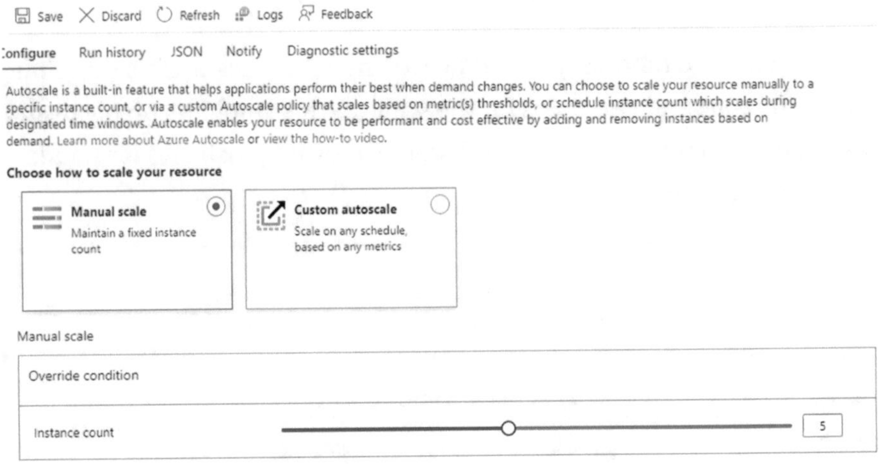

Figure 4-36. *The Manual Scale setting can instantly set the number of active instances*

Additional Settings and Configurations

In addition to the issues already covered, there are a few other things to know as I close this look at Azure App Services. This final section hits on a few of the remaining critical points and leaves a couple of remaining blades for you to examine on your own should you desire to do so.

Networking

One of the remaining critical sections is the Networking blade. While default app services deployed to the public web are great and you won't really need this page, for those who are deploying to a more restricted scenario or a scenario where load-balancing and additional traffic hops are important, the Networking blade will help you see important settings for your app service.

Inbound IP Address

The first important setting is for inbound traffic. Specifically, your inbound IP address. Every app service gets one, and only one, inbound IP address. This address will not change unless you delete the application or delete or renew the SSL bindings for the application (see Figure 4-37).

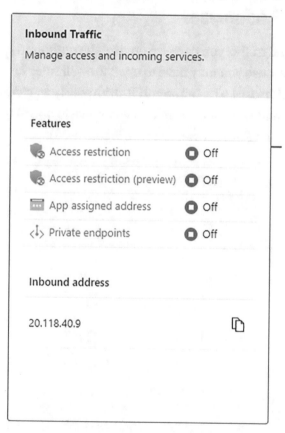

Figure 4-37. *The inbound address; other options exist for managing inbound traffic to your application*

Additional capabilities exist to lock down access just like you can do for a deployed VM with an NSG. On the app service, you can set the rules for your public-facing website and the backing management page

(yourwebsite.scm.azurewebsites.net). The management page is where
you can see the files that are deployed, as well as run other commands
against the web application. This page can also be reached via the left-
navigation menu for Advanced Tools on the App Service blade in the portal
in Azure.

Outbound IP Addresses

Like the inbound traffic, you can also control the outbound traffic. This
is important because you may have to open firewall rules for each of the
outbound IP addresses. The outbound IP addresses can change when you
delete and re-create an application or if you move to one of the higher P2,
P3, or Isolated tiers from a lower tier (see Figure 4-38).

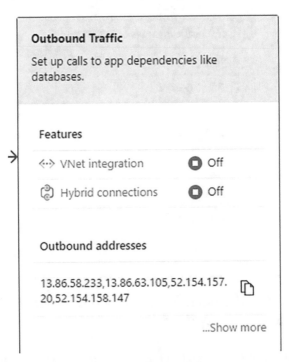

Figure 4-38. The outbound IP addresses on the Networking blade for
an app service

Certificates and TLS/SSL

Additional settings can be configured regarding the TLS/SSL settings for your application. For example, in the past, you could easily require HTTPs only and set the minimum TLS version from the TLS/SSL Settings page. This page is likely going away in the future, as the Certificates page is now in preview and the settings just mentioned were available under the app service configuration.

On the TLS/SSL settings options, you can also add Private and Public certificates and buy a new certificate. Finally, once you have a certificate, you can add the host and thumbprint. These operations are all moving to the Certificates blade, where the certificates will be managed. You can bring your own certificates generated by the app service, you can host certificates in Key Vault, or you can just upload the certificate to the Certificates blade (see Figure 4-39).

Figure 4-39. *The Certificates blade*

A Few Things Not Covered in this Chapter

This study of App services could continue for another 40 pages, but at this point the major things you need to be in command of have been covered. There are just a few other concepts you can look at on your own. A few of the remaining blades are self-explanatory, while others might require a bit of research. The following left-navigation items are worth exploring for a few minutes:

- Backups

- Custom Domains

- Resource Health

Review Your Learning

As an additional challenge, consider the following questions and determine how you would approach potential solution(s). You can find answers to these questions in Appendix A at the end of this book.

1) What is the relationship between App Service Plans and App Services? Can an App Service have more than one App Service Plan? Can an App Service Plan have more than one App Service? What are some considerations when the relationship goes beyond 1:1?

2) Where do you choose which operating system will be utilized? Where do you configure the choice for code vs. container vs. static?

3) Which plan is the entry-level plan that offers scaling? Which plan is the entry-level plan for deployment slots? Which plans can have a custom domain for hosting? What is the minimal plan level to implement private networking?

4) What are some considerations for creating autoscaling rules?

5) Can an App Service Plan and the app service be deployed into different regions?

6) How do you implement security around the application regarding HTTP/HTTPS, TLS levels, and certificates? How do you enforce certain security levels for clients? Can you deny traffic that is not utilizing HTTPS?

7) Where can you go to check the status of your website deployments?

8) How do you create custom variables and settings? Where should you set environment variables? Where should you add connection strings?

Complete the Azure App Service Web Apps Learn Modules

To fully learn the material, I recommend taking the time to also complete the MS Learn modules for Create Azure App Service web apps found here:

- Create Azure App Service web apps: `https://learn.microsoft.com/en-us/training/paths/create-azure-app-service-web-apps/`

Chapter Summary

In this chapter, you learned about working with the Azure App Service for hosting web applications. A number of the major services within the app service ecosystem were addressed and you should be well positioned to utilize app services and understand the components that make Azure App Service so popular for hosting web solutions.

After working through this chapter and the Microsoft Learn module, you should be on track to be in command of the following concepts as you learn about Azure and prepare for the AZ-204 Exam:

- Create and provision App Services, utilizing various App Service Plans.

- Implement basic CI/CD in GitHub actions/how to deploy your code.

- Leverage the correct App Service Plan for testing, and understand where plan offerings gain features like deployment slots and the ability to scale.

- Utilize metrics to configure automatic scaling of your web solution.

- Utilize environment variables and connection strings.

In the next chapter, you learn about working with the Azure Container ecosystem, including the Azure Container Registry, Azure Container Instances, and Azure Container Apps.

CHAPTER 5

Azure Container Ecosystem: Azure Container Registry, Azure Container Instances, and Azure Container Apps

If you have been working in Microsoft technologies for some time, you may have little exposure to containers. In some cases, it's possible that you've never been exposed to containers at all. Additionally, you might be in a scenario where you feel that you will never need containers. If this describes you, this chapter can help you realize the power and potential of containerized applications.

© Brian L. Gorman 2023
B. L. Gorman, *Developing Solutions for Microsoft Azure Certification Companion*,
Certification Study Companion Series, https://doi.org/10.1007/978-1-4842-9300-3_5

Other developers may have been working with containerized applications for a long time at this point. For such developers, this chapter might be more of a review than anything, and just enough to help you know the major pieces of the Azure Container Ecosystem that you are expected to be familiar with for the AZ-204 Exam.

Four Important Things to Know About Containers

In any event, it's important to understand a couple of things about containers: .

1. Containers are for everyone.

2. Containers are not "microservices" or "cloud-native applications," but they are often utilized in microservice architectures and cloud-native applications.

3. Containers are agnostic to their hosting platform.

4. Containers can have a steep learning curve (much like GIT).

Containers Are for Everyone

At this point, you can host applications in a container from just about every major tech stack. Additionally, they are generally lightweight and easy to run, and they can provide a more stable hosting environment for your application.

Containers Are Not Microservices or Cloud-Native Applications

It's important to note that containers are not "microservices" and cloud-native applications do not have to be containerized. That being said, a lot of the time these terms are used to refer to containerized applications. Indeed, you can host code in an Azure Function as a microservice. You can also have cloud-native serverless applications that do not utilize containers. However, containers do work well for cloud-native applications, and they are a very rewarding choice due to the ability to run tools according to their own needs without interfering with other applications.

Containerized Applications Are Agnostic to Their Hosting Platform

As long as your hosting provider can run containers, you can run your application, regardless of the underlying operating system, in a VM or on a platform service, and even across a multi-cloud scenario. This is typically accomplished by having the Docker runtime installed on the host, and the container runs inside the Docker runtime. Therefore, any host that has Docker can host containers.

Containers and the Container Ecosystem Have a Steep Learning Curve

There is a fairly steep learning curve when it comes to working with containers. However, this learning curve is no different than having to learn how to configure a VM with IIS or build networking and hosting for an on-premises application, or even learning GIT.

In the end, the cost of learning is recouped when you get the flexibility to deploy to any VM that has a hosting runtime or in any cloud platform that can run containers. The power and flexibility of containers is easily leveraged in cloud solutions.

Hosting Containers in Azure

There are a number of ways to host containers in Azure. For the AZ-204
Exam, a couple of key technologies need to be examined. This chapter
looks at the ability to utilize the Azure Container Registry (ACR) for hosting
images. Additionally, you'll see how easy it is to quickly host a container on
a public-facing URL with Azure Container Instances (ACI). You'll also take
a quick look at two other major container technologies in Azure—Azure
Kubernetes Service (AKS) and Azure Container Apps (ACA).

Before diving into the specifics of Azure, however, let's take a short look
at the tools you need to get up and running with containers. Complete
training on working with containers, the commands for Docker, and other
critical concepts for container development are outside of the scope of this
book, so if you need that level of training, consider going through some
introductory training from docker.com's getting started tutorial, found at
`https://docs.docker.com/get-started/`.

Windows Subsystem for Linux (WSL)

Assuming that most of you reading this book aren't on a Mac or Linux
would be foolish. However, if you are on Mac or Linux, it's generally
much easier for you to get up and running with Docker to utilize Linux
containers.

For those of you who are on a Windows machine, you will want to
make sure that you have the Windows Subsystem for Linux installed.
For almost every scenario, when developing with containers, you should
endeavor to use Linux containers. For more information on getting
WSL on your Windows machine, you can review this link: `https://
learn.microsoft.com/windows/wsl/install`. The time to use Windows
containers is useful in scenarios such as when you are running legacy
Windows solutions such as the .NET Framework 4.8 (or earlier).

No matter what machine you are on, as long as you are not working for a large organization with more than 250 employees or making more than $10 million USD in revenue, I recommend utilizing Docker Desktop, which can be found at `https://www.docker.com/products/docker-desktop/`.

If you do not qualify for the free Docker Desktop, consider another tool like Rancher Desktop, which can be found at `https://rancherdesktop.io/`. Either way, having a visual tool to help with your container development is a great way to get going without needing to know all the low-level commands directly, especially when you are new to containers.

Docker

All containers are just a running version of an image. For a container to work, however, it must have a runtime in which it operates. One of the benefits of containers is that they are platform agnostic. It does not matter if the box has a Windows OS, Ubuntu, or some other version of Linux, or macOS. No matter what, if the machine is running Docker, your containers will just work.

If you install Docker and Docker Desktop, you'll have the ability to easily run your containers. On Windows machines you can even switch between Linux and Windows containers. Even so, you should always endeavor to use Linux containers unless that is not possible (for example, the .NET Framework 4.8 and previous versions require Windows containers). All .NET core versions will run on Linux containers. In general, Linux containers are more efficient. In addition to being more efficient, the container ecosystem is native to Linux whereas the Windows ecosystem typically requires more configuration. For example, running containers on a Windows Server is not as straightforward as running containers on Ubuntu.

You can typically install Docker from a package manager like HomeBrew or Chocolatey. On Linux, simple commands to install Docker get you up and running with containers in no time. If you've never

installed Docker before, follow the instructions on getting Docker Desktop
from `https://docs.docker.com/desktop/`.

When your installation is completed, you can see your Docker version
by typing the `docker  -v` command or by reviewing it in Docker Desktop
(see Figure 5-1).

Figure 5-1. *The Docker version can be queried with a simple
command or by looking at the version in Docker Desktop*

Images

Once Docker is up and running on your machine, you will create an image
for your application. The image is created by utilizing a Dockerfile. The
Dockerfile has all of the important information about the application,
including build instructions, any dependency information, and additional
information about the ports to connect to the container as well as any
networking or database information.

After creating your code, you configure the Dockerfile, and then you
can create an image with this simple build command:

```
docker build -t your-image-name .
```

You must include the final period or the build of the image will not
succeed. Building the image results in an image of the application. Each
image then can be hosted in one or more containers. Figure 5-2 shows

the command for building an application to an image called my-simple-website. The command used is

```
docker build -t my-simple-website .
```

Note that the trailing . is expected as part of the command. Also note that this command would work on either Dockerfile, whether you are utilizing the .NET 6 or .NET 7 version of the project. If you want to use both, of course you will want to use a different name for each image, or perhaps a version tag in the image name at a minimum.

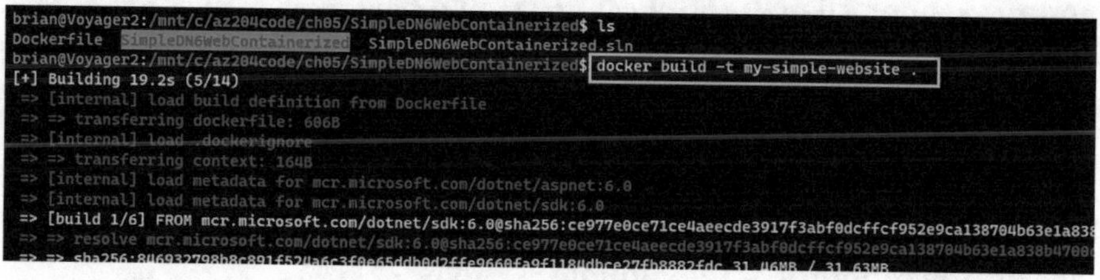

Figure 5-2. *The command to build an image from a Dockerfile*

After building the image, you can list the image by using the docker images command. This shows the image name in the list of images as well as in the Images tab in Docker Desktop (see Figure 5-3).

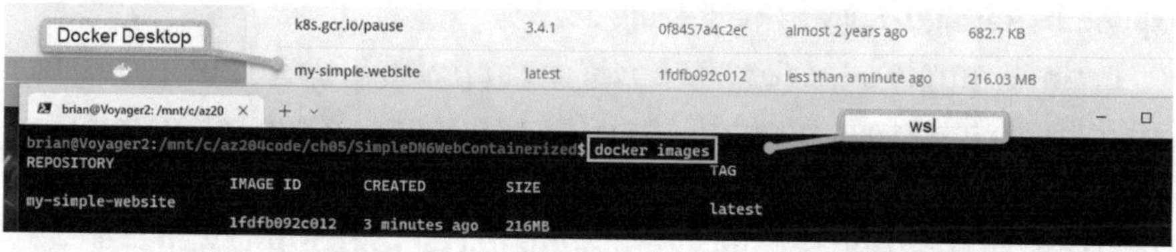

Figure 5-3. *The images are listed using the docker images command*

Containers

Once you have built your image, the next step is to run the image in a container. As mentioned, the same image can run in many containers. This

is where the power of containerization can be leveraged. To run multiple
versions of a website, you need multiple VMs hosting each website, or at a
minimum, you need to manage a number of virtual directories.

On a traditional VM, multiple sites might also interact and interfere
with one another. For example, if you have a Java application and a
.NET application, you need both runtimes. You also could have multiple
versions of each runtime. To host both applications, you may need an
Apache Tomcat server and IIS. Putting all of this on one machine with one
OS means any time either of the application runtimes or hosting engines
require a reboot, all of the applications would be down. With containers,
putting multiple versions and runtimes side-by-side is no concern at all.
When one container needs to be updated, you just update the image, stop
the existing container, and then spin up a new container. There is also no
concern for any side effects of the various potential conflicts for interaction
between the runtimes or the runtime versions.

To run the container, you need to use a command to put any
information into the container that you want to leverage during the
runtime. You also need to point the ports from your host machine to the
ports exposed by the Dockerfile. Typically, this is run with at least ports
in a command such as `docker run -dp <local-port>:<entry-port-
exposed> <image-name>:<version>`.

In the example code for this book, the app also has two environment
variables, so those can be added into the command. If you build the
Dockerfile for either the .NET 6 or the .NET 7 version with the name `my-
simple-website`, then the final command to run the sample app is as
follows:

```
docker run --env SimpleWebShared_MySimpleValue='ENV: Simple
Shared Value' --env SimpleWebShared_MySecretValue='ENV: Simple
Secret Value'  -dp 8080:80 my-simple-website
```

The creation of the container and resulting running container
information is shown in Figure 5-4.

Figure 5-4. *The container is created with the docker container run
[options] image-name command, and the resulting container is
shown from Docker Desktop and by running the docker container
ls command*

The container is now hosted and running and can be reached via
port 8080 on the localhost. Additionally, the environment variables were
injected at the time of the container creation. It's important to note that
these environment variables are immutable. If they needed to change, you
would need to run a new container and destroy the old one. Also note that
listing the containers is easily accomplished with the docker container
ls command and containers are easily managed in Docker Desktop, as
shown in Figure 5-4.

After you create the container, the hosted site is easily reviewed by
navigating to the localhost on the mapped port per the creation command,
as shown in Figure 5-5.

SimpleDN6WebContainerized   Home   Privacy

Simple DN6 Web Containerized

Get Started with Docker and C# ASP.Net 6 here

My Simple value shared

ENV: Shared Simple Value

My Simple secret shared

ENV: Simple Secret Value

Figure 5-5. *The exposed port is mapped and the site is visible by navigating to the public port on the localhost*

Now that there is an image that is tested and working, you can utilize the image in the various platform solutions in Azure.

Azure Container Registry

The first major technology in Azure that you need to be familiar with is the Azure Container Registry (ACR). A container registry is a place where you can centralize your custom images to be utilized by other developers and services. Similar to how you push your code to a centralized GIT repository like GitHub, you will push images to the container registry. Developers and services can then pull the image and utilize it locally or within the service's hosting environment. In a similar manner to how you can tag commits as a release, you can create multiple versions of an image and tag each version so that different versions of the image can be run in local containers or by services in Azure, just by utilizing the version number.

DockerHub is one of the most popular image container registries, and you can easily use DockerHub from within Azure on various Azure services. DockerHub can also store images as public or private images, with individual repositories for each image. One limitation of DockerHub, however, is that you can't utilize a private network within Azure so your images would be on the DockerHub ecosystem. Even if you make your

repositories private, you still need to have communication outside of your
network and your images are not completely under your control.

Within Azure, you can create one or more Azure Container Registries.
Within Azure, your images can easily be kept private, and you do not
have to connect to a third-party solution to utilize the images in the
Azure Container Ecosystem. Furthermore, with the ACR you can leverage
Role-Based Access Control (RBAC) from within your subscription, easily
granting permissions like push or pull to individuals or groups. Your ACR
can also be provisioned in a private network and configured with no ability
to reach your code from outside of your Azure network.

Service Tiers

Azure Container Registry has three tiers available for use—Basic, Standard,
and Premium. As with any Azure service offering, when it's time to sit for
the AZ-204 Exam, it's always a good idea to know when you would want or
need to choose each specific tier.

Basic

The Basic tier is best utilized for development and simple testing
workloads. Basic tiers have the same capabilities as the other tiers, but
you are limited when it comes to storage capacity and overall throughput
to the registry. Additionally, Basic tier ACRs are limited to a single region,
cannot leverage availability zones, and have no ability to utilize any private
networking capabilities.

Storage for your images in the ACR in the Basic tier is limited to start
with about ten gigabytes (10 GB) and can be expanded to a maximum of
about twenty terabytes (20 TB) overall. This amount of storage is not too
bad for the basic tier for basic workloads. For example, the image size for
the sample default web is around 220 MB for either runtime.

Throughput in the Basic tier is limited to 1,000 read and 100 write
operations per minute. Upload and Download are capped at 10 and 30
Mbps, respectively. Finally, the Basic tier only allows for two webhooks.

Standard

The Standard tier is similar to the Basic tier, but the amount of storage and
throughput is increased, as are various other settings. As with the Basic tier,
the Standard tier cannot be utilized outside of one region, cannot leverage
availability zones, and no networking capabilities are enabled at this tier.

Storage in the Standard tier is limited to start with about 100 GB and
can also be expanded to the upper limit of around 20 TB. Read throughput
is limited to 3,000 operations and write is limited to 500 operations per
minute. Upload and download are limited to 20/60 Mbps, respectively. The
Standard tier can have up to ten webhooks.

Premium

The Premium tier is the only choice when you need to utilize private
networking. Additionally, the Premium tier allows for leveraging regional
availability zones or multi-regional scenarios. Premium is also the only tier
where you can create your own encryption keys for your images.

With the Premium tier, you get nearly 500 GB of included storage with
the same ability to expand to nearly 20 TB of total storage. In the Premium
tier, your image pull/push operations can be completed at 10,000 read
operations and 2,000 write operations per minute, respectively. Download
and upload throughput are also maximized in the Premium tier at 50 Mbps
up and 100 Mbps down. You can have up to 500 webhooks on your ACR in
the Premium tier.

Finally, there is currently an additional feature to scope permissions
for access similar to Shared-Access Signature (SAS) tokens for storage, with
permissions and time limitations at the repository level in public preview

for the Premium tier. While the public preview tier doesn't guarantee this feature will make it to general availability, that would be the next step should the feature be fully released.

Additional Information

Additional information regarding the ACR service tiers can be found at https://learn.microsoft.com/azure/container-registry/container-registry-skus.

Image Storage

As mentioned, if you want to store your image in availability zones or multiple regions, you'll want to leverage a Premium tier container registry, as the Basic and Standard tiers don't have this capability.

One of the nice things about the container registry is that no matter what tier you use, your images are encrypted at rest. If you want to enable the ability to use your own encryption key, you need to deploy in the Premium tier.

Deploy an Azure Container Registry

Deploying a new container registry is very easy to do, once you know which features you want. As outlined, Basic is great for development and Standard will likely be sufficient for production workloads. If you want networking or redundancy, choose Premium. For this book, I deploy as a Basic tier registry.

To get started, search for container registries in the Azure Portal, then start the process of creating a new container registry.

As with any service, you need the subscription, a resource group, and the region to which you want to deploy. You must also set the public-facing URL for the repository. This repository name is limited to [a-zA-Z0-9]* with a minimum of 5 characters and a maximum of 50 characters (see Figure 5-6).

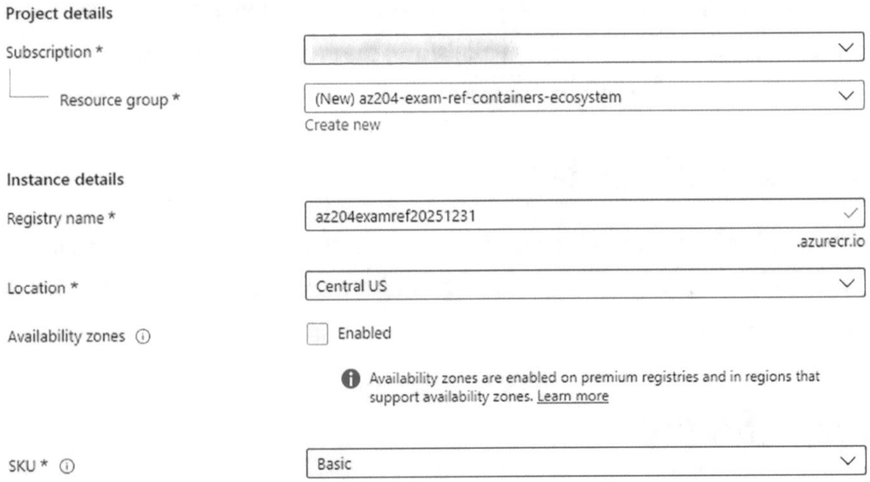

Project details

Subscription *

Resource group *   (New) az204-exam-ref-containers-ecosystem
Create new

Instance details

Registry name *   az204examref20251231
.azurecr.io

Location *   Central US

Availability zones (i)   ☐ Enabled

ⓘ Availability zones are enabled on premium registries and in regions that
support availability zones. Learn more

SKU * (i)   Basic

Figure 5-6. *The container registry is created with a valid name and
SKU in a region on your subscription*

Since the Basic tier doesn't allow for networking or changing any
encryption settings, there is nothing else to configure unless you are using
a tagging strategy. Clicking Review+Create. Create deploys the container
registry.

Push an Image to the Container Registry

Once the registry is created, you can set your local machine to push images
to the registry with a few commands. Detailed instructions can be found
on your container registry in the Quick Start blade, as shown in Figure 5-7.

Figure 5-7. *Instructions to push to your container registry can be found on the Quick Start blade in your deployed registry*

If you are an owner of the Azure subscription or at least the Azure Resource Group where the ACR is provisioned, or if you have the correct RBAC permissions (such as `AcrPush`), then you can likely get by with just logging into Azure. If the registry is locked down, however, you might need to use the administrator login. Roles for the registry are shown in Figure 5-8.

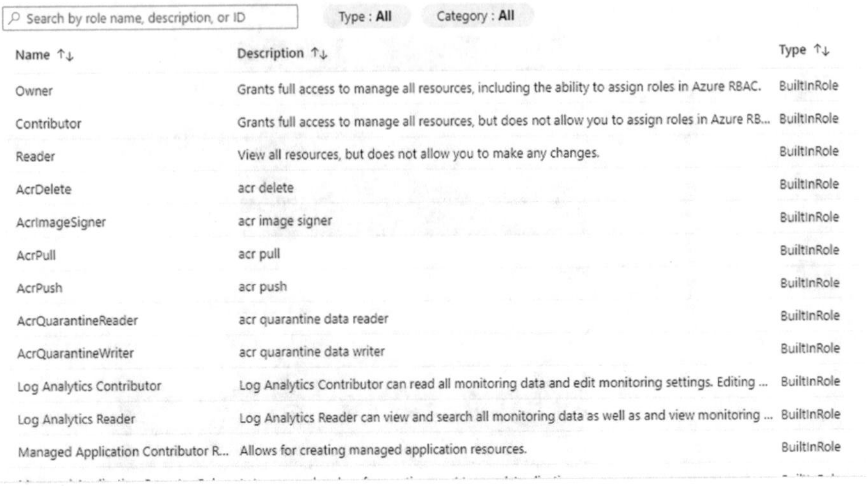

Search by role name, description, or ID   Type : All   Category : All

Name ↑↓	Description ↑↓	Type ↑↓
Owner	Grants full access to manage all resources, including the ability to assign roles in Azure RBAC.	BuiltInRole
Contributor	Grants full access to manage all resources, but does not allow you to assign roles in Azure RB...	BuiltInRole
Reader	View all resources, but does not allow you to make any changes.	BuiltInRole
AcrDelete	acr delete	BuiltInRole
AcrImageSigner	acr image signer	BuiltInRole
AcrPull	acr pull	BuiltInRole
AcrPush	acr push	BuiltInRole
AcrQuarantineReader	acr quarantine data reader	BuiltInRole
AcrQuarantineWriter	acr quarantine data writer	BuiltInRole
Log Analytics Contributor	Log Analytics Contributor can read all monitoring data and edit monitoring settings. Editing ...	BuiltInRole
Log Analytics Reader	Log Analytics Reader can view and search all monitoring data as well as and view monitoring ...	BuiltInRole
Managed Application Contributor R...	Allows for creating managed application resources.	BuiltInRole

Figure 5-8. *There are additional roles that can be assigned to Azure AD users for specific permissions on the registry*

Log in to Your Registry from Your Local Machine

Begin by logging into Azure with the `az login` command and then run the command to log in to the `docker login <yourrpositorynamehere>.azurecr.io` registry. If you're prompted for a username and password, you'll have to get them from your Access Keys blade, as shown in Figure 5-9.

az204examref20251231 | Access keys
Container registry
Search
Overview
Activity log
Access control (IAM)
Tags
Quick start
Events
Settings
Access keys
Encryption
Registry name
az204examref20251231
Login server
az204examref20251231.azurecr.io
Admin user
Enabled
Username
az204examref20251231
Name
Password
Regenerate
password
password2

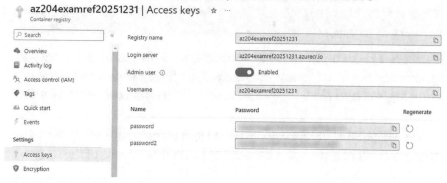

***Figure 5-9.** The Access Keys with the administrator login enabled allow you to log in from your local machine to your container registry*

When you log in, you won't see your password, but it will tell you that you logged in successfully, as shown in Figure 5-10.

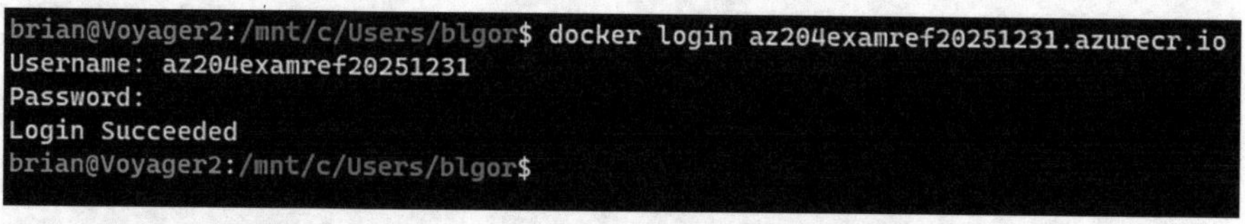
brian@Voyager2:/mnt/c/Users/blgor$ docker login az204examref20251231.azurecr.io
Username: az204examref20251231
Password:
Login Succeeded
brian@Voyager2:/mnt/c/Users/blgor$

***Figure 5-10.** The login is successful using the administrator login from the registry*

Tag Your Image with Your Registry Name and a Version Number

Next, you'll want to tag the image with your registry name. You should also put a version number on the tag (see Figure 5-11). The tag command is just `docker tag <image-name> <registry-name>.azurecr.io/<image-name>:<version>`.

```
brian@Voyager2:/mnt/c/Users/blgor$ docker tag my-simple-website az204examref20251231.azurecr.io/my-simplewebsite
brian@Voyager2:/mnt/c/Users/blgor$ docker tag my-simple-website az204examref20251231.azurecr.io/my-simplewebsite:v1
brian@Voyager2:/mnt/c/Users/blgor$
```

Figure 5-11. *In order to push your image to the Azure Registry you need to tag the local image correctly. This figure shows the image being tagged and then tagged a second time with a version number*

I've tagged this image twice so that I can push to the default latest version as well as a stamped version (v1) with this release of the image.

Push Your Tagged Image to the Registry

Once the image is tagged, you can push it to the registry. To push the image, run the `docker push <tagged-image-name>:<version>` command (see Figure 5-12).

```
brian@Voyager2:/mnt/c/Users/blgor$ docker push az204examref20251231.azurecr.io/my-simplewebsite
Using default tag: latest
The push refers to repository [az204examref20251231.azurecr.io/my-simplewebsite]
7b7c9e942dd7: Pushed
e44791b1c65b: Pushed
5b010387857f: Pushed
e53e70a3c1a5: Pushed
7c74681f0f33: Pushed
55125ebb8920: Pushed
a12586ed027f: Pushed
latest: digest: sha256:07e354b7a61c7094a8f8b5601da93754dc875b55f4ef53c44b70799303d499fa size: 1789
brian@Voyager2:/mnt/c/Users/blgor$ docker push az204examref20251231.azurecr.io/my-simplewebsite:v1
The push refers to repository [az204examref20251231.azurecr.io/my-simplewebsite]
7b7c9e942dd7: Layer already exists
e44791b1c65b: Layer already exists
5b010387857f: Layer already exists
e53e70a3c1a5: Layer already exists
7c74681f0f33: Layer already exists
55125ebb8920: Layer already exists
a12586ed027f: Layer already exists
v1: digest: sha256:07e354b7a61c7094a8f8b5601da93754dc875b55f4ef53c44b70799303d499fa size: 1789
brian@Voyager2:/mnt/c/Users/blgor$
```

Figure 5-12. *The tagged images can be pushed to the Azure Container Registry with the docker push command*

With the image pushed, you can review it in the ACR by clicking the Repositories blade, as shown in Figure 5-13.

Figure 5-13. *The image is successfully pushed to the ACR with the
latest and the v1 versions*

Automated Build Tasks

In some scenarios, you might want to utilize the ability to build your
images in Azure in the ACR. You can set triggers for changes to GIT
branches or, if you have an image hierarchy when the base image is
updated, you can ensure that the dependent images are built.

In addition to build tasks, there are also tasks to send information
regarding billing and costs for the registry, as well as tasks like running unit
tests or automating a workflow around your container.

If you want more information on how to set up a build that is utilized
when the code for the image is updated at GitHub, you can find a tutorial
at `https://learn.microsoft.com/azure/container-registry/`
`container-registry-tutorial-build-taskh`.

Azure Container Instances

The next major technology you want to be in command of for the AZ-204 is
the Azure Container Instances (ACI). Like Azure App Service, the ACI is a
platform service that allows you to deploy a containerized solution quickly
and easily, without having to worry about setting up an infrastructure.

Creating and working with an ACI deployment is incredibly easy, and
you can do it from the portal, with the AZ CLI from within the portal, or
from your local machine. When creating with a script or using the AZ CLI,
you need to configure all the options at the time you are ready to deploy.

There are two important notes that you should remember about
the ACI. The first is that when you deploy, your image will be hosted in
the ACI as a container, and it will be immutable. That means that any
environment variables must be set at the time of deployment, and any
changes require destroying and re-creating the container. The second note
is that immediately after deployment, you'll have a public-facing URL for
the hosted application. However, the public-facing URL will not leverage
HTTPS by default. If you want to leverage HTTPS, you need to set that up
yourself.

Deploy from the Container Registry

With the AZ-204 Exam being for developers, it's likely that you'll need to be
in command of the AZ CLI and/or PowerShell commands to accomplish
tasks in Azure. For this reason, this section first deploys an ACI using the
AZ CLI, and then it shows you how this can easily be done from the portal.

Deploying with the AZ CLI

In the portal from the cloud shell, you can easily deploy an ACI with your
image from your ACR using the AZ CLI commands (the script can be found
in the materials for this chapter). Figure 5-14 shows the script execution in
the portal.

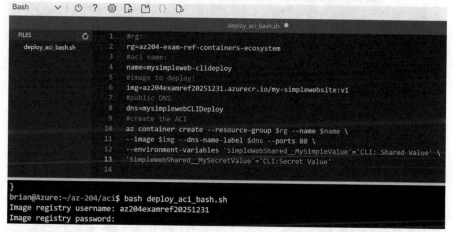

Figure 5-14. *The AZ CLI can be used to deploy a new ACI instance
using an image from your repository*

For additional reference, the script follows:

```
#rg:
rg=az204-exam-ref-containers-ecosystem
#aci name:
name=mysimpleweb-clideploy
#image to deploy:
img=az204examref20251231.azurecr.io/my-simplewebsite:v1
#public DNS
dns=mysimplewebCLIDeploy
#create the ACI
az container create --resource-group $rg --name $name
--image $img --dns-name-label $dns --ports 80 --environment-
variables 'SimpleWebShared__MySimpleValue'='CLI: Shared Value'
'SimpleWebShared__MySecretValue'='CLI:Secret Value'
```

Once the solution is deployed, the Fully-Qualified Domain Name
(FQDN) and Public IP Address (PIP) will be shown in the output (see
Figure 5-15).

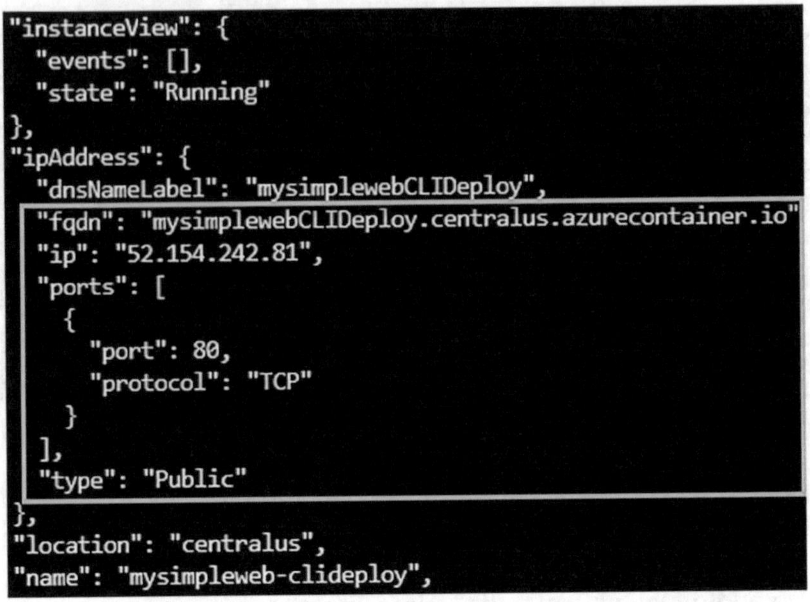

```
"instanceView": {
  "events": [],
  "state": "Running"
},
"ipAddress": {
  "dnsNameLabel": "mysimplewebCLIDeploy",
  "fqdn": "mysimplewebCLIDeploy.centralus.azurecontainer.io"
  "ip": "52.154.242.81",
  "ports": [
    {
      "port": 80,
      "protocol": "TCP"
    }
  ],
  "type": "Public"
},
"location": "centralus",
"name": "mysimpleweb-clideploy",
```

Figure 5-15. *The PIP and FQDN are shown in the successful output from the CLI deployment*

You can then use either the PIP or the FQDN to review the solution from any public web browser, as shown in Figure 5-16. You can also browse to the deployed resource and get its public URL there. Using the portal is examined in the next section.

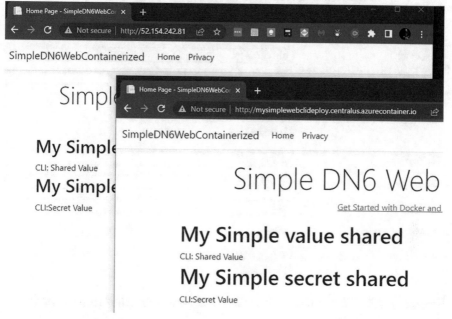

Figure 5-16. *The website is up and running as a valid ACI after deployment and is reached via the FQDN or the PIP from the deployment information*

Deploying from the Portal

Deploying from the portal is quick and easy. You select the common items of subscription, resource group, and region. You also need to name the ACI, which must be all lowercase letters or numbers and can have dashes as long as the dash is not the first or last character. The maximum name length is 63 characters. In the portal, you can easily select your image from the container registry using the provided drop-downs (see Figure 5-17).

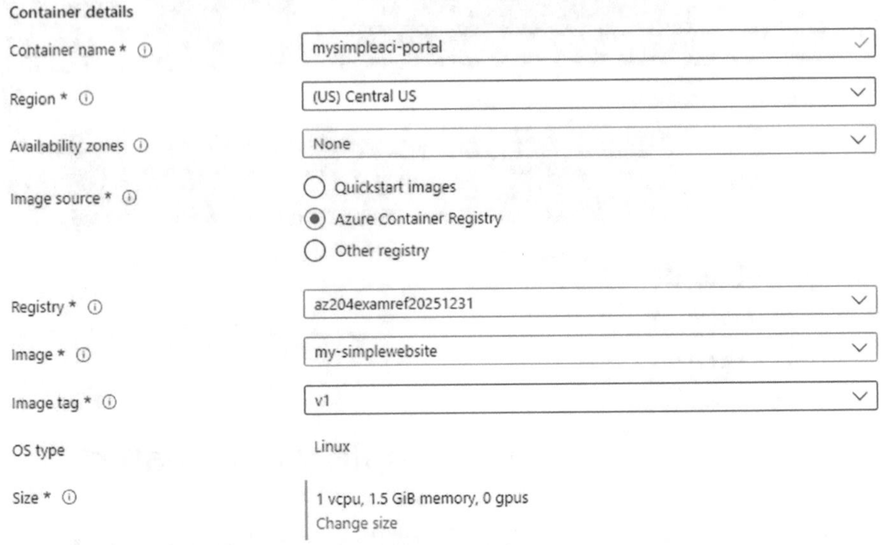

Container details

Container name * ⓘ	mysimpleaci-portal
Region * ⓘ	(US) Central US
Availability zones ⓘ	None
Image source * ⓘ	◯ Quickstart images ◉ Azure Container Registry ◯ Other registry
Registry * ⓘ	az204examref20251231
Image * ⓘ	my-simplewebsite
Image tag * ⓘ	v1
OS type	Linux
Size * ⓘ	1 vcpu, 1.5 GiB memory, 0 gpus Change size

Figure 5-17. *The container instance is easily created with simple
drop-downs in the portal*

Remember not to just create this ACI right away. If you want to
configure other settings like the environment variables, you need to do that
before you deploy or you will be out of luck and will need to delete the ACI
and redeploy it.

Networking

On the Networking blade, you can configure the settings for public
or private networking, the DNS label, and the ports to expose (see
Figure 5-18).

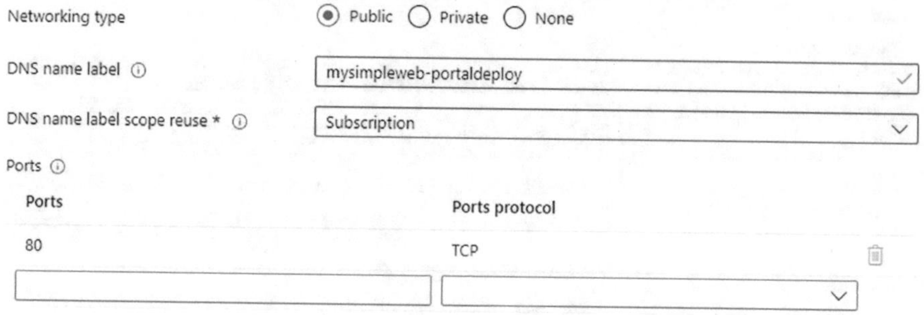

Networking type   ● Public   ○ Private   ○ None

DNS name label ⓘ   mysimpleweb-portaldeploy   ✓

DNS name label scope reuse * ⓘ   Subscription   ⌄

Ports ⓘ

Ports   Ports protocol

80   TCP   🗑

[   ]   [⌄]

Figure 5-18. *The Networking blade allows configuration for the*
public or private access, the DNS label, and the ports to expose

Restart Policy and Environment Variables

On the Advanced blade, you can configure the Restart Policy to restart On
Failure, Always, or Never (see Figure 5-19).

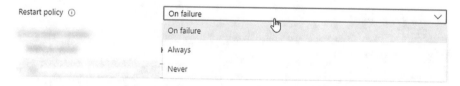

Restart policy ⓘ   On failure   ⌄

                                         On failure

                                       ⊦ Always

                                       ⊤ Never

Figure 5-19. *The Restart Policy can be On Failure, Always, or Never*

The environment variables are also configured on the Advanced
tab. As you create the variables here, you can mark them as secure. All
that means is that they will be obfuscated from viewing and logging (see
Figure 5-20).

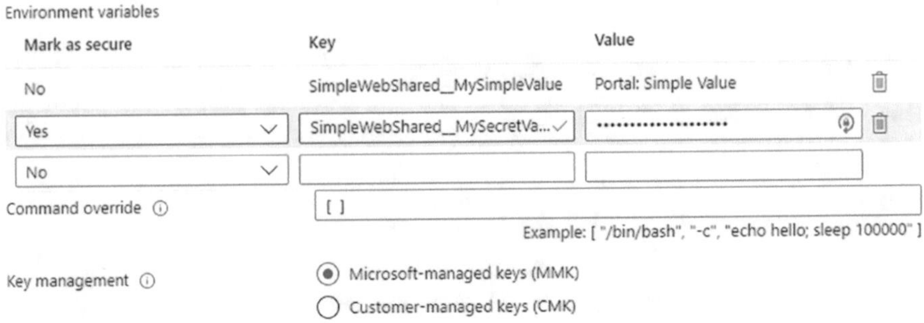

Environment variables

Mark as secure	Key	Value	
No	SimpleWebShared__MySimpleValue	Portal: Simple Value	🗑
Yes ⌄	SimpleWebShared__MySecretVa... ✓	••••••••••••••••••••	💬 🗑
No ⌄			

Command override ⓘ   [ ]

Example: ["/bin/bash", "-c", "echo hello; sleep 100000"]

Key management ⓘ   ⦿ Microsoft-managed keys (MMK)
                       ○ Customer-managed keys (CMK)

Figure 5-20. *The Environment Variables can be configured on the
Advanced tab and can be marked as secure*

From the Advanced tab, you can run a command on the start of the
container and utilize your own encryption key if you want. With everything
configured, you can then deploy and review the site from either the PIP or
the FQDN found on the Overview blade, as shown in Figure 5-21.

Figure 5-21. *The FQDN and the PIP can be found on the Overview
blade once the container instance is deployed*

You can then review the site from any public browser by visiting either
the FQDN or the PIP (see Figure 5-22).

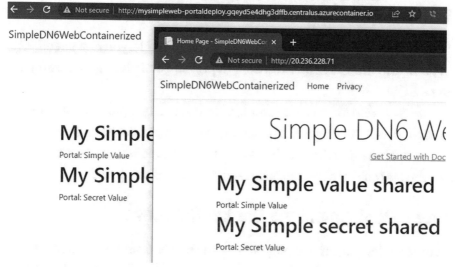

Figure 5-22. *The deployment from the portal is shown, with similar results as the CLI deployment*

Container Groups

In some instances, one container might not be enough to serve your application. Perhaps you would like to sidecar another container to host a database or a logging solution for your application.

When you have a solution that has a couple of containers that need to share a lifecycle, you can utilize container groups with the ACI. The containers are then grouped together under the same DNS and public IP address. The container group can also share storage and networking so that they can communicate with one another and persist some information in storage.

To deploy a container group, you need to use an Azure Resource Manager (ARM) template, a Docker Compose file, or a YAML manifest file. The YAML manifest file is similar to how you might deploy solutions with Kubernetes and is a solid choice for creating a container group. The Docker Compose file requires leveraging your container registry and is likely the easiest way to deploy a container group.

Group Deployment via a YAML File

In order to leverage the deployment with a YAML file, you first need
to configure the YAML file. You then deploy the container group using
the AZ CLI.

If you would like to try a sample where you can deploy a container
group to the ACI using a YAML file, there is a great tutorial on this in the
Learn documents at `https://learn.microsoft.com/azure/container-`
`instances/container-instances-multi-container-yaml`.

Group Deployment via Docker Compose

In order to leverage the deployment with Docker Compose, you must have
a container registry. Then you configure the deployment with a Docker
Compose file. You use the Docker Compose file to build and push the
image to your ACR. You then have to create an Azure Context; you can
then use the Docker Compose with your context to deploy the container
group application to the ACI.

If you want to try a sample where you can deploy a container group
to the ACI using Docker Compose, there is a great tutorial on this in the
Learn documents at `https://learn.microsoft.com/azure/container-`
`instances/tutorial-docker-compose`.

Persistent File Shares

In order to work with state or store information past the lifecycle of the
container, you need to mount some type of shared network storage. With
ACI, you can use Azure File Storage to mount a persistent storage solution.

First, you create the storage account, then when you deploy your
solution with the CLI, you can add the connection information for the file
storage as part of the deployment. This command, from `https://learn.`
`microsoft.com/azure/container-instances/container-instances-`

volume-azure-files#deploy-container-and-mount-volume---cli, shows the `container create` cli command with values for mounting the persistent storage:

```
az container create \
    --resource-group $ACI_PERS_RESOURCE_GROUP \
    --name hellofiles \
    --image mcr.microsoft.com/azuredocs/aci-hellofiles \
    --dns-name-label aci-demo \
    --ports 80 \
    --azure-file-volume-account-name $ACI_PERS_STORAGE_
      ACCOUNT_NAME \
    --azure-file-volume-account-key $STORAGE_KEY \
    --azure-file-volume-share-name $ACI_PERS_SHARE_NAME \
    --azure-file-volume-mount-path /aci/logs/
```

Containers in Azure App Services

App Services were covered in detail in the last chapter. However, using containers in App Services is also something that you might need to be familiar with for the exam. Even so, knowing that the next step in the container ecosystem is to leverage app services is a great thing for your career.

As mentioned, utilizing ACI is great to get up and running and for simple container workloads. However, there were a couple of simple limitations, including lack of a built-in HTTPS certificate and an inability to reset the container with a new environment variable. While app services are not going to be your go-to choice for large container workloads that require a lot of orchestration, they are a great middle ground that can be much less expensive than a full Kubernetes instance and a bit more robust than container instances.

By utilizing an App Service Linux plan, you can easily deploy your containers from your container registry (see Figure 5-23).

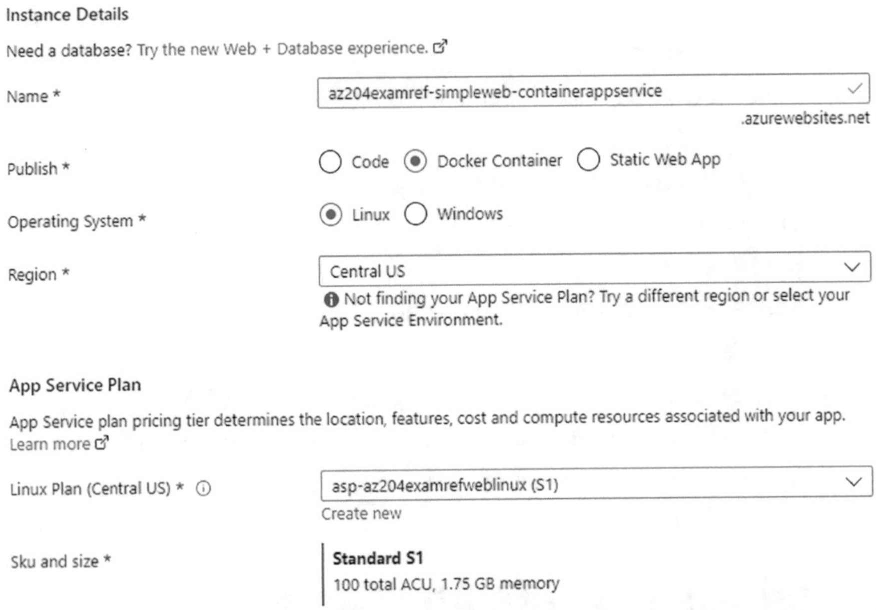

Instance Details

Need a database? Try the new Web + Database experience. ☐

Name * | az204examref-simpleweb-containerappservice   ✓ |
                                                                  .azurewebsites.net

Publish *   ○ Code ⦿ Docker Container ○ Static Web App

Operating System *   ⦿ Linux ○ Windows

Region * | Central US   ⌄ |
                            ❶ Not finding your App Service Plan? Try a different region or select your
                            App Service Environment.

App Service Plan

App Service plan pricing tier determines the location, features, cost and compute resources associated with your app.
Learn more ☐

Linux Plan (Central US) * ⓘ | asp-az204examrefweblinux (S1)   ⌄ |
                            Create new

Sku and size * | **Standard S1**
                            | 100 total ACU, 1.75 GB memory

Figure 5-23. *Utilization of a container from an Azure App Service is easily configured in the portal on a Linux App Service Plan*

Basics   Docker   Networking   Monitoring   Tags   Review + create

Pull container images from Azure Container Registry, Docker Hub or a private Docker repository. App Service will deploy
the containerized app with your preferred dependencies to production in seconds.

| Options | Single Container | ⌄ |
| Image Source | Azure Container Registry | ⌄ |

Azure container registry options

Registry *	az204examref20251231	⌄
Image *	my-simplewebsite	⌄
Tag *	v1	⌄
Startup Command ⓘ		

Figure 5-24. *Wiring up your app service from your container registry
is easy with the Azure App Service*

As with ACI, you simply need to select the image from your ACR along
with the tag and you can then deploy directly to the app service utilizing
the image from your registry.

As with any app service, you can easily configure inbound and
outbound network traffic or just host on the public Azure Internet
backbone. Monitoring your app is slightly more involved with containers
than in a traditional application in app services. If you want to leverage
Container Insights and Application Insights, you need to make sure to add
the Application Insights SDK to your container.

Once your application is configured, you have the full ability
to leverage the benefits of a deployed app service and the ease and
convenience of hosting your container for deployment. Along with
this, you can leverage the ability to have slots, built-in HTTPs, and
configurations that can "orchestrate" the containers a bit. You'll
immediately note that your application is now hosted with a default
HTTPS setting so there is no concern, even though your container only
exposed port 80. Azure App Service takes care of the SSL binding for you
(see Figure 5-25).

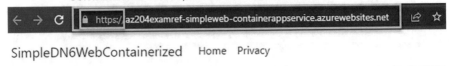

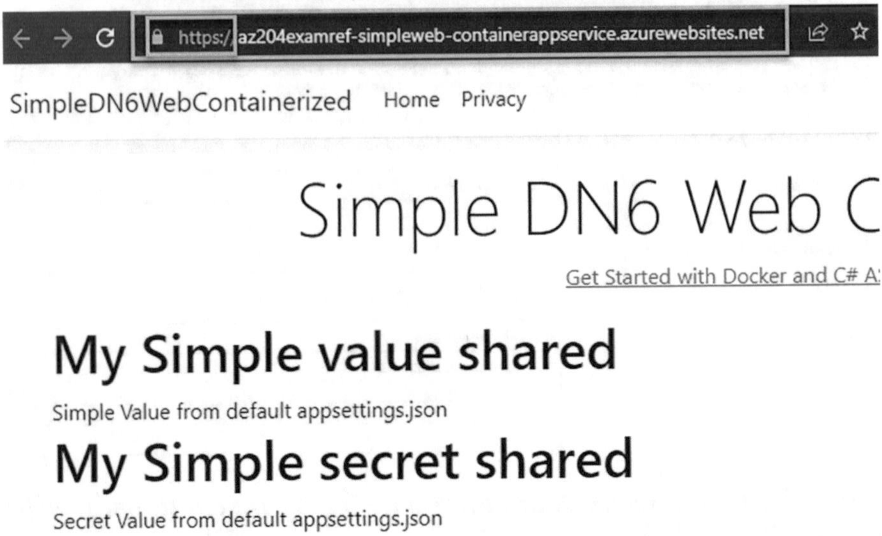

https://az204examref-simpleweb-containerappservice.azurewebsites.net
SimpleDN6WebContainerized
Home
Privacy
Simple DN6 Web C
Get Started with Docker and C# A
My Simple value shared
Simple Value from default appsettings.json
My Simple secret shared
Secret Value from default appsettings.json

***Figure 5-25.** The SSL is automatic with Azure App Service, so your application is already behind the HTTPS protocol*

With ACI, if the environment variable changes, you must destroy and rebuild the ACI. With app services, just set the new value in the configuration, as shown in Figure 5-26.

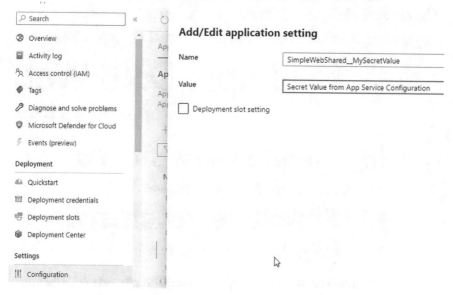

Figure 5-26. *The App Service configuration can easily inject
environment variables into your hosted containers*

Save the changes; the app service will then manage the lifecycle of the
container with the new environment variable (see Figure 5-27).

SimpleDN6WebContainerized   Home   Privacy

Simple DN6 Web

Get Started with Docker and

My Simple value shared

Simple Value from App Service Configuration

My Simple secret shared

Secret Value from App Service Configuration

Figure 5-27. *The variables are injected and the site restarts without having to be totally destroyed and re-created*

Additional Services

This final section of the chapter is completely optional. As of the time of this writing, there should not be any deep need to know how to work with Azure Container Apps (ACAs) or Azure Kubernetes Service (AKS).

Indeed, these topics are extremely complex and already have books written on each of the individual services. As each service is presented, additional resources will be given if you are interested in learning more about one or both of the services. The learning curve for these solutions is incredibly steep and it is a substantial jump for traditional Windows developers with little-to-no container experience.

However, the trend in the industry seems to be clearly leading in this direction. As solutions become more platform-agnostic, containerized solutions are proving to be highly desirable. As with anything, containerized solutions have some issues that arise when applications scale to production workloads. While container instances and even app services can host containerized applications, more powerful solutions need to be utilized to orchestrate hundreds to thousands of active containers with varying levels of resource needs and different access for users via roles and routes.

Azure Kubernetes Service (AKS) was the leading tool for orchestration of containers (managing lifecycle, running health check probes, and ensuring deployment across a pool of servers). AKS is still likely to be the number one choice for container orchestration in Azure. However, Azure Container Apps is a new player in this space, and it promises to give you the ability to utilize the power of Kubernetes without having to know how to actually do Kubernetes.

Azure Kubernetes Service

Kubernetes has a number of key components, and this book in no way is going to be sufficient to explain them all to you. Instead, consider this a high-level overview or baseline understanding so that you can at least have a general idea of what Kubernetes is trying to do for your applications and your organizations.

To begin, consider the traditional network and application. You would have your own VMs for your Web and Data layers. These would be in pools behind load balancers, public and private. Additionally, you'd have firewall and routing rules so that only some users can get through and they would be directed to your applications according to the request they make.

Kubernetes is essentially the same thing, only it's all configured in the Kubernetes service with YAML files. You create namespaces to group applications together. You create an ingress to route the public traffic to various services like a load balancer, which then can direct traffic to nodes within the pool (backed by VMs that you don't have to manage). The containers then are hosted on these nodes in things called *pods*. Each of these pods can be one or more containers. There are health checks and liveness probes that you can get by default or configure to ensure that your app is started and that it is responsive. You configure how many versions of the app you want with replica sets and you can be assured that Kubernetes is going to keep that many active, healthy containers up and running. If one goes bad, Kubernetes just blows it away and starts a new one without you having to manage it.

You can easily change configurations by interacting with the service via a CLI tool called kubectl and you can easily scale in/out with rules. You can also have a ridiculously large number of backing VMs so that you can handle the workload of your entire organization in one Kubernetes cluster. You can also split your workloads into separate clusters if you want to ensure that applications/clients cannot possibly interact or harm other applications/clients.

In summary, AKS is simply all the power of traditional infrastructure in the cloud with simple configurations that allow you to leverage massive scale effectively and easily, designed for orchestration around your containerized applications.

If you want more about AKS, you can find out more at `https://learn.microsoft.com/training/modules/intro-to-kubernetes/`.

Azure Container Apps

Kubernetes is great, but Kubernetes is also hard. I know I just made it sound like a breeze, but there really are some tricky parts to it, like configuring an ingress correctly, mapping services for load balancers to applications, and other initial configurations.

If you want all the power of Kubernetes but want to leverage it in a way that gives you a managed service where you don't have to do a lot of the underlying configuration, then you should consider working with Azure Container Apps.

With just a few lines of code, you can get up and running and have a serverless cloud-native solution without a lot of the learning curve required for Kubernetes, while still getting a lot of the benefits that come with a full Kubernetes deployment.

If you want to know more about Azure Container Apps, you can read more at https://learn.microsoft.com/azure/container-apps/overview. Additionally, the learn module for this unit contains a simple introductory exercise to learn about Container Apps, specifically around Deploying, AuthZ and AuthN, Secrets, and Dapr.

Review Your Learning

As an additional challenge, consider the following questions and determine how you would approach potential solution(s). You can find answers to these questions in Appendix A at the end of this book.

1) Which runtime is required to host containers?

2) What is the purpose of the Azure Container Registry (ACR)? How do you interact with the ACR from your local machine?

3) What do the following terms mean: Dockerfile, image, and container? How does each play a part in the containers ecosystem?

4) Can you change the variables in a running container instance? Can you change the variables of a container hosted in Azure App Service? What about Kubernetes or Azure Container Apps?

5) Can you have an Azure Container Instance running on a private network?

6) How do you authenticate against the ACR? Can you get granular per-user control over individual images within an ACR?

7) Can the ACR run automated builds and deployments for your images?

8) Can a container instance communicate with other Azure services such as an Azure SQL Server?

9) Can a container instance host multiple containers?

Complete the Three AZ-204: Implement Containerized Solutions Modules

To fully learn the material, I recommend taking the time to also complete the three MS Learn modules for Implement Containerized Solutions found here:

- Manage container images in Azure Container Registry `https://learn.microsoft.com/etraining/modules/ publish-container-image-to-azure-container- registry/`

- Run container images in Azure Container Instances: `https://learn.microsoft.com/training/modules/ create-run-container-images-azure-container- instances/`

- Implement Azure Container Apps: `https://learn. microsoft.com/en-us/training/modules/implement- azure-container-apps/`

In addition to these two modules, I also recommend taking a look at the following modules and documents to get your feet wet on the remaining technology solutions for containerized/cloud-native applications in Azure:

- Deploy and run a containerized web app with
  Azure App Service: `https://learn.microsoft.`
  `com/training/modules/deploy-run-container-`
  `app-service/`

- `https://learn.microsoft.com/azure/container-`
  `apps/quickstart-portal`

- Deploy a containerized application on Azure
  Kubernetes Service: `https://learn.microsoft.com/`
  `training/modules/aks-deploy-container-app/`

Chapter Summary

In this chapter, you learned about working with containers and utilizing
the two main services for the AZ-204 Exam—the Azure Container Registry
and the Azure Container Instances. In addition to these two services, you
also saw how to deploy a container to an Azure App Service for additional
power. The final part of the chapter introduced you to two technologies
that are not necessarily on the exam but need to be on your radar—Azure
Container Apps and Azure Kubernetes Service.

After working through this chapter and the Microsoft Learn module,
you should be on track to be in command of the following concepts as you
learn about Azure and prepare for the AZ-204 Exam:

- Work with .NET code in a container.

- Create an image and a container locally.

- Deploy an Azure Container Registry.

- Publish an image to the Azure Container Registry.

- Control access to images within the ACR using RBAC.

- Utilize versioning in your images.

- Publish an Azure Container Instance by using the image from an ACR.

- Publish an Azure App Service by leveraging an image from an ACR.

- Publish an Azure Container Apps instance that leverages an image from a Container Registry.

In the next chapter, you learn about working with Azure Functions as a solution to deploy standalone code, simple APIs, and microservices into your Azure subscription.

CHAPTER 6

Implement Azure Functions

Do you want to write code for a microservices solution without having to utilize containers? Are you looking for a quick and easy API solution that can be public or private? Would you like to break up your monolithic application and get portions of your solution hosted independently with the ability to update the code quickly without having to wait for entire development cycles to complete? Maybe you just want to move some server-based solutions to the serverless cloud for quick file processing or other code-heavy solutions that can stand alone. If so, Azure Functions is a great option for you!

Azure Functions are easy to use and test. You will find the barrier to entry lies more in the ability to get your organization to buy into the viability of Azure Functions as a solution, rather than creating and using the actual solutions.

At a high level, you can get started building serverless solutions by writing code directly against SDKs or by leveraging bindings to integrate with other Azure services quickly and easily, including Blob Storage, Azure Service Bus, and Azure Cosmos DB.

This chapter looks at the basics of Azure Functions and explains how to start working with them via code. It also discusses triggers, using tools to test your function apps, and bindings to other Azure services. You'll then finish up with a look at Azure Durable Functions and the various patterns you need to be in command of before sitting for the AZ-204 Exam.

© Brian L. Gorman 2023
B. L. Gorman, *Developing Solutions for Microsoft Azure Certification Companion*,
Certification Study Companion Series, https://doi.org/10.1007/978-1-4842-9300-3_6

A Quick History of Azure Functions

Azure Functions were originally created to be stateless with a maximum runtime of five minutes. In the original implementations, if you created an Azure Function, it would automatically die after five minutes. This was both a limitation of the execution environment and a safety feature to ensure that you didn't accidentally run up a gigantic bill with an infinite loop in a function that never died. The stateless nature of an Azure Function was designed to make sure that nothing had to be persisted across the execution of functions.

All of this worked great, and this is technically still the backbone of Azure Functions. If you create an Azure Function app without doing any additional settings, you will be utilizing these same constraints and operational features as per the original design of Azure Functions.

As modern development continues to evolve and cloud migration has been gaining steam for many years, operational features that have become necessary to serverless workflows are now additional features in Azure Functions. The major changes came with the release of Durable Functions, which allow functions to run from just a few seconds to infinity, and created some other useful workflows that you'll learn about later in the chapter. The other feature added by Durable Functions is persistent state, which exists even through the restart of an Azure Function application.

Both non-durable and durable functions can exist in the same function app, as the durable nature of a function is defined by the code of the function and not any settings in the Azure service itself.

One limitation you need to be aware of is that, except in very early versions of Azure Functions prior to version 2, all functions in an Azure Function app must be in the same language. Therefore, unless you are working on a legacy Azure Function app, if you need some of your functions to run Java, others to run JavaScript, and even others to run .NET, you need to create a new function app for each language.

There is a final thing that can trip up development on function apps early on. If the code is developed in the portal (you can write function code from your browser in the portal), you should not try to work with the code from a local development machine, and working as a team on the solution can get tricky. If your team is developing the function app locally and utilizing GitHub or Azure Repos (or another SCM solution), you should not expect to be able to also utilize the portal for development for that solution. Once you've wired up your app with automated deployments, the portal will display a message that states, "Your app is currently in read only mode because you have source control integration enabled".

For the most part, you'll likely want to develop locally and utilize source control with automated deployments, but it can be nice to test a few things just by developing them in the portal. There are additional considerations that you will do in the portal as well, such as setting integrations for bindings. The integrations can be modified in the portal regardless of whether the solution was built in the portal or from a local machine utilizing source code. Bindings are discussed in detail later in the chapter.

Creating an Azure Function

Getting started with Azure Functions is simple, but it requires a couple of steps if you are going to develop locally and publish to the cloud. The first step is to create a function app in your Azure subscription. After creating the function app, you need to develop the code locally and publish to Azure.

As mentioned, options exist to develop directly in the cloud via the portal, but it's likely desirable to develop mostly from your local machine (especially when working with others). Therefore, this book focuses on local app development. If you want to see more about development from the Azure Portal, you can review an example from Microsoft Learn: `https://learn.microsoft.com/azure/azure-functions/functions-create-function-app-portal`. Looking through that example is worth your time to also get a quick look at some simple debugging and testing from the portal.

The rest of this chapter deploys an Azure Function app in the portal but uses local development tools to build the solution. Eventually a GitHub Action will be utilized to deploy the application to Azure. The code created in this chapter is available with the materials for this book for you to review and try on your own.

Name the Function App

As with many of the other services so far, the function app must have a unique public-facing domain name that is comprised of the name of your application with `.azurewebsites.net` added to the end.

The name of the application must be between 2 and 64 characters, can't start or end with a hyphen, and must contain only alpha-numeric characters and/or hyphens (see Figure 6-1).

Figure 6-1. *Naming a new Azure Function app*

Publish

The options to publish your application include choosing Code or a Docker Container. For this book, the application will use code, but you can also work with a Docker container.

If you choose to use a Docker deployment, the portal deployment is a bit confusing. You will just deploy with the sample QuickStart using a single container, then after deployment, choose the Registry source and other important information about your image, as shown in Figure 6-2.

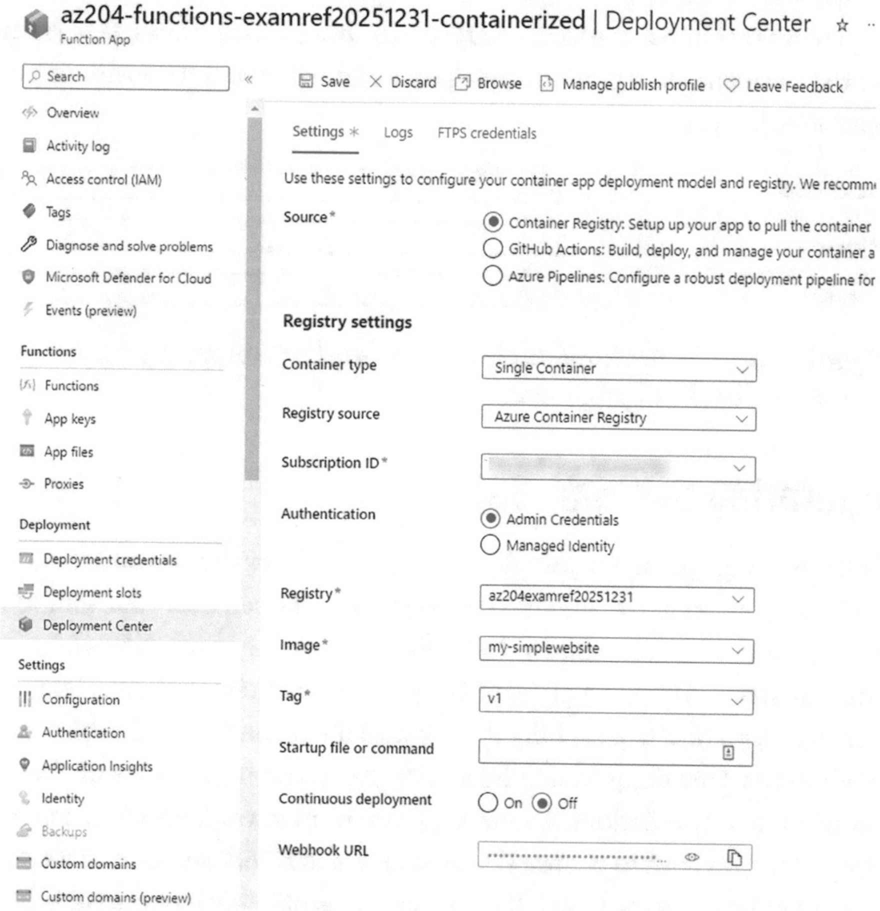

Figure 6-2. *Deploy your Azure Function with the Docker option and then configure the deployment after the resource has been provisioned*

Runtime Stack

As with other services, you have a number of choices for your runtime stack, with available options of .NET, Node.js, Python, Java, PowerShell, or a Custom Handler.

Once you choose the stack, you have to choose an appropriate version for the stack and then pick an appropriate region for your deployment (see Figure 6-3).

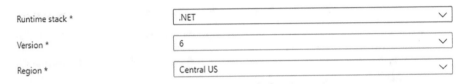

Figure 6-3. *The runtime stack, version, and region are set on the Basics tab for the deployment*

Operating System (OS)

The operating system for your deployment is another choice you have to make, so you need to make sure the OS you choose can host your solution. The system will recommend a choice for you based on your choice of runtime stack. With most of the offerings, you could choose Linux. For this deployment, I'm just going to stick with the recommended choice of Windows. One thing about Linux OS is that you cannot work with the portal to modify functions. Therefore, if you want to work on a function in the portal, you have to choose Windows. For a .NET 6/7 solution, you can use either Windows or Linux. If your solution is utilizing Python, Node.js, or Java, Linux is likely your first choice.

Hosting Plans

As with Azure App Services, Azure Functions need a hosting plan. The default plan is the Consumption tier, which has a minimal fee for storage and offers up to a million requests against your functions before you incur any charges. The Consumption tier is typically called the "serverless" tier—it's listed as Consumption (Serverless) in the options. The great thing about this plan is that it is extremely inexpensive. Indeed, you can get up to a million requests per month without paying for the resource. You will see a nominal fee for the backing storage account, however. As long as you don't go crazy, that storage fee is generally negligible. One drawback for the consumption plan is that the consumption tier does not have an option to keep the solution warm, so there can be some side effects or latency concerns if the app hasn't been used in a while.

When an application has to "warm up" before it can serve requests, this is known as a "cold start." Typically, a cold start happens when an app has been idle for around 20 minutes; however with a function app, this can actually happen for any request. In some instances, therefore, as the request may have to wait for the application to start, a 404 error can potentially happen if the request times out while the function app is warming up, even when the request is to a valid endpoint. For heavy workloads, or when a cold start is unacceptable, the consumption plan is likely not the correct choice for your solution. In these cases, you have a couple of other options.

The first option is the Premium plan, which offers a shared hosting solution that is production worthy and gives you additional options like the ability to use a virtual network and the ability to host multiple function applications. The Azure Functions Premium plan is much more expensive, and you pay by execution time against the CPU and memory. Typical prices are listed on the pricing page: https://azure.microsoft.com/pricing/details/functions/#pricing.

Another type of deployment can be used for your function application, which is to just deploy an App Service plan. As with the App Service, an App Service plan can be selected to give additional power and tools for your use. One of the main benefits of an App Service plan is the ability to utilize the Always On option that exists for typical production-ready app service plans, meaning that you'll never encounter any issues with cold starts. Pricing and available resources are determined by the App Service plan, so although you are paying for this service no matter what, you will have a more predictable bill on this plan than on a Premium or Consumption plan.

There are two final options for hosting, which you may need to be aware of for the exam. The first is the ability to host a function application in Kubernetes, where everything from compute to cost is dictated by the Kubernetes deployment. The second option is the ability to create an App Service Environment (ASE) and use that environment to host the function application.

For learning purposes and for many scenarios, the correct choice is to utilize the Consumption tier, as shown in Figure 6-4.

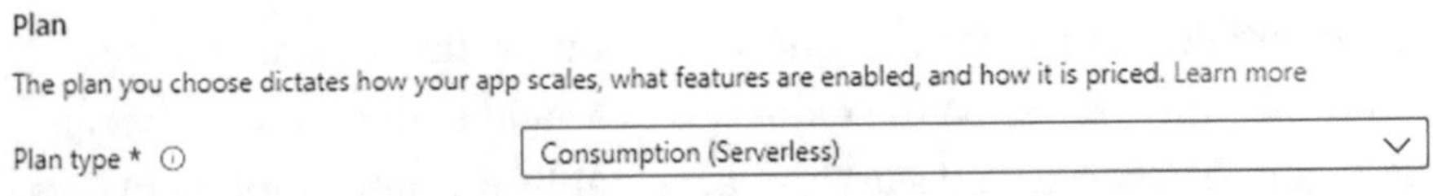

Plan

The plan you choose dictates how your app scales, what features are enabled, and how it is priced. Learn more

Plan type * ⓘ   Consumption (Serverless)   ⌄

Figure 6-4. *The Consumption tier is extremely popular due to the low cost and low barrier of entry for working with serverless Azure Functions*

Backing Storage

Every Azure Function app must have a backing storage account. When the backing storage is created, a number of services are automatically created within the storage account to service the function app. Additionally, the storage account is where your deployed solution is stored. Figure 6-5 shows the creation of the backing storage during the function app creation in the portal.

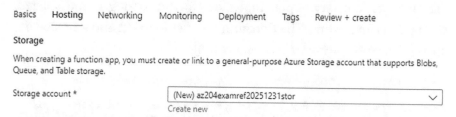

Figure 6-5. *All Azure Function apps must have a backing storage account to service the application, which can be previously existing or created new during deployment*

The backing storage account must be a general purpose storage account with the ability to support Blob, Queue, and Table storage. This account is necessary to keep track of important operational considerations such as monitoring and logging of executions and managing the triggers. Additionally, the function app uses queues to manage long-running processes, and to resume executions when the process is interrupted. The backing storage is also responsible for state management.

Since the storage is so important for a function app, it is considered bad practice to have more than one function app using the same storage account (even though you can do this), and the general recommendation is to create a one-to-one relationship between storage accounts and function apps. For more information on storage considerations with Azure Functions, you can review this learn document: `https://learn.microsoft.com/azure/azure-functions/storage-considerations`.

Networking

If you need to utilize a private network, you have to choose the Premium tier, an Azure App Service plan that allows for networking, or the Isolated/ASE options for hosting. The Consumption tier function app is hosted on the public Azure backbone (see Figure 6-6).

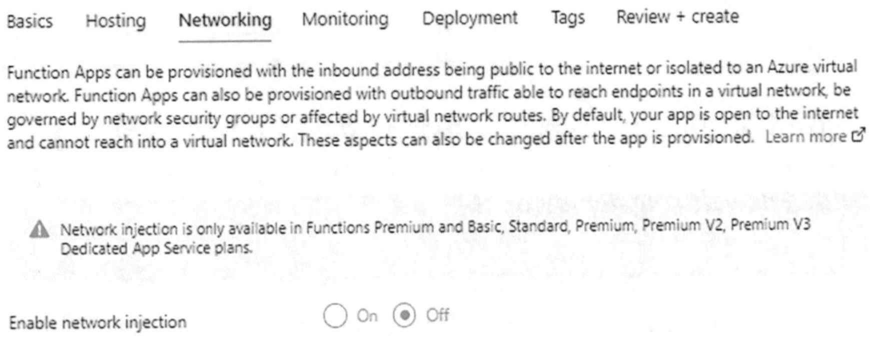

Basics   Hosting   **Networking**   Monitoring   Deployment   Tags   Review + create

Function Apps can be provisioned with the inbound address being public to the internet or isolated to an Azure virtual network. Function Apps can also be provisioned with outbound traffic able to reach endpoints in a virtual network, be governed by network security groups or affected by virtual network routes. By default, your app is open to the internet and cannot reach into a virtual network. These aspects can also be changed after the app is provisioned. Learn more ⌕

⚠ Network injection is only available in Functions Premium and Basic, Standard, Premium, Premium V2, Premium V3 Dedicated App Service plans.

Enable network injection   ◯ On ◉ Off

Figure 6-6. *Consumption function apps cannot utilize a private network*

Monitoring

Azure Application Insights give powerful tools for instrumenting and error logging. As with the Azure App Service, utilizing Application Insights gives you the ability to not only get the typical information about an Azure Function Application, but also allow you to further instrument your code for additional logging and tracing (see Figure 6-7).

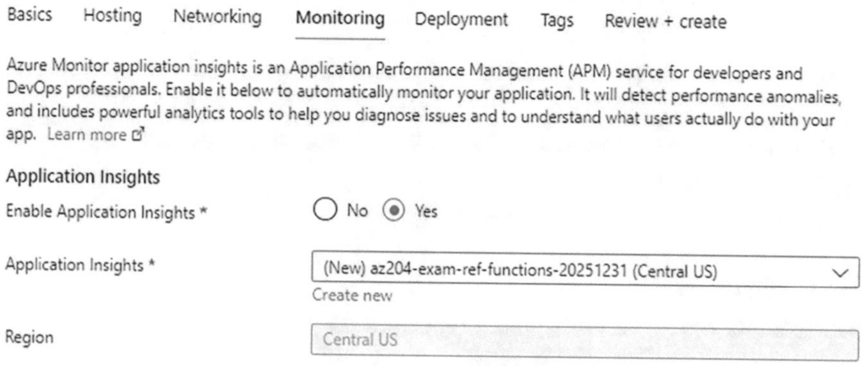

Basics   Hosting   Networking   **Monitoring**   Deployment   Tags   Review + create

Azure Monitor application insights is an Application Performance Management (APM) service for developers and DevOps professionals. Enable it below to automatically monitor your application. It will detect performance anomalies, and includes powerful analytics tools to help you diagnose issues and to understand what users actually do with your app. Learn more ☐

Application Insights

Enable Application Insights *   ○ No ⦿ Yes

Application Insights * | (New) az204-exam-ref-functions-20251231 (Central US)   ⌄ |
                                 Create new

Region | Central US |

Figure 6-7. *The Monitoring option includes the ability to easily enable a new or existing Application Insights instance within the same region as the Azure Function app*

Deployment Options

Until recently, it was not possible to enable CI/CD on an Azure Function app. Recent changes have made this possible as of around October of 2022. If you want to enable GitHub Actions during provisioning of the application, you can wire up your GitHub account and choose the organization (which is either a full team or can also be just your own GitHub account), repository, and branch from which to deploy.

Often, it is easier to just deploy the function application and then later come back to the Deployment Center and wire up the CI/CD after you've created code at GitHub for the function application. Figure 6-8 shows keeping the option disabled during deployment. I'll be circling back to this once the application is deployed and the code is created to enable the CI/CD via the Deployment Center from the provisioned function app.

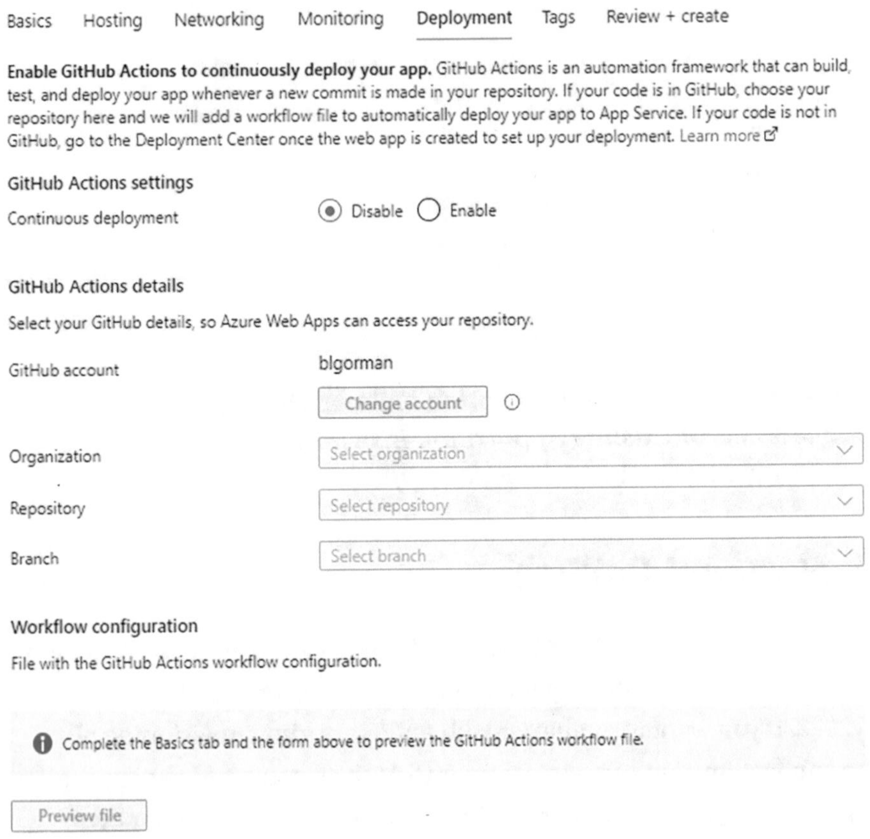

Basics   Hosting   Networking   Monitoring   Deployment   Tags   Review + create

Enable GitHub Actions to continuously deploy your app. GitHub Actions is an automation framework that can build, test, and deploy your app whenever a new commit is made in your repository. If your code is in GitHub, choose your repository here and we will add a workflow file to automatically deploy your app to App Service. If your code is not in GitHub, go to the Deployment Center once the web app is created to set up your deployment. Learn more ☐

GitHub Actions settings

Continuous deployment   ⊙ Disable   ◯ Enable

GitHub Actions details

Select your GitHub details, so Azure Web Apps can access your repository.

GitHub account   blgorman

                                [Change account]   ⊙

Organization   [Select organization   ⌄]

Repository   [Select repository   ⌄]

Branch   [Select branch   ⌄]

Workflow configuration

File with the GitHub Actions workflow configuration.

ℹ Complete the Basics tab and the form above to preview the GitHub Actions workflow file.

[Preview file]

Figure 6-8. *Deployment is not enabled during provisioning in this example. If you already have code ready to go, you would be able to enable this option and connect to the correct source to automatically create a CI/CD GitHub Action*

In addition to using the built-in deployments, a GitHub Action YAML script is included with the resources for easily deploying the solution to your own function app by creating an empty action in GitHub and filling in the variables. If you choose to use the script, you can either utilize Azure to create the script and replace the contents, or you can download the Publish Profile for the function app, put the XML into a GitHub Secret, create a new action manually, and then set the variables appropriately in the script.

Slots

After the Azure Function app is deployed, you can configure the deployments and you will also note that even on the Consumption plan, the Azure Function app gets the ability to have two slots. If you need more than two slots, you must utilize an Azure App Service plan, such as the Standard tier or better, where you can get five or more slots depending on the SKU you choose for deployment.

Figure 6-9 shows a staging slot on the consumption plan created for the Azure Function app as deployed. During creation of the staging slot, you also need to enable the ability to use slots. Doing this gives a warning that you will have to reset any secrets.

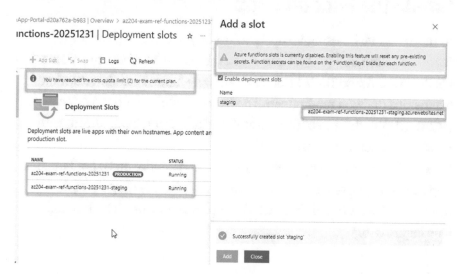

Figure 6-9. *The creation of a slot is easily accomplished, and the consumption tier allows for up to two total slots. Enabling the utilization of slots gives you the power for modern deployments in your function app solutions*

Creating the Application Code

To examine the remaining features of the Azure Function application, it will be highly beneficial to utilize code and create a couple of functions as you work through the material.

For this book, I'm focusing on C#.NET and therefore the application will be written in that runtime language. The functionality of most of this code is basic enough that you should be able to port it to your language of choice should you want to deploy with another runtime language such as Java, JavaScript, or Python.

Create the Function App

In this book, I'll be using Visual Studio, but you can easily work with Azure Function apps in VS Code if you prefer. For VS Code, make sure that you have the Azure Tools extensions and any Azure Function Runtime extensions that you might need. The Learn modules for the AZ-204 Exam (see the link at the end of the chapter) include a quick walkthrough on creating a function app with VS Code.

For this example, I open Visual Studio and choose an Azure Function app project. I just store the code locally, and after creating a simple function, I push to GitHub for CI/CD deployment with a GitHub Action (see Figure 6-10).

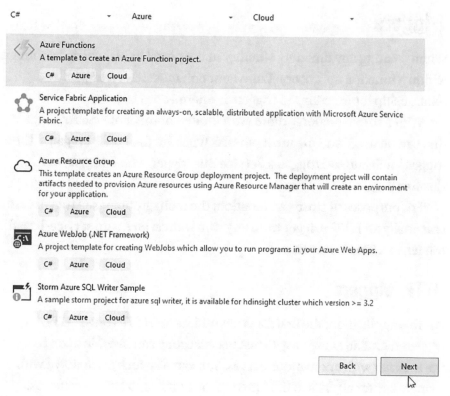

Figure 6-10. *Visual Studio has a template for the Azure Function App Project type, which is used to create a new Function App project*

Function Apps and Functions

It's important to note that in order to run code in an Azure Function, the function code must be contained within an Azure Function application. Therefore, the function app can have many Azure Functions in it, and each Azure Function can have one (and only one) parent function app. The function app is deployed as a single unit, so all of its functions are deployed at the same time. This means that even if you only change one of the functions, the entire application is deployed to Azure to affect changes.

Triggers

When creating any function, whether in the portal or in local development within a function app, every Azure Function must have a trigger. The relationship for functions to triggers is one-to-one (1:1).

With Azure Functions, there are a limited number of types of triggers that can be used, and the most popular types are the HTTP trigger, a Timer trigger, an EventGrid trigger, a Service Bus trigger, a Blob trigger, or a Cosmos trigger.

For purposes of close examination, the main groupings of triggers are essentially an HTTP trigger from any web source, an Azure service-based trigger, or a Timer trigger.

HTTP Triggers

For this application, the first function utilizes an HTTP trigger. HTTP-triggered functions are easy to test because they can be wide open to the Internet with anonymous access. You can also lock them down with a single key for all calls to the function, or, in more complex scenarios, you can utilize a key but also lock down the function app to only allow authorized access (with or without a function key).

When creating the function app in Visual Studio, every function gives you the option to choose your trigger. Figure 6-11 shows the choice of an HTTP trigger from among other options.

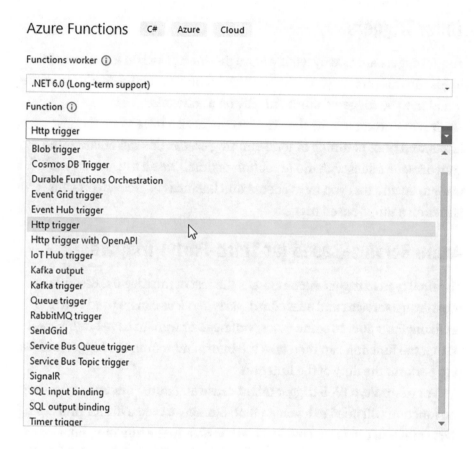

Figure 6-11. *The first function is created with an HTTP trigger for easy testing and utilization via a simple HTTP endpoint for the function*

It is important to note that HTTP functions can only have one new request per second, so if you get a flood of requests, your function app could get bogged down or start responding with a 429 to the requestor. If you need to consider a throttling strategy, Azure API Management (covered in Chapter 11) is a viable solution. You can also consider the option of limiting requests in the host.json file for the Azure Function app.

Timer Triggers

Timer triggers are exactly what you might think based on the name of the trigger. In this option, you can use CRON syntax to set the operation of the function to be triggered automatically on a schedule.

It is important to note that Timer triggers also have some request limits, and poor planning or long-running executions can create some concurrency issues with the execution of timer-based triggers, so you'll want to ensure that you have checks and balances in place to prevent issues on a timer-based trigger.

Azure Service-Based (or Third-Party) Triggers

The final type of trigger encompasses the rest of the triggers. Essentially, most Azure services and a few third-party services can be used to trigger an Azure Function. In some cases, you need or want to have bindings set so that the function can then take the information from the trigger and use it to perform the duty of the function.

For example, a Blob trigger might cause an Azure Function to fire, and the function will need to leverage Blob Storage to read a file for processing. To do this, you can write code against the SDK in the function, but a binding would make it very easy to work against the Azure service (see the section entitled "Bindings" for more information).

Another example might be a Cosmos DB triggered function. This function might be utilized to help monitor and work with the Cosmos data utilizing the Cosmos DB change feed. When changes happen in one Cosmos document, the result can ripple through other documents. The change feed in Cosmos is set to make sure that the data is correctly updated across all documents. This is incredibly important since Cosmos is not a relational database and a lot of denormalized data needs to be kept in sync. Utilization of a Cosmos DB trigger with the change feed to execute code from an Azure Function is the workflow of choice for this scenario.

Authorization Levels

Every Azure Function must be set to have one of five authorization levels. They are Anonymous, Function, Admin, System, and User. You can create a function with any of the five options, and you can easily change the option after creation of the function via the declaration of the function in code.

Anonymous

As implied by the name, a function with anonymous access will have a public-facing endpoint that can be called by any request without an additional filtering to block the request.

Function

When you choose to utilize the Function authorization level, the function will still have a public-facing endpoint, but all requests to the endpoint must pass a secret token, either via the query string or through the request headers. Failure to utilize the token in one of these two ways will result in a 404 error.

It is also important to make a security callout here. Utilization of a function token is not an entirely secure solution. While using a token does ensure that simple requests to the endpoint would be blocked, this solution is only as secure as your worst player who has knowledge of the function token.

When using a Function token, all of your clients will share the same function key and, as soon as the token is leaked or posted online, the function is no more secure than an anonymous function. If this happens, you can at least rotate the keys to help mitigate this solution, but then, once again, you must distribute this new key to any clients. Until they update their processes, they cannot utilize your function. When you need a more secure solution, the Azure API Management service will quickly be the service of choice. (API Management is covered in more detail in Chapter 11.)

The deployment of the first function in this demonstration utilizes function-level authorization (see Figure 6-12).

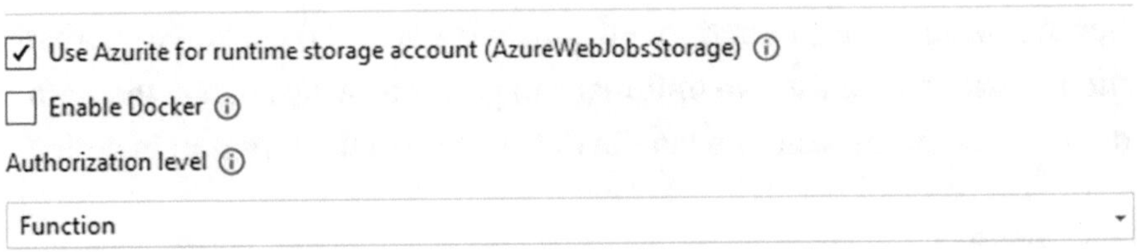

☑ Use Azurite for runtime storage account (AzureWebJobsStorage) ⓘ

☐ Enable Docker ⓘ

Authorization level ⓘ

Function ▾

Figure 6-12. *The function is created with function-level authorization*

Admin

The admin authorization level means that a shared admin token can be used to access this function and any other functions in the Azure Function app (host-level). This is essentially the master key for the application and should be treated as you would treat any secret that you do not want to expose to the public.

Once again, for reasons mentioned, utilization of a single token, especially one with access to all the functions, should not be considered a secure solution.

System

The system authorization level is primarily internal to Azure. This is typically used to work with extensions and APIs in Azure, such as the durable tasks extension, or to handle triggers into the function from systems like the Event Grid.

User

The user authorization level allows for individual roles and identities to execute functions.

The Default HTTP Trigger Function

For purposes of quick examination and learning, the sample function app for this chapter has retained a simple HTTP triggered function. This function has no input or output bindings (see the next section). The function can be easily triggered via an HTTP endpoint with function-level authorization.

The function has a simple name—Function1—and the name is restated as a C# attribute on the function declaration. In the declaration, you'll note the trigger is an HttpTrigger, and the AuthorizationLevel is Function (set from an enumeration with five options).

The function declaration also declares HTTP verbs like get and post, with a default route set to null. What this means is that you can alter the request to only work on GET or POST verbs, and you can also respond to both, as in the case of this function. The route being null means that there are no other considerations other than the default endpoint of the function name.

If you want to further qualify the request with route paths, you can do that by changing null to the path. For example, Route = "api/subgroup/{id:int?}" would only allow the function to respond to the request if the route matches that pattern, including an optional integer ID for further segregation.

The input parameters for the request body (HttpRequest req) and an ability to log to the function runtime (ILogger log) are also present in the default signature for the default function. The following code snippet shows the default function declaration in more detail:

```
public static class Function1
{
    [FunctionName("Function1")]
    public static async Task<IActionResult> Run(
```

```
    [HttpTrigger(AuthorizationLevel.Function, "get",
    "post", Route = null)] HttpRequest req,
    ILogger log)
{
```

Immediately following the declaration is the use of the logger and the request body/query string information passed in. The function then determines if the user has passed a variable in the query string or the request body for the value name. If so, the name is displayed in an output message. If not, the output message states that the function was triggered successfully, but a name was not provided and should be passed in the body or the query string for the request.

```
log.LogInformation("C# HTTP trigger function processed a
request.");
```

```
string name = req.Query["name"];
```

```
string requestBody = await new StreamReader(req.Body).
ReadToEndAsync();
dynamic data = JsonConvert.DeserializeObject(requestBody);
name = name ?? data?.name;
```

```
string responseMessage = string.IsNullOrEmpty(name)
    ? "This HTTP triggered function executed successfully. Pass
    a name in the query string or in the request body ..."
    : $"Hello, {name}. This HTTP triggered function executed
    successfully.";
```

```
return new OkObjectResult(responseMessage);
```

.NET 7 Changes

As I'm working through the final edits for this book, .NET 7 has been released, and the default function is different. They've changed a number of things in the latest release. One important change is the introduction of isolated functions. When you create your application now, you can choose to run in an Isolated Worker. If you are going to deploy .NET 7 (or in the upcoming .NET 8), at the time of this writing you must choose to deploy as isolated functions.

The ability to use isolated functions allows you to run your functions in a version that is different from the host application version. This also means your functions are executing in a different thread than the host process, which should result in fewer conflicts. Additionally, due to this new functionality, you can now run code from the .NET Framework (version 4.8) in your Azure Functions.

With these changes also comes new code for the default function template. The Isolated .NET 7 function includes a factory for logging with dependency injection, and the code for Function1 just returns a simple message: "Welcome to Azure Functions!".

```
private readonly ILogger _logger;

public Function1(ILoggerFactory loggerFactory)
{
    _logger = loggerFactory.CreateLogger<Function1>();
}

[Function("Function1")]
public HttpResponseData Run([HttpTrigger(AuthorizationLevel.
Function, "get", "post")] HttpRequestData req)
{
    _logger.LogInformation("C# HTTP trigger function processed
    a request.");

    var response = req.CreateResponse(HttpStatusCode.OK);
```

```
response.Headers.Add("Content-Type", "text/plain;
charset=utf-8");

response.WriteString("Welcome to Azure Functions!");

return response;
}
```

GetTopMovies Function

Another simple HTTP Trigger function is included in the starter application. You do not need it for this chapter, but it will be leveraged in Chapter 11 when working with APIM. Feel free to uncomment this function as well or leave it commented; it is up to you. If you are creating from scratch, consider ignoring this function for now.

Deploy the Function App

You have two options for deployment, which are to deploy manually or by utilizing automated CI/CD.

Right-Click and Publish from Your Local Environment

It is entirely possible to deploy your solution quickly and easily to Azure by using the Publish tools in either Visual Studio or Visual Studio Code. If you do not want to utilize CI/CD then this is a viable option. It is not very likely that you would be required to know CI/CD in detail for the AZ-204 Exam, as that is more of a topic for the AZ-400 Azure DevOps Expert Exam. Therefore, feel free to publish from your local machine to save time, or wire up the CI/CD from GitHub. Either way, as long as your code publishes, you will be able to learn appropriately.

Assuming that just about everyone can utilize the right-click and publish option without much trouble, I've chosen not to highlight it here. If you need more information, you can find a tutorial at `https://learn.microsoft.com/azure/azure-functions/functions-develop-vs?tabs=in-process#publish-to-azure`. Furthermore, if you run into trouble using GitHub Actions or another CI/CD process, you may find that deploying with the right-click and publish method ensures that your project is working, and the problem is in the deployment.

Deploying with CI/CD

A better solution for deployment of your application is to deploy to GitHub and utilize GitHub Actions to deploy it. The sample code project for this chapter has the final version of all the code shown and used in this chapter. For simplicity, the starter package has everything commented out, so the additional functions for Durable Functions and EventGrid trigger don't cause you initial deployment issues. It is important to note that if you switch to .NET 7, you'll also need to update `FUNCTIONS_WORKER_RUNTIME` in the `local.settings.json` file in the project and in the Function Configuration in Azure to use `dotnet-isolated` instead of `dotnet`.

Adding your code to GitHub is outside of the scope of this book and it is assumed you can manage this on your own. If you need help, refer to documentation at `https://docs.github.com/repositories/creating-and-managing-repositories/creating-a-new-repository`. You can easily make your own project or just use the sample project if you want to practice working with Azure.

Once you have created your repository, go back to the function app and configure the repository for automated deployment from the Deployment Center blade. Doing this will generate a deployment via GitHub Actions.

For the purpose of further examination of the concept of modern deployments (outside of the scope of the AZ-204 but good for every developer to know), you can wire the deployment to a staging slot (slots are discussed in Chapter 4). Figure 6-13 shows the deployment selections from within the portal on a staging slot that was created in the function app.

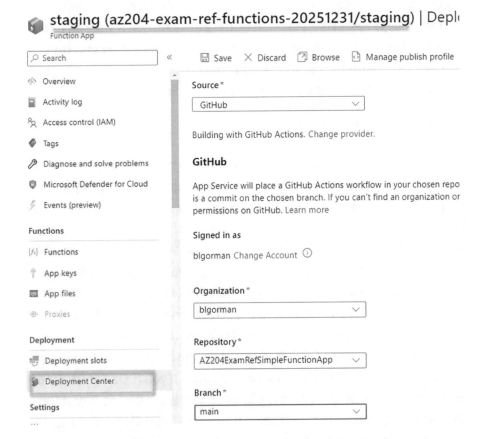

Figure 6-13. *Deploy from GitHub using the built-in deployment functionality*

One additional thing to note is that even the Consumption function app gets two total slots, so you can do this without having to purchase a more expensive offering. You also don't have to use GitHub, as you can also easily deploy your code from BitBucket or Azure Repos or potentially another external Git repository (such as GitLab).

When you save the settings, a new GitHub Action is created for you and the code is automatically deployed. This default deployment does include the use of the `publish-profile` (the XML settings can be downloaded from the Manage Publish Profile link, also shown in Figure 6-13 but not highlighted—it's at the top right). The publish profile is an XML file that contains all the information to deploy a function app. To utilize it in the action, you need to download the file, then copy the XML from inside the file and place it in a GitHub Action Secret. More information on working with GitHub Action Secrets can be found at `https://docs.github.com/actions/security-guides/encrypted-secrets`.

The default deployment in the generated YAML also builds on a Windows agent. Switching to an Ubuntu agent tends to lead to a more efficient build in your actions (see Figure 6-14). The YAML file is stored in your GitHub repository in the `.github/workflows` folder. The sample code also contains a default workflow that you can update and utilize from your own repository with your own publish profile, which is stored in your GitHub Secrets for the Actions on your repository.

Figure 6-14. *The Ubuntu agent is orders of magnitude faster than the Windows agent to build and deploy .NET to Azure*

Test the Function App

To work with the function in Azure, once the function app is deployed, you can easily trigger the function for testing from within the portal. To do this, navigate to your deployed function app, select the staging slot if you are using a slot or the production slot if you are not using slots, select the functions, and then drill into the Function1 function. Once in the function, select the Code + Test option, as shown in Figure 6-15.

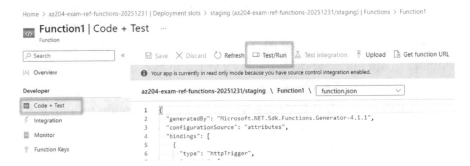

Figure 6-15. *The Azure Functions can be easily tested from within the portal using built-in tools when the trigger is an HTTP trigger [Note: at the time of this writing there is a bug in the portal for Isolated Functions and you can't use the Test/Run for Isolated functions. You can still run them from their function URL or via PostMan or cURL requests].*

Once in the function for Code+Test, choose Test/Run to open the dialog for testing. This function can be done as GET or POST, so you can leave POST selected. For the Key, select Default (Function Key). If you are working with .NET 6, add a query parameter with Name set to name and Value set to az204examRef. Then choose the Run button. Figure 6-16 shows the result of executing the function in a .NET 6 Function App from within the portal with the query string parameter name set as directed.

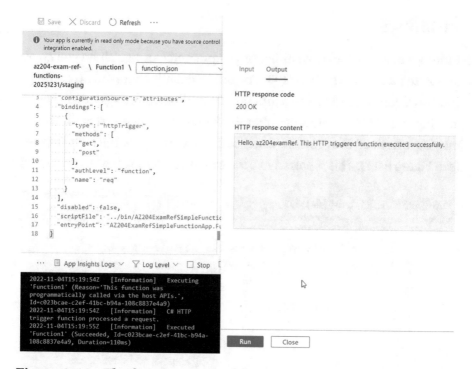

Figure 6-16. *The function is tested from the portal and easily triggered. Also note the output for the logging is shown as the function runs*

Additionally, for testing, you can just navigate to the public-facing endpoint with the function key and/or you can trigger this function easily from a tool such as PostMan or via a simple cURL request. Remember that if you update the route, you need to reflect the full route from your PostMan or cURL. Also note that currently if you are working with an Isolated Worker Runtime, you may find that you won't be able to test in the portal. If that is the case, you should still be able to make calls to the functions via PostMan or cURL, or by just placing the function URL into a browser and navigating to the function endpoint.

Bindings

Bindings in Azure have two directions: Input and Output. When you create an Azure Function with an HTTP Trigger, by default, there are no bindings set. However, you can create a function that utilizes bindings or you can add input and output bindings after the function has been created. You may have noticed the previous function has a binding for the httpTrigger (see Figure 6-17). This is stored in a file called function.json in the portal.

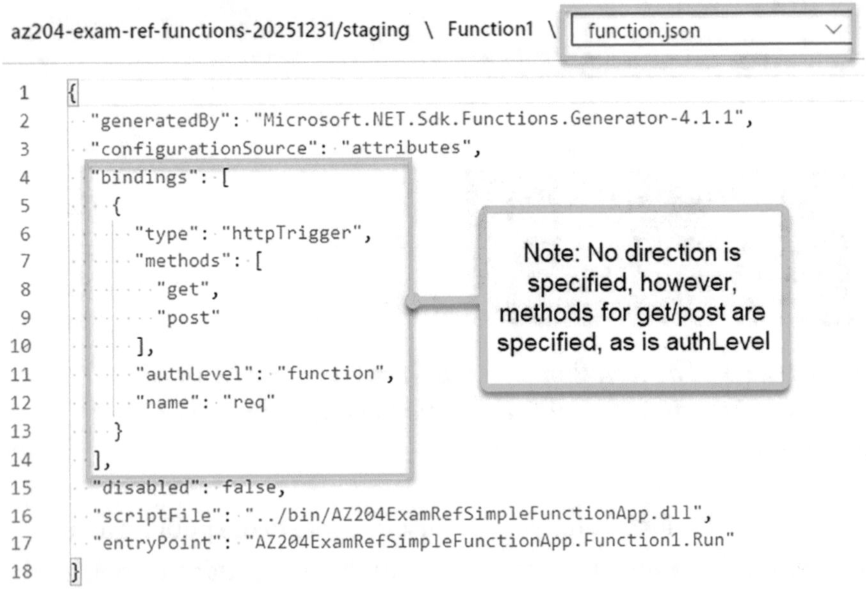

```
   az204-exam-ref-functions-20251231/staging  \  Function1  \  function.json                    ∨

1    {
2        "generatedBy": "Microsoft.NET.Sdk.Functions.Generator-4.1.1",
3        "configurationSource": "attributes",
4        "bindings": [
5            {
6                "type": "httpTrigger",
7                "methods": [
8                    "get",
9                    "post"
10               ],
11               "authLevel": "function",
12               "name": "req"
13           }
14       ],
15       "disabled": false,
16       "scriptFile": "../bin/AZ204ExamRefSimpleFunctionApp.dll",
17       "entryPoint": "AZ204ExamRefSimpleFunctionApp.Function1.Run"
18   }
```

Note: No direction is specified, however, methods for get/post are specified, as is authLevel

Figure 6-17. *The binding for the function is stored in the function. json file on the Azure Portal*

When it comes to the AZ-204 Exam, you should be prepared to look at different `function.json` files and/or in code signatures of function app functions and be able to discern binding information, including type and purpose, such as whether the binding is an input binding, an output binding, or both.

The interesting thing about bindings is that they make it so you don't need to write the plumbing to connect to services. Instead, you can just utilize the incoming bindings to get information. For example, getting a file that is uploaded to Blob Storage is fairly straightforward. You could wire up a Blob trigger and utilize that, but working with code seems to work better if you utilize the EventGrid trigger, and then wire up the event from Blob Storage via the EventGrid trigger. When you do this, you can use a Blob Storage input binding to easily get information about an uploaded blob.

Create a Function with an Input Binding to Blob Storage

If you are using the sample code, you can simply uncomment the `ProcessExcelToCosmos` function. If you are building from scratch, create a new function called `ProcessExcelToCosmos` using the EventGrid trigger type (see Figure 6-18).

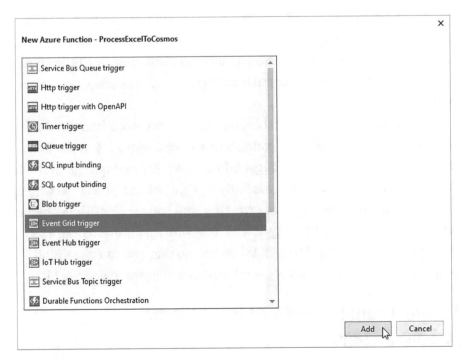

Figure 6-18. *Create a new function utilizing the EventGrid trigger*

After creating the function, add the blob binding to the function declaration. You can then utilize the blob in the function with code as follows:

```
[FunctionName("ProcessExcelToCosmos")]
public static void Run([EventGridTrigger]EventGridEvent
eventGridEvent,
        [Blob(blobPath: "{data.url}", access: FileAccess.Read,
            Connection = "myStorageConnection")] Stream
            fileToProcess,
        ILogger log)
{
    log.LogInformation(eventGridEvent.Data.ToString());
    log.LogInformation($"FileInfo: {fileToProcess.Length}");
}
```

Push the function to GitHub to deploy to Azure, and then swap so that this code makes it to the Production slot. While that deploys, consider the signature of this function. Instead of an `HttpTrigger`, you have an `EventGridTrigger`. This trigger type indicates that the way this function will be fired is when the event grid sends a notification that the event has been fired. Additionally, there is an input binding for the Blob Storage based on the path, with read access. Of particular concern is the `myStorageConnection` variable. For this to work, the function app must have that variable configured correctly. To run locally, you also need to add this to your local user secrets.

Of course, you need a storage account with a container that you can upload files into. Create a storage account and get the primary connection string for the storage account. To make sure this works in both slots, you need to also add the configuration setting to the production slot for the `myStorageConnection` connection string (found under the Access Keys blade in your storage account), which would ideally be a second storage account so that you can trigger it independently for each environment. For purposes of this learning, wiring up events to the production slot only is sufficient, as wiring them up to both production and staging would just be repeating the same actions. Adding your storage account connection string to the function app on either the main deployment or the staging slot is easily accomplished, as shown in Figure 6-19, where the setting is added as an application setting.

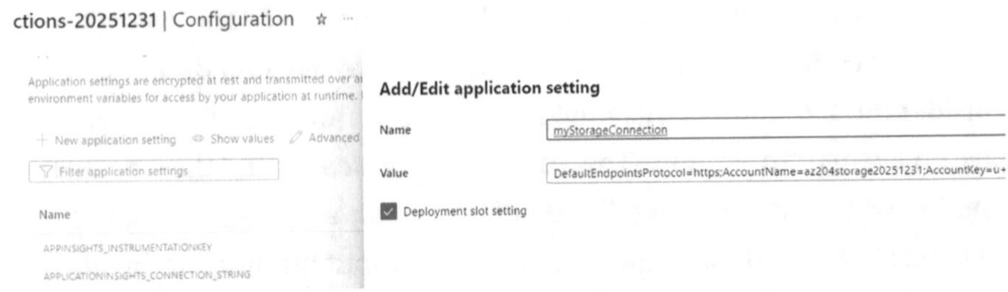

Figure 6-19. *Make sure to set the connection string information for your Azure Storage Account where the file will be uploaded so the function app can connect to the storage account*

With the application deployed and the Event Grid Trigger function set to the Production slot and the connection string set in the application settings, you can now create the EventGrid subscription. For this, you need to go to the storage account where you will upload the sample data Excel sheet (found in the resources for this chapter). On the Storage Account blade, click Events, and then click the +Event Subscription button, and although it may seem like the right thing at this time, do *not* click the Azure Function option (see Figure 6-20).

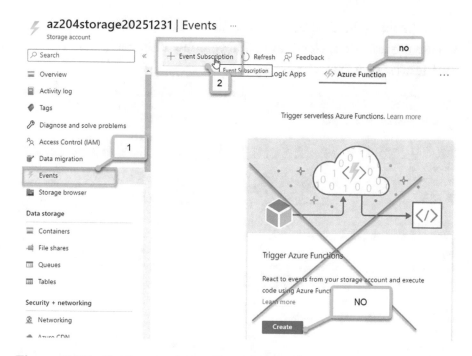

Figure 6-20. *Setting an Azure Function as the target for an Event subscription from within the Azure Storage Account*

On the Create Event Subscription blade, enter the following details:

- Name: `az204-exam-ref-blob-events`

- Event Schema: Event Grid Schema

- Topic Type: Storage Account (already set)

- Source Resource: `<your storage account>` (already set)

- System Topic Name: `az204-exam-ref-events`

- Filter to Event Types: Blob Created

For the Endpoint details, select the Azure Function option,
then use the provided selections to find your function that has an
EventGridTrigger (as in Figure 6-21).

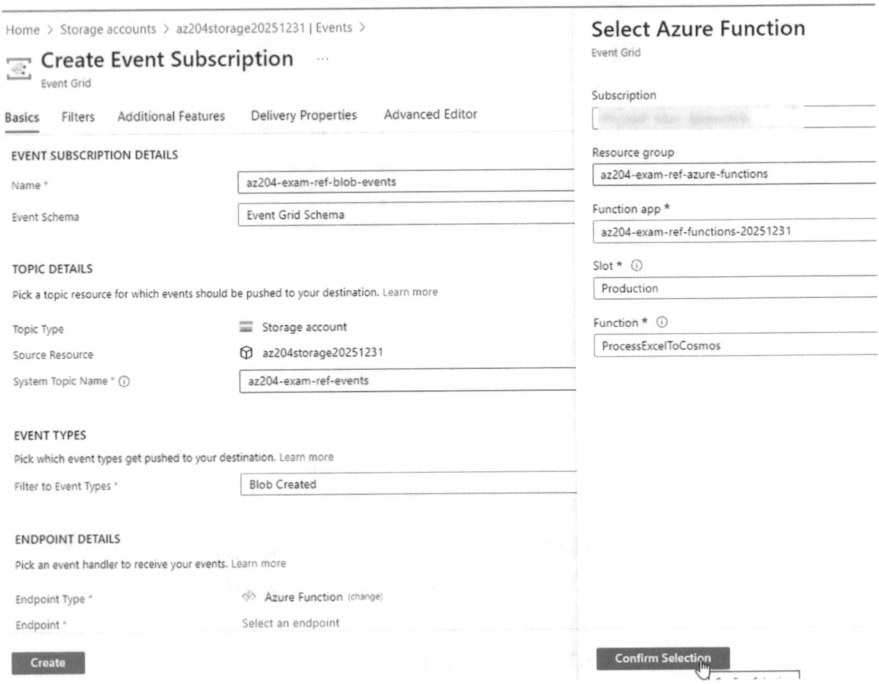

Figure 6-21. *Utilize the Create Event Subscription blade to set the
subscription for responding to blob-created events in your storage
account and triggering your Azure Function*

Confirm and then create the subscription. You'll see it listed in the
events for the storage account once it is set correctly (see Figure 6-22).

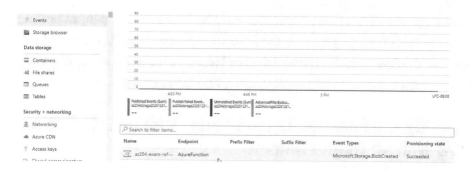

Figure 6-22. *The event subscription is listed in the Events blade for the storage account*

To test that everything is working, navigate to the deployed function and then open the Monitor tab to watch the logs for trigger and processing events. In another window, upload your file to your Blob Storage container and watch the function app respond (as shown in Figure 6-23).

Figure 6-23. *The function app responds to the event. The input binding for the Azure Function allows the Blob Storage to be easily accessed to get the file as a stream*

When you dropped the file into Azure Storage, Azure Monitor fired an event to monitor and respond to the blob-created event. Because you also set the event grid to watch for this event and handle it, you can now publish that event to subscribers to further process the information. The function binding for the event grid lets you set the function as the subscriber, and the `EventGridTrigger` on the function is fired, which propagates information to the function. The function has an input binding on the Blob Storage, and with the information about the file passed by the event, the function can retrieve the file for read access, parse the file, and work with the data to eventually push it into Cosmos DB.

Modify the Function to Parse and Push Data to Cosmos DB with an Output Binding

To work with the file, you can utilize the stream from the incoming blob and then parse it out and put the information into Cosmos. To do that, you need an object to build and map the parsed data, and a Cosmos DB account with a container. You also need to set up a Cosmos DB output binding to put the data into Cosmos.

Before deploying any changes, make sure you have a Cosmos DB database you can use, with a database named SampleDataItems and a container named Items, which has a partition key of /Title. Get the connection string for the Cosmos DB instance. You need the name of the database and the container for the binding information, as well as the connection string setting (found under the Keys blade in your Cosmos DB instance), which is similar to the connection string setting for the Blob Storage.

Put the connection string value into your Azure Function on the configuration page in a key named myCosmosConnection. On the function app's Configuration blade, you'll then have both settings in the application settings. Additionally, you need to add the setting to your local user secrets to run the function locally.

The sample application has the remaining additional code, including the output binding for the Cosmos DB in the function declaration, which adds the Cosmos DB binding to the existing function declaration:

```
[FunctionName("ProcessExcelToCosmos")]
        public static async Task
        Run([EventGridTrigger]EventGridEvent eventGridEvent,
```

```
    [Blob(blobPath: "{data.url}", access:
    FileAccess.Read,
        Connection = "myStorageConnection")] Stream
        fileToProcess,
    [CosmosDB(
        databaseName: "SampleDataItems",
        collectionName: "Items",
        ConnectionStringSetting =
        "myCosmosConnection")]
        IAsyncCollector<SampleDataItem>
        sampleDataItemDocuments,
        ILogger log)
{
```

This code adds the output binding to Cosmos DB, making the
connection using the connection string entered into the application
settings. The fields for databaseName and collectionName give you
the ability to tell the binding exactly what database and container
to target for operations against the Cosmos DB instance. The
sampleDataItemDocuments will essentially be a list of all the data from
Excel modelled into the SampleDataItem type and can be pushed into
cosmos vial the IAsyncCollector<T> binding.

Additionally, the code to easily write all the documents from the
parsed data is as follows:

```
var parseResults = ParseFile.ParseDataFile(ms);
foreach (var pr in parseResults)
{
    log.LogInformation($"Adding {pr.Title} to cosmos db output
    documents");
    await sampleDataItemDocuments.AddAsync(pr);
}
```

The best part of all of this is that, thanks to the output binding, you don't have to write any SDK code and it just works. If you didn't have the output binding, you could utilize the Cosmos DB SDK directly, but you'd need to configure the code similar to code in Chapter 2—first establishing the connection, then getting the database and container clients set, and finally performing `Insert/Upsert` operations.

This simple example illustrates the power of using input and output bindings with your Azure Functions. The input binding allows direct interaction with the Blob Storage without writing SDK code. The output binding allows direct interaction with Cosmos DB without writing SDK code. The output and documents from Cosmos are highlighted in Figure 6-24.

Figure 6-24. *The function handles the Blob Storage-created event, parses the file, and loads the data into Cosmos DB using an EventGrid trigger, an input binding for Blob Storage, and an output binding for Cosmos DB*

The function.json File

With the input and output bindings in place and the Event Grid trigger to handle the Blob Storage-created event, there are now a number of important details to review in the `function.json` file in Azure.

Navigate to the function.json file that is available on the Function blade in the portal under the Code + Test option. Reviewing the file shows the following JSON:

```
"bindings": [
    {
        "type": "eventGridTrigger",
        "name": "eventGridEvent"
    },
    {
        "type": "blob",
        "connection": "myStorageConnection",
        "blobPath": "{data.url}",
        "access": 1,
        "name": "fileToProcess"
    },
    {
        "type": "cosmosDB",
        "connectionStringSetting": "myCosmosConnection",
        "databaseName": "SampleDataItems",
        "collectionName": "Items",
        "createIfNotExists": false,
        "useMultipleWriteLocations": false,
        "useDefaultJsonSerialization": false,
        "name": "sampleDataItemDocuments"
    }
],
```

As you can see, the important information here shows the trigger and the two bindings for the blob and Cosmos DB bindings. One problem here is that for some reason the binding direction does not go along with .NET projects, and this can cause some confusion. The code is working, but the `function.json` file should have direction values for the input and output parameters. If you look at the Integration blade for the function, you will likely see a warning "The following bindings are missing the required direction property and may have been placed incorrectly...", as shown in Figure 6-25.

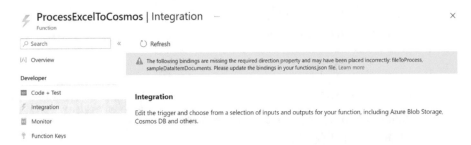

Figure 6-25. *Function binding direction is missing on autodeployed .NET Function apps*

The bindings are shown on the Integration blade as well, but are not assigned (see Figure 6-26).

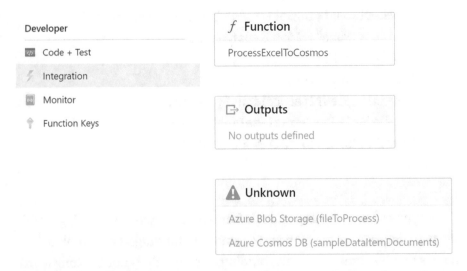

Figure 6-26. *The bindings are present, but are not correctly associated with the function by direction of in and out*

The text that is in the image is the text quoted previously. I realize it might be difficult to read in this text, but the blade shows that the bindings aren't found and the two bindings are listed in the Unknown box.

You can fix this by allowing your code to be modified and then diving into the debug console. To do this, first you need to make sure you aren't in write-only mode. If you have a setting on your function app called WEBSITE_RUN_FROM_PACKAGE with a value of 1 (see Figure 6-27), then you are in write-only mode, because you right-clicked and published. If you want to modify this file, you need to remove that. To be honest, if you are doing this, you should not try to modify this file, as the package deployment will be off track. If you have deployed from CI/CD via GitHub or another solution, this setting is not present in your function app. I've published from GitHub so I can show how to modify this file in this book.

myCosmosConnection	Hidden value. Click to show value	App Service
myStorageConnection	Hidden value. Click to show value	App Service
WEBSITE_CONTENTAZUREFILECONNECTION:	Hidden value. Click to show value	App Service
WEBSITE_CONTENTSHARE	Hidden value. Click to show value	App Service
WEBSITE_RUN_FROM_PACKAGE	1	App Service

Connection strings

Figure 6-27. If you are manually deploying you may have an entry for WEBSITE_RUN_FROM_PACKAGE. If this is present, you can't modify the files in the KUDU command debugger. You can try to change this to 0 and modify the files, but it will likely not work very well after you do that

If you deployed with CI/CD, navigate to the Debug Console, which is found by going into the Kudu tools. To get there, navigate to the root of your Azure Function app in your browser and place .scm between the name of your function app and azurewebsites.net (such as https://az204-exam-ref-functions-20251231.scm.azurewebsites.net/) and then choose the Debug Console ➤ CMD. Navigate into your site folder, then the wwwroot folder, then the function folder, then finally select the function.json file. Once you're in the function.json file, add the direction parameters for the bindings, as shown in Figure 6-28.

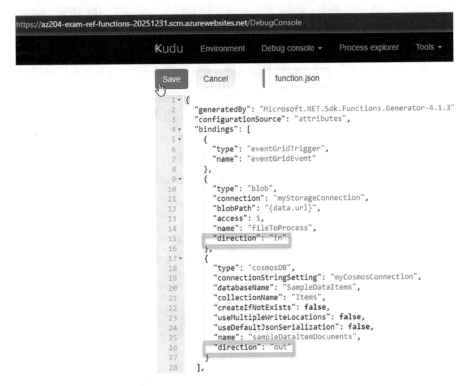

Figure 6-28. *Manually fixing the direction parameter in the function. json file*

Completing this modification and saving the file will allow the Integration page to work as expected (see Figure 6-29).

Figure 6-29. *The Integration page now works as expected, showing the input and output bindings in the correct locations*

The changes are temporarily great because that is how the solution should work, but the solution is working even without the changes. Unfortunately, this issue seems to be a bug in the portal for Azure that has been ongoing. What's worse is that the next time you change the code and redeploy the application, the bindings will once again lose their directional indicator in the portal. Therefore, there is no reason to worry about updating the binding direction for the purposes of the functionality of the application, but now you know how to update the binding direction should you choose to do so.

For the AZ-204 Exam, it's important you are fully aware of the importance of bindings and their directions, so this was a good chance to see this concept up close and personal. No matter what, you need to understand that the function.json file *should* always show the direction of the bindings, and you should be able to discern the purpose and direction of a binding based on the JSON in that file because of these settings. Each function.json file is the settings file for the specific function itself, and defines the things like the bindings, the triggers, and other settings related to the trigger and status of the function. For example, you can set schedule information on a Timer trigger, connection information for Blob Storage and Cosmos DB as shown in this chapter, and you can even set a flag to disable the function completely in the function.json file.

WebJobs vs. Functions

Azure App Services have an option that is similar to a function app in Azure. The option on an app service is the Azure WebJob. To keep this section very short and simple, WebJobs are housed within an existing app service and are capable of doing most of the things that Azure Functions can do. In fact, Azure Functions are built on top of WebJobs. Utilization of the Event Grid trigger in the previous app required the WebJobs extension.

WebJobs can run like CRON jobs and can run similar to a Windows service in a manner that runs essentially infinitely. Original Azure Functions were not designed to do this. Azure Functions can return output and take the best parts of WebJobs and allow you to build independent units of work around the functions. This also allows for more flexibility when it comes to choice of programming language and independent development lifecycles and scaling for the function app.

Durable Functions

As mentioned, durable functions were invented to make it possible to write Azure Functions that maintain state and that don't have a limited scope on the amount of time that they can execute.

The remainder of is chapter focuses on the purpose, creation, and utilization of Azure Durable Functions.

Task Hubs

Each durable function must be part of a task hub. In the task hub, you have all of the functions for a single durable function application. Everything about the task hub is handled in Azure Storage. You must have a different task hub name for each of your durable function applications. You can therefore share the same backing storage account across multiple durable function applications as long as they have different names. The task hub name is declared in the host.json file.

Each function app has its own host.json file. The host.json file is the main for the entire function app to allow for configuration. Whereas the function.json file is specific to the function for which it is associated, the host.json file contains the settings for the entire function app. As the function app is utilizing Application Insights, that information is also included so that all functions can leverage the insights without having to individually configure the settings.

Since the host.json file can store settings for all functions, it's easy to ensure that the function app has a unique extensions:durableTask: hubName value. The task hub name can also wreak havoc when you have slots. To make the task hub name work with slots, the easiest solution is to put the entry into the host.json file as a variable, and then set the task hub name in the application configuration for both the function and the production slots. The host.json file would then look similar to the following:

```
{
  "version": "2.0",
  "logging": {
    "applicationInsights": {
      "samplingSettings": {
        "isEnabled": true,
        "excludedTypes": "Request"
      }
    }
  },
  "extensions": {
    "durableTask": {
```

```
        "hubName": "%mytaskhub%"
    }
  }
}
```

Because the sample application needs to work out of the box, I hardcoded the AZ204ExamRefFunctionsDT value into the host.json file in the provided resources. If you are deploying to slots, you will want to change that setting now to reflect the previous entry, then use the continuing information to complete the process of making it unique for each slot.

With the settings in place, after deployment, make sure to update the staging slot and the production slot with an appropriate unique value in the application configuration. A good value is something like examreftaskhubproduction (see Figure 6-30).

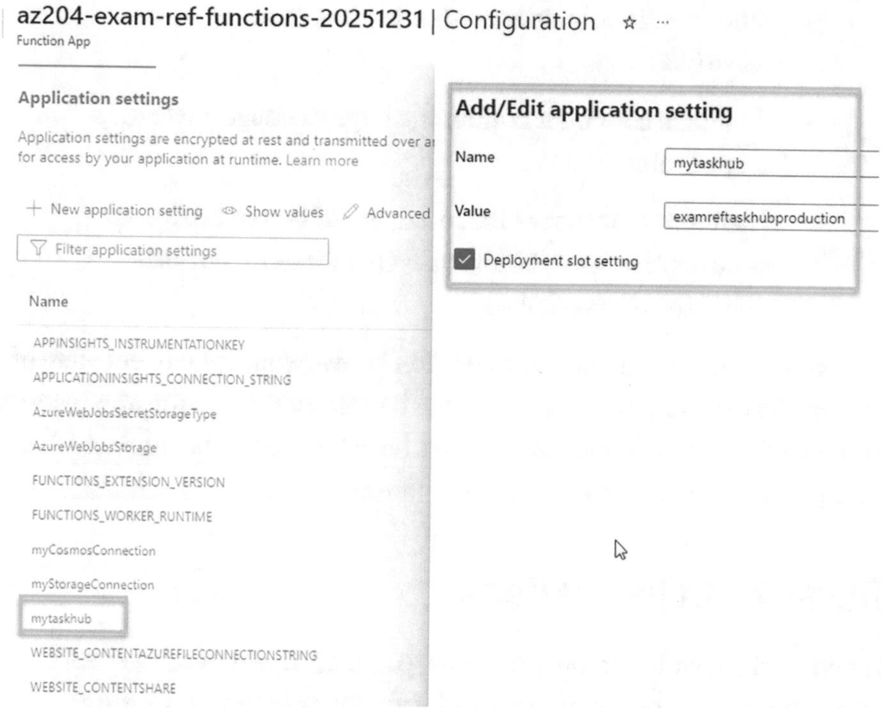

Figure 6-30. *The task hub name is configured on each slot as an environment variable named mytaskhub*

Storage Resources

When you deploy an Azure Function app with durable functions, a number of resources are automatically provisioned to back the durable function app. These include:

- One or more control queues

- One work-item queue

- One history table

- One instances table

- One storage container containing one or more
  lease blobs

- A storage container containing large message payloads,
  if applicable

- (Reference: `https://learn.microsoft.com/training/ modules/implement-durable-functions/4-durable- functions-task-hubs`)

These resources are how the solution knows what the current state of the entities are, how orchestrations can be restarted when the app restarts, and how the system knows which tasks have been executed and which are yet to be completed (via history and queues).

Durable Orchestrations

When working with durable functions, you may have a need to keep state or you might be creating an entire workflow for a step-by-step process. Durable orchestrations can be procedural or simple interactions with entities in state. You can trigger one or more functions either synchronously or asynchronously. With the flexibility of durable functions, you can have processes that run for a few seconds or for as long as you need them to. With the ability to persist state, you can also expect your entities to hold state even when the function app has been restarted.

Durable Function Types

When working with durable functions, it's important to understand the purpose of each of the major parts of the durable-function ecosystem. By understanding what each type within the ecosystem is for, you can easily start to build out the durable functions.

Orchestrator Functions

Orchestrator functions are the brains of the operations. When you want to run any of the design patterns around durable functions, the orchestrator is going to be the function you start and then you will utilize the pattern from within the orchestrator. Orchestrator functions can easily interact with the other types in the durable function ecosystem, including Activity functions, Clients, and Entities.

Every run of any orchestration needs an instance ID. If unset, the orchestration ID will be a GUID that is automatically generated. However, most of the time you will provide your own orchestration identity. The orchestration identity allows your context to be unique to the task hub so each run can be tracked, reported, logged, and executed to completion.

Orchestrator functions are triggered by Orchestrator Trigger Bindings.

Activity Functions

In a long-running orchestration or just a short function that needs to be executed by an orchestrator, you can use Activity functions. Activity functions called by an orchestrator are guaranteed to execute at least once. Activity functions run with a parameter for the `DurableActivityContext`. You can only pass one parameter to your activity functions, so if you need to pass more than one, you have to pass a complex object.

Entity Functions

Just like a class in your normal code, you need something to hold state. The Entity function is designed to work with properties and state to persist past the execution of a function. You can use code to call to an entity function from the orchestrator function or from a client function.

Entity functions are triggered by an Entity Activation Trigger.

Client Functions

Client functions can be utilized to trigger orchestrator and entity functions. The client function interacts with the task hub to get messages to then trigger either orchestrator or entity functions.

The client function can be any regular function with any regular trigger type. Inside the client function, you can interact with the client or the entity function with the durable client binding.

Patterns

For the AZ-204 and in real-world applications, there are a number of patterns that you need to be in command of. These patterns typically apply to specific scenarios, but you will also find ways to adapt them or combine them for your applications.

Function Chaining

The first pattern with durable functions is the Function Chaining pattern, which is how you can process functions in a serial (chain) pattern. To make the Function Chaining pattern work, you set any regular function to call the orchestrator function for the chain. Uncomment the ChainFunctionOrchestrator function in the sample files or create the orchestrator function by creating a new function and using the Durable Functions Orchestration option if you are creating your project from scratch (see Figure 6-31).

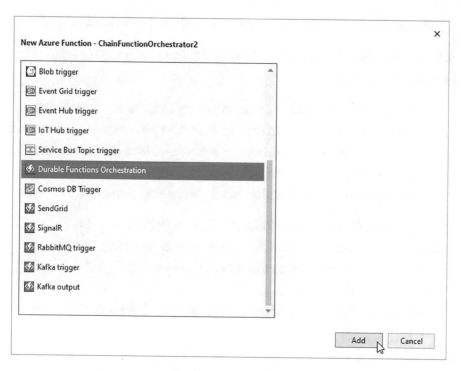

Figure 6-31. *The Durable Functions Orchestration function type can be easily created and it contains a sample function utilizing the Function Chaining pattern*

Within the orchestrator function, you can chain as many function calls as needed to complete your work. The default Orchestrator Function builds a complete sample for you. The signature of the function is as follows:

```
[FunctionName("ChainFunctionOrchestrator")]
public static async Task<List<string>> RunOrchestrator(
    [OrchestrationTrigger] IDurableOrchestrationContext context)
{
```

The body of the function has repeated calls to a function in a chain:

```
outputs.Add(await context.CallActivityAsync<string>(nameof(Say
Hello), "Tokyo"));
```

These functions are called asynchronously by default. Note that you can pass only one parameter to the function, and you wouldn't have to call the same function as in this example. Each consecutive call can call any function with an `ActivityTrigger`.

Also notice the starter function has the following signature:

```
[FunctionName("ChainFunctionOrchestrator_HttpStart")]
public static async Task<HttpResponseMessage> HttpStart(
    [HttpTrigger(AuthorizationLevel.Anonymous, "get", "post")]
    HttpRequestMessage req,
    [DurableClient] IDurableOrchestrationClient starter,
    ILogger log)
{
```

Which utilizes the `IDurableOrchestrationClient`. The orchestration client can call to the orchestrator function or entity functions. In this case, the call is to the orchestrator function:

```
string instanceId = await starter.StartNewAsync("ChainFunctionO
rchestrator", null);
```

Fan-out/Fan-In

Another common pattern is to process workloads in parallel. In the Fan-Out/Fan-In pattern, you create an orchestrator function that uses parallel tasks to call to multiple functions to run in parallel.

When the functions are all complete, you can either end the orchestration or you can call to a final function. For example, you might want to process files in bulk batches. Perhaps you set a batch size of ten and you then start the orchestration. The first function gathers each of the next ten files to process and then orchestrates a run of a function to process each of the files as ten parallel file processing functions. When they are all completed, a final function can be triggered, or the process can terminate.

In this example, you would have returned something like a string for each file to process and conglomerate that into a list of string. For the trivial example that follows, a simple int is returned to set the number of "files" that need to be processed, a worker function does some work, and the end result sums it all up. Your workload in the real world might keep track of how many files were processed based on the return from the original function, and you might not need to sum anything up.

To create this example function, you can uncomment the function code in the sample application, or you can just create a new orchestration trigger function called FanInFanOutOrchestrator and replace the code as follows:

```
[FunctionName("FanInFanOutOrchestrator")]
public static async Task<int> RunOrchestrator(
    [OrchestrationTrigger] IDurableOrchestrationContext context
    , ILogger log)
{

    // Initialize: Get a number of work items to process in
    parallel:
    var workBatch = await context.CallActivityAsync<int>("First
    Function", 0);

    log.LogInformation($"Starting the fan out/in orchestration
    with {workBatch} workload function calls");

    //use parallel tasks to fan out and call n operations
    simultaneously
    var parallelTasks = new List<Task<int>>();
```

```
for (int i = 1; i <= workBatch; i++)
{
    Task<int> nextWorker = context.CallActivityAsync<int>("
    WorkloadFunction", i);
    parallelTasks.Add(nextWorker);
}

log.LogInformation("Parallel Tasks completed!");
// Aggregate all N outputs and send the result to Final
Function.

await Task.WhenAll(parallelTasks);

//get the total from all execution calculations:
var total = parallelTasks.Sum(w => w.Result);

log.LogInformation($"Total sent to final function: {total}");
await context.CallActivityAsync("FinalFunction", total);

return total;
}
```

You also need to set an environment variable named NumberOfWorkerFunctions to make sure that the function executes at least one time—set the value to any integer for testing.

The workload functions don't have to be the same, even though this illustration is calling the same workload function. For this illustration, the code is completed by writing a couple of additional functions—the FirstFunction, the WorkloadFunction, and the FinalFunction. These functions are called by the orchestration to show the fan-out/fan-in operation in detail.

```
[FunctionName(nameof(FirstFunction))]
public static int FirstFunction([ActivityTrigger] int starter,
ILogger log)
```

```
{
    //do some setup work here, other startup function tasks
    var numberOfWorkersToProcess = starter;
    try
    {
        bool success = int.TryParse(Environment.GetEnvironmentV
        ariable("NumberOfWorkerFunctions")
                                            , out numberOfWorkers
                                              ToProcess);
    }
    catch (Exception ex)
    {
        log.LogError("The environment variable
        NumberOfWorkerFunctions is unset!", ex);
    }

    log.LogInformation($"Current number of workers
    {numberOfWorkersToProcess}.");
    return numberOfWorkersToProcess;
}

[FunctionName(nameof(WorkloadFunction))]
public static int WorkloadFunction([ActivityTrigger] int
nextWorkload, ILogger log)
{
    //do the work
    var computed = nextWorkload * 2;
    log.LogInformation($"Current detail {nextWorkload} |
    Computed: {computed}.");
    return computed;
}

[FunctionName(nameof(FinalFunction))]
```

```
public static int FinalFunction([ActivityTrigger] int total,
ILogger log)
{
    //complete the work here
    log.LogInformation($"Final Function [value]: {total}.");
    return total;
}

[FunctionName("FanInFanOutOrchestrator_HttpStart")]
public static async Task<HttpResponseMessage> HttpStart(
    [HttpTrigger(AuthorizationLevel.Anonymous, "get")]
    HttpRequestMessage req,
    [DurableClient] IDurableOrchestrationClient starter,
    ILogger log)
{

    // Function input comes from the request content.
    string instanceId = await starter.StartNewAsync("FanInFanOu
    tOrchestrator", null);

    log.LogInformation($"Started orchestration with ID =
    '{instanceId}'.");

    return starter.CreateCheckStatusResponse(req, instanceId);
}
```

Once everything is working, you can open each function for monitoring in the portal, kick off the first function, and see all of them execute successfully (see Figures 6-32 through 6-35).

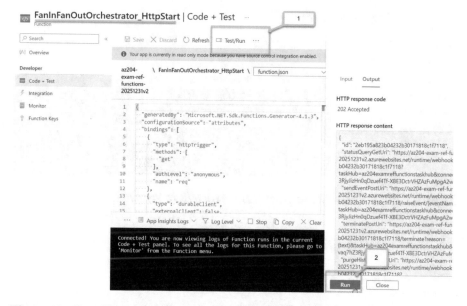

Figure 6-32. *The orchestration is triggered to start the fan-out process*

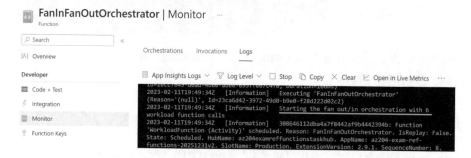

Figure 6-33. *The fan-out orchestrator triggers multiple worker functions.*

Figure 6-34. *The worker functions execute in parallel*

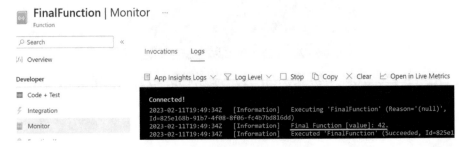

Figure 6-35. *The final function is executed and the sum is calculated from the prior runs*

Async HTTP APIs

Another pattern that is useful is the Async HTTP APIs pattern. In this scenario, you are likely making a call to a long-running process and need to go idle until that process has completed. Once the process completes, you would then want to continue with your orchestration or set some process indicator as complete. For more information regarding implementation of the Async HTTP APIs pattern, review the documentation at `https://learn.microsoft.com/azure/azure-functions/durable/durable-functions-http-features?tabs=csharp`.

Monitor

In some instances, you need to provide regular polling to find out if a process or workload has completed. Unlike the Async pattern, this pattern does poll against an endpoint to check for some sort of status indicator. More information about the monitor pattern can be found at `https://learn.microsoft.com/azure/azure-functions/durable/durable-functions-monitor?tabs=csharp`.

Human Interaction

The Human Interaction pattern is useful when you have a scenario that requires approval and you need to make sure the approval is handled within a set amount of time. When the approval has not been handled in a set amount of time, the solution can escalate to another function path or notify another party for approval. For more information about the Human Interaction plan, review this document: `https://learn.microsoft.com/azure/azure-functions/durable/durable-functions-phone-verification?tabs=csharp`.

Aggregator

The final pattern at the time of this writing is the Aggregator pattern. This pattern is useful for aggregating information over a period of time. This pattern utilizes a durable entity to store the state, such as a billing scenario where you need to track usage or some other metric for clients for the month. The state can be persisted in an entity and utilized to keep track of the information for each client for the current month. Information about the pattern can be found at `https://learn.microsoft.com/azure/azure-functions/durable/durable-functions-overview?tabs=csharp#aggregator`.

Review Your Learning

As an additional challenge, consider the following questions and determine how you would approach potential solution(s). You can find answers to these questions in Appendix A at the end of this book.

1) What is the purpose of the host.json file? What is the purpose of a function.json file? What information can be determined from each?

2) What is a Function trigger? What kinds of triggers are available? How can each be utilized?

3) What plans are available for Azure Function apps and what are some of the considerations for each? Can you use slots in function apps? Can you put your function app on a private network?

4) What is an input binding? What is an output binding? What are some advantages to working with bindings?

5) What is an Isolated Worker runtime and how does it change the operations of a function app?

6) What are the various authentication modes for an Azure Function? What are some security considerations for each mode?

7) What is the difference between a regular Azure Function and a Durable Azure Function? What are the types of Durable Functions and when can each be used?

8) What are the patterns associated with Durable Functions and what is an example of each pattern?

Complete the AZ-204: Implement Azure Functions

To fully learn the material, I recommend taking the time to also complete the MS Learn modules for Implement Azure Functions found here:

- Explore Azure Functions: `https://learn.microsoft.com/training/modules/explore-azure-functions/`

- Develop Azure Functions: `https://learn.microsoft.com/training/modules/develop-azure-functions/`

- Implement Durable Functions: `https://learn.microsoft.com/training/modules/implement-durable-functions/`

Chapter Summary

In this chapter, you learned about working with Azure Functions, including the concepts of triggers and bindings. A practical example then showed you how to work with Blob Storage and Cosmos DB. You then learned about the purpose of durable functions with orchestrations and the various design patterns associated with durable function workloads.

After working through this chapter and the Microsoft Learn modules, you should be on track to be in command of the following concepts as you learn about Azure and prepare for the AZ-204 Exam:

- Work with Azure Functions, including creating and deploying to Azure.

- Understand what triggers are available and how to use them, including HTTP, `EventGrid`, and Schedule (Timer).

- Leverage input and output bindings from Azure Functions.

- Work with Azure Durable Functions.

- Understand the different aspects/types of durable functions, such as Orchestration, Entity, and Activity.

- Know the patterns associated with Azure Durable Functions, such as fan-out/fan-in, function chaining, and the various monitoring/polling and continue patterns for long-running processes.

In the next chapter, you learn about working with authentication and authorization in your Azure solutions.

PART III

Implement Azure Security

CHAPTER 7

Implement User Authentication and Authorization

Identity, access, and authorization within Azure applications has never been something to take lightly. As threats have continued to increase and security concerns have become paramount, one could argue that this topic is the most important aspect of any of the topics on the exam and in your day-to-day development work.

Getting started and working with identity, for all its complexities and importance, is very well done, which makes the developer experience enjoyable. You don't have to be too worried about doing it wrong, as for the most part it won't work unless you do it correctly, and with just a couple of simple steps you can set it up correctly.

To get started, it's important to understand a couple of critical security considerations when working with Azure regarding signing in to your account. These considerations are multi-factor authentication and unusual sign-in attempts.

© Brian L. Gorman 2023
B. L. Gorman, *Developing Solutions for Microsoft Azure Certification Companion,*
Certification Study Companion Series, https://doi.org/10.1007/978-1-4842-9300-3_7

Multi-Factor Authentication (MFA)

Over the past five to ten years, information protection and user authentication have become much more robust and easier to manage via tools like Microsoft Sentinel, Microsoft Defender, and the general Microsoft Identity and M365 solutions available to organizations.

One of the most critical aspects of user security is multi-factor authentication. While the possibility of not utilizing MFA still exists, you should expect that it will not be an option to skip or disable MFA in the next few years.

MFA exists to help solve the problem of authorizing the correct user. Typically this is accomplished with something you know (like a password) and something you have (like a phone or a Rivest-Shamir-Adleman—RSA—hardware dongle) that can generate a verifiable code. Sometimes you can leverage a text message or phone call to perform MFA, although those methods are generally not as secure. This is because it is a lot easier to intercept a phone call or socially engineer an improper response to the challenge, or the user might accidentally approve the request without thinking about it, which is generally easier and more common than it is to generate a key that matches a specific encryption algorithm.

Conditional Sign-in/Risky Sign-in Detection

Another key concept that Azure has implemented is the ability to detect unusual or risky sign-in attempts. This can be configured by administrators or might be automatically triggered in some instances.

Typically, an organization might lock down IP addresses or regional access to help prevent users from signing in from unauthorized locations. For example, only allowing logins from the North American region would mean that no users physically located outside of Mexico, the United States, or Canada would be able to log in using your Azure credentials.

However, this might also be as strict as you typically logging in from a physical building in one city, then traveling a few hundred miles away and attempting to log in. Microsoft might detect your unusual sign-in and issue additional challenges for you to log in to your account.

Authentication and Authorization

Before starting with identity and access, it's important to define the difference between authorization and authentication.

To visualize the difference, think about the government-issued license that allows you to drive. If you don't have something like a driver's license, think about a passport. Either way, there are specific pieces of information on them that validate who you are. For example, when you take the AZ-204 Exam, you need a photo ID of some sort. When you are taking the exam from a remote location, I highly recommend using a passport if possible. If not, you need your government issued ID (i.e., your driver's license) and a credit card or other validation to prove who you are. One look at the ID and it will be clear that your name and photo are shown, which can be used to authenticate that you are the person you say you are. If the photo or the name does not match, you can't be authenticated.

In other words, Authentication (AuthN) is the concept of proving you are who you say you are. In Azure and application terms, this might be your login with a password and two-factor authentication.

Once you are authenticated, you are able to validate that you should be viewing the subscription, driving the car, or taking the test. However, additional permissions are generally required in order to proceed with more advanced operations. This additional access is provided by rules for Authorization (AuthZ) on your user or application credentials.

For example, specific drivers' licenses have additional permissions to drive large vehicles, and even further permissions allow driving large vehicles with hazardous chemicals in tow. Not just anyone has permission to drive around with a cargo that could spill and cause environmental or health emergencies. The driver must first prove they know what they are doing and become authorized with a Commercial Driver's License (CDL), which is required in the United States to drive specific vehicles above a certain size on business-related trips. Additionally, a Hazardous-Materials (HazMat) authorization can be added to the CDL, which means that in addition to the regular driver's license and the ability to drive specific commercial vehicles, the specific identified (authenticated) driver is authorized to drive a large commercial vehicle hauling hazardous materials that could pose an ecological or biological threat if spilled or mishandled.

Primary Authorization Roles in Azure

All Azure subscriptions and resource groups have four key authorization roles that you need to be in command of (among others, at a minimum you need to know these well). The four key roles are:

- Reader
- Contributor
- User Access Administrator
- Owner

The Reader Role

The first authorization role is the *Reader* role. In this role, the authenticated user becomes authorized to read the resources at the resource-group level or the subscription level. Readers can only view resources and settings for the resources. Readers cannot modify, change, delete, or provision resources. Readers cannot change anything about permissions on anything in the subscription.

The Contributor Role

The second role assignment is the *Contributor* role. This authorization tier gives users the ability to read and modify resources within the resource group(s) or subscriptions to which they have been granted access as a contributor. Contributors can also deploy new resources to any group or subscription on which they are granted authorization. Contributors cannot change any permissions or assign any new roles to users within the groups or subscriptions on which they are authorized.

The User Access Administrator Role

The third role assignment is the *User Access Administrator* role. In this role, an authorized user can grant and revoke role access to other users. This can be at a resource-group level or across the subscription. User access administrators cannot do anything with resources within an Azure subscription outside of assigning permissions for reader/contributor/owner/custom/additional roles.

The Owner Role

The fourth role assignment is the *Owner* role. This role is essentially God mode on the resource-level assigned. A user can be the owner of a subscription, where they have full control over the subscription, including user access, resource management, additional role creation, and other powerful abilities such as canceling the subscription. In other scenarios, a client or contractor might be an owner of just a resource group, so that the authorization gives that user tools to do their work just for the resource group while making sure they do not have permission to modify other settings in the subscription. This role assignment is highly useful for governance as well, as you can lock down the group and subscription with policies and be confident the owner of that group cannot change policies and will be limited to only deploying resources approved by your governance strategy.

Requiring Authentication

In Azure, you'll quickly find that a number of the public-facing resources can be easily locked down for authentication. When you enable authentication on the application, the users who browse to your public-facing resource must first validate who they are in order to proceed to the application.

By default, a public-facing resource, such as the Azure App Service, does not have any authorization turned on. This means your initial deployment is wide open to the entire public Internet (unless you provisioned on a private network). Once you enable authorization, users cannot utilize your application. This authorization is outside of the scope of any roles and/or user registrations in your application, but you can utilize the Microsoft Identity platform within your application as well. You'll get a chance to dive deeper with a closer look at authorization in Azure on a web application later in this chapter.

For example, an Azure App Service, as deployed in Chapter 4, is currently wide open to the public Internet (hosted at a public URL such as https://az204examref20251231.azurewebsites.net/) (see Figure 7-1).

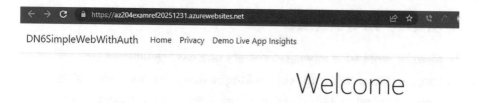

Learn about building Web apps with ASP.NET Core.

My Simple value shared

Shared Value from production slot Configuration Application Settings

My Simple secret shared

Secret Value from production slot Configuration Application Settings

Figure 7-1. *The Azure App Service can be accessed from the public Internet when deployed with default settings*

With no further changes, this application can be locked down to users in the tenant with a simple configuration change. On the App Service blade in the portal, on the left side, is a navigation item for Authentication. When you click the button for Authentication, you have an option to add an identity provider, as shown in Figure 7-2.

Figure 7-2. *The Authentication has an option to add an identity provider*

Identity Providers

An *identity provider* is any service that manages credentials for a person, service, or other object. As long as that person/service/object can be referenced as a unique digital presence, then the identity can be authenticated. Furthermore, that identity can be authorized to have rights.

It is entirely possible for you to provide your own identity solution. However, in most cases, you will be better off leveraging a pre-built identity solution. For example, ASP.NET MVC has ASP.NET identity baked in. This is an authentication and authorization base than can stand on its own, and you don't have to write anything.

As you'll see later in this chapter, however, there are many times you want to integrate the identity of your users from another platform, such as Microsoft, Facebook, Apple, GitHub, or another solution that serves as a valid identity provider.

Within Microsoft, the identity is managed using Microsoft Graph. Specifically, for Azure solutions, you'll utilize Azure Active Directory (Azure AD). Microsoft Graph provides information about what "scopes" within the identity your application needs access to. For example, you might choose the user scope to get just the email address, or you might go deeper into the graph and find deeper information such as the channels in Teams that a user has access to. The concept of Microsoft Graph and scopes are both addressed later in the chapter.

Other providers also have a similar feature to Microsoft Graph, along with scopes for permissions that your application needs to effectively work with the user.

Integrated Providers

When adding an identity provider, you have a number of default providers from which to choose. Most of these are well-known. For example, Microsoft, Apple, Facebook, GitHub, Twitter, and Google can all be easily used for authentication to view the application. It is important to remember that this is only the first step for authentication and authorization in the application. The application has no current ability to leverage this authentication by default for further authorization. Identity providers are shown in Figure 7-3.

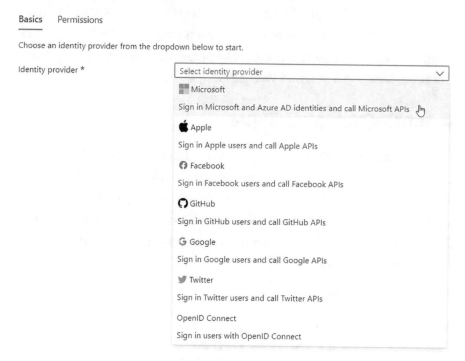

Figure 7-3. *The identity provider can be easily selected for the Azure App Service*

Choosing Microsoft as the identity provider is the easiest way to get started, as the application will just work with your tenant and doesn't require any additional configuration at a third-party site. Using something like Google or Facebook will likely require you to set up an application in their unique developer tools portal and to wire up the generated app ID and secret from that environment to work with your tenant in Azure.

Creating a New App Registration

After selecting Microsoft, you need to create a new app registration and set the name and supported account types. App registrations are covered in more detail shortly, including how to create them from the Azure CLI. For this first look, you'll create the new application for an Azure App Service. It's important to note that the app registration can be used for many types of applications in addition to the Azure App Service apps, including Azure Functions, Desktop Apps, and Web APIs.

Supported Account Types

You can leverage the platform for your single tenant only, any Azure account, any personal Microsoft account, or a combination of any Azure directory and personal accounts. Depending on who you want to let in, this is a very important choice. In this option, only users from my Azure AD directory (including guest users) will be allowed to authenticate on the web application (see Figure 7-4).

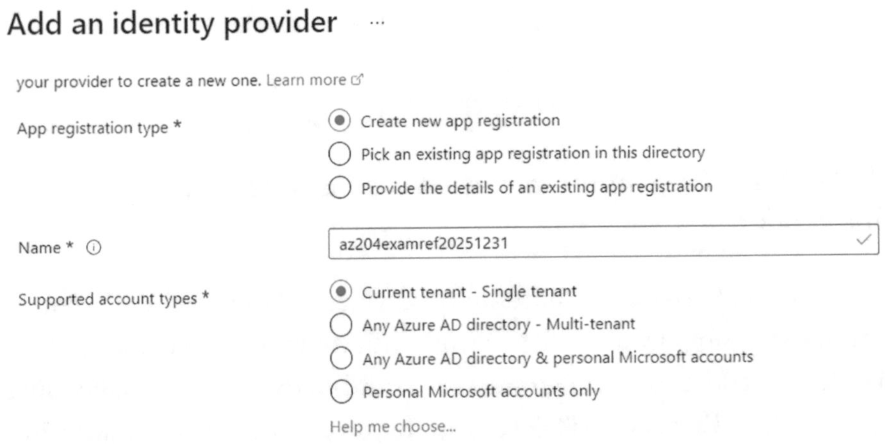

Figure 7-4. *Adding an identity provider starts by creating an app registration and selecting which account types are allowed to authenticate*

These account types will leverage OAuth 2.0 in order to connect to and interact with the Microsoft identity platform.

Authentication Settings

For the authentication settings, you can choose to still allow unauthenticated access, which might be necessary—perhaps for a single-page application (SPA) or a public-facing home page that you want the world to be able to access without signing in. The additional settings determine what happens when unauthenticated users visit the main site. The 302 will redirect them to an authorization endpoint, allowing the users to sign in, grant permissions to their account via scopes (scopes are discussed in the next section for permissions), and then proceed to the application. The 401 will block further access (no chance to log in), as will a 403 or a 404. You can also store the application tokens to allow Azure to manage the refresh of your authentication tokens on your application. For most scenarios, utilize the token store (see Figure 7-5).

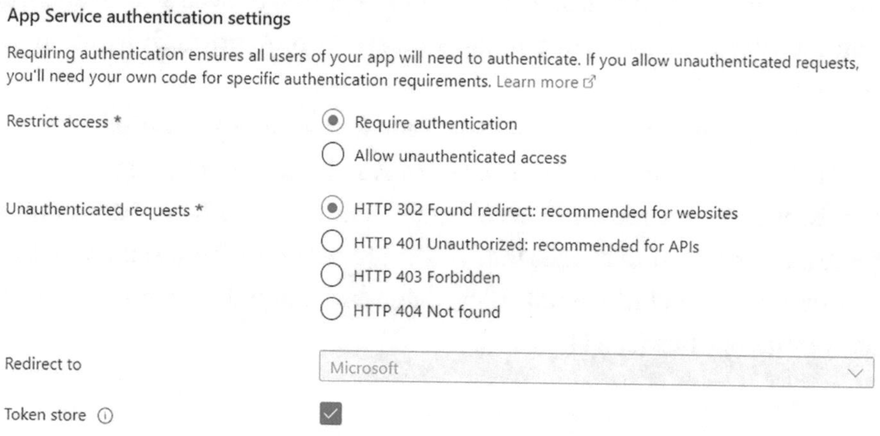

App Service authentication settings

Requiring authentication ensures all users of your app will need to authenticate. If you allow unauthenticated requests, you'll need your own code for specific authentication requirements. Learn more ⌐

Restrict access *	◉ Require authentication
	○ Allow unauthenticated access
Unauthenticated requests *	◉ HTTP 302 Found redirect: recommended for websites
	○ HTTP 401 Unauthorized: recommended for APIs
	○ HTTP 403 Forbidden
	○ HTTP 404 Not found
Redirect to	Microsoft ⌄
Token store ⓘ	☑

Figure 7-5. *The authentication settings allow you to require authentication and determine how to handle traffic from users or other applications that are not signed in*

Permissions

For all app registrations at this time, permissions are handled in Microsoft Graph. If you have a legacy Azure application, you might encounter some permissions in an older system; however, most applications have likely been migrated to Microsoft Graph at this time. By default, the minimal scope for authentication is selected, which requires users to consent to let your application read their profile through the User.Read permission. In general, your application should only request the scopes that are needed to do the work required of the application. If you request too many scope permissions, users might become wary of giving consent.

You can add permissions at any point; however, changing permissions requires users to sign in again and authorize any additional scopes you've added, so you should not do this often. Some permissions that are elevated also require an administrator to approve the ability to authenticate with those permissions. On some permission strategies, the application needs to know about all of the available permissions at creation. Other times, you might come back and add scopes. How you approach these scope requests is entirely dependent on your application and your Azure authorization strategies.

For simplicity, selecting just User.Read is easiest to get started. If you want to look at others, you can click the + Add Permission button. If you do this, ensure that you don't accidentally remove User.Read. Additional interesting permission scopes that you might request for interactions with your user might include Email, Files, Calendar, Schedule, Teams, or one of many other options (see Figure 7-6).

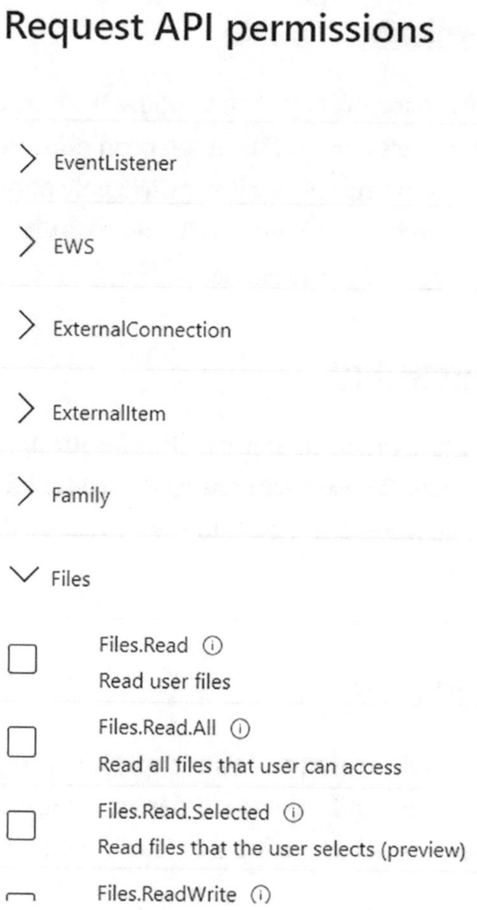

Request API permissions

> EventListener

> EWS

> ExternalConnection

> ExternalItem

> Family

∨ Files

☐   Files.Read ⓘ
    Read user files

☐   Files.Read.All ⓘ
    Read all files that user can access

☐   Files.Read.Selected ⓘ
    Read files that the user selects (preview)

☐   Files.ReadWrite ⓘ

Figure 7-6. *Requesting additional permissions (scopes) for the user to authorize, thereby allowing your application to have more access to user information*

Caution   Reviewing additional permissions and clicking Discard will actually remove the User.Read permission. If you do this, make sure to add the User.Read permission back before proceeding.

Delegated Permissions

There are two types of permissions that you can choose from when working with scopes in Microsoft Graph. The first type of permissions are delegated permissions. These permissions allow your application to run and send requests as the signed-in, authenticated user. The User.Read permission is one of the delegated permissions.

Application Permissions

Application permissions allow you to set permissions for the application to run without a signed-in user. These permissions are useful for a service layer or other middleware solution that needs to perform activities regardless of user presence.

Required Sign-In

Now that the app registration is created and your application requires authentication, visiting the site requires users to sign in. An anonymous request will be met with an immediate redirect to log in, as shown in Figure 7-7.

Figure 7-7. *The application will no longer allow anonymous access. Navigating to the site requires the user sign-in to authenticate and be able to access the application*

Note that in the dialog shown in Figure 7-7, there is information about the application, your sign-in information, and the scopes to which the application wants to access. If the application has a number of scopes, this list could be very long, which might scare off some users. For this reason, and in the spirit of least privilege, it is generally best to keep the list of required scopes as minimal as possible.

Consent on Behalf of Your Organization

If you are the administrator of the Azure subscription, you may also see a checkbox to Consent on behalf of your organization. Checking this box will automatically consent for all users in the organization, and they will not need to accept the permission scopes as presented.

If any scopes are added later, the users must accept scope changes at their next login. Once again, an administrator can delegate consent for the entire organization.

One final note is that you can accept the scopes back in the Authentication tab for the application. Navigating back and selecting Edit on the identity provider for the Authentication section allows you to modify permissions. When the organization admin can accept scopes for all users, a checkbox will appear and you can check Grant Admin Consent for Default Directory. Checking this box will allow the administrator to accept the scopes for all users in the current tenant directory (see Figure 7-8).

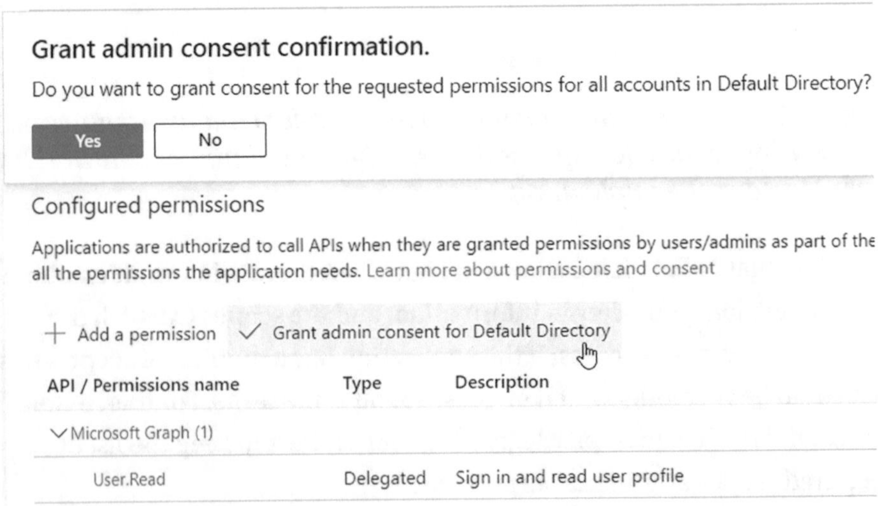

Grant admin consent confirmation.

Do you want to grant consent for the requested permissions for all accounts in Default Directory?

Yes	No

Configured permissions

Applications are authorized to call APIs when they are granted permissions by users/admins as part of the all the permissions the application needs. Learn more about permissions and consent

+ Add a permission   ✓ Grant admin consent for Default Directory

API / Permissions name	Type	Description
⌄ Microsoft Graph (1)		
User.Read	Delegated	Sign in and read user profile

Figure 7-8. *Admin consent can be granted from within the Authorization section of the application*

Once the administrator grants permissions, users will not be presented with a login dialog and any user signed in to the tenant can review the application. If a user is not signed in to the tenant or the request is anonymous, it will still require an authorized user to sign in to view the website.

Leverage the Microsoft Identity in Your Application

With the authorization requirement now in place on the Azure App Service, it is very straightforward to start working with the identity for your logged-in user as part of the Azure App Service.

Unfortunately, using the same app registration utilized for Authorization onto the platform service will not work. To remedy this situation, another app registration is required. Once this is created, you need to make a small code change and configure a couple of secrets. Then the Application will allow for user authorization from the signed-in Azure user.

One of the awesome features of the Azure App Service is the fact that the headers for your user claims are passed directly to the application. As your users authenticate, the OAuth tokens are stored and refreshed in a token store in Azure Storage, and the identity information is sent through the headers into the application.

Create an Additional App Registration

For this app registration, name the application something global like AuthorizeMicrosoftTenantUsers. Select the option for Accounts in Any Organizational Directory (...) and then enter a Web Redirect URI of your application localhost with a port, followed by /signin-microsoft.

While it seems tedious to do this for yet another endpoint, the two endpoints conflict when in the same app registration and the authorization will not work for your application (see Figure 7-9).

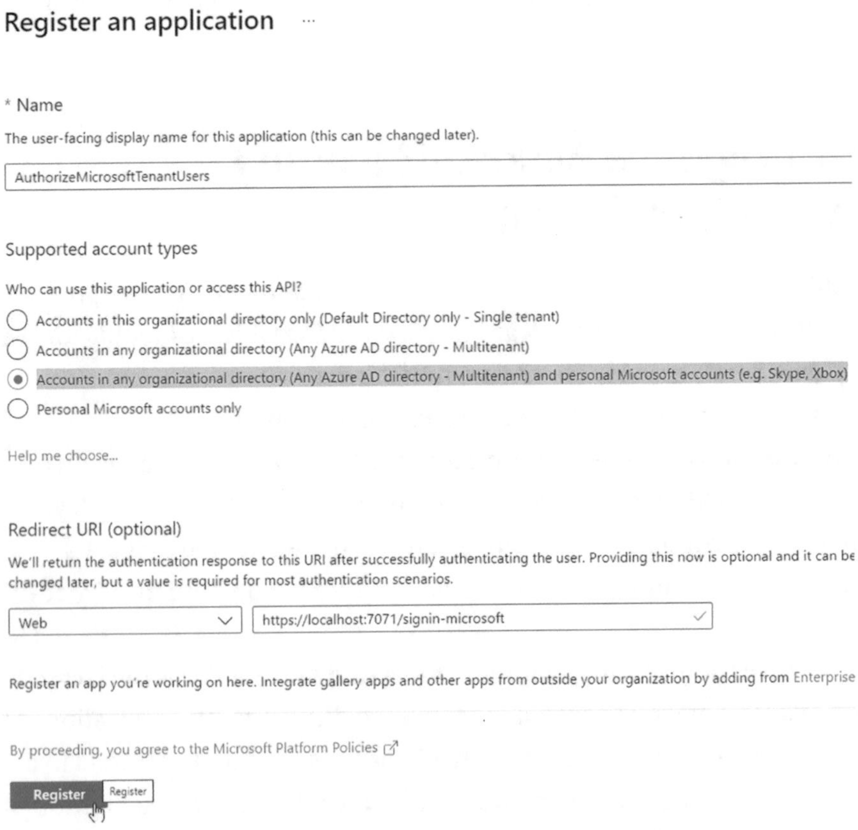

Register an application   ⋯

* Name

The user-facing display name for this application (this can be changed later).

AuthorizeMicrosoftTenantUsers

Supported account types

Who can use this application or access this API?

○ Accounts in this organizational directory only (Default Directory only - Single tenant)

○ Accounts in any organizational directory (Any Azure AD directory - Multitenant)

◉ Accounts in any organizational directory (Any Azure AD directory - Multitenant) and personal Microsoft accounts (e.g. Skype, Xbox)

○ Personal Microsoft accounts only

Help me choose...

Redirect URI (optional)

We'll return the authentication response to this URI after successfully authenticating the user. Providing this now is optional and it can be changed later, but a value is required for most authentication scenarios.

| Web ⌄ | https://localhost:7071/signin-microsoft | ✓ |

Register an app you're working on here. Integrate gallery apps and other apps from outside your organization by adding from Enterprise

By proceeding, you agree to the Microsoft Platform Policies ☐

Register   Register

Figure 7-9. *The second application registration is completed for the user authorization into the web application for registration on the app itself*

Add a Redirect URI to the App Registration

For the sign-in to work, the app registration needs to know where to redirect the OAuth workflow. In the previous step, the redirect for localhost was created, but an additional redirect is needed for the production app and another one for any slots as well. Get the URL of the production app and staging slot and append the same /signin-microsoft to the end of the URLs. Then add them as additional redirects under the Authentication blade on the app registration (see Figure 7-10).

Figure 7-10. *The User Authorization endpoint is added for the sign-in redirect on the production web application*

Get the Application (client) ID for this app registration from the Overview blade. You need it for authorization in the .NET Web application (see Figure 7-11).

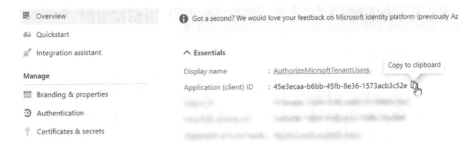

Figure 7-11.   *The Application (client) ID is critical to allow the authorization to work successfully*

Add a Client Secret to the App Registration

In addition to the application ID, you also need a client secret for the authorization to work. You will then store the Client ID and the Client Secret in your local user secrets. After deployment, you'll need to configure these in the app service for the solution to work as expected. Under Certificates & Secrets in the App Registrations blade, select + New Client Secret. Name the secret something like WebAuth and then add it with an expiration of an appropriate amount of time. When the secret is created, immediately record the value of the secret (this is the only time you can see it). The Secret ID is irrelevant; you only need the secret value (review Figure 7-12).

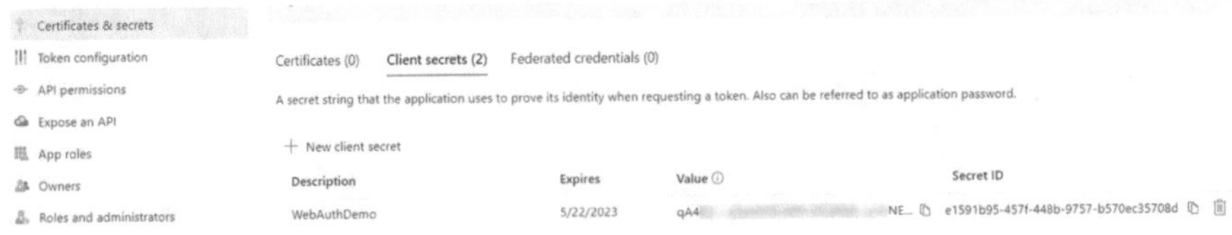

Figure 7-12.   *The client secret is created for use in the authorization code*

Add a NuGet Package

To make the Microsoft Authentication work in your .NET application, you need to add the `Microsoft.AspNetCore.Authentication.MicrosoftAccount` NuGet package to the project. Make sure to add the appropriate version to your application for the runtime of the application, whether that is 6, 7, or another version.

Add the Authentication Code to the Application

With the settings configured, you can now add the code to the application to ensure that the application can register users and utilize authorization on that user for specific roles in the application.

The following code must be uncommented or added to the solution in the `Program.cs` file to enable Microsoft authorization:

```
builder.Services.AddAuthentication().
AddMicrosoftAccount(options => {
    options.ClientId = builder.Configuration["MicrosoftSignIn:
    ClientId"];
    options.ClientSecret = builder.Configuration["MicrosoftSign
    In:ClientSecret"];
});
```

The best place to add the code is after this line of code: `builder.Services.AddDatabaseDeveloperPageExceptionFilter();`

In addition to adding the code, you must add the client ID and the client secret to the user secrets file, with entries to match the expected code to work from your local machine. Once deployed, you also need to have these values set in your app service configuration (or some combination that may include Azure Key Vault and/or Azure App Configuration).

```
"MicrosoftSignIn": {
    "ClientId": "your-client-id",
    "ClientSecret": "your-client-secret"
  }
```

Add Configuration Values to App Service and Slot

Make sure to add both values to both the Production and Slot App Configuration sections on the Azure App Service. If you fail to do this, the application will not load after deployment.

Register the Users

Run the application and validate that you can register your user identity with the application. Once that's done, you are able to leverage your user identity for authorization within the application.

Make sure to push all the changes and deploy the application. Don't forget to swap slots to get the latest version to production. You can then test your authorization schema on your deployed instance. The flow should prompt for the users to log in, similar to Figure 7-13.

Figure 7-13. *The login process is complete, and utilization of your identity via Microsoft Identity in the web application should now be working*

Service Principals

In contrast to a user identity, an identity known as a *service principal* might be utilized for assigning Role Based Access Control (RBAC) permissions, authentication, and other authorized activities within your Azure tenant. One drawback to a service principal is that anyone with the key and secret for a service principal can leverage it as a form of pass-through authentication (operating as the service principal, not as yourself).

Service principals are automatically created when an app registration is created. Once the service principal is created, the App Registration blade can be used to further modify the service principal.

One common use of a service principal is for deployment to Azure from a GitHub Action or from an Azure DevOps pipeline. In some cases, you may need to run an action that will deploy an entire volatile environment and then publish the application. In other cases, simply publishing the application will be enough. Even though you can publish the application via the publish profile, you may want to add the additional security for deployment of your application via a service principal.

Leverage a Service Principal in GitHub Actions

To be clear, the actual implementation from GitHub Actions is a bit beyond what you will likely encounter on the AZ-204 Exam. However, creating a service principal for access to your Azure tenant from GitHub Actions can be accomplished using the Azure CLI, and may be something you'll need to be in command of.

To set up a deployment from GitHub into your Azure tenant, begin by running the following command in the Azure CLI to generate a service principal (the create_service_principal.sh script is found in the resources for this chapter, also shown in Figure 7-14):

```
rg=az204-exam-ref-authnauthz
subId=$(az account show --query 'id' --output tsv)
appName=deployment-sp-20251231

az ad sp create-for-rbac \
--name $appName --role contributor
--scopes /subscriptions/$subId/resourceGroups/$rg
```

Figure 7-14. *The script can be easily run to create a new service principal in Azure*

Note   For this to work for a specific preexisting application, make sure to leverage the correct resource group when creating your service principal.

Once the script is completed, the output will show the important information about the app registration. You can save it from the output (shown in Figure 7-15), or you can always just get information that matters from the App Registration blade in the portal.

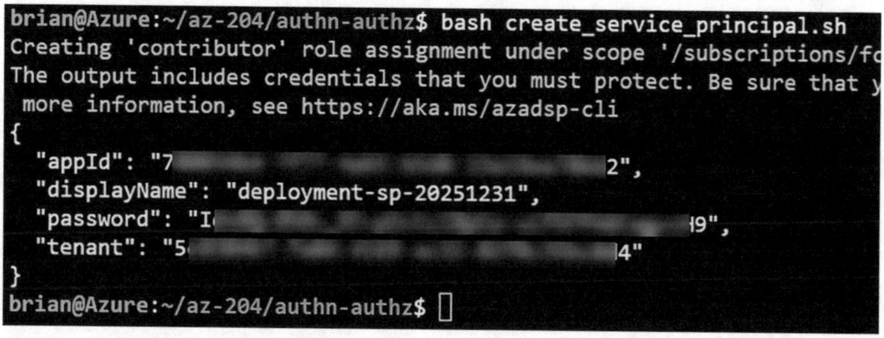

```
brian@Azure:~/az-204/authn-authz$ bash create_service_principal.sh
Creating 'contributor' role assignment under scope '/subscriptions/fd
The output includes credentials that you must protect. Be sure that y
 more information, see https://aka.ms/azadsp-cli
{
  "appId": "7                              2",
  "displayName": "deployment-sp-20251231",
  "password": "I                         49",
  "tenant": "5                          4"
}
brian@Azure:~/az-204/authn-authz$ 
```

Figure 7-15. *The output of the CLI command includes the important information about the service principal*

Add Federated Credentials

In order for the deployment from a pipeline to work, you have to set up a secret in the App Registration. To do this, navigate in the portal to the newly created app registration. On the App Registration blade for the service principal/app you just created, select the left-navigation item for Certificates & Secrets. Here you will set any certificates and secrets for the app, including the Federated Credentials required to execute deployments from a GitHub Action (see Figure 7-16).

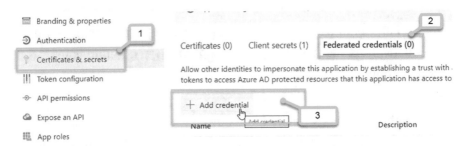

Figure 7-16. *The blade is shown to add secrets and certificates, including Federated Credentials, which are required for authorization from a GitHub Actions pipeline*

When adding a Federated Credential, you have many options, including GitHub Actions, Kubernetes, or even any other OpenID connect provider (see Figure 7-17).

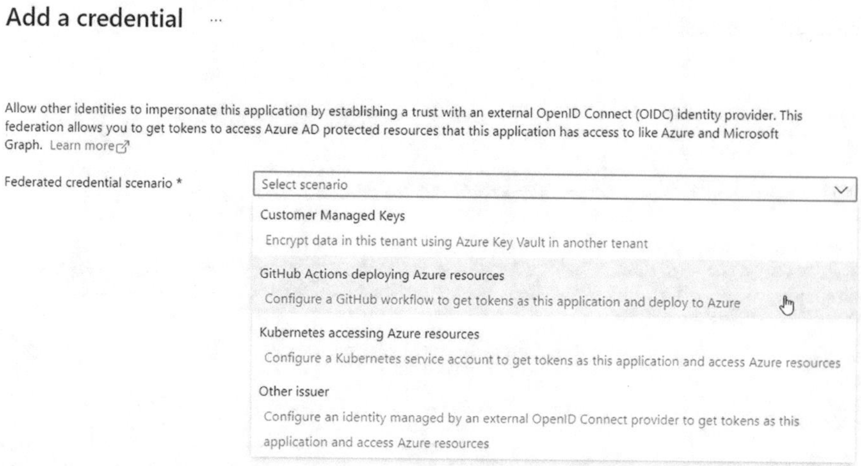

Add a credential ...

Allow other identities to impersonate this application by establishing a trust with an external OpenID Connect (OIDC) identity provider. This federation allows you to get tokens to access Azure AD protected resources that this application has access to like Azure and Microsoft Graph. Learn more⊡

Federated credential scenario *

Select scenario ⌄

Customer Managed Keys

Encrypt data in this tenant using Azure Key Vault in another tenant

GitHub Actions deploying Azure resources

Configure a GitHub workflow to get tokens as this application and deploy to Azure

Kubernetes accessing Azure resources

Configure a Kubernetes service account to get tokens as this application and access Azure resources

Other issuer

Configure an identity managed by an external OpenID Connect provider to get tokens as this application and access Azure resources

Figure 7-17. *Federated Credentials can be used for a deployment scenario or access from other services*

In the GitHub Actions connection, set information that will connect your specific account and repository for this Federated Credential. The Entity Type and Environment Name are critical to your GitHub Action to be able to deploy via this service principal. The critical path information is captured in the final Subject Identifier value (see Figure 7-18).

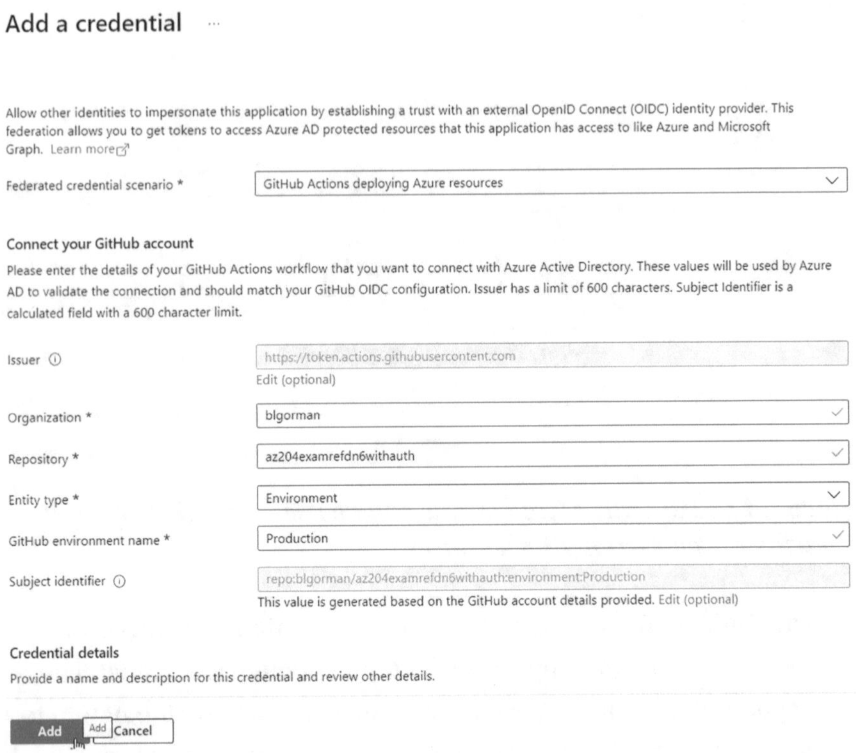

Add a credential   ...

Allow other identities to impersonate this application by establishing a trust with an external OpenID Connect (OIDC) identity provider. This federation allows you to get tokens to access Azure AD protected resources that this application has access to like Azure and Microsoft Graph. Learn more

Federated credential scenario *   GitHub Actions deploying Azure resources   ∨

Connect your GitHub account

Please enter the details of your GitHub Actions workflow that you want to connect with Azure Active Directory. These values will be used by Azure AD to validate the connection and should match your GitHub OIDC configuration. Issuer has a limit of 600 characters. Subject Identifier is a calculated field with a 600 character limit.

Issuer ⓘ   https://token.actions.githubusercontent.com
                                   Edit (optional)

Organization *   blgorman   ✓

Repository *   az204examrefdn6withauth   ✓

Entity type *   Environment   ∨

GitHub environment name *   Production   ∨

Subject identifier ⓘ   repo:blgorman/az204examrefdn6withauth:environment:Production
                                   This value is generated based on the GitHub account details provided. Edit (optional)

Credential details

Provide a name and description for this credential and review other details.

    Add   [Add] Cancel

***Figure 7-18.** The Federated Credential is correctly configured for the application service principal*

The rest of the deployment is handled by the YAML in the GitHub Action and is outside the scope of the AZ-204 Exam. However, the YAML would need to look similar to the following for deploying an ARM template to the resource group using the authorization created previously:

```
- name: 'Az CLI login'
      uses: azure/login@v1
      with:
        client-id: ${{ secrets.AZURE_CLIENT_ID }}
        tenant-id: ${{ secrets.AZURE_TENANT_ID }}
        subscription-id: ${{ secrets.AZURE_SUBSCRIPTION_ID }}
```

```
# Deploy ARM template
- name: Run ARM deploy
  uses: azure/arm-deploy@v1
  with:
    subscriptionId: ${{ secrets.AZURE_SUBSCRIPTION_ID }}
    resourceGroupName: ${{ secrets.AZURE_RG_NAME }}
    template: ./azure-deploy-dev-env.json
    parameters:
      webAppName=az204ref-${{ env.CURRENT_BRANCH }}-dev
```

Note that you would need to set secrets for the client ID created for the service principle (the Application ID on the App Registration blade) along with your tenant and subscription information. Again, this is outside of the scope of the AZ-204 Exam, so this is here just to help enhance the purpose of the client ID/app registration/service principal.

Managed Identities

Another common use for a service principal is to grant one or more deployed infrastructure or platform services access to other services in Azure. This can be accomplished with a type of service principal also known as a managed identity. Managed identities are the recommended resource used to grant specific permissions for one or more resources via RBAC to other resources within the Azure tenant.

One of the most common scenarios where managed identities are utilized is to allow an application to get secret information from Azure Key Vault and/or Azure App Config. This scenario is also covered in detail in the next chapter on implementing secure cloud solutions. In that chapter, you also learn more about managed identities.

Authorization Flows

Another important concept that you need to be in command of for the AZ-204 Exam is the ability to discern the correct authorization flow for your solution. Each of these authorization flows is examined in the next few sections.

Authorization Code

In the Authorization Code flow, a user typically starts by logging in to your web application. This application then sends a request to the authorization endpoint, which causes the user to redirect to the login endpoint and enter their credentials (and give any consent to scopes if necessary). The authorization endpoint then sends a token back to the web app to work on behalf of the user. The web app then sends the authorization token along with the application client ID and secret to the token endpoint, where everything is validated. Upon validation, the validated access token is sent to the web app and the app can then make requests with the access token.

More information about this flow (including a nice diagram of the flow) can be found at `https://learn.microsoft.com/azure/active-directory/develop/v2-oauth2-auth-code-flow`.

This workflow scenario is similar to utilization of authorization on the web application described earlier, where the users now have to log in to the Azure tenant in order to be able to access the application.

Client Credentials

In the client credentials authorization flow, an administrator preconfigures the authorization for the application and generally issues the client credentials flow for use between services or applications. This workflow allows the service to then be able to operate without a user present. More information about this workflow can be found at `https://learn.microsoft.com/azure/active-directory/develop/v2-oauth2-client-creds-grant-flow`.

This scenario is similar to utilization of a system-managed identity to allow an application to get secrets from Key Vault. The administrator sets the RBAC permissions against the managed identity and the application can get information regardless of the level of authorization for the user, or without a user being present in the case of services, WebJobs, or background processes.

Device Code

The Device Code workflow allows you to authorize a device on your solutions from another device. The easiest way to envision this process is any time you've utilized Amazon Prime, Hulu, YouTube, or another streaming service on your Smart TV and the service gave you a code that was displayed on the screen. You then logged in to the service from your laptop or smartphone and authorized the TV to utilize the service from your account. This type of authorization is also highly useful in IoT scenarios.

You can read more about the device code authorization flow at `https://learn.microsoft.com/azure/active-directory/develop/v2-oauth2-device-code`.

Implicit

The Implicit workflow is going away, so you won't want to use this on future applications. This workflow requires cookies on the client machine and is/was highly useful for working with single-page JavaScript applications to allow your solution to be more secure by not having refresh tokens that could be intercepted. The recommended flow is to migrate your SPA solutions to utilize the Authorization Code workflow.

You can read more about the implicit workflow as well as view the official workflow diagram at `https://learn.microsoft.com/azure/active-directory/develop/v2-oauth2-implicit-grant-flow`.

Integrated Windows

The Integrated Windows workflow is used with domain-joined machines, allowing them to authenticate with the Azure Active Directory. In this workflow, the token is granted to the machine and then the applications on the machine can leverage the user credentials. This is accomplished without any interaction from the user.

You can read more about the workflow and view an awesome visualization of this workflow at `https://learn.microsoft.com/azure/` `active-directory/develop/msal-authentication-flows#integrated-` `windows-authentication-iwa`.

Interactive and Non-Interactive

The difference between interactive and non-interactive workflows is whether or not a user is prompted for interaction. This could be signing in or providing additional information to resolve MFA or risky sign-on/conditional sign-on challenge questions.

In the non-interactive workflow, the system tries to do things without input from the user with regards to authorization. In a non-interactive workflow, if things require interaction then the interaction can be sent for input from the user.

The recommended approach is to try to work without interaction from the user and only utilize user interaction when necessary. This scenario typically utilizes token caching to avoid interaction with the user as much as possible.

On-Behalf-Of

In the On-Behalf-Of flow, a middleware application needs to act as the user to a third-party or other solution. In this scenario, the client calls to the application endpoint and the application then leverages the same user credentials as the client's logged-in user. This is done by getting the user access token and executing on behalf of the user. The application doesn't need to have any specific roles, and therefore only the access and permissions available to the client user are available to the executing middleware.

More information and a visualization of this workflow can be found at `https://learn.microsoft.com/azure/active-directory/develop/v2-oauth2-on-behalf-of-flow`.

Username/Password

The Username/Password workflow is also known as Resource Owner Password Credentials (ROPC). In this workflow, the password for the user is managed by the application. This workflow is therefore not very secure and you should try to avoid using it as long as another viable solution exists.

More information and a visualization of this workflow can be found at `https://learn.microsoft.com/azure/active-directory/develop/v2-oauth-ropc`.

Shared Access Signatures

Shared Access Signatures (SAS) are a critical part of giving temporary or delegated access to items in Azure Storage. SAS tokens were mentioned and discussed in Chapter 1 on Azure Blob Storage. SAS tokens are also critical when working with Event Hub and Service Bus in the final chapters of this book. The following is a general summary of what you need to know about SAS tokens in the scope of the AZ-204 Exam:

- Individual tokens generated off the account key cannot be revoked (the key can be rotated, however, invalidating the SAS token).

- Tokens have scope and permissions, as well as start and expiration dates.

- You should be able to discern the exact specifications from the token, including the type of storage, start and end dates, and permissions authorized by an SAS token.

- Tokens have a signature that is based on the key and token settings. Users trying to use an URL hijack attack on your tokens will not succeed, as the signature will not match.

- You can create policies at the account level to issue tokens en masse. This is both more secure and more manageable from an administrative viewpoint.

- Policies set the permissions, start and end dates, and what services are accessible for all tokens.

- You can revoke all tokens in a policy at once if there is a need to do so without having to rotate your account access keys.

- For Event Hub and Service Bus, you create SAS tokens to allow for publish, consume, and/or management permissions around your topics and subscriptions.

Identity and Authorization in Applications

The remainder of this chapter covers the utilization of the Microsoft Authentication Library (MSAL) and the Microsoft Graph SDK.

It is important to note that in order to work with either the MSAL library or the Microsoft Graph SDK, you must have an app registration set up in Azure.

Create the App Registration

If you are going to test this code with a desktop application or a console application, you should set up your application to have one public client with a redirect to `http://localhost`. This is not intuitive, since your application will be a desktop/console application without any web interaction.

Name your application, set the supported account types, and then create a public client/native redirect URI with the value of `http://localhost`, as shown in Figure 7-19.

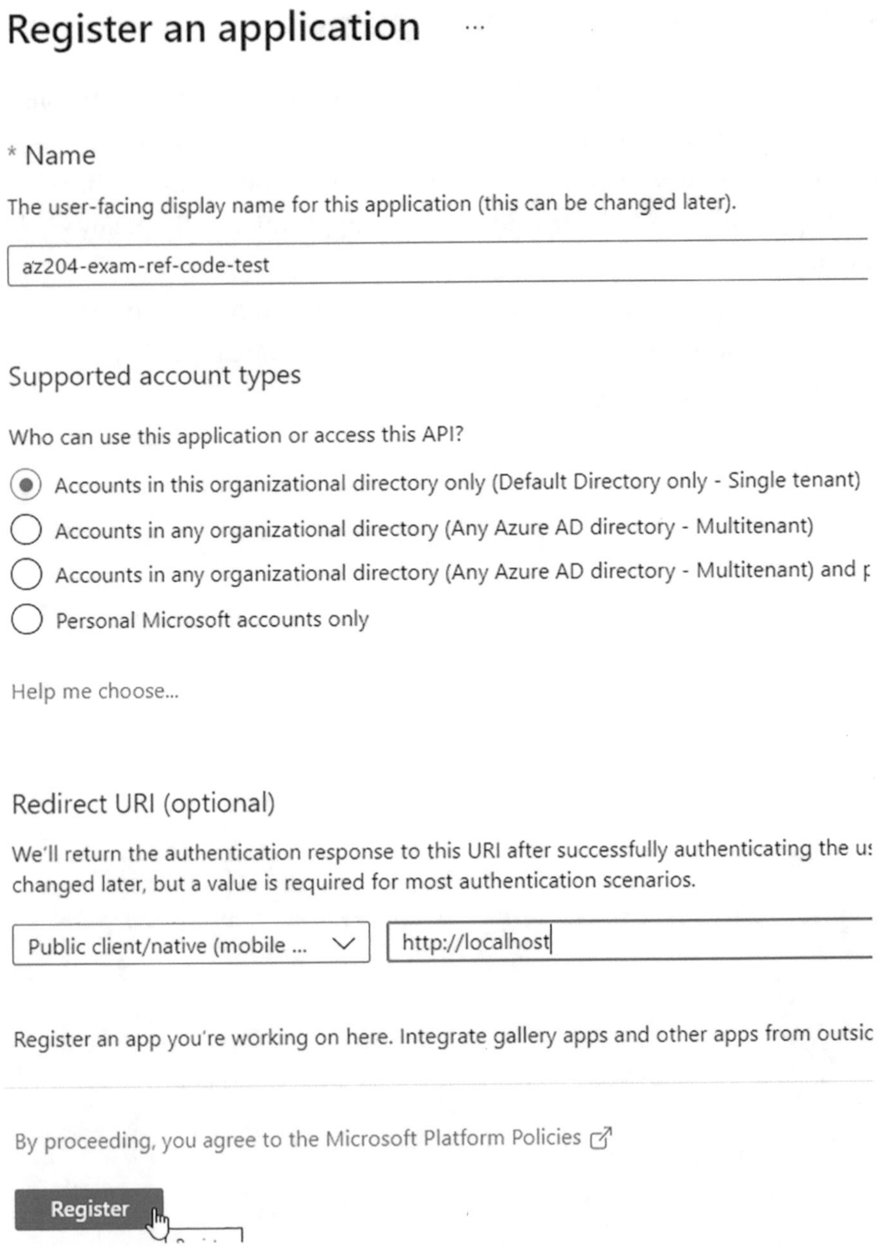

Register an application   ...

* Name

The user-facing display name for this application (this can be changed later).

az204-exam-ref-code-test

Supported account types

Who can use this application or access this API?

- (●) Accounts in this organizational directory only (Default Directory only - Single tenant)
- ( ) Accounts in any organizational directory (Any Azure AD directory - Multitenant)
- ( ) Accounts in any organizational directory (Any Azure AD directory - Multitenant) and ｆ
- ( ) Personal Microsoft accounts only

Help me choose...

Redirect URI (optional)

We'll return the authentication response to this URI after successfully authenticating the u:
changed later, but a value is required for most authentication scenarios.

| Public client/native (mobile ...   ∨ | http://localhost |

Register an app you're working on here. Integrate gallery apps and other apps from outsic

By proceeding, you agree to the Microsoft Platform Policies ⟋

Register

Figure 7-19. *The app registration for testing is easily configured with a public client and a redirect URI of* http://localhost

Once the application is registered, you need to note the application (client) ID and your tenant ID. Those will be two key values for working with code to integrate with Microsoft Identity in your code.

Working with the Microsoft Authentication Library (MSAL)

The solution files for this activity can be found in the repository for this book and are adapted based on materials found at https://learn. microsoft.com/azure/active-directory/develop/desktop-app- quickstart?pivots=devlang-uwp. However, key components of working with MSAL to get a user logged in are highlighted here. This application code is very minimal, but it is enough to get you authenticated in Azure and retrieve an authorization bearer token for your user account.

One notable piece of information is that you need the NuGet package for the Microsoft.Identity.Client.

Build the Application

The first step for this solution is to build the application using PublicClientApplicationBuilder. Utilize the following code to initialize the application variable:

```
//create the application:
var msalAPP = PublicClientApplicationBuilder
              .Create(clientId)
              .WithAuthority(AzureCloudInstance.AzurePublic,
              tenantId)
              .WithRedirectUri("http://localhost")
              .Build();
```

Note that this code creates the client application based on the client ID and the tenant ID. What's interesting is the authority location—`AzureCloudInstance.AzurePublic`. The scope dictates which cloud to use, as there are many sovereign cloud regions to choose from (see Figure 7-20).

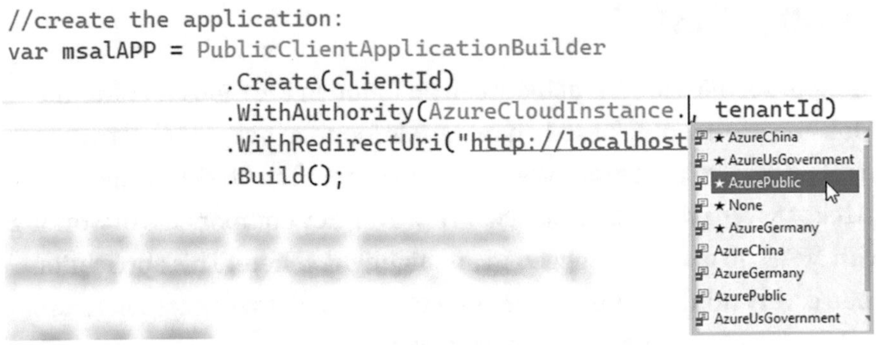

```
//create the application:
var msalAPP = PublicClientApplicationBuilder
            .Create(clientId)
            .WithAuthority(AzureCloudInstance.|, tenantId)
            .WithRedirectUri("http://localhost
            .Build();
```

Figure 7-20. The authority can be one of many public or sovereign clouds

Set the Scopes

Once you have created the application, you need to set the scopes for the permissions you are requesting. As with the choices earlier, there are many permissions (scopes) that you can leverage here, but the more you choose, the more consent you need from the user. For this application, the scopes are `User.Read` and `Email`, as shown in this code:

```
//set the scopes for user permissions:
string[] scopes = { "user.read", "email" };
```

When selecting scopes, you can choose delegated (user permissions) or application permissions. Typical user permissions allow you to do things with the users' account information. Application permissions are for things like agreements and interacting with other Azure Services (see Figure 7-21).

Request API permissions

×

< All APIs

Microsoft Graph
https://graph.microsoft.com/ Docs ⤢

What type of permissions does your application require?

Delegated permissions	Application permissions
Your application needs to access the API as the signed-in user.	Your application runs as a background service or daemon without a signed-in user.

Select permissions   expand all

🔍 Start typing a permission to filter these results

Permission	Admin consent required
> AccessReview	
> Acronym	
> AdministrativeUnit	
> AgreementAcceptance	
∨ Agreement	
☐ Agreement.Read.All ⓘ Read all terms of use agreements	Yes
☐ Agreement.ReadWrite.All ⓘ Read and write all terms of use agreements	Yes
> APIConnectors	

Figure 7-21. *Scopes can be user-based or application-based and give access to abilities for the authorized application against the user account or other Azure services*

Get Your Access Token

When the application runs, with the msalAPP and scopes ready to go, the code can easily get the access token with the following code:

```
//get the token
var result = await msalAPP.AcquireTokenInteractive(scopes).
ExecuteAsync();
```

Print the Token

You would not really want to print the token, but for this application, it won't hurt just to see it. This token is your full credential, so protect it as such. The token is already in the result variable, so just debug and review it or print it:

```
//print token
Console.WriteLine($"Your Token: {result.AccessToken}");
```

Run and Grant Permissions

With the code completed, run the solution and grant permissions, as shown earlier and again in Figure 7-22.

 Microsoft

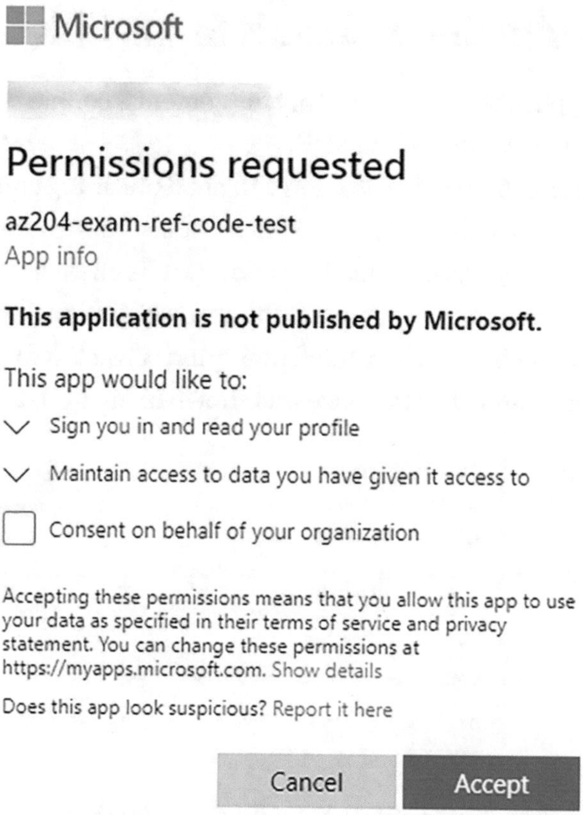

Permissions requested

az204-exam-ref-code-test
App info

This application is not published by Microsoft.

This app would like to:

∨   Sign you in and read your profile

∨   Maintain access to data you have given it access to

☐   Consent on behalf of your organization

Accepting these permissions means that you allow this app to use
your data as specified in their terms of service and privacy
statement. You can change these permissions at
https://myapps.microsoft.com. Show details

Does this app look suspicious? Report it here

Cancel   Accept

Figure 7-22. *The application asks for credentials and consent for the requested scopes when it is run*

The token prints as expected, as shown in Figure 7-23.

Figure 7-23. *The access token is retrieved as expected*

Working with the Microsoft Graph SDK

In the same application, you can easily implement a couple of changes to get information using the Graph SDK.

To get started, the app registration will need one thing configured. For this application, the code will use a Device Code authorization flow, and therefore the app registration needs to allow public client flows. To do this, enable it in the portal by going to the app registration, then selecting the Authentication blade. Then scroll down and select Yes for Enable the Following Mobile and Desktop Flows, as shown in Figure 7-24.

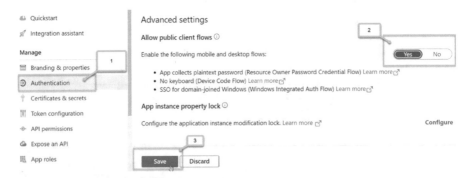

Figure 7-24. *Enabling public client flows so the device code authorization will work from the console app for Microsoft Graph*

Additionally, you need to bring in NuGet packages for `Microsoft.Graph`, `Microsoft.Graph.Core`, and `Azure.Identity` for this to work as expected.

Build the Application

Building the application utilizes the exact same code:

```
//create the application:
var graphAPP = PublicClientApplicationBuilder
            .Create(clientId)
```

```
.WithAuthority(AzureCloudInstance.AzurePublic,
tenantId)
.WithRedirectUri("http://localhost")
.Build();
```

Set the Scopes

Scopes are set exactly the same for this interaction:

```
//set the scopes for user permissions:
string[] scopes = { "user.read", "email" };
```

Create Device Code Credential

This workflow uses the Device Code credential. In this workflow, you have to navigate to the device code endpoint and then enter a code to continue. The credential is created by first composing credential options with the tenant and client IDs. Then create the credential with the options as a parameter:

```
//create the DeviceCodeCredential
var credentialOptions = new DeviceCodeCredentialOptions() {
TenantId = tenantId, ClientId = clientId };
var credential = new DeviceCodeCredential(credentialOptions);
```

Figure 7-25 shows the device code login request from the application.

Figure 7-25. *Using the device code flow requires navigating to a browser and entering a code, then logging in to your account*

Create the Graph Service Client

Once the credentials are set, you can create the client with a single line of code, passing the credentials and the scopes to the client constructor:

```
// Create a graph service client
var gsc = new GraphServiceClient(credential, scopes);
```

Get the Me Object

Finally, a simple call to the graph service client for the Me object will allow the code to get information about the logged-in user from Microsoft.Graph:

```
var myInfo = await gsc.Me.Request().GetAsync();
Console.WriteLine($"{myInfo.GivenName} ${myInfo.Surname}");
```

Figure 7-26 shows the expected output.

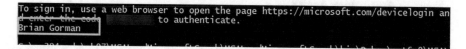

Figure 7-26. *The graph client gets information about the logged-in user and the app prints it, as expected*

Review Your Learning

As an additional challenge, consider the following questions and determine how you would approach potential solutions. You can find answers to these questions in Appendix A at the end of this book.

1) What is authentication? What is authorization? How are they different? Which one must exist for the other to work?

2) What are the various ways a user can satisfy MFA sign-in requirements? Are some more secure than others? When MFA is turned on, in what scenarios will the user always receive a second challenge for sign-in?

3) What are the four primary roles that can be used for subscription and/or resource group management? Which role should you give to a guest on your subscription? What about a guest on a specific resource group? What if the guest needs to modify resources in a specific resource group?

4) What is the purpose of an identity provider? What is a scope?

5) What are the various authorization flows? What is an example of each?

6) What is a service principal? Can you sign in to Azure using a service principal?

7) What are the various boundaries for Azure Cloud Offerings? What is a sovereign region? Can you cross boundaries with an Identity?

Complete the AZ-204: Implement User Authentication and Authorization

To fully learn the material, I recommend taking the time to also complete the MS Learn modules for implementing user authentication and authorization found here:

- Explore the Microsoft identity platform: `https://learn.microsoft.com/training/modules/explore-microsoft-identity-platform/`

- Implement authentication by using the Microsoft Authentication Library: `https://learn.microsoft.com/training/modules/implement-authentication-by-using-microsoft-authentication-library/`

- Implement Shared Access Signatures: `https://learn.microsoft.com/training/modules/implement-shared-access-signatures/`

- Explore Microsoft Graph: `https://learn.microsoft.com/training/modules/microsoft-graph/`

Chapter Summary

In this chapter, you learned about working with user access for authentication and authorization, as well as identity management. You also learned about working with identity in Azure with Microsoft Graph and MSAL using .NET.

After working through this chapter and the Microsoft Learn modules, you should be on track to be in command of the following concepts as you learn about Azure and prepare for the AZ-204 Exam:

- Authenticate and authorize users with the Microsoft identity platform

- Understand basic RBAC via Azure Active Directory, including the four main roles

- Work with Shared Access Signatures (also covered in Chapters 1, 12, and 13)

- Work with MSAL and Microsoft Graph via .NET using an app registration with the appropriate client and tenant IDs

In the next chapter, you learn about implementing secure cloud solutions with Azure Key Vault, the Azure App Service, and integration with managed identities and RBAC for users and platform service authorization within Azure.

CHAPTER 8

Implement Secure Cloud Solutions

Assuming you worked through the other chapters, it is likely that you have deployed resources to Azure, specifically around the Azure App Service. If you didn't work through the previous chapters, it's still likely that you have a pretty good handle on working with Azure App Services if you are planning to sit for the AZ-204 Exam. If so, then you are in a good place to start putting the finishing touches on the solution with some security and interaction within Azure Services.

If you didn't work through previous chapters or are fairly new to working with Azure App Services, review Chapter 4 on creating Azure App Service Web Apps before reading this chapter. Specifically, deploying the application from that chapter will position you with code for working with the Azure platform services targeted in this chapter.

As a TL/DR on that, if you get the starter files for this chapter and deploy to an Azure App Service, you will be ready to go. For the App Service, I recommend using an S1 Tier with slots so you can see the secrets and settings in various environments. However, if you want to do this with an F1 tier for cost considerations, you can do so and just utilize the secrets from your single Production slot. Of course the free tier will not have slots so you won't have any slot swapping or deploying to staging in that scenario.

© Brian L. Gorman 2023
B. L. Gorman, *Developing Solutions for Microsoft Azure Certification Companion*, Certification Study Companion Series, https://doi.org/10.1007/978-1-4842-9300-3_8

As another reminder, the solution files leverage an Azure SQL Server for Identity and Entities, so you need to ensure that is also set up with the correct connection string information in the App Service Connection Strings settings.

As you work through this chapter, you'll get a chance to enhance the default web application to add integration with the Azure App Configuration, and then ultimately to leverage secrets from the Azure Key Vault. Both platform services require authorization and Role Based Access Control (RBAC). As you'll see later in the chapter, the Azure Key Vault will also utilize additional policies for various levels of access to secrets within the vault.

Through the sample application code, you will see how to connect your user and the provisioned app service to the Azure App Configuration. You'll also learn about managed identities, where you'll see how to connect your web applications and developers to get secrets from your Azure Key Vault or settings from the app configuration on an as-needed basis.

The three services and resource types mentioned previously are the main learning goals for this section of the AZ-204 Exam. By the end of this chapter, combined with the identity information from the previous chapter, you will be in a very good place to develop secure applications within Azure.

As Azure Key Vault and Azure App Configuration both require the utilization of managed identities for authorization, the first thing you need to be in command of is what managed identities are and how to use them in your Azure tenant.

Managed Identities

Within Azure, there are two different types of managed identities for use in your solutions. The first type of managed identity is the system-assigned identity. The second type is the user-assigned identity.

System-Assigned Identities

System-assigned managed identities are useful when you have a one-to-many relationship where you have one application that needs to have RBAC permissions on one or more other services. System-assigned identities are enabled on the Identity blade for the service (such as App Service, Function Apps, Azure App Config, Cosmos DB, and Virtual Machines).

Once you've enabled an identity on an Azure service, that identity can be used as a principal within Azure to administer role-based access to other services. With system-assigned identities, if you delete the service, the identity will also be deleted, thereby removing any associated permissions since no identity remains for authorization.

Creating a system-managed identity for a resource is simple, as is shown in Figure 8-1.

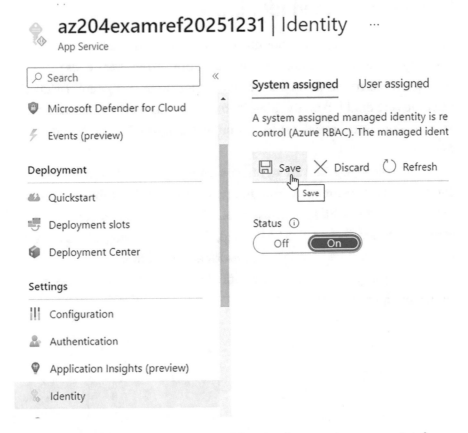

Figure 8-1. *It's easy to turn on an identity for any Azure service from the Service blade, under the Identity left-navigation item*

After creating the system-managed identity, the app service will then be able to connect to other resources in Azure with appropriate permissions via RBAC.

Later in the chapter, a system-managed identity such as the one created previously, will be required to authorize the app service for permissions in both the Azure App Configuration and Azure Key Vault. If you want, you can go ahead and create the managed identity now on your Azure App Service.

User-Assigned Identities

User-Assigned identities are useful when you have a many-to-many relationship between resources and services in Azure and the permissions that they need.

For example, consider a fleet of virtual machines (VMs) that are serving your database layer for a critical line-of-business application. In this scenario, you might need to authorize all VMs to have access to read secrets from Key Vault for working with encrypted columns or possibly your applications may need to interact with Azure Storage or another Azure service. Since each machine needs the exact same permissions, creating one-off system-assigned identities would be tedious and error-prone. Additionally, any new machine would need to also create each permission individually for every system-managed identity. Therefore, creating a user-assigned identity is ideal in this scenario. With a user-assigned identity, you can create the identity and assign all permissions to the single identity, then just associate the shared user-assigned identity to each appropriate resource.

To use a user-assigned identity, you must first generate a new user-assigned identity, which you might do with the Azure CLI. The following script could be used to generate an identity:

```
rg=az204-exam-ref-securesolutions
name=fleetVMSIdentity
az identity create --name $name --resource-group $rg
```

You could then assign the identity to appropriate resources by selecting the managed identity in the portal on each resource, or by running another script to assign the identity to the appropriate resources.

User-assigned identities have a lifespan that is not dependent on the resources to which they are assigned. Even if every VM in this scenario were deleted, the identity would live on, as would its associated permissions in the Azure tenant. Therefore, if you are cleaning up resources that use this identity and all of the associated resources are deleted, you must also delete the user-assigned managed identity resource to prevent the identity and permissions from remaining orphaned and active in your tenant, which could pose a security risk.

This book does not go deeper into creating user-managed identities. The official Microsoft Learn material for this chapter does include the "Implement Managed Identities" learning module, which has extensive information on utilizing user-managed identities with virtual machines, and is therefore a great place to learn more about user-managed identities.

Azure Key Vault

Keeping information secret is paramount in modern applications. It is commonly accepted that information—such as connection strings, passwords, third-party API keys, and other critical secrets—should never be directly placed into your source code or checked into your repository at GitHub or any other remote repository.

Additional security considerations are also present with certificates used for secure communication and authentication over the web via Secure Socket Layer (SSL) communications and Transport Layer Security (TLS). These certificates have to be protected and also need to be maintained.

A final area of concern are the keys used to encrypt documents, drives, Azure resource data, and columns in databases. These encryption keys are also critical to both protect and maintain.

Azure Key Vault is an Azure resource that is designed to provide a secure, centralized location for managing your keys, secrets, and certificates.

When creating an Azure Key Vault, you need to name the vault a unique name for use as part of the domain name in the pattern `https://your-vault-name.vault.azure.net`. All of the resources in the vault will have a URI from this domain.

As with any other resource, you also need to choose the subscription, resource group, and region for the deployment of the vault (see Figure 8-2).

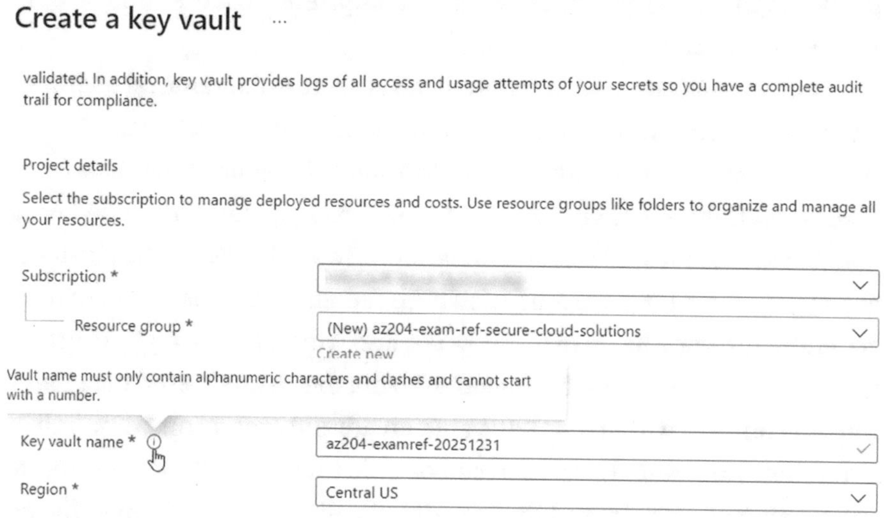

Create a key vault ⋯

validated. In addition, key vault provides logs of all access and usage attempts of your secrets so you have a complete audit trail for compliance.

Project details

Select the subscription to manage deployed resources and costs. Use resource groups like folders to organize and manage all your resources.

Subscription *	⌄
Resource group *	(New) az204-exam-ref-secure-cloud-solutions ⌄
	Create new

Vault name must only contain alphanumeric characters and dashes and cannot start with a number.

Key vault name * ⓘ	az204-examref-20251231 ✓
Region *	Central US ⌄

Figure 8-2. Creating a vault begins with the subscription, resource group, and vault name

Centralized Storage

While it is possible to localize secrets and thereby keep them off of developer machines and out of your Git repositories, some solutions do not centralize this functionality. Even if the solution is centralized, it is not necessarily secured with full RBAC to prevent unauthorized access.

With Azure Key Vault, you can create a solution where only a few trusted members of your organization ever have direct access to the value of a secret, certificate, or key. This is a great thing for both the team and the developers. Additional controls can be put in place with the centralized storage solution to ensure that rotation of keys has a minimal impact on any applications or resources that rely on the key, secret, or certificate.

The centralized location of the Azure Key Vault provides an extra layer of protection knowing that a custom solution was not implemented for a specific application that could be lost or compromised if the codebase is corrupted or stolen.

Another consideration for centralized storage is the removal of any specific knowledge requirements to manage the secrets. For example, if all of your secrets are stored in the etcd vaults for your Kubernetes clusters (all Kubernetes clusters have a default key-value store called etcd available to them where secrets can be stored specifically for the cluster), then anyone who needs to administer the secrets would also need to have an underlying knowledge of Kubernetes, and would also need to know how to manage secrets in the cluster utilizing the cluster's etcd backing store. In contrast, with Azure Key Vault, an administrator can know little or nothing about Kubernetes and still be able to manage the secrets for the organization effectively, and the containers within the Kubernetes clusters just need to communicate with Azure Key Vault effectively to utilize the secrets.

Azure Key Vault Tiers

There are two tiers that you can select from when creating an Azure Key Vault. The first tier is the Standard Key Vault, and the second tier is the Premium Key Vault. Unlike most offerings in Azure, the pricing for both tiers is similar, so your selection will mostly come down to what you want to do with the Key Vault service. Selecting the tier is available when you create the vault, as shown in Figure 8-3.

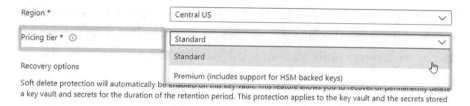

Figure 8-3. The Pricing tier is selected during creation of the key vault

Standard Key Vault

The Standard Key Vault is used to provide protection for your keys, certificates, and secrets using a software-based encryption key.

Premium Key Vault

The Premium Key Vault can provide the software-based encryption key and can also utilize Hardware Security Modules (HSMs) to back the encryption. While this is greatly simplified and not all-encompassing, you can think of this as something like a specific serial number from a tamper-proof, isolated hard drive that is leveraged for generating encryption keys. Without this additional security measure available, the decryption of the information cannot be performed. Only when the HSM is available for validation can the key be decrypted.

Data Retention

With Key Vault, you can select the ability to retain data for a specific number of days, and you can also specify whether you want extra protection to prevent accidental purging of data. The default settings are 90 days of retention with purge protection disabled. Minimum retention is 7 days.

You should be advised that enabling purge protection means you can't completely delete a vault or any of its data for that minimum number of days, since the purge protection will prevent the data from getting deleted until the soft-delete minimum number of days have passed. Additionally, you cannot change the policy to disable purge protection once the vault is created with purge protection enabled (see Figure 8-4).

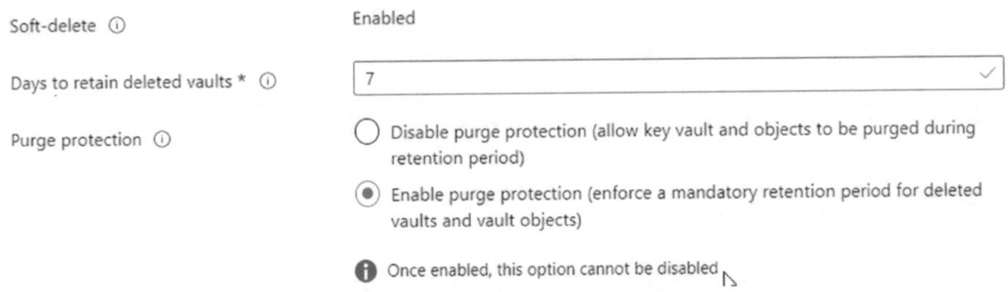

Soft-delete ⓘ   Enabled

Days to retain deleted vaults * ⓘ   7 ✓

Purge protection ⓘ   ◯ Disable purge protection (allow key vault and objects to be purged during retention period)

◉ Enable purge protection (enforce a mandatory retention period for deleted vaults and vault objects)

ℹ Once enabled, this option cannot be disabled

Figure 8-4. A vault is created with a minimum of 7 days of retention time and when purge protection is enabled it cannot be disabled

Although Figure 8-4 shows the purge protection on, when you are on a trial subscription or just creating a temporary resource for learning purposes, I recommend leaving the setting on Disable Purge Protection so that you can clean up your resources when you are done testing/learning.

Access Policy

The Access Policy is the most important functionality of the Key Vault for allowing other resources and users to review, modify, or delete information from the vault. There are two permission models to choose from—Vault Access Policy and Azure Role-Based Access Control.

If you want to manage access policies directly within the vault, or when you just want to manage vault secrets for an application, then select the Vault Access Policy. If you want to allow direct access to manage vault secrets across multiple vaults or provide the ability to set various levels of access for different resource groups, subscriptions, or management groups, then use the RBAC-Based Access Control. Choosing the Azure RBAC Access Control will eliminate the ability to define any access or policies when creating the vault.

When creating the vault with a vault access policy, you can set the permission model and you can also give specific access for resources like virtual machines, ARM templates, and Disk Encryption.

Additionally, during the vault creation, you can set access policies for user principals as well as system- or user-managed identities. By default, the subscription owner will be listed with permissions on Keys, Secrets, and Certificates. While you can add other principals with access here, you can also manage policies after vault creation (see Figure 8-5).

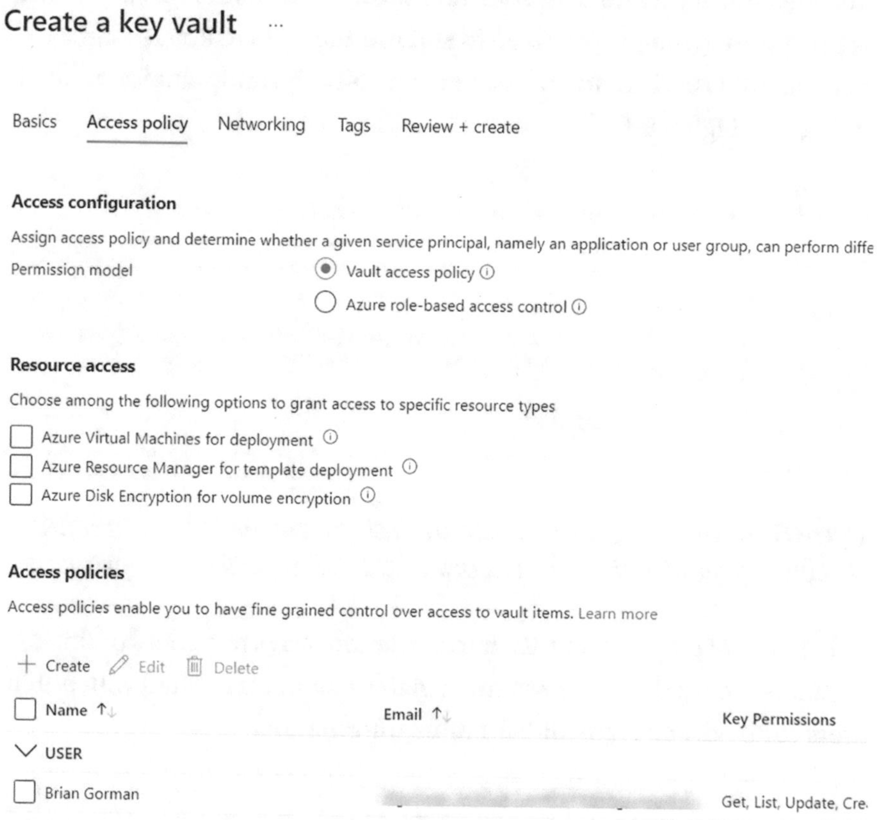

Create a key vault   ⋯

Basics   **Access policy**   Networking   Tags   Review + create

Access configuration

Assign access policy and determine whether a given service principal, namely an application or user group, can perform diffe

Permission model   ⦿ Vault access policy ⓘ

                                      ◯ Azure role-based access control ⓘ

Resource access

Choose among the following options to grant access to specific resource types

☐ Azure Virtual Machines for deployment ⓘ
☐ Azure Resource Manager for template deployment ⓘ
☐ Azure Disk Encryption for volume encryption ⓘ

Access policies

Access policies enable you to have fine grained control over access to vault items. Learn more

＋ Create   ✎ Edit   🗑 Delete

☐ Name ↑↓   Email ↑↓   Key Permissions

∨ USER

☐ Brian Gorman   Get, List, Update, Cre.

Figure 8-5. *The Key Vault is created with a vault access policy and default policies and access*

Network Access

As with other Azure resources, you can create the Key Vault with public access, or you can only allow access to the vault via your private Azure networks. You can also utilize the private endpoint to allow a private connection to the Key Vault on your network.

If you do create a private endpoint, you need to have created your virtual network with a DNS Zone, and then you can set the endpoint to be integrated into a private DNS zone for routing your traffic. Failure to create the private zone means you need to add routing rules to any resources directing traffic and/or add a host file to resolve the endpoint for network routing (see Figure 8-6).

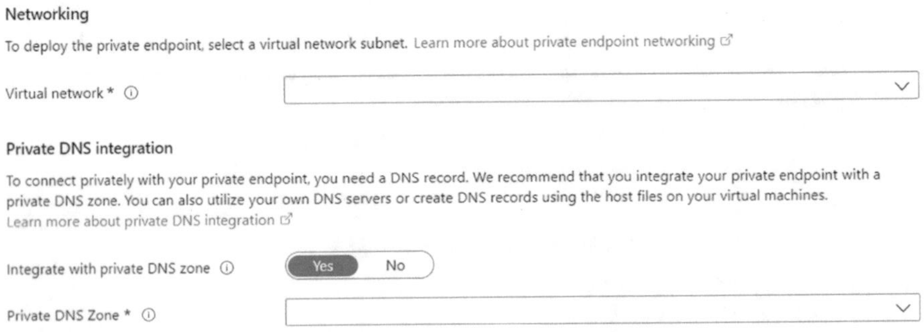

Networking

To deploy the private endpoint, select a virtual network subnet. Learn more about private endpoint networking ☐

Virtual network * ⓘ

Private DNS integration

To connect privately with your private endpoint, you need a DNS record. We recommend that you integrate your private endpoint with a private DNS zone. You can also utilize your own DNS servers or create DNS records using the host files on your virtual machines. Learn more about private DNS integration ☐

Integrate with private DNS zone ⓘ   `Yes` No

Private DNS Zone * ⓘ

Figure 8-6. *Creating a private endpoint for the vault recommends utilizing a prebuilt virtual network and DNS zone to work properly*

For ease of creation for this demonstration, no private networking or endpoints are used. The vault shown in this chapter is created with public access enabled. See Figure 8-7 for more information.

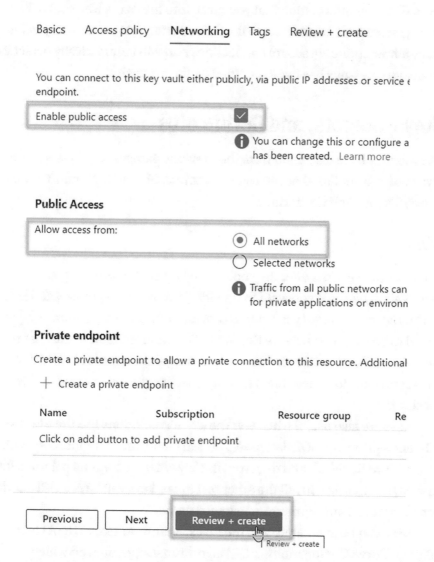

Create a key vault   ...

Basics   Access policy   **Networking**   Tags   Review + create

You can connect to this key vault either publicly, via public IP addresses or service e
endpoint.

Enable public access   ☑

            🛈 You can change this or configure a
              has been created. Learn more

Public Access

Allow access from:
            ◉ All networks
            ○ Selected networks

            🛈 Traffic from all public networks can
              for private applications or environn

Private endpoint

Create a private endpoint to allow a private connection to this resource. Additional

  + Create a private endpoint

Name	Subscription	Resource group	Re

Click on add button to add private endpoint

Previous	Next	**Review + create**

                        Review + create

Figure 8-7. *The Key Vault is created with public access enabled on all
networks*

Data Encryption

By default, all information that you place into the Azure Key Vault will be encrypted at rest. In addition to the default encryption, Azure Key Vault only allows traffic via secure connections and will automatically detect if a transport message has been modified while in transit.

Keys, Secrets, and Certificates

As you may have discerned from the previous paragraphs, there are three types of information that you can protect in an Azure Key Vault. They are Keys, Secrets, and Certificates.

Keys

Many Azure services offer the choice of using an Azure-managed encryption key or, if you want to provide your own, a user-managed key. In any scenario where you want to provide your own encryption key, you need to do this via the Azure Key Vault. For example, later in the chapter, you'll see how to create an Azure App Configuration resource, which can be set to allow for a user-managed key, just like the one created in this section.

Keys are also useful when you want to use solutions like the Always-On encryption in a SQL database. You can create an encryption key within your Azure Key Vault and then use that key when encrypting columns from any SQL Table. As with all the other resources, keys will have a URI, so you need to use an appropriate and allowed name.

Keys can be generated with the Rivest Shamir Adleman (RSA) or Elliptic Curve Cryptography (ECC) algorithm. Depending on which algorithm you choose, you can also choose the key size or curve name. Either type provides an optional activation date and an optional expiration date. The key can also be set as enabled or disabled. Additionally, you can put tags on the keys to group them logically for your own records. In general, they both have equivalent protection, but ECC uses a shorter key, which can lead to better performance.

A final option lets you create an automatic rotation policy, but you need to remember to choose this option with caution. A rotation policy is great for Azure resources that will automatically utilize the new key, but this could cause some significant management for applications or databases that wouldn't just automatically accept the new key. During rotation, you can set the automation to be enabled or disabled. You also set the amount of time the policy will be valid and configure the rotation time. Figure 8-8 shows the blade to create a rotation policy.

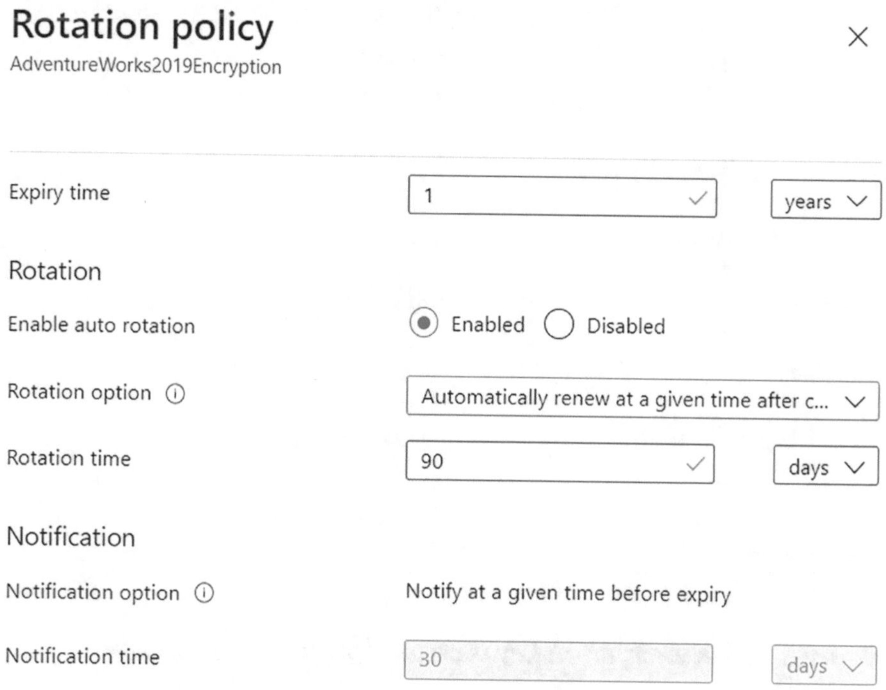

Rotation policy   ✕
AdventureWorks2019Encryption

Expiry time	1	✓	years ∨

Rotation

Enable auto rotation	⦿ Enabled ◯ Disabled		
Rotation option ⓘ	Automatically renew at a given time after c... ∨		
Rotation time	90	✓	days ∨

Notification

Notification option ⓘ	Notify at a given time before expiry		
Notification time	30		days ∨

Figure 8-8. *The rotation policy can be created to rotate the key for a specific policy length at specified intervals if desired*

Generating a key without a rotation policy for use in encrypting database columns is shown in Figure 8-9.

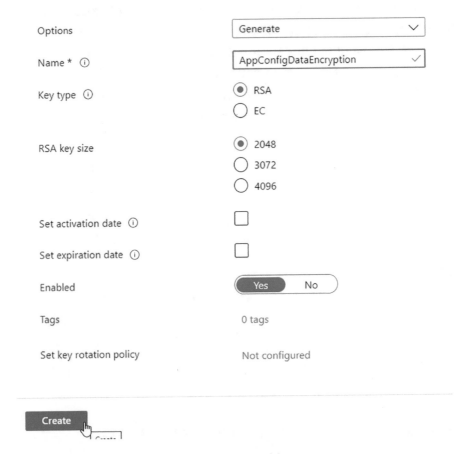

Figure 8-9. *An encryption key is created for use in always-on encryption*

Once created, the key can be easily managed in the Azure Portal, and users or services can access the key via the vault policies (policy management is explained later in the chapter).

Secrets

Secrets are likely the most common resource that application developers need to work with in an Azure Key Vault. Secrets include any information in your application that needs to be configured but protected, such as connection strings, API keys, IP addresses, or any other volatile secret information. Secrets are stored as text and can be easily versioned.

You can create secrets in the portal, via automation, through the REST API, or via the Azure CLI. Using the Azure CLI to create secrets is part of the official material in the Microsoft Learn modules, and you should make sure to run through that information to be familiar with the commands. In this book, you learn how to create a secret using the portal, as shown in Figure 8-10.

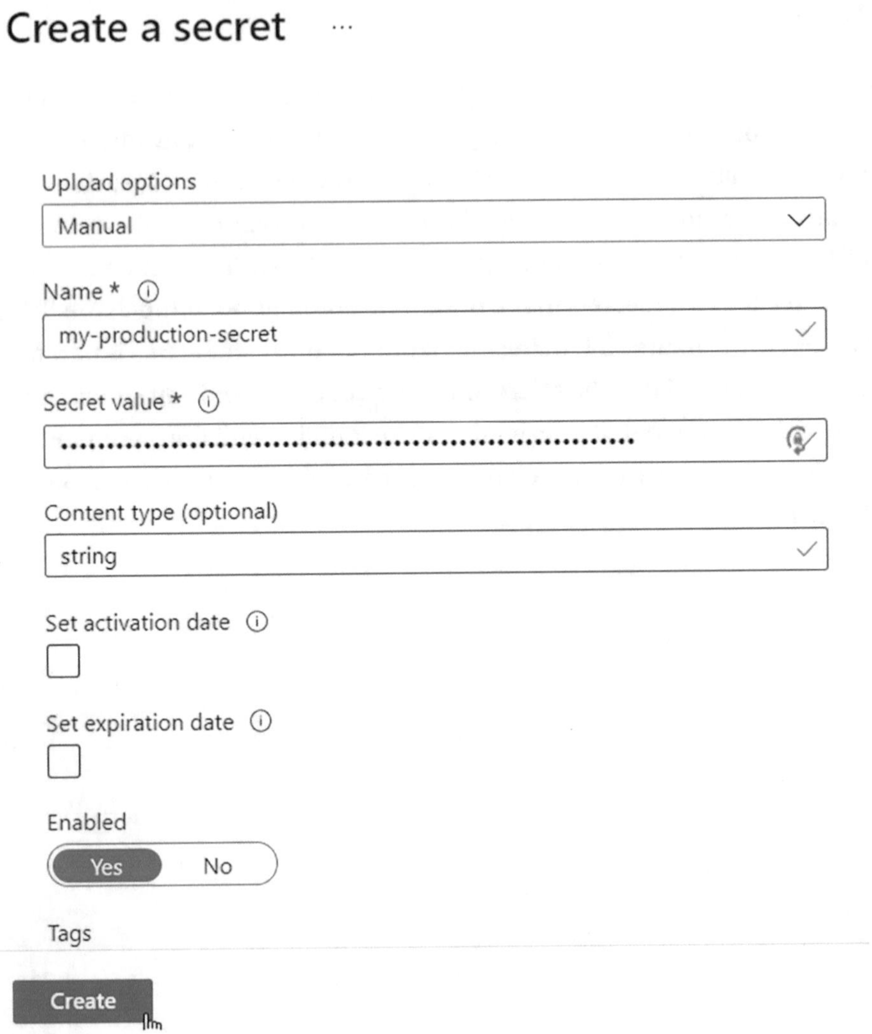

Create a secret   ...

Upload options

Manual

Name * ⓘ

my-production-secret

Secret value * ⓘ

••

Content type (optional)

string

Set activation date ⓘ

☐

Set expiration date ⓘ

☐

Enabled

Yes   No

Tags

Create

Figure 8-10. A secret is created in the Key Vault with the name my-production-secret

As with the key, the secret can have an optional start and end date and can be set to enabled or disabled during creation. The secret can also be tagged for organizational purposes.

Once the secret is created, it can be viewed through commands or via the portal by authorized users, but the value is immutable. If the value needs to change, a new version of the secret needs to be created. You can allow secrets to be used with multiple versions of the secret active at the same time. Each version of the secret will have its own URI based on the version number of the secret. If no version number is specified, then the most-recently-created secret is selected. Previous versions of the secret must be specified by version in the URI for utilization. To get the full secret identifier, browse to the secret in the vault and then select the version. Each version gets its own secret identifier (see Figure 8-11).

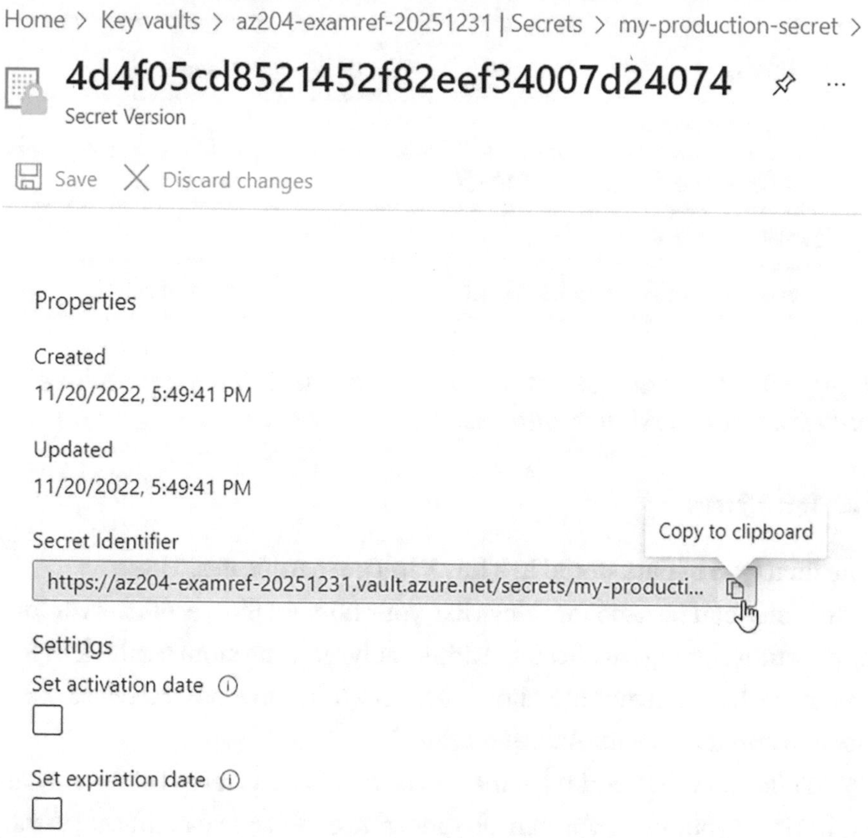

Home > Key vaults > az204-examref-20251231 | Secrets > my-production-secret >

4d4f05cd8521452f82eef34007d24074 ✗ ⋯
Secret Version

💾 Save   ✕ Discard changes

Properties

Created
11/20/2022, 5:49:41 PM

Updated
11/20/2022, 5:49:41 PM

Secret Identifier   Copy to clipboard

https://az204-examref-20251231.vault.azure.net/secrets/my-producti... 📋

Settings

Set activation date ⓘ
☐

Set expiration date ⓘ
☐

Figure 8-11. Each version of a secret has its own secret identifier and can be retrieved in the portal

To invalidate a secret with no expiration date, set the secret as disabled via commands or from the portal. A secret set to disabled or with an expiration date in the past can no longer be retrieved for utilization by applications or systems within Azure. (Figure 8-12 shows the original secret set to disabled.)

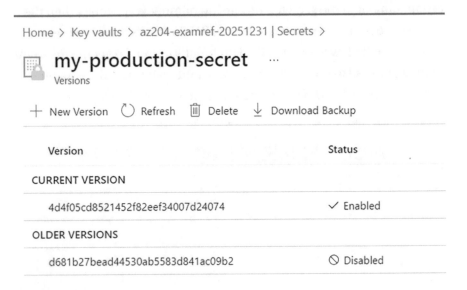

Figure 8-12. *A vault secret is shown with multiple versions where only the latest version is enabled*

Certificates

The final type of data stored in a Key Vault are certificates. These certificates can be used for things like your domain SSL certificates or for application signing certificates. Additionally, you can store certificates for use in public client authorization (such as IoT, web, or other devices that need to connect to your Azure solutions).

While you will likely be adding official certificates created at a certificate authority to your vault, you can also generate a self-signed certificate within the Key Vault for use in testing and other non-public scenarios.

To create the certificate, you must give it a valid name (as with other vault resources). Additionally, you must provide a full "X.500" distinguished name for the certificate, add any DNS names to the certificate as required, give it a validity period, and set the content type for the certificate (see Figure 8-13).

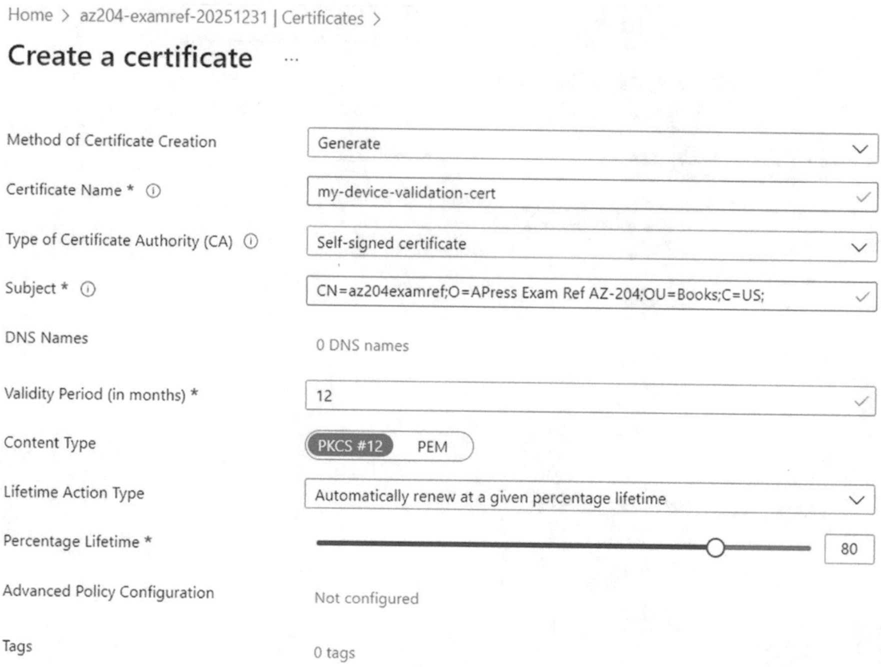

Home > az204-examref-20251231 | Certificates >

Create a certificate   ...

Method of Certificate Creation	Generate
Certificate Name * ⓘ	my-device-validation-cert
Type of Certificate Authority (CA) ⓘ	Self-signed certificate
Subject * ⓘ	CN=az204examref;O=APress Exam Ref AZ-204;OU=Books;C=US;
DNS Names	0 DNS names
Validity Period (in months) *	12
Content Type	PKCS #12 PEM
Lifetime Action Type	Automatically renew at a given percentage lifetime
Percentage Lifetime *	80
Advanced Policy Configuration	Not configured
Tags	0 tags

Figure 8-13. *A self-signed certificate is easily generated in the Azure Key Vault*

Additional options exist to auto-renew the certificate once the expiration date is approaching and more options for an advanced policy configuration can be added. Advanced policy configuration allows for things like changing the key size, reusing the key, choosing the key generation algorithm, and making the key exportable (see Figure 8-14).

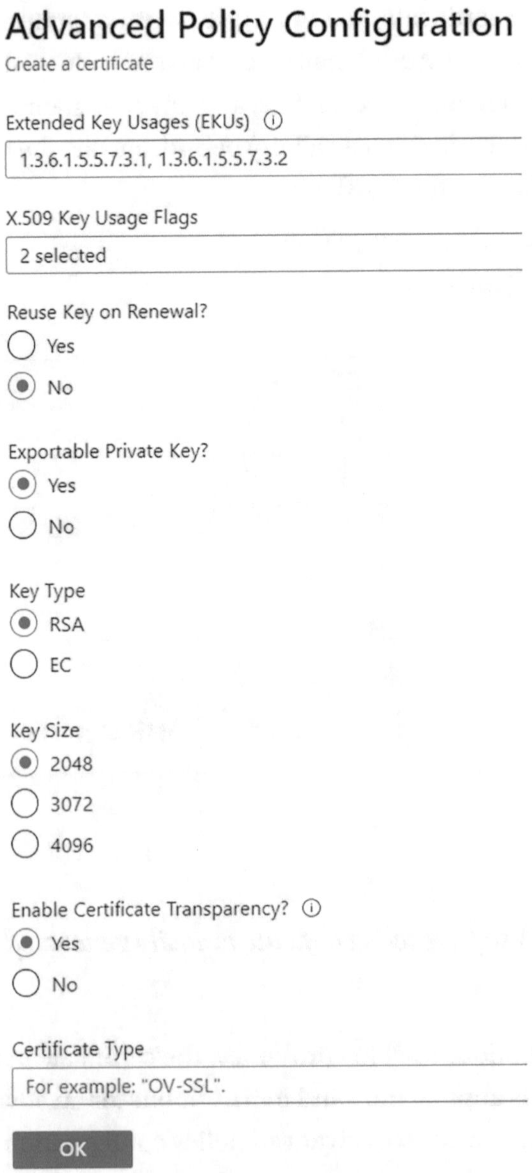

Advanced Policy Configuration

Create a certificate

Extended Key Usages (EKUs) ⓘ

1.3.6.1.5.5.7.3.1, 1.3.6.1.5.5.7.3.2

X.509 Key Usage Flags

2 selected

Reuse Key on Renewal?

○ Yes

⦿ No

Exportable Private Key?

⦿ Yes

○ No

Key Type

⦿ RSA

○ EC

Key Size

⦿ 2048

○ 3072

○ 4096

Enable Certificate Transparency? ⓘ

⦿ Yes

○ No

Certificate Type

For example: "OV-SSL".

OK

Figure 8-14. *Additional options for certificate generation can be optionally configured when necessary*

Note that it can take a few minutes to generate a new certificate in Azure.

Access Policies

When utilizing the Azure Vault Policies to manage your access, you need to know exactly which policies are necessary and for which user or applications.

Policy management allows you to give specific permissions on one or more of the storage types to any principal. You can get as granular as you need to at the permissions level within the vault policies. It is important to note, however, that this policy assignment means that any principal with the policy set to allow access can do this for all of the keys, secrets, or certificates in that vault. For example, the policies cannot be configured for specific secrets so an application with permission to "get" a secret can get any secret in the vault, not just one specific secret.

Therefore, if you need to segregate applications from secrets, the safest approach is to create separate vaults for the various security levels. For example, you might create a vault for each environment, so that there is never any concern that a test application is reading a production value.

Create an Access Policy

When you're managing access through the vault policies and it's time to give access to one of your secrets, certificates, or keys, you must create the appropriate access via a new policy. Start by navigating to the Access Configuration blade in the vault. Once on the Configuration blade, you can change your permission model or grant default access to a few resources as was available during creation. To create policies in the vault policies strategy, just click the Go to Access Policies button. Here you will see all of your current access policies. Click the Create button to start creating a new policy (see Figure 8-15).

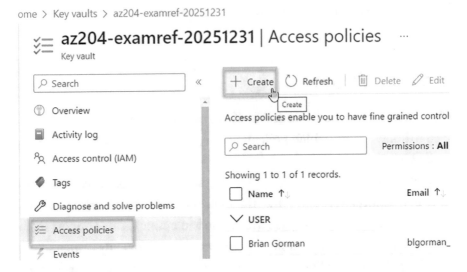

Figure 8-15. *Use the Access Policies blade to create new policies*

Earlier in the chapter you saw the creation of a managed identity for the App Service named az204examref20251231. To give this app service the ability to get (read) secrets, click the + Create button, then select Get from Secret Permissions, as shown in Figure 8-16.

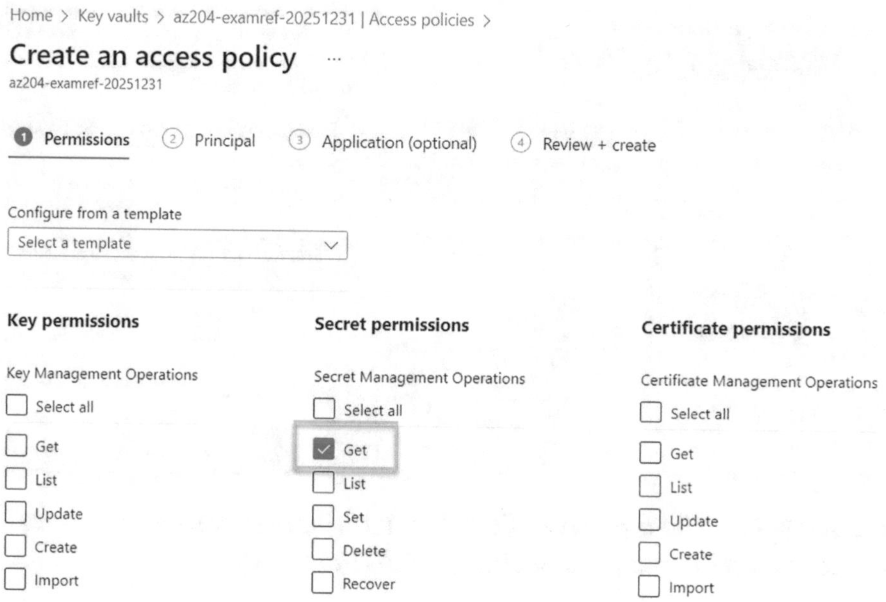

Home > Key vaults > az204-examref-20251231 | Access policies >

Create an access policy   ...

az204-examref-20251231

① **Permissions**   ② Principal   ③ Application (optional)   ④ Review + create

Configure from a template

| Select a template | ∨ |

Key permissions

Key Management Operations

☐ Select all

☐ Get

☐ List

☐ Update

☐ Create

☐ Import

Secret permissions

Secret Management Operations

☐ Select all

☑ Get

☐ List

☐ Set

☐ Delete

☐ Recover

Certificate permissions

Certificate Management Operations

☐ Select all

☐ Get

☐ List

☐ Update

☐ Create

☐ Import

Figure 8-16. *Adding the Get permission for secrets on the Vault Access Policy*

On the Principal tab, type the name of the app service you want to authorize (remember that the app service won't show up until it has a system-managed identity assigned). When selecting the principal, make sure to select the entry that has the ID that matches the managed identity that was created on the app service. Figure 8-17 shows selecting the correct principal lined up with another window to validate that the Client ID matches.

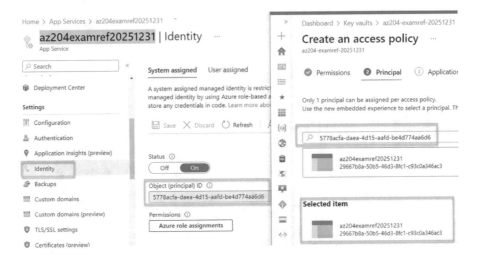

Figure 8-17. *The Identity Object ID is validated and used to choose the correct principal for association with the policy*

On the next screen, you can choose an application one is if not already chosen. Here, the application is already chosen so the policy can move through creation.

You might have also noticed that only the Get permission was granted. Why not grant the List permission as well? It's critical to note that the Get permission will allow the application to get any secret from this vault, so long as it has the correct secret URI. If the application knows the name of a secret, it can request the value of the secret. Without the permission to List, the application must explicitly know the names of any secrets that it will leverage. If you grant the List permission, you open a huge security risk in your application, because the application could iterate all of the vault secrets and get any values that are present for any secret. Therefore, you should not grant the List permission when all that is needed is access to one to a few secrets to which the application can be directly aware of by name.

Once the application (or any principal) is granted access, the specific principal and permissions will show up on the Policies blade, as shown in Figure 8-18.

Figure 8-18. *The policies that exist are listed on the main blade for the Access Policies, including the recently created permission for the app service*

Connect to Azure Key Vault From Azure App Service

With the access policy set, it is fairly easy to connect to the Key Vault from the Azure App Service. In order to do this, you don't even need to make any code changes.

Previously in the book, the app service was deployed and configuration values were set for the app service called az204examref20251231. In that app service, two configuration values were created—one for SimpleWebSha red:MySimpleValue and another for SimpleWebShared:MySecretValue.

As a quick refresher, these values are just pulled into the front page on the default application, and you can easily see the current values from the configuration when browsing to the application (see Figure 8-19).

Figure 8-19. *The application renders the values from the configuration, as previously deployed*

Configure the Application to Read From Key Vault

As stated, this will only work when you have created a service principal as a system-managed identity on the app service and then have given the app service the authorization to get secrets from the Key Vault.

Previously in the Key Vault, a secret was created with two versions and only the latest version was left in the enabled state. Using the URI of the secret, which is something similar to `https://az204-examref-20251231.vault.azure.net/secrets/my-production-secret/4d4f...`, the configuration can now be set to read from the Key Vault.

On the Configuration blade for the application, for the secret value, changing the value to read from your Key Vault secret is as easy as placing the following value into the value already set in the App Service Configuration settings:

```
@Microsoft.KeyVault(SecretUri=https://<your-vault-name-here>.
vault.azure.net/secrets/<your-secret-name-here>/<secret-
version-number-here>)
```

Once you set the secret to read from the Key Vault, click the Save button to make the changes take effect. When the changes are applied, you will get a visible indication in the Configuration section if you have the correct URI and access permissions. You may have to wait a minute and click Refresh to see it. Figure 8-20 shows the indicator when either the URI or the access permissions are not set correctly.

Figure 8-20. *Access to the Key Vault secret is not configured correctly so the page shows a red X next to the Key Vault Reference*

As of this moment, the secret will not display and you'll instead see the full link to the Key Vault setting. You will get a chance to leverage the secret later via the Azure App Configuration and Key Vault.

If you want to enable this right now to see direct connection to the Azure Key Vault, you just need to add the access policy in the Key Vault for the managed identity of your web application.

Navigate to the Identity blade on your application and copy the Object (principal) ID to your clipboard (see Figure 8-21).

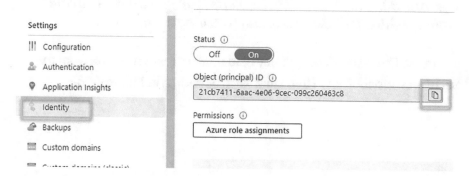

Figure 8-21. *Getting the object (principal) ID for the identity to use in a Key Vault Policy in the next step*

To complete the association, navigate to the secret in the Key Vault and select Access Policies; then select + Create to add a new policy (see Figure 8-22).

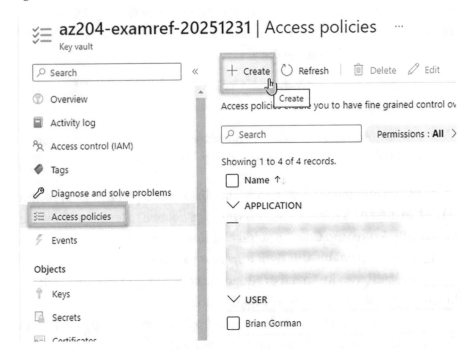

Figure 8-22. *The Access Policies blade is open with the + Create option highlighted. Use this to start creating a new policy*

In the Create an Access Policy blade, select the Get option from the Secret Permissions list. Then click Next, as shown in Figure 8-23.

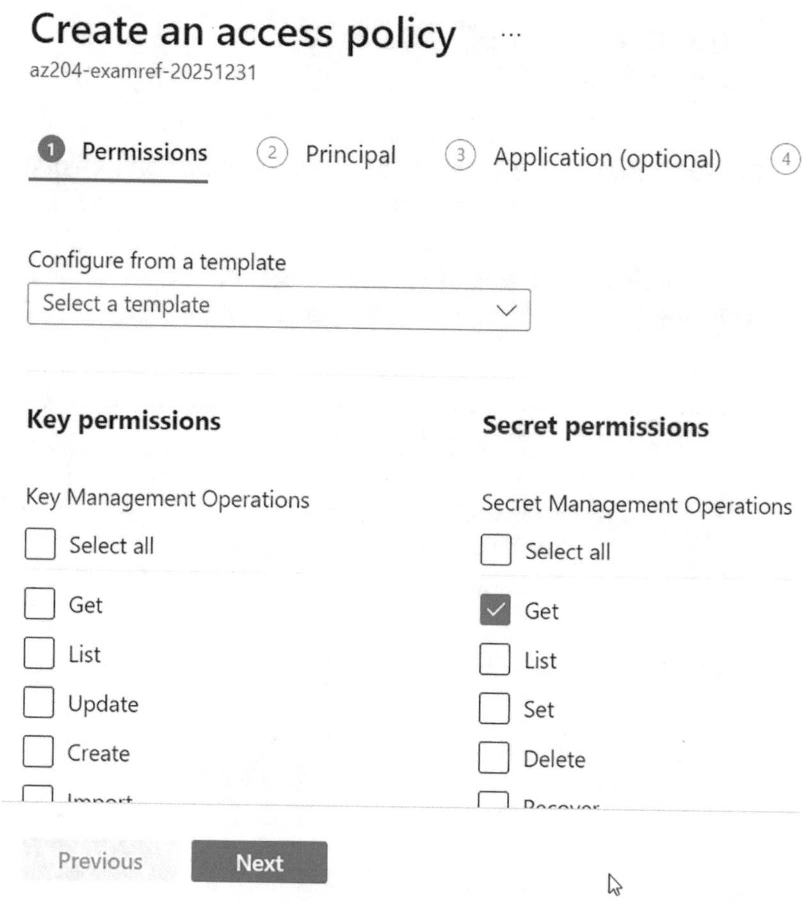

Create an access policy ...

az204-examref-20251231

1 Permissions   ② Principal   ③ Application (optional)   ④

Configure from a template

Select a template   ⌄

Key permissions

Key Management Operations

☐ Select all

☐ Get

☐ List

☐ Update

☐ Create

☐ Import

Secret permissions

Secret Management Operations

☐ Select all

☑ Get

☐ List

☐ Set

☐ Delete

☐ Recover

Previous   **Next**

Figure 8-23. The Get permission is selected for the secrets only

On the Principal tab, enter the Object (Principal) ID that you copied from the app service. Select the object that matches that Object (Principal) ID. Click Next, then continue through to create the association, as shown in Figure 8-24.

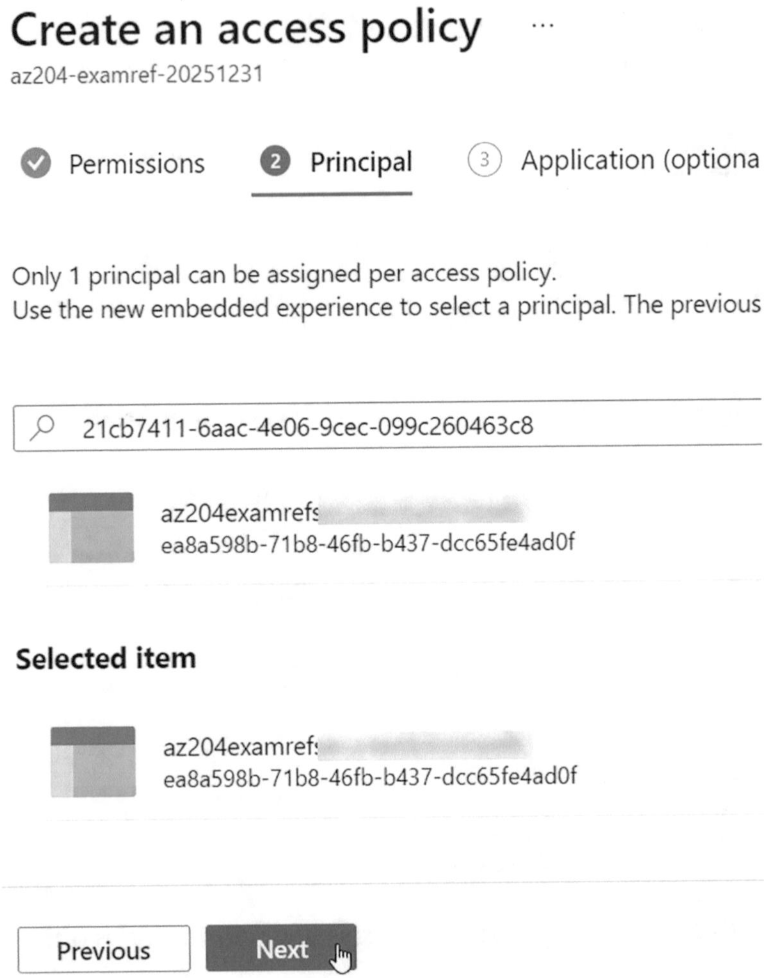

Create an access policy   ...

az204-examref-20251231

✓ Permissions   ② **Principal**   ③ Application (optiona

Only 1 principal can be assigned per access policy.
Use the new embedded experience to select a principal. The previous

> 🔍 21cb7411-6aac-4e06-9cec-099c260463c8

az204examref:
ea8a598b-71b8-46fb-b437-dcc65fe4ad0f

Selected item

az204examref:
ea8a598b-71b8-46fb-b437-dcc65fe4ad0f

Previous   Next 🖑

Figure 8-24. *The policy is created to map the Get secret credential to the managed identity for the app service. This will allow the app service to read the secret value*

With everything in place, the solution should now show a green checkmark for the secret in the App Service Configuration settings (see Figure 8-25). If, for some reason, there are problems, try restarting the web application to see if it can pick up on the connection. Also, you will need to double-check all of your settings to ensure you don't have any typos or any unsaved blades.

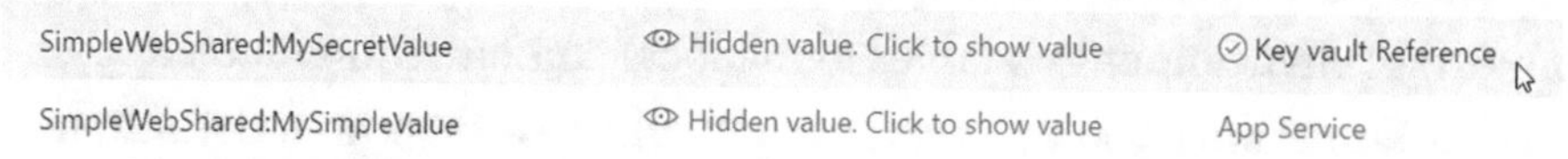

| SimpleWebShared:MySecretValue | 👁 Hidden value. Click to show value | ⊘ Key vault Reference |
| SimpleWebShared:MySimpleValue | 👁 Hidden value. Click to show value | App Service |

Figure 8-25. *The Key Vault secret is able to be retrieved and the green checkmark indicates successful configuration*

When things are working, the reference will show as a green checkmark next to the Key Vault Reference text. Then you can review the application and see the secret value, as shown in Figure 8-26.

My Simple value shared

Shared Value from production slot Configuration Application Settings

My Simple secret shared

This is the latest version of a secret stored in Key Vault as "my-production-secret"

Figure 8-26. *The value is retrieved from the Azure Key Vault once permissions and settings are configured without having to make any changes to code*

Azure Application Configuration

Most modern applications require secrets for things like the database connection string and third-party API keys. Additional settings may be required to toggle features on and off, or to provide general environment settings that aren't necessarily secrets, such as a path for images or other public documents.

Centralized Configuration

The Azure Application Configuration is a resource in Azure that lets you share settings across multiple applications. In Chapter 4, you saw how to set environment variables in the local configuration for an app service. Sometimes you will need to share those settings across multiple applications or share the same setting but have slightly different setting values across environments like development and production.

For these scenarios, the Azure App Configuration lets you centralize the management of environment variables, database, and other shared secrets and environment-specific configuration values with a shared key.

An important caveat to call out immediately here is that App Configuration is not designed to protect secrets or sensitive information. If you have a secret such as a password or connection string or a third-party API key that needs to be protected, the best solution is the Azure Key Vault. Using the Key Vault via the App Configuration is the best solution for protecting your secrets and for sharing the configuration settings to get the secret across applications. You will get a chance to see how to leverage Key Vault via the App Configuration from your app service in the last section of this chapter.

Azure Managed Service

The Azure App Configuration is a platform service in Azure, so utilizing this service gives you a guaranteed SLA for availability, the ability to back up your solution for regional failover and resiliency, and RBAC control for access to the app configuration values.

Creating a New Azure App Configuration

To create a new app configuration in the portal, navigate to the App Configuration blade and select + Create. As always, select your subscription and resource group, as well as the location for the resource.

To name the configuration, once again you must find a unique name that can be a public-facing URL.

The next step is to choose the correct tier, either Free or Standard. The Free tier is limited in throughput and can only house one configuration, whereas the Standard tier has much more throughput and an unlimited number of configuration resources. Additionally, the Free tier does not have an SLA and the Standard tier has an SLA of three nines (99.9 percent). Figure 8-27 includes the start of creating an app configuration.

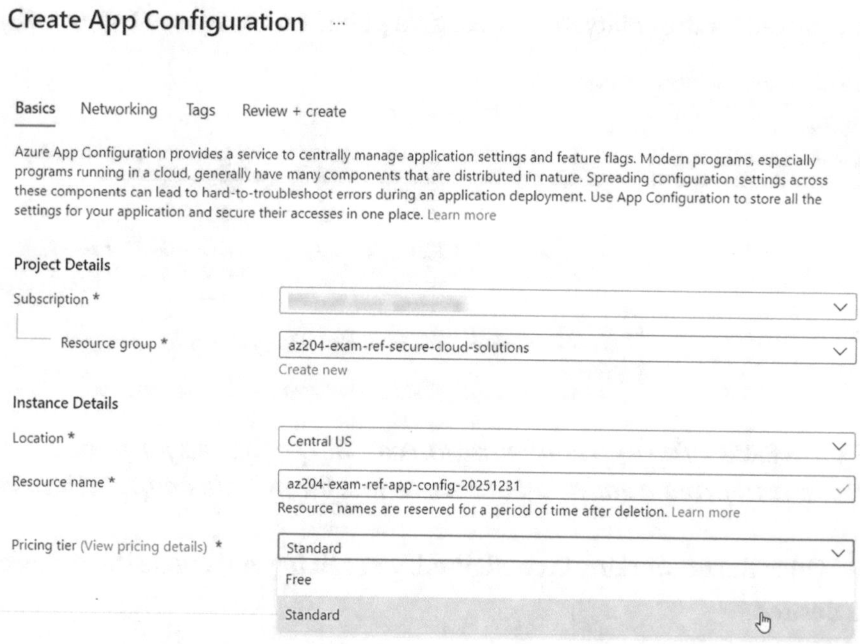

Create App Configuration ...

Basics Networking Tags Review + create

Azure App Configuration provides a service to centrally manage application settings and feature flags. Modern programs, especially programs running in a cloud, generally have many components that are distributed in nature. Spreading configuration settings across these components can lead to hard-to-troubleshoot errors during an application deployment. Use App Configuration to store all the settings for your application and secure their accesses in one place. Learn more

Project Details

Subscription *

Resource group *   az204-exam-ref-secure-cloud-solutions
Create new

Instance Details

Location *   Central US

Resource name *   az204-exam-ref-app-config-20251231
Resource names are reserved for a period of time after deletion. Learn more

Pricing tier (View pricing details) *   Standard

Free

Standard

Figure 8-27. *Starting to create a new app configuration resource*

During creation, if you choose the Free tier, you can't select any backup replication or recovery options. If you select the Standard tier, you can choose to utilize Geo-Replication and set recovery options, such as how long to retain data (up to seven days). In the Standard tier, you can also enable purge protection, similar to the creation of the Key Vault. Finally, and perhaps most importantly, if you want to have your data encrypted, you need to utilize the Standard tier.

A Standard tier app configuration cannot be scaled down to a Free tier, but you can scale a Free tier up to Standard tier at any point.

Networking

As with other services, the app configuration can have a public endpoint or can be accessed via a private endpoint. During creation you can select an automatic detection where the app configuration will be public-facing unless a private endpoint is present. After creation, simply choose enabled or disabled for the ability to connect via a public endpoint (see Figure 8-28).

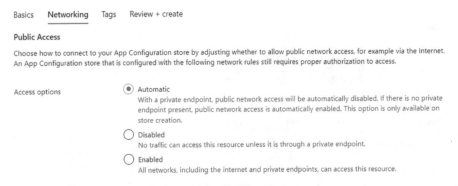

Figure 8-28. *The app configuration can be configured for public access and private endpoint access, or just for private endpoint access*

Once the networking is configured, you can tag and create the resource as desired.

Data Encryption

As with Key Vault, the app configuration values are encrypted both in transit and at rest when deployed in the Standard tier. Your application configuration values are therefore protected against unauthorized access and attacks like man-in-the-middle and packet sniffing.

Create a System-Managed Identity

To be able to work with encryption and for later use to connect to Key Vault (or other Azure resources), you need to ensure the app configuration has its own system-managed identity. As with the App Service and other Azure resources, creating a system-managed identity is easily accomplished on the Identity blade for the app configuration, as shown in Figure 8-29.

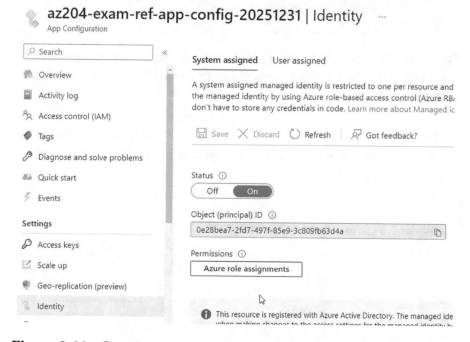

Figure 8-29. *Creating a system-managed identity on the app configuration is done in the same manner as for the app service, although this time from the App Configuration blade*

Customer-Managed Key

On the Encryption blade, you can choose to manage the encryption with a customer-managed key. In order to make this work, you need an Azure Key Vault, the app configuration must be Standard tier and have a managed identity, and the Key Vault must have a policy allowing the managed identity to get, wrap, and unwrap keys.

To connect to Key Vault so you can get secrets when using the app configuration, add the appropriate permissions for the app configuration to the Key Vault policies for Key permissions (see Figure 8-30).

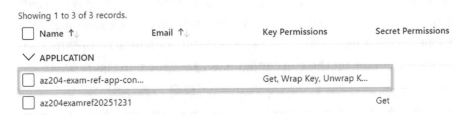

Figure 8-30. *The Key Vault is set to allow the app configuration to use a key from the vault for encryption of the app configuration data at rest and in transit*

Once the policy is active, you can create the connection for the app configuration to Azure Key Vault for encryption on the Encryption blade, as shown in Figure 8-31.

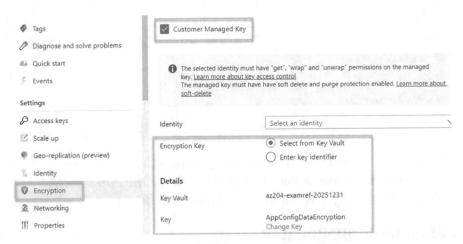

Figure 8-31. *The key is set to utilize the customer-managed key from Key Vault*

Attempting to save these changes might cause an error if the Key Vault is not configured for soft delete and purge protection. Upgrading the vault gives you the ability to save the changes, as shown in Figure 8-32.

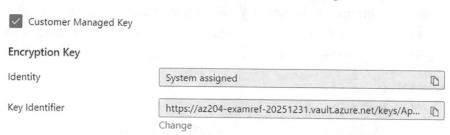

Figure 8-32. *With the vault upgraded, the customer-managed key can be used for data encryption*

Note   In order to utilize customer-managed keys for encryption, the vault must be configured to ensure that soft delete and purge protection are enabled. Updating the Key Vault for purge protection is a one-way operation and cannot be undone once updated.

Utilizing the customer-managed key gives you full control over the rotation strategy for the key.

Keys and Values

Within the app configuration, you can start creating your configuration settings for use in your applications. This is done with Keys and Values. Typically, the Key will be the flat string that you also utilize in your app secrets file on your machine, using colons to group the data together. For example, you might group keys similar to the following entries:

```
WebApp:ConnectionString:SqlServer
WebApp:ConnectionString:Cosmos
```

This grouping of keys allows for ease of maintenance on configuration settings, either in your local user secrets or as the key for the entry in the Azure App Configuration. In your appsettings files, you can use the previous groupings, or you might choose to expand them to a more familiar JSON look, as follows: (Note that this is for the user-secrets.json or appsettings.json files only, not the app configuration.)

```
"WebApp" {
    "ConnectionString": {
        "SqlServer": "some connection string...",
        "Cosmos": "another connection string..."
    }
}
```

When you create keys in the Azure App Configuration, you can choose from a typical key-value pair or from a key-vault reference. The key-value pair (shown in Figure 8-33) allows for simple creation, but should not be utilized for secrets.

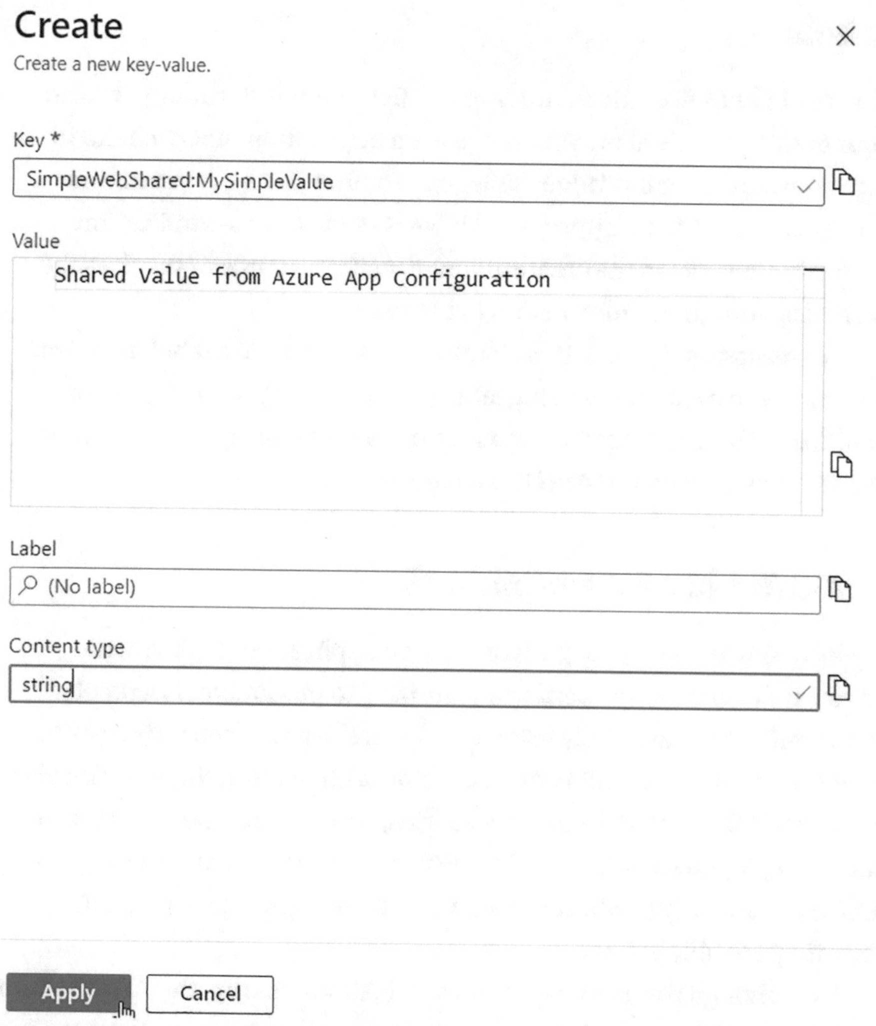

Create

×

Create a new key-value.

Key *

SimpleWebShared:MySimpleValue   ✓ 📋

Value

```
    Shared Value from Azure App Configuration
```

📋

Label

🔍 (No label)   📋

Content type

string   ✓ 📋

Apply   Cancel

Figure 8-33. *Creating a key-value in the app configuration to replace the configuration value for the app service simple shared, non-secret value*

Labels

One major benefit of the Azure App Configuration is the ability to label your entries. Labels allow you to create an application that can read from the same configuration value across environments. As the environment setting is changed, the appropriate label is read, and the application correctly connects to the environment-specific resource or displays the correct environment information to the user.

For reasons of brevity, this chapter doesn't include a label. However, you can learn more about using labels from Azure App Configuration at `https://learn.microsoft.com/azure/azure-app-configuration/howto-labels-aspnet-core?tabs=core5x`.

Feature Flag Management

If you've started down the path of modern application deployments or you are in an environment where moving to production is a regular occurrence, you have likely leveraged feature flags to ensure that your application does not deploy to production with new functionality that is not fully implemented. In other scenarios, you may also be looking at a canary deployment or ring deployments where you want to manage the ability to have only a subset of your users working against new features until they are fully vetted.

Even though this is a chapter on application security, this is really your only chance to take a look at the Azure App Configuration, so I wanted to talk about these feature flags briefly at this time.

Feature flags give you the ability to deploy to production quickly and easily with your application code in any state, while also making sure features are not reachable until you are ready for users to see the new functionality.

Azure App Configuration is the tool of choice in Azure to manage these scenarios around feature flags.

Within App Configuration, when you navigate to the Feature Manager blade, you can start creating features that can be easily toggled and configured as expected.

Create a Feature Flag

In the Feature Manager, select + Create to create a new feature flag. Check the Enable box and give the flag a valid name such as az204-feature-flag-demo. This flag name will be referenced in code, so keep that in mind when creating it.

Additional options exist to create feature filters. This is where you can get very specific as to the deployment settings, including the geographic locations or specific devices, targeting a percentage or specific group, and making this available only during specific time windows.

Figure 8-34 shows a simple feature flag creation without any custom filters. You can learn more about using filters at https://learn. microsoft.com/azure/azure-app-configuration/howto-feature-filters-aspnet-core.

Create ...

Create a new feature flag

A feature flag is a variable with a binary state of on or off. It allows you to activate or deactivate features in your application without deploying new code. This can dynamically administer a feature's lifecycle. Learn more

Enable feature flag

Details

Feature flag name * ⓘ   az204-feature-flag-demo

Key ⓘ   .appconfig.featureflag/   az204-feature-flag-demo

Label   🔎 (No label)

Description   Description

Feature filters

A Feature filter consistently evaluates the state of a feature flag. Our feature management library supports three types of built-in filters: Targeting, TimeWindow, and Percentage. Custom filters can also be created based on different factors, such as device used, browser types, geographic location, etc. Learn more

Use feature filter

[Apply]   [Discard]

Figure 8-34. A feature flag is easily created in the Azure App Service. Feature filters are optional and can be used to specify more precise targets for the feature to be accessible

Feature Flag Configuration

Most configurations in Azure can be configured in bulk. The feature flag configuration is no different. When you are in the Feature Manager, you can select the Advanced Edit option on any feature, and you will get the JSON representation for the feature. For example, a feature that is not enabled for 50 percent default targeting could have the following JSON representation:

```
{
    "id": "az204-feature-flag-filtered",
    "description": "A filtered feature flag",
```

```
    "enabled": false,
    "conditions": {
        "client_filters": [
            {
                "name": "Microsoft.Targeting",
                "parameters": {
                    "Audience": {
                        "Users": [],
                        "Groups": [],
                        "DefaultRolloutPercentage": 50
                    }
                }
            }
        ]
    }
}
```

If you want more information on working with feature flags, you can review this tutorial: https://learn.microsoft.com/azure/azure-app-configuration/quickstart-feature-flag-aspnet-core?tabs=core6x.

Connecting an App Service Web Application to an Azure Application Configuration

In the previous sections, an Azure App Configuration was deployed and the simple shared value for configuration was set to map to the same setting currently deployed in the previously deployed Azure App Service.

As with the utilization of settings from the Azure App Service to Azure Key Vault, a few things need to be configured correctly on the permissions front. Additionally, using the Azure App Configuration requires a code change to allow the app service to correctly connect to the app configuration and read values.

Configure the Security Settings

To get started, the Azure App Service must have a managed identity. This should be done already, as it was necessary for connecting to the Azure Key Vault. To complete the setup, you need to make sure three things are configured—the role for the app service against the app configuration, the configuration setting in the app service, and a code change to the application to allow for connecting to and reading from the app configuration.

Add a New Role Assignment

Navigate to the Azure App Configuration and select the Access Control (IAM) blade. On this blade, select + Add Role Assignment to begin the process of adding the app service to the correct role.

On the Add Role Assignment blade, select App Configuration Data Reader, as this role will give the application the ability to read values from the app configuration's key-values and key-vault references (see Figure 8-35).

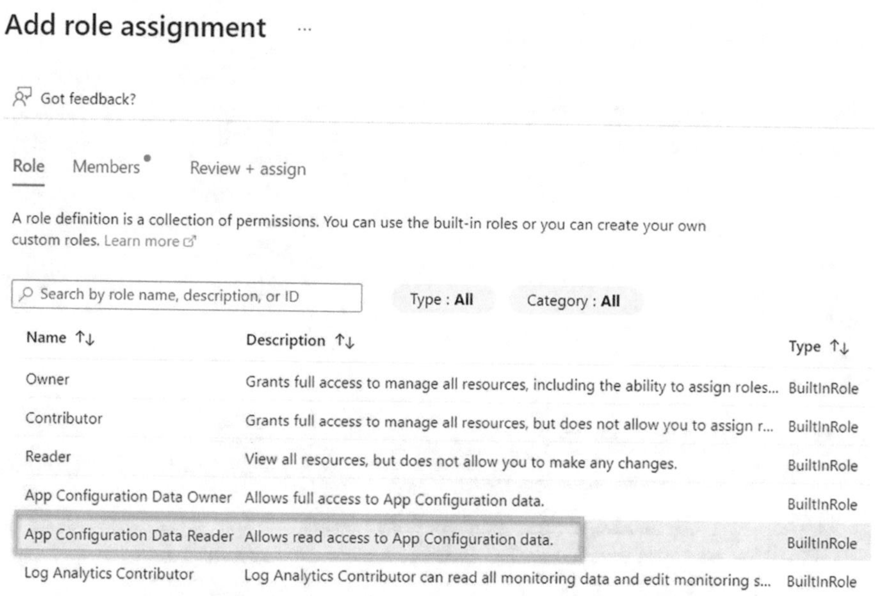

Add role assignment   ...

R͞ Got feedback?

Role   Members *   Review + assign

A role definition is a collection of permissions. You can use the built-in roles or you can create your own custom roles. Learn more ☐

Name ↑↓	Description ↑↓	Type ↑↓
Owner	Grants full access to manage all resources, including the ability to assign roles...	BuiltInRole
Contributor	Grants full access to manage all resources, but does not allow you to assign r...	BuiltInRole
Reader	View all resources, but does not allow you to make any changes.	BuiltInRole
App Configuration Data Owner	Allows full access to App Configuration data.	BuiltInRole
App Configuration Data Reader	Allows read access to App Configuration data.	BuiltInRole
Log Analytics Contributor	Log Analytics Contributor can read all monitoring data and edit monitoring s...	BuiltInRole

Search by role name, description, or ID   Type : **All**   Category : **All**

Figure 8-35. *Add the App Configuration Data Reader role for a new role assignment*

On the Members blade, utilize the managed identity for the app service. For this service, you can select directly from the available managed identities (see Figure 8-36).

Add role assignment ...

Got feedback?

Role   Members*   Review + assign

Selected role

App Configuration Data Reader

Assign access to

○ User, group, or service principal

● Managed identity

Members

+ Select members

Name	Object ID	Type
No members selected		

Description

Optional

Review + assign	Previous	Next

Got feedback?

Subscription *

Microsoft Azure Sponsorship

Managed identity

App Service (2)

Select ⓘ

Search by name

LicensePlateAdminWeb20231231blg
/subscriptions/

Selected members:

az204examref20251231
/subscriptions/

Select	Close

Figure 8-36. *Add the managed identity to the role assignment*

Review and assign the role for the App Configuration Data Reader to your app service. Note that you also need to assign the role to any slots you are utilizing.

Update the Azure App Service Configuration

This update is going to be a bit different than the standard updates prior to this update. Typically, you would utilize an endpoint for a specific configuration URI or a Secret URI. To make Azure App Configuration work, however, you just point the value for the configuration to the app configuration endpoint and the code will do the rest of the work. Find the endpoint for your app configuration and return to the app service to update the settings.

In the Azure App Service, on the Configuration blade, change the value for the SimpleWebShared:MySimpleValue key to point to the endpoint for the deployed Azure App Configuration resource (found on the Overview blade). This endpoint will be similar to https://<your-app-config>. azconfig.io (see Figure 8-37).

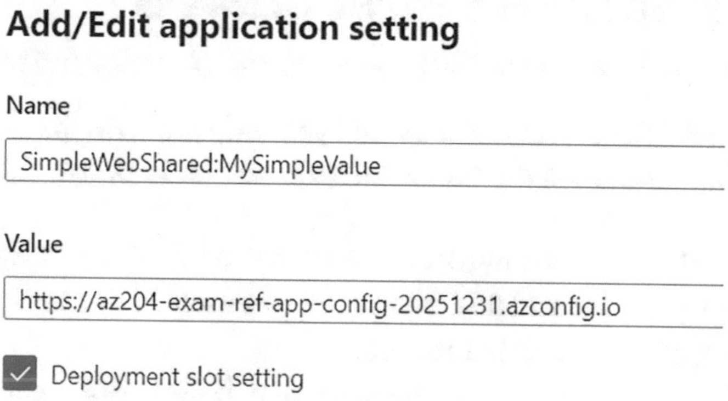

Add/Edit application setting

Name

SimpleWebShared:MySimpleValue

Value

https://az204-exam-ref-app-config-20251231.azconfig.io

☑ Deployment slot setting

Figure 8-37. The configuration value points to the endpoint for the Azure App Configuration resource

Make sure to save the settings and ensure that the value is updated by navigating away from the configuration settings on the app service and returning to the blade to validate that the changes were saved (unsaved changes generate a warning when you navigate away from the blade).

Update the Application Code to Connect to Azure App Configuration

The final step to make this connection work is to update the application code and redeploy it to your app service. Currently, if you saved changes in the previous step, the app service configuration variable was updated, and the value was set to read from the app configuration resource. Additionally, the app configuration has granted data reader rights to the application. The value is not displayed, however, without a code change. (Navigating to the page currently displays the URL of the app configuration, as shown in Figure 8-38.)

My Simple value shared

https://az204-exam-ref-app-config-20251231.azconfig.io

My Simple secret shared

This is the latest version of a secret stored in Key Vault as "my-production-secret"

Figure 8-38. *The secret is not shown yet, only the URL for the app config. This is because the code change is not yet in place*

In the default application provided for use in this study, navigate to the Program.cs file and find the section commented out for the ConfigureAppConfiguration section.

In this section, uncomment the block so that the configuration settings will be leveraged correctly. Do not yet uncomment the lines for the config where the Key Vault settings are utilized (that will come in the next section). If you are writing the code yourself, the code you need to add is as follows:

```
builder.Host.ConfigureAppConfiguration((hostingContext,
config) =>
{
    var settings = config.Build();
    var env = settings["Application:Environment"];
    if (env == null || !env.Trim().Equals("develop",
    StringComparison.OrdinalIgnoreCase))
    {
        //requires managed identity on both app service and
        app config
        var cred = new ManagedIdentityCredential();
        config.AddAzureAppConfiguration(options =>
                options.Connect(new Uri(settings["AzureApp
                ConfigConnection"]), cred));
    }
```

```
    else
    {
        var cred = new DefaultAzureCredential();
        config.AddAzureAppConfiguration(options =>
            options.Connect(settings["AzureAppConfig
            Connection"]));
    }
});
```

Note that this code checks your local device to see if you have a setting for Application:Environment set to develop. If you want to connect from your local machine, make sure to add that setting to your usersecrets. json file (do not put in the appsettings.json file or it will be pushed to your Azure deployment). In your local secrets, you also need to put the actual connection string to the app configuration and your developer identity (default Azure credential) needs to have the appropriate rights on the app configuration resource as a App Config Data Reader (see Figure 8-39).

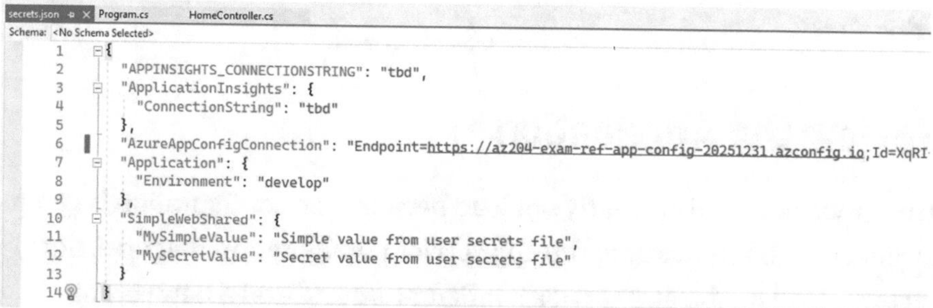

Figure 8-39. To run from a local development environment, some secrets must be added to the application secrets for environment and the Azure App Configuration connection string

> **Note**   The App Configuration connection string can be retrieved from the portal on the Access Keys left-navigation menu item. Unlike the app service, which just leverages the endpoint, the local device must use the entire connection string.

An additional change is needed to make sure the code compiles. You must uncomment the using statement for using Azure.Identity at the top of the Program.cs file. The package is already imported to the default project, otherwise you would also need to get the package from NuGet.

It is a good idea to run the project locally to ensure the code changes build and run and that the app configuration code is correctly implemented without the Key Vault references at this point. Troubleshooting in Azure might be less than trivial to discern errors if the problem is something with the build or access to the app configuration.

Once you are sure that the settings can be read from your Azure App Configuration in your local environment, publish your changes to deploy to Azure and remember to swap the changes to production if you are using slots.

Review the Application

The application will currently not load because the configuration is going to look for a different key in the app service configuration that does not yet exist. Update the app service configuration and add a new setting called AzureAppConfigConnection as per the code you just added to the application. Then set the value to the endpoint for the App Configuration as you did for the simple value key previously (see Figure 8-40).

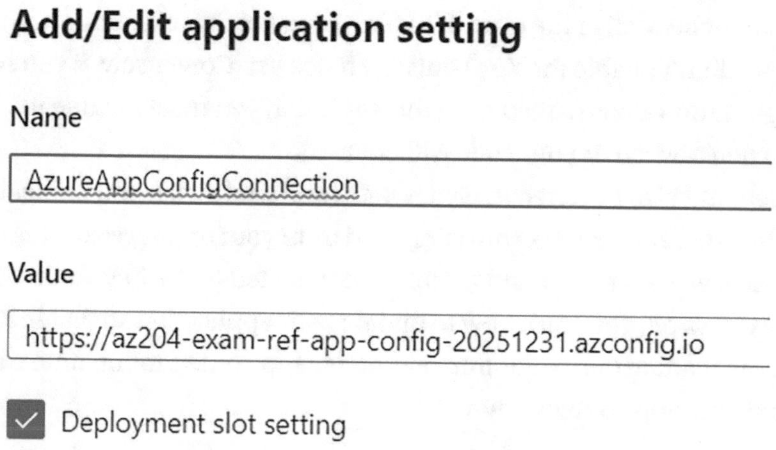

Add/Edit application setting

Name

> AzureAppConfigConnection

Value

> https://az204-exam-ref-app-config-20251231.azconfig.io

✓ Deployment slot setting

Figure 8-40. *The app service config needs this final application setting to make sure the code can correctly connect to the app configuration in Azure per the code settings*

With all the changes to the code made and the settings configured correctly, your application should now be displaying the default text for the simple, non-secret value from the Azure App Configuration on your main page (see Figure 8-41).

My Simple value shared

Shared Value from Azure App Configuration

My Simple secret shared

This is the latest version of a secret stored in Key Vault as "my-production-secret"

Figure 8-41. *The application now shows the value from the app configuration via the settings and code changes applied in this section*

If you continue to get a 500.30 - ASP.Net Core app failed to start message, you can be certain something is incorrect in your Program. cs file with the implementation of the app configuration code. Make sure to double-check all of the code. If you're using the default solution, ensure that you didn't enable the Key Vault reference yet. Conversely, if you set configuration values to read from the Key Vault, you must include the Key Vault code portion or your code will not work.

It should also be noted in Figure 8-41 (and likely what you are seeing) that the Key Vault value is still being read from your app service. This is because it was set earlier and is directly connected to the Key Vault. In the next section, you learn how to update your application so that the app service is reading the values from either the app configuration or the Key Vault via the app configuration.

Connect to Azure Key Vault Through Azure Application Configuration

Connecting to the Azure Key Vault via the Azure Application Configuration requires all of the security settings configured in the previous examples. In order to read from the Key Vault, the app service and the app configuration both need to have Get access on the secrets at the Vault, which means the App Service and the App Configuration both need to have a managed identity configured. The code also needs to read from the app configuration as per the settings in the previous example.

Additionally, to complete this activity, the app configuration must add a reference to the Key Vault secret, and the code must be updated to leverage the Key Vault secret. In order to run the application locally, the developer also needs to be able to read from the Key Vault secrets. For this reason, consider a development and a production label that gives the developer access to only the development secret.

Make the Code Change

To expedite this example, start with the code change. In the application, uncomment the lines of code that reference the Key Vault and comment out the original code that connects without the `.ConfigureKeyVault` setting (or just delete the two lines in each block that leverage the app configuration without the Key Vault reference).

For reference, the new code should be as follows (commented code deleted for brevity and clarity):

```
if (env == null || !env.Trim().Equals("develop",
StringComparison.OrdinalIgnoreCase))
{
    var cred = new ManagedIdentityCredential();
    config.AddAzureAppConfiguration(options =>
        options.Connect(new Uri(settings["AzureAppConfig
        Connection"]), cred).ConfigureKeyVault(kv => {
        kv.SetCredential(cred); }));
}
else
{
    var cred = new DefaultAzureCredential();
    config.AddAzureAppConfiguration(options =>
        options.Connect(settings["AzureAppConfigConnection"])
                    .ConfigureKeyVault(kv => {
                    kv.SetCredential(cred); }));
}
```

Make sure the code can be built successfully on your local machine, and then push your changes for deployment. The setting is not yet in the Azure App Configuration, so testing locally is not currently possible.

Update Azure App Configuration

In the Azure App Configuration, add a new Key Vault Reference setting. For this setting, name the key exactly as the original secret was named: `SimpleWebShared:MySecretValue`. For the key, select the appropriate secret from the drop-down menu and select either the latest or the current version. Utilization of the latest will allow for rotation without concern (see Figure 8-42).

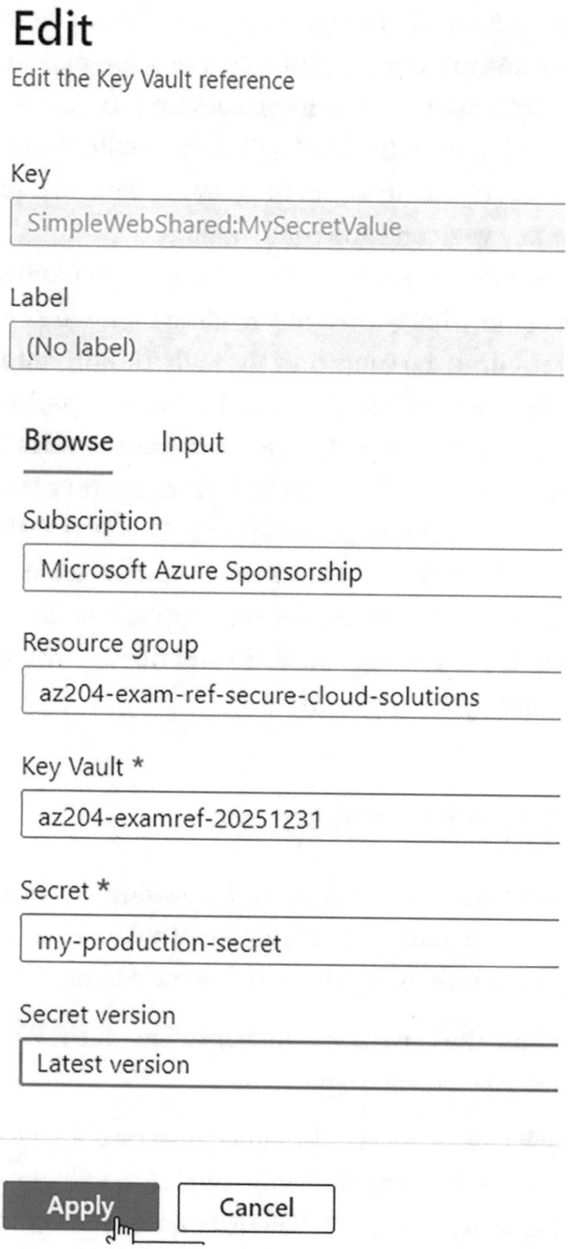

Edit

Edit the Key Vault reference

Key

SimpleWebShared:MySecretValue

Label

(No label)

Browse   Input

Subscription

Microsoft Azure Sponsorship

Resource group

az204-exam-ref-secure-cloud-solutions

Key Vault *

az204-examref-20251231

Secret *

my-production-secret

Secret version

Latest version

Apply   Cancel

Figure 8-42. *The configuration is set with the Key Vault reference to reveal the secret*

By now the code should have deployed, so perform the swap if you are using slots. Feel free to test locally from your development environment as well. If the application fails locally, make sure your Azure principal is set with Get permission on the Key Vault. If the application fails at the Azure App Service, ensure that your `Program.cs` file is correctly leveraging credentials for Key Vault and app configuration.

Finally, to see this in action, you must disable the App Service configuration setting that is currently reading from the Key Vault to ensure you are getting the value only through the app configuration. As with the value for `SimpleWebShared:MySimpleValue`, update `Simple WebShared:MySecretValue`, replacing the current value of `@Microsoft.KeyVault(SecretUri=....)` with the public endpoint of the App Configuration (exactly the same as the value for `SimpleWebShared:MySimpleValue`). Once that is done, save everything and wait for the app service to restart. Finally, review your application to ensure that you have the ability to leverage the Key Vault through the Azure App Configuration from your app service.

Review Your Learning

As an additional challenge, consider the following questions and determine how you would approach potential solution(s). You can find answers to these questions in Appendix A at the end of this book.

1) What are the two types of managed identities? When would you use each type?

2) Which type of managed identity must be manually deleted? Which type is tightly coupled to a single instance of a resource? Which can be reused across multiple resources?

3)   What are the three types of information that can be stored securely in an Azure Key Vault? What is a common use for each type of information stored?

4)   How can you prevent your Azure Key Vault from being deleted by accident? What about keys?

5)   Can you have multiple versions of a secret active at the same time?

6)   What are two ways a secret can exist in the vault but also be unusable?

7)   What is the purpose of an access policy in Azure Key Vault? Can you get fine-grained access-level control to individual secrets?

8)   Why might a developer choose to implement the Azure App Configuration?

Complete the AZ-204: Implement Secure Cloud Solutions

To fully learn the material, I recommend taking the time to also complete the MS Learn modules for Implement Secure Cloud Solutions found here:

- Implement Azure Key Vault: https://learn.microsoft.com/ training/modules/implement-azure-key-vault/

- Implement managed identities: https://learn. microsoft.com/training/modules/implement- managed-identities/

- Implement Azure App Configuration: https://learn. microsoft.com/training/modules/implement-azure- app-configuration/

Chapter Summary

In this chapter, you learned about creating secure cloud solutions with Azure. To build secure solutions, you learned about creating managed identities for authorization of Azure resources within the Azure tenant. You then learned about Key Vault and how to leverage a vault to store keys, certificates, and secrets. Finally, you saw how the Azure App Configuration can be used to share settings across your Azure tenant, and you learned how to work with the Azure App Configuration in your .NET applications.

After working through this chapter and the Microsoft Learn modules, you should be on track to be in command of the following concepts as you learn about Azure and prepare for the AZ-204 Exam:

- Create secure applications using keys, secrets, and certificates in the Azure Key Vault, either directly in your code, via the AZ CLI, via configuration settings, and/or via the Azure App Configuration.

- Implement access policies for Key Vault keys, secrets, and certificates.

- Share configuration data in the Azure App Configuration.

- Utilize feature flags with the Azure App Configuration.

- Determine which managed identity to use in specific scenarios, how to implement both types (system and user) of managed identities and which ones have independent lifecycles and abilities to be shared across resources.

In the next chapter, you learn about caching and content delivery for your Azure solutions with the Azure CDN and Azure Cache for Redis.

PART IV

Monitor, Troubleshoot, and Optimize Azure Solutions

CHAPTER 9

Implement Caching for Solutions

Up to this point, every request made on your website is going directly to your Azure App Service instance. This includes all of the dynamic content such as calls to authenticate the user. This also includes the delivery of all of the content that is static, such as the images, Cascading Style Sheets (.css) files, and JavaScript (.js) files.

In addition to static content, your solution must make a database call every time some content that rarely changes is leveraged.

Both scenarios are fine with smaller workloads, but if the workload increases on the database or the number of calls to the static content grows, you may have to implement options to keep your solutions responsive. For these and similar scenarios, there are ways that you can optimize your content delivery within the Azure ecosystem.

In this chapter, you take a look at two critical services in Azure for delivering static content and cached content to provide an optimal workflow. You'll see that the number of database calls can be greatly reduced by utilizing Azure Cache for Redis (Redis Cache) and the delivery of static content can be handled by distributing assets to the Azure Content Delivery Network (CDN).

© Brian L. Gorman 2023
B. L. Gorman, *Developing Solutions for Microsoft Azure Certification Companion*,
Certification Study Companion Series, https://doi.org/10.1007/978-1-4842-9300-3_9

Benefits of Caching

With these scenarios in mind, it's easy to discuss a couple of the benefits that you will get by leveraging caching of content or data in your solutions.

Data Stored in Local Memory

One major benefit of caching is the ability to have data stored in local memory for the application. In the previous scenario, data that is fairly constant with little change should not be fetched repeatedly from the data store. However, the implementation did not leverage caching and therefore needs to make a database call every time the data is requested by a client application.

When your solution caches the data, you can retrieve data from your local memory without having to go back to the database repeatedly, thereby reducing the workload on your database server.

Retrieve and Mutate Data Quickly

Another benefit of caching data or content is the ability to get and manipulate the localized version of the data quickly.

In certain scenarios, you could allow the user to manipulate the state of the data or content. Rather than waiting for the data to post, update, and then be confirmed, this solution can manage the data in the cache and then update it using an asynchronous operation.

This ability to work in memory and manage state or content locally means your solution might be able to eliminate many bottlenecks involving reading and writing to other services.

Server Offload, High Throughput

Not having to make a round trip to the centralized provider (like Azure Storage or Azure SQL) can make your application more responsive due to no latency and no waiting for queries to complete.

By utilizing cache, you can remove the burden of calls that ordinarily have to be handled by the centralized servers since the data or content can be leveraged from cache.

Benefits of Delivering Static Content via the CDN

Along with caching your data and content in memory, it is also possible to leverage a Content Delivery Network (CDN) to quickly serve the information or content. Using a CDN has a number of potential benefits, discussed next.

Higher Throughput

Once your data is cached at a CDN, your solutions don't need to make requests back to the centralized location. In most scenarios, edge or point-of-presence (PoP) nodes are available that are geographically distributed closer to the client users.

It is important to call out the fact that as humans we often think of "closer" as a physical distance. While it's true that most of the time the nodes that are physically closer to a user will also provide the best throughput, there are scenarios where delivery from a node that is physically farther away results in a lower latency. In these scenarios, even though the distance is greater, it is the lowest latency that should be thought of as "closer."

Resiliency

Once you've implemented a CDN solution, your content is essentially resilient to failure due to the distributed nature of the CDN. Even if the default region where your images or other static content is stored goes down, as long as the data has been cached at the edge nodes, the application can still render the data to the client (provided the application is still available).

Server Offload

As with the caching solution, the CDN allows for many requests that would ordinarily need to be handled at the central server to be offloaded to the edge nodes. This can free up resources and allow your solutions to be more responsive to the user.

Azure Content Delivery Network (CDN)

In order to prepare for the AZ-204 Exam, it's important to be familiar with the Azure Content Delivery Network (CDN). This section walks through the main features of the Azure CDN and explains how you can create a profile and leverage storage from a CDN endpoint.

CDN Profiles

To work with the Azure CDN, you need to create a CDN Profile. You can do this either by setting up a storage account and then leveraging CDN from the storage account, or by creating a standalone CDN profile. For an even more robust solution, you can deploy an Azure Front Door instance.

Limitations

CDN Profiles are limited in a few ways, including the total number of PoP nodes and how many custom domains you can point to a single profile. You can therefore create multiple profiles if needed. Additionally, profiles can only be associated with one of the available tiers, so if you want to leverage different tiers or providers, you need multiple profiles.

Azure Front Door CDN

Although the Azure Front Door is not necessarily part of the current AZ-204 Exam material, the utilization of a Front Door solution is important when it comes to utilizing static content on a CDN in Azure. Since the Front Door is a bit out of scope, this section just takes a quick look at the service creation, but you won't deploy or use it in this study. Instead, you'll see how to deploy a classic Microsoft CDN Profile. If you want to dive deeper, consider starting at https://learn.microsoft.com/azure/frontdoor/create-front-door-portal.

The Azure Front Door gives you the best production-level solution that also has much more robust security and traffic routing capabilities as part of the Front Door service. The Front Door service is a bit more expensive than just utilizing a CDN from storage, but the benefits far outweigh the costs in a production solution.

To get started, you create a new Front Door deployment by navigating to the Front Door and CDN Profiles blade. There, you can select + Create to add a new profile. Once you are looking at the offerings, you can see options for the Front Door as well as the Explore Other Offerings panel (see Figure 9-1).

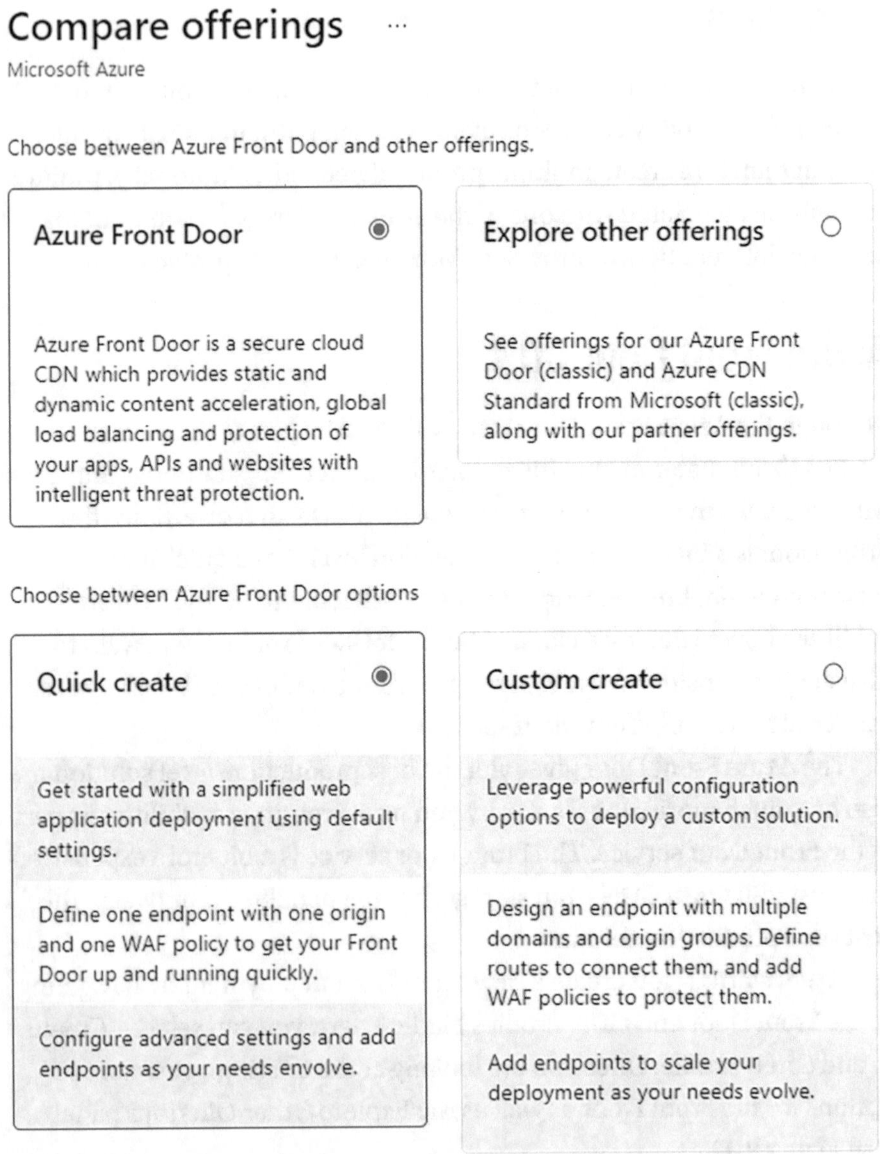

Compare offerings   ...

Microsoft Azure

Choose between Azure Front Door and other offerings.

Azure Front Door ⦿	Explore other offerings ○
Azure Front Door is a secure cloud CDN which provides static and dynamic content acceleration, global load balancing and protection of your apps, APIs and websites with intelligent threat protection.	See offerings for our Azure Front Door (classic) and Azure CDN Standard from Microsoft (classic), along with our partner offerings.

Choose between Azure Front Door options

Quick create ⦿	Custom create ○
Get started with a simplified web application deployment using default settings.	Leverage powerful configuration options to deploy a custom solution.
Define one endpoint with one origin and one WAF policy to get your Front Door up and running quickly.	Design an endpoint with multiple domains and origin groups. Define routes to connect them, and add WAF policies to protect them.
Configure advanced settings and add endpoints as your needs envolve.	Add endpoints to scale your deployment as your needs evolve.

Figure 9-1. *The Front Door and CDN Profiles Create operation is in progress with choices for the Front Door or other offerings*

At the time of this writing, when you choose the Explore Other Offerings panel, you will see the classic Front Door as well as the traditional Azure CDN offerings from Microsoft, Verizon, and Akamai (see Figure 9-2).

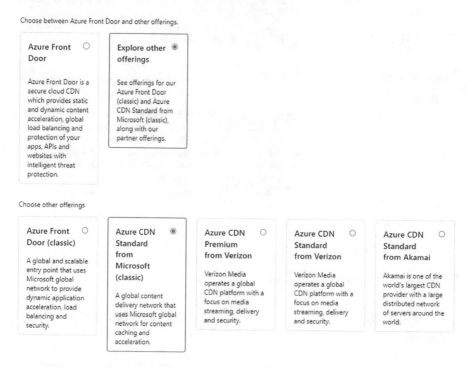

Figure 9-2. *The other offerings include the traditional (classic) offerings for Front Door and Azure CDN*

Creating a Microsoft Standard CDN Profile

Continuing with the creation process, make sure to utilize the Azure CDN Standard as shown in Figure 9-2 by clicking the Create button on that blade. The Basics blade then requires a subscription, resource group, and region. Additionally, you must set a name for the profile (see Figure 9-3).

Basics   Tags   Review + create

Project details

Select the subscription to manage deployed resources and costs. Use resource groups like folders to organize and manage all your resources. Learn more ☐

Subscription *	Microsoft Azure Sponsorship ⌄
└─ Resource group *	(New) az204-exam-ref-cdn-caching ⌄
	Create new
Resource group region * ⓘ	Central US ⌄

Profile details

Name *	az204-exam-ref-cdn ✓
Region	Global
	ⓘ CDN profiles are global resources that work across Azure regions
Pricing tier *	Microsoft CDN (classic) ⌄
	View full pricing details ☐

Endpoint settings

Create a new CDN endpoint	☐

Figure 9-3. *Creating a CDN Profile*

The final step is to choose one of the product offerings, as shown in Figure 9-4.

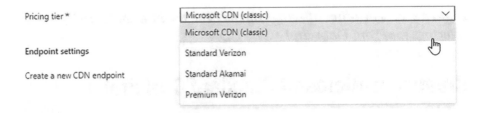

Figure 9-4. *The product offerings are available for selection during the CDN Profile creation*

Optionally, you can create a new CDN endpoint during the initial creation, but you can always add endpoints later. Once the profile is deployed, it can be leveraged for creating new CDN endpoints and caching content globally for use in your solutions. If you're following along, go ahead and create the CDN Profile now.

Product Offerings

Whether you are using the Front Door creation or just want to deploy a classic Azure CDN Profile, you have four product offerings from which to choose. They are shown in Figure 9-2 and Figure 9-4, and are Microsoft Standard, Verizon Standard, Verizon Premium, and Akamai Standard.

The offerings do have some differences, with the most notable differences being the size of files you can use (Akamai is better with smaller files) and the ability to implement solutions with URL redirect, mobile device rules, header settings, and caching rules, as well as a couple of additional options that are only available at the Premium tier.

Create an Endpoint

In order to work with the CDN once it's deployed, you need at least one endpoint. The *endpoint* is a resource that provides content to be delivered, often from your subscription but optionally from another service or endpoint outside of your Azure subscription. Endpoints can be one of the following:

- Storage (Azure Storage)

- Storage static website (storage-based static site)

- Cloud service (another Azure Cloud Service)

- Web App (Azure App Service Web Apps)

- Custom origin (any public origin, including non-Azure sources)

Endpoints are easily created in the portal. On the CDN Profile blade, select + Endpoint. When the Endpoint blade comes up, you need to configure it with a name, then select from one of the origin types listed previously.

For this demonstration, I chose Storage and selected a storage account that I previously created. I also only include the /images folder. The settings are shown in Figure 9-5.

Add an endpoint   ✕

Allows configuring content delivery behavior and access.

Name *

az204cdn20251231

.azureedge.net

Origin type *

Storage

Origin hostname * ⓘ

az204storage20251231.blob.core.windows.net

Origin path ⓘ

/images

Origin host header ⓘ

az204storage20251231.blob.core.windows.net

☑ HTTP port ⓘ

80

☑ HTTPS port ⓘ

443

Optimized for ⓘ

General web delivery

Figure 9-5. *Creating the endpoint for the CDN Profile*

Creating an endpoint can take a few minutes and propagating the data can take up to ten minutes. Once the endpoint is working, blobs that were accessible via the storage endpoint should now be accessible from the CDN endpoint. For example, an image (found at `https://www.pexels.com/photo/photo-of-moon-47367/`) with this path `https://az204storage20251231.blob.core.windows.net/images/pexels-pixabay-47367.jpg` is now available at `https://az204cdn20251231.azureedge.net/images/pexels-pixabay-47367.jpg`. Essentially, the blob storage endpoint is just replaced with the CDN endpoint for serving the image.

Caching Rules

Caching rules are used to define the lifecycle of your cached content as well as how you handle requests—specifically if you want to consider the query string or not.

There are ways to implement rules for the solution as provided by each provider. Rules can be global or custom.

For the Microsoft CDN, the rules are done in the Rules engine, and for the other offerings, they are available in similar tools. You can easily create rules from the Rules Engine blade in the Azure CDN (see Figure 9-6).

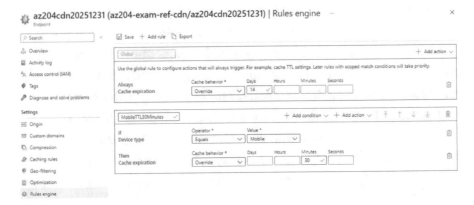

Figure 9-6. *CDN endpoints can have rules configured for many things, including overrides on TTL*

Global Caching Rules

Global caching rules affect all of the cached content on a single endpoint. If a global caching rule is present, it takes precedence over every other directive other than a custom caching rule for lifecycle management of the cache objects.

Typical uses for global caching rules would be to set a default Time-To-Live (TTL) for the cache, ensuring that items go stale after an expiration date. In Figure 9-6, the default TTL of seven days is overridden to 14 days. This is for all cached items on this endpoint.

Custom Caching Rules

Custom caching rules allow you to configure specific rules based on the route or extension for content. As these rules are typically more specific, they take precedence over global caching rules.

Typical use of custom rules would be to allow content that rarely changes or is larger in size to have a longer lifecycle. For example, a folder with documents that only get updated at the start of a new fiscal year may be allowed to cache for a longer duration since the data won't be stale for an entire year. In Figure 9-6, a rule is created to expire the cache on mobile devices after 30 minutes.

Query String Caching

If you've been in web development for some time, you've likely enjoyed the scenario where a JavaScript or CSS file was updated and deployed, but client browsers have cached the file locally, and therefore the users don't get the expected content. Having been in that scenario, you likely have utilized a solution where the file is appended with a query string that has some sort of version number or timestamp.

For example, site.css might be site.css?v1.0 and site.js might be site.js?v20251231. The reason for the query string is to force the clients to download the script or styles on the next deployment by changing the version number. By changing the query string, the content appears to be new on the client and the browser automatically fetches the new version of the file.

CDN query string caching is essentially for this type of scenario, with a couple of baked-in options that you can configure via rules. The rules are: *ignore query strings, bypass caching for query strings*, and *cache every unique URL*. Figure 9-7 shows the configuration for the endpoint.

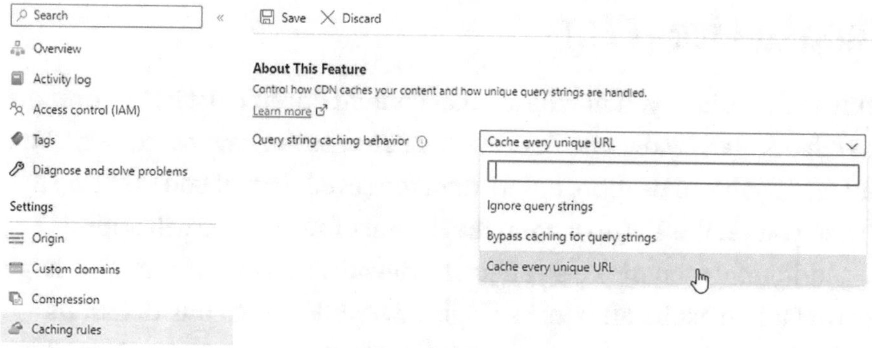

Figure 9-7. *Setting the caching rules to cache every unique URL*

Ignore Query Strings

If you create the rule to ignore query strings, you essentially cache the object by the default route and any version or other query string information is not considered when evaluating content for updating.

Even though the query string is ignored here, the content still adheres to the predetermined TTL.

Bypass Query String Caching

If you set the rule to bypass the query string caching, then no caching will take place and all of the requests for the content will go to the server. Since there is no caching here, there is no concern with stale or expired content and no need to configure TTL on the content.

Cache Unique Query Strings

Caching unique query strings is similar to the solution for the changing files. In this solution, however, consider that this path and query string combination is not just for static files that need to be versioned, but could be for caching the result or content for specific routes with filters set by the user. If there are a number of possible content results for a path based on these filters, you will definitely want this option.

Time to Live (TTL)

Time to live is how you make sure that content doesn't just live forever on the edge nodes. By default, Azure has a TTL of seven days on content. You can modify this to be more or less than the seven days. If you don't set a TTL or you set the TTL to 0, then the default of seven days will apply.

Additional scenarios also affect the default storage. For example, large files default to expire after just a single day, while other considerations like live or on-demand video—which is typically buffered—can have the buffered data cached for an entire year by default.

Purging Content

Even with TTL and versioning, sometimes your best solution is to clear out the nodes and start over, or to just delete some content that is no longer needed.

Purging the content can be done for all content or for specific content as needed. This operation can be accomplished via code in .NET or by running commands utilizing the Azure CLI. Additionally, you can purge the endpoint content via the portal, as shown in Figure 9-8.

Figure 9-8. *You can easily purge endpoint content from the portal*

Point of Presence (PoP)

The Azure CDN works by having edge nodes distributed geographically for serving the cached static content. When you create your Azure CDN Profile, you get the ability to manage the nodes. These nodes are called Point of Presence (PoP) nodes. Often the PoP nodes are referenced as edge nodes. PoP nodes are set in specific cities for each geographic region.

Order of Operations

When utilizing the Azure CDN, it's important to understand how the content is cached and how the client gets the data. This is mostly intuitive, but bears enough weight to make sure it's very clear. The order of operations is the following:

- Step 1: The user makes a request to the page that requires cached content.

- Step 2: The PoP node checks if it has the content. If not (i.e., this is the first request or the TTL has expired), then the PoP requests the content from the central source.

- Step 3: The content is sent to the PoP from the central source.

- Step 4: The PoP caches the content locally.

- Step 5: The PoP returns the content to the client, who can see the content as requested.

- Step 6: Second and consecutive requests within the TTL for the document are made to the application.

- Step 7: The PoP has the content and returns from the cache to the client without making a request to the server.

If you want to see a detailed diagram of this flow, review this Microsoft Learn document and scroll down just a bit: https://learn.microsoft.com/azure/cdn/cdn-overview.

Pre-Loading Content

As explained in the PoP section, the first request for static content requires a call to the server to get the content. In some scenarios, you may want to mitigate the latency caused by this request to the server.

To avoid the scenario where a user or client request has to wait for content to be propagated to the edge node via the request, you can manually force the data to be present on the node by pre-loading the content. For some endpoints, you can navigate to the edge node in the portal and load the content manually.

Geo-Filtering Content

Another nice feature of the CDN is the ability to configure *geo-filtering* for the CDN content. This is a simple solution that allows you to configure a single allow or deny rule. For example, you might only allow content delivery for a single country, or for a group of countries via this rule. In contrast, you might leave it open to all but a few countries (see Figure 9-9).

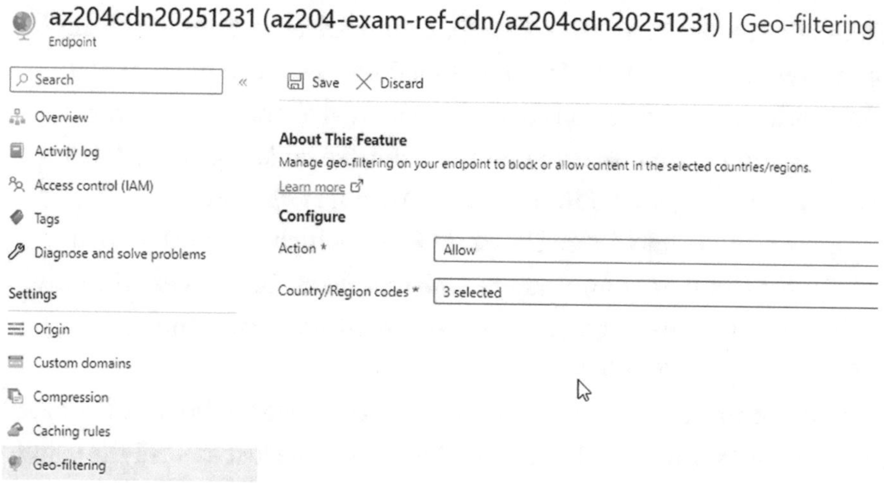

Figure 9-9. *The geo-filtering rule allows configuration of an allow or deny list of locations*

Interact with the Azure CDN via .NET Code

Working with the Azure CDN from code is not trivial, in that you must have active credentials, you will likely need to create an app registration and authenticate via that registration, a storage account origin, and you must utilize the `Azure.ResourceManager.Cdn` library to work with the CDN Profiles and Endpoints from code.

If you want to review how to work with the CDN from code, you can review this resource: `https://github.com/Azure/azure-sdk-for-net/blob/main/sdk/cdn/Azure.ResourceManager.Cdn/samples/Sample1_ManagingCdnOriginGroups.md`.

Additionally, the MS Learn Modules for this section include additional sample code for you to review, although, at the time of this writing, the samples on MS Learn currently utilize the `Microsoft.Azure.Management.Cdn.Fluent` library, which is marked as deprecated.

Caching for Optimization

The static content in a CDN clearly has some advantageous effects on optimization for delivery of content that doesn't change often. When it comes to content that does have the potential to change or is from a dynamic source, such as user input or database tables, caching data or settings can be a great addition to optimize your solutions.

Before diving into Azure Cache for Redis, which is a focal point of the AZ-204 Exam, it's important to note that Redis Cache is not the only caching solution. In fact, you can create an in-memory cache with the .NET IMemoryCache object.

The IMemoryCache object can be injected into controllers and utilized to cache user settings or data from a database table just as easily as using Redis Cache. However, Redis Cache can provide some additional benefits as it's more than just a basic caching solution. For example, IMemoryCache objects can't execute in transactions, and IMemoryCache objects will be stored in the application memory, which could be limited or cause some other performance issues.

If you want to learn more about working with IMemoryCache, you can review this Microsoft Learn document: https://learn.microsoft.com/ aspnet/core/performance/caching/memory?view=aspnetcore-7.0.

Redis Cache

Redis Cache is a standalone solution that is developed and sold by Redis Labs. It is available as an open source solution, which can be utilized without cost, and as an Enterprise solution, which provides additional features and also has a cost associated with it. Redis also has its own cloud solution where you can purchase a Redis Cache instance on the Redis cloud if you want to work with Redis but host outside of Azure for some reason.

In addition to the Redis cloud, you can also set up your own Redis servers and maintain them. Configuring and supporting an Enterprise server is not trivial, but is also not outside the ability of most IT professionals.

Utilizing Azure Cache for Redis will merge the best of both worlds, with a preconfigured solution that is managed by Azure with all of the power and capabilities of a complete Redis Cache solution.

Azure Cache for Redis

Azure Cache for Redis is the recommended solution for a robust caching solution within Azure, and you need to be familiar with the service and how to implement .NET code against Azure Cache for Redis as part of the AZ-204 Exam.

Azure Cache for Redis is a preconfigured solution that has several tiers that offer various throughput and distribution options, as well as the ability to leverage Redis modules.

Provisioning Azure Cache for Redis is easily accomplished in the portal and typically takes about 15 minutes to fully provision and deploy across the Azure ecosystem.

Cache Types

When deploying the Azure Cache for Redis instance, after selecting your subscription, resource group, and region, you need to provide a valid unique name that will be accessible via the public endpoint of your name followed by `redis.cache.windows.net`. With all of that configured, you need to choose the appropriate cache type.

Figure 9-10 shows the creation of an Azure Cache for Redis instance at the Basic tier with the option C0. This is the least expensive and lowest performance tier you can buy in Azure.

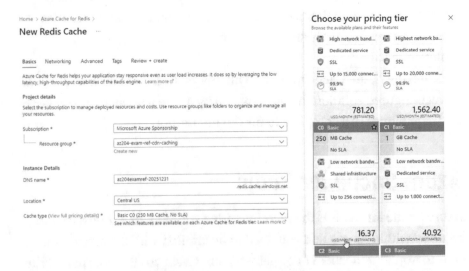

Figure 9-10. *Deploying the Basic C0 tier Azure Cache for Redis instance*

The following choices exist for creating an Azure Cache for Redis instance: Basic, Standard, Enterprise, and Enterprise Flash. Within each cache type, there are tiers that allow your solution to have various levels of throughput, memory, distribution, and resiliency.

Open Source Redis

The cache types available that utilize the open source version of Redis Cache are Basic, Standard, and Premium. All distinct data from this section is available at https://azure.microsoft.com/pricing/details/cache/.

Basic Cache

The Basic Cache type is the entry-level version of Azure Cache for Redis. You will only use this for development and testing purposes. This tier has no resiliency, as it is implemented on only one virtual machine. If that single machine is down, you have no access to your cache. As such, there is no SLA for this version of Azure Cache for Redis. This basic implementation can have from 250 MB to 53 GB of memory. The basic cache instance can connect a maximum of 256 clients with a maximum of 20,000 connections. You can also connect to this cache via an Azure private link network connection. There is no capability to use this cache type on a virtual network (see Figure 9-11).

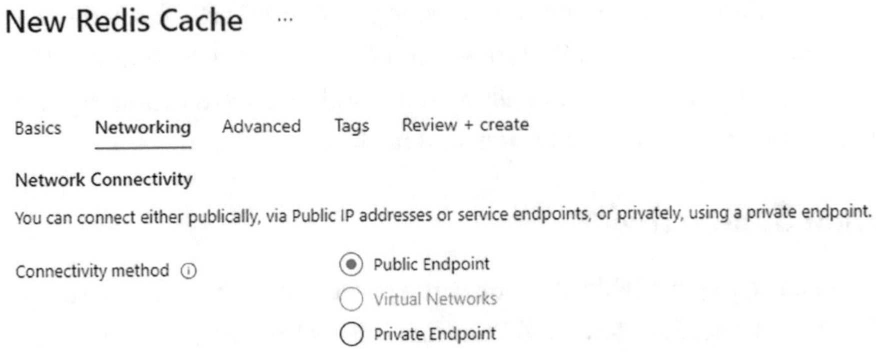

New Redis Cache   ⋯

Basics   **Networking**   Advanced   Tags   Review + create

Network Connectivity

You can connect either publically, via Public IP addresses or service endpoints, or privately, using a private endpoint.

Connectivity method ⓘ

- ⦿ Public Endpoint
- ◯ Virtual Networks
- ◯ Private Endpoint

Figure 9-11. *The Basic tier only allows for implementation with a public endpoint or a private endpoint for network isolation. You cannot deploy to a virtual network at this tier*

Additional options exist for all tiers when deploying. In Figure 9-12, the options are shown to choose the version of Redis to implement. Typically, you would use the latest version. Additionally, you can expose the instance via a non-TLS port. The reason this option exists is to allow Redis tools to connect to the instance. Unless you need to directly connect with a Redis tool or a client that doesn't work with TLS, you should leave this option unchecked.

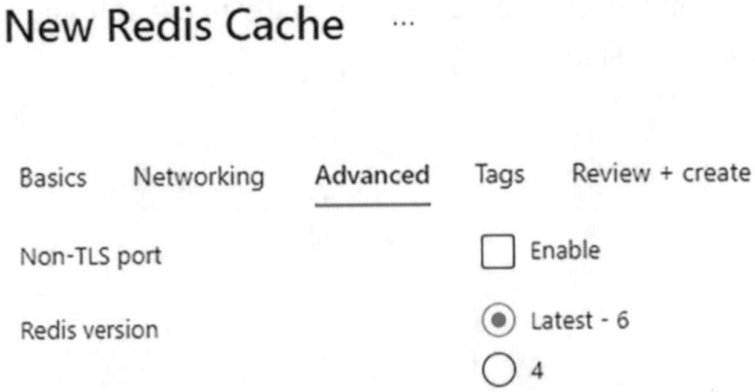

New Redis Cache   ⋯

Basics   Networking   **Advanced**   Tags   Review + create

Non-TLS port   ☐ Enable

Redis version   ⦿ Latest - 6
                            ◯ 4

Figure 9-12. *The Advanced options offer the ability to leverage an older version of Redis and enable a non-TLS port*

Standard Cache

Azure Cache for Redis in the Standard tier offers the same throughput, networking, private link, memory, and connection offerings as the Basic tier. The standard cache is implemented in multiple virtual machines, however, so this is the first tier that offers an SLA, which is three nines (99.9 percent). With the implementation of multiple virtual machines, you get replication and failover, but you do not get any zone redundancy within regions in the standard cache. Additionally, this tier does not offer any geo-replication or the ability to exist on a virtual network.

Premium Cache

Azure Cache for Redis in the Premium tier has quite a bit more power than the previous offerings. At the Premium level, you get the same replication and failover as with Standard, but you are now implemented on much more powerful virtual machines, and you get zone redundancy and geo-replication in an active-passive configuration. Most importantly, this is the only offering where you can create the instance on a virtual network in Azure.

The SLA for this tier is also just three nines, but the memory size is higher, from 6 GB to 120 GB of memory. This tier can also leverage up to 7,500 clients with 40,000 active connections. Finally, this tier can take advantage of Redis data persistence and Redis cluster functionality.

Enterprise Redis

Azure Cache for Redis at the Enterprise level allows you to leverage the full benefits of Redis Enterprise. At this level, there are two offerings within Azure—Enterprise and Enterprise Flash.

Enterprise Cache

Azure Cache for Redis Enterprise gives you all of the benefits of an Azure-managed service with a fully-implemented and managed installation of Redis Enterprise. At this tier, you get an SLA of five nines (99.999 percent). This tier also gives you full ability to have replication and failover, zone redundancy, and geo-replication in an active-active configuration. You also get the ability to leverage Redis data persistence and clustering. The memory size is 12-100 GB and the connection limits are 50,000 clients, with up to 200,000 active connections.

The main benefit of this tier on the Enterprise level is the ability to leverage Redis modules. These modules are powerful tools to handle additional workloads. For example, you can leverage RediSearch to gain powerful query tools into your cache. You may also leverage RedisTimeSeries to do things like take a time-series analysis of data that is being pushed into Redis in an IoT streaming scenario. Other modules include RedisJSON and RedisBloom, both of which are available on this tier. Redis on Flash (storing your data into a database on persistent storage) is not available on this tier. You cannot utilize this tier in a virtual network.

Enterprise Flash Cache

Azure Cache for Redis in the Enterprise Flash version is a lightweight implementation of Redis Enterprise built for storing massive amounts of data at an affordable price, which is available with the Redis on Flash module from Redis Enterprise. In this offering, you get persistence to a disk instead of just volatile RAM. This persistence is typically less expensive and much more durable. However, there can be some performance implications of utilizing persistent storage instead of just having data in-memory.

Like the regular Enterprise offering, you get an SLA of five nines, all the same replication and redundancy offerings and configurations, the same amount of connections, and the ability to leverage RediSearch and RedisJSON. RedisBloom and RedisTimeSeries are not available on this tier. You also cannot utilize this tier in a virtual network. Limits on this tier are much higher for memory, ranging from 384 GB to 1.5 TB due to the ability to offload to persistent storage.

Caching Patterns

As you are implementing cache and preparing for the AZ-204 Exam, there are a couple of caching patterns that you need to be aware of and potentially able to implement at a minimal level. Redis Cache and Azure Cache for Redis give you a great ability to implement these patterns in your solutions.

Data Cache (Cache-Aside)

Caching your data is probably the most common use of any cache implementation, whether you are using Redis or not. In one of the examples later in this chapter, you see an implementation of the Cache-Aside pattern using Azure Cache for Redis.

To implement this pattern, you generally need to write code to read and write data to and from cache while also keeping it fresh with the database. For example, any form that takes an address for someone from the United States typically requires all 50 states, as well as potentially D.C., Puerto Rico, and any other U.S. territories to be available in a drop-down list. The likelihood of this data changing throughout the year is about .0000001 percent (this is a made-up number, of course). Considering that the data doesn't change often, if ever, it doesn't make sense to query all the way to the database every time a page needs to render the data. For this reason, the first call to get the data makes the call to the database and then adds information to the cache. From then on, the second and consecutive calls will just leverage the data from the cache, easing the burden on your database servers and also increasing the responsiveness of the pages to the clients.

When data does change, your code needs to make sure to invalidate the cache so that the next request will refresh the data. Additionally, cache typically has a time-to-live (TTL) that can be configured as data is written to the cache. If the TTL expires, then the next request will refresh the data.

Content Cache

As you saw earlier with the CDN, you can choose to cache content that is static so that the server doesn't need to continually serve this content to the user. This Content Cache pattern is the same whether using the CDN or using a service like Azure Cache for Redis.

The interesting thing to remember about Redis Cache is that you can store cache items as binary byte arrays, which could provide for better performance and consume less size and throughput while giving you full control of all the bits. You can also serialize objects to JSON and store that data, which can be highly useful as a type of NoSQL store.

Session Store

In the web development world, sessions are mostly a necessary evil. The stateless nature of the web combined with our ever-present desire to store state leads to things like needing to manage if a user is signed in or perhaps give the user an ability to configure individual settings for a site. In these scenarios, a cookie typically can be used, and the cookie then either stores the settings or a session token; the user information for a client can then be validated by sending this session token along with any request.

With Azure Cache for Redis, you can leverage the idea of session storage and eliminate the need for cookies on a client machine. This implementation can also be useful for things like managing the active user credentials. With Azure Cache for Redis, you can also get similar functionality to the implementation of a Cosmos DB, so those same types of implementations might also be useful for things like storing user choices for settings and configuration or potentially tracking user actions throughout the site.

Messaging

The messaging pattern is the ability to disconnect operations from the client to the server. This pattern allows for the client to operate independently of any backend processing. Additionally, this pattern allows either side to scale at will and only when necessary.

When a solution is not decoupled, you must have backend processing in place at the correct level to handle load as requests come in from the frontend. If your frontend gets a spike, your backend must handle it accordingly. If the level of load cannot be handled, the frontend can become unresponsive to the user. Giving the frontend the ability to operate and take requests as fast as possible can be the difference between a few dollars and a few million dollars in sales, depending on what you sell and how many sales you would lose if the system were too slow.

By creating a message queue, you can take incoming requests as fast as possible and then process them on the backend when available. This is typically called "temporal decoupling." Additionally, the frontend or the backend can scale independently so that they can process workloads in a cost-effective manner without causing problems for the user.

In Chapter 13, you look at using Service Bus and Azure Storage for message queueing solutions within the Azure ecosystem. There you learn more about the internal workings of messages and how to interact with them in Azure.

Another example of this implementation could be to leverage a message queue within your Azure Cache for Redis implementation. You would need to write the appropriate code to issue commands against your Redis queue. If you are interested in looking into this in more detail, consider reviewing this document: `https://learn.microsoft.com/azure/architecture/solution-ideas/articles/messaging`.

Transactions

Most seasoned developers should be in command of the idea of a transaction, executed by starting the transaction, issuing commands, and then committing the transaction when there are no errors and data integrity is maintained.

Utilizing transactions from Azure Cache for Redis is possible, which allows you to create batch transactions against your cache instance. This can be highly useful to make sure to keep things synchronized. In the case where something can't be performed, you don't end up with cached data that is not accurately representing data from an underlying data store.

Networking

As mentioned, in the various types of cache, only the Premium tier allows you to utilize a private network within Azure for caching your data. All other tiers require that you connect via a private endpoint if you want to ensure that your network traffic is isolated.

Utilizing a private network ensures that your data is not available over the public Internet, which can be considered more secure. This could be an important requirement for compliance and can be used to ensure that interaction with the cached content works only from other solutions on the same network.

Clustering

In typical instances of Azure Cache for Redis, data is placed on a single node, and as long as that node is available, you can get your data. Clustering gives you the ability to place your data on multiple nodes, and essentially split your data across the nodes. This is a very beneficial practice for resiliency of your data, as more nodes means better availability and potentially better throughput to the end user. An additional consideration here is that sharding your data leads to a greater ability to scale your solutions.

When I'm training AZ-204 live, I always like to show one potential concern with the ability to cluster data. The concern is the overall cost. Earlier, an instance was provisioned that runs a little less than $20 per month. However, at the Enterprise level, costs are much higher, as shown in Figure 9-13.

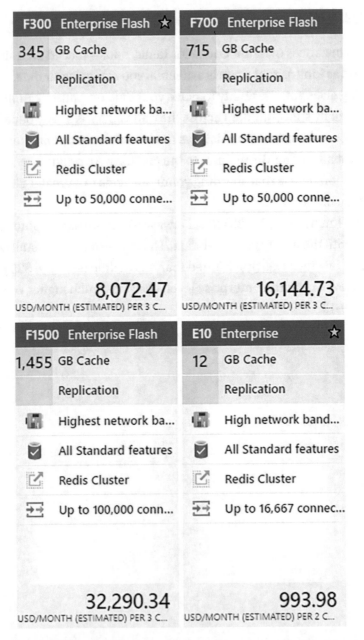

Figure 9-13. *Enterprise Azure Cache for Redis can be much more expensive with increased options*

To be clear, it's not the cost that is concerning here: the cost is based on getting some super powerful enterprise-level features. What's concerning is when you start to shard this out and choose to do this on up to ten nodes. You pay the same price for each node, and you can do the math on the numbers multiplied by ten, per month. Again, this is not to say you wouldn't have a use case where that performance is necessary, but more to just be that little warning voice: make sure you don't just randomly deploy to ten nodes, because you will be paying for each node.

Redis Commands

There are several common commands that you will want to be aware of as you prepare to implement Azure Cache for Redis and also as part of your journey toward the AZ-204.

To make this section useful and memorable, the commands are presented alongside code that implements the commands, and a sample project is available for you to practice the commands.

The following sections give you a quick overview of some of the commands available for use against a Redis Cache, which can also be found in the comprehensive list at https://redis.io/commands/. As the interaction for the .NET client will happen via the StackExchange. Redis NuGet package, you may also find the documentation at https://github.com/StackExchange/StackExchange.Redis/blob/main/src/StackExchange.Redis/Enums/RedisCommand.cs.

Despite all of the commands available, you just need to work with a few of them to be ready for most usage scenarios and the AZ-204 Exam. Before getting started with commands, you have to connect to the Azure Cache for Redis instance.

Working with Redis Cache via .NET

To work with the cache, you must compose an object and connect to the database, and then you can issue commands. To connect to the database, you must have a connection string. The connection string is easily found in the portal on the provisioned instance via the Access Keys blade, as shown in Figure 9-14.

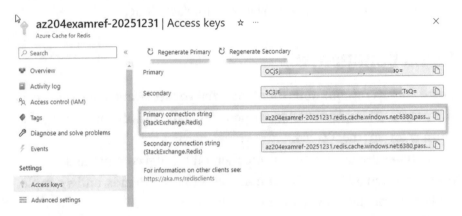

Figure 9-14. *The connection string information is easily found in the Access Keys blade in the Azure Portal for the deployed Azure Cache for Redis instance*

Redis Connection String Information

The instance has a Primary and a Secondary key, both of which can be recycled easily. The connection string is the name of the deployed cache (i.e., az204examref-20251231.redis.cache.windows.net) followed by the typical Redis access port of 6380, then the password (which is just the primary or secondary key), then a setting to ensure SSL is set to true by default and a setting to abort connections if the cache is unreachable set to false by default. For example, something like this with a valid name and password for your instance:

```
your-instance-name.redis.cache.windows.net:6380,password=your-
primary-or-secondary-key,ssl=True,abortConnect=False
```

The practice project expects you to put the connection string into your user secrets file with JSON, as follows:

```
"AzureSettings": {
    "RedisCache": {
        "ConnectionString": "your-connection-string"
    }
}
```

With that in place, you can execute the creation of the database object and connect to it.

Create the Connection Multiplexer and Connect

To connect to the database, you need to make sure your project has included the StackExchange.Redis NuGet package (already included in the sample application).

Always remember that most things in Azure require a hierarchy and Azure Cache for Redis is no different. Here, first you create the connection object as a ConnectionMultiplexer, then connect it to a single command in the pattern ConnectionMultiplexer.Connect(your-connection-string). The connection multiplexer allows for reusing connections (similar to a database connection pool). In the sample application, reading from the user secrets, the ConnectionMultiplexer object can be created as follows:

```
private static Lazy<ConnectionMultiplexer> redisConnection= new
Lazy<ConnectionMultiplexer>(() =>
{
    var redisConnectionString = _configuration["AzureSettings:
    RedisCache:ConnectionString"];
    return ConnectionMultiplexer.Connect(redisConnection
    String);
});
```

Create the Database Object

With the connection object, you can easily get a reference to the database:

```
var db = redisConnection.Value.GetDatabase();
```

This object stored in the db variable is of type StackExchange.
Redis.IDatabase. The IDatabase object db can use synchronous and
asynchronous commands.

Run the Commands

Once you have the database object, you can run commands. The following
commands are important enough for the exam to be mentioned here,
but this is not an all-inclusive list. It is also important to note that these
commands may not be part of your exam and your exam may potentially
contain a command not listed in these examples.

PING/PONG

The first command you should run is the PING command, which should
elicit a PONG response (see Figure 9-15).

```
// Simple PING command
var cacheCommand = "PING";
Console.WriteLine("\nCache command   : " + cacheCommand);
Console.WriteLine("Cache response : " +
db.Execute(cacheCommand).ToString());
```

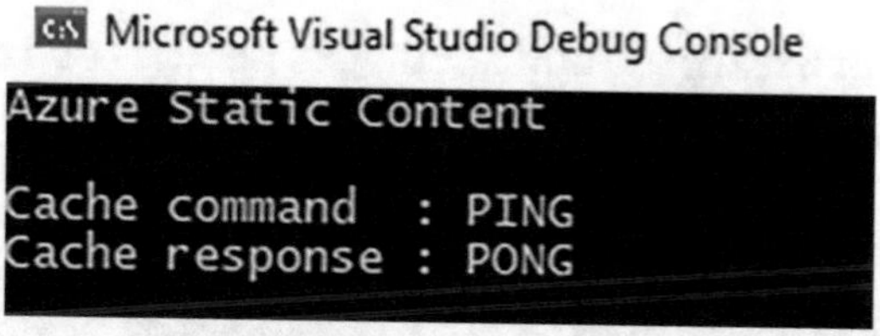

Figure 9-15. *The PING/PONG command is executed to prove access to the cache is working as expected*

StringSet

To store information in the cache, you can simply send information as a string, including the key and the value with the method StringSet, passing the key and value as the first and second parameters to the method.

For example, the cache key of "Message" and the string "Hello! The cache is working from a .NET console app!" can be stored with the following code:

```
var key = "Message";
var msg = "Hello! The cache is working from a .NET
console app!";
Console.WriteLine("Cache response : " + db.StringSet(key, msg).
ToString());
```

The output is shown in the next command.

StringGet

To get information from the cache as a string, simply call the StringGet method with the key as the first and only parameter.

```
var msgValue = db.StringGet(key);
Console.WriteLine($"Message Retrieved: {msgValue}");
```

The output for StringSet and StringGet per the code examples is shown in Figure 9-16.

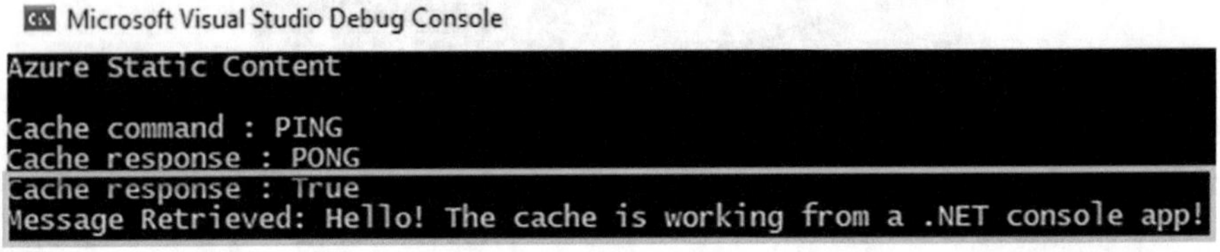

Figure 9-16. *The StringSet and StringGet methods allow the storage and retrieval of key-value pairs in the Azure Cache for Redis instance via the StackExchange.Redis NuGet package*

Store Serialized JSON

With the same commands, you can easily take this to the next level and store serialized JSON for use in your applications. The following code illustrates this option (note that all code necessary is included in the sample project, including a SecretAgent class):

```
SecretAgent agentBond =  new SecretAgent("007", "James Bond", 36);
db.StringSet("a007", JsonConvert.SerializeObject(agentBond));

Console.WriteLine("Agent Info:");
var cachedAgentBond = JsonConvert.DeserializeObject<SecretAgent
>(db.StringGet("a007"));
Console.WriteLine(cachedAgentBond);
Console.WriteLine($"Name: {cachedAgentBond.Name}");
```

This code functionality can be seen in Figure 9-17.

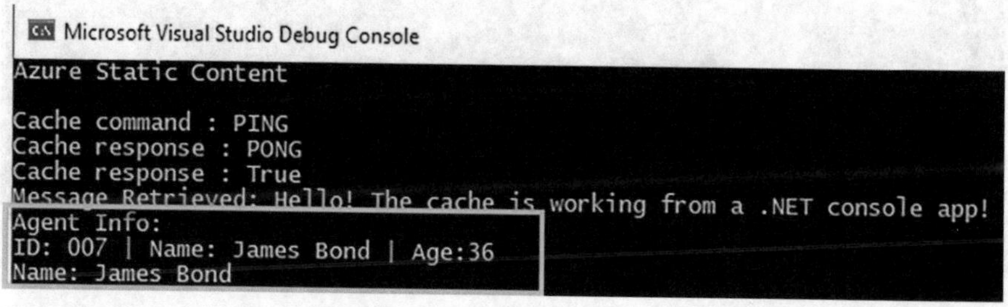

Figure 9-17. *Serialized JSON is easily stored as a string in the Redis Cache instance*

List All Clients

You may be required to discern which clients are connected to your Azure Cache for Redis instance. To do this, you can get a full list of all clients and iterate it with the following code (the output is shown in Figure 9-18):

```
var clientList = db.Execute("CLIENT", "LIST").ToString().
Replace("id=", "|id=");
Console.WriteLine($"Cache response : \n{clientList}");
var clients = clientList.Split("|");
foreach (var client in clients)
{
    if (string.IsNullOrWhiteSpace(client)) continue;
    Console.WriteLine("Next Client:");
    Console.WriteLine(client.Replace("|id=", "id="));
}
```

```
Cache response :
|id=51553 addr=169        86:51937 fd=13 name=VOYAGER2(SE.Redis-v2.6.80.25426) age=0 idle=0 flags=P db=0 sub=2 psub=0 m
ulti=-1 qbuf=0 qbuf-free=0 argv-mem=0 obl=0 oll=0 omem=0 tot-mem=20504 ow=0 owmem=0 events=r cmd=subscribe user=default
numops=6
|id=51554 addr=169        86:51938 fd=12 name=VOYAGER2(SE.Redis-v2.6.80.25426) age=0 idle=0 flags=N db=0 sub=0 psub=0 m
ulti=-1 qbuf=26 qbuf-free=32742 argv-mem=10 obl=0 oll=0 omem=0 tot-mem=61466 ow=0 owmem=0 events=r cmd=client user=defau
lt numops=15

Next Client:
id=51553 addr=169        86:51937 fd=13 name=VOYAGER2(SE.Redis-v2.6.80.25426) age=0 idle=0 flags=P db=0 sub=2 psub=0 mu
lti=-1 qbuf=0 qbuf-free=0 argv-mem=0 obl=0 oll=0 omem=0 tot-mem=20504 ow=0 owmem=0 events=r cmd=subscribe user=default n
umops=6

Next Client:
id=51554 addr=169.       6:51938 fd=12 name=VOYAGER2(SE.Redis-v2.6.80.25426) age=0 idle=0 flags=N db=0 sub=0 psub=0 mu
lti=-1 qbuf=26 qbuf-free=32742 argv-mem=10 obl=0 oll=0 omem=0 tot-mem=61466 ow=0 owmem=0 events=r cmd=client user=defau
t numops=15
```

Figure 9-18. *The clients connected are iterated via code*

Additional Commands Not Shown

In addition to the commands shown, you could take some time to try other commands against your Azure Cache for Redis instance. Look through the commands listed on the db object to see commands for batching\ transactions, using hashes to set and get, resetting and removing keys, and using streams to add, get, and remove.

Cache-Aside in an ASP.Net MVC Application

Working with Azure Cache for Redis from a traditional MVC application is a bit more involved than you might think it would be based on the previous commands. The reason it is more difficult than expected is because getting the Redis Cache constructed for utilization an injectable object requires a bit more work from a connection helper class. Some of this work is technically out of scope for the AZ-204 Exam, but I've decided to include it because I believe it is useful for any .NET developer working on traditional web solutions.

To conclude this chapter, modifications to the sample web project used in previous chapters will enable Azure Cache for Redis and utilize the Cache-Aside pattern to store information for the United States. If you've been working along, feel free to utilize the code you already have in place. If you skipped to this chapter, make sure you provision an Azure App Service and utilize the Chapter 9 starter files. Note that the starter files have everything commented out so that there won't be any conflicts for things like Key Vault and/or App Configuration settings that were created in the previous chapters.

Utilize User Secrets

To make this work with the .NET MVC project, you need to set the connection information in your local user secrets (usersecrets.json) file. You then need to place the connection string information into your Azure Key Vault, your Azure App Configuration, or just into the configuration of the app service before deploying the solution. Ideally, you would protect your information other than the Redis instance name by putting the connection information into an existing Key Vault (refer to Chapter 8 for information on working with the Key Vault).

The settings you need are the same connection string information retrieved for the previous application and the instance name for easily leveraging it in code. The two settings necessary are shown here, with the recommendation that you store the first two in your Key Vault.

```
"Redis": {
  "ConnectionString": "your-cache-name.redis.cache.windows.
  net:6380,password=your-primary-key,ssl=True,abortConnect=
  False",
  "RedisInstanceName": "your-cache-name"
}
```

Set the connection information locally for testing and utilize Key Vault from the app service or app config in Azure (see Figure 9-19).

Figure 9-19. *The Connection String information should be leveraged from the Azure App Service via a secret stored in Key Vault*

With Azure, if you don't have an Azure Key Vault, be extremely careful where you store this information, as this connection string is valid for connecting to your cache for any application from any source. You can also rotate the keys after you complete the training if you're concerned about having exposed the secret.

Inject Redis Cache into the Application

Included in the sample application is a class called RedisConnection. The RedisConnection class is from the official samples found at https://github.com/Azure-Samples/azure-cache-redis-samples/blob/main/quickstart/aspnet-core/ContosoTeamStats/RedisConnection.cs. This connection object allows the connection multiplexer to be configured and used as a singleton within the .NET application.

In the Program.cs file, uncomment the code for working with Redis. In the project, notice there is a second controller for working with the states. This StatesCachedController is configured to leverage a provisioned Redis Cache instance. Review the Program.cs code.

After configuration, the Program.cs file should have code that gets the connection string information and the instance name from the configuration file or settings based on the two keys:

```
Redis:ConnectionString
Redis:InstanceName
```

Additionally, the code to inject the StackExchangeRedisCache and the singleton for the connection is now turned on:

```
builder.Services.AddStackExchangeRedisCache(options =>
{
    options.Configuration = builder.Configuration.GetConnection
    String(redisCNSTR);
    options.InstanceName = redisInstanceName;
});
```

```
//Direct access to the cache
builder.Services.AddSingleton(async x => await RedisConnection.
InitializeAsync(connectionString: redisCNSTR));
```

Review the Controller Code

After uncommenting the code as directed, the StatesController.cs file should now have two methods—one to AddOrUpdateCache and the other to GetStatesFromCache. These two methods utilize serialized JSON and the methods StringSetAsync and StringGetAsync:

```
private async Task<List<State>> AddOrUpdateStatesInCache()
{
    var states = await GetStates();
    var statesJSON = JsonSerializer.Serialize(states);

    //add to cache
    _redisConnection = await _redisConnectionFactory;
    await _redisConnection.BasicRetryAsync(async (db) =>
                await db.StringSetAsync(STATES_KEY,
                statesJSON));

    return states;
}

private async Task<List<State>> GetStatesFromCache()
{
    _redisConnection = await _redisConnectionFactory;
    var result = (await _redisConnection.
    BasicRetryAsync(async (db) =>
                await db.StringGetAsync(STATES_KEY))).
                ToString();

    if (string.IsNullOrWhiteSpace(result))
    {
```

```
        return await AddOrUpdateStatesInCache();
    }

    var data = JsonSerializer.Deserialize<List<State>>(result);
    return data;
}
```

A third method to InvalidateStates is used to clear the cache using the KeyDeleteAsync method:

```
private async Task InvalidateStates()
{
    _redisConnection = await _redisConnectionFactory;
    await _redisConnection.BasicRetryAsync(async (db) => await
    db.KeyDeleteAsync(STATES_KEY));
}
```

Each of the original controller methods to interact with states data is updated to work against the cache and only make calls to the database as required.

Run the Code

To prove this works as expected, open SSMS, turn on SQL Profiler, and watch as your database is accessed only when necessary. You will still be able to interact with the data as required on any page, but the requests won't happen after the first query to get all states until the state data is invalidated by a change from the user.

Note that the states are accessible on the States controller, which doesn't have a link. If you want to add a link, feel free to do so, or just go to the home link and navigate to https://localhost:7137/States (change it to your own port or URL if somehow different). The result is a Cache-Aside implementation on states that doesn't require multiple database calls once the first call is made until the state data is edited and saved or states are added or deleted (see Figure 9-20).

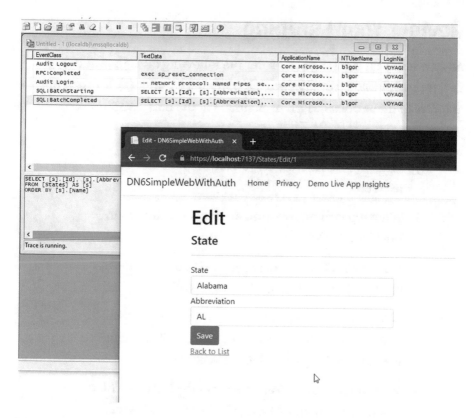

Figure 9-20. *The states data is now implemented in the Azure Cache for Redis instance and is leveraged from the .NET Core MVC Application*

Additional Resources

This code is adapted from a talk I did a while back for the Redis User Group. To prepare for that talk and to build that code, I leveraged a number of resources. If you want to, you can review all of my information on this public GitHub link, which includes detailed information about where I got the sample code and additional Learn modules that I utilized to build this solution:

```
https://github.com/blgorman/UsingRedisWithAzure/blob/main/
RedisNotes.md
```

Review Your Learning

As an additional challenge, consider the following questions and determine how you would approach potential solution(s). You can find answers to these questions in Appendix A at the end of this book.

1) What are some benefits of caching?

2) What is a CDN? How do you implement a CDN in Azure?

3) What types of information are ideal candidates to host on a CDN?

4) How does a CDN work in relation to user requests, serving data, and Time-To-Live (TTL)?

5) What are some reasons you would choose to use IMemoryCache instead of Redis Cache? Why might you choose Redis over IMemoryCache?

6) What offerings are available for Redis Cache? Which can be implemented on a private network? Which offerings leverage Redis modules (RediSearch, etc.)?

7) What are some of the basic commands to work with Redis?

8) How do you interact with Redis Cache from .NET code?

Complete the AZ-204: Integrate Caching and Content Delivery Within Solutions

To fully learn the material, I recommend taking the time to also complete the MS Learn modules for Integrating Caching and Content Delivery within solutions found here:

- Develop for Storage on CDNs: `https://learn.microsoft.com/training/modules/develop-for-storage-cdns/`

- Develop for Azure Cache for Redis: `https://learn.microsoft.com/training/modules/develop-for-azure-cache-for-redis/`

Chapter Summary

In this chapter, you learned about working with the Azure CDN and Azure Cache for Redis to optimize your solutions and deliver content efficiently by caching static content.

After working through this chapter and the Microsoft Learn modules, you should be on track to be in command of the following concepts as you learn about Azure and prepare for the AZ-204 Exam:

- Work with Azure Cache for Redis, including how to leverage TTL and expiration of THE cache, as well as how to set, update, and purge cache data via the `StackExchange.Redis` NuGet package.

- Understand different caching patterns, including Cache-Aside, Session Store, Messaging, and utilization of transactions.

- Leverage the Azure Cache for Redis to store key-value
  pairs and understand the limitations of using keys
  within Redis, specifically remembering to use a key that
  is small but effective at describing/grouping the data.

In the next chapter, you learn about supporting and troubleshooting your Azure solutions using metrics, queries, dashboards, ping tests, and log data with Application Insights, Kusto Queries, dashboards, and the Azure Log Analytics Workspace.

CHAPTER 10

Troubleshoot Solutions by Using Metrics and Log Data

Your application is deployed, and everything seems to be going well for many days. Suddenly, you start getting calls from your users due to errors with the application. If only you had some way to be notified when pages are not responsive, files are missing, network traffic isn't responding, databases aren't working, or servers are overloaded. The good news, of course, is that you do have a way to know this information, and it's generally very easy to implement. In fact, some things are already implemented for you just by deploying your solutions to Azure.

However, what is the best approach for you when things do start to go poorly? If you've set everything up correctly, you can utilize metrics and logs together to send alerts and do postmortem queries to both be notified when a problem is happening in real-time and to review the logs from your solution within Azure to determine what was going on leading up to, during, and even after the event.

© Brian L. Gorman 2023
B. L. Gorman, *Developing Solutions for Microsoft Azure Certification Companion*,
Certification Study Companion Series, https://doi.org/10.1007/978-1-4842-9300-3_10

Additionally, you can use instrumentation like Application, Container, or VM Insights and visualization tools like Power BI, Grafana, and/or Azure Dashboards to make timely and effective decisions for scaling, responding to problems, or other implementations like discerning the usage patterns of your clients.

In this chapter, you learn about the tools and services available within Azure for instrumentation and monitoring your solutions via Application Insights from within a .NET application. You also discover how Azure logs events and other information to Log Analytics. Additionally, you see how to create availability tests and display relevant metrics and queries in a dashboard.

Azure Monitor

Azure Monitor is the backbone of the entire monitoring and alerting solution in Azure. Within Azure, every event that takes place, from powering on a virtual machine to deleting a storage account to restarting an Azure Function App, is uniquely logged. These logged events can then be queried for analysis. Without even doing anything additional on your subscription, most solutions have a number of baked-in metrics for making critical decisions around the performance of the service. These default metrics are typically leveraged when creating autoscaling rules. In addition to events and default metrics, your applications can track custom telemetry by instrumentation with the Application Insights SDK, which can be accomplished from either the server-side code or client-side scripts.

After data is collected into logs (stored in a Log Analytics Workspace), the Azure Monitor ecosystem provides tools to query the logs in the portal, which allows you to create powerful visualizations on the data. Finally, with the same telemetry that is useful for autoscaling scenarios, the telemetry can be utilized to send alerts to stakeholders or can be monitored to trigger remediation actions for known issues.

Within Azure Monitor, there are four main types of information, two of which are generally critical for any solution. The four types are as follows:

- Metrics

- Logs

- Traces

- Changes

Of these metrics, the two that your solutions will likely leverage the most for performance and issue analysis are metrics and logs.

Metrics

Metrics are numbers that can be calculated and represent the state of a service or provisioned resource at a specific point in time. Whenever a solution is deployed in Azure, regardless of anything else you do, there are typically some default metrics that will be logged within Azure Monitor, and all you need to do is discern what interesting information you want to review in order to utilize metrics.

For example, a deployed virtual machine will automatically have metrics around things like memory and CPU utilization. The utilization could be the exact current utilization percentage at this moment, or it could be the average utilization percentage over the last hour. The importance and concern around metrics will always be up to you and your team, but in almost every scenario you would need, Azure is already logging the data. Figure 10-1 shows a graph that highlights the average CPU utilization for a VM over the past ten minutes.

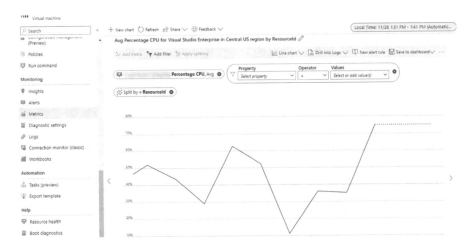

Figure 10-1. *Metrics are gathered on any deployed virtual machine with no additional configuration necessary*

Once again, the metrics are already present, the only thing that was necessary was creating an interesting view of those metrics. The example in Figure 10-2 shows the number of requests that were good and bad against the Key Vault instance deployed in Chapter 8.

Overview	Failures					
Subscription	↑↓ Requests ↑↓	Requests timeline	Request failures ↑↓	Average latency ...↑↓	Saturation	
∨	114		8	99.5ms	✓ 0%	
∨ az204-examref-20251231 (8)	113		8	99.5ms	✓ 0%	
authentication	5		5		✓ 0%	
secretget	26		3	41.15ms	✓ 0%	
keyget	46		-	78.39ms	✓ 0%	
keyunwrap	23		-		✓ 0%	
vaultget	9		-	18.56ms	✓ 0%	
secretlist	2		-	99.5ms	✓ 0%	
secretlistversions	1		-		✓ 0%	
secretset	1		-	99ms	✓ 0%	

Figure 10-2. *Metrics are gathered on resources without any interaction. Here, requests against a Key Vault instance are tracked without any configuration*

Logs

Logs are verbose pieces of information that are generated within Azure or by custom telemetry from your solutions. In a log entry, information is typically gathered to specify the type of information along with details about what happened during the telemetry event.

Within Azure, the Log Analytics Workspace is the place where logs are conglomerated. You can then drill into the logs for your Azure subscription and run custom queries to determine what happened during an event or specific sets of information, like the number of exceptions that have occurred for a new deployment in the first hour of operation. Figure 10-3 shows exceptions in the scope of Application Insights that occurred more than an hour ago.

Figure 10-3. *Logs contain information that can be queried based on interesting concerns*

In Figure 10-4, the cryptography exception is expanded to show that logs keep track of quite a bit more information than just a simple metric.

```
1
2  exceptions
3  | where timestamp < ago(1h)
4
```

Results   Chart

timestamp [UTC]	problemId	type	assembly	method
⌄ 11/22/2022, 6:54:08.559 AM	System.Security.Cryptography....	System.Security.Cryptography....	Microsoft.AspNetCore.DataPr...	Microsoft.AspNe
timestamp [UTC]	2022-11-22T06:54:08.5598475Z			
problemId	System.Security.Cryptography.CryptographicException at Microsoft.AspNetCore.DataProtection.KeyManagement.KeyRingBased			
type	System.Security.Cryptography.CryptographicException			
assembly	Microsoft.AspNetCore.DataProtection, Version=6.0.0.0, Culture=neutral, PublicKeyToken=adb9793829ddae60			
method	Microsoft.AspNetCore.DataProtection.KeyManagement.KeyRingBasedDataProtector.UnprotectCore			
outerType	Microsoft.AspNetCore.Antiforgery.AntiforgeryValidationException			
outerMessage	The antiforgery token could not be decrypted.			
outerAssembly	Microsoft.AspNetCore.Antiforgery, Version=6.0.0.0, Culture=neutral, PublicKeyToken=adb9793829ddae60			
outerMethod	Microsoft.AspNetCore.Antiforgery.DefaultAntiforgeryTokenSerializer.Deserialize			
innermostType	System.Security.Cryptography.CryptographicException			
innermostMessage	The key {dd...32} was not found in the key ring. For more information go to http://aka.ms/d			

***Figure 10-4.** The log entries contain a great deal of information about each logged event*

Traces

Traces are typically used to track user interaction with pages or additional instrumentation that you want to record based on page flow or any other information that might help diagnose errors.

Traces are implemented via instrumented code and can be added to a single app or can be instrumented across microservices or other disconnected/distributed workflows. Figure 10-5 shows messages being logged from the Azure App Service when the solution is instrumented to utilize the TrackTrace() command.

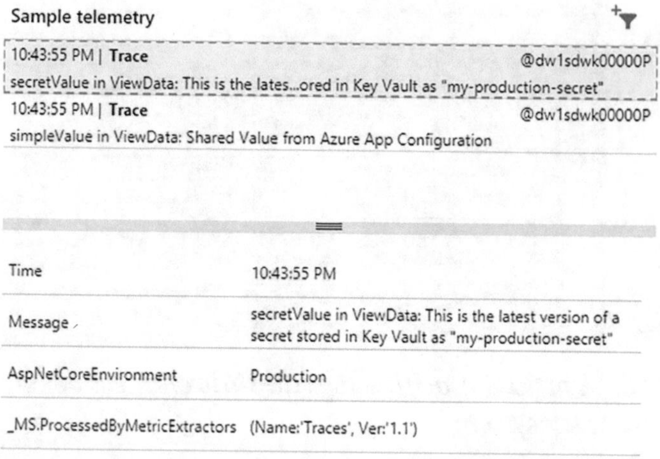

Sample telemetry

10:43:55 PM | **Trace**   @dw1sdwk00000P
secretValue in ViewData: This is the lates...ored in Key Vault as "my-production-secret"
10:43:55 PM | **Trace**   @dw1sdwk00000P
simpleValue in ViewData: Shared Value from Azure App Configuration

Time	10:43:55 PM
Message	secretValue in ViewData: This is the latest version of a secret stored in Key Vault as "my-production-secret"
AspNetCoreEnvironment	Production
_MS.ProcessedByMetricExtractors	(Name:'Traces', Ver:'1.1')

Figure 10-5. *Application Insights telemetry can utilize the TrackTrace() command to log additional information from user interactions or application operations*

Changes

Change Analysis is utilized to view the logged events that have happened on your Azure subscription that have mutated the state of any resource.

For example, Figure 10-6 shows changes on the Azure subscription for the state of a virtual machine as it was shut down and deallocated (shown as the top two changes that are tracked in Figure 10-6).

Figure 10-6. *A virtual machine logs all state changes as part of the Azure Monitor ecosystem*

Different Components of Azure Monitor

As you've seen, Azure Monitor has several useful tools that are baked in without having to do any sort of additional configuration. Since these tools are baked in, there is no additional cost associated with them. However, if you are concerned about cost, be aware that logging events and telemetry into Log Analytics does have an associated cost. Therefore, if you start logging terabytes (TBs) of data, you will incur fees associated with the ingestion of that data. Along with the default telemetry recorded in Azure Monitor for any Azure subscription, there are additional tools and services that you can utilize to enhance your solutions for monitoring and troubleshooting. These tools are as follows:

- Insights

- Visualizations

- Analytical tools

- Alerts and autoscaling

- Integrations and automation

Insights

Within Azure Monitor, there are several tools for instrumentation that give additional insights into various platform solutions. These insights are as follows:

- Application Insights
- Virtual Machine Insights
- Container Insights
- Network Insights

Typically, utilizing these insights requires additional work and/or instrumentation to record the additional metrics and logs. For example, later in this chapter, you see how easy it is to leverage Application Insights from a .NET application. Although it is not trivial, you can also utilize Container Insights to monitor your Kubernetes and Azure Container Instances. Virtual Machine Insights can be installed via the portal, as shown in Figure 10-7. Network Insights are typically ready to go with your networks and help you validate things like IP Flow and client connections via Network Security Groups (NSGs).

Figure 10-7. *Virtual Machine Insights can be easily installed on a virtual machine from the Azure Portal*

Once you've decided to enable insights, you need to create a collection rule. For VM Insights, you can place your VM Insights in a Log Analytics Workspace, or you can use the Default Azure Monitor space (see Figure 10-8). Application and Container Insights are best stored in a Log Analytics Workspace as well.

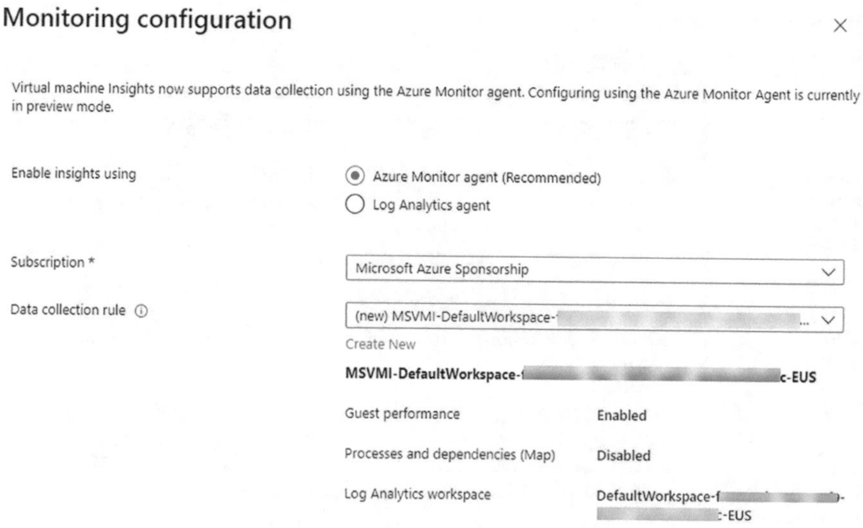

Monitoring configuration   ✕

Virtual machine Insights now supports data collection using the Azure Monitor agent. Configuring using the Azure Monitor Agent is currently in preview mode.

Enable insights using   ⦿ Azure Monitor agent (Recommended)
                                         ◯ Log Analytics agent

Subscription * | Microsoft Azure Sponsorship   ⌄ |

Data collection rule ⓘ | (new) MSVMI-DefaultWorkspace-   ... ⌄ |
                                         Create New
                                         MSVMI-DefaultWorkspace-   **c-EUS**

                                         Guest performance   Enabled

                                         Processes and dependencies (Map)   Disabled

                                         Log Analytics workspace   DefaultWorkspace-f   )-
                                                                        c-EUS

Figure 10-8. *Configuration of the VM Insights creates the logging and directs to the log store of your choice*

You can review the machines that are currently being monitored under the Azure Monitor Insights, as shown in Figure 10-9.

Figure 10-9. *Azure Monitor has a number of blades in the portal to easily review resources that are instrumented with insights*

Visualizations

Every metric and log that is recorded can be visualized in charts or graphs in the portal. Alternatively, the metric or log data can be listed with the information the entry contains in the portal (and can be found via Kusto Queries). However, sometimes it's important to get all the information quickly and make it readily available for your users to make informed decisions quickly. In those scenarios, you'll likely want to leverage one or more of the more powerful visualization tools.

Tools for visualization include but are not limited to the following:

- Azure Workbooks

- Azure Dashboards

- Power BI

- Grafana

You get a chance to see the creation of an Azure Dashboard later in the chapter, in the Kusto Queries section. The visualization tools are discussed in more detail in the last part of this chapter.

Tools for Analysis

For analysis, you'll leverage one of the three main built-in services with Azure Monitor. These analysis services are as follows:

- Metric Explorer
- Log Analytics
- Change Analysis

The Log Analytics blade is a major part of this chapter and is discussed a few times in upcoming sections. You've already seen the Change Analysis screen when talking about the deallocation of a virtual machine. Similar to the Insights view, Monitor has a Metrics blade that lets you set scope and determine any metrics for the subscription (see Figure 10-10).

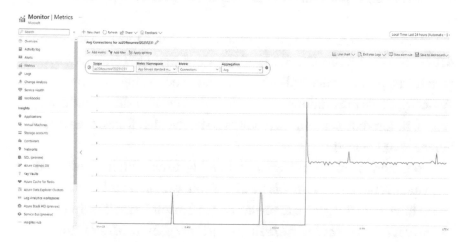

Figure 10-10.   *The Metrics blade in Azure Monitor lets you select any scope in your subscription and home in on a specific resource for visualizing the data*

Ability to Respond

With metrics available, you can set thresholds to monitor your solutions and respond when things are not handling load appropriately. This can be done by creating autoscaling rules.

In another scenario, perhaps you want to notify your development team when something is happening that is of concern. For example, perhaps you want to send an alert when a solution has recorded too many exceptions in the past hour. This scenario is examined later in the chapter in the Kusto Queries section.

Integrations

In more advanced scenarios, you might need to mitigate some issue by running a custom block of code or performing a workflow to send an email or kick off other processes. In these scenarios, you can leverage an Azure Logic App to perform operations to mitigate and/or remediate a problem, send an email, or perform other automated responses to problems or threats.

In addition to Azure Logic Apps, you might build integrations with Azure Functions or even make a call to a third-party API endpoint when certain key performance indicators are met or are failing to be met. Typically, these integrations are handled via a custom alert. For the alert action, rather than sending an email or SMS, the alert triggers the Azure Function or Logic App.

Utilization of an Azure Logic App to mitigate conditions or respond to an alert is not covered in this text, so if you want more information about how to do this, you can review this Microsoft Learn link: `https://learn.microsoft.com/azure/azure-monitor/alerts/alerts-logic-apps?tabs=send-email`.

Utilizing Application Insights

One of the primary concerns for the AZ-204 Exam is your ability to leverage Application Insights from within a .NET application. The first thing you need to do is "instrument" the code by adding the Application Insights tools into your application. For .NET, this is easily accomplished. A demonstration of this is covered in the section on implementing Application Insights.

With the instrumentation in place, you need to be aware of how to utilize code to log information, exceptions, and/or create your own custom tracking events.

The next section covers the basic creation and utilization of Application Insights. It's important to note that the sample application already has some insights in place and is likely already logging telemetry to your Azure App Service. Unless you specifically set the solution to provision without Application Insights, the telemetry necessary is already present in the application. Additionally, your app service deployment should have configured your instrumentation key into the Azure App Service Configuration Application settings (see Figure 10-11).

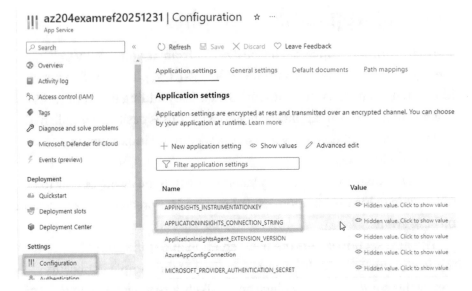

Figure 10-11.   *The app service configuration is already set during deployment unless you deployed without Application Insights*

While this is perfect for your trusted production application, what about insights from your development machine? The interesting thing about Application Insights is that the telemetry can be logged from any host, even if the host is outside of Azure—as long as the application is instrumented correctly (an example is shown in the next section).

To do this, you need to deploy a new Application Insights instance in Azure to store telemetry data from your development machine so that the development telemetry is not contained in the same place as your production telemetry. At this point, you should utilize the workspace-based Application Insights and you can create a new Log Analytics Workspace or share an existing one. Figure 10-12 shows the Creation blade of a new Application Insights instance for tracking developer machine metrics.

Application Insights ⋯

Monitor web app performance and usage

Basics   Tags   Review + create

Create an Application Insights resource to monitor your live web application. With Application Insights, you have full observability into your application across all components and dependencies of your complex distributed architecture. It includes powerful analytics tools to help you diagnose issues and to understand what users actually do with your app. It's designed to help you continuously improve performance and usability. It works for apps on a wide variety of platforms including .NET, Node.js and Java EE, hosted on-premises, hybrid, or any public cloud. Learn More

PROJECT DETAILS

Select a subscription to manage deployed resources and costs. Use resource groups like folders to organize and manage all your resources.

Subscription * ⓘ	⌄
└─ Resource Group * ⓘ	(New) az204-exam-ref-monitoring ⌄
	Create new

INSTANCE DETAILS

Name * ⓘ	DefaultWebDeveloperInsights ✓
Region * ⓘ	(US) Central US ⌄
Resource Mode * ⓘ	Classic **Workspace-based**

WORKSPACE DETAILS

Subscription * ⓘ	Microsoft Azure Sponsorship ⌄
└─ *Log Analytics Workspace ⓘ	DeveloperLogs [centralus] ⌄

Figure 10-12. *The Application Insights for developer machine metrics is configured for creation*

Once the instance is created, navigate to the resource, get the connection string and instrumentation key from the Overview blade, and record that information for use in your application. These settings will be manually configured into the application user secrets on the developer machine.

Implementing Application Insights in .NET

To implement the Application Insights SDK for instrumentation, you can easily just right-click the project in Visual Studio and select Add ➤ Application Insights Telemetry (see Figure 10-13).

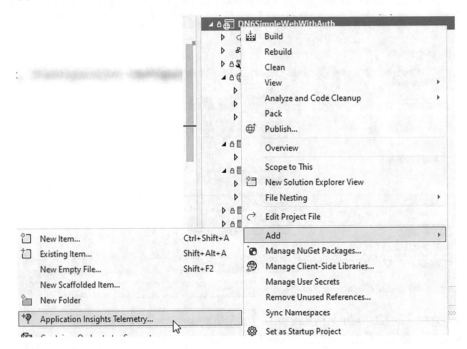

Figure 10-13. *Adding the Application Insights instrumentation to a .NET application is easily accomplished in Visual Studio*

While you can select a local version and just utilize local Application Insights, I've personally found it easier to configure directly to Azure on the dependency connection dialog, especially when it comes to then deploying into Azure, as there is no doubt that the insights are being recorded in Azure. Additionally, working in Azure means your insights will be persistent and able to be queried in the Azure Portal (see Figure 10-14).

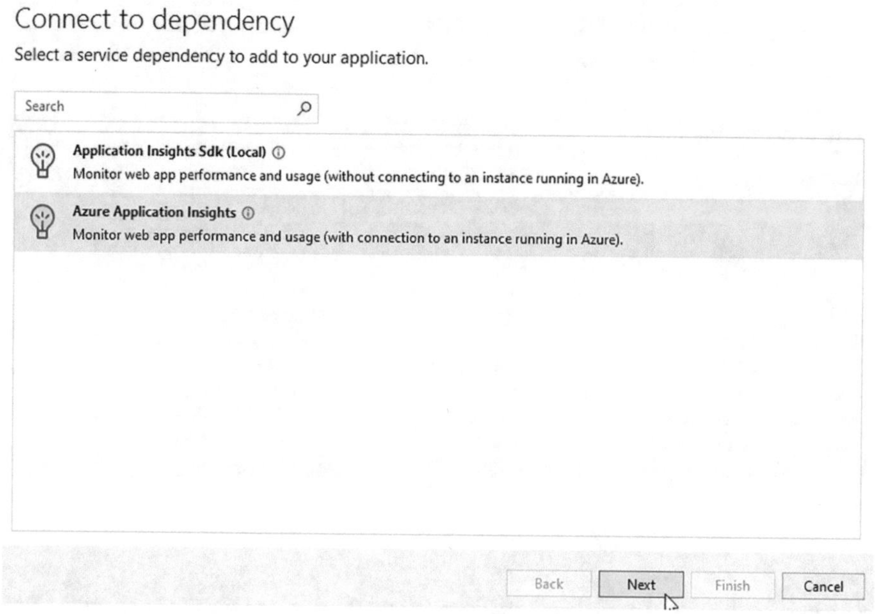

Connect to dependency

Select a service dependency to add to your application.

Search	🔎

Application Insights Sdk (Local) ⓘ
Monitor web app performance and usage (without connecting to an instance running in Azure).

Azure Application Insights ⓘ
Monitor web app performance and usage (with connection to an instance running in Azure).

Back   **Next**   Finish   Cancel

Figure 10-14. *The Connect to Dependency blade has options for local or Azure-based insights. I recommend you choose Azure Application Insights here*

With the Azure option selected, the next screen requires you to log in to your Azure account, and, once logged in, you will then select the specific Application Insights to which you want to connect your application. Here, I select the DefaultWebDeveloperInsights that was created previously, as shown in Figure 10-15.

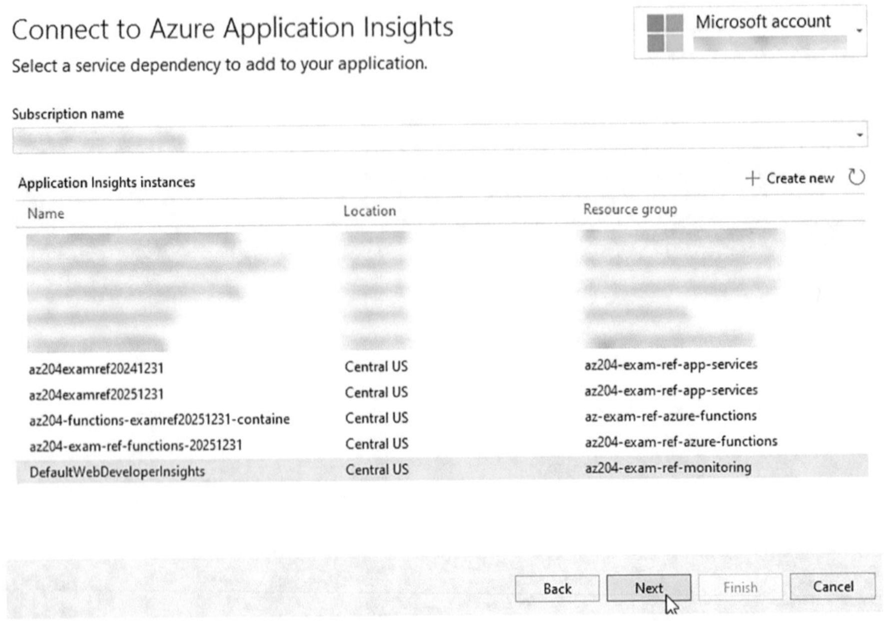

Figure 10-15. *Log in and then select the correct Application Insights instance*

On the Connect to Azure Application Insights dialog, leave the default settings (see Figure 10-16).

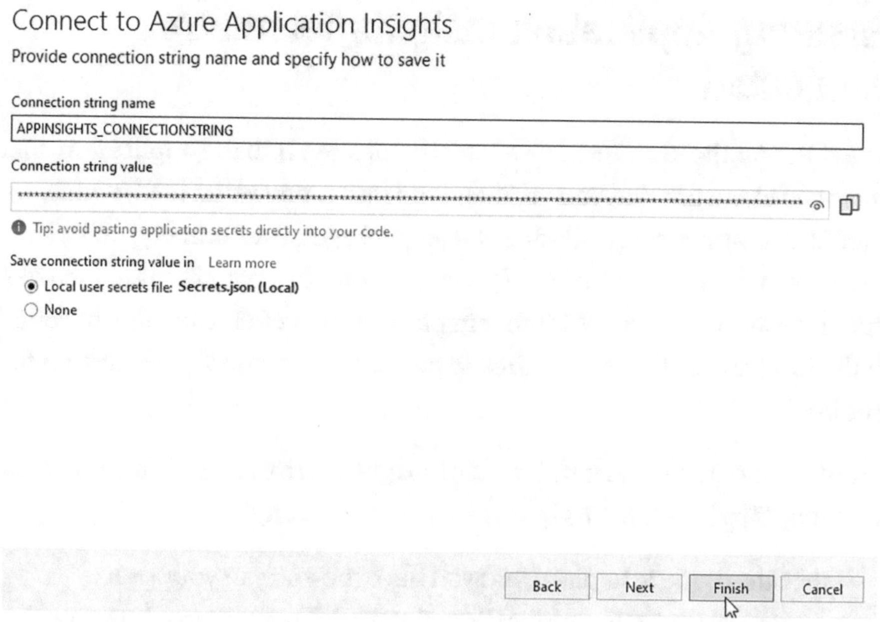

Connect to Azure Application Insights

Provide connection string name and specify how to save it

Connection string name

APPINSIGHTS_CONNECTIONSTRING

Connection string value

•• ⊙ ⧉

ⓘ Tip: avoid pasting application secrets directly into your code.

Save connection string value in   Learn more

⦿ Local user secrets file: **Secrets.json (Local)**

◯ None

Back	Next	Finish	Cancel

Figure 10-16. *The final dialog lets you set the connection string directly into the user secrets file*

Note   Even though the solution says it will leverage the `Secrets.json` file, for unknown reasons you'll get your instrumentation key set into your `appsettings.json` file as well. Be sure to move this setting to the secrets file and remove any other configuration information in the user secrets file generated around Application Insights. Do not to push any secrets to GitHub or Azure DevOps by accident.

Ensuring Application Insights Telemetry Is Injected

To get the Application Insights telemetry injected into the application, first you need to ensure that you've added the instrumentation SDK, which should also bring in any missing NuGet packages. Additionally, make sure you moved the configuration information from the appsettings.json file into the user secrets file. With that in place, add the following line of code to the Program.cs file (this is already present in the sample application for this book):

```
builder.Services.AddApplicationInsightsTelemetry(builder.Config
uration["ApplicationInsights:ConnectionString"]);
```

Once that code is in place and you have the entry in your user secrets, you can test your application. Before doing that, note how the telemetry client is injected into controllers now that Application Insights is configured as a service for your web application (see Figure 10-17).

```
private readonly ILogger<HomeController> _logger;
private readonly TelemetryClient _telemetryClient;
private readonly IConfiguration _configuration;
private readonly IUserRolesService _userRolesService;

0 references | 0 exceptions - live
public HomeController(ILogger<HomeController> logger, TelemetryClient telemetryClient, IConfigi
{
    _logger = logger;
    _telemetryClient = telemetryClient;
    _configuration = configuration;
    _userRolesService = userRolesService;
}
```

Figure 10-17. *The telemetry client is injected into the controller*

Within the controller are a couple of methods to show how you can easily leverage Application Insights from the code. The first is in the Index method, where both secrets are traced using _telemetryClient. TrackTrace("...").

The second and third telemetry instrumentation statements are for tracking an event and tracking an exception in the DemoLiveInsights method. The code is as follows:

```
public IActionResult DemoLiveInsights()
{
    _telemetryClient.TrackEvent("EventTracked: Demo Live
    Insights Viewed");
    try
    {
        throw new Exception("All exceptions can be easily
        tracked!");
    }
    catch (Exception ex)
    {
        _telemetryClient.TrackException(ex);
    }
    return View();
}
```

With the code in place, along with injection, you can review the information in Live Metrics in Azure, even when you are utilizing the code from your local development machine.

Reviewing Live Metrics

When an application is properly instrumented with Azure Application Insights, you can review the live metrics in real-time in Azure. To view live metrics, start the local application, then navigate in the portal to the Application Insights blade for the developer insights instance.

Requests

The Live Metrics view has several metrics automatically configured and available, including Request Rate, Request Duration, and Request Failure Rate for incoming requests.

Dependencies

For outgoing requests, note that Figure 10-18 validates the default outgoing requests are shown for Dependency Call Rate, Dependency Call Duration, and Dependency Call Failure Rate.

Exceptions

The Live Metrics view also includes a view of the exception rate, along with information about the health of the application. See Figure 10-18.

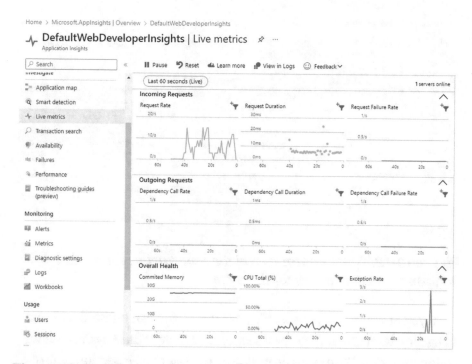

Figure 10-18.   *The Live Metrics include a number of line charts showing active information on the web solution*

Page Views/Server Performance

Just below the Live Metrics navigation item, the Performance navigation item lets you see the overall performance of the server and even see the performance of specific operations. You can use this to determine any bottlenecks in your network traffic, or potentially you might notice a route that is getting an extraneous number of executions and look for any bugs that might be calling the route too many times (or perhaps find options to cache the result of the route). Figure 10-19 shows the Performance blade for your review.

Figure 10-19. *The Performance blade shows active routes and performance information for the server*

If you are interested in specific page views, you can utilize the Events navigation item under the Usage section and filter to the Any Page View option under the Who Used drop-down. The User Flows section is also nice if you want to see how users are interacting with your site and what happens before and after pages are visited or events are fired.

User/Session Counts

Additional information on the Application Insights blade allows you to drill in and see the number of active users and sessions. This information isn't super exciting on a single developer machine, but you can imagine how useful this might be on a production application (see Figure 10-20).

Figure 10-20.   *The users and sessions can be viewed in the Application Insights blade*

Live Tracking of Trace, Event, and Exceptions

Another benefit of the live tracking of your application is you can instantly review any trace, event, and exception information that is being instrumented from your code. In the sample application, navigation to the home page will generate a couple of traces to log information about the configuration values retrieved. On the Demo Live App Insights blade, you can quickly and easily see the logging of events and exceptions. The live metrics are instantly shown as they occur, as shown in Figure 10-21.

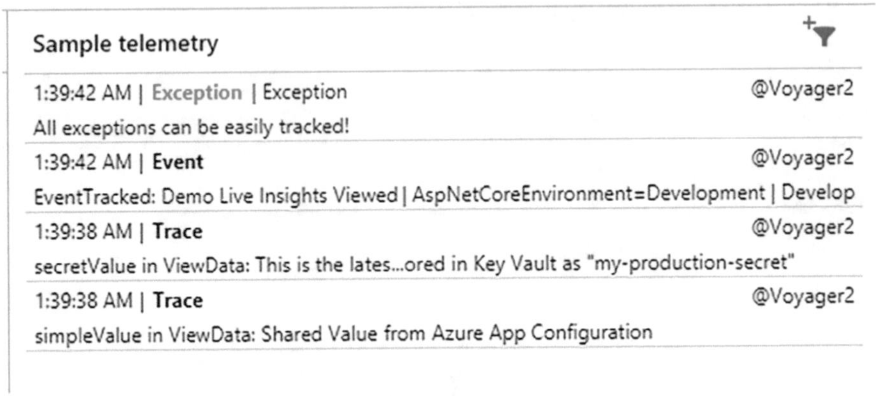

Sample telemetry	✚ 🝙
1:39:42 AM | Exception | Exception	@Voyager2
All exceptions can be easily tracked!	
1:39:42 AM | Event	@Voyager2
EventTracked: Demo Live Insights Viewed | AspNetCoreEnvironment=Development | Develop	
1:39:38 AM | Trace	@Voyager2
secretValue in ViewData: This is the lates...ored in Key Vault as "my-production-secret"	
1:39:38 AM | Trace	@Voyager2
simpleValue in ViewData: Shared Value from Azure App Configuration	

Figure 10-21. *Live Metrics instantly shows events, exceptions, and trace logs for review*

Client-Side JavaScript and AJAX Requests

In many scenarios, you'll need to instrument your application from the client side to enhance your monitoring. This is especially useful in a Single Page Application (SPA). To do this, you need to add a simple script to the client side of your application and include your instrumentation key in the JavaScript.

You can find more information about using Application Insights from the client-side at `https://learn.microsoft.com/azure/azure-monitor/app/javascript?tabs=snippet#snippet-based-setup`.

Performing Availability Tests

Availability tests are critical to determining if a problem is occurring before getting the influx of calls from users because pages are unresponsive. There are a number of tests that you can utilize, and for the AZ-204 Exam and in your day-to-day work, it's likely important to discern which type of test you would want to implement for various scenarios. All tests are found under the Availability blade, which is under the Investigate heading in your Application Insights instance (see Figure 10-22).

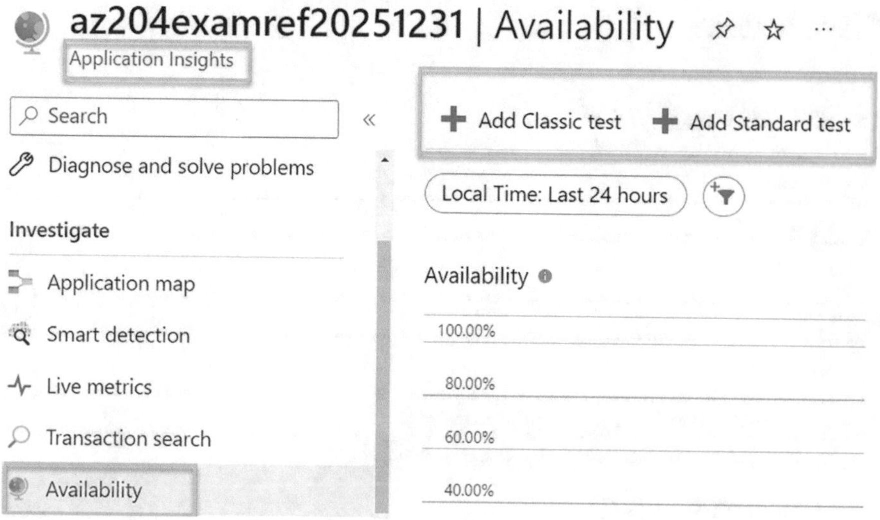

Figure 10-22. *The Availability blade in the Application Insights instance contains the ability to create tests for availability on your deployed applications*

URL Tests (Classic Test)

The simplest availability test just pings the URL that you specify. If no response is received, the test fails. You configure how often to test and how many failures to get in a row before sounding the alarm (see Figure 10-23).

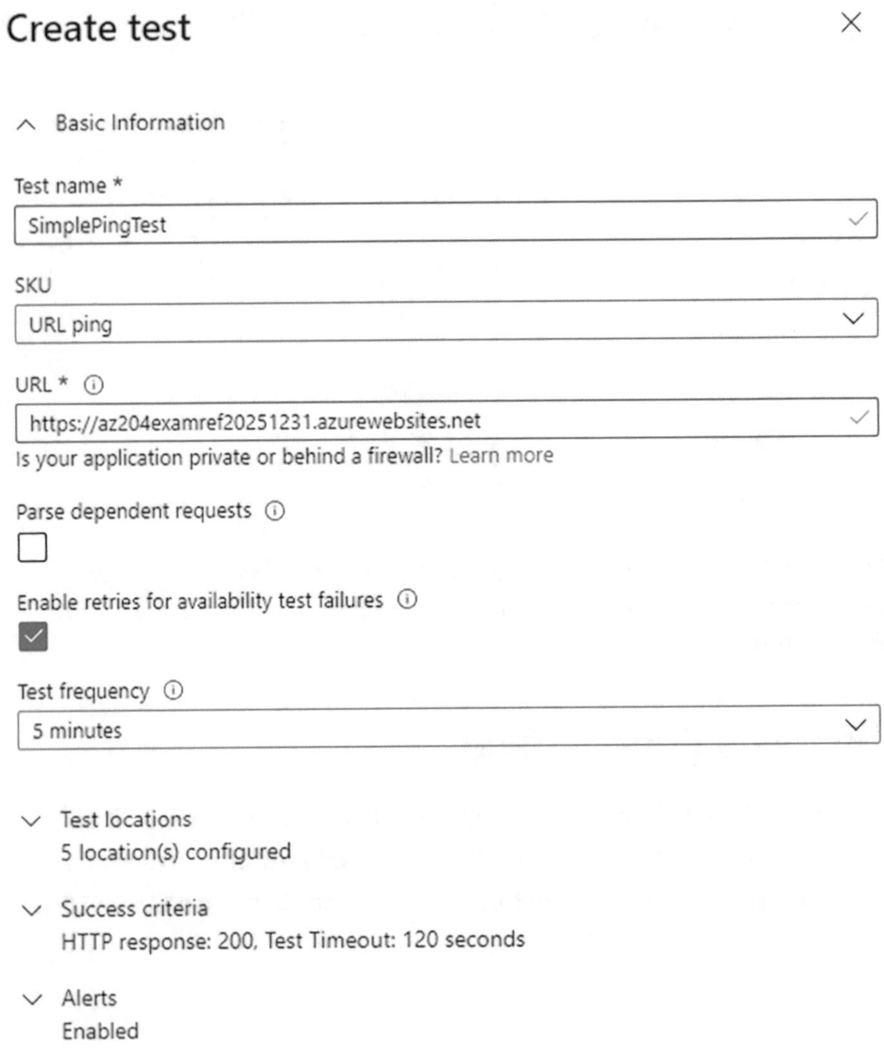

Create test ✕

⌃ Basic Information

Test name *

| SimplePingTest | ✓ |

SKU

| URL ping | ⌄ |

URL * ⓘ

| https://az204examref20251231.azurewebsites.net | ✓ |

Is your application private or behind a firewall? Learn more

Parse dependent requests ⓘ

☐

Enable retries for availability test failures ⓘ

☑

Test frequency ⓘ

| 5 minutes | ⌄ |

⌄ Test locations
    5 location(s) configured

⌄ Success criteria
    HTTP response: 200, Test Timeout: 120 seconds

⌄ Alerts
    Enabled

Figure 10-23. *Creating a simple URL PING test*

Standard Test

In many scenarios, you need to validate health in addition to availability. For example, consider an API endpoint that is returning data from a database. Perhaps you want to validate that the data is included in the response. In another scenario, you might need to get various results based on information you pass in the header of the request. In these scenarios, you can utilize a standard test. Standard tests can also be used to validate SSL validity.

Custom Testing with TrackAvailability()

A third type of test can be used for tracking availability via custom code. This test can be more complex because you control the code, so this test requires a code change.

In the appkication's code, you can create a call to your telemetry object's `TrackAvailability` method. This allows you to trace the availability of a specific route or method with much greater detail as to the information involved in the request.

You can learn more about these tests at `https://learn.microsoft. com/azure/azure-monitor/app/availability-azure-functions`.

Application Map

Once an application has Application Insights telemetry, Azure will automatically start graphing resource dependencies. After the application is utilized for a few minutes and dependencies are leveraged, the Application Map can be an invaluable resource for reviewing the network traffic and identifying any bottlenecks. Figure 10-24 shows the Application Map after a few requests are made and the user logs in to the website.

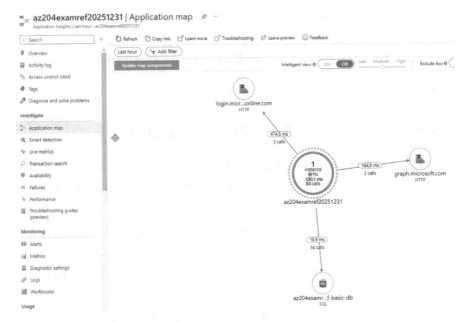

Figure 10-24. *The Application Map tracks dependency information automatically once an application is configured correctly for Application Insights*

Kusto Queries

Within Azure there are a couple of times that using Kusto Queries is expected. The most important place this is used when preparing for the AZ-204 Exam is in Log Analytics to gather information about your applications from insights. If you get deeper into security and study for other security exams, Kusto will be used for scenarios like threat-hunting in Microsoft Defender (see this link for more information: `https://learn.microsoft.com/microsoft-365/security/defender/advanced-hunting-query-language?view=o365-worldwide`).

Kusto can be an incredibly frustrating language for traditional T-SQL developers because everything will feel a bit backwards as to the composition of a query. For example, a time-series event that happened within the last hour in T-SQL would be something like WHERE `timeField` > `DATEADD(hh, -1, GETDATE())`. In Kusto, the query is something similar to this:

```
traces
| where timestamp > ago(1h)
```

Note that the timestamp is part of the event, and the query is looking for traces that happen since "1 hour ago until now".

To run queries, you want to be set to the scope of the Application Insights instance where the events, traces, and exceptions are happening. On the Insights instance, select the Logs navigation item to run queries.

There are two types of queries that perform differently based on their usage: log-based and pre-aggregated time-series.

Log-Based Metrics

Log-based metrics require a query to gather the data and are therefore a bit slower due to fetching data and conglomerating it as the query is executed.

Pre-Aggregated Time-Series

Pre-aggregated time-series metrics are conglomerated as they happen, so these queries are highly performant.

Creating an Alert Based on a Query

Typically, you will create alerts in Azure to handle notification of problems within a solution or group of solutions. These alerts are part of the Azure Monitor ecosystem. You can create alerts on any events within Azure, and alerts require three things.

- A signal

- An action group to notify

- How to notify the action group

Signals

Signals are the condition to monitor. One signal can be a metric threshold, such CPU utilization above 85 percent or memory utilization above 75 percent. Another signal might be based on a query, for things like too many exceptions in the last hour. Yet another signal might be based on a custom log entry, where the alert is fired because a critical failure has occurred.

Action Groups

Action groups are simple groups that need to be notified based on common concerns. This could be a set of web administrators for a web solution, database administrators for database alerts, and could even be for security concerns. Based on the type of alert, the action group allows the appropriate users to get notifications.

Notification Methods

When a signal fires, the action group is notified. The notification methods are configured in the action group, but it's important enough to separate this out to know the ways notifications can be sent. Notifications can currently be sent via the following methods:

- Email

- SMS

- Push notifications

Additionally, notifications or responses can be configured to accomplish further tasks associated with the alert, such as:

- Trigger an Azure Function

- Trigger an Azure Logic App

- Place information into your IT Service Manager ticketing system (ITSM)

- Send an event to the Azure Event Hub

- POST information to a webhook

- Run an Azure Automation Runbook

For this example, a custom query is created to generate an alert.

Create the Query

Open the Logs blade in the Application Insights and create the following query to test that it is valid:

```
exceptions
| where timestamp > ago(4h)
| count
```

Note that you may need to trigger some exceptions if none are showing up. Assuming the count is greater than zero, you can create an alert rule. Click + New Alert Rule in the Query Editor, as shown in Figure 10-25.

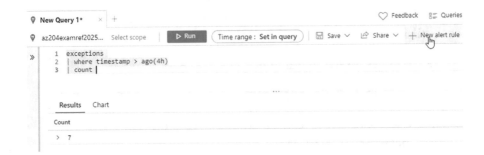

Figure 10-25. *Creating a new alert rule from a valid query*

Set the Alert Condition

Most of the information will fill in automatically when you create the rule this way, but if you were creating the rule from scratch, you'd have to add the query on this blade.

The `Measure` alert condition will be set to the count, with an aggregation type of `Total`. You can set the granularity to make sense for this alert. Perhaps the best implementation is to aggregate results every 30 minutes and then run the montor to fire only every 30 minutes to avoid noise in your alert channels, while potentially keeping the costs down. Truly, the costs around an alert are not individually excessive. (They are usually around $0.10/alert, but can range to a higher number based on frequency and the types of operations in the alert signal.)

For testing, set the aggregation and evaluation values to five minutes. For the operator, set the value to Greater Than, and put a threshold value of five as well, so if there are more than five exceptions in the previous four hours, every five minutes you'll get an alert (see Figure 10-26).

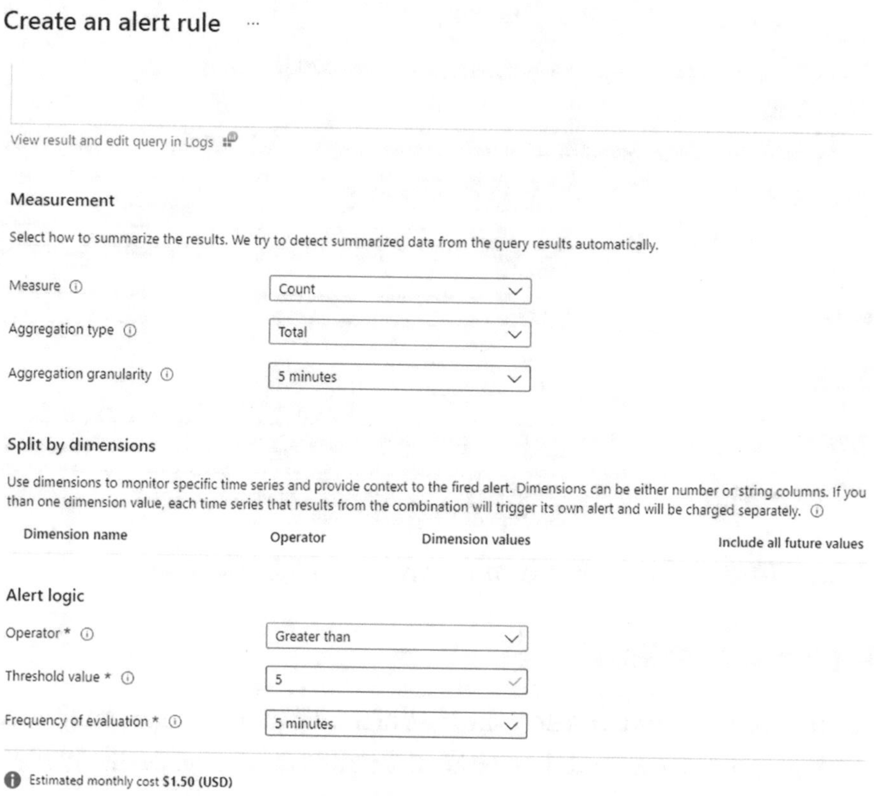

Create an alert rule   ...

View result and edit query in Logs 🗗

Measurement

Select how to summarize the results. We try to detect summarized data from the query results automatically.

Measure ⓘ	Count ⌄
Aggregation type ⓘ	Total ⌄
Aggregation granularity ⓘ	5 minutes ⌄

Split by dimensions

Use dimensions to monitor specific time series and provide context to the fired alert. Dimensions can be either number or string columns. If you than one dimension value, each time series that results from the combination will trigger its own alert and will be charged separately. ⓘ

| Dimension name | Operator | Dimension values | Include all future values |

Alert logic

Operator * ⓘ	Greater than ⌄
Threshold value * ⓘ	5 ✓
Frequency of evaluation * ⓘ	5 minutes ⌄

ⓘ Estimated monthly cost $1.50 (USD)

Figure 10-26. *The alert signal is the query, and the evaluation is configured with an estimated cost of $1.50 per month*

Create the Actions

To get the action set, you need to create and select an action group, and you need to determine who is in the action group and what the notification channel will be.

Set the Basics

For the basics, configure the name and display name in the subscription and resource group for the correct region (see Figure 10-27).

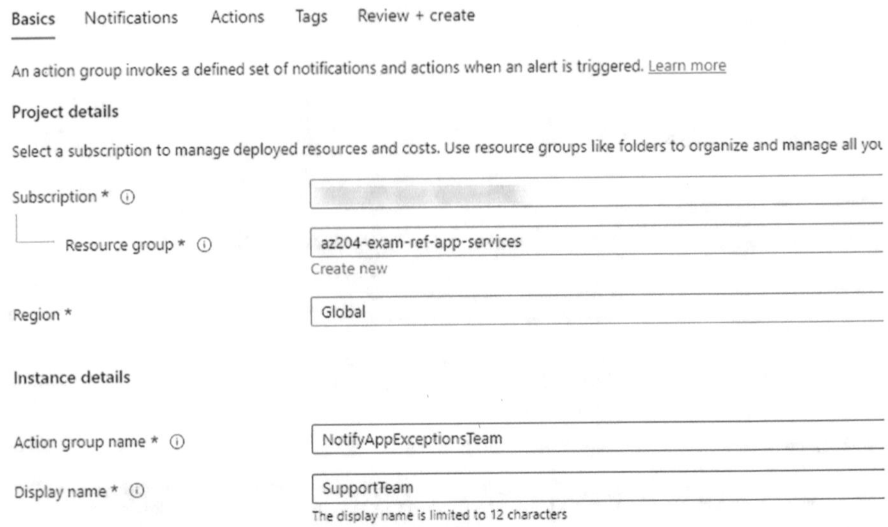

Basics   Notifications   Actions   Tags   Review + create

An action group invokes a defined set of notifications and actions when an alert is triggered. Learn more

Project details

Select a subscription to manage deployed resources and costs. Use resource groups like folders to organize and manage all you

Subscription * ⓘ

Resource group * ⓘ   az204-exam-ref-app-services
                            Create new

Region *   Global

Instance details

Action group name * ⓘ   NotifyAppExceptionsTeam

Display name * ⓘ   SupportTeam
                            The display name is limited to 12 characters

Figure 10-27.   *The action is configured on the Basics tab*

Set the Notifications

On the Notifications tab, select the type of notification, such as email/SMS
message/push/voice, and then name the notification type. On the blade,
enter any email and/or SMS information (see Figure 10-28).

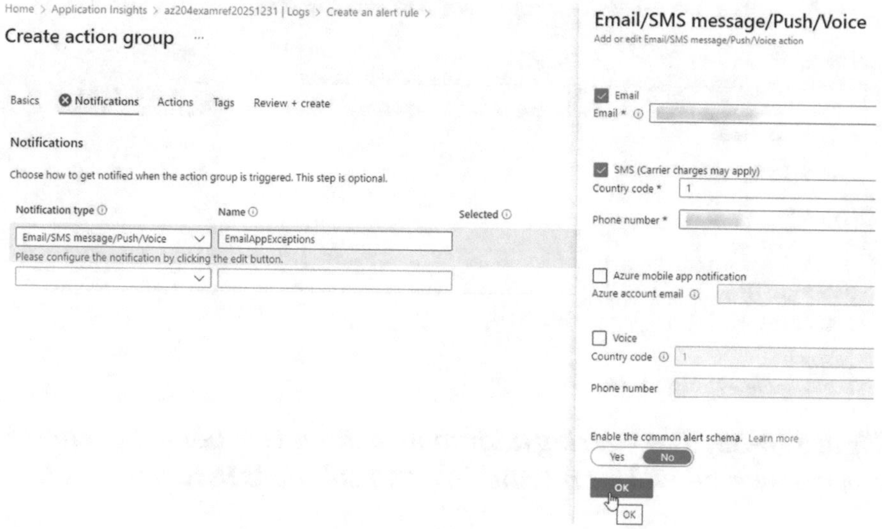

Figure 10-28. *The notifications are configured for the new alert*

Configure the Actions

In addition to email/SMS, you can configure additional options as
mentioned earlier. For this alert rule I'm not creating any additional
actions. Now that you've seen this operationally, you should be in
command of the idea of what it takes to utilize these alerts with various
actions like triggering an Azure Function or Logic App, sending an event to
the Event Hub, or posting to another webhook endpoint (see Figure 10-29).

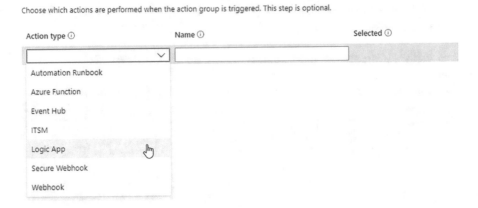

Figure 10-29. *Configuring additional actions is optional but can be a very powerful tool for monitoring your solutions in Azure*

With the options selected, complete the creation of the action group. Once the group is created, it will be associated with the rule you are in the process of creating (see Figure 10-30).

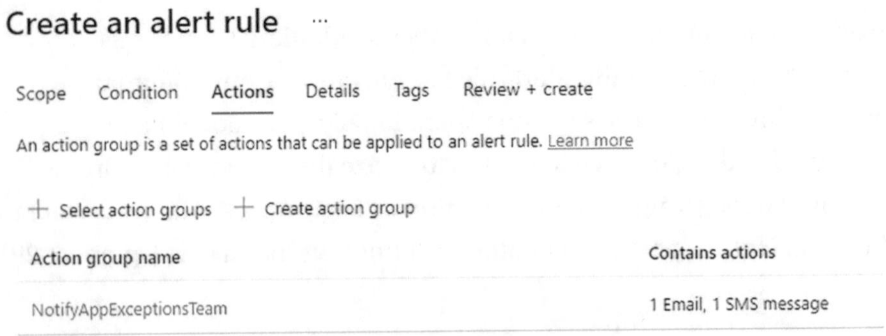

Figure 10-30. *The alert rule is configured with the newly created action group*

Details

When configuring the Details section, you can choose a specific severity level from 0 (critical) to 4 (verbose) and then name the rule and give it a description. Make sure to also set your region for the rule. Additionally, you can configure advanced options around the rule and give metadata around the rule for your own custom properties. Figure 10-31 shows the configuration of the rule before creation.

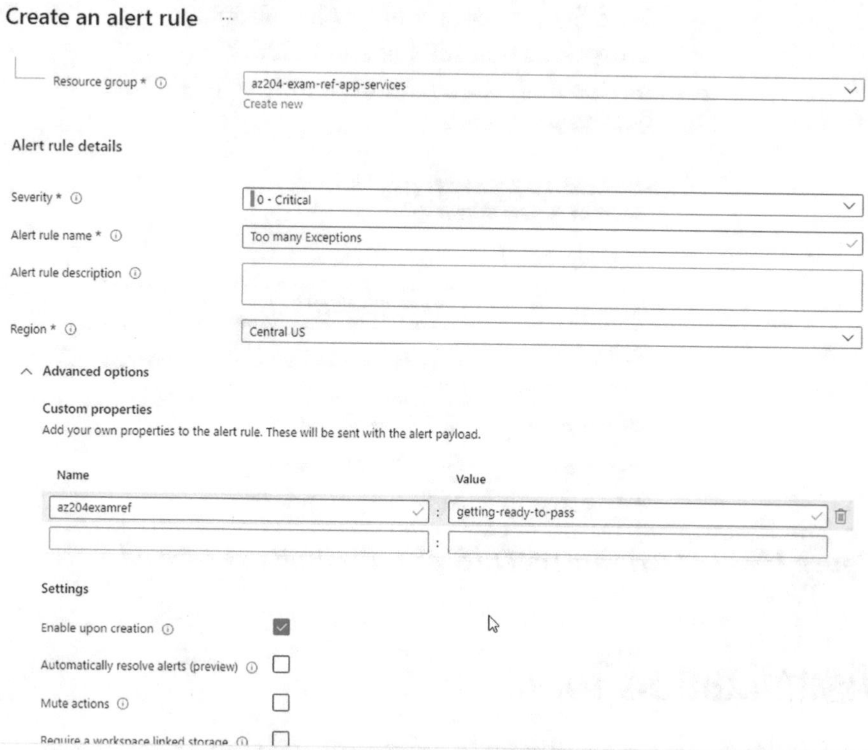

Figure 10-31. *Configuring the rule is completed*

Complete the rule, and you should start getting some email and/or SMS notifications after about ten minutes or so, provided you have greater than five exceptions in the last four hours. The SMS and email alerts are both shown in Figure 10-32.

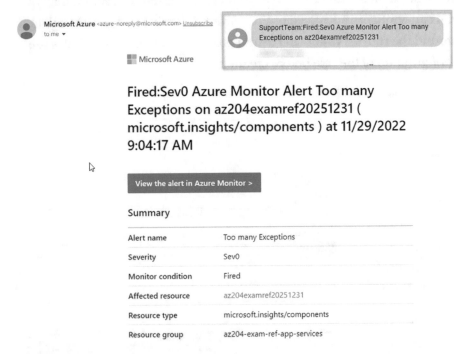

Figure 10-32. *Alerts are sent to SMS and email as expected*

Visualization Tools

The last thing that you need to be in command of for the AZ-204 Exam when it comes to monitoring your solutions is how to visualize the data. Throughout this chapter you've seen some of the charts and logs that can be utilized, but what do you do when you need to get a single pane of glass to view all the information that is critical to you at once? You need to create some sort of business dashboard.

Power BI

The tool that might be the most integrated into your current workflows and team ecosystems is likely Power BI. Power BI is a Microsoft solution, and you can get a free trial to learn how to use Power BI for building powerful dashboards if you want to try it out. You should not need to know how to create a Power BI dashboard for this exam, but it will likely be more important to understand how to build visualizations as you move toward the AZ-400 Exam for DevOps if that is your next step.

Third-Party Solutions/Grafana

As an alternative to Power BI, you could consider creating dashboards in a third-party solution such as Grafana. Once again, this is a bit beyond the scope of the AZ-204 Exam.

Workbook

A third option in Azure is to create an Azure Monitor Workbook. Creating a workbook is typically outside of the scope of the AZ-204 Exam, but is important enough to review, and would likely be within scope for the AZ-400 DevOps Exam and the AZ-305 Architect Exam. For more information on creating a workbook, review the following link: `https://learn.microsoft.com/azure/azure-monitor/visualize/workbooks-create-workbook`.

If you click Pin To and select Workbook and then send the time and query as parameters and part of the workbook, you can easily create a workbook similar to the one shown in Figure 10-33.

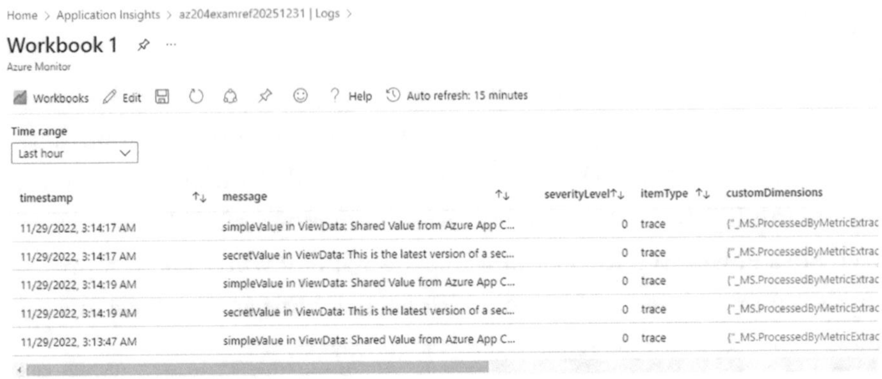

Figure 10-33. *A workbook can easily be created for viewing data*

One nice thing about the workbook is it obfuscates the query and can be set to auto-refresh at specified intervals.

Azure Dashboard

A final option for creating a visualization is within an Azure Dashboard. This is the easiest way to create a visualization for Azure Monitor and is baked into your Azure subscription.

Create a Dashboard Based on a Query

To get started, return to the logs for the Application Insights and create the same query as before, but change the query to `traces` instead of `exceptions`. Change the timestamp to `> ago(1h)`.

With the query set, select Pin To and then select Azure Dashboard. Select Create New and Shared, then name the dashboard something like `Traces for Default Web` (see Figure 10-34).

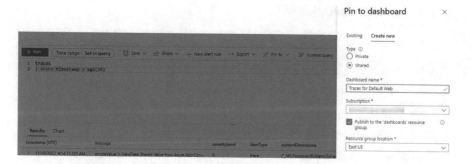

Figure 10-34. *The query is pinned to a new shared dashboard*

Publish the dashboard, then navigate to it under the Shared dashboards for the subscription. You will see your query results on the dashboard. You can now add queries to this dashboard or wire up metrics from any Application Insights to create a powerful single-pane-of-glass view to monitor your solution (see Figure 10-35).

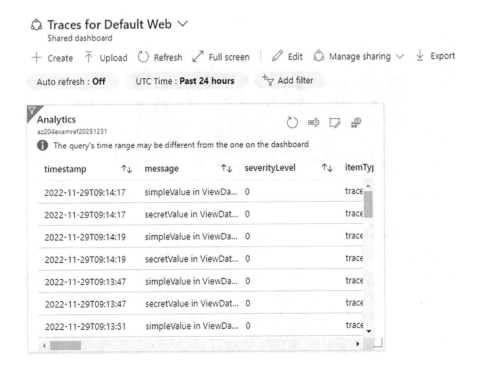

Figure 10-35.   *The Azure Dashboard shows the results of the query*

Complete the AZ-204: Instrument Solutions to Support Monitoring and Logging

To fully learn the material, I recommend taking the time to also complete the MS Learn module for Instrument Solutions to Support Monitoring and Logging found here:

- Monitor App Performance: https://learn.
  microsoft.com/training/modules/monitor-app-
  performance/

Review Your Learning

As an additional challenge, consider the following questions and determine how you would approach potential solution(s). You can find answers to these questions in Appendix A at the end of this book

1) What types of information can be monitored? Do you have to do anything to get monitoring in your Azure subscription?

2) What are the major components of Azure Monitor?

3) Do your web solutions automatically get monitoring? If so, is there additional monitoring you can implement? If so, how do you do this for a typical .NET application?

4) What types of information can be utilized with Application Insights? What are some of the other types of insights available and what are they for?

5) What is an availability test? How do you create a test to check if your website is responding?

6) What is the purpose of the Application Map? What do you have to do to get it to work with your solutions?

7) What is a Kusto Query? How do you run a custom Kusto Query? How do you use a custom query to trigger an alert?

8) What are the three main aspects of creating an alert? Do alerts always cost the same? What are some of the actions for notification/remediation/tracking of alerts that you can take?

9) What are some of the main ways to visualize information from Azure Monitor? Are there any default visualizations that you can leverage? What are the benefits of creating more robust visualizations?

10) Where in Azure can you create visualizations? What are some additional tools that allow you to create visualizations?

Chapter Summary

In this chapter, you learned about instrumenting your solutions with Application Insights to allow your team to troubleshoot your application performance, create a dashboard that lets you quickly see your app performance, use Kusto Queries to look for issues in your app, perform URL PING tests, and review the Application Map.

After working through this chapter and the Microsoft Learn modules, you should be on track to be in command of the following concepts as you learn about Azure and prepare for the AZ-204 Exam:

- Instrument your applications to use Azure Application Insights.

- Leverage the Azure Log Analytics Workspace with Kusto Queries to query log data for display on dashboards.

- Know which types of dashboards and tools you can use and which scenarios to use them in (the difference between metrics and logs, static and dynamic dashboards).

- Utilize Application Insights to trace through your application resources, view request metrics, and find bottlenecks with the Application Map.

- Create and utilize standard and URL PING tests to determine the ongoing health of a website. Create and utilize an alert when the site is not healthy.

- Create and utilize alerts, specifically how do you create them and how do you notify users (both how and where do you do this).

In the next chapter, you learn about implementing an API solution to group your APIs for proper customer access on a single application URL, while obfuscating the backend details from the customers with Azure API Management.

PART V

Connect to and Consume Azure Services and Third-Party Services

CHAPTER 11

Implement API Management

Consider the scenario in your organization where you have multiple function apps, app services, and/or containerized solutions exposed on multiple public-facing endpoints. In this scenario, clients must be aware of your entire API offerings, and you really don't have a lot of control over how they interact with these various APIs.

Overview

API Management (APIM) is a tool that is designed to help you bring all your APIs together under one façade. With APIM, you can give your clients only one public-facing URL, and you can completely decouple your backend operations from their requests, meaning that you are free to update the APIs as necessary and the client may never know anything about where or how the information is retrieved—they simply make the same call they've always made.

Additional benefits of the APIM implementation are discussed as you journey through this chapter. Some of these benefits are the reduction of attack surface, the ability to version your APIs, and the ability to group and control access to all your APIs into one centralized management solution.

© Brian L. Gorman 2023
B. L. Gorman, *Developing Solutions for Microsoft Azure Certification Companion*, Certification Study Companion Series, https://doi.org/10.1007/978-1-4842-9300-3_11

Prerequisites

If you are going to work through this chapter, make sure you've deployed the Azure Function App as per Chapter 6. The code for the Azure Function App is included with the resources for the book, both in Chapter 6 and in this chapter. Alternatively, you can create a much simpler app that just has a couple of functions for use in this chapter if you haven't worked through Chapter 6 or just want to practice creating a simple function app.

For this chapter, you need two functions: Function1 and GetTopMovies. Function1 is just the default function created with any Azure Function App (using .NET 6 or previous) that takes the parameter for name in the query string or in the request body. If you use the newer .NET 7, it will be just fine as well, but you won't have any parameter for name in Function1 for .NET 7. GetTopMovies is just a function that returns a list of movies (or really, any list of objects as JSON; see Figure 11-1).

Figure 11-1. *This chapter focuses on a function app with at least two functions. Here, the GetTopMovies function is tested to validate the list of movies is returned*

To make this as simple as possible, the resources for this chapter use the completed function app from Chapter 6 and a starter function app using .NET 6 and a starter function app using .NET 7. All of the solutions contain the necessary start conditions, as mentioned. Your main job, therefore, is to make sure you have one of them deployed. For extra practice, you can choose to deploy all of them and make API endpoints to each one. Each project also contains a YAML file if you want to automate your deployment, or you can right-click and publish to your Function App at Azure.

One final note here. As of the writing of this chapter, functions that utilize the Isolated Worker Process cannot be tested from within the portal. This seems to be a known bug that is not getting addressed. If you deploy the .NET 7 Isolated Function App, you can still run the functions by accessing the URL for the function, you just may not be able to test them in the portal. I've also tried to call out differences, but in case I missed any or it isn't clear, the default function in .NET 6 has a `querystring` or body parameter for name that toggles the response to show the name or ask for the name. The default function for .NET 7 just responds with `Welcome to Azure Functions` and that is all it does.

Resource Group

In contrast to previous chapters, this chapter starts by deploying a new APIM instance. When you deploy the APIM, you need to have a preexisting Application Insights instance.

For this reason, begin this provisioning process by creating a resource group. Name the resource group something like `az204-exam-ref-apim` and set the group to the region of your choice. For practice, consider performing this step using the Azure CLI with a command like `az group create --name az204-exam-ref-apim --location centralus`. When completed, validate that you have the group as expected (see Figure 11-2).

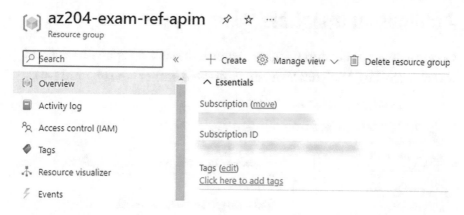

Figure 11-2. The resource group was created as expected

Log Analytics Workspace

Assuming you will want to utilize Application Insights, you need a Log
Analytics Workspace to store the data from the Application Insights. Create
a new Log Analytics Workspace named something like `az204-exam-`
`ref-apim-analytics`. Ensure the workspace is created (similar to the
deployment shown in Figure 11-3).

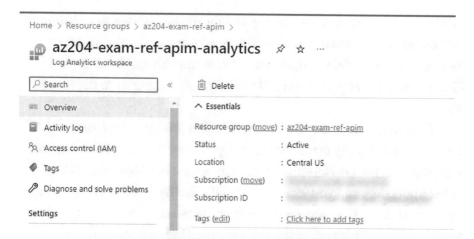

Figure 11-3. The Log Analytics Workspace was created as expected

Application Insights

Create a new Application Insights instance that is workspace-based and leverage the Log Analytics Workspace created earlier (see Figure 11-4).

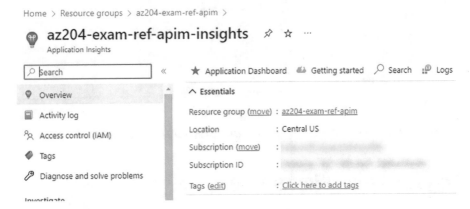

Figure 11-4. An Application Insights resource is provisioned prior to provisioning the APIM instance

Creating an APIM Instance

A couple of the examples for policy and the developer web application will require an instance that is on the Developer tier. Deploying at any tier other than the Consumption tier will require about 45 minutes. A Consumption tier application will take about five minutes to deploy at the most.

If you don't mind skipping a couple of the examples and/or you just need to move quickly through this, or if you want to minimize costs, you can deploy at the Consumption tier. You will not be able to throttle by subscription key and you won't get a public-facing Developer Portal for your APIM at the Consumption tier. Everything else should pretty much work in a similar manner to the Development tier deployment.

APIM Basics Tab

On the Basics tab, select your subscription and resource group, along with a region. For the resource name, use a unique name such as az204-exam-ref-apim-development. While you should use your organization name and email, you can put anything you want in those two fields (see Figure 11-5).

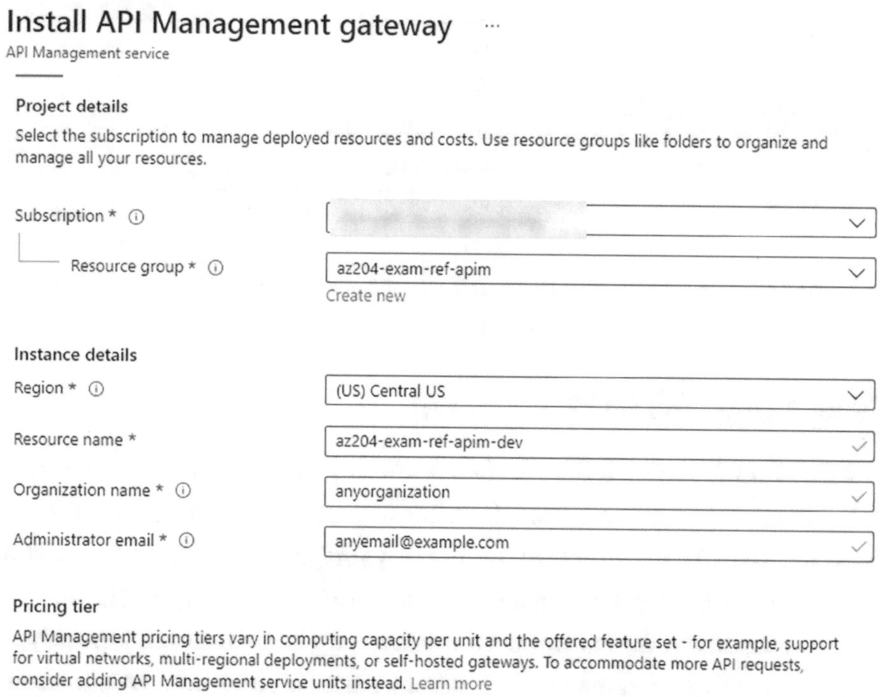

Install API Management gateway ...
API Management service

Project details

Select the subscription to manage deployed resources and costs. Use resource groups like folders to organize and manage all your resources.

Subscription * ⓘ	
Resource group * ⓘ	az204-exam-ref-apim
	Create new

Instance details

Region * ⓘ	(US) Central US
Resource name *	az204-exam-ref-apim-dev
Organization name * ⓘ	anyorganization
Administrator email * ⓘ	anyemail@example.com

Pricing tier

API Management pricing tiers vary in computing capacity per unit and the offered feature set - for example, support for virtual networks, multi-regional deployments, or self-hosted gateways. To accommodate more API requests, consider adding API Management service units instead. Learn more

Figure 11-5. The basic configuration is complete other than the tiers

APIM SKUs (Tiers/Offerings)

There are a number of tiers that you can choose from on the APIM deployment. As mentioned, the Consumption tier is relatively inexpensive and deploys in a matter of a couple of minutes. The other tiers have additional offerings and considerations, and they take about 45 minutes to deploy.

For this demonstration, I'm using a Development tier. If you want to select the Development tier and move on (rather than wait for the deployment to complete), submit to deploy the APIM, then come back to review the different options on the tiers. Pricing tiers are shown as the available options in Figure 11-6.

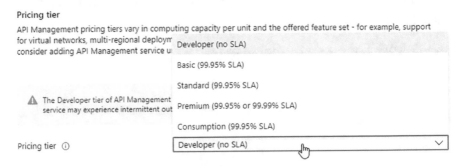

Figure 11-6. *The pricing tiers are shown as the available options when creating a new APIM instance*

Consumption (99.95 Percent SLA)

The Consumption tier is the serverless offering for APIM that allows you to have around a million free calls to the service and then runs about four cents per 10,000 calls after that. At this tier, you get a bit of an SLA, but you don't have the ability to be on a private network or have any isolation.

The reason the Consumption tier can get up and running so quickly is that it is on a shared gateway, and therefore doesn't have to provision and deploy a new gateway.

Developer (no SLA)

The Developer tier is really meant for testing and prototyping a solution and is not intended to be used for production. There is no SLA on this tier, and it costs about seven cents per hour to run a developer tier APIM. The Developer tier is the first tier that gets a Developer Portal for creating a public-facing page with information about your APIs and the ability to request a subscription to utilize the APIs. The Developer tier is limited to 500 requests per second.

Basic (99.95 Percent SLA)

The Basic tier is the entry-level production tier that uses a shared gateway. This tier cannot be isolated on a private network and has no ability to leverage Azure AD on the Developer Portal. This tier costs 21 cents per hour. The basic tier can scale to two instances, which allows for a throughput of 1,000 requests per second.

Standard (99.95 Percent SLA)

The Standard tier is designed for small to medium production workloads and runs at $0.95 per hour. The standard tier can scale to four instances and has a throughput of 2,500 requests per second. Azure AD can be used with the Developer Portal at this tier.

Premium (99.95 or 99.99 Percent SLA)

The Premium tier is for medium to large production workloads and runs at $3.83 per hour. This tier can scale to 12 units per region, and it is the first production-ready tier to offer options for utilization of availability zones and private networking. The Premium tier has a throughput of 4,000 requests per second and runs on a self-hosted gateway. The ability to utilize a self-hosted gateway allows for secure connection to hybrid networks (on-premises) and multi-cloud networks.

APIM Monitoring Tab

On the Monitoring tab, select your predeployed Application Insights, as shown in Figure 11-7.

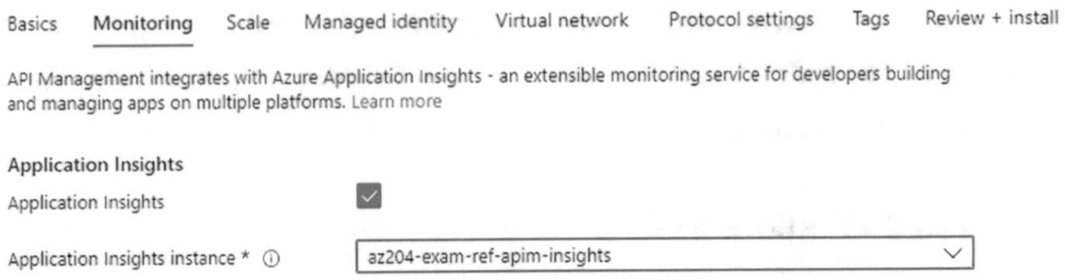

Basics   **Monitoring**   Scale   Managed identity   Virtual network   Protocol settings   Tags   Review + install

API Management integrates with Azure Application Insights - an extensible monitoring service for developers building and managing apps on multiple platforms. Learn more

Application Insights

Application Insights   ☑

Application Insights instance * ⓘ | az204-exam-ref-apim-insights   ⌄ |

Figure 11-7. The Monitoring tab gives you the ability to implement a preexisting Application Insights instance

APIM Scale Tab

At the Developer and Consumption tiers, no scaling is possible. On higher tiers, you can create additional units (at additional cost, of course). Additional units provide additional hardware for your APIM solution to handle more requests per second (this increases your throughput). Figure 11-8 shows how you can choose up to ten "units" on the Premium tier.

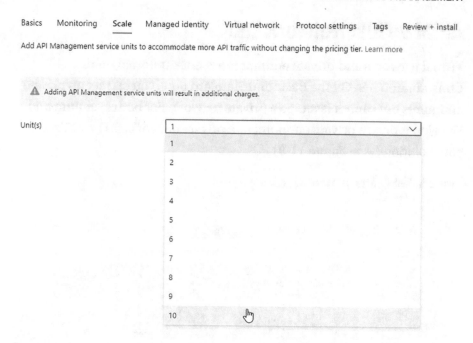

Figure 11-8. *The higher tiers allow additional units to be provisioned for scaling your workloads to increase the number of requests per second that your APIM solution can handle*

APIM Managed Identity

You can (and likely will) want to create a managed identity for the APIM instance. This can be accomplished after deployment, however. For this reason, skip through the Managed Identity tab when deploying and assign the Managed Identity when it is needed.

APIM Virtual Network Tab

Virtual networks and private endpoints are not supported on the Consumption tier. On the Basic and Standard tiers, you can set up private endpoints but cannot leverage a private network. For both Premium and Developer tiers, a private endpoint or a private network can be utilized in your solutions (see Figure 11-9).

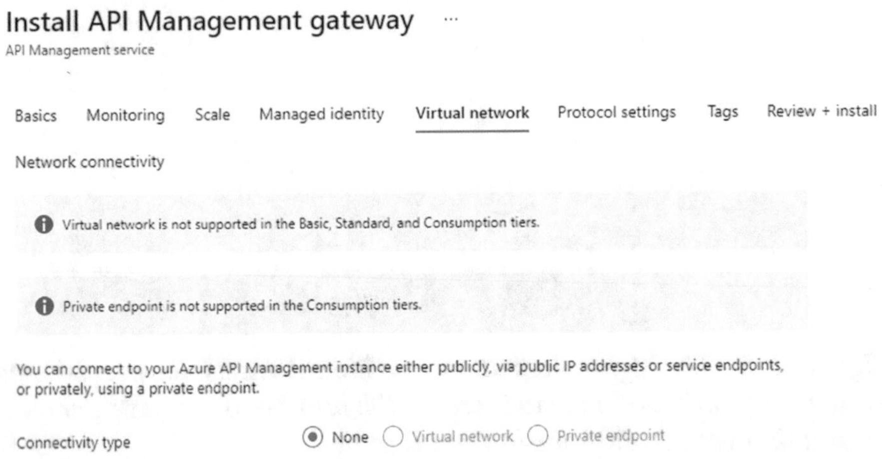

Figure 11-9. *The networking options are limited in tiers other than Developer and Premium*

APIM Protocol Settings

The protocol settings allow you to configure additional options for connecting with and utilizing traffic (or securing traffic) to and from your APIM. Unless you need additional functionality, just leave the additional protocol settings unchecked (see Figure 11-10).

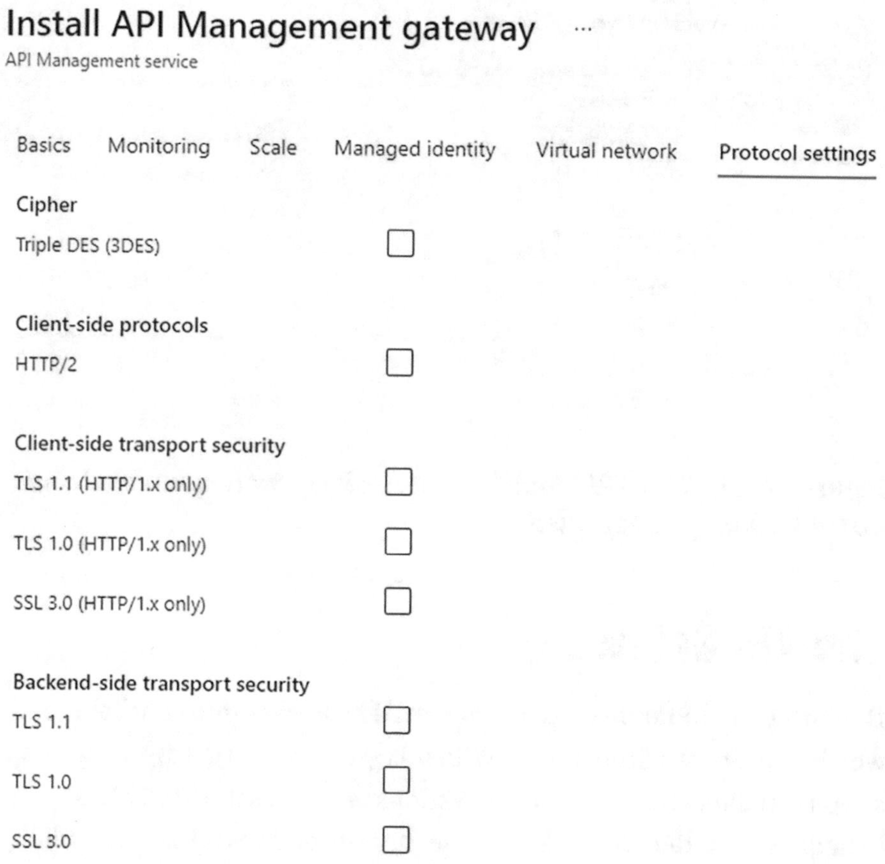

Install API Management gateway ...
API Management service

| Basics | Monitoring | Scale | Managed identity | Virtual network | Protocol settings |

Cipher

Triple DES (3DES) ☐

Client-side protocols

HTTP/2 ☐

Client-side transport security

TLS 1.1 (HTTP/1.x only) ☐

TLS 1.0 (HTTP/1.x only) ☐

SSL 3.0 (HTTP/1.x only) ☐

Backend-side transport security

TLS 1.1 ☐

TLS 1.0 ☐

SSL 3.0 ☐

Figure 11-10. *The protocol settings can be left to the default settings*

Go ahead and start the deployment of the APIM instance. As mentioned, this may take a significant amount of time for the non-Consumption tiers to establish public gateway access. When completed, validate that your APIM instance is up and running as expected (see Figure 11-11).

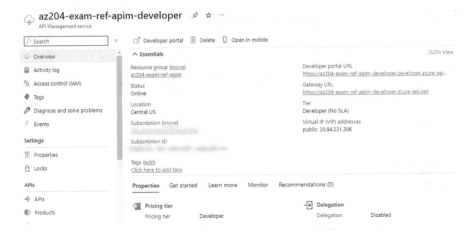

Figure 11-11. *The API Management deployment is completed and up and running as expected*

The API Gateway

Deploying the APIM instance creates an API Gateway into your solution, which is one centralized façade. With this gateway, you get layer 7 routing so you can direct traffic by route to various backend services. This is incredibly important for APIs because the bulk of the work is based on the route provided. If the gateway only gave layer 4 routing, then the only thing that could be used to direct traffic would be the IP address, which wouldn't work for a route-based API call. With the gateway in place, the clients simply have to manage the single point of entry and then any unique routes they have been authorized to utilize via products and/or subscriptions in the API Management solution (products and subscriptions are covered later in the chapter).

Entry Point for All Requests

Since the clients have only one public URL to remember, they don't have to manage a number of individual endpoints. This makes their integrations with your solutions much easier for your clients and your team to manage. While the clients only have one entry point, you also have just a single control plane on which you need to manage their access.

When the client request comes in, based on the URL and any authentication you have in place, your solution then routes their requests to the appropriate services and returns the data from the solution to the client.

Essentially, the API Gateway acts as a reverse proxy. By allowing your solutions to easily send data to the clients while also managing what access clients have in the solution, you can be assured that you are also protecting other data from incorrectly being accessed by your clients.

Gateway Routing

As stated, the API Gateway operates on layer 7 routing, so the requests can be directed based on the path, not just on IP address (which would be a limitation of layer 4 routing).

Benefits of a Centralized Gateway

The centralized gateway means that you only have one entry point to manage access and the client only has one entry point to which they send requests. This is a benefit for both you and your clients, as you can easily allow or deny requests as appropriate, and the client doesn't have to manage multiple endpoints.

Route Aggregation

Another benefit of this solution is the ability for the client to make one call and your solution to be able to make multiple calls to different backend services, conglomerate the data, and return the result.

For example, instead of the client needing to call to three calculation functions individually, the client calls to one endpoint, which could leverage a backend service like an Azure durable function that implements a fan-out pattern. When the request fans back in and the data is summarized, the client gets the result and doesn't have any concern about the various services needed to create the desired result.

Decouple Backend Services from Clients

With the use of APIM, your backend services are now completely independent of the client. As mentioned, the client just calls to the façade, and your APIM manages the routing of the traffic. This could be to a legacy service or to the latest version of a new implementation. The client is agnostic to the backend services, and they are able to be interchanged without breaking client applications.

SSL Termination (SSL Offload)

Although SSL termination is more likely a concern for network administrators, as a developer you may be put in charge of managing the SSL for a solution. With multiple backend services that are public-facing, each would need SSL management. With APIM, you can have the entry-point on SSL and then all the backend services can send traffic without SSL since the traffic is on the Azure backbone once it's routed from inside the APIM instance.

Reduced Attack Surface

With multiple public services, you also have multiple security concerns. While you will still have plenty of security concerns even with an APIM solution, the fact that you no longer have to manage multiple public entry points can give you a lot more control and ability to monitor your solutions for security risks.

Logging and Monitoring

The centralized nature of this solution also means that all requests can be easily logged and any issues that happen in the service can be monitored and mitigated.

Response Caching

With response caching, you can reduce the latency for calls to your APIs by caching responses so that the second and consecutive calls to the endpoint don't need to call to the backend service. An additional benefit of this is not just the latency improvements, but the reduced workload on your backend services.

Validation of Tokens and/or Certificates

With APIM, your solution can create additional security by requiring the clients that connect to utilize JSON Web Tokens (JWT) for authorization or you can implement a full client/server certificate authorization solution.

Administering APIs in the Azure Portal

Hopefully your APIM solution is deployed by now or at least is getting close to being available. In the next few sections in this chapter, you're to learn how to create and work with the various moving pieces of APIM to create a solution that exposes only the appropriate data to various clients. To follow along, make sure you have a completely deployed APIM instance.

APIs

At the heart of the APIM solution is the ability to have one or more APIs. Each of these APIs will expose various operations via endpoints to the clients.

Create an API

To get started, navigate into your APIM instance and select the APIs blade. On the APIs blade, select + Add API. Within the portal, under Create from Azure Resource, select Function App to start the process of creating an API that leverages an Azure Function App (see Figure 11-12).

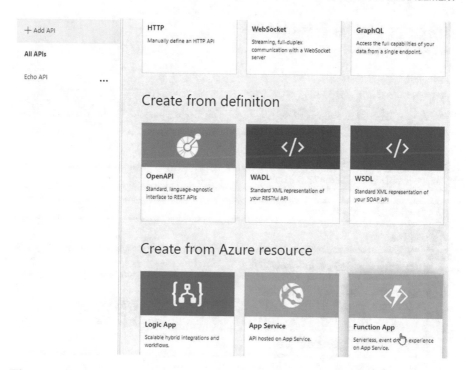

Figure 11-12. *Start the process of creating an API from an Azure Function App*

When the Create from Function App dialog comes up, choose the Browse button to select your Azure Function App. In the Import Azure Functions section, find the function app deployed to your subscription from Chapter 6 or from the discussion at the start of this chapter. Note that once you select the function app, all of the available functions are listed. For this first API, just select the Function1 function and leave the rest unchecked (see Figure 11-13).

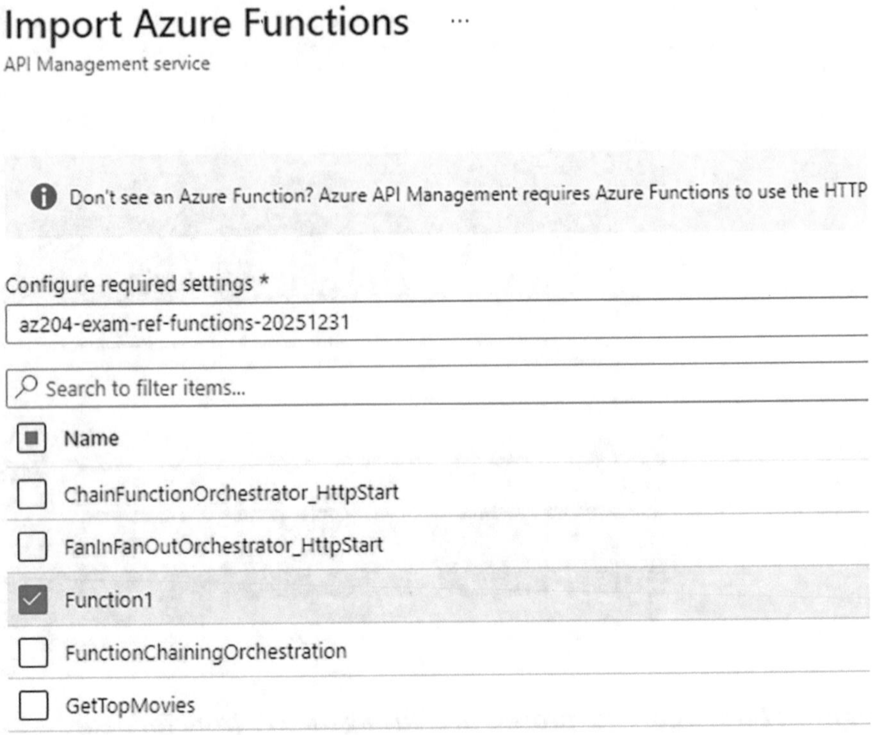

Import Azure Functions   ⋯

API Management service

ℹ️ Don't see an Azure Function? Azure API Management requires Azure Functions to use the HTTP

Configure required settings *

az204-exam-ref-functions-20251231

🔍 Search to filter items...

☑	Name
☐	ChainFunctionOrchestrator_HttpStart
☐	FanInFanOutOrchestrator_HttpStart
☑	Function1
☐	FunctionChainingOrchestration
☐	GetTopMovies

Figure 11-13. *Import the Azure Function called Function1*

If you aren't seeing your Azure Function, note that there is a nice informational block at the top of the settings that makes a profound statement about the fact that API Management requires Azure Functions to use the HTTP trigger with either a Function authorization or Anonymous authorization.

With the function selected, when you return to the dialog box, change the Display Name to Public. For the URL suffix, change the value to public (see Figure 11-14).

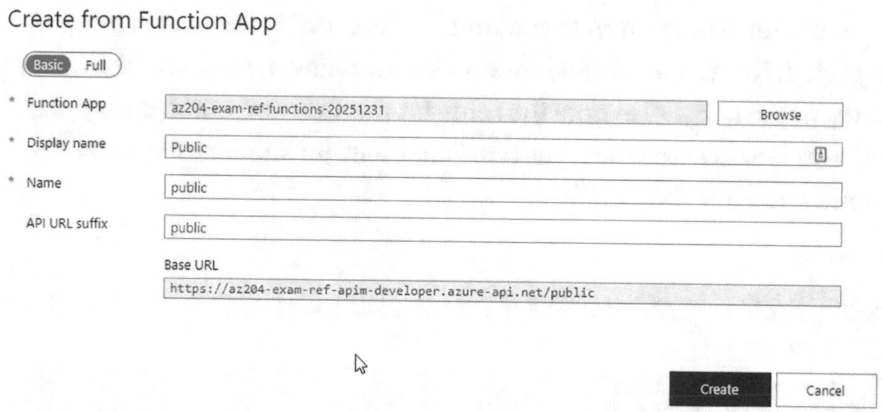

Create from Function App

(Basic) Full

* Function App   az204-exam-ref-functions-20251231   Browse

* Display name   Public   ⊞

* Name   public

  API URL suffix   public

                      Base URL
                      https://az204-exam-ref-apim-developer.azure-api.net/public

                                                                          Create   Cancel

Figure 11-14. *Setting the values to map this single function to a*
public offering

Click the Create button to create the API. This will generate the Public
API and you will see the Function1 entry. With the GET option selected,
choose the Test blade in the top-center area of the APIM API blade (see
Figure 11-15).

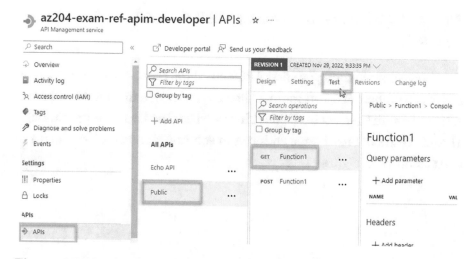

Figure 11-15. *Starting the test to validate that the solution is working*

Click the Send button to see your function call being made as expected. Notice the output is asking for the name to be part of the query string or the body. Also note the route for this function is `https://your-apim-url.azure-api.net/public/Function1` (or similar). Figure 11-16 shows these details.

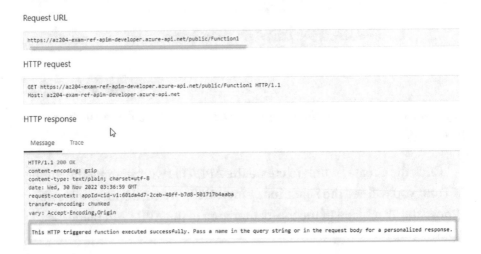

Request URL

```
https://az204-exam-ref-apim-developer.azure-api.net/public/Function1
```

HTTP request

```
GET https://az204-exam-ref-apim-developer.azure-api.net/public/Function1 HTTP/1.1
Host: az204-exam-ref-apim-developer.azure-api.net
```

HTTP response

Message   Trace

```
HTTP/1.1 200 OK
content-encoding: gzip
content-type: text/plain; charset=utf-8
date: Wed, 30 Nov 2022 03:36:59 GMT
request-context: appId=cid-v1:601da4d7-2ceb-48ff-b7d8-501717b4aaba
transfer-encoding: chunked
vary: Accept-Encoding,Origin
```

```
This HTTP triggered function executed successfully. Pass a name in the query string or in the request body for a personalized response.
```

Figure 11-16. *The APIM endpoint is able to execute the function as expected*

You've now created your first API. Repeat the process and create a new API for customers at an endpoint called `customers`. In the new Customers API, make sure to select both `Function1` and `GetTopMovies` as operations. The end result of this change within your solution should look similar to what is shown in Figure 11-17.

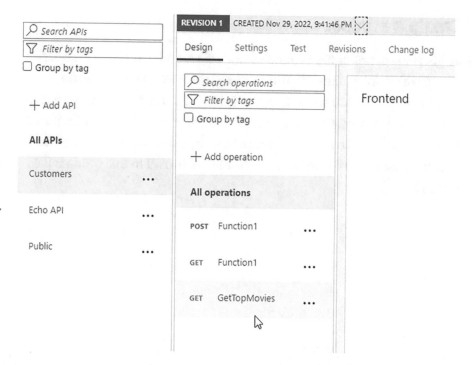

Figure 11-17. *The Customers API is created with additional methods*

Test the GetTopMovies function to ensure the data is returned as expected.

Products

Products within APIM give you the ability to create offerings for clients that allow them to leverage one or more APIs via the product.

For example, you can have a product that only exposes the Public API, and you can have a product that exposes the Public and the Customers API. In this scenario, the Public API is unnecessary since the same endpoint is exposed in the Customers API, but you'll get a chance to group into a product anyway for practice and understanding.

Create a Product

To get started, under the Products blade, click Add to create a product.

For the display name on this product, call it Everyone. Give the product a description such as `Any API that is free should be grouped into this product`. Check the Published tab and uncheck the Requires Subscription box. Leave everything else as is, but under the APIs at the bottom, choose the + symbol and add the Public API to this product (see Figure 11-18).

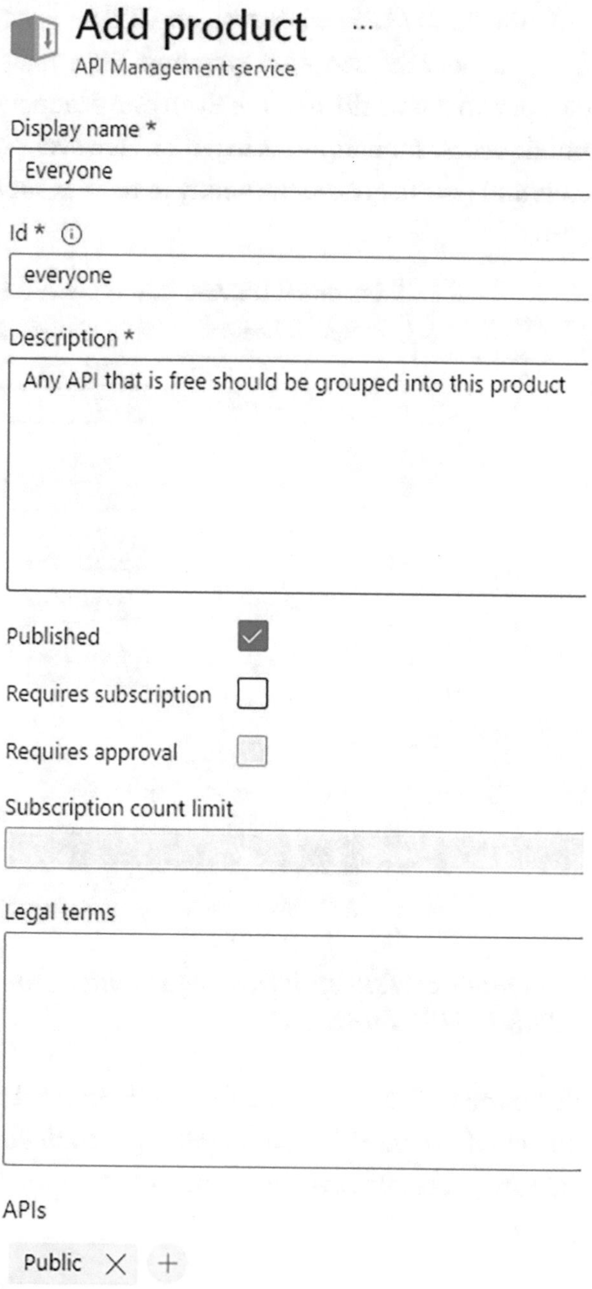

Add product ...

API Management service

Display name *

Everyone

Id * ⓘ

everyone

Description *

Any API that is free should be grouped into this product

Published   ☑

Requires subscription ☐

Requires approval   ☐

Subscription count limit

Legal terms

APIs

Public ✕ +

Figure 11-18. *Creating the Everyone product with the Public API in a scenario where no subscription is required*

Drill back into the Public API and then select GET for Function1. On the Settings blade, uncheck Subscription Required. Essentially, this public endpoint is now open to the world, and the Everyone product is just a nice way to group public access for endpoints together. However, you can also see that both APIs and products have the ability to require subscriptions (see Figure 11-19).

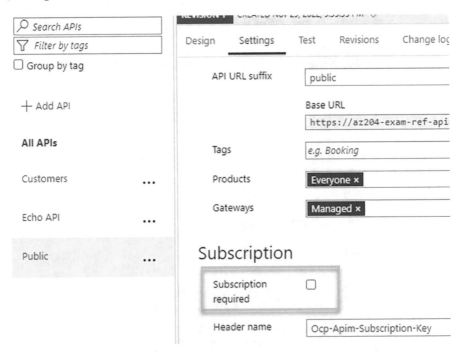

Figure 11-19. *Remove any subscription requirement from the GET method of the Public API's Function1*

Get the URL for the GET operation on the Public API and run it in a browser or from PostMan or curl. When everything is configured correctly, you should be able to get results, even without an Azure function key (see Figure 11-20).

Hello, az204examref. This HTTP triggered function executed successfully.

Figure 11-20. *The endpoint for the public façade is working with no authorization or subscription required*

If you tried to access the endpoint on the GetTopMovies function from the Customers API, you'd get an error about no subscription key, as shown in Figure 11-21.

Figure 11-21. *You can't access the Customers API without a subscription key*

To get ready for subscriptions, first create a second product called Clients with a description of Paying Customers and give it access to both APIs (Customers and Public). Make sure the product is published and that it requires a subscription (see Figure 11-22).

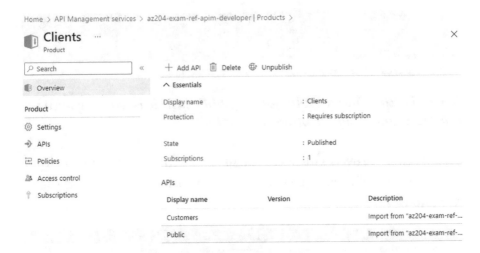

Figure 11-22. *The Clients product is created, and it exposes both the Public and the Customers APIs*

Subscriptions

As noted, even having APIs exposing endpoints through products will not be enough to allow access to the API endpoint. To get full access, clients must utilize a subscription key that will be sent in the request headers.

You can create one or more subscriptions on any product. The one thing to note is that all subscriptions must have a unique base name, but the public name can be reused. For example, in Figure 11-23, a common display name of Standard is chosen but the name of the product is tagged with the unique prefix of the product name as ClientsStandard so that the name of this subscription will be unique across all products.

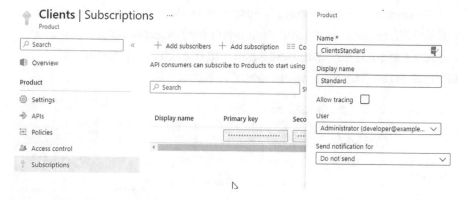

Figure 11-23. *Creating a subscription in the Clients product*

Create Two Subscriptions

In the Clients product, click Subscriptions. By default, a subscription is already created. However, the best practice here is to create a new subscription for each subscription level. At the top, click + Add Subscription. Name the subscription ClientsStandard and give it a display name of Standard. Then select the Administrator and Do Not Send (see Figure 11-23).

Complete the operations to create the subscription. Repeat the operation to create a second subscription called ClientsPremium with a display name of Premium. Once both subscriptions are created, click Show/Hide Keys in the ellipses on the far right. Record the primary key for both subscriptions somewhere on your computer (such as in a new text document in Notepad) that you can easily reference later for Copy/Paste operations.

Send a Request

For this next part, you need to be able to send a request and you need to add a request header to make the call work with the subscription. You can send the request however you are comfortable, as long as you can inject the header.

My favorite tool for testing is PostMan. In PostMan, I can place the public URL of the request and then inject my headers easily. If you used the API endpoint for customers again and tried the GET method of GetTopMovies, PostMan would look like Figure 11-24.

Figure 11-24. *The original request via PostMan is denied due to the missing subscription key, just as was shown from the browser earlier*

To either of the subscription keys you recorded, add a new header into the request called ocp-apim-subscription-key and the value of the subscription key. The request should now return results, as you are successfully using the subscription key (see Figure 11-25).

Figure 11-25. *The ocp-apim-subscription-key header allows your request to work with the subscription key in the Standard or Premium level on the Clients product in the APIM instance*

Developer Portal

The Developer Portal allows client developers to explore your public-facing APIs and subscribe and get a key or request approval to get a key.

Click the Developer Portal link at the top of the APIs blade above all the APIs (note, if you are on the Consumption tier, then you won't have a Developer Portal). You will be brought to a Content Management System (CMS), where you can administer how clients will view your portal website. Click the airplane icon and then choose the Publish Website operation (see Figure 11-26).

Figure 11-26. *The Developer Portal allows you to create a client experience for accessing APIs. First you must publish the site*

Public API Documentation

With the site published, you can navigate to it. On the APIM instance, on the Overview blade, get the URL for the Developer Portal and navigate to it (don't be surprised if this page looks awful right now).

Find the link to Explore APIs. When you click the APIs, you should at least see the APIs that you created (see Figure 11-27).

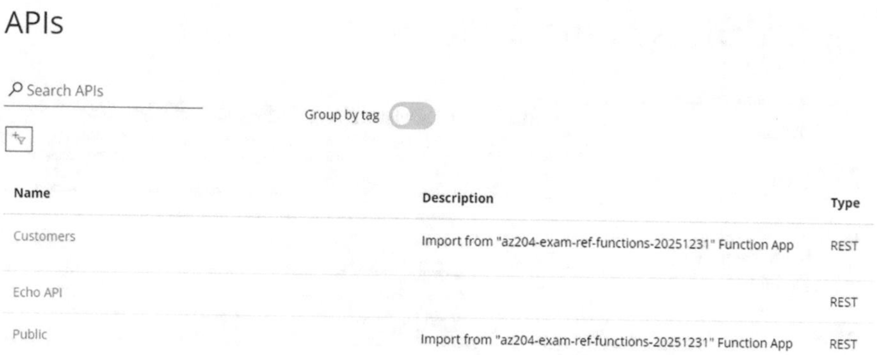
APIs
Search APIs
Group by tag
Name
Description
Type
Customers
Import from "az204-exam-ref-functions-20251231" Function App
REST
Echo API
REST
Public
Import from "az204-exam-ref-functions-20251231" Function App
REST

***Figure 11-27.** The APIs for your solution are listed on the Developer Portal*

Groups

Groups exist by default in the Developer Portal for Administrators, Developers, and Guests. By utilizing groups, you can easily set boundaries on who can see which products for requesting subscriptions.

Expose APIs via Products to Groups

Review the page from an incognito window. You will only see the Echo API listed. This is because all of the products and APIs created have been set to Administrator only. You can change the access control under the products to show additional APIs if you want to expose them to the public. Changing the access control here is likely not what you want to do, but for learning purposes, adding guests to the product will let anyone see your offerings (see Figure 11-28).

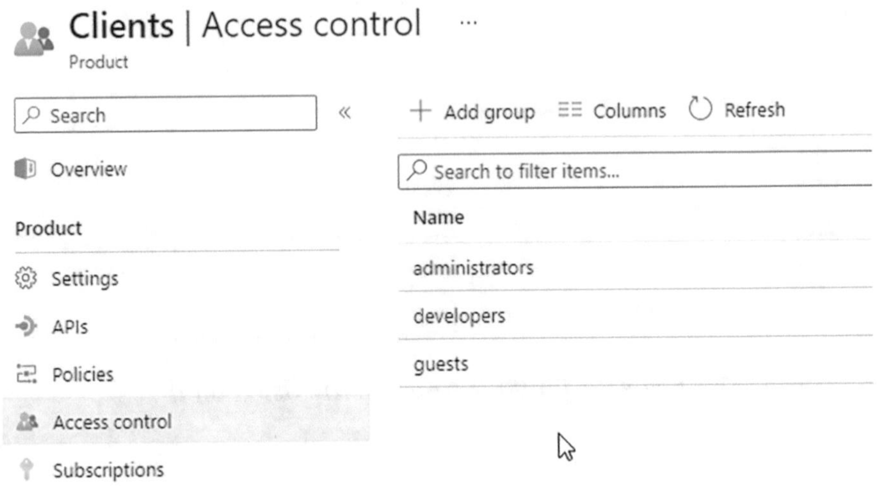

Figure 11-28. *The access control is set to allow everyone to be able to get access to the subscriptions for the Clients product*

Register Developers

Reviewing the solution in the incognito window now will show all the APIs, and a Subscribe button will be shown (see Figure 11-29).

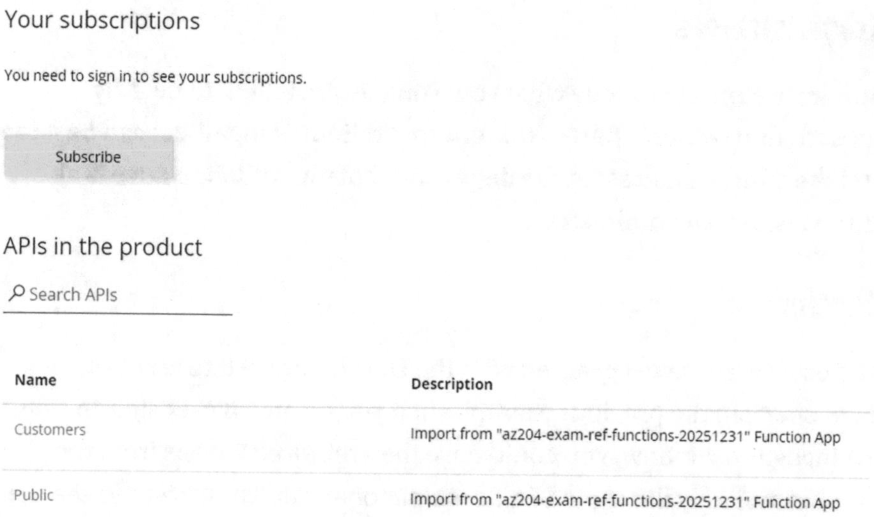

CHAPTER 11   IMPLEMENT API MANAGEMENT

Your subscriptions

You need to sign in to see your subscriptions.

Subscribe

APIs in the product

🔎 Search APIs

Name	Description
Customers	Import from "az204-exam-ref-functions-20251231" Function App
Public	Import from "az204-exam-ref-functions-20251231" Function App

Figure 11-29. *The client developer can request a subscription to be generated for their use against this product*

This APIM instance was purposefully left open. In the real-world, you'd perhaps allow anyone to automatically get a subscription to the Everyone product, but the Clients product would require invite or approval only. Getting a subscription would require signing up and logging in to the site. Once that's done, a request would be automatically approved and that user would get a subscription key for use against the APIM instance.

Default Groups

As you saw, the three default groups will always exist and they cannot be changed. They are Administrators, Developers, and Guests. Default groups cannot be removed from the solution.

Administrators

Administrators are exactly what you would expect them to be. Any subscription owner is part of this group. Additional members can be added and the admin email set at the deployment of the APIM instance is also automatically an administrator.

Developers

Any users who have registered with the Developer Portal are set as developers. In the previous example, had you created a user sign-in from the incognito window, you could have then removed Guests from the product and only the signed-in developer or administrator would see the API products.

Developers can also be managed from the Active Directory for some tiers, and the Administrator can also create and register developers.

Guests

Any anonymous user is treated as a guest on the Developer Portal. This is why the Echo API that is available to guests was immediately available in the incognito window, and why adding the Guests group allowed you to see the Clients product.

Custom Groups

As with any solution at Azure, you can create your own groups for management in the Developer Portal. Once you add your custom group, you can then add users to that group. Here, you might create a group for auditing or some other read-only purpose that would allow members to view metrics, data, and authorized users but not actually call the APIs and get a result.

Utilizing Policies

With the APIM instance created, some routes in place, products to manage groupings of APIs, APIs to route requests, and operations to make specific calls to backend services, the last piece of the APIM ecosystem that you need to be in command of is the ability to manipulate requests from the frontend as they go to the backend services.

Policies are XML documents that exist at every level in the APIM solution to give you inheritance and the ability to be more specific for each individual operation, API, or all APIs.

The rest of this chapter looks at utilizing policies to control operations within the deployed APIM instance.

Inject/Decorate Information in Request/ Response

Drill into the Public API and get the URL for the GET operation on Function1 operation via the Settings tab. This is the default function that requires a query string or request body that contains a name in .NET 6 (or just shows that the function is working in .NET 7). Make a call to the endpoint (it should be open, as previously set) and review the result. You should see the friendly ... pass a name in the query string.... message for .NET 6 (or Welcome to Azure Functions! for .NET 7) (see Figure 11-30).

Figure 11-30. *The request requires a query string parameter or request body for the name to show*

In the APIM, on the GET request for Function1, select the Design tab, and then click the + Add Policy button on the Inbound request (see Figure 11-31).

Figure 11-31. *Inject a policy into the Inbound request*

A number of options exist, including Filter IP Addresses, Limit Call Rate, Mock Responses, Set Query Parameters, Set Headers, and more, including a spot to create other policies. The interesting one here is Set Query Parameters. Select that box to start the process of creating an injected query parameter.

When the Inbound Processing dialog box appears, add the Name as name and the Value as name has been set by policy in APIM. Leave the Action as override, then save the setting, as shown in Figure 11-32.

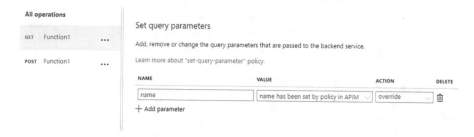

Figure 11-32. *Adding an override for the query string parameter name by policy*

After saving, click the setting. You will see everything you just created in the XML for the policy (see Figure 11-33).

Figure 11-33. *The policy is set as XML and you can edit the values here just as easily as when using the baked-in tools*

With this policy saved and in place, make the call again from the client to see the result. Of course, now you will see the value for name no matter if the name is passed or not from the client side (see Figure 11-34).

Figure 11-34. *The query string parameter is overridden by policy in the APIM instance*

Injecting a parameter is extremely useful if a secret code, such as a third-party API key or other setting, needs to be passed to the backend API and you don't want to expose that information to the clients of your APIM solution.

Rate Limit

Rate limiting is another tool you can use from the APIM policies. For example, consider the two subscriptions. You may want to set rate limits on the GetTopMovies operation for the Standard vs the Premium subscriptions. Note that rate limiting by subscription key is not available at the Consumption tier level. Rate limiting is incredibly useful to prevent bad players from accessing your API too often. If a rate limit is reached, the client will receive a 429 - Too Many Requests response from your APIM solution.

On the GetTopMovies operation, select the policies again and choose the Limit Call Rate option. On the blade, set the Number of Calls to 5 and the Renewal Period in Seconds to 60 seconds. Select API Subscription as the Counter Key and then use Any Request as the Increment Condition (see Figure 11-35).

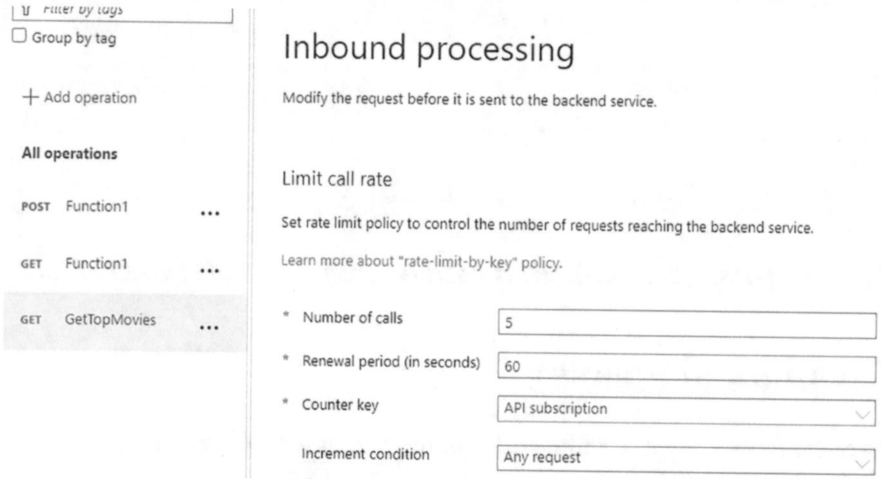

Figure 11-35. *The rate limiting policy is set to be created*

Save the new policy, then utilize PostMan or another tool or command of your choice to send requests to the GetTopMovies endpoint with the subscription key in place. It won't matter which subscription you use, because you've blocked them all with the previous settings. Even the Premium subscription would get a 429 error for too many requests, as shown in Figure 11-36.

Figure 11-36. *The rate limit is easily exceeded for any subscription*

Conditional Policies

In order to limit by a specific key, you have to essentially use an `if` condition, just like you would in any code-based scenario. In the APIM policies, this is done via conditions with the verb `choose` instead of `if` or `case`. Like SQL, the `choose` verb is followed by `when`. The final condition is `otherwise`.

Update the XML, replacing the rate-limit entry for the policy with the following:

```
<choose>
    <when condition="@(context.Subscription.Key ==
    "premium-key-here")">
        <rate-limit-by-key calls="20" renewal-period="60"
        counter-key="@(context.Subscription.Id)" />
    </when>
    <when condition="@(context.Subscription.Key ==
    "standard-id-here")">
```

```
            <rate-limit-by-key calls="10" renewal-period="60"
            counter-key="@(context.Subscription.Id)" />
        </when>
        <otherwise>
            <rate-limit-by-key calls="5" renewal-period="60"
            counter-key="@(context.Subscription?.Key ??
            "anonymous")" />
        </otherwise>
    </choose>
</inbound>
```

Make sure to update the subscription key for each condition to the appropriate subscription ID from the creation of the two subscriptions earlier in the chapter. Once completed, return to your tool of choice and blast your endpoint with requests, validating that the Premium subscription can get to 20 requests before receiving a 429 response and the Standard subscription can get to ten requests before receiving a 429 response.

IP Address Restrictions

Rate limiting by subscription is great, but what if it's not everyone on the subscription but perhaps it's one bad developer who made a mistake, or a bad player who just wants to take you down? Instead of blocking the entire subscription, another option is to block by IP address. IP addresses can be blocked by range or by a specific IP address. Additionally, IP addresses can be allowed by range, meaning that you can prevent all other IP addresses from executing your APIs (see Figure 11-37).

Inbound processing

Modify the request before it is sent to the backend service.

Filter IP addresses

Set filtering of incoming requests based on allowed or blocked IP addresses.

Learn more about "ip-filter" policy.

(**Allowed IPs**   Blocked IPs)

IP ADDRESS FROM	IP ADDRESS TO	DELETE
10.10.0.0	10.10.255.255	🗑

+ Add IP filter

Figure 11-37. *Filtering by IP enables you to allow and deny requests based on a range of IP addresses*

Validate Certificates

So far you've locked down requests by subscription key and by rate limiting and IP address. However, what happens when someone has a valid subscription key that they should not have access to? In that scenario, you need to authenticate the client before allowing the request to continue.

Within the APIM instance, you can use policies to validate certificates in one of many ways. Note that the examples that follow in this section are all available at `https://learn.microsoft.com/azure/api-management/api-management-howto-mutual-certificates-for-clients`.

For the most part, the following code is exactly as it is shown on the website, with a few tweaks, such as a separate issuer and subject, which are utilized simply for learning purposes.

Issuer (Certificate Authority)

The first way you can validate a certificate with a policy is based on the issuer. In this case, your policy would look as follows:

```
<choose>
    <when condition="@(context.Request.Certificate == null ||
    !context.Request.Certificate.Verify() || context.Request.
    Certificate.Issuer != "trusted-issuer")" >
        <return-response>
            <set-status code="403" reason="Invalid client
            certificate" />
        </return-response>
    </when>
</choose>
```

Thumbprint

As with the issuer, you can check the thumbprint as follows:

```
<choose>
    <when condition="@(context.Request.Certificate == null ||
    !context.Request.Certificate.Verify() || context.Request.
    Certificate.Thumbprint != "DESIRED-THUMBPRINT-IN-UPPER-
    CASE")" >
        <return-response>
            <set-status code="403" reason="Invalid client
            certificate" />
        </return-response>
    </when>
</choose>
```

Subject

Another example is to validate by subject:

```
<choose>
    <when condition="@(context.Request.Certificate == null ||
    !context.Request.Certificate.Verify() || context.Request.
    Certificate.SubjectName.Name != "expected-subject-name")" >
        <return-response>
            <set-status code="403" reason="Invalid client
            certificate" />
        </return-response>
    </when>
</choose>
```

Validate Against Uploaded Certificates

If you upload a certificate to APIM, you can validate client certificates against the uploaded certificate:

```
<choose>
    <when condition="@(context.Request.Certificate == null
    || !context.Request.Certificate.Verify()  || !context.
    Deployment.Certificates.Any(c => c.Value.Thumbprint ==
    context.Request.Certificate.Thumbprint))" >
        <return-response>
            <set-status code="403" reason="Invalid client
            certificate" />
        </return-response>
    </when>
</choose>
```

Validate by JWT

Another common authorization scenario is to validate users by JSON Web Tokens. The utilization of JWT for authorization is less than trivial. If you want to learn more about this, specifically how to use JWTs to authenticate by specific HTTP verb, review this document (which includes an inbound policy): `https://learn.microsoft.com/azure/api-management/policies/authorize-request-based-on-jwt-claims`.

Which Is Better (JWT or Certificates)?

This is the million-dollar question. On the one hand, it may be easier to utilize JWT for authentication. Once implemented, the solution can easily be validated and is highly reusable for many clients. The JWT is designed to share enough information about the user to make the appropriate authentication/authorization checks. However, JWT may not be as secure as using a certificate can be. With a certificate, you also have to make sure to keep the certificates secure and the client needs to have a valid leaf certificate that allows the solution to authenticate the client and allow the requests. You'll likely need to store your certificates in Azure Key Vault and rotate them regularly.

In the end, the solution of choice will be up to you and your team. Do you want a lightweight and easy way to allow clients to authenticate, or do you need the best security, including encryption? Based on factors like these, you'll need to decide which approach your solution needs to implement.

Mock Responses for Testing

Just like you can create mock data in typical unit tests, you can utilize a mock response policy to send fake or mocked response codes back to the client for testing purposes.

Authenticate to the Backend

One final scenario that is likely a bit outside the scope of the AZ-204 Exam but good to know is how to authenticate your APIM against a resource at Azure.

In general, consider the scenario where your Azure Function App requires authentication. This means that even with a valid function key, unless the request also includes a valid bearer token in the header, the request is rejected. Once a user or entity is logged in or has a valid managed identity, the authorization can be validated.

To make everything work, the first step is that the function app or other endpoint resource must be registered as an application in your subscription. This will give the application a client ID. Additionally, the endpoint resource must require authorization so that anonymous requests are rejected.

With that in place, the APIM itself must have a managed identity so that it can be authenticated in the Azure tenant. Unfortunately, it's not as easy as working with the Key Vault, where the function app or other resource can create an access policy. In the case of the APIM authentication, after the configuration is set up, a policy must be added to all requests going against the locked-down backend in APIM.

The policy must set information utilizing the client ID of the endpoint resource application. The policy is simple, and it is created in the inbound policies for ALL APIs. To implement the policy, simply add the following to the `ALL APIs` inbound policies:

```
<authentication-managed-identity resource="client-id-of-
endpoint-app" />
```

With that policy in place, the APIM instance can utilize its system-managed identity to authenticate and make calls against the locked-down endpoint resource.

Review Your Learning

As an additional challenge, consider the following questions and determine how you would approach potential solutions. You can find answers to these questions in Appendix A at the end of this book.

1) What are the different offerings within APIM for deployment of solutions? Which tier(s) get a Developer Portal?

2) Why do some tiers deploy quickly while others take 30-45 minutes to deploy? Which tier(s) get a self-hosted gateway? Why might a self-hosted gateway be important?

3) What is an API within APIM?

4) What is a product within APIM?

5) What is a subscription within APIM? Is the subscription applied to the API or the product? How does this enhance your solution?

6) What is a policy? How do you utilize policies? Where can you apply policies and in what directions? What is the inheritance precedence of policies?

7) What are two ways to validate client requests outside of subscriptions? Which is considered more secure?

Complete the AZ-204: Implement API Management Learn Module

To fully learn the material, I recommend taking the time to also complete the MS Learn module for AZ-204: Implement API Management found here:

- Export API Management: `https://learn.microsoft.com/training/paths/az-204-implement-api-management/`

Chapter Summary

In this chapter, you learned about working with the Azure API Management to create a centralized façade on the Public APIs. The benefits of this approach were examined, and you saw how to utilize the API Management solution to present one public endpoint with multiple routes to various backend services. You also learned about using policies to intercept and decorate the requests on the incoming request or the outgoing response. Additionally, you learned about working with groups, products, and subscriptions to create various levels of access to your API Management. Within the APIM instance, you can block or throttle requests by IP address, and at the development tier or better, you can also use policies along with subscription keys to perform operations like rate-limiting and throttling.

After working through this chapter and the Microsoft Learn module, you should be on track to be in command of the following concepts as you learn about Azure and prepare for the AZ-204 Exam:

- Create and work with APIM via the Azure Portal.

- Know the difference and hierarchy of APIs, operations, subscriptions, and products.

- Understand and leverage policies to perform common
  operations like validation of tokens or certificates,
  inject or modify the requests and responses, or throttle
  (rate-limit) requests.

In the next chapter, you learn about working with event-driven
solutions in the Azure ecosystem, specifically around the Azure Event Hub
and Azure Event Grid.

Develop Event-Based Solutions

When I first started learning about Azure, one thing that was more confusing than most things was the purpose and reasoning for both an Event Grid and an Event Hub. In fact, I was unsure what either service was, when to use which service, and even if they were dependent on one another (such as questions as to whether all event hubs must have an event grid, or vice versa). Perhaps you are in a similar position related to these services as you are studying for your AZ-204 Exam. I hope this chapter will eliminate any questions about what these services are for, how they work, and when to use each one. In any event, this chapter presents two major technologies for event-based solutions in Azure—Azure Event Hubs and Azure Event Grid.

Event Hub vs Event Grid

Before going further, I'll give you a spoiler alert on the questions you may have based on the first paragraph. To be clear from the start, the Azure Event Grid and Azure Event Hubs offerings are both standalone services in Azure and are independent of one another as offerings in Azure. Where it does get somewhat confusing is that you can combine them in solutions at times, such as sending a single event into an event hub or perhaps

© Brian L. Gorman 2023
B. L. Gorman, *Developing Solutions for Microsoft Azure Certification Companion,*
Certification Study Companion Series, https://doi.org/10.1007/978-1-4842-9300-3_12

putting a service like Stream Analytics behind the ingested data at a hub and sending custom events to the event grid based on queries against the stream from within Stream Analytics.

At the highest level, to keep the two services separate in your learning and while you sit for the AZ-204 Exam, you can think of these two services separately by always remembering how each is designed to be utilized.

The Azure Event Grid service is for working with one-off events that are either system generated or custom events created by you. These events are the result of some singular event at a specific point in time, generated by a specific resource or from within a specific application.

The Azure Event Hub service is used to ingest a massive number events from a stream, generally hundreds to hundreds of thousands of events per minute from many disparate sources. This service could be reporting telemetry, logging data, or some combination of information that is consistently streamed and needs to be analyzed, reported, or responded to.

Azure Event Hubs

The primary reason for utilizing Azure Event Hubs is to ingest streaming data as it is produced. At capacity, an event hub has the capability to ingest (ingress) over one million events per minute and can egress nearly four times that number.

In a typical architecture, events are produced and ingested into Azure Event Hubs, either with Advanced Messaging Queuing Protocol 1.0 (AMQP) or via Apache Kafka 1.0. With the event hub, events are available for playback from one to ninety days, depending on the tier of the event hub.

Event-Driven Architecture

With Azure Event Hubs, you can implement a full event-driven architecture to work with events in a distributed environment at scale and at massive capacity.

In an event-driven architecture, events are gathered, and information is analyzed or conglomerated to discern appropriate additional actions. Once the analysis of the event is completed, then typically a follow-up action needs to take place. This follow-up action can be automated or may also be a process that requires manual intervention.

For example, you might create a fleet of IoT devices to monitor the temperature and air quality in hospital operating rooms for your organization's 150 hospitals in the central United States. In this case, you'll likely have millions of telemetry data points coming in at regular intervals throughout the day. When data is outside of a normal threshold, it's critical to make that information available to someone who can remediate the solution. This can be accomplished by sending an alert, or it might be automated through a function or Logic App, or could even be sent as information to a custom webhook endpoint.

As a side note, an IoT solution such as this would likely utilize the Azure IoT Hub, which is out of scope for the AZ-204 Exam (but not the AZ-220 IoT Specialization). The IoT hub is a subset of the event hub. As such, the code you write against the IoT hub can leverage the same event hub SDK code that you would use to write code against Azure Event Hubs.

In any event-driven architecture, regardless of the various implementations, there are a few important concepts and terms critical to the solution that you need to be in command of. These concepts and terms are:

- Producer

- Receiver

- Partition

- Consumer

- Consumer group

- Checkpointing

- Client

Producer

The producer is the source of the event. This could be logs from an application, telemetry from devices, or any other stream of data that needs to be captured for analysis.

Receiver

The receiver is the tool or tools that are responsible for the ingress (intaking/processing) of the data. In this architecture, the receiver is the event hub, and the data is received in either the Kafka 1.0 or Advanced Message Queuing Protocol (AMQP) 1.0 data format.

The Kafka 1.0 format is based on Apache Kafka, which is one of the major players in big-data streaming solutions. If you are interested in knowing more about Apache Kafka, you can read more at `https://kafka.apache.org/10/documentation.html`. Other than knowing the Kafka 1.0 protocol is offered and the fact that Azure Event Hubs can ingest data just like a Kafka cluster would be able to, additional information regarding Apache Kafka is out of scope for the AZ-204 Exam.

The AMQP 1.0 data format is an international standard messaging protocol, which, according to the documentation (see `https://learn.microsoft.com/azure/service-bus-messaging/service-bus-amqp-overview?#amqp-10-technical-features`), is approved by ISO and IEC in the ISO/IEC 19454:2014 Standard.

Partition

Internally to the hub, the data can be grouped into one or more partitions. These partitions record the data in the order of events grouped by a specific partition key. Although you can code your solution to write directly to a partition, the correct way to send data to the event hub via code is to send with the partition key and let your event hub handle which partition to write the data on. The number of partitions for any event hub is set during creation of the hub and cannot be changed after creation. The maximum number of partitions is 32, but this can be increased via a request to support if necessary.

Consumer

The consumer is the application or service that is reading and processing events. Later you'll see this done with a .NET application. Additionally, the event hub created will be capturing data to an Azure data lake storage account.

Consumer Group

When it comes to reading the data, a consumer is required. However, in order for the hub to allow multiple readers to review the streams without affecting each other, there is a feature called consumer groups. An event hub can have up to 20 consumer groups, and each group can have five concurrent readers. The recommendation is to only have one active reader per consumer group if possible. Due to the ability to replay the data from the event hub over time, there is a concept known as checkpointing.

Checkpointing

Checkpointing essentially allows each consumer group to have a specific marker in the stream, which points to the last event processed. Therefore, each consumer group can replay data for sliding window analysis at will, or the consumer can just pick up processing where the last consumer left off in the case of resuming the processing of data.

Client

The client for the event hub is the SDK that can be used for reading and writing to the event hub. In this chapter, you see the .NET SDK for event hubs being utilized. Other SDKs exist for Java, Python, JavaScript, Go, and C.

Creating an Event Hub Namespace in Azure

To get started creating an event hub, note that the first thing you need to do is create a namespace. What's most interesting here is the URL that will be the namespace for the hub. Even though this is an event hub, and you might expect the URL to be something like yourhub.eventhubs.windows.net, what you'll see is that the URL is actually yourhub.servicebus.windows.net. You'll get a chance to learn more about Azure Service Bus in the next chapter. For now, just note this oddity on the URL for the event hubs.

To create your hub namespace, select your subscription and resource group as expected, then give your hub namespace a useful and unique name, like az204examref-event-hub-namespaceYYYYMMDD. Choose the appropriate location and then discern the appropriate pricing tier (see Figure 12-1).

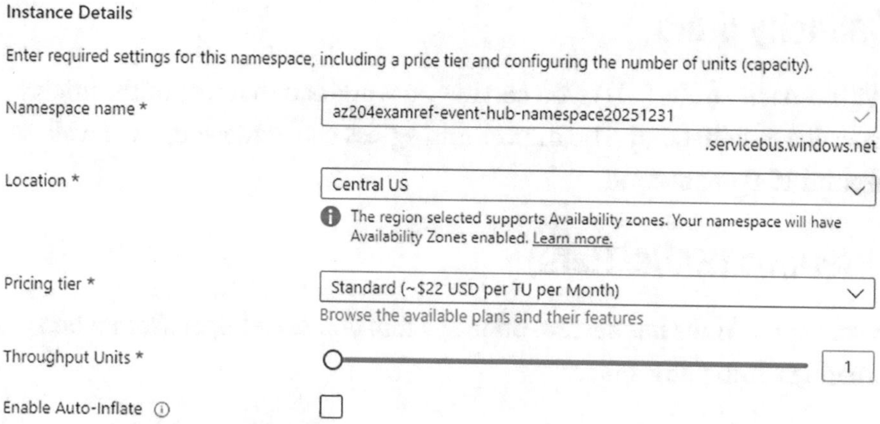

Instance Details

Enter required settings for this namespace, including a price tier and configuring the number of units (capacity).

Namespace name *	az204examref-event-hub-namespace20251231 ✓
	.servicebus.windows.net
Location *	Central US ⌄
	ⓘ The region selected supports Availability zones. Your namespace will have Availability Zones enabled. Learn more.
Pricing tier *	Standard (~$22 USD per TU per Month) ⌄
	Browse the available plans and their features
Throughput Units *	○————————————————— 1
Enable Auto-Inflate ⓘ	☐

Figure 12-1. *The basics for an event hub namespace are set*

Due to the desire to demonstrate capture, this hub is provisioned at the Standard tier, but the workload will be minimal, so one throughput unit (TU) with no scaling is sufficient.

Throughput Units (TU)

The throughput unit is used in the Basic and Standard tiers, and it is a pre-purchased compute resource to process data for the event hub(s) in your namespace. This is done on a shared architecture in Azure. Capacity for a single TU on ingress is 1MB/second or 1,000 events per second and 2MB/second or 4,096 events per second on egress.

Processing Units (PU)

Similar to a TU, the processing units (PU) are compute resources offered in the Premium tier for event hubs. This offering is isolated to its own CPU and memory. The capacity for processing is dependent on your workload and can be from 5-10 MB/second on ingress and 10-20MB/second on egress.

Capacity Units

With capacity units (CU), you can have a workload that responds quickly to scale when needed. The ingress and egress can achieve upper levels around 1GB per second.

Offerings (SKUs/Tiers)

Azure Event Hubs has several offerings that you can choose from when creating a hub namespace.

Basic

As the entry-level tier, the Basic hub tier offers a maximum retention period of one day and only allows up to 84 GB of storage. You cannot capture to storage at this tier, nor can you leverage Apache Kafka, and you won't be able to forgo sharing the schema on your data.

Standard

The Standard tier gives you the ability to capture data, utilize Kafka, and leverage the schema registry to forgo the need to exchange schema information. At this tier, additional charges can apply if you add data capture. Event data can be stored up to seven days, and the max amount of storage is also capped at 84 GB.

Premium

The Premium tier has everything that the Standard tier offers but prices for ingress and capture are included in the overall cost. Event data retention is up to 90 days, and the storage capacity is 1 TB per processing unit (PU).

Dedicated

The Dedicated tier is the most expensive tier by far and offers everything the Premium tier offers with capacity set to 10 TB per capacity unit (CU). At the Dedicated tier, you are reserving the resources as dedicated to your tenant. Ingress and egress at this tier are much higher, so you can do massive amounts of data processing.

Advanced Settings

The Advanced settings for the hub allow you to select a Minimum TLS Version and decide whether or not to utilize Local Authentication (SAS tokens). Figure 12-2 shows the Advanced tab with default settings selected.

Basics   **Advanced**   Networking   Tags   Review + create

Security

Minimum TLS version ⓘ

Version 1.2   ⌄

ⓘ Increasing the minimum TLS version will prevent connections using a lower
TLS version from connecting to this namespace. Learn more

Local Authentication ⓘ   (**Enabled**   Disabled)

Figure 12-2. *Creating a hub namespace on the Advanced tab*

Networking

As with other solutions in Azure, you can utilize private access for your hub namespace to configure the private endpoint connections for the hub. For this demonstration, public access is sufficient.

Creating a Data Lake Storage Account and Container

When creating a hub in the next sections, the event hub will leverage the ability to automatically capture data. In order to do this, you need to have the storage account and container provisioned before provisioning the hub. For big data pipelines, you generally want data lake storage. Therefore, make sure to provision the account with a hierarchical namespace on the Advanced tab, as shown in Figure 12-3.

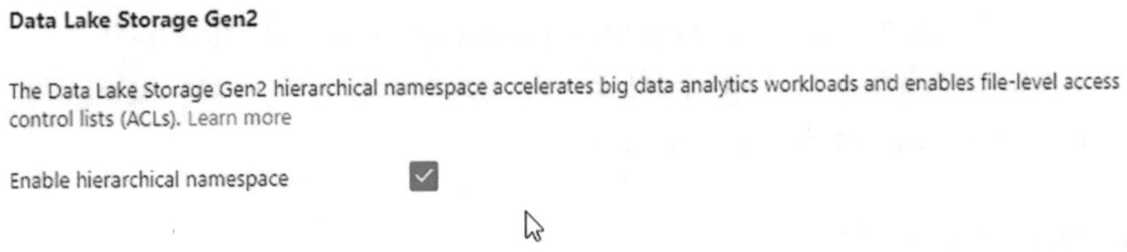

Data Lake Storage Gen2

The Data Lake Storage Gen2 hierarchical namespace accelerates big data analytics workloads and enables file-level access control lists (ACLs). Learn more

Enable hierarchical namespace   ☑

Figure 12-3. Creating an Azure Data Lake hierarchical storage account

Within the new storage account, create a container named eventdata or something similar to store the captured event data.

Creating an Event Hub in Azure

Once the namespace is created, you can create one or more event hubs in the namespace. Use the + Event Hub from the Namespace blade to create a new hub. Give the hub a reasonable name, and then set the partition count from 1-32 and message retention from 1-7 days (as shown in Figure 12-4).

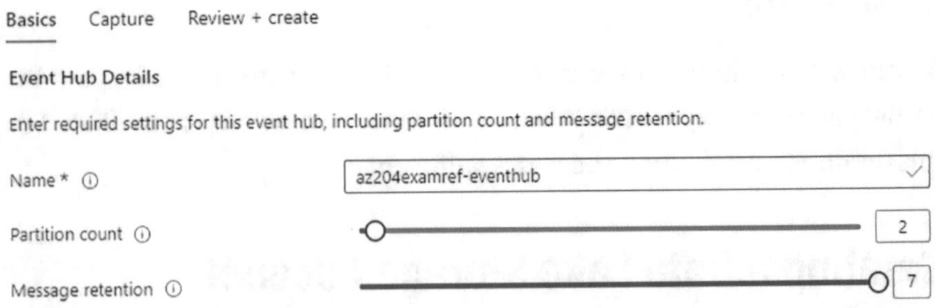

Basics   Capture   Review + create

Event Hub Details

Enter required settings for this event hub, including partition count and message retention.

Name * ⓘ	az204examref-eventhub	✓
Partition count ⓘ	○—————————	2
Message retention ⓘ	——————————○	7

Figure 12-4. Creating a new event hub in the event hub namespace

Event Hub Capture

With the hub created, you can capture your data automatically to storage. Typically, for a big data pipeline, you'll want this to be hierarchical, so you would use Azure Data Lake Storage (which is just blob storage with the data lake feature enabled). Select On to start configuration of the capture.

The event hub capture process will capture data automatically at a specified interval of a specified number of minutes or at a specific amount of data (size in MB), whichever comes first.

Time Window (Minutes)

This is the number of minutes that can expire before data is captured. This will automatically create a file every *n* minutes if the data size window is not met in that time period. The default of five minutes is sufficient for this demonstration.

Size Window (MB)

This is the maximum amount of data to ingest before capturing to storage. The size window will only trigger if the overall data reaches a set amount before the time window expires. The default of 300 MB is sufficient for this demonstration.

Emit Empty Files

As mentioned previously, it is generally easier for your downstream processing to handle data even if there are empty files due to the fact that your system will not have to discern if data is missing (i.e., there was data but no file was emitted). For this reason, the default and the recommended approach is to emit empty files, leaving this box unchecked.

Capture Provider

The capture provider has two options. The typical Storage Account (Gen 2) or the older Data Lake (Gen 1). If you created a new account, select the Storage Account option. Only select the Data Lake option if you have an older, Azure Gen 1 Data Lake Storage, account to which to capture your data.

Azure Storage Container

This is just a regular blob storage container inside your Gen 2 hierarchical Azure Storage account.

File Name Formats

Unless you have a structure in place, there is no reason to change these settings. They will capture data in a way that allows the data to be in folders based on the date of capture.

Review and Create the Event Hub

Figure 12-5 shows the completed capture information.

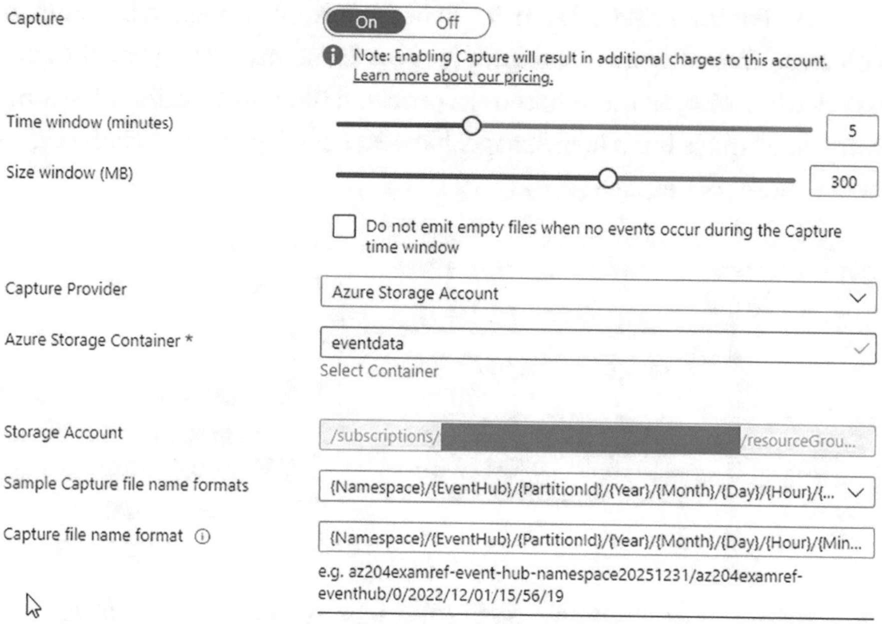

Capture	On Off

Note: Enabling Capture will result in additional charges to this account. Learn more about our pricing.

Time window (minutes)	5
Size window (MB)	300

☐ Do not emit empty files when no events occur during the Capture time window

Capture Provider	Azure Storage Account ∨
Azure Storage Container *	eventdata ✓

Select Container

Storage Account	/subscriptions/ ▓▓▓▓▓▓ /resourceGrou...
Sample Capture file name formats	{Namespace}/{EventHub}/{PartitionId}/{Year}/{Month}/{Day}/{Hour}/{... ∨
Capture file name format ⓘ	{Namespace}/{EventHub}/{PartitionId}/{Year}/{Month}/{Day}/{Hour}/{Min...

e.g. az204examref-event-hub-namespace20251231/az204examref-eventhub/0/2022/12/01/15/56/19

Figure 12-5. *Completed capture information*

Working Against an Event Hub with .NET

The next part of this chapter discusses how to connect clients to the hub and send and consume data.

.NET Client for Sending Events to the Hub

The sample code for this chapter includes clients to send and receive data to and from the event hub.

Shared Access Signatures

In order to connect to the Event Hub, the client could be authenticated. However, for ease of use and configuration, you can connect via Shared Access Signatures (as long as you left that enabled when creating the solution). For the AZ-204 Exam, it will be important enough to be familiar with these shared access signatures for events and messaging and they are easy to work with, so the solutions as provided utilize SAS authentication. Every namespace has a RootManageSharedAccessKey that has all the rights on the entire namespace (see Figure 12-6).

Figure 12-6. *The RootManageSharedAccessKey can do all things against all hubs in the namespace, so you should rarely use this and you should never share it*

Note   SAS authentication can be handled at the namespace level for all hubs in the namespace, or it can be at the specific hub level for granular control.

Data Roles

To set the signatures and roles in Azure, it's important to be aware of three levels of control. They are Owner/Manage, Sender/Send, and Listener/Listen.

Owner

If you want to manage the hub via code but want to limit this to a specific hub rather than using the root key for the namespace, create an SAS token in the hub with Manage capability. Go to the hub and create a new SAS policy called HubOwner. Note that checking the Manage option automatically selects Send and Listen without the ability to remove those options, so the Owner policy can be used to manage the hub and also to ingress and/or egress data to the hub (see Figure 12-7).

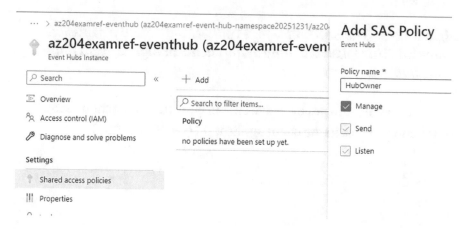

Figure 12-7. *The SAS policy for the owner with the Manage, Send, and Listen capabilities selected*

Sender

Within the hub or at the root level, you can create a specific SAS policy for producing events. Figure 12-8 shows creating a policy named Producer specifically for az204examref-eventhub.

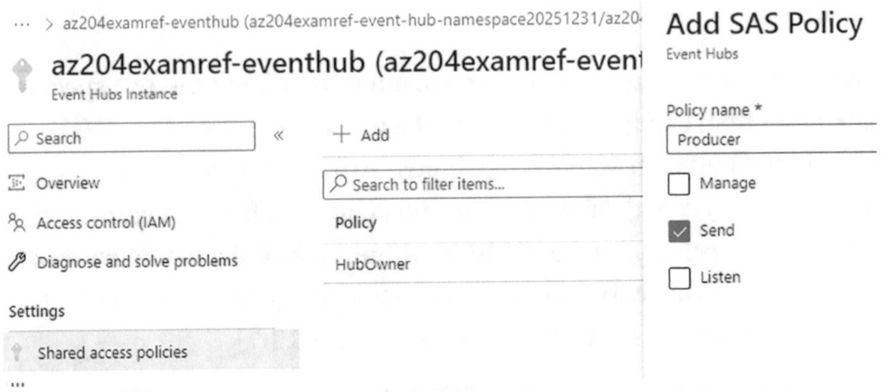

Figure 12-8. *The SAS policy for Producer with Send permission is created. This token will only allow clients to ingress event data to the hub*

After creating the policy, make sure to copy the connection string information for use in the client application (see Figure 12-9).

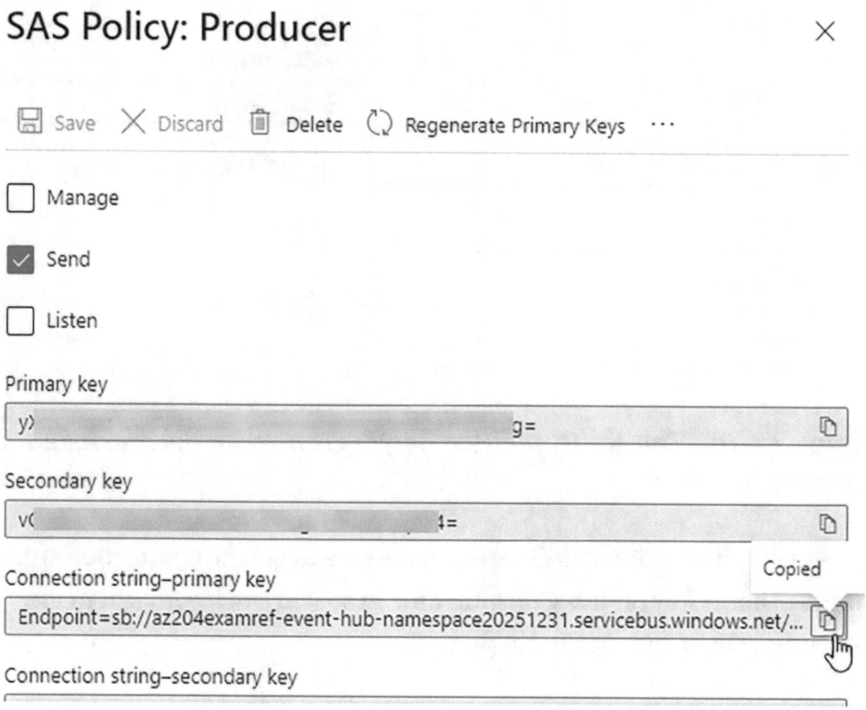

SAS Policy: Producer   ✕

🖫 Save   ✕ Discard   🗑 Delete   ⟳ Regenerate Primary Keys   ⋯

☐ Manage

☑ Send

☐ Listen

Primary key

| y⟩   g= | 🗐 |

Secondary key

| v(⼯= | 🗐 |

Connection string–primary key   Copied

| Endpoint=sb://az204examref-event-hub-namespace20251231.servicebus.windows.net/... | 🗐 |

Connection string–secondary key

Figure 12-9. *Get the connection string for the new Producer SAS token*

Listener

As with the Producer, you'll likely want your clients that are listening to only be able to consume event data. Create another SAS token named Consumer that has only the ability to listen (see Figure 12-10).

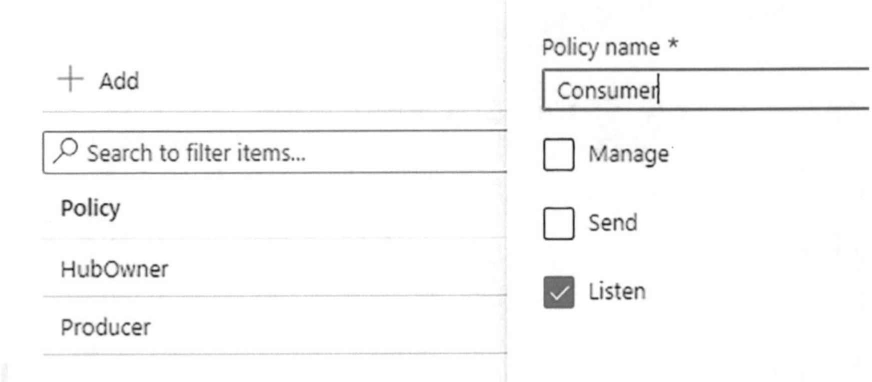

Figure 12-10. *The ability to listen only is granted on the SAS token named Consumer*

As with the Producer SAS token, make sure to get the connection string for the primary key on this Consumer token so you can leverage it in the Consumer client later in the chapter.

.NET Event Producer

The sample code has two client applications. The first application is the producer and is in the project called WorkingWithEventHub. In this producer, you will need to set the connection information to utilize the SAS token for the Producer created previously. Note that you could use the Manage token or the Root token, but the best choice is to limit privilege to only allow the client to send data to the hub.

Set the ConnectionString and Name in Secrets.json

Manage the user secrets in the WorkingWithEventHub project to add the connection string. If you don't have the connection string handy, go back to the hub and select the Producer SAS token you created previously.

Additionally, add the name of the hub to the secrets file. Your secrets file should be similar to what is shown in Figure 12-11.

```
secrets.json  ⊕ ✕  usersecrets-example.txt    ConfigurationB...erSingleton.cs    Program.cs
Schema: <No Schema Selected>
   1    ⊟{
   2    ⊟    "EventHub": {
   3              "ConnectionString": "Endpoint=sb://az204examref-event-hub-namespace20251231.servicebus.windows.net/;Shared
   4              "Name": "az204examref-eventhub"
   5         }
   6    }
```

Figure 12-11. *The event hub Producer client connection information is set in the secrets.json file*

Code to Produce Events

To publish data from this client application, the code leverages the EventHubProducerClient object, which needs the connection string and the event hub name. Remember that the connection string must have the Send permission as part of the SAS token or this client won't be able to send data to the hub.

```
producerClient = new EventHubProducerClient(_
eventHubConnectionString, _eventHubName);
```

For simplicity, this application does nothing more than send trivial practice apps available from Microsoft Learn. A batch of data is created and sent based on your specified number of events, producing the data in the hub. Note that the data is encoded as binary by the application into an EventData object.

```
using EventDataBatch eventBatch = await producerClient.
CreateBatchAsync();

for (int i = 1; i <= _numberOfEvents; i++)
{
    var log = GenerateNewLogMessage();
    if (!eventBatch.TryAdd(new EventData(Encoding.UTF8.
    GetBytes($"Event {i}: {log}"))))
    {
        // if it is too large for the batch
```

```
        throw new Exception($"Event {i} is too large for the
        batch and cannot be sent.");
    }
}
```

Once the batch is created, the data is sent via the Producer client:

```
try
{
    // Use the producer client to send the batch of events to
    the event hub
    await producerClient.SendAsync(eventBatch);
    Console.WriteLine($"A batch of {_numberOfEvents} events has
    been published.");
}
finally
{
    await producerClient.DisposeAsync();
}
```

Run the client application to send the batch data to the hub. Validate that a success message is generated in the client application (see Figure 12-12).

Figure 12-12. *Success message shows that the events have been published*

Note that you can also see this information on the Event Hub blade (see Figure 12-13).

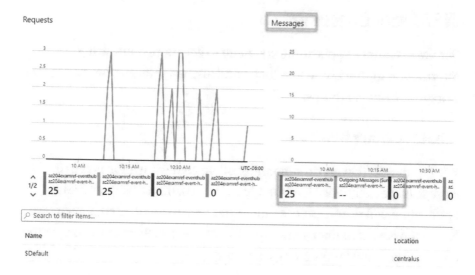

Figure 12-13. *The event hub has ingressed 25 messages*

Wait for five minutes. The automatic capture will run and the data will be captured to your data lake storage container (see Figure 12-14).

Figure 12-14. *The data is captured to storage automatically*

The data is stored as `.avro` files, which is a binary file protocol commonly utilized in Big Data pipelines. You can download the file if you want, but viewing it will not be very useful in its binary state.

.NET Event Consumer

For the consumer application, you need to get connection string information for the Listen SAS token and also get information for another storage account container.

Create Another Container

While you would likely do something other than store information in storage (especially since it is already captured), this consumer client application will simply process and move data to another container. Name the new container something like processedeventdata and get the connection string for the storage account.

Update User Secrets for the Client Application

For the client application, update the user secrets with the Listen SAS token connection string, event hub name, storage account connection string, and the container name. Your secrets.json file for the EventHubConsumer app should be similar to what is shown in Figure 12-15.

Figure 12-15. *The Consumer secrets are set to consume the events and send the results to storage*

Consume Events

To consume the event messages from the event hub, the EventProcessorClient is used. This consumer client will use the DefaultConsumerGroup. The storage client information is also set for use during processing:

```
// Read from the default consumer group: $Default
string consumerGroup = EventHubConsumerClient.
DefaultConsumerGroupName;
_storageClient = new BlobContainerClient(_
blobStorageConnectionString

                                    , _blob
                                    ContainerName);

// Create an event processor client to process events in the
event hub
_processor = new EventProcessorClient(_storageClient,
consumerGroup

                        , _eventHubConnectionString,
                        _eventHubName);
```

If you want to use another consumer group, you can create one and use it. Also note that this EventProcessorClient is set to leverage storage by reading from the consumer group on the hub via the Listen SAS token connection string.

After setting the processor, handlers are added to process events and errors:

```
// Register handlers for processing events and handling errors
_processor.ProcessEventAsync += ProcessEventHandler;
_processor.ProcessErrorAsync += ProcessErrorHandler;
```

Next, the processor is started. The application waits 30 seconds and stops processing, just for the academic nature of the application. In the real world, you may never stop processing on a dedicated consumer.

I'll leave the code examination for error handling to you (it's academic and trivial here). For the processing, note the ability to get the data from the message as expected; this client is automatically ingesting to storage as a way to manage the processed information.

```
var eventArgsMessageData = eventArgs.Data.Body.ToArray();
var eventArgsMessageString = Encoding.UTF8.GetString(eventArgs
MessageData);

// Write the body of the event to the console window
Console.WriteLine($"\tReceived event:
{eventArgsMessageString}");

// Save the data to a text file at Storage:
var fileName = $"{DateTime.Now.ToString("yyyy.MM.dd_")}
{r.Next(1000, 1999)}.txt";
var blobClient = _storageClient.GetBlobClient(fileName);

using (var ms = new MemoryStream(eventArgsMessageData))
{
    await blobClient.UploadAsync(ms, true);
}

// Update checkpoint in the consumer group so that the app
processes
// only new events the next time it's run
await eventArgs.UpdateCheckpointAsync(eventArgs.
CancellationToken);
```

Run the application (right-click and select Debug ➤ Start New Instance) to consume the 25 events generated earlier (see Figure 12-16).

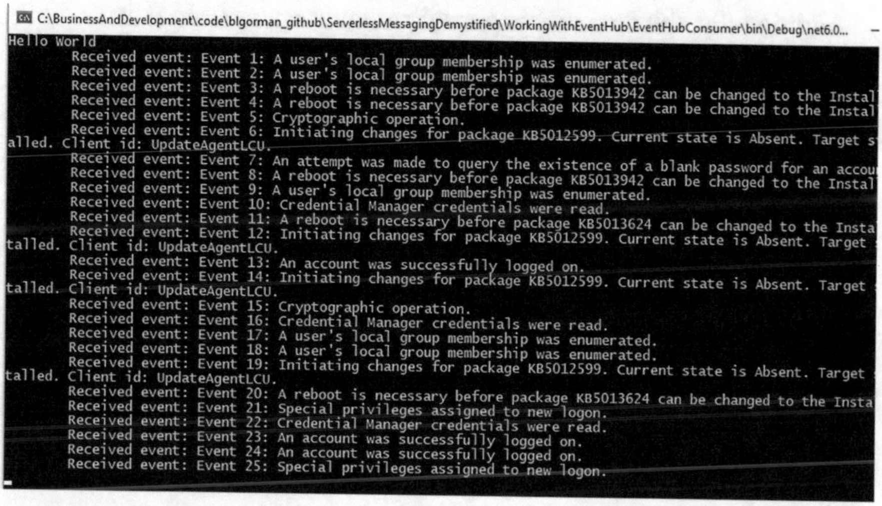

Figure 12-16. *The data is removed from the hub during processing and this application is sent to Azure Storage*

Note that autocapture and even the processing did not remove these event messages from the event hub, but this processing has moved the Checkpoint so the messages are effectively "removed" from the hub for the $Default consumer group.

If you explore the storage, you'll see that the container is storing information about the checkpoint for the $Default consumer group (see Figure 12-17).

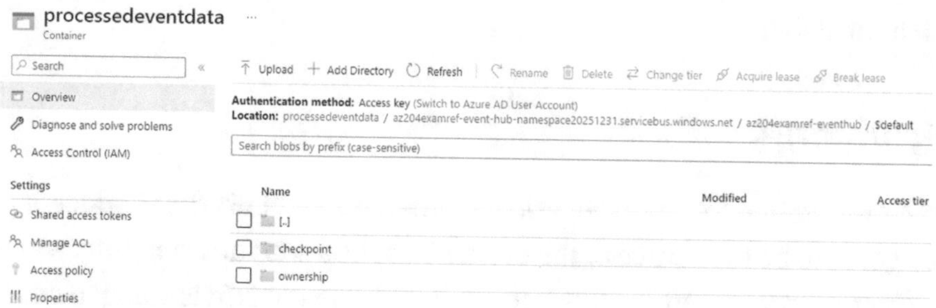

Figure 12-17. *The consumer group checkpoint is stored in storage*

Additionally, the data was exported as expected, as shown in Figure 12-18.

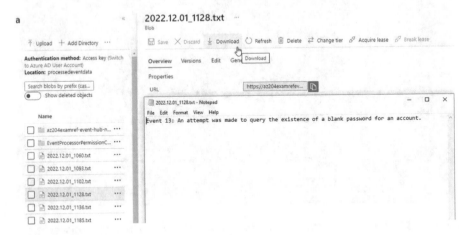

Figure 12-18. *The data was exported, and you can easily review it since the data is stored as simple text files*

Azure Event Grid

If you've completed other chapters in this book, you likely read the Azure Functions chapter, where a storage event was created on an upload of a new file, and the event triggered an Azure Function via the event grid trigger. In this chapter, you get another chance to look at the event grid in a bit more detail.

Producers

In consideration for the event grid, as with the event hub, the producers are going to be the source of the events. In contrast to the event hub, where each producer streams events into the hub, the event grid is going to be a single event generated by a producer. Each time an event happens, you can respond to the event directly by subscribing to the event topic.

Event producers can be anything within Azure, such as the blob storage events for create, delete, and modify. Additional sources (producers) can be things like virtual machine started/stopped events, messages received in the message bus topic or queue, or even things like a user signed in to Azure create events that can be leveraged. You can also create custom events (more on this later).

Consumers

The consumer of an event grid event is any client application or service in Azure that has correctly subscribed to the event. When the event is raised, Azure Event Grid broadcasts the event data to all subscribers. This means a single event can be handled by more than one application or service.

Typical responses to an event might be an Azure Function (see Chapter 6), Logic Apps (shown later in this chapter), automation runbooks, storage, event hubs, or any custom webhook endpoint or third-party API endpoint.

Concepts

Within the Azure Event Grid ecosystem, there are generally five things that you need to be in command of. They are events, sources, topics, subscriptions, and handlers.

Events

When it comes to Azure events in the event grid, every event has common information associated with it. This information is always in a JSON document and you can leverage this information to handle the event in various manners. Each JSON document contains the same information (covered in detail under the upcoming "Event Schema" section). The first callout here is the data section, which contains the event information from the producer.

One thing that is important to note before going forward is that the size of the data for the event is limited to 64 KB without fee and a max size of 1 MB. Events larger than 64 KB will incur a fee. As a quick first investigation into whether to use messages or events in your solutions, make a note that data in an event is supposed to be informational only, whereas data in a message (covered in the next chapter) will typically contain both information and state. For example, a blob storage event contains only the URL to the file (not the file contents), whereas a message might contain the URL to the file and one or more of the rows of data from the file, as well as any other important information for use in a distributed transaction.

Another distinction between messages and events is that typically the event grid doesn't care if you do anything with the information sent via an event. Once the event is registered as delivered, it's forgotten about (fire-and-forget). In contrast, messages and message brokers typically have some concern as to the processing of the message.

Sources

As mentioned, sources for the event are just the solution or system where the event was generated.

Topics

In my opinion, one of the more difficult things to understand about events (and messages in the next chapter) is the concept of topics, simply because of the obscurity of the naming. What exactly is a "topic" after all?

To make this easier, you can think of a topic such as a general "today's topic of discussion is anything related to" either "the reduction of the overall acreage of rainforests globally" or "the scores from each game in the world cup during round two." If your events are focused on something that is related, that is the concept of what a topic should do, it's better to group related events in Azure Event Grid.

For example, responding to blob storage events on a specific storage account is a topic. Another example might be custom events from your major line-of-business application. Likely the subscriber only cares about one of those, not both, so routing all of the events from both producers into the same topic would be a poor design choice. Those events should be properly grouped as individual topics so that interested parties could subscribe to the topics that make sense for their day-to-day operations.

Subscriptions

Once a topic is created, any consumer can subscribe to the topic to respond to the event. A topic can have multiple subscribers, and each subscriber can respond to all events individually. Additionally, subscribers can use filtering to only respond to events within the topic that concern their purpose (filtering is covered later).

For example, consider the blob storage account. On the created event, a Logic App and an Azure Function are both subscribing to the topic and therefore responding to the event and can use the information from the event individually. Perhaps the function app is parsing the file if it a *.csv or *.xlsx file, and perhaps the Logic App is doing something else with the file if it is an image file like a *.jpg or *.png file. Maybe they both do something with the information. The operation and handling of the events by one or more subscribers is entirely up to you as the developer.

Handlers

The event handlers are the applications or systems that subscribe to topics and then continue the processing of the event.

Event Schema

Every event that is generated has the same schema within Azure. This makes it universally easier to process events across your subscription, and also allows for filtering of events. The event schema is JSON and contains the following items:

- ID

- Topic

- Subject

- Event type

- Event time

- Data

- Data version

- Metadata version

The schema is JSON and is formatted as follows (from `https://learn.microsoft.com/azure/event-grid/event-schema`, which you can review for more information):

```
[
  {
    "topic": string,
    "subject": string,
    "id": string,
    "eventType": string,
    "eventTime": string,
    "data":{
      object-unique-to-each-publisher
    },
    "dataVersion": string,
```

```
    "metadataVersion": string
  }
]
```

ID

Every event has its own unique ID, which is required on all events. Typically, you don't have a lot of concern about this property in your event handling solutions. The ID is generated in system events and can be anything you want in custom events.

Topic

The topic in an event grid schema is not actually required. Most of the time, however, you will have the topic for the event included in the schema.

As you may have already gathered, there are two types of topics that can be utilized—system and custom.

System Topics

System topics are any topics that are generated by solutions within the Azure ecosystem. For example, a blob storage account might have a topic associated with it. In this scenario, any subscriber could get all the events raised by the storage account.

Custom Topics

Custom topics are any event topic you create to handle custom event data. For example, you might create a custom topic to respond to a button-press event in one of your applications. When the user presses the button, your code raises a custom event for the topic with the payload as expected by your application event handlers. The event is then sent to the event grid and can be handled by any subscribers.

Subject

The subject is one of the required fields. This subject has relevant data from the producer to the event subject. For example, this might be the path to the file when a blob is created, or it could be a path to a route for your custom event.

Type

The event type is required and is based on the event itself and can be used to filter handling. The common example continually mentioned here is blob storage. Within blob storage, you have many event types, including blob created and blob deleted. If the event handler doesn't care when blobs are deleted, then it will filter to only the event types it does care about.

Time

The time field is required and is the date and time (timestamp) to mark the exact moment when the event was created.

Data

The data for an event is not required, but when present, it is in the JSON schema, formatted as JSON within the data section. This is where the meat of the event information resides for use by handlers. For example, here is the sample body for an event that contains data regarding a blob storage created event (note the data section, which contains metadata info about the blob, including the url, but is *not* the full file):

```
{
    "topic": "/subscriptions/..../resourceGroups/az204-exam-
    ref-apim/providers/Microsoft.Storage/storageAccounts/
    az204examrefstor20251231",
```

```
  "subject": "/blobServices/default/containers/anycontainer/
  blobs/SampleData.xlsx",
  "eventType": "Microsoft.Storage.BlobCreated",
  "id": "56175e60-f01e-0057-0de4-30f0d306be43",
  "data": {
    "api": "PutBlob",
    "clientRequestId": "d179b80a-8ecc-44f5-8aab-dda658fc5010",
    "requestId": "56175e60-f01e-0057-0de4-30f0d3000000",
    "eTag": "0x8DAFEFB97E7C92E",
    "contentType": "application/vnd.openxmlformats-office
    document.spreadsheetml.sheet",
    "contentLength": 9154,
    "blobType": "BlockBlob",
    "url": "https://az204examrefstor20251231.blob.core.windows.
    net/anycontainer/SampleData.xlsx",
    "sequencer": "00000000000000000000000000001580500000000
    00007203",
    "storageDiagnostics": {
      "batchId": "dcf8dc55-f006-0068-00e4-303870000000"
    }
  },
  "dataVersion": "",
  "metadataVersion": "1",
  "eventTime": "2023-01-25T17:42:56.5147822Z"
}
```

(A similar data sample is also shown in Figure 12-33 at the end of the chapter.)

Again, it is critical that events are treated as information only about a specific happening at a specific date and time.

For example, an event might be information that a rocket was launched by SpaceX on October 8th 2022 at 18:05 from Launchpad CCSFS SLC 40. All of that "event" data can easily be sent in JSON form within the 1 MB Limit (and likely under the 64KB limit where no additional charges are incurred). There is no concern as to what happened next on the launch— whether it was successful, returned, crashed, orbited, went to mars, or anything else. All that matters is the event that happened, and that is all the data has made available. Any subscribers could report that the launch had happened and get information from the data payload as to the event type and launchpad details.

Versions (Data/Metadata)

Version information for data and metadata are not required fields (these two entries are combined for brevity in this book). The event grid schema is determined by the event grid, and currently only has the one version (which contains all of these properties). If you want to give your data a version, the producer of the event can put a data version on the event data.

Subscribing to Topics

As mentioned, to set up events, you must create a topic in the event grid that responds to the events (otherwise events are ignored). Once a topic is created, one or more handlers can subscribe to the topic.

Filtering Data

In most scenarios, the handler doesn't need to respond to every event. In certain scenarios, your solution may even rely on filtering to prevent certain processing from happening.

For example, consider a solution that needs to notify fans of the world cup about the scores of today's games. Consider a scenario where the fans only want to get live updates for specific teams in the world cup, but they want the ending score for all games. For simplicity, assume this is as simple as the fan selecting to get score updates and then selecting to get detailed updates from the game where teams are France vs Poland, and another subscriber wants the updates from the USA vs Netherlands game. Each fan can filter by team and get detailed updates, and the fact that they subscribed means they get final scores for all games. Event data is similar to this. Certain events can be handled based on the filters set in the subscription.

Filter by Subject

One way to filter data is by the subject. This might include a filter where the subject starts with some key string like "images" or is in a specific container in a storage account like ../images/uploads. The filter here can also be concerned only with the end of the subject (such as the extension) to handle, such as *.jpg or *.xlsx only.

Filter by Type

Another important way to filter data is to key on the type. This is similar to the ongoing example where the type is something like the BlobCreated event type on the blob storage account. All other event types would be ignored. Another might be to key on only the type for events involving virtual machines where the type is machine deallocated.

Filter by Conditions

An advanced way to work with events is to leverage some conditional logic in your event filter. In these filtered queries, you set some conditions which evaluate the data property and discern if the event should trigger the handler.

The conditions you can filter on include a number of operator types involving checking a data field or the subject for some evaluation that results in a Boolean true/false value. A comprehensive list can be found at https://learn.microsoft.com/azure/event-grid/event-filtering.

For example, you can check the data on a field named length to see if the length is greater than or equal to 150 (an arbitrary value) with the following advanced filter in the subscription:

```
"advancedFilters": [{
    "operatorType": "NumberGreaterThanOrEquals",
    "key": "data.length",
    "value": 150
}]
```

Another example lets you check the data field fileURL for ends with *.jpg as follows:

```
"advancedFilters": [{
    "operatorType": "StringEndsWith",
    "key": "data.fileURL",
    "values": "jpg"
}]
```

Event Delivery

Unless certain scenarios are encountered (see the next section on retry policies), Azure Event Grid will attempt to deliver an event indefinitely until the event is acknowledged as delivered.

Retry Policies

When you create a subscription, you can set a maximum number of retries or a time limit to limit the number of attempts, and there are specific error codes that the system will know can never be resolved. They will be immediately placed in the dead-letter queue or dropped completely if you haven't configured dead-lettering for the topic.

Error Codes that Immediately Cancel Retry

The following codes are unresolvable with time, so the Event Grid immediately dead-letters or drops the event when any of the following error codes occur:

- 400: Bad request
- 401: Unauthorized (webhook only)
- 403: Forbidden
- 404: Not Found
- 413: Request Entity Too Large

Maximum Number of Attempts

When you create the subscription, you can set the maximum number of retry attempts to a valid number between 1 and 30.

Maximum TTL

When you create the subscription, you can set the maximum time to retry for an event from 1 to 1,440 minutes.

Dead-Letter

If you want to ensure that no event is ever lost, you can create a dead-letter policy on the subscription. Typically, the events that are sent to dead-letter are stored in an Azure Storage account. You configure the storage settings upon creation of the topic (see Figure 12-19).

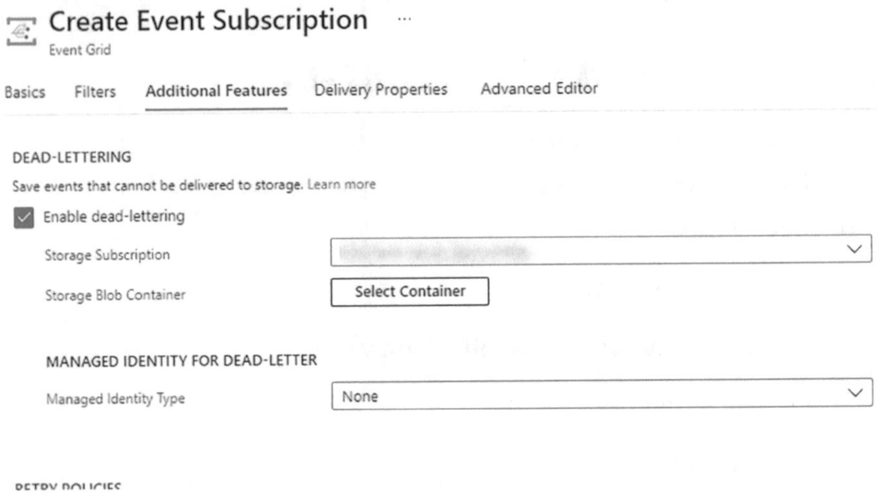

Figure 12-19. *The subscription for an event allows configuration of the dead-lettering policy*

Responding to an Event with a Logic App

To complete this chapter, you look at creating a simple event subscription on a storage account to run a Logic App upon a blob upload.

Leverage the Storage Account

Earlier in this chapter, you created a storage account. For simplicity, you can leverage that for this activity. Navigate to that storage account. On the storage account, make sure to record the name of the account as well as either the primary or secondary key for access (you can get these from the Access Keys left-navigation menu). When you have that information ready, then click the Events left-navigation menu (see Figure 12-20).

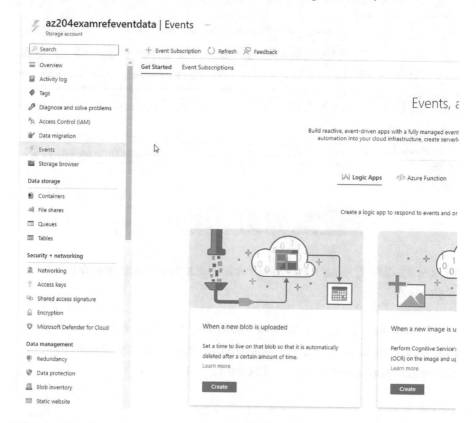

Figure 12-20. *Starting the process of creating a new Logic App on a blob-created event*

Add a Subscription

Click the Create button with Logic Apps selected. This will direct you to the page to create a new Logic App. In order to make the event subscription and get set up, the Logic App requires you to sign in (potentially you could leverage a managed identity for some of this as well).

Add your sign-in information for the storage account, as shown in Figure 12-21.

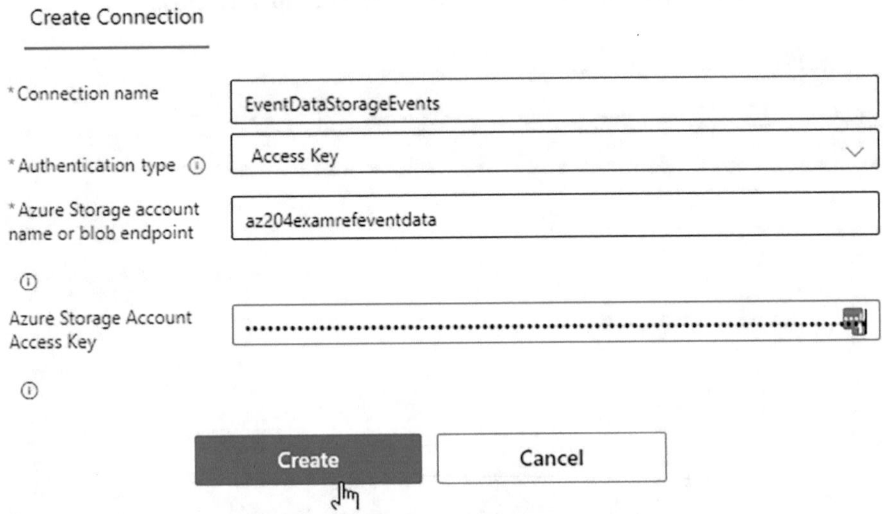

Create Connection
_____

* Connection name	EventDataStorageEvents
* Authentication type ⓘ	Access Key ⌄
* Azure Storage account name or blob endpoint	az204examrefeventdata
ⓘ	
Azure Storage Account Access Key	••
ⓘ	

[Create]   [Cancel]

Figure 12-21. *Create a connection to the storage account for the Logic App*

For the event grid, you have to sign in or you could use a previously built service principal or user-assigned managed identity. Sign in to authorize Azure Event Grid (see Figure 12-22).

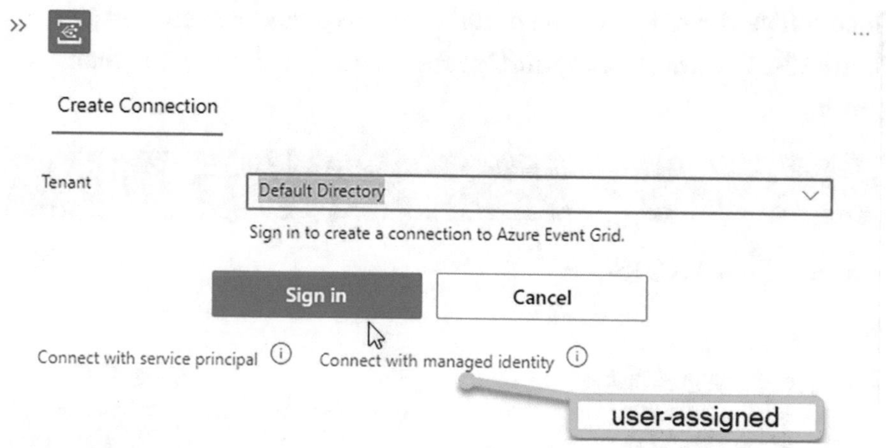

Figure 12-22. *The event grid requires authentication. For this demonstration, use your user account. For production-ready uses, consider the other two options*

Once both connections are built, click Continue, as in Figure 12-23.

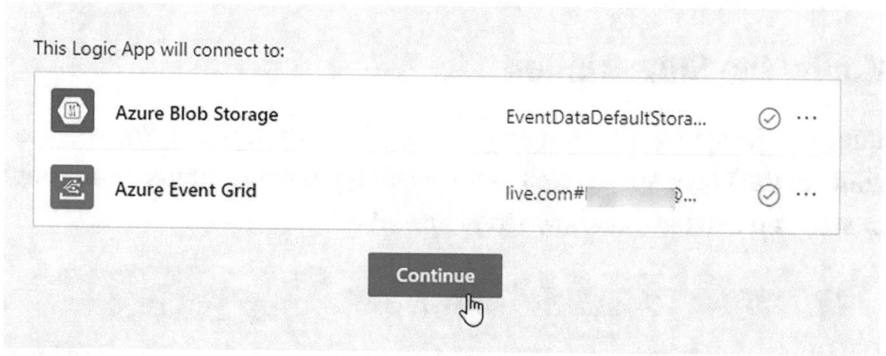

Figure 12-23. *The connections are good, so it's time to create the Logic App*

Once the Logic Apps Designer comes up, immediately save the Logic App to create the endpoint and not lose anything. Name the Logic App something like az204storageevents. You can't change the name of a Logic App after you save it, so make sure you name it properly right away.

Once you've created it and the portal confirms it has been created (see Figure 12-24), navigate away and ignore the You'll lose your changes warning.

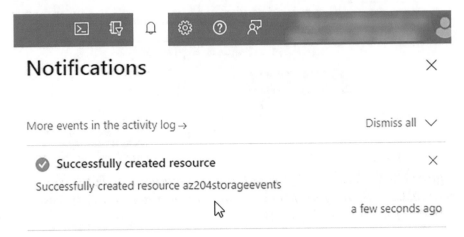

Figure 12-24. *The Logic App is successfully created, but the portal won't realize it so you need to get out and come back to this view*

Modify the Subscription

Return to the storage account and review your subscriptions. You will see a link for the Logic App, as well as the event types being filtered (currently created and deleted), as shown in Figure 12-25.

Figure 12-25. *The Logic App subscription is set on the Events blade for the storage account*

In the subscription, change the filters to only trigger on Blob Created. Note that you can also add subject filtering and advanced filters here. You don't need any, but it's important to note this screen so you can see where those filters are applied. See Figure 12-26 for details.

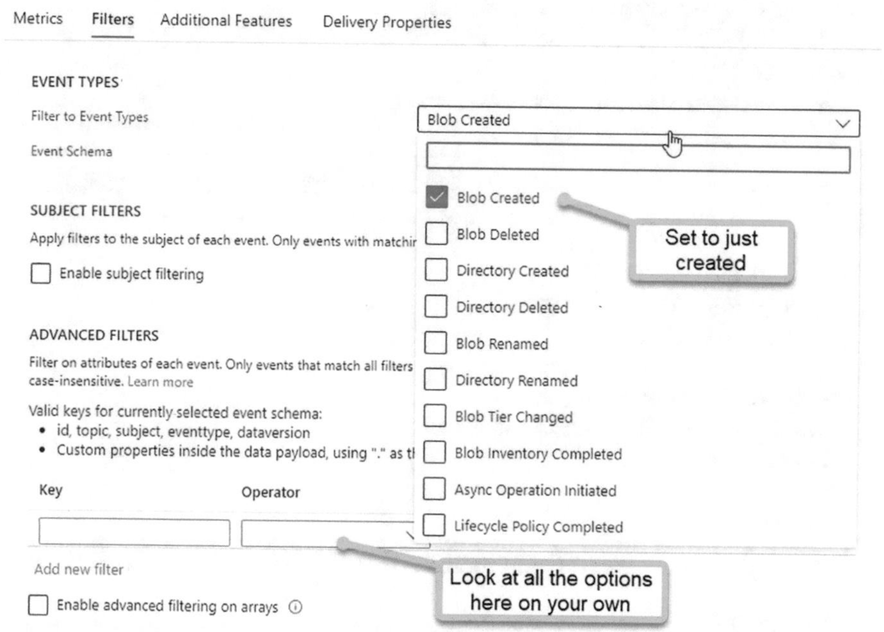

Metrics   **Filters**   Additional Features   Delivery Properties

EVENT TYPES

Filter to Event Types

Blob Created

Event Schema

SUBJECT FILTERS

Apply filters to the subject of each event. Only events with matchir

☐ Enable subject filtering

☑ Blob Created

☐ Blob Deleted

☐ Directory Created

Set to just created

☐ Directory Deleted

ADVANCED FILTERS

Filter on attributes of each event. Only events that match all filters case-insensitive. Learn more

☐ Blob Renamed

☐ Directory Renamed

Valid keys for currently selected event schema:
- id, topic, subject, eventtype, dataversion
- Custom properties inside the data payload, using "." as tl

☐ Blob Tier Changed

☐ Blob Inventory Completed

Key   Operator

☐ Async Operation Initiated

☐ Lifecycle Policy Completed

Add new filter

Look at all the options here on your own

☐ Enable advanced filtering on arrays ⓘ

Figure 12-26. *You can modify the filters for the subscription in the Event Subscription blade*

Add a subject filter to only process .txt files, as shown in Figure 12-27.

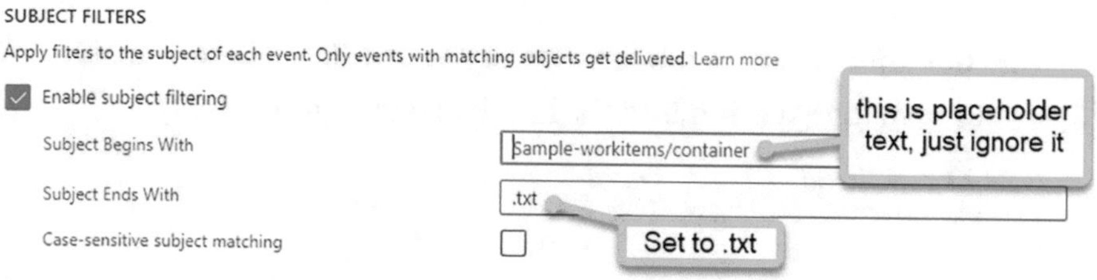

SUBJECT FILTERS

Apply filters to the subject of each event. Only events with matching subjects get delivered. Learn more

☑ Enable subject filtering

Subject Begins With   Sample-workitems/container

this is placeholder text, just ignore it

Subject Ends With   .txt

Case-sensitive subject matching   ☐

Set to .txt

Figure 12-27. *Filter events to only process .txt files*

Make sure to save any changes.

Continue looking at the subscription to review the Additional Features blade, as discussed (see Figure 12-28).

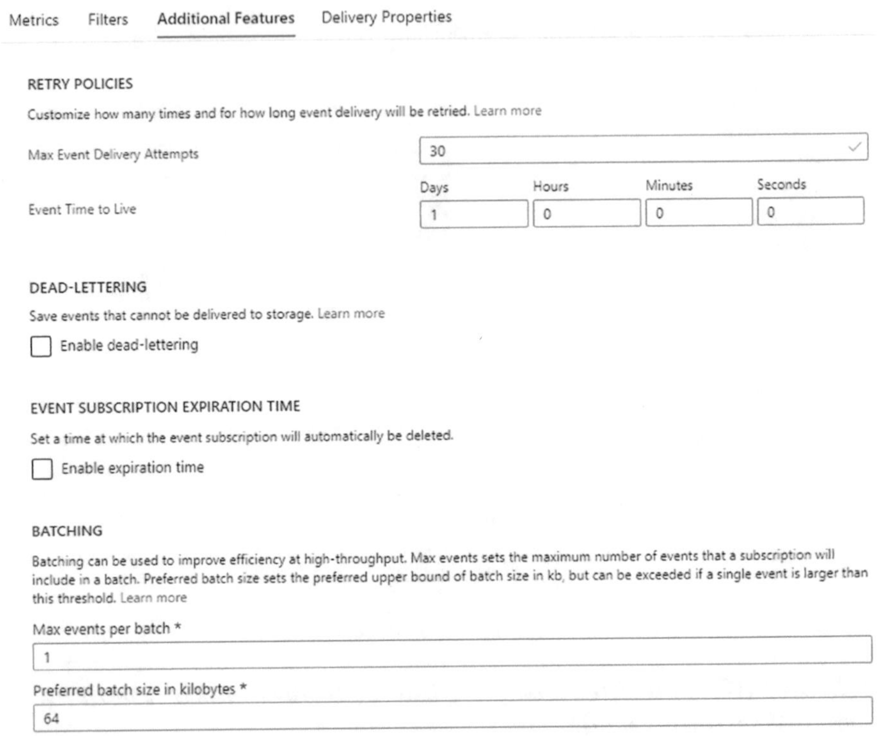

Metrics   Filters   **Additional Features**   Delivery Properties

RETRY POLICIES

Customize how many times and for how long event delivery will be retried. Learn more

Max Event Delivery Attempts

	Days	Hours	Minutes	Seconds
Max Event Delivery Attempts	30			
Event Time to Live	1	0	0	0

DEAD-LETTERING

Save events that cannot be delivered to storage. Learn more

☐ Enable dead-lettering

EVENT SUBSCRIPTION EXPIRATION TIME

Set a time at which the event subscription will automatically be deleted.

☐ Enable expiration time

BATCHING

Batching can be used to improve efficiency at high-throughput. Max events sets the maximum number of events that a subscription will include in a batch. Preferred batch size sets the preferred upper bound of batch size in kb, but can be exceeded if a single event is larger than this threshold. Learn more

Max events per batch *

1

Preferred batch size in kilobytes *

64

Figure 12-28. *The Additional Features blade includes dead-lettering and retry policy configurations*

Note that there is also a tab for Delivery Properties, where you can inject your own information into the headers (see Figure 12-29).

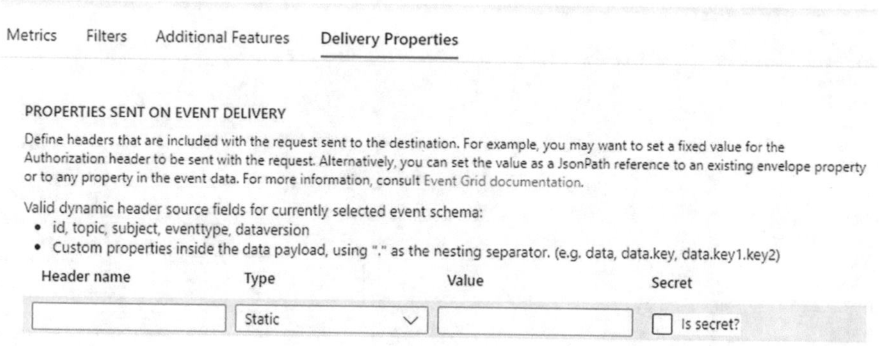

Metrics   Filters   Additional Features   **Delivery Properties**

PROPERTIES SENT ON EVENT DELIVERY

Define headers that are included with the request sent to the destination. For example, you may want to set a fixed value for the Authorization header to be sent with the request. Alternatively, you can set the value as a JsonPath reference to an existing envelope property or to any property in the event data. For more information, consult Event Grid documentation.

Valid dynamic header source fields for currently selected event schema:
- id, topic, subject, eventtype, dataversion
- Custom properties inside the data payload, using "." as the nesting separator. (e.g. data, data.key, data.key1.key2)

Header name	Type	Value	Secret
	Static ⌄		☐ Is secret?

Figure 12-29. *The Delivery Properties blade allows you to add other headers to the event if you want, and you can make them secret*

Modify the Logic App

Return to the Logic App. The default Logic App has a path that runs for 30 days. You will want to delete this. Also, you'll see that the Logic App was triggered potentially by the autocapture from the event hub (depending on how long you took in the previous steps). Cancel any runs that are in progress.

In the Logic App Designer, delete the condition and everything that is under it. Change the When a Resource Event Occurs option to have only the event type of blob created (see Figure 12-30).

Figure 12-30. *The Logic App with the condition deleted and the type set to create only*

This Logic App is now complete for this demonstration, but you can play around with it more if you want to do something like send an email to yourself via SendGrid or Outlook, or if you want to process the file further. There are over 200 connectors available for you to choose to work with the file, and the data you need will be in the JSON schema. Let's run a few that only process text files as expected to prove this.

Test the Logic App Event Handler

To test the Logic App event handler, you can manually upload any text file to the storage account. An easier solution is to open the event hub app from earlier in the chapter and change the value to produce five or so events, then run it and then run the consumer. When the five or so text files are created, the Logic App should fire once for every new text file created (if you deleted your hub before this or are using a fresh storage account, just manually upload a text file to any blob storage container in the account).

Your end result should show that the Logic App has been triggered by the event as many times as you uploaded a new file to storage with a *.txt extension (see Figure 12-31).

Figure 12-31. *The storage account upload triggered the event that was handled in the Logic App for every text file uploaded*

Review the Logic App Data

Open any of the successful runs and review the data in the run. You should be able to see the event grid data schema in the body of the data for the run, as shown in Figure 12-32.

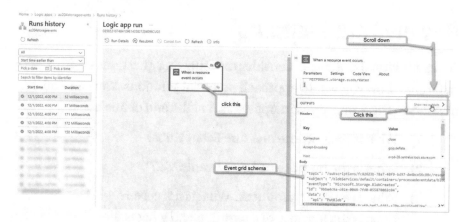

Figure 12-32. *The Logic App executed and you can review the run data, where you can see the details of the event schema*

If you click Show Raw Outputs, you can see much more information about the data, as shown in Figure 12-33.

```
"body": {
    "topic": "/subscriptions/                              /resourceGroups/az204-exam-ref-eventbasedsoluti
    "subject": "/blobServices/default/containers/processedeventdata/blobs/2022.12.01_1523.txt",
    "eventType": "Microsoft.Storage.BlobCreated",
    "id": "9bbe4c9a-c01e-0046-7fd0-055878062c04",
    "data": {
        "api": "PutBlob",
        "clientRequestId": "d1c8caf0-bef7-4403-a70e-9b145ba0f79e",
        "requestId": "9bbe4c9a-c01e-0046-7fd0-055878000000",
        "eTag": "0x8DAD3E77E63FA45",
        "contentType": "application/octet-stream",
        "contentLength": 50,
        "blobType": "BlockBlob",
        "blobUrl": "https://az204examrefeventdata.blob.core.windows.net/processedeventdata/2022.12.01_1523.txt",
        "url": "https://az204examrefeventdata.blob.core.windows.net/processedeventdata/2022.12.01_1523.txt",
        "sequencer": "00000000000000000000000000001b98f00000000000036c4",
        "identity": "$superuser",
        "storageDiagnostics": {
            "batchId": "d8b6864c-5006-006b-00d0-05eb0b000000"
        }
    },
    "dataVersion": "",
    "metadataVersion": "1",
    "eventTime": "2022-12-01T22:00:43.77628Z"
```

Figure 12-33. *The entire event schema is easily viewed in the Logic App run raw outputs blade*

Review Your Learning

As an additional challenge, consider the following questions and determine how you would approach potential solutions. You can find answers to these questions in Appendix A at the end of this book.

1) What is the purpose of Azure Event Hubs?

2) What is the purpose of Azure Event Grid?

3) What is an event producer? What is a receiver? What is the purpose of a partition and what is the maximum number of partitions you can have? What is a consumer? What is a consumer group? How many readers can you have per consumer group? What is checkpointing?

4) How do you work with .NET code to send and receive events?

5) What is an event topic? What is an event subscription?

6) What is a dead-letter event?

7) What are some ways to utilize event subscriptions to respond to events?

Complete the AZ-204: Develop Event-Based Solutions

To fully learn the material, I recommend taking the time to also complete the MS Learn module for AZ-204: Develop Event-Based Solutions found here:

- Explore Azure Event Grid: `https://learn.microsoft.com/training/modules/azure-event-grid/`

- Explore Azure Event Hubs: `https://learn.microsoft.com/training/modules/azure-event-hubs/`

Chapter Summary

In this chapter, you learned about working with event-based solutions, including working with Azure Event Hubs and Azure Event Grid. You should now have a general understanding of when to use each, and the moving parts and pieces associated with each type of event solution in Azure.

After working through this chapter and the Microsoft Learn modules, you should be on track to be in command of the following concepts as you learn about Azure and prepare for the AZ-204 Exam:

- Know the difference between the Event Grid and the Event Hub.

- Recognize reasons to utilize each (Event Grid/ Event Hub).

- Understand SAS tokens and their purpose for Send/ Listen/Manage.

- Work with the Event Hub SDK to publish and consume data using Event Hub.

- Recognize basic pipeline structure for Big Data, including hot and cold path storage with automatic capture for hierarchical cold storage.

- Create and subscribe to events within the Azure Portal.

- Respond to events such as blob storage created to launch an Azure Function, a Logic App, or send data to another API webhook endpoint.

In the next (and final) chapter, you complete this book and your AZ-204 study by learning about working with messaged-based solutions in the Azure ecosystem using Azure Service Bus Queues, Azure Service Bus Topics, and the Azure Storage Queue.

Develop Message-Based Solutions

You've made the move to a serverless architecture, or you've decided to "microservice all the things". You're in the middle of implementing your solution and you realize that creating events is great for fire-and-forget type of scenarios, and the fact that you can process an Excel file when it hits storage is great. Everything is working as expected, and you've gone live. What you forgot was that the end of the month processing is about to kick off, on a Friday, and you'll have about 250-300 Excel files coming in from 3:00 PM until 5:00 PM.

The fact that all the files are coming in isn't terrible. Your function can scale up at will and the processing will work great. That is until the backend service that is handling the data as it's placed into an Azure SQL server starts to get bogged down, and your Azure Function will be throwing an error for every new file because the backend database can't keep up. One good thing about this scenario is that the order of the processing isn't important, so at least you don't need to manage that in this scenario, but you can foresee some upcoming issues where the order could be critical.

© Brian L. Gorman 2023
B. L. Gorman, *Developing Solutions for Microsoft Azure Certification Companion*,
Certification Study Companion Series, https://doi.org/10.1007/978-1-4842-9300-3_13

After some research, you learn that your best option is to implement some messaging to decouple the processing of the files from storing the data in the backend database.

Overview

Queues and messaging services give you the benefit of being able to decouple your various applications, which is sometimes called "temporal decoupling" or "load leveling." By placing the correct information into a message and sending to the queue, your application can offload the work and your frontend or processing units can run just as quickly as before, just sending the information to the service bus or storage queue to continue the processing without getting bogged down, even when the backend processes or downstream services can't keep up with the load.

Within the messaging ecosystem in Azure, especially when concerned with what might be on the AZ-204 Exam, you need to be in command of three messaging solutions. The three services are Azure Service Bus Queues, Azure Service Bus Topics, and Azure Storage Queues. Which service you choose to implement will be based on the needs of your solution and the functionality that each service provides. For the exam, and to make your decision when creating your solutions, you need to know which features and options are available for each of the three services. Before taking a look at the services, it's important to cover a couple of basic concepts for working with messaging solutions. These concepts are:

- First in/first out (FIFO) processing
- Load leveling
- Loose coupling

First In/First Out (FIFO)

In computer science, there are a couple of major terms for data structures in regard to processing order. The concept of first in/first out (FIFO) is important for queueing. When it comes to FIFO operations in these Azure messaging solutions, the only service that can guarantee FIFO processing is the Service Bus Queue, and that's only when you utilize sessions. Therefore, if you need to have a guaranteed processing of messages in the order they are received, you must use Service Bus Queue with sessions.

What's funny to me is that even though the Storage Queue is literally named "queue," the processing cannot be guaranteed to be in order, which, in my mind, is the critical function of a queue For example, you waited in line for three days for those Taylor Swift tickets, so they better not just let someone just waltz up to the window and buy better tickets before you even get a chance, right?

Load Leveling

As mentioned, one of the major benefits of working with messaging is the concept of load leveling, which eliminates any chance that the client solution will be bogged down by backend processing. In the Azure messaging ecosystem, you can accomplish load leveling with any of the three messaging solutions, so this benefit has no deterministic effect on your overall solution architecture where load leveling is concerned.

Loose Coupling

Another benefit of working with messaging solutions is the loose coupling that you get by nature in a distributed system. The solution on the consumer side of the queue can be reworked and deployed at will and the solution on the producer side of the queue can also be reworked and deployed at will. In both scenarios, as long as the message structure and payload are the same, the producer or the consumer doesn't have any dependency or concern on the architecture of the other side of the message broker.

As with load leveling, loose coupling is a benefit that you can get from any of the three solutions, so there is no benefit or drawback to choosing any of the options when it comes to achieving loose coupling.

Working with Azure Storage Queue

Azure Storage Queue is simple enough to implement and utilize, so it's a great starting place for looking at these three solutions. It's important to remember that Azure Storage Queue cannot guarantee order, and it can't guarantee at-most-once delivery without additional work to implement the functionality on your part.

When to Use Azure Storage Queue

When it comes to Azure Storage Queue, there are a couple of scenarios where it will be the only choice.

For example, consider a scenario where you have a massive amount of message data. The Storage Queue is the only place where you can store over 80 GB of message data. Another situation that requires utilization of the Storage Queue is when you need to keep track of all the transactions against the queue or if you need to have some sort of indication as to the progress of message processing (such as the ability to set a checkpoint in Azure Event Hubs, but typically just one long-running process around a message on the storage queue where one message processing operation can be continued if a timeout or other error happens).

Azure Storage Queue Features

Azure Storage Queue has several features and benefits that make it an attractive option with a lower barrier to entry than Azure Service Bus. However, there will be scenarios where Storage Queue is not the correct solution, and these are addressed later in the chapter with discussions on the appropriate utilization of Service Bus Queues.

Access via HTTP/HTTPS

One benefit of storage queues is their ability to produce and consume messages via the HTTP/HTTPS protocol. Storage queues work well with HTTP/HTTPS, whereas service buses use AMQP protocols, which don't play well over HTTP/HTTPS.

Message Size (64 KB)

When working with Azure Storage Queue, the maximum size of the message is limited to 64 KB. This is not intuitive, since the max size for a Service Bus message is larger (256 KB or 100 MB, discussed later in the chapter). You might be tempted to think that storage would have larger message sizes since it is, by nature, storage. Make sure to not get tripped up on this point. A very important part of your job (and this certification) is to discern when to use a service and the size of the message is absolutely critical to ascertaining which service you should choose..

Massive Amounts of Messages (>80 GB)

Although the storage queue has a smaller maximum message size, the storage queue itself can store massive amounts of messages. If you have more than 80 GB of data that needs to be retained, then Azure Storage Queue is your only viable option (other than perhaps creating multiple service bus namespaces and queues).

Storage Queue URL

While it's not really a feature, it's important to remember that the type of storage for anything in the storage ecosystem is easily identifiable by the URL. In the case of the storage queue, the URL is `https://your-storage.queue.core.windows.net/queue-name`.

Operations

When working with the Azure Storage Queue, all operations will take two steps or more to process a message. This is done in a lease and delete approach. In contrast, you'll see that Service Bus Queue provides a similar option to this approach (Peek Lock), as well as an option to receive and delete with one command (which is not an option with Azure Storage Queue).

Lease the Queue Message

The first step is to get a lease on the message from the queue. This lease is typically valid for 30 seconds. In that time, no other process can access the message being processed.

Renew the Lease

Whenever the processing is going to take more than the original lease time, and the process needs to continue working on the message, and the process has not encountered an unrecoverable error, then the consumer client needs to send a command to renew the lease with Azure Storage Queue. If the consumer fails to do this, the message will be put back into the queue. The maximum amount of time you can renew a lease is for seven days.

Delete the Message

After a message is successfully processed, it needs to be deleted from the queue. Failure to send the command to delete the message will mean that eventually the message will be back in the queue and could be processed a second time.

At-Most-Once

As seen in these last three sections, Azure Storage Queue does not have the ability to immediately remove a message at the same time as the message is being retrieved. For this reason, there is no At-Most-Once guarantee. While you could get the message and immediately delete it, there is still not a solid guarantee on At-Most-Once for all messages. Therefore, if you want At-Most-Once delivery guaranteed, your best choice is Azure Service Bus Queue.

Message Retention

The messages in Azure Storage Queue are only retained for seven days. After seven days, messages in the queue are automatically deleted.

Working with Storage Queue in .NET

To work with Azure Storage Queue, you just need to create a queue and then you can leverage the code samples from this chapter to see how to work with the .NET SDK in order to add and receive messages in Azure Storage Queue.

Create an Azure Storage Queue

To create an Azure Storage Queue, you just need to leverage an existing Azure Storage Account or create a new one. On the Storage Account blade, select the Queues left navigation, then select + Queue (see Figure 13-1).

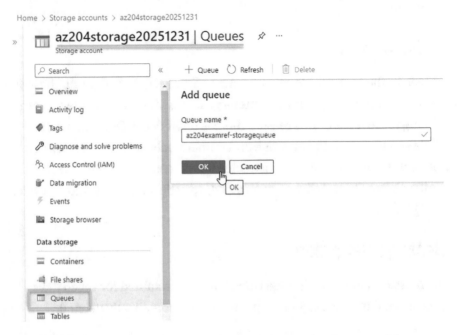

Figure 13-1. *Creating an Azure Storage Queue in the portal is very straightforward*

Just give the queue any name, such as az204examref-storagequeue. Remember that the name must be able to be reached via a public-facing web address, so it must be compliant with web domain naming rules. Creating the queue also shows the full URL after creation (see Figure 13-2).

Figure 13-2. *The full URL for the storage queue is shown. It may seem simple, but this is a critical part of working with the queue over HTTP/HTTPS should you desire to do so*

If you're annoyed at the level of attention to the URL at this point, I apologize. I just need to convince you that this attention to detail is something to keep in mind and it's very easy to forget if the first part of the URL is the storage account name or if it is the queue name. Hopefully at this point you won't ever need to question what goes where in the URL ever again.

NuGet Packages

In order to work with the code against the Azure Storage Queue, you need the Azure.Storage.Queues NuGet package.

Get the Connection String

For the SDK, you can connect via the Azure Storage Account connection string, just as if you were going to work against blob or table storage. Get the connection string from the Access Keys page on your Storage account (see Figure 13-3).

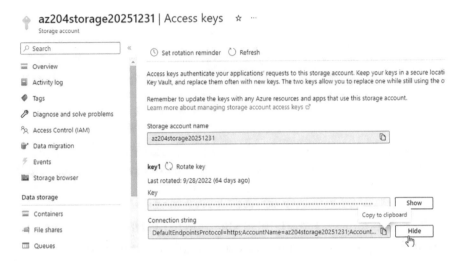

Figure 13-3. *The Access Keys page on your Storage account contains the connection string*

Add the connection string to your local user secrets file. In addition, put the name of your queue into the local secrets file (see Figure 13-4).

Figure 13-4. *Ensuring the connection string and queue name are in your local secrets file*

Compose the Client

As the pattern has been in other instances, start by creating your client object as a new QueueClient:

```
_sqClient = new QueueClient(_sqConnectionString, _sqName);
```

Next, ensure that the queue is created. This command is idempotent and won't hurt you if the queue already exists:

```
await _sqClient.CreateAsync();
```

Send Messages to the Queue

When you send messages to the queue, you can get a receipt back from the queue as to the success of the send operation. To add a message to the queue, utilize the QueueClient object and leverage the SendMessageAsync command. Note that the object is serialized by the code before sending to the queue.

```
var movies = GetMovies();
var receipts = new List<SendReceipt>();

foreach (var movie in movies)
{
    receipts.Add(await _sqClient.SendMessageAsync(JsonConvert.
    SerializeObject(movie)));
}
```

Receipts have several properties, and you can analyze the receipts to see the message IDs and expiration times if you want or need to do so (see Figure 13-5).

SendReceipt	SendReceipt.MessageId	SendReceipt.InsertionTime	SendReceipt.ExpirationTime	SendReceipt.PopReceipt	SendReceipt.TimeNextVisible
Azure.Storage.Queues.Models.SendReceipt	0438a859-8354-47ee-a33b-944637e25c3e	12/2/2022 3:58:12 PM +00:00	12/9/2022 3:58:12 PM +00:00	AgAAAAMAAAAAAAAAK6HD4WYG2QE=	12/2/2022 3:58:12 PM +00:00
Azure.Storage.Queues.Models.SendReceipt	013527f8-81a5-40c9-8aa0-7c6f4adfa8d1	12/2/2022 3:58:12 PM +00:00	12/9/2022 3:58:12 PM +00:00	AgAAAAMAAAAAAAAAO//W4WYG2QE=	12/2/2022 3:58:12 PM +00:00
Azure.Storage.Queues.Models.SendReceipt	a20b16a6-b847-4738-b703-cd7da25ceaf8	12/2/2022 3:58:12 PM +00:00	12/9/2022 3:58:12 PM +00:00	AgAAAAMAAAAAAAAApIXc4WYG2QE=	12/2/2022 3:58:12 PM +00:00
Azure.Storage.Queues.Models.SendReceipt	b49c937c-908d-4648-831d-6a880b59e1f0	12/2/2022 3:58:13 PM +00:00	12/9/2022 3:58:13 PM +00:00	AgAAAAMAAAAAAAAAlPrh4WYG2QE=	12/2/2022 3:58:13 PM +00:00
Azure.Storage.Queues.Models.SendReceipt	f9452992-2cf4-4c5d-b513-9399fa1e5f82	12/2/2022 3:58:13 PM +00:00	12/9/2022 3:58:13 PM +00:00	AgAAAAMAAAAAAAAAHfn4WYG2QE=	12/2/2022 3:58:13 PM +00:00

Figure 13-5. *You can analyze the receipts for information like the message ID and expiration time*

Peek at the Messages

You can peek at messages in the queue using Azure Storage Queue. When you peek at a message, you can review it without removing it from the queue. To complete the operation, you can peek at the messages with the following code, utilizing the PeekMessagesAsync command:

```
PeekedMessage[] peekedMessages = await _sqClient.
PeekMessagesAsync(maxMessages: 10);

foreach (PeekedMessage peekedMessage in peekedMessages)
{
    // Display the message
    Console.WriteLine $"MessageId: {peekedMessage.MessageId} |
    Message: {peekedMessage.MessageText}");
}
```

For the peeked messages, you can specify a number (i.e., 10), and you can see the message text and the message ID with the peekedMessage.MessageText and peekedMessage.MessageId commands, respectively (see Figure 13-6).

Figure 13-6. *The messages are shown, and you can see the ID and the text of the messages by peeking at each message*

Update a Message in the Queue

In some cases, you may need to update a message in the queue. You can do this in Azure Storage Queue. Using the message ID from the message receipts, you can update it to a new value:

```
// Update a message using the saved receipt from sending
the message
var newMovie = new Movie() { Id = "235234QAW", MPAARating = "PG-13"
                           , Title = "Top Gun: Maverick",
                           ReleaseYear = 2022 };
await _sqClient.UpdateMessageAsync(receipts[0].MessageId
                               , receipts[0].PopReceipt
                               , JsonConvert.
                               SerializeObject(newMovie));
```

Receive but Leave the Messages

With Storage Queue, you have two operations that must be performed together to remove a message from the queue. The two operations are essentially to lease and/or delete the messages. For this operation, you can read all the messages, and if you don't delete them, they stay in the queue. The code to get the messages leverages the client. It calls the ReceiveMessagesAsync method and sets the number of messages to get at one read:

```
var messages = await _sqClient.ReceiveMessagesAsync(maxMess
ages: 20);

foreach (var m in messages.Value)
{
    var qMovie = JsonConvert.DeserializeObject<Movie>(m.Body.
    ToString());
```

```
Console.WriteLine($"Received Message deserialized to Movie
{qMovie.Title}");
}
```

This shows a max of 20 messages, which includes all the movies from the queue, as shown in Figure 13-7.

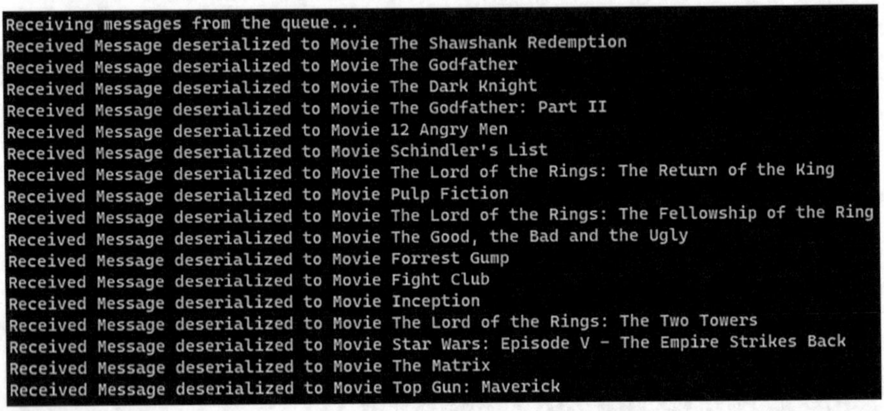

Figure 13-7. *All of the messages are retrieved from the storage queue*

Extend the Lease

As mentioned, you can extend your lease on the object by setting the object visibility (see Figure 13-8). Be very careful here, however. If you set the lease to one hour from now as in this code, if your code breaks or can't be continued, you could lose your reference and ability to work with those messages for the next hour.

```
TimeSpan ts = new TimeSpan(1);
foreach (QueueMessage message in messages.Value)
{
    Console.WriteLine($"Renewing Lease for 1 hour on {message.
    MessageId}");
```

```
        await _sqClient.UpdateMessageAsync(message.MessageId
                                    , message.PopReceipt
                                    , message.Body, ts);
    }

    foreach (QueueMessage message in messages.Value)
    {
        Console.WriteLine($"Message: {message.MessageId} " +
                    $"Next visible on: {message.
                    NextVisibleOn}");
    }
```

```
Renewing Lease for 1 hour on b474e9a5-d3eb-48ab-b8c1-0a57006a1ff9
Renewing Lease for 1 hour on 3a8a5b00-15a9-4407-ae3a-99527550122d
Renewing Lease for 1 hour on 5ee23a09-0090-4ea5-8100-c47bed6f6275
Renewing Lease for 1 hour on 2e434801-8401-4f50-b995-03218717fdd7
Renewing Lease for 1 hour on 13d9800e-8cf0-49a7-9358-e01d4294a2c6
Renewing Lease for 1 hour on f175e0ae-3875-4b77-a878-4ac0a0699bb8
Renewing Lease for 1 hour on 1f8849f4-c5eb-48ec-8e3e-4d66969397c0
Renewing Lease for 1 hour on 8d99969f-03b3-4eae-b4a5-af32a7214b97
Renewing Lease for 1 hour on def3cf95-0fb0-45d8-a5d6-d5f1524516f0
Renewing Lease for 1 hour on 29a50e45-d80c-47c4-8c10-a4e5a743e511
Renewing Lease for 1 hour on c1b2192d-956a-4f68-a139-2124d69518ee
Renewing Lease for 1 hour on 0603c352-0bc1-4da6-8344-52f9c4171eac
Renewing Lease for 1 hour on 890e9822-fd29-4ebe-b777-9b2eb93a9f9f
Renewing Lease for 1 hour on 576e3576-2ff1-4879-96c7-28dd6e7f052d
Renewing Lease for 1 hour on 004d4965-4428-469e-b9eb-fbb63f2e4dd4
Renewing Lease for 1 hour on 08917077-8a6d-4014-a205-bb329ebaea88
Renewing Lease for 1 hour on 178d6f15-026c-46b3-9b32-3c140a0a59ec
Renewing Lease for 1 hour on 1cbbca3c-90b1-435d-831c-3fb82aa55ead
Renewing Lease for 1 hour on 1e59db14-ba1b-4a61-be01-3074b891213e
Renewing Lease for 1 hour on 268b1c38-57f4-476b-bb8a-c8b977975c52
Message: b474e9a5-d3eb-48ab-b8c1-0a57006a1ff9 Next visible on: 12/2/2022 4:23:49 PM +00:00
Message: 3a8a5b00-15a9-4407-ae3a-99527550122d Next visible on: 12/2/2022 4:23:49 PM +00:00
Message: 5ee23a09-0090-4ea5-8100-c47bed6f6275 Next visible on: 12/2/2022 4:23:49 PM +00:00
Message: 2e434801-8401-4f50-b995-03218717fdd7 Next visible on: 12/2/2022 4:23:49 PM +00:00
Message: 13d9800e-8cf0-49a7-9358-e01d4294a2c6 Next visible on: 12/2/2022 4:23:49 PM +00:00
Message: f175e0ae-3875-4b77-a878-4ac0a0699bb8 Next visible on: 12/2/2022 4:23:49 PM +00:00
Message: 1f8849f4-c5eb-48ec-8e3e-4d66969397c0 Next visible on: 12/2/2022 4:23:49 PM +00:00
Message: 8d99969f-03b3-4eae-b4a5-af32a7214b97 Next visible on: 12/2/2022 4:23:49 PM +00:00
Message: def3cf95-0fb0-45d8-a5d6-d5f1524516f0 Next visible on: 12/2/2022 4:23:49 PM +00:00
Message: 29a50e45-d80c-47c4-8c10-a4e5a743e511 Next visible on: 12/2/2022 4:23:49 PM +00:00
Message: c1b2192d-956a-4f68-a139-2124d69518ee Next visible on: 12/2/2022 4:23:49 PM +00:00
Message: 0603c352-0bc1-4da6-8344-52f9c4171eac Next visible on: 12/2/2022 4:23:49 PM +00:00
Message: 890e9822-fd29-4ebe-b777-9b2eb93a9f9f Next visible on: 12/2/2022 4:23:49 PM +00:00
Message: 576e3576-2ff1-4879-96c7-28dd6e7f052d Next visible on: 12/2/2022 4:23:49 PM +00:00
Message: 004d4965-4428-469e-b9eb-fbb63f2e4dd4 Next visible on: 12/2/2022 4:23:49 PM +00:00
Message: 08917077-8a6d-4014-a205-bb329ebaea88 Next visible on: 12/2/2022 4:23:49 PM +00:00
Message: 178d6f15-026c-46b3-9b32-3c140a0a59ec Next visible on: 12/2/2022 4:23:49 PM +00:00
Message: 1cbbca3c-90b1-435d-831c-3fb82aa55ead Next visible on: 12/2/2022 4:23:49 PM +00:00
Message: 1e59db14-ba1b-4a61-be01-3074b891213e Next visible on: 12/2/2022 4:23:49 PM +00:00
Message: 268b1c38-57f4-476b-bb8a-c8b977975c52 Next visible on: 12/2/2022 4:23:49 PM +00:00
```

Figure 13-8. *Leases are extended by setting the visibility of the message*

It is also important to note that the messages cannot be deleted once leased for another hour (until the lease expires), even if you have a handle on the message. Once you set the visibility, you are essentially making it so that the queue can't see or alter messages. If you run this code and then try to delete any message immediately after extending the lease, you get an error, as shown in Figure 13-9.

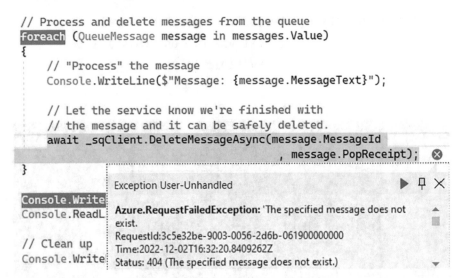

Figure 13-9. *The message is not visible so the program can't delete it, and you get an error message showing this fact*

Delete Messages from Storage Queue

To delete messages from Azure Storage Queue, you just need to leverage the DeleteMessageAsync call with the message ID and pop receipt:

```
foreach (QueueMessage message in messages.Value)
{
    // "Process" the message
    Console.WriteLine($"Message: {message.MessageText} processed" +
                        $", now deleting...");
```

```
// Let the service know we're finished with
// the message and it can be safely deleted.
await _sqClient.DeleteMessageAsync(message.MessageId
                                  , message.PopReceipt);
}
```

The messages are deleted, as shown in Figure 13-10.

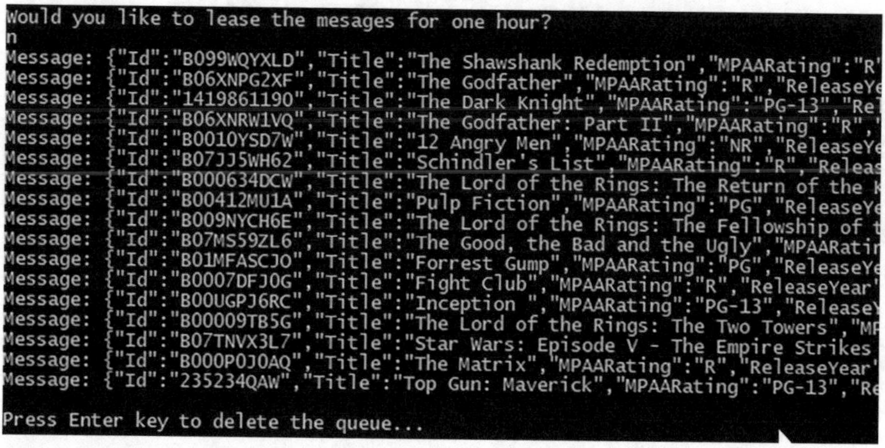

Figure 13-10. *The messages are deleted from the queue*

Delete the Queue

You can use code to delete the queue. If you want to do this, leverage the
DeleteAsync method as follows:

```
await _sqClient.DeleteAsync();
```

Working with Azure Service Bus

Compared to Azure Storage Queue, working with Azure Service Bus takes
a bit more to get up and running. Additionally, the Service Bus Queue and
Topics will likely incur more charges by default than Storage Queue.

Tiers

Service Bus has three tiers—Basic, Standard, and Premium. For testing, you'll use Basic, which is inexpensive, but for production, you'll want to use Standard or Premium to get the best consistency and latency, both of which have some dedicated monthly charges. It should be noted that the official recommendation is to use Premium for production scenarios due to the potential for variable throughput and latency at the standard level.

As you deploy a new instance of Service Bus, you'll note that you first need a Service Bus namespace (just like with the Event Hub from the previous chapter). However, this URL will actually be for a Service Bus instance, so the Service Bus namespace URL makes much more sense in this case. For this demonstration and any testing solution, the Standard tier is sufficient (if you don't need topics, then use the Basic tier).

For more information and a comparison of the service offerings, take a quick look at the chart offered at https://azure.microsoft.com/pricing/details/service-bus/. Also, reference Figure 13-11.

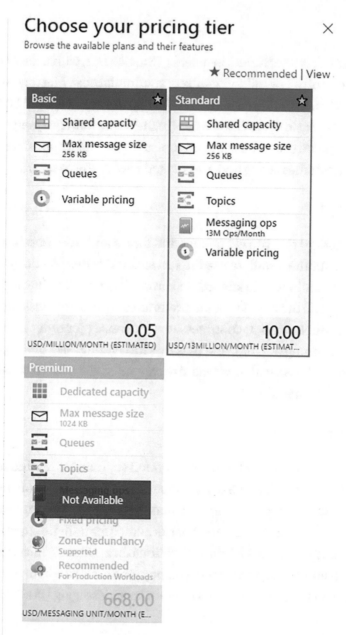

Figure 13-11. *The tier can be changed from Basic to Standard or back once deployed. The Premium offering is not available once the Service Bus has been deployed at the Basic tier*

Basic

The Basic tier is a serverless instance of Service Bus, with a lower cost of entry. It can do a few million requests at minimal cost. Message size is limited to 256 KB, and all service bus instances cannot exceed 80 GB of storage. The Basic tier is comparable to the Azure Storage Queue, offering the basic queue capabilities but no topics (topics are responsible for pub/sub-multicast messaging and are covered later in the chapter).

Standard

At the Standard tier, you get queues and topics and pay a baseline, entry-level price for the month to use the service. At this tier, you do get variable throughput and variable latency, so you can't get predictable performance. You also get all the benefits of the premium service like transactions, automatic duplicate detection, sessions (necessary for order guarantee and long-running polling), and message forwarding. Size limits are the same as with Basic, with message size capped at 256 KB and 80 GB max storage for the namespace.

Premium

The Premium offering is the recommended solution for production scenarios. You get all of the benefits/features of Service Bus on an isolated tier, and your message size can be a massive 100 MB. With Premium tier offerings, you get guaranteed performance for both throughput and latency, and you can set additional options for resiliency, including failover to another region (where you pay for the service in that region as well). The Premium tier also supports Java Messaging (JMS) 2.0. See Figure 13-12.

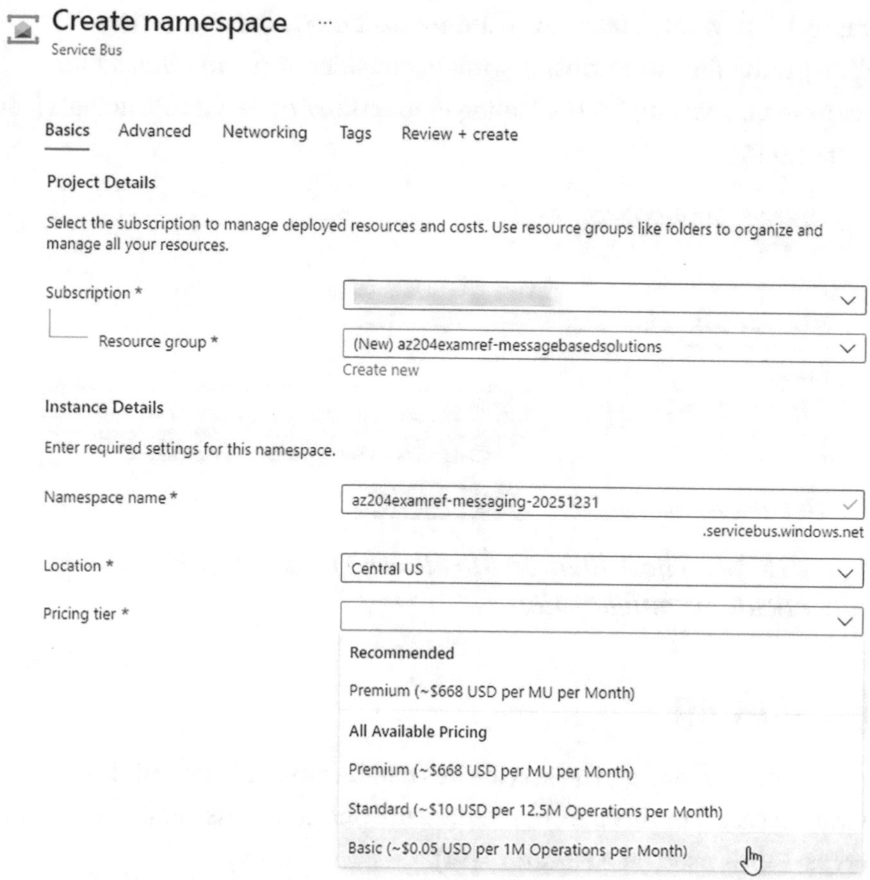

Create namespace ...
Service Bus

Basics   Advanced   Networking   Tags   Review + create

Project Details

Select the subscription to manage deployed resources and costs. Use resource groups like folders to organize and manage all your resources.

Subscription *

Resource group *   (New) az204examref-messagebasedsolutions
                         Create new

Instance Details

Enter required settings for this namespace.

Namespace name *   az204examref-messaging-20251231
                                                        .servicebus.windows.net

Location *   Central US

Pricing tier *

                         Recommended

                         Premium (~$668 USD per MU per Month)

                         All Available Pricing

                         Premium (~$668 USD per MU per Month)

                         Standard (~$10 USD per 12.5M Operations per Month)

                         Basic (~$0.05 USD per 1M Operations per Month)

Figure 13-12. *The Service Bus Namespace is created on the pricing tier (all queues and topics share this tier pricing and compute)*

Initially, I deployed this test instance on the Basic tier, then scaled up to Standard for the ability to leverage topics.

Advanced Tab

During deployment, as with the deployment of the Event Hub Namespace, you'll choose the minimum TLS version and the ability to do local authentication (this is the same SAS token capabilities seen in the previous chapter). You want to leave local authentication on for this testing. In future production scenarios, you might consider implementing a more secure solution using RBAC, Managed Identities, or Service Principals (see Figure 13-13).

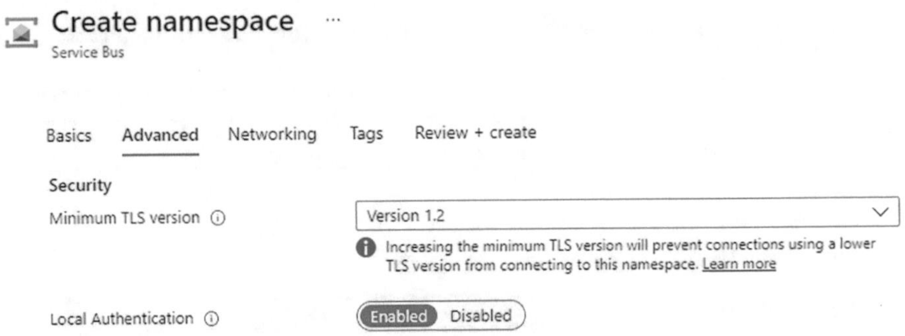

Create namespace ...
Service Bus

Basics   Advanced   Networking   Tags   Review + create

Security

Minimum TLS version ⓘ

Version 1.2 ⌄

ⓘ Increasing the minimum TLS version will prevent connections using a lower TLS version from connecting to this namespace. Learn more

Local Authentication ⓘ   (Enabled   Disabled)

Figure 13-13. *The Advanced tab allows TLS and local authentication configuration*

Networking

As with other offerings, the service bus can be created with Public or Private access. For this demonstration, the public-access version of Azure Service Bus is used (see Figure 13-14).

Basics   Advanced   **Networking**   Tags   Review + create

Network connectivity

You can connect to this namespace either publicly, via public IP addresses or service endpoints, or privately, using a private endpoint.

ⓘ Private access is only available on Premium namespaces.

Connectivity method   ⦿ Public access
                           ◯ Private access

Figure 13-14. *Networking can be leveraged if you want to keep your service bus on a private virtual network*

The Service Bus Namespace is then deployed to be utilized later in the chapter.

When to Use Azure Service Bus

As with the Azure Storage Queue, your job here is to know when to leverage Service Bus over Storage Queue. Hopefully, as this chapter has already discussed several reasons for using Storage Queue, the choice will become more evident as you continue to learn about the features each offers.

Features

As Service Bus is the message broker of choice within Azure that is a bit more involved and expensive, there are several powerful messaging features that you can leverage in your solutions available through Service Bus.

Message Size (Up to 256 KB or 100 MB)

Message size in Azure Service Bus is typically 256 KB, but at the Premium tier you can have messages up to 100 MB. For most scenarios, 100 MB of data is an excessive amount of data. However, consider the cases where you may need to pass an entire document or relevant state information for a system. In those scenarios, you might need 4 MB or more. In other scenarios, you may be looking to pass along information from an email, which might have attachments.

Although Outlook currently limits attachments to 20 MB, if the email has a few attachments you would be better served if you can keep them all together. All of that being said, even though you can send up to 100 MB messages, it is highly recommended that you keep your messages small. For the previous cases, a pattern known as the "claim check" is a better solution. In that pattern, you send information in the message that allows you to get the data from another place, such as Azure Storage. For more information, you can review this document: https://learn.microsoft.com/azure/architecture/patterns/claim-check.

Sessions (Long-Polling and Guaranteed FIFO)

To achieve true FIFO processing, the Service Bus offering must implement *sessions*. The Session feature is also useful for implementing long-polling solutions, which is essentially like streaming messages into your client, rather than the client continually fetching (polling) the messages. Note that this is not the same as streaming data into an event hub.

Duplicate Detection

With Service Bus at Standard or Premium tiers, you get automatic duplicate detection. This is incredibly useful to ensure that data can be resent if there is an error, and no side-effects occur if the message is already present.

Transactions

Another powerful feature of Service Bus is the ability to batch operations into *transactions*. This feature makes it possible to ensure that you get all-or-none operations for grouping messages or processing.

Moving messages within Service Bus is also transactional, so if a message is forwarded or moved to the dead-letter queue, the operation is transactional to ensure that messages are not lost during these operations.

Opaque Binary Payload

Service Bus is agnostic regarding your message payload. This is a great thing because it means you can serialize your data on your services, send the data, and get the data back to complete the operation by deserializing the data. In the middle, Service Bus does its own serialization to make your payload binary, and you don't have to interact with that at all. The content of your message therefore has no effect on the processing at Service Bus, and your data is opaque as far as Service Bus is concerned.

Auto-Forwarding

This advanced feature allows you to build a chain of queues that can be used for advanced processing scenarios. As long as the queues or topics are in the same namespace, you can forward from one to another. This can be useful for a fan-out scenario, similar to fan-out on Azure Durable Functions. Another useful benefit this can give you is the ability to build a massive messaging system where senders and consumers are decoupled and independent of one another.

Dead-Lettering

As with events, messages are supposed to be delivered to a consumer at some point. With messaging, in contrast to events, the dead-letter queue is automatically utilized in your solution. Messages are moved to this queue when they can't be delivered and then you can look at these messages to try to resubmit or correct any issues.

Dead-letter messages will never expire, and, in contrast to how you work with messages in Azure Storage Queue, you can utilize both approaches to receive queue messages where you either peek at and then delete the message, or you just receive and delete the message with one operation.

Another interesting fact is that one of the main reasons messages move to the dead-letter queue is due to the fact that messages can expire before delivery. Since messages never expire from the dead-letter queue, you will then need to purposefully interact with the dead-letter queue to remove these messages, if desired.

Batching

If you want to improve your overall Service Bus performance, you can enable batching at the subscription and topic level. This means that as your clients send in requests to write messages or delete them, Service Bus is internally batching the operations. Rather than running 100 individual delete requests, Service Bus might receive 100 requests and then execute them in a batch.

When batching is enabled (which it is by default on your queues and topics), your clients typically see no latency issues and you don't have to worry about losing any data in the process.

Auto-Delete on Idle

Imagine a scenario where you need to quickly queue several messages and then once they are all processed, the queue is no longer needed (perhaps a nightly batch process). In this scenario, you can configure the queue to be deleted once it's been idle for a specified time interval, such as one hour. While the batch is active, the queue is alive. As soon as the batch is completed and one hour has passed since the last message was received, the queue is completely deleted.

At-Most-Once Delivery

Azure Storage Queue is unable to guarantee at-most-once delivery. With Azure Service Bus, you can utilize this functionality. It is important to note that if you do use this functionality, if something goes wrong during processing of the message, there is no chance for recovery. Essentially, since the message is retrieved using the Receive and Delete option, on read the message is immediately deleted from the queue so that At-Most-Once delivery is achieve. If something goes wrong, the message is lost forever since it no longer exists in the queue.

At-Least-Once Delivery

All three messaging services have At-Least-Once capability. All this means is that your message will exist at least until it is read, and then another manual operation will be required to remove it from the queue. Service

Bus may be more useful to you in this category over storage queues because the storage queue has a Time To Live (TTL) of just seven days. After seven days, messages are purged from the Azure Storage Queue forever.

With Azure Service Bus, expired messages are moved to the dead-letter queue. Therefore, if a message expires before being removed, you still don't lose the data.

Technically, neither solution has delivered "at least once" in this scenario (the message was never delivered in either scenario after all). However, the fact that the message still exists in the Service Bus dead-letter queue means that you didn't lose the history of the unprocessed message, which could be extremely important.

Filtering

Another advanced and powerful feature of Service Bus is the ability to filter your messages. If you worked through the previous chapter on events, then you are aware of what it means to have a separation of concerns on messages based on some filters. With Service Bus, you can use filtering to only review the items from the queue or topic that you are concerned with.

Later in the chapter, you get to see this in action when a topic is given a number of movies, and three separate consumers care only about certain movies that meet either family or non-family rating criteria (such as only the movies rated G). Filtering allows the exact same result set to be viewed differently across three subscriptions with only relevant entries present.

Queues and Topics

Within Azure Service Bus, the two services you need to be in command of are queues and topics. At the high level, *queues* are singular entities. *Topics* are publish and subscribe (pub/sub) and have all the capabilities of queues but can be multicast. The concept of multicasting a message just means that delivery of one message can be received by multiple clients at the same time or asynchronously. As with the filtering scenario, a single message queue can be read in different ways by different clients. One message can therefore be received by one or more clients.

Queues

Working with queues is available at all tiers in Service Bus and is going to follow along with all the other tenets you've likely seen throughout this book in terms of composition. For example, you start with the Azure Service Bus namespace, then add a queue, similar to how you create an Azure Storage Account and then add a storage queue. The code composition pattern of starting from the top level and composing objects that are more specific follows these same patterns.

Receive Mode

Within the queue ecosystem, as mentioned previously, there are two ways to receive data. The first method is the At-Most-Once approach of Receive and Delete. The second method is the At-Least-Once approach of Peek and Lock.

Receive and Delete

The first mode you can utilize to get items from the queue is Receive and Delete. To utilize this mode, set the receive options on creation of the client similar to the following code:

```
var sbpo = new ServiceBusProcessorOptions();
sbpo.ReceiveMode = ServiceBusReceiveMode.ReceiveAndDelete;
var processor = client.CreateProcessor(_sbQueueName, sbpo);
```

It is important to note that this read mode has no fault tolerance because once you receive the message in this mode, it is also deleted from the queue. If something goes wrong, you lose the message forever.

`ServiceBusReceiveMode.ReceiveAndDelete` is the mode you want to use to when you need to implement At-Most-Once processing.

Peek Lock

To enable the message to remain in the queue until you want to delete it, you want to implement a Peek and Delete strategy. To accomplish this, utilize the `ServiceBusReceiveMode.PeekLock` option. In this option, you get At-Least-Once delivery, and you can then process the message.

Messages are read and passed to a processing method via an event handler. Once the message is completely processed, you then need to make a second call to delete the message from the queue. The second call is to a method called `CompleteMessageAsync`, which deletes the message from the queue.

Working with Service Bus Queue in .NET

To get started here, grab the starter code for the `ServiceBusQueue` project. This project will reference the NuGet package `Azure.Messaging.ServiceBus` in the publisher and the consumer projects.

Configure a Queue

In addition to the project, you need to create a queue in Azure. You can name the queue whatever you like, something like `az204examrefqueue`. You can leave all the default settings (optionally, you could make the message TTL just a couple of days instead of 14 since this is a test instance), but take a minute to review all the settings to see how they line up with a few of the features already discussed in this chapter, such as duplicate detection, auto-delete, sessions, dead-lettering, and auto-forwarding (see Figure 13-15).

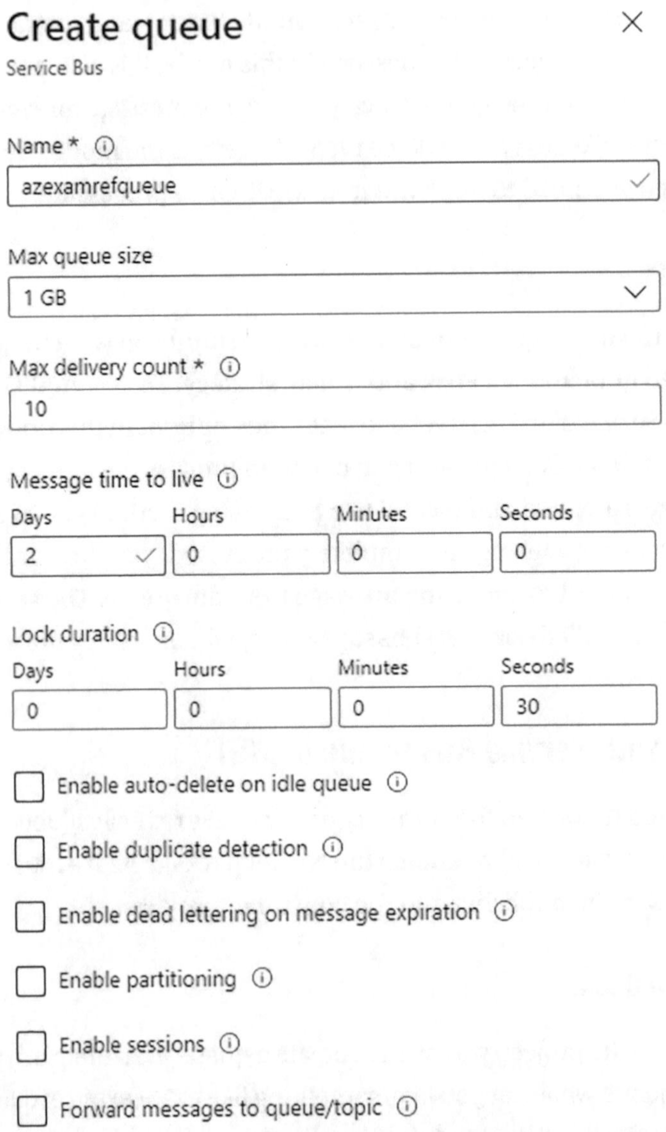

Create queue   ✕

Service Bus

Name * ⓘ

azexamrefqueue   ✓

Max queue size

1 GB   ⌄

Max delivery count * ⓘ

10

Message time to live ⓘ

Days	Hours	Minutes	Seconds
2 ✓	0	0	0

Lock duration ⓘ

Days	Hours	Minutes	Seconds
0	0	0	30

☐ Enable auto-delete on idle queue ⓘ

☐ Enable duplicate detection ⓘ

☐ Enable dead lettering on message expiration ⓘ

☐ Enable partitioning ⓘ

☐ Enable sessions ⓘ

☐ Forward messages to queue/topic ⓘ

Figure 13-15. *Creating a default queue for use in testing. No additional options are configured, but TTL is reduced to two days*

Shared Access Policies

If you worked through the previous chapter, you're fully aware of Shared Access Policies. These policies allow your consumers to read only and your producer to write only.

Drill into the new queue and select the left-navigation item for Shared Access Policies, then click + Add. Create a policy called Consumer with Listen access (see Figure 13-16).

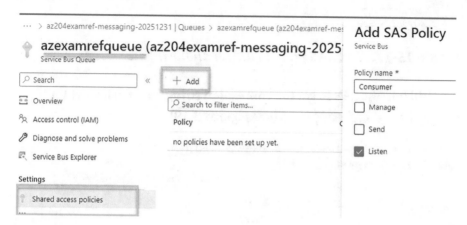

Figure 13-16. *Creating the Consumer SAS policy for the new queue*

Make sure to record the connection string information for the new policy. You'll need it in your consumer application.

Create another policy called Producer with Send access. Of course, if you are going to modify the queue structure or properties, you would need a policy with manage rights as well. Creating a manage policy is beyond the needs of this example, but you are welcome to create it for practice if you like. Figure 13-17 shows the two policies that are necessary to complete this example.

🔑 azexamrefqueue (az204examref-messaging-20251231/azexam
Service Bus Queue

🔍 Search	«
⊟⊟ Overview	
🔏 Access control (IAM)	
🩺 Diagnose and solve problems	
🖥️ Service Bus Explorer	

Settings

🔑 Shared access policies

➕ Add	
🔍 Search to filter items...	
Policy	**Claims**
Consumer	Listen
Producer	Send

Figure 13-17. *The SAS policies are set on the queue*

Drill into the SAS to get the connection string for each if you don't already have them ready to go (see Figure 13-18).

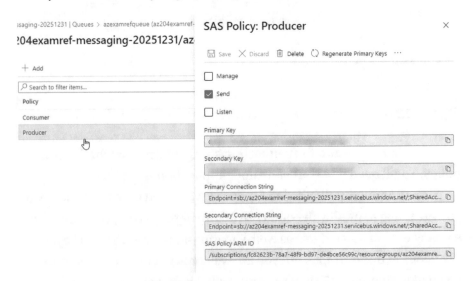

Figure 13-18. *The SAS tokens have connection strings. You need each to have the appropriate access to send or receive messages to and from the queue*

Update User Secrets

Update the user secrets for the Publisher and the Consumer projects. Utilize the examples to get the format and information you need for each (see Figure 13-19).

```
secrets.json* ↔ ✕  usersecrets-example.txt      Program.cs      usersecrets-example.txt      ServiceBusQue...nsumer.csproj      ServiceBusQueu...blisher.csproj      Program.cs
Schema: <No Schema Selected>
1    {
2        "ServiceBus": {
3            "WriteOnlyConnectionString": "Endpoint=sb://az204examref-messaging-20251231.servicebus.windows.net/;SharedAccessKeyN
4            "QueueName": "azexamrefqueue"
5        }
6    }
```

Figure 13-19. *The Producer app is ready to go with user secrets updated*

Make sure you have updated secrets for the Publisher and the Consumer applications with the correct SAS token connection string and queue name information.

Publish Messages to the Queue

To publish messages to the queue, the Publisher project highlights the way to send data. First, however, you must compose the object (just like every other SDK you've seen in the Azure ecosystem):

```
var client = new ServiceBusClient(sbConnectionString);
var sender = client.CreateSender(sbQueueName);
```

With the ServiceBusClient you create Sender. This Sender object is then used to send messages in a ServiceBusMessageBatch with a using statement:

```
using ServiceBusMessageBatch messageBatch = await sender.
CreateMessageBatchAsync();
```

Next, the TryAddMessage method adds the message to the batch:

```
foreach (var m in theMovies)
{
    var moviesJSON = JsonConvert.SerializeObject(m);

    if (!messageBatch.TryAddMessage(new ServiceBusMessage(mov
    iesJSON)))
    {
        // if an exception occurs
        throw new Exception($"Exception has occurred adding
        message {moviesJSON} to batch.");
    }
}
```

Finally, the SendMessagesAsync method is utilized to send messages:

```
try
{
    await sender.SendMessagesAsync(messageBatch);
    Console.WriteLine($"Batch processed {messageBatch.Count}
    messages " + $"to the queue for movie review list");
}
```

Run the Producer to put messages into the Service Bus Queue.
Provided everything is set correctly, you should see that 17 messages were
sent to the queue. You can also see that the queue has 17 messages in it if
you view it in the portal (see Figure 13-20).

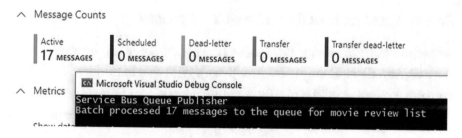

Figure 13-20. *The queue received all 17 messages*

Service Bus Explorer

A new feature has recently been added to Azure Service Bus in the portal. You can navigate to the Service Bus Explorer, and you can actually review the data in your queue using the At-Least-Once PeekLock Read-and-Delete approach (see Figure 13-21).

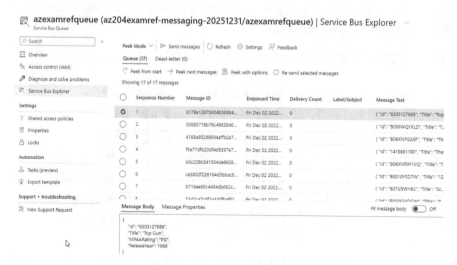

Figure 13-21. *The Service Bus Explorer lets you examine messages in the queue in a way that leaves the messages in the queue*

Receive Messages from the Queue with a Consumer

As mentioned, the Service Bus Queue is really designed for just one downstream dependency (not a multicast). With that in mind, the consumer client should typically read the messages and process them.

To get started reading the messages, the client needs to be created:

```
var client = new ServiceBusClient(_sbConnectionString);
```

Next, you can optionally set options for PeekLock or ReceiveAndDelete, depending on how you want to proceed. If you use PeekLock, which doesn't explicitly remove messages at the time of the read, the messages will remain in the queue. If you use ReceiveAndDelete, then the messages will be received and removed at the same time.

Either way, you need to use the client to create a processor. The code contains one processor that utilizes PeekLock and another that runs the ReceiveAndDelete operations:

```
sbpo.ReceiveMode = ServiceBusReceiveMode.ReceiveAndDelete;

var processor = client.CreateProcessor(_sbQueueName
                               , new ServiceBus
                               ProcessorOptions() {
                                       ReceiveMode =
                                       ServiceBus
                                       ReceiveMode.
                                       PeekLock
                               });
var processorReceiveAndDelete = client.CreateProcessor
(_sbQueueName, sbpo);
```

For demonstration purposes, both types of read operations are created in the previous code, but only the PeekLock processor is used in the remaining code (it requires the additional completion to remove the message from the queue). Feel free to experiment with this on your own for additional learning. The At-Most-Once approach is utilized in the final example later in the chapter.

Process Messages

Similar to event processing, the client processor will use a callback function as an event handler to respond to messages for processing. An additional method is leveraged to record any errors:

```
// add handler to process messages
processor.ProcessMessageAsync += MessageHandler;

// add handler to process any errors
processor.ProcessErrorAsync += ErrorHandler;
```

Processing is then started and continues until stopped:

```
await processor.StartProcessingAsync();
```

This academic app just stops after a minute. In the real world, you likely would just let it run indefinitely, or as necessary for your solution. The code to end message processing is as follows:

```
await processor.StopProcessingAsync();
```

The Code to Process Messages

The code required to process messages is as follows:

```
private static async Task MessageHandler(ProcessMessageEvent
Args args)
{
    string body = args.Message.Body.ToString();
    Console.WriteLine($"Received: {body}");

    var movie = JsonConvert.DeserializeObject<Movie>(body);
    await WriteMessageToConsole(movie);
```

```
// complete the message. message is deleted from the queue.
await args.CompleteMessageAsync(args.Message);
}
```

Note the final line of code with the call to the `CompleteMessageAsync` method is how the message is deleted from the queue in the `PeekLock` processing flow. Additional options exist on the `args` object that instead allow you to renew, defer, or abandon the message.

Complete the Processing

Run the consumer application to view the output for `PeekLock` and then run the `args` command at the end for complete message to remove it from the queue (see Figure 13-22).

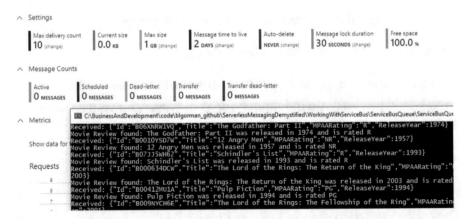

Figure 13-22. *The queue was able to be read and the messages are removed as expected*

Topics

The final area of concern in the Azure messaging ecosystem is Azure Service Bus Topics. Topics are the pub/sub solution for multicasting messages to multiple consumers. Additionally, topics allow consumers to filter their feeds to only receive the messages that concern them.

Pub/Sub

The major benefit of topics over queues, as mentioned, is the pub/sub nature of topics. With this feature, each topic is a standard queue but each subscriber gets all the benefits of essentially viewing their own version of the main queue. These subscriber queues do not affect each other, so consumer A can remove messages from their queue and consumer B would still have those messages available until consumer B has processed the message.

Filtering

Another major benefit of topics is their ability to filter the data. As the consumer, an application may only be concerned about a subset of the messages in the queue. It would be extraneous and perhaps even dangerous if the consumers can review all of the messages in the queue.

For example, consider a scenario where you have the world cup example from the previous challenge. The data for every team is available in queues that store the stats for every game. However, one consumer only cares about one or two countries and just wants the data from those games. Using filtering, the consumer can get only the pertinent messages regarding games of interest, and all other messages are ignored.

An additional scenario might be your company publishing feed data to clients. Perhaps you only want some specific clients—like your best customers—to see the best sales offers, and so you configure their queue to pick those offers up in the messages from their product offers queue. Clients who do not meet a certain sales threshold do not see those offers in their product offers queue.

Working with Service Bus Topics in .NET

The sample application for this final project is a bit more involved, as there are three clients. Grab the sample code for the chapter for WorkingWithServiceBusTopics and open the solution, then look at the ServiceBusAdministrator project.

Get Started with the Administration Project

To make this administration project work, you need to create and/or get a root-level SAS token for the administrator and run that project, which will create your pub/sub topics and subscriptions.

Root-Level Administrator Token

Navigate in Azure to your Service Bus instance. On the Shared Access Policies blade, select RootManageSharedAccessKey and get the secondary connection string for this. (Use the primary for production, use secondary for testing and development; if it gets exposed by accident you can then just rotate it quickly and production will be unaffected in theory.) See Figure 13-23.

Figure 13-23. *Getting the root management key for the entire service bus instance. This is the God Mode key and should be well protected. Do not check this key into your code or push it to GitHub under any circumstances*

Set Secrets for the Administrator Project

Use the connection string to configure the secrets for the Administrator project in the solution, as illustrated in Figure 13-24.

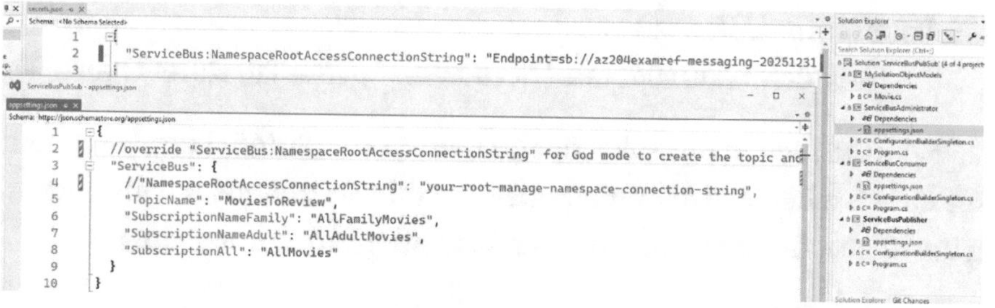

Figure 13-24. *The Root Manage Shared Access Key is added to the user secrets*

Commands from the Admin Program

Within the Administrator program, first, as always, an object hierarchy is established:

```
adminClient = new ServiceBusAdministrationClient(_
sbConnectionString);
```

Next, the program checks to see if the topic for MoviesToReview exists.

```
var existingTopic = await adminClient.GetTopicAsync(_sbTopicName);
```

If not, the topic is created using the following line of code:

```
await adminClient.CreateTopicAsync(_sbTopicName);
```

Next, each of the subscriptions is created if they don't exist with similar commands:

```
var anExistingSubscription = await adminClient.
GetSubscriptionAsync(_sbTopicName, _sbSubscriptionAllMovies);
```

and

```
await adminClient.CreateSubscriptionAsync(
        new CreateSubscriptionOptions(_sbTopicName, _
sbSubscriptionAllMovies),
        new CreateRuleOptions("AllMovies", new TrueRuleFilter()));
```

Note the filter in this subscription is set to TrueRuleFilter. Essentially, this filter is a Boolean filter that, when the value is true, gets all the entries in the queue. Compare that to this subscription creation statement:

```
await adminClient.CreateSubscriptionAsync(
        new CreateSubscriptionOptions(_sbTopicName, _
sbSubscriptionAdultMovies),
        new CreateRuleOptions("AllAdultMovies"
                        , new SqlRuleFilter("MPAARating='PG-13'
OR MPAARating = 'R'")));
```

Note this subscription uses SqlRuleFilter, which checks to see what the rating is within the message. Only movies that are rated PG-13 or R are selected in this subscription.

The filters used previously are built-in and can be selected. The options for filtering include the previously shown Boolean and SqlRuleFilter, as well as a Correlation filter. The conditions of the filter are set by you. Boolean and SqlRuleFilters are both utilized in the code examples.

The Correlation filter is a bit more involved and is not shown in the code. With the Correlation filter, you can create a set of conditions that must be matched in order for the filter to select the message for your queue. The following properties can be matched when using a Correlation filter:

- ContentType
- Label

- MessageId

- ReplyTo

- ReplyToSessionId

- SessionId

- To

- Custom properties defined by you

If you want to know more about using filters, you can review this document on Microsoft Learn: https://learn.microsoft.com/azure/service-bus-messaging/topic-filters#filters.

Execute the Administration Program

With everything in place, you can now execute the administration program to create the topic and subscriptions. Figure 13-25 shows the execution of the program and the result in the portal with the topic and all subscriptions.

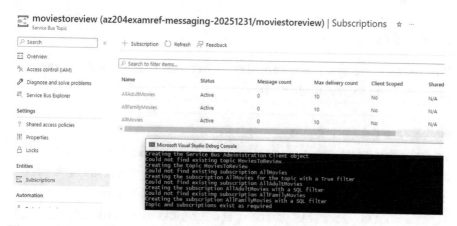

Figure 13-25. *The topic and subscriptions are created*

Note that you can drill into the subscriptions to see more information and/or configure them in Azure as well (see Figure 13-26).

Figure 13-26.   *The filter can be reviewed and modified from within the portal*

Publish Messages

Publishing messages is accomplished with the ServiceBusPublisher program from the example projects.

Producer and Consumer Tokens

To make this work, you need a write-only (Send) SAS token for the topic. Navigate to the portal, drill into the topic, and then select the left-navigation menu item called Shared Access Policies. Note that you can use a token from any level, but you can get as granular as the specific topic, all topics, or for the entire namespace with your SAS tokens.

This token should be specifically for the moviestoreview topic. Of course, using the most specific access level is much more secure, as this token won't work on other topics or queues (whereas a namespace-level token could work on any of the queues).

By now you should be familiar with tokens, and you should likely realize you will need the Listen token in a minute for the final part of the solution. Therefore, you can create both tokens now and then just record the connection strings for each token to use as needed (see Figure 13-27).

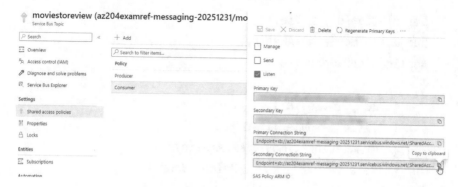

Figure 13-27. *The SAS tokens for Send and Listen are added, and connection strings are recorded for future use*

Send Messages

To put this all together, pretend that you are working for the last Blockbuster video store on Earth, and you have created this program that allows users to review the movie catalog. The first thing you need to do is load all the available rentals. This is done by sending data to the topic.

The first thing you need to do is establish the hierarchy, which includes the ServiceBusClient and Sender (similar to sending to a queue):

```
_sbClient = new ServiceBusClient(_sbConnectionString);
_sbSender = _sbClient.CreateSender(_sbTopicName);
```

Next, you get all the movies and send them one-by-one to the topic with the following code:

```
var message = new ServiceBusMessage(
                    Encoding.UTF8.GetBytes(
                        JsonConvert.SerializeObject(movie)))
{
    CorrelationId = movie.Id,
    Subject = movie.MPAARating,
    ApplicationProperties =
    {
        { "Id", movie.Id },
        { "Title", movie.Title },
        { "MPAARating", movie.MPAARating },
        { "ReleaseYear", movie.ReleaseYear }
    }
};
await sender.SendMessageAsync(message);
```

Note the use of the Subject field to store the movie's Motion Picture Association of America (MPAA) rating. This is how the filters will retrieve the correct messages.

Run the Program

With everything in place, run the program to send the movies that are available to rent into the topic for consumption by subscribers. Figure 13-28 shows how each of the movies is added to the topic, and Figure 13-29 shows that you can go to the portal and review the data to see that the subscriptions have different amounts of data in them, based on the ratings filter.

```
Service Bus Pub/Sub producer started
Sending all movies to the topic...
All messages sent.
All movies added to the topic
Press any key to end the application
Sent movie to topic with id: B07MS59ZL6, Title: The Good, the Bad and the Ugly, MPAARating: R, ReleaseYear: 1966
Sent movie to topic with id: B00412MU1A, Title: Pulp Fiction, MPAARating: PG, ReleaseYear: 1994
Sent movie to topic with id: B06XNRW1VQ, Title: The Godfather: Part II, MPAARating: R, ReleaseYear: 1974
Sent movie to topic with id: B01MFASCJO, Title: Forrest Gump, MPAARating: PG, ReleaseYear: 1994
Sent movie to topic with id: B001OYSD7W, Title: 12 Angry Men, MPAARating: NR, ReleaseYear: 1957
Sent movie to topic with id: B077TNVX3L7, Title: Star Wars: Episode V - The Empire Strikes Back, MPAARating: PG, ReleaseYear: 1980
Sent movie to topic with id: B00OPOJOAQ, Title: The Matrix, MPAARating: R, ReleaseYear: 1999
Sent movie to topic with id: 6305127689, Title: Top Gun, MPAARating: PG, ReleaseYear: 1986
Sent movie to topic with id: B07JJ5WH62, Title: Schindler's List, MPAARating: R, ReleaseYear: 1993
Sent movie to topic with id: B009NYCH6E, Title: The Lord of the Rings: The Fellowship of the Ring, MPAARating: PG-13, ReleaseYear: 2001
Sent movie to topic with id: 1419861190, Title: The Dark Knight, MPAARating: PG-13, ReleaseYear: 2008
Sent movie to topic with id: B00UGPJ6RC, Title: Inception, MPAARating: PG-13, ReleaseYear: 2010
Sent movie to topic with id: B0007DFJ0G, Title: Fight Club, MPAARating: R, ReleaseYear: 1999
Sent movie to topic with id: B000634DCW, Title: The Lord of the Rings: The Return of the King, MPAARating: PG-13, ReleaseYear: 2003
Sent movie to topic with id: B06XNPG2XF, Title: The Godfather, MPAARating: R, ReleaseYear: 1972
Sent movie to topic with id: B099WQYXLD, Title: The Shawshank Redemption, MPAARating: R, ReleaseYear: 1994
Sent movie to topic with id: B00009TB5G, Title: The Lord of the Rings: The Two Towers, MPAARating: PG-13, ReleaseYear: 2002
```

Figure 13-28. *The movies are loaded into the service bus topic*

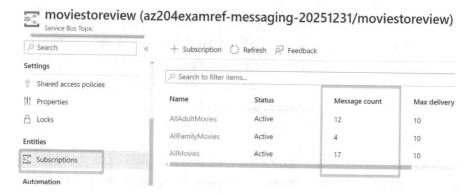

Figure 13-29. *The messages are distributed to the appropriate subscriptions based on the preapplied filters*

Consume Messages

The rentals are all in place, and now, say you have a couple of customers in the store. You need to help them find a movie, so you ask them what kind of movie they want. The first customer conveniently lets you know that they want "a family" movie. Customer two is looking for "an adult movie— no not that kind of adult movie, just not a kids or family movie." Customer three asks to see all the movies. You are in luck, because, wouldn't you know it, this is just how you set up the subscriptions.

Update the Secrets

For purposes of brevity, and because it's been covered numerous times, including in the "Publishing Messages" section, I'll assume you can now quickly and easily update the secrets file for the Consumer app with the Listen SAS token for the moviestoreview topic.

Compose the Hierarchy

To connect and read from the topics, you need to create the ServiceBusClient and ServiceBusReceiver objects:

```
_sbClient = new ServiceBusClient(_sbConnectionString);
_sbReceiver = _sbClient.CreateReceiver(_sbTopicName, subChoice
            , new ServiceBusReceiverOptions() {
                ReceiveMode = ServiceBusReceiveMode.
                ReceiveAndDelete
            });
```

The interesting things to note here are that the subChoice variable is set based on which subscription to review. The options are presented in a switch in the program and are read from the general appsettings.json file:

```
_sbConnectionString = _configuration["ServiceBus:ReadOnlySASCon
nectionString"];
_sbTopicName = _configuration["ServiceBus:TopicName"];
_sbSubscriptionFamilyMovies = _configuration["ServiceBus:Subscr
iptionNameFamily"];
_sbSubscriptionAdultMovies = _configuration["ServiceBus:Subscri
ptionNameAdult"];
_sbSubscriptionAllMovies = _configuration["ServiceBus:Subscrip
tionAll"];
//...other code
switch (choice)
{
```

```
case 1:
    Console.WriteLine("You have chosen all movies");
    subChoice = _sbSubscriptionAllMovies;
    break;
case 2:
    Console.WriteLine("You have chosen the family movies");
    subChoice = _sbSubscriptionFamilyMovies;
    break;
case 3:
    Console.WriteLine("You have chosen the adult movies");
    subChoice = _sbSubscriptionAdultMovies;
    break;
default:
    Console.WriteLine("You have chosen poorly. All movies
    selected by default");
    break;
}
```

Also note that the receive mode is set to ReceiveAndDelete, which, as you know from earlier, means that this is an At-Most-Once delivery. The reason this is interesting because it illuminates the deletion of entries and how, even when they are removed from one subscription, they are still available to the other subscriptions that have not yet consumed the messages. Therefore, you can be confident that each subscription is independently affected and can't interfere with other subscriptions.

Receive All Messages

As the program runs, you can pretend to be one of the customers and get a subset of the movies. This is done with the ReceiveMessageAsync command against the correct subscription:

```
while (true)
{
```

```
        var receivedMessage = await receiver.
ReceiveMessageAsync(TimeSpan.FromSeconds(10));
        if (receivedMessage != null)
        {
            foreach (var prop in receivedMessage.ApplicationProperties)
            {
                Console.Write("{0}={1},", prop.Key, prop.Value);
            }
            Console.WriteLine("CorrelationId={0}", receivedMessage.
            CorrelationId);
            receivedMessages++;
        }
        else
        {
            // No more messages to receive.
            break;
        }
    }
}
```

Run the Program for All Movies

The first run of the program should use the AllMovies subscription. This will prove that the others are not affected by removing all the movies from one subscription. Figure 13-30 shows all the movies from the AllMovies subscription, and the portal shows that no more movies exist in that subscription after the ReceiveAndDelete At-Most-Once delivery has completed, as shown in Figure 13-31.

```
Service Bus Pub/Sub consumer started
************************************************************************
Which type of movies do you want to review?
************************************************************************
* 1 - All movies
* 2 - Family movies
* 3 - Adult movies
************************************************************************
1
You have chosen all movies
Receiving all messages from your chosen subscription
Id=B06XNRW1VQ,Title=The Godfather: Part II,MPAARating=R,ReleaseYear=1974,CorrelationId=B06XNRW1VQ
Id=B00412MU1A,Title=Pulp Fiction,MPAARating=R,ReleaseYear=1994,CorrelationId=B00412MU1A
Id=B01MFASCJO,Title=Forrest Gump,MPAARating=PG,ReleaseYear=1994,CorrelationId=B01MFASCJO
Id=B07MS59ZL6,Title=The Good, the Bad and the Ugly,MPAARating=R,ReleaseYear=1966,CorrelationId=B07MS59ZL6
Id=B009NYCH6E,Title=The Lord of the Rings: The Fellowship of the Ring,MPAARating=PG-13,ReleaseYear=2001,CorrelationId=B009NYCH6E
Id=B0010YSD7W,Title=12 Angry Men,MPAARating=NR,ReleaseYear=1957,CorrelationId=B0010YSD7W
Id=6305127689,Title=Top Gun,MPAARating=PG,ReleaseYear=1986,CorrelationId=6305127689
Id=B06XNPG2XF,Title=The Godfather,MPAARating=R,ReleaseYear=1972,CorrelationId=B06XNPG2XF
Id=B07TNVX3L7,Title=Star Wars: Episode V - The Empire Strikes Back,MPAARating=PG,ReleaseYear=1980,CorrelationId=B07TNVX3L7
Id=B00009T85G,Title=The Lord of the Rings: The Two Towers,MPAARating=PG-13,ReleaseYear=2002,CorrelationId=B00009T85G
Id=B00OPOJOAQ,Title=The Matrix,MPAARating=R,ReleaseYear=1999,CorrelationId=B00OPOJOAQ
Id=B000634DCW,Title=The Lord of the Rings: The Return of the King,MPAARating=PG-13,ReleaseYear=2003,CorrelationId=B000634DCW
Id=B0007DFJOG,Title=Fight Club,MPAARating=R,ReleaseYear=1999,CorrelationId=B0007DFJOG
Id=B099WQYXLD,Title=The Shawshank Redemption,MPAARating=R,ReleaseYear=1994,CorrelationId=B099WQYXLD
Id=1419861190,Title=The Dark Knight,MPAARating=PG-13,ReleaseYear=2008,CorrelationId=1419861190
Id=B07JJ5WH62,Title=Schindler's List,MPAARating=R,ReleaseYear=1993,CorrelationId=B07JJ5WH62
Id=B00UGPJ6RC,Title=Inception,MPAARating=PG-13,ReleaseYear=2010,CorrelationId=B00UGPJ6RC
Received 17 messages from subscription.
Would you like to run the program again [y/n]?
```

Figure 13-30. *The AllMovies subscription has cleared all entries and delivered all 17 messages to the client*

+ Subscription   ○ Refresh   ⌨ Feedback

🔍 Search to filter items...

Name	Status	Message count
AllAdultMovies	Active	12
AllFamilyMovies	Active	4
AllMovies	Active	0

Figure 13-31. *The portal shows that the other subscriptions still contain relevant messages, but the AllMovies subscription has no more messages that have not been consumed after the execution*

Repeat the Run for Each Subscription

To finalize this learning, run the program two more times to review each subscription and ensure the filtering works as expected (see Figure 13-32).

Name	Status	Message count	Max delivery count	Client Scoped
AllAdultMovies	Active	0	10	No
AllFamilyMovies	Active	0	10	No
AllMovies	Active	0	10	No

```
Microsoft Visual Studio Debug Console
Service Bus Pub/Sub consumer started
************************************************************************************
Which type of movies do you want to review?
************************************************************************************
* 1 - All movies
* 2 - Family movies
* 3 - Adult movies
************************************************************************************
2
You have chosen the family movies
Receiving all messages from your chosen subscription
Id=B00412MU1A,Title=Pulp Fiction,MPAARating=PG,ReleaseYear=1994,CorrelationId=B00412MU1A
Id=B01MFASCJO,Title=Forrest Gump,MPAARating=PG,ReleaseYear=1994,CorrelationId=B01MFASCJO
Id=B07TNVX3L7,Title=Star Wars: Episode V - The Empire Strikes Back,MPAARating=PG,ReleaseYe
L7
Id=6305127689,Title=Top Gun,MPAARating=PG,ReleaseYear=1986,CorrelationId=6305127689
Received 4 messages from subscription.
Program completed
```

Figure 13-32. *The movies can be listed by their filter, as expected. This image shows the FamilyMovies subscription output. Once the program has run for all subscriptions, no messages remain in any of the filtered subscriptions*

Review Your Learning

As an additional challenge, consider the following questions and determine how you would approach potential solution(s). You can find answers to these questions in Appendix A at the end of this book.

1) What is the maximum size of an Azure Storage Queue message? What is the maximum size of an Azure Service Bus message?

2) Which service can store more than 80 GB of data?

3) Which service can guarantee order?

4) Which service(s) can guarantee At-Most-Once delivery? Which service(s) can guarantee At-Least-Once delivery?

5) What is the difference between PeekLock and ReceiveAndDelete?

6) What are the various types of filters available for filtering messages? How do you leverage a filter for a subscription? What does it mean to multicast? If topics are multicast, can a message be read more than once? If possible, how or why is this possible?

7) What are the various levels of SAS tokens? What token can do everything on the Service Bus deployment? What is/are the benefit(s) of using granular SAS tokens?

Complete the AZ-204: Develop Message-Based Solutions Learn Module

To fully learn the material, I recommend taking the time to also complete the MS Learn module for AZ-204: Develop Message-Based Solutions found here:

- Discover Azure Message Queues: https://learn. microsoft.com/training/modules/discover-azure-message-queue/

Chapter Summary

In this chapter, you completed your study for the AZ-204 Exam: Developing Solutions for Microsoft Azure by learning about the messaging options of Service Bus Queue, Service Bus Topic/Subscription Pub/ Sub, and Azure Storage Queues. In the process, you have gained enough information to discern when to use each of the solutions and what kinds of features each has to offer for the various scenarios you will encounter in your development work.

After working through this chapter and the Microsoft Learn module, you should be on track to be in command of the following concepts as you learn about Azure and prepare for the AZ-204 Exam:

- Work with Azure Storage Queue, including creating and deleting a queue and using an At-Least-Once approach to publish and consume messages.

- Work with Azure Service Bus Queue, including creating and deleting a queue, and using either an At-Least-Once or an At-Most-Once approach to publish and consume messages.

- Understand the limitations of the sizes of messages and queues.

- Understand which transport protocols can be used against which queues.

- Utilize Service Bus Topics to create a pub/sub queue solution.

- Utilize filters to get only the messages that are important to your specific consumer applications.

Book Wrap-Up

I hope you have enjoyed working through this book. I've put a lot of time into building the solutions to help you get some really solid experience with the concepts and techniques needed to develop solutions in Azure, and so you're prepared to sit for the AZ-204 Exam. I am honored that you gave me the opportunity to be a part of your journey.

It is my sincere hope that this material also has positioned you to have the confidence and skills to sit for the AZ-204 Exam and pass it. I encourage you to not be afraid of the exam, but to get ready and sit for it. When you do pass the exam, and if this book was a big help/part of your journey, I would be very grateful if you would let me know and/or if you would be willing to post something on any of your social media channels such as Twitter, LinkedIn, or another social media provider. Feel free to tag me as well, if you want to (@blgorman on Twitter).

On another note, if you did give this book a sincere work through and you are unable to pass the exam, I would appreciate it if you reach out to me (`www.linkedin.com/in/brianlgorman/` is easiest) and let me know about your experience. I would love to have the chance to work with you to get you to the peak and help you plant the flag of the AZ-204 certification on your resume.

With that being said, it's time to wrap this journey up. I appreciate your sincere efforts and I am so grateful to have had the chance to lead you through this material. All the best to you in the future, and now, go pass that exam!

APPENDIX A

Answers to the "Review Your Learning" Questions and Additional Links

This appendix contains my thoughts regarding each of the questions for the "Review Your Learning" sections at the end of every chapter. There are some questions that include thoughts that I have, and those should be taken as such—simply my thoughts. However, the majority of the questions have a precise answer that can be validated via documentation and the Microsoft Learn materials for this exam.

Additionally, you will find links to the Microsoft Learn modules for each chapter conveniently listed here. There are also a couple of extra links for your review to aid in your final exam preparation.

I hope you find these questions and reviews useful as a final part of your study for the AZ-204 Exam.

Chapter 1: Azure Storage

Chapter 1 is about Azure Storage. Specifically, Azure Blob Storage.

© Brian L. Gorman 2023
B. L. Gorman, *Developing Solutions for Microsoft Azure Certification Companion*,
Certification Study Companion Series, https://doi.org/10.1007/978-1-4842-9300-3

Review Your Learning

The questions and answers from the "Review Your Learning"
section follow:

1) How do you access a specific private blob and all
private blobs in a container from the public URL?

   In order to access a private blob via the public URL,
   you need to have a valid SAS token. As a reminder,
   the SAS token contains the access permissions,
   effective date range, and a signature to validate
   that the token is valid. The signature is generated
   from one of the Storage Account Access Keys.
   `https://learn.microsoft.com/azure/cognitive-services/translator/document-translation/how-to-guides/create-sas-tokens`

2) What are some scenarios where you might make
blobs public?

   This is one of those scenarios that is up to you, but
   essentially making a blob public means that anyone
   could access the blob with the public URL. Good
   use cases for this include hosting common images
   or documents that need to be served from a web
   page. `https://learn.microsoft.com/azure/storage/blobs/anonymous-read-access-overview`

3) Can you put an Azure Storage account inside a
private network?

   Yes, you can have storage that is only accessible
   from within a private network via private endpoints.
   `https://learn.microsoft.com/azure/storage/common/storage-private-endpoints`

4) What is the maximum size of a blob?

The current maximum size of a block blob in Azure
Storage is 190.7 TiB and an append blob can be 195
GiB. This is based on the blob being composed of
50,000 blocks of sizes up to 4000 MiB for a block
blob and 4 MiB for an append blob. `https://`
`learn.microsoft.com/azure/storage/blobs/`
`scalability-targets`

5) How do you move blobs from one tier to another?

You can move blobs from one tier to another by
selecting any blob from the storage account in the
portal and selecting the Change Tier option. You can
then move the blob into another tier. Additionally,
you can move the blob to a new tier via PowerShell
and the Azure CLI. `https://learn.microsoft.`
`com/azure/storage/blobs/access-tiers-`
`online-manage`

Remember: Moves from hot to cool, hot to archive,
cool to hot, and cool to archive are performed
immediately. Moves from archive to any other tier
are not performed immediately.

6) Describe the process of rehydration of a blob from
archive storage to any other tier?

In order to restore a blob from archive storage to
the hot or cold tier, you must copy the blob to a new
hot or cool tier blob or change the tier on the blob
and wait for it to be rehydrated. Currently, it can
take up to 15 hours to rehydrate a blob. However,
in some cases you may be able to pay more to get

a high-priority rehydration, where you get a blob
rehydrated that is under 10 GB in size in less than
one hour. https://learn.microsoft.com/azure/
storage/blobs/archive-rehydrate-overview

Learn Modules

AZ-204: Develop Solutions That Use Blob Storage Learning Path

To fully learn the material, I recommend taking the time to also complete
these Microsoft Learn modules, found in the learning path (https://
learn.microsoft.com/training/paths/develop-solutions-that-use-
blob-storage/):

- Explore Azure Blob Storage: https://learn.
  microsoft.com/en-us/training/paths/develop-
  solutions-that-use-blob-storage

- Manage the Azure Blob Storage lifecycle: https://
  learn.microsoft.com/training/modules/manage-
  azure-blob-storage-lifecycle

- Work with Azure Blob Storage: https://learn.
  microsoft.com/en-us/training/modules/work-
  azure-blob-storage

Chapter 2: Cosmos DB and Table Storage

Chapter 2 covers what it takes to work with the Azure Cosmos DB and the
Azure Table Storage offerings.

Review Your Learning

The questions and answers from the "Review Your Learning" section follow:

1) What is a logical partition in Cosmos DB? What are some good and bad partitions for write-heavy and read-heavy databases?

    A logical partition is how the data is segregated within the physical partitions in Cosmos DB. For write-heavy databases, the logical partition should typically be based on some value with a high cardinality (like a unique ID or email address) so that the data will spread evenly over the partitions. On a read-heavy database, you should use the best partition you can find with unique values, but you should consider the where clause in your read operations. When data is going to be queried with a where clause, it will often be the case that utilization of the field being queried against can make a good partition so that data will be grouped together for efficiency. https://learn.microsoft.com/azure/cosmos-db/partitioning-overview

2) What is a physical partition in Cosmos DB? What are the physical partition limits?

    A physical partition is the actual storage mechanism for the data. Physical partitions can contain one or more logical partitions. The limits that require multiple physical partitions are the RU limit of 10,000 for a physical partition and/or total

storage of 50 GB of data per partition. `https://`
`learn.microsoft.com/azure/cosmos-db/`
`partitioning-overview`

3) Can a Cosmos DB be accessed from a private
network?

Yes, you can connect to a Cosmos DB database
from a private network using Azure Private Link.
`https://learn.microsoft.com/en-us/azure/`
`cosmos-db/how-to-configure-private-endpoints`

4) What is the maximum size of a Cosmos DB
document?

The maximum size of a typical document is 2 MB for
a regular Cosmos DB Account. The size is larger for
Mongo DB, which allows a 16 MB document size.
`https://learn.microsoft.com/azure/cosmos-db/`
`concepts-limits`

5) How do you calculate an RU?

An RU is calculated based on the memory, CPU, and
IOPS required to read the data. A common example
is 1 RU equals the cost to read 1 KB of data using the
index and partition. This is the best performance
you could get on a read. `https://learn.`
`microsoft.com/azure/cosmos-db/request-units`

6) When working with code against the Cosmos
Database, what are two different ways to connect to
the account using keys?

You can connect the SDK for Cosmos DB to your
Cosmos DB Account in .NET code by composing
a client with the account endpoint and an access

key, or you can connect via the account connection
string. `https://learn.microsoft.com/azure/`
`cosmos-db/nosql/how-to-dotnet-get-started`

7) What does it take to migrate a table storage
application to a Cosmos DB Table API application?

To migrate an application that utilizes Azure Table
Storage to Azure Cosmos DB, all you need to do
is change the connection string and point to the
correct Cosmos DB. This is possible because the
SDK code is the same for the Cosmos Table API and
Azure Table Storage, and the migration can happen
by simply changing the connection string. `https://`
`learn.microsoft.com/dotnet/api/overview/`
`azure/data.tables-readme`

Learn Modules

AZ-204: Develop Solutions That Use Azure Cosmos DB

To fully learn the material, I recommend taking the time to also complete
these Microsoft Learn modules, found in the learning path (`https://`
`learn.microsoft.com/training/paths/az-204-develop-solutions-`
`that-use-azure-cosmos-db/`):

- Explore Azure Cosmos DB: `https://learn.microsoft.`
  `com/training/modules/explore-azure-cosmos-db`

- Implement partitioning in Azure Cosmos DB: `https://`
  `learn.microsoft.com/en-us/training/modules/`
  `implement-partitioning-azure-cosmos-db/`

- Work with Azure Cosmos DB: `https://learn.`
  `microsoft.com/training/modules/work-with-`
  `cosmos-db/`

Chapter 3: Infrastructure as a Service (IaaS) Solutions

Chapter 3 kicks off the look at important infrastructure tools in Azure. Because the infrastructure system is large, this first look concentrates only on the first part, which includes virtual machines (VMs) and Azure Resource Manager (ARM) templates (with a little Bicep thrown in for good measure).

Review Your Learning

The questions and answers from the "Review Your Learning" section follow:

1) What is a VM Availability Set? What is a VM Scale Set? How are VM Scale Sets and VM Availability Sets different? When would you use one over the other?

   A VM Availability set is a VM that is provisioned across fault and update domains in an Azure Data Center. A VM Scale Set is used to replicate a number of identical VMs, typically to handle load balancing.

   An availability set is great if you just need to keep a VM active in case of a simple failure within a single data center. `https://learn.microsoft.com/azure/`
   `virtual-machines/availability-set-overview`

The Scale Set is more redundant, as it can span zones within the region and also spans fault domains within the single data center(s). https://learn.microsoft.com/azure/virtual-machine-scale-sets/overview

2) What are some of the main groups of VM compute configurations?

The compute configurations are generally broken up by letter, with A being for test, B for burstable (batch processing), D for general purpose (dev/small production), E for memory optimized, F for compute optimized, and G for memory and storage optimized. There are many other groups, including some high-compute scenarios and some GPU-based scenarios for Big Data. https://azure.microsoft.com/pricing/details/virtual-machines/series

3) Which Azure disks are managed? Which are potentially unmanaged? What are some considerations to remember when utilizing an unmanaged disk?

All SSD disks are managed by Azure. The only option for unmanaged disks that currently remains is a standard 7200 RPM hard drive. If you choose to utilize an unmanaged disk, you must also encrypt it and maintain backups, as well as manage the page blob for the disk in Azure Storage. If you utilize a managed disk, Azure manages all of the encryption and storage details for you. https://learn.microsoft.com/azure/virtual-machines/managed-disks-overview

4) How do you limit traffic to and from a VM in Azure?
What are some common ports to be aware of?

Inbound and outbound traffic for a VM can be
managed by using Network Security Groups (NSGs)
that are attached to the Network Interface Card
(NIC) or the subnet of a virtual network. `https://`
`learn.microsoft.com/azure/virtual-network/`
`network-security-groups-overview`

Ports to be aware of as a developer include the
common port 3389 for Remote Desktop (RDP) to
Windows boxes and port 22 for Secure Shell (SSH) to
Linux boxes. Additionally, HTTP is exposed on port
80, HTTPS via port 443, MySQL communications
typically happen on port 3306, and MS SQL utilizes
port 1433. There are many more ports to consider,
but these are the ones I recommend knowing very
well should you need to administer a VM for web
development in most languages.

5) Which resources in Azure are necessary to deploy a
VM with a desired configuration? What are the steps
to ensure a VM has a feature enabled?

To deploy a VM with Desired State Configuration
(DSC), you need to create a PowerShell (PS) script.
With the PS script, you use Azure Automation to
create a manifest and then deploy the manifest into
Azure Automation. Once the DSC is set in Azure
Automation, you associate any VMs to ensure that
the DSC is run against the VM. `https://learn.`
`microsoft.com/azure/virtual-machines/`
`extensions/dsc-overview`

6) What are the main sections of an ARM template?
How do you create and work with variables?

The main sections of an ARM template are the
parameters, variables, functions, resources,
and outputs. Typically, an ARM template will
use parameters to make the solution reusable.
Additionally, you can leverage variables that either
modify the parameters (such as adding a unique
value to a string) or are just internal variables.
Parameters and variables are both accessed with
a special square braces string in the JSON file and
are referenced by type and name. For example, a
variable named `storageAccountName` would be
referenced as `[variables('storageAccountNa`
`me')]`. `https://learn.microsoft.com/azure/`
`azure-resource-manager/templates/template-`
`tutorial-create-first-template`

7) Working with Bicep, how do you configure a
deployment for a new resource? How do you use
variables?

Bicep is less verbose than ARM and uses a
more straightforward syntax. `https://learn.`
`microsoft.com/azure/azure-resource-manager/`
`bicep/quickstart-create-bicep-use-visual-`
`studio-code`

You can create a new resource by declaring it in the
template with the name of the resource. You can
easily just declare variables within the template
much like regular code. `https://learn.microsoft.`
`com/azure/azure-resource-manager/bicep/`
`variables`

8) What is the difference between an incremental and a complete template deployment?

An incremental deployment will only modify the resources or deploy the resources that are configured within the template. A complete deployment will both modify and deploy resources as configured in the template and also remove any resources in the resource group that are not explicitly defined in the template. `https://learn.microsoft.com/azure/azure-resource-manager/templates/deployment-modes`

Learn Modules

AZ-204: Implement Infrastructure as a Service Solutions (Modules 1 and 2)

To fully learn the material, I recommend taking the time to also complete the first two Microsoft Learn modules for Implement Infrastructure as a Service Solutions, found in this learning path (`https://learn.microsoft.com/en-us/training/paths/az-204-implement-iaas-solutions`):

- Provision virtual machines in Azure: `https://learn.microsoft.com/training/modules/provision-virtual-machines-azure/`

- Create and deploy Azure Resource Manager templates: `https://learn.microsoft.com/training/modules/create-deploy-azure-resource-manager-templates`

Chapter 4: Azure App Service Web Apps

Chapter 4 examines the concept of deploying a public-facing web app with traditional code.

Review Your Learning

The questions and answers from the "Review Your Learning" section follow:

1) What is the relationship between App Service Plans and App Services? Can an App Service have more than one App Service Plan? Can an App Service Plan have more than one App Service? What are some considerations when the relationship goes beyond 1:1?

   The App Service Plan determines the compute and cost, as well as the region and the operating system. `https://learn.microsoft.com/azure/app-service/overview-hosting-plans`

   An App Service can have many App Services but each App Service can only have one App Service Plan. `https://learn.microsoft.com/azure/app-service/overview`

   You might put more than one App Service into a plan for optimizing your Azure spend on test instances. Just remember that all App Services within a plan will share the compute dictated by the App Service Plan, so if one becomes a hog of resources that could be bad for the others.

2) Where do you choose which operating system will
    be utilized? Where do you configure the choice for
    code vs. container vs. static?

    The operating system, region, and compute settings
    of the configuration of the App Service Plan. The
    choice to deploy code vs. container vs. static
    websites is part of the App Service configuration
    (review the links in Question 1 for more
    information).

3) Which plan is an entry-level plan that offers scaling?
    Which plan is an entry-level plan for deployment
    slots? Which plans can have a custom domain
    for hosting? What is the minimal plan level to
    implement private networking?

    Scaling can happen manually in the shared
    Basic Dedicated (B1) tier, with up to three active
    instances. However, it is more likely that you
    would implement scaling in the Standard (S1 and
    better) tier or better, where you can have up to ten
    instances, and you can create autoscaling rules. The
    Standard (S1 and better) tier is also the first plan
    to get deployment slots (it gets five). The Custom
    domain is available on all but the free tier. `https://`
    `azure.microsoft.com/en-us/pricing/details/`
    `app-service/windows/`

    In order to use virtual networks, you must be in a
    dedicated compute pricing tier (not free). `https://`
    `learn.microsoft.com/en-us/azure/app-service/`
    `overview-vnet-integration`.

4) What are some considerations for creating autoscaling rules?

Always remember two things when creating autoscaling rules. First, make sure to create rules in pairs—one rule to scale out and another to scale back in. Next, also make sure to create a range in the metric being used as the determinant so that the scale-in will take place without immediately requiring a scale-out operation. Additional considerations include making sure to utilize the correct metric for the scaling operation. `https:// learn.microsoft.com/azure/architecture/best- practices/auto-scaling`

5) Can an App Service Plan and the App Service be deployed into different regions?

No. The App Service Plan determines the region, and the App Service is dependent on the plan. If you want to create a high-availability, multi-region deployment, you must have individual App Service Plans. `https://learn.microsoft.com/azure/ architecture/reference-architectures/app- service-web-app/multi-region`

6) How do you implement security around the application regarding HTTP/HTTPS, TLS levels, and certificates? How do you enforce certain security levels for clients? Can you deny traffic that is not utilizing HTTPS?

All of the security settings for an App Service are configured in the App Service Configuration. You can set all of the information via the portal

or use tools like the Azure CLI to configure
that app service. `https://learn.microsoft.`
`com/azure/app-service/configure-`
`common?tabs=portal#configure-app-settings`

7) Where can you go to check the status of your website
deployments?

You can review the deployments in the Deployment
Center under the app service in the portal.
`https://learn.microsoft.com/shows/azure-`
`friday/an-overview-of-azure-app-service-`
`deployment-center`

8) How do you create custom variables and settings?
Where should you set environment variables?
Where should you add connection strings?

Variables and connection strings are created
on the configuration blade for the app service.
Environment variables are typically utilized in the
Application Settings portion of the App Service
Configuration, whereas connection strings are
added to the Connection Strings section. `https://`
`learn.microsoft.com/azure/app-service/`
`reference-app-settings`

Learn Modules

Complete the Azure App Service Web Apps Learn Modules

To fully learn the material, I recommend taking the time to also complete
the Microsoft Learn modules for Create Azure App Service Web Apps from

this learning path (https://learn.microsoft.com/en-us/training/paths/create-azure-app-service-web-apps/):

- Explore Azure App Service: https://learn.microsoft.com/training/modules/introduction-to-azure-app-service/

- Configure web app settings: https://learn.microsoft.com/training/modules/configure-web-app-settings

- Scale apps in Azure App Service: https://learn.microsoft.com/training/modules/scale-apps-app-service/

- Explore Azure App Service Deployment Slots: https://learn.microsoft.com/training/modules/understand-app-service-deployment-slots/

Chapter 5: Azure Container Ecosystem (Container Registry and Container Instances)

Chapter 5 is the second part of the infrastructure information that developers need to be in command of for the AZ-204 Exam. This portion deals with the Azure Container Registry and Azure Container Instances. Note that Azure Container Apps and Azure Kubernetes Service are not in scope for the AZ-204 at the time of this writing (but you may still want to familiarize yourself with these services as a cloud application developer).

Review Your Learning

The questions and answers from the "Review Your Learning" section follow:

1) Which runtime is required to host containers?

   The runtime most commonly used to host containers is Docker. `https://docs.docker.com/ get-started/`

2) What is the purpose of the Azure Container Registry (ACR)? How do you interact with the ACR from your local machine?

   The Azure Container Registry (ACR) is used to create repositories, which are deployable images you have pushed to the ACR. Any deployment that leverages containers can then pull the image from the ACR for deployment. `https://learn. microsoft.com/azure/container-registry/ container-registry-intro`

3) What do the following terms mean: Dockerfile, image, and container? How does each play a part in the containers ecosystem?

   A Dockerfile is the file you create with your code that tells Docker how to create an image. An image is the build of the application using a layered approach based on the instructions in the Dockerfile. Once an image is created, you can run the image in any number of containers. Containers are separate versions of the application built and deployed, typically exposing a port and running the application as developed by you and built into the deployable image artifact. `https://docs.docker.com/get-started/02_our_app/`

4) Can you change the variables in a running container instance? Can you change the variables of a container hosted in Azure App Service? What about Kubernetes or Azure Container Apps?

Containers are immutable, so you cannot change the variables in an Azure Container Instance (ACI) that is deployed from the portal. To change the variable, you either need to delete and redeploy the ACI or potentially connect to the container and run some commands to modify values from inside the running container. `https://learn.microsoft.com/azure/container-instances/container-instances-environment-variables`

An Azure App Service adds a layer of orchestration in that you can change a setting on the configuration of the app service and the Azure App Service will restart the container with the new variable information injected into the new container. You do not need to delete the app service for this to take place. `https://learn.microsoft.com/azure/app-service/configure-custom-container`

While Kubernetes or Azure Container Apps are out of scope, those systems are specifically designed to orchestrate container lifecycle, so you would have no problem changing settings and the deployed solution would orchestrate new containers to

handle the new variable information. `https://
learn.microsoft.com/azure/aks/intro-
kubernetes`

5) Can you have an Azure Container Instance running
   on a private network?

   Yes, you can deploy the ACI instance into a private
   network, either a new or existing one. You can also
   create a private endpoint to connect to the ACI
   from a virtual network. `https://learn.microsoft.
   com/azure/container-instances/container-
   instances-vnet`

6) How do you authenticate against the ACR? Can you
   get granular per-user control over individual images
   within an ACR?

   You can authenticate to the Azure ACR via RBAC
   as your own principal, as a service principal, or
   you can use the registry administrator credentials.
   Individuals can be limited to push and/or pull
   operations based on role membership or their
   identity principal. `https://learn.microsoft.com/
   azure/container-registry/container-registry-
   authentication`

7) Can the ACR run automated builds and
   deployments for your images?

   Yes, ACR has the ability to build images with ACR
   tasks. `https://learn.microsoft.com/azure/
   container-registry/container-registry-
   tasks-overview`

8) Can a container instance communicate with other Azure services such as an Azure SQL Server?

Yes, as long as the ports are open on the services and connection information is in place with appropriate settings, the container can easily work with a service such as Azure SQL Server and Azure SQL Server Managed Instances. additionally, you can set the managed identity on a container instance to allow communication with other Azure services. `https://learn.microsoft.com/azure/container-instances/container-instances-managed-identity`

9) Can a container instance host multiple containers?

Yes, it is common to *sidecar* a container with an application container into what is called a container group. This is easily accomplished in Azure Container Instances using YAML. `https://learn.microsoft.com/azure/container-instances/container-instances-multi-container-yaml`

Learn Modules

AZ-204: Implement Infrastructure as a Service Solutions Modules (Modules 3 and 4)

Complete the AZ-204 Microsoft Learn path (`https://learn.microsoft.com/en-us/training/paths/az-204-implement-iaas-solutions/`), Modules 3 and 4:

- Manage container images in Azure Container Registry: `https://learn.microsoft.com/training/modules/publish-container-image-to-azure-container-registry/`

- Run container images in Azure Container Instances:
  `https://learn.microsoft.com/training/modules/`
  `create-run-container-images-azure-container-`
  `instances/`

Learn Modules for Optional/Additional Learning

- Deploy and run a containerized web app with Azure
  App Service: `https://learn.microsoft.com/en-`
  `us/training/modules/deploy-run-container-`
  `app-service/`

- Quickstart: Deploy your first container app using the
  Azure Portal: `https://learn.microsoft.com/en-us/`
  `azure/container-apps/quickstart-portal/`

- Deploy a containerized application on Azure
  Kubernetes Service: `https://learn.microsoft.`
  `com/en-us/training/modules/aks-deploy-`
  `container-app/`

Chapter 6: Implement Azure Functions

Chapter 6 covers Azure Functions, including regular functions and Azure
Durable Functions.

Review Your Learning

The questions and answers from the "Review Your Learning"
section follow:

1) What is the purpose of the `host.json` file? What is the purpose of a `function.json` file? What information can be determined from each?

   The `host.json` file is utilized for the function app settings for the entire host application, and includes information like the runtime of the host, the runtime version, and logging information. The `function.json` file is specific to a single function and has information like the input and output bindings, the trigger, and any other information like connection settings and the function entry point. `https://learn.microsoft.com/azure/azure-functions/functions-reference`

2) What is a Function trigger? What kinds of triggers are available? How can each be utilized?

   The Function trigger is how the function is kicked off to run. There are a number of triggers that you need to be in command of, including, timer triggers (using CRON job settings), HTTP triggers using GET and/or POST requests, and various triggers from other Azure services like the `EventGridTrigger` or `ServiceBusTrigger`. `https://learn.microsoft.com/azure/azure-functions/functions-triggers-bindings`

3) What plans are available for Azure Function Apps and what are some of the considerations for each? Can you use slots in function apps? Can you put your function app on a private network?

The Function App Plan offerings include the
Consumption plan, which gives one million free
requests and incurs a minimum storage charge.
When the Consumption plan is not enough, you can
utilize an App Service Plan to host your functions.
You can also use an App Service Environment,
and you can even host Azure Functions in Azure
Kubernetes Service. `https://learn.microsoft.`
`com/azure/azure-functions/functions-scale`

Function apps can utilize slots. `https://learn.`
`microsoft.com/azure/azure-functions/`
`functions-deployment-slots`

The Consumption tier includes two slots, and any
hosting in App Service Plans would allow for slots as
long as the plan offers slots.

You can use your Function app in a private network
as long as it is not in the Consumption tier. `https://`
`learn.microsoft.com/en-us/azure/azure-`
`functions/functions-networking-options`

4)   What is an input binding? What is an output
binding? What are some advantages to working with
bindings?

Input bindings allow your Function app to connect
to other Azure Services and receive data from them.
Output bindings allow you to send data to other
Azure services. Utilization of the bindings allows
you to not have to wire up the plumbing of the
SDK code to connect and work with the services.
`https://learn.microsoft.com/azure/azure-`
`functions/functions-triggers-bindings`

5) What is an Isolated Worker Runtime and how does that change the operations of a Function app?

Isolated Worker Runtimes (Processes) are new to Azure functions and allow your Function app host to be written in one language (such as .NET 6 or .NET 7) and run functions in another language (such as the .NET Framework 4.8). `https://learn.microsoft.com/azure/azure-functions/dotnet-isolated-process-guide`

6) What are the various authentication modes for an Azure Function? What are some security considerations for each mode?

There are a few authentication modes, including Anonymous, Function Key, and Admin Key. In the Anonymous mode, anyone with the link can execute the function. In the Function Key authorization, anyone with the link and the token can execute the function. With the Admin token, any functions in the application can be executed. `https://learn.microsoft.com/java/api/com.microsoft.azure.functions.annotation.authorizationlevel?view=azure-java-stable`

7) What is the difference between a regular Azure Function and a Durable Azure Function? What are the types of Durable Functions and when can each be used?

"Regular" Azure Functions are stateless. Durable Azure Functions maintain state and have persistence even past the recycling of the Function App. The types and features of durable functions

can be reviewed here: https://learn.microsoft.
com/en-us/azure/azure-functions/durable/
durable-functions-types-features-overview.

8) What are the patterns associated with Durable
    Functions and what is an example of each pattern?

    The patterns were covered in the text, and they
    are Function Chaining, Fan-Out/Fan-In, Async
    HTTP APIs, Monitoring, Human Interaction, and
    Aggregator. Examples were mentioned and you
    can review this link: https://learn.microsoft.
    com/azure/azure-functions/durable/durable-
    functions-overview?tabs=csharp#application-
    patterns.

Learn Modules

AZ-204: Implement Azure Functions

Review the following Microsoft Learn modules (https://learn.
microsoft.com/en-us/training/paths/implement-azure-functions/):

- Explore Azure Functions: https://learn.microsoft.
  com/training/modules/explore-azure-functions/

- Develop Azure Functions: https://learn.microsoft.
  com/training/modules/develop-azure-functions/

- Implement Durable Functions: https://learn.
  microsoft.com/training/modules/implement-
  durable-functions

Chapter 7: Implement User Authentication and Authorization

Chapter 7 covers how to create code to work against identity and the Microsoft Graph.

Review Your Learning

The questions and answers from the "Review Your Learning" section follow:

1) What is authentication? What is authorization? How are they different? Which one must exist for the other to work?

    Authentication is "who you are." Authorization is "what you can do." Authentication allows you to be identifiable and the authorization uses that identity to allow you to do things within systems. You cannot have authorization without authentication.
    https://learn.microsoft.com/azure/active-directory/develop/authentication-vs-authorization

2) What are the various ways a user can satisfy MFA sign-in requirements? Are some more secure than others? When MFA is turned on, in what scenarios will the user always receive a second challenge for sign-in?

    Users can provide MFA credentials by proving who they are and something they are or have and/or something they know. Usually this means signing in with a user ID and password, then providing a token or an answer to a challenge question. In Azure, you can use tokens from an authenticator app, get a text message, or get a phone call.

A challenge will always be issued if the sign-in is considered "risky." This can happen if the user is outside of normal regions, signs in from a strange IP address, or uses a new device. https://www.microsoft.com/en-us/security/business/identity-access/azure-active-directory-mfa-multi-factor-authentication

3) What are the four primary roles that can be used for subscription and/or resource group management? Which role should you give to a guest on your subscription? What about a guest on a specific resource group? What about if the guest needs to modify resources in a specific resource group?

The four primary roles are Owner, Contributor, Reader, and User Access Administrator. Guests can be a contributor on a resource group, and a reader on the subscription. When resources need to be modified, the Contributor role is best. In order to assign user access, the user must be in the Owner or User Access Administrator role. https://learn.microsoft.com/azure/role-based-access-control/built-in-roles

4) What is the purpose of an identity provider? What is a scope?

An identity provider is a service that provides authentication for users. The main providers that you might encounter are Microsoft, Google, Facebook, Apple, Okta, and a few others. Within identity providers, a scope is utilized to request access to information associated with the identity. For example, you might ask for the ability to get the user's email address, and perhaps more information. Scope can also extend to things like "Friends" on Facebook. Remember that the more scope your application requests, the less likely users are to agree to allow you to authorize their accounts. `https://learn.microsoft.com/azure/active-directory/external-identities/identity-providers`

5) What are the various authorization flows? What is an example of each of them?

The main types of authorization flows you need to be in command of are the Authorization Code, Implicit, Client Credentials, On-Behalf-Of, and Device Code. Review this document for more information and examples of each: `https://learn.microsoft.com/azure/active-directory/develop/authentication-flows-app-scenarios?#scenarios-and-supported-authentication-flows.`

6) What is a service principal? Can you sign in to Azure using a service principal?

A service principal is an identity object within Azure, and it can be used to assign permissions, typically by adding the principal to roles and policies. Typically, you don't directly sign in to Azure with a service principal. Instead, your solutions utilize the service principal to authenticate. For example, a service principal allows your application to have GET access to secrets in Azure Key Vault, or a service principal allows your Azure DevOps Pipeline to log in and deploy resources into a specific resource group. `https://learn.microsoft.com/powershell/azure/create-azure-service-principal-azureps?view=azps-9.3.0`

7) What are the various boundaries for Azure Cloud Offerings? What is a sovereign region? Can you cross boundaries with an identity?

There are a few boundaries based on the different offerings. The offerings are Azure Public, Azure Government for the U.S. Government, Azure Germany for German government, and Azure China for the Chinese regions. You cannot cross the boundaries of an Azure sovereign region into another Azure offering. `https://learn.microsoft.com/azure/cloud-adoption-framework/migrate/azure-best-practices/multiple-regions`

Learn Modules

AZ-204: Implement User Authentication and Authorization

Review the following Microsoft Learn modules (https://learn. microsoft.com/en-us/training/paths/az-204-implement-authentication-authorization/):

- Explore the Microsoft Identity platform: https:// learn.microsoft.com/training/modules/explore-microsoft-identity-platform/

- Implement authentication by using the Microsoft Authentication Library: https://learn. microsoft.com/en-us/training/modules/ implement-authentication-by-using-microsoft-authentication-library

- Implement shared access signatures: https://learn. microsoft.com/en-us/training/modules/implement-shared-access-signatures/

- Explore Microsoft Graph: https://learn.microsoft. com/en-us/training/modules/microsoft-graph/

Chapter 8: Implement Secure Cloud Solutions

Chapter 8 wraps up the look at security by showing you how to create secure solutions within Azure. Specifically, concepts like managed identities are used, and then Key Vault is explored. Along with Key Vault, the Azure App Service is also utilized to round out the learnings of working with various solutions in Azure in a secure manner.

Review Your Learning

The questions and answers from the "Review Your Learning"
section follow:

1) What are the two types of managed identities? When
   would you use each type?

   The two types of managed identities are system-
   assigned and user-assigned identities. Use system-
   assigned identities for one-to-one relationships
   between services and identity. Use user-assigned
   identities to manage the same authorization and
   settings for a number of resources (such as a fleet
   of VMs). `https://learn.microsoft.com/azure/`
   `active-directory/managed-identities-azure-`
   `resources/overview`

2) Which type of managed identity must be manually
   deleted? Which type is tightly coupled to a single
   instance of a resource? Which can be reused across
   multiple resources?

   The user-assigned identity must be manually
   removed since it is not associated directly with a
   resource. The system-assigned identity is tightly
   coupled to a single resource so it is removed once
   the associated service is removed. Use the user-
   assigned identity to manage multiple resources. See
   the link in Question 1 for more information.

3) What are the three types information that can be
   stored securely in an Azure Key Vault? What is a
   common use for each type of information stored?

Three types of information that you can store in
an Azure Key Vault are Certificates, Keys, and
Secrets. Certificates are great for authorization of
devices for web or IoT scenarios. Keys are used to
encrypt data, information, or resources. Secrets
can store common settings like connection strings
and passwords. `https://learn.microsoft.com/`
`azure/key-vault/general/about-keys-secrets-`
`certificates`

4) How can you prevent your Azure Key Vault from
being deleted by accident? What about keys?

Azure Key Vault utilizes soft-delete to prevent
accidental deletion of the vault and keys. You can
read more about soft-delete and the upcoming
changes that will make it required for all vaults here:
`https://learn.microsoft.com/azure/key-vault/`
`general/soft-delete-overview`.

5) Can you have multiple versions of a secret active at
the same time?

Yes, secrets receive a version and you can have
multiple versions active at the same time. `https://`
`learn.microsoft.com/en-us/azure/key-vault/`
`secrets/about-secrets`

6) What are two ways a secret can exist in the vault but
also be unusable?

A secret will exist in the vault until it is deleted.
If you want to make a secret unusable without
deleting it, set an expiration date. Once it reaches
the expiration date, the secret will no longer work.

If you want to immediately disable a version of a
secret, you can toggle the Enabled value on the
secret in the vault via the portal or via PowerShell
or the Azure CLI. `https://learn.microsoft.com/`
`en-us/dotnet/api/microsoft.azure.commands.`
`keyvault.setazurekeyvaultsecret.disable`

7) What is the purpose of an access policy in Azure Key
    Vault? Can you get fine-grained access level control
    to individual secrets?

    Access policies allow for RBAC-based authorization
    on the vault. This layer of security gives granular
    control to allow individual identities to be
    authorized for specific actions such as GET secrets.
    `https://learn.microsoft.com/azure/key-vault/`
    `general/assign-access-policy`

    It's important to remember that the permissions
    are for *all* of the entities in the vault. For example,
    GET on Secrets means that the authorized identity
    can read *any* of the secrets in that vault. This is why
    you should not give LIST permission to an identity,
    and it also means you need to use separate vaults to
    create security boundaries as appropriate.

8) Why might a developer choose to implement the
    Azure App Configuration?

    The Azure App Configuration is a great service
    for sharing configuration settings across multiple
    applications. Additionally, the Azure App Configuration
    is the tool of choice for managing feature flags within
    an Azure App Service. `https://learn.microsoft.com/`
    `azure/azure-app-configuration/overview`

Learn Modules

AZ-204: Implement Secure Cloud Solutions

Review these modules for the Microsoft Learning Path for Implementing Secure Cloud Solutions (https://learn.microsoft.com/en-us/training/paths/az-204-implement-secure-cloud-solutions/):

- Implement Azure Key Vault: https://learn.microsoft.com/training/modules/implement-azure-key-vault/

- Implement managed identities: https://learn.microsoft.com/training/modules/implement-managed-identities/

- Implement Azure App Configuration: https://learn.microsoft.com/training/modules/implement-azure-app-configuration

Chapter 9: Implement Caching for Solutions

Chapter 9 explores caching and CDN solutions within Azure.

Review Your Learning

The questions and answers from the "Review Your Learning" section follow:

1) What are some benefits of caching?

    When you cache information, you get improved application performance and you can offload work that ordinarily has to go to the server or centralized

location of the application. You also generally gain
in latency since the information doesn't need to
make roundtrips to the centralized application
servers. `https://learn.microsoft.com/en-us/`
`azure/architecture/framework/scalability/`
`optimize-cache`

2) What is a CDN? How do you implement a CDN
in Azure?

A CDN is a content delivery network. The CDN is
implemented by creating a CDN Profile and then
setting the endpoints. For example, you can use
Azure Front Door to create the CDN profile and then
have the static web content served that is housed
in an Azure Storage account. `https://learn.`
`microsoft.com/azure/cdn/cdn-overview?toc=%2F`
`azure%2Ffrontdoor%2FTOC.json`

3) What types of information are ideal candidates to
host on a CDN?

Static resources such as images and documents that
need to be served to users.

4) How does a CDN work in relation to user requests,
serving data, and Time-To-Live (TTL)?

Time-To-Live is generally configured by the
application. The data is first retrieved from the
central location and then housed in the PoP (Point
of Presence) edge endpoints until the data is
invalidated or the Time-To-Live expires. Review the
link in Question 2 to see the flow in a nice image.

5) What are some reasons you would choose to use
   IMemoryCache instead of Redis Cache? Why might
   you choose Redis over IMemoryCache?

   IMemoryCache is a built-in .NET solution object,
   and it doesn't require any additional configuration
   or services to work. Redis Cache is a powerful and
   robust caching solution that can also be replicated
   globally. If you need simple caching, you might
   leverage IMemoryCache. If you need a robust
   solution with the ability to be highly available and
   have additional tools, you'll likely want to leverage
   Redis Cache. https://learn.microsoft.com/en-
   us/azure/architecture/best-practices/caching

6) What offerings are available for Redis Cache? Which
   can be implemented on a private network? Which
   offerings leverage Redis modules (RediSearch, etc.)?

   Redis Cache for Azure has an open source and an
   Enterprise tier. To utilize networking and the Redis
   modules, you need to implement the Enterprise
   tier. https://learn.microsoft.com/azure/azure-
   cache-for-redis/cache-overview#service-tiers

7) What are some of the basic commands to work
   with Redis?

   There are a number of commands. Within the
   Azure ecosystem, however, the main commands
   are StringSet and StringGet. https://learn.
   microsoft.com/azure/azure-cache-for-redis/
   cache-dotnet-core-quickstart#executing-
   cache-commands

8) How do you interact with Redis Cache from
.NET code?

Utilize the StackExchange.Redis NuGet package
and compose the cache object hierarchy, then issue
commands. https://learn.microsoft.com/en-us/
azure/azure-cache-for-redis/cache-web-app-
aspnet-core-howto

Learn Modules

AZ-204: Integrate Caching and Content Delivery Within Solutions

Review the Microsoft learning path for Integrating Caching and Content
Delivery (https://learn.microsoft.com/en-us/training/paths/
az-204-integrate-caching-content-delivery-within-solutions/):

- Develop for Storage on CDNs: https://learn.
  microsoft.com/training/modules/develop-for-
  storage-cdns/

- Develop for Azure Cache for Redis: https://learn.
  microsoft.com/training/modules/develop-for-
  azure-cache-for-redis/

Chapter 10: Troubleshoot Solutions by Using Metrics and Log Data

Chapter 10 covers working with Application Insights, PING tests, alerts,
and also takes a short look at setting up dashboards and working with
Kusto queries.

Review Your Learning

The questions and answers from the "Review Your Learning" section follow:

1) What types of information can be monitored? Do you have to do anything to get monitoring in your Azure subscription?

   Within the Azure Monitor ecosystem, you can monitor metrics and logs. Technically, you can also monitor and respond to events as well, but for this chapter the main concepts are metrics and logs, with some concern about traces and changes. Azure Monitor is automatically included and will be running on your subscription with no required configuration on your part. `https://learn.microsoft.com/azure/azure-monitor/overview` Some services do require additional agents, such as applications, VMs, and containers.

2) What are the major components of Azure Monitor?

   The major components are the source of the metric, log, or event, the type of the monitored data (i.e., metric/log), and the target service being monitored.

3) Do your web solutions automatically get monitoring? If so, is there additional monitoring you can implement? If so, how do you do this for a typical .NET application?

   Azure App Service does have monitoring without any automatic configuration. However, you are likely going to want to instrument Application

Insights on your solutions (or container or VM
insights depending on your architecture). Adding
the insights will give you additional monitoring
and the ability to create custom logs and traces.
`https://learn.microsoft.com/azure/azure-`
`monitor/app/asp-net-core`

4) What are the types of information that can be
   utilized with Application Insights? What are some
   of the other types of insights available and what are
   they for?

   Once you've instrumented Application Insights,
   you can utilize code to track events, traces,
   exceptions, and metrics. Additional Insights exist
   for containers, VMs, and networks. The insights
   give you additional tools that allow you to leverage
   visualizations, perform better logging, and have
   a better understanding of the workflows in your
   applications. You can then write queries and create
   dashboards or view application maps. `https://`
   `azure.microsoft.com/products/monitor`

5) What is an availability test? How do you create a test
   to check if your website is responding?

   An availability test is just a way to determine if a web
   page is responding. Within Application Insights,
   you can use URL tests, standard tests, and more.
   `https://learn.microsoft.com/azure/azure-`
   `monitor/app/monitor-web-app-availability`

6) What is the purpose of the Application Map?
   What do you have to do to get it to work with your
   solutions?

The Application Map shows the requests and
latency between Azure solutions utilized from
within your application. You don't have to do
anything other than instrument Application
Insights; the system will do the rest. `https://`
`learn.microsoft.com/azure/azure-monitor/`
`app/app-map`

7) What is a Kusto Query? How do you run a custom
Kusto Query? How do you use a custom query to
trigger an alert?

Kusto Queries utilize the Kusto Query Language
(KQL) to perform analysis against Azure Monitor
Logs. This can be done to find information about
your solutions and to perform threat hunting.
`https://learn.microsoft.com/azure/azure-`
`monitor/logs/log-query-overview?WT.mc_id=AZ-`
`MVP-5004334`

You can use a Kusto Query as the signal to
determine if an alert should fire.

8) What are the three main aspects of creating an alert?
Do alerts always cost the same? What are some of
the actions for notification/remediation/tracking of
alerts that you can take?

To create an alert, you need a metric or log entry
to monitor as the "signal." You then need an action
group to determine who to notify, and you need
the ways to notify the group (i.e., SMS or email).
Additionally, you can perform a POST to a webhook
with alert information, trigger Azure Functions or
Logic Apps, and automatically create entries in your

ITSM solutions. `https://learn.microsoft.com/`
`azure/azure-monitor/alerts/alerts-overview`

Alerts vary in cost depending on the signal and
other factors. `https://learn.microsoft.com/`
`azure/azure-monitor/alerts/tutorial-`
`log-alert`

9)   What are some of the main ways to visualize
     information from Azure Monitor? Are there any
     default visualizations that you can leverage?
     What are the benefits of creating more robust
     visualizations?

     By default, the App Service has a number of
     visualizations on metrics, but custom visualizations
     give you more information about your solutions.

10)   Where in Azure can you create visualizations? What
      are some additional tools that allow you to create
      visualizations?

      You can utilize a number of tools to visualize data.
      The easiest is to leverage an Azure Dashboard.
      `https://learn.microsoft.com/azure/azure-`
      `portal/azure-portal-dashboards` Other tools
      such as Power BI and Grafana can also be used to
      visualize data.

Learn Modules

AZ-204: Instrument Solutions to Support Monitoring and Logging

Review these Microsoft Learn modules (`https://learn.microsoft.`
`com/en-us/training/paths/az-204-instrument-solutions-support-`
`monitoring-logging/`):

- Monitor App Performance: `https://learn.`
  `microsoft.com/training/modules/monitor-app-`
  `performance`

Chapter 11: Implement API Management

Chapter 11 looks at creating an API Management solution on the
Developer tier so you can see a bit about the Developer website in addition
to the basic API Management solution.

Review Your Learning

The questions and answers from the "Review Your Learning"
section follow:

1) What are the different offerings within APIM
   for deployment of solutions? Which tier(s) get a
   Developer portal?

   The different offerings include a Consumption
   tier, the Developer tier, then Basic, Standard,
   and Premium. All tiers except consumption get

a developer portal. `https://learn.microsoft.`
`com/en-us/azure/api-management/api-`
`management-features`

2) Why do some tiers deploy quickly while others take
   30-45 minutes to deploy? Which tier(s) gets a self-
   hosted gateway? Why might a self-hosted gateway
   be important?

   The Consumption tier uses a shared gateway, so it
   can deploy very quickly. All other tiers use a gateway
   that has to be deployed, which takes around 30-45
   minutes (this is similar to the time required to
   deploy a VPN Gateway into a private network).
   The Developer and Premium tiers get a self-hosted
   gateway, which is useful to connect to private
   networks in a hybrid scenario, either on-premises
   or in a multi-cloud scenario. `https://learn.`
   `microsoft.com/azure/api-management/api-`
   `management-key-concepts#self-hosted-gateway`

3) What is an API within APIM?
   Within the API Management solution, an API is
   a group of operations that are typically related.
   `https://learn.microsoft.com/azure/api-`
   `management/import-and-publish`

4) What is a product within APIM?
   A product is a grouping of one or more APIs, used
   to expose operations as a solution to your clients.
   `https://learn.microsoft.com/azure/api-`
   `management/api-management-howto-add-products`

5) What is a subscription within APIM? Is the
subscription applied to the API or the product? How
does this enhance your solution?

A subscription allows you to create a token for
clients to use on your API Management solution to
authorize requests and prove that the client should
be able to execute the API. Developers can use the
subscription key to make requests, and you can use
the key to manage the throughput and access for the
developers. https://learn.microsoft.com/azure/
api-management/api-management-subscriptions

6) What is a policy? How do you utilize policies? Where
can you apply policies and in what directions? What
is the inheritance precedence of policies?

Policies are XML documents that create additional
functionality on request. You can apply policies
on request, during backend processing, and on
response. Policies can be applied for all APIs,
for a single API, and at the operation level. More
recent policies supersede any base policies (i.e., an
operation policy supersedes the All APIs policy).
https://learn.microsoft.com/azure/api-
management/api-management-howto-policies

7) What are two ways to validate client requests outside
of subscriptions? Which is considered more secure?

Two ways to validate clients are JWTs (https://
learn.microsoft.com/azure/api-management/
validate-jwt-policy) and Certificates (https://

learn.microsoft.com/azure/api-management/
api-management-howto-mutual-certificates-
for-clients).

Certificates are considered more secure, but it may
be easier to implement solutions with JWTs.

Learn Modules

AZ-204: Implement API Management

Review these Microsoft Learn modules (https://learn.microsoft.com/
en-us/training/paths/az-204-implement-api-management/):

- Export API Management: https://learn.microsoft.
  com/training/modules/explore-api-management/

Chapter 12: Develop Event-Based Solutions

Chapter 12 is all about leveraging events in Azure with Azure Event Hub
and Azure Event Grid.

Review Your Learning

The questions and answers from the "Review Your Learning"
section follow:

1) What is the purpose of the Azure Event Hubs?

    Azure Event Hubs is designed to ingress millions of
    records of streaming data per minute for Big Data
    pipelines. https://learn.microsoft.com/azure/
    event-hubs/event-hubs-about

2) What is the purpose of the Azure Event Grid?

   Azure Event Grid is designed to handle single events by allowing a producer to publish the event and subscribers to respond to the event. https://learn.microsoft.com/azure/event-grid/overview

3) What is an event producer? What is a receiver? What is the purpose of a partition and what is the maximum number of partitions you can have? What is a consumer? What is a consumer group? How many readers can you have per consumer group? What is checkpointing?

   A producer is the source of the event and the receiver is the service that responds to the event. https://learn.microsoft.com/en-us/azure/event-hubs/event-hubs-features Partitions group data together to easily allow consumers to read the data. The Event Hub has a maximum of 32 partitions. A consumer group is one to five applications that are reading the same data from within the hub. A checkpoint is a pointer to the last event that was consumed.

4) How do you work with .NET code to send and receive events?

   As with other solutions, you compose the objects in a .NET project and leverage the SAS token to gain permissions to send or receive (or do both). https://learn.microsoft.com/en-us/azure/event-hubs/event-hubs-dotnet-standard-getstarted-send

5) What is an event topic? What is an event
   subscription?

   Within Event Grid, a topic is an endpoint that allows
   publishing of a particular group of events. `https://`
   `learn.microsoft.com/en-us/azure/event-grid/`
   `post-to-custom-topic` An event subscription
   is utilized to consume the events as they are
   published. `https://learn.microsoft.com/azure/`
   `event-grid/receive-events`

6) What is a dead-letter event?

   A dead-letter event is an event that was published
   but never delivered. `https://learn.microsoft.`
   `com/azure/event-grid/manage-event-delivery`

7) What are some ways to utilize event subscriptions to
   respond to events?

   You can set subscriptions in the Azure Portal to
   respond to events for things like Blob Storage
   created events or VM State Change events
   (i.e., power up/down). You can respond with a
   subscription that triggers an Azure Function or
   an Azure Logic App, or you can place message
   information into Azure Service Bus when an event is
   fired for distributed processing in your solutions.

Learn Module

AZ-204: Develop Event-Based Solutions

Review these Microsoft Learn modules (https://learn.microsoft.com/
training/paths/az-204-develop-event-based-solutions/):

- Explore Azure Event Grid: https://learn.microsoft.
  com/training/modules/azure-event-grid

- Explore Azure Event Hubs: https://learn.microsoft.
  com/training/modules/azure-event-hubs

Chapter 13: Develop Message-Based Solutions

The final chapter of the book is about message-based solutions, leveraging
Azure Service Bus and Azure Storage Queue.

Review Your Learning

The questions and answers from the "Review Your Learning"
section follow:

1) What is the maximum size of an Azure Storage
   Queue message? What is the maximum size of an
   Azure Service Bus message?

   The maximum size of a storage queue message is
   64 KB. https://learn.microsoft.com/azure/
   storage/queues/storage-queues-introduction
   The maximum size of a typical Service Bus Message
   is 256 KB, but it can be up to 100 MB in size. Even

though it can be larger, Microsoft recommends
keeping your service bus message size less than
or equal to 1MB. `https://learn.microsoft.`
`com/azure/service-bus-messaging/service-`
`bus-quotas`

2) Which service can store more than 80 GB of data?

The service that can store more than 80 GB of data is
the Azure Storage Queue.

3) Which service can guarantee order?

The service that can guarantee order is the Azure
Service Bus.

4) Which service(s) can guarantee At-Most-Once
delivery? Which service(s) can guarantee At-Least-
Once delivery?

All services can guarantee At-Least-Once delivery.
Only Azure Service Bus can guarantee At-Most-
Once delivery.

5) What is the difference between `PeekLock` and
`ReceiveAndDelete`?

The difference is in how the messages are
processed. With `PeekLock`, the message is read
from the queue but is left in place, and it has to
be completed later in order to be deleted (which
also means it could potentially be read by another
consumer). `https://learn.microsoft.com/`
`en-us/azure/service-bus-messaging/message-`
`transfers-locks-settlement#peeklock`

With the `ReceiveAndDelete` operation, the message
is read and deleted at the same time from the queue.
This operation guarantees At-Most-Once delivery,
but it can also result in a loss of data. `https://`
`learn.microsoft.com/azure/service-bus-`
`messaging/message-transfers-locks-settlement`
`#receiveanddelete`

6) What are the various types of filters available for
filtering messages? How do you leverage a filter for
a subscription? What does it mean to multicast? If
topics are multicast, can a message be read more
than once? If possible, how or why is this possible?

Service Bus offers SQL filters, Boolean filters, and
Correlation filters. To leverage a filter, you create one
when you create the subscription. Any consumers
of the subscription automatically benefit from
the filter.

Multicasting means you can publish once and
consume with multiple clients. With multicasting,
messages are designed to be read by multiple
consumers so they are read more than once in their
various subscriptions. To prevent duplicate reads
on a single subscription, use the `ReceiveAndDelete`
approach (but remember that the other
subscriptions still read the message individually).
`https://learn.microsoft.com/en-us/azure/`
`service-bus-messaging/topic-filters`

7) What are the various levels of SAS tokens? What
token can do everything on the Service Bus
deployment? What is/are the benefit(s) of using
granular SAS tokens?

As with Event Hubs, the Service Bus has SAS tokens
available for Send, Listen, and Manage. There is also
a RootManage SAS token that allows all the topics
and queues to be leveraged with that single key.
Using a granular approach ensures that keys are
limited to the scope they should have, such as only
sending to one topic with no ability to send to the
wrong topic or listen for messages. `https://learn.`
`microsoft.com/azure/service-bus-messaging/`
`service-bus-sas.`

Learn Modules

AZ-204: Develop Message-Based Solutions

Review these Microsoft Learn modules (`https://learn.microsoft.com/`
`en-us/training/paths/az-204-develop-message-based-solutions/`):

- Discover Azure Message Queues: `https://learn.`
  `microsoft.com/training/modules/discover-azure-`
  `message-queue/`

Conclusion

I hope this appendix has been useful in helping to solidify your knowledge
and preparing you for the AZ-204 Exam.

Index

A

© Brian L. Gorman 2023
B. L. Gorman, *Developing Solutions for Microsoft Azure Certification Companion*,
Certification Study Companion Series, https://doi.org/10.1007/978-1-4842-9300-3

N

Q

T

Printed in the United States
by Baker & Taylor Publisher Services